Devolution and British Politics

DATE DUE

FEB 1 0 2007	
MAR 2 6 2011	

We work with leading authors to develop the
strongest educational materials in politics,
bringing cutting-edge thinking and best learning
practice to a global market.

Under a range of well-known imprints, including
Longman, we craft high quality print and
electronic publications which help readers to
understand and apply their content,
whether studying or at work.

To find out more about the complete range of our
publishing please visit us on the World Wide Web at:
www.pearsoned.co.uk

Devolution and British Politics

Edited by

MICHAEL O'NEILL

Harlow, England • London • New York • Boston • San Francisco • Toronto • Sydney • Singapore • Hong Kong
Tokyo • Seoul • Taipei • New Delhi • Cape Town • Madrid • Mexico City • Amsterdam • Munich • Paris • Milan

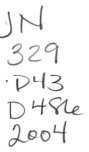

Pearson Education Limited
Edinburgh Gate
Harlow
Essex CM20 2JE
England

and Associated Companies throughout the world

Visit us on the World Wide Web at:
www.pearsoned.co.uk

First published 2004

ISBN 0 582 47274 1

British Library Cataloguing-in-Publication Data
A catalogue record for this book is available from the British Library

Library of Congress Cataloging-in-Publication Data
A catalog record for this book is available from the Library of Congress

10 9 8 7 6 5 4 3 2 1
08 07 06 05 04

Typeset in 10/13pt Palatino by
Printed and bound in Malaysia

The publisher's policy is to use paper manufactured from sustainable forests.

For Richard, Matthew, Karen and Helen

'A state without the means of some change is without the means of its conservation'

Edmund Burke [1790]

Contents

List of tables

List of contributors

David Baker is Senior Lecturer in the Department of Politics and International Studies at the University of Warwick. He is also co-founder (with Professor Andrew Gamble) and Co-director of the joint Members of Parliament Project. He has published extensively in the field of British political parties with particular regard to the issue of Britain and European Union. He is currently working on a major book dealing with the many competing and conflicting models of fascism.

Eberhard Bort is the Academic Co-ordinator of the Institute of Governance and a Lecturer in Politics at the University of Edinburgh. His recent publications include: (ed., with Malcolm Anderson), *The Frontiers of Europe* (London: Pinter, 1998), *The Irish Border: History, Politics, Culture* (Liverpool University Press, 1999); (ed., with Russell Keat), *The Boundaries of Understanding* (Edinburgh: ISSI, 1999); (ed., with Neil Evans), *Networking Europe: Essays on Regionalism and Social Democracy* (Liverpool University Press, 2000); (with Malcolm Anderson), *The Frontiers of the European Union* (Basingstoke: Palgrave, 2001); *Commemorating Ireland: History, Politics, Culture* (Dublin: Irish Academic Press, 2004).

Antonia Dodds is Lecturer in Politics at the University of Edinburgh currently completing a doctoral thesis at the University of Leeds on Scottish nationalism. Her recent publications include: 'The Exception to the Rule: Nineteenth Century Scotland and the Causes of National Movements', in Catherine DiDomenico, Alex Law, Jonathan Skinner, Mick Smith (eds), *Boundaries and Identities: Nation, Politics and Culture in Scotland* (Dundee: University of Abertay Press, 2001).

James Hunter is Senior Lecturer in Public Policy in the Nottingham Graduate School for Social and Policy Research at the Nottingham Trent University.

Michael Keating is Professor of Regional Studies at the European University Institute, Florence, and Professor of Scottish Politics at the University of Aberdeen. He has taught at the universities of Strathclyde and Western Ontario and is the author of numerous books and articles on urban and regional politics and nationalism.

Andrew Massey is Professor of Government at the University of Portsmouth. His recent research/publications include: (with R.A.W. Rhodes, P. Carmichael, J. McMillan), *Decentralising the Civil Service: From Unitary State to Differentiated Polity in the United Kingdom* (Buckingham: Open University Press, 2003).

Janet Mather is Senior Lecturer in Politics at Manchester Metropolitan University. Her recent publications include: *The European Union and British Democracy: Towards Convergence* (Basingstoke: Macmillan, 2000).

Janice McMillan is Senior Lecturer in Public Service Management, Newcastle Business School, Northumbria University. Her research interests are public administration and public policy. Recent publications include: (with R.A.W. Rhodes, P. Carmichael, A. Massey), *Decentralising the Civil Service: From Unitary State to Differentiated Polity in the United Kingdom* (Buckingham: Open University Press, 2003).

Michael O'Neill is Jean Monnet Professor of EU Politics at the Nottingham Trent University. He has published extensively on European politics and is currently working on a study of European citizenship and political identity.

David Seawright is Senior Lecturer in British Politics in the School of Politics and International Studies (POLIS), at the University of Leeds. He is the author of *An Important Matter of Principle*, about the postwar decline of the Scottish Conservative and Unionist Party, and co-editor of *Britain For and Against Europe*.

Christopher Stevens is Principal Lecturer in Politics at the Christ Church University College, Canterbury. He has published on grassroots political behaviour, working-class Conservatism and electoral sociology, and is now engaged in research on regional governance.

Rick Wilford is Professor of Politics at Queen's University Belfast. He is currently co-coordinator of the Monitoring Devolution in Northern Ireland project, co-funded by Leverhulme and the ESRC. Recent publications include: *Aspects of the Belfast Agreement* (Oxford University Press, 2001). He is currently working on a study of the Northern Ireland Assembly established in 1998.

Acknowledgements

This book has deep roots, both scholarly and personal. Firstly, it reflects a long-standing academic curiosity about the peculiar fabric of the British polity, the cultural cement and the affective bonds that have bound and continue to hold these islands and their respective peoples together as a United Kingdom. Relations, albeit, that have been shaped and are sustained in the spirit of creative tension, a condition familiar to mature polities and one aptly expressed in the epithet of the Roman poet Horace as *concordia discors*. This exploration of the special nature of these long-standing but far from sclerotic political and cultural relations has, too, an emotional resonance. One that is grounded in the sensibilities of a native Scotsman born of an English mother and with long-standing Irish ancestry who was schooled and went to university in England. This quest to better understand the workings of the British polity, its cultural fabric and social make-up as much as its merely institutional arrangement is timely. The idea for this book was conceived in the immediate aftermath of the re-imagining of the British state that followed the historic devolution of 1998. We are now a full five years into the new British politics: an opportune moment for reflection, review and evaluation.

The task of producing a book invariably accumulates substantial debts and even more so in the collective endeavour that is an edited volume. My principal debts are to my fellow contributors whose common fund of political wisdom and expertise has made this project possible. They have laboured without complaint to write to a narrow brief dictated by this editor and the outcome of their efforts adds much to our knowledge of the politics of the United Kingdom. I am likewise grateful to the staff at Longman Pearson for the light but constructive editorial hand with which they have guided the project from its conception and over its gestation.

There are debts closer to home that must be acknowledged. The pressures that accompany committed scholarship and research are mitigated by a particularly supportive and amicable working environment in my department at the Nottingham Trent University. I would make particular mention here of Professor Paul Periton whose good humour and encouragement makes for a working environment especially conducive to scholarly pursuits. Professor David Webb, Dean of the Faculty of Economics and Social Science likewise actively cultivates a serious research culture, by both his example and personal encouragement. I am particularly grateful to my good colleague and valued friend Professor Lawrence Wilde, who is always generous of both time and spirit, constructive in his criticism, perceptive in his observations, and supportive beyond the call of duty. A number of my colleagues and friends, both in Nottingham and further afield, have taken the time from busy lives to reflect on and to offer helpful comment on this project, and especially on my own contributions to this book. I am grateful to each one of them for their valued assistance in shaping the ideas expressed herein. It goes without saying that any errors or shortcomings that remain are entirely the responsibility of the editor.

Many and varied influences are brought to bear, contribute over a working lifetime to the processes by which intellectual curiosity is honed into the capacity and commitment to research one's hunches about how politics works and then to write about them. I am singularly fortunate in this regard. I have been particularly reminded over the course of this past year of very early but nonetheless important debts to people who contributed much to my academic development and personal well-being at the outset of my academic career. Notable in this regard are Linda Eldred who was there as a very dear friend and stalwart support at the start of the journey, the apprenticeship years, and my sixth form tutor John Sutton, an inspiring teacher and an early mentor.

To research, write and certainly to edit a book is consuming of both time and emotional energy. Time spent in the library, in the archives and at the desk is time not spent elsewhere. There are silent witnesses to this endeavour on whom these costs mostly fall. As always, my family have been the mainstay of this effort and without their encouragement and support this project could not have been brought to a successful conclusion. I dedicate this book to the four young people who keep me sane, who connect me with the real world beyond the library and the study, and who unfailingly bring laughter and a sense of fun to my door. They give me a due sense of proportion, and constantly remind me about what really matters in life. These are precious gifts, the emotional ballast of, the indispensable balance to, my professional activities. This book is about the future of the British state as much as it is about its past condition and present circumstances. It is fitting, then, that it should be dedicated to four of the nicest, most energetic, warmhearted and thoughtful youngsters who have citizenship of the remarkable island kingdom that is the subject of this book. I am very proud of them and I trust they will continue to keep me fully engaged in the affairs of this twenty-first century, intellectually curious and duly reflective about its current issues. My greatest debt is to my wife Wendie without whose good counsel and practical support, nothing would ever happen. No tentative 'first thoughts' or mere jottings on the notepad would ever travel the long and arduous road to completion and publication.

Michael O'Neill
Screveton, Nottinghamshire

PUBLISHER'S ACKNOWLEDGEMENTS

We are grateful to A.P. Watt on behalf of Vernon Bogdanor for permission to include extracts from *Devolution in the United Kingdom* by Vernon Bogdanor (2001).

Every effort has been made by the publisher to obtain permission from the appropriate source to reproduce material which appears in this book. In some instances we have been unable to trace the owners of copyright material, and we would appreciate any information that would enable us to do so.

Introduction

THE IDEA OF THE UNION STATE

Political development in Britain during the historic phases of nation building and democratisation was presided over by a centralised and unitary state. The annexation of the principality of Wales by England in 1536, the union of the two kingdoms of Scotland and England (1707), and the eventual colonisation of Ireland (where a union of parliaments was 'agreed' in 1800 and implemented in 1801) established a union state in Britain.[1] A unionist tradition became part of the national ideology, embedded in the official mindset of the political elite, a facet of Whig statecraft but also from the later eighteenth century more widely manifested in popular political culture.[2] Political scientists and sociologists have made much of the underlying social homogeneity of British society after some two hundred years of industrialisation, a variable that 'must also be taken into account in identifying the components of the anti-territorial bias' of British politics since the foundation of the United Kingdom.[3]

Political authority, fiscal prerogative and legal sovereignty were vested in Parliament – arrangements sustained by a widely accepted national identity and giving rise to a homogeneous if adversarial political culture. But this union state also implied acceptance of the idea of national unity, a cultural reflex rooted in the abiding assumptions about national power of the English elite, and for a long time subscribed to by their regional counterparts too. These arrangements were embedded over time in a composite national identity, a mindset whereby regional elites were assimilated into metropolitan political culture.[4]

The union state was the formal embodiment of this process of nation building, confirming a common political identity and an overarching national interest that superseded merely territorial interests. In this narrative of national statecraft, government managed the economy, making authoritative policy decisions on behalf of British society from the political centre geographically located in a national, indeed for some two centuries an imperial, capital. The writ, legitimacy and authority of these arrangements ran throughout the land without exception. The principle of indivisible sovereignty was established by practice and precept, and was famously captured in Blackstone's pronouncement (1765) that 'what the parliament doth, no authority upon earth can undo'.[5]

Needless to say, this idea was challenged by its opponents, and not least in the non-English territories, but at the outset without having any significant impact. In the opinion of one recent commentator, opponents of home rule for the historical territorial parts of the Union perceived such political aspirations to be a threat to the construction of a new homogeneous British national identity, 'a partnership of three kingdoms, a partnership of four nations'. This unity of purpose 'was to be achieved not by absorbing the identity of these different nations into one undifferentiated whole, but by explicitly recognizing that Britain was a multinational state, and devising institutions which allowed the various identities of her component nations to be expressed'.[6] Distinctive territorial identities were duly acknowledged by special governance arrangements, for Scotland and later for Northern Ireland. Scotland's history as an independent kingdom and the voluntary union of the crowns in 1603 both ensured a stronger residual identity there and warranted greater political autonomy when the union bargain was negotiated. There was, too, a separate legal system, distinct local government and education arrangements, Scottish banknotes, a national press and its own established church.

Regional elites were nevertheless readily absorbed into a metropolitan political culture though assimilation was modulated by a genuflection towards 'local colour'.[7] Residual differences of accent or other distinctive cultural attributes were thus overlaid by a prevailing and predominant Britishness.[8] Regional interests, wherever they arose, were, according to the prevailing orthodoxy, deemed to be properly represented at the centre by territorial elites participating in the management of national affairs.

Of course, the notion of cultural equivalence was much less a priority in the nation-building process than were altogether more mundane considerations. Calculations of self-interest as much as cultural propinquity played a part in cementing the British project. As public expenditure markedly increased as a proportion of gross domestic product, the case for territorial interaction with the centre was sustained by central government's adoption of fiscal procedures ensuring that the 'other nations' received a greater share of state largesse than was demographically justified. Other factors, too, have added impetus to the centripetal dynamic of unionism. Amongst these are a majority electoral system and a party system dominated by two class-based parties both committed, if in varying degrees, to a centralised union state and with active macro-economic management and some redistribution of wealth through a welfare state organised on the principle of universal benefits.[9] The distribution of parliamentary seats reinforced these bonds by favouring the territorial nations, Scotland being proportionately over-represented, seats to population share, by some 20 per cent.

The success of national integration notwithstanding, the cement binding the Union remained a matter of abiding concern for those preferring a significant degree of territorial self-determination. To this extent, the issues raised in the current debate on devolution are hardly novel. They have been a constant refrain of opponents of the union state project, and indeed of those who would discredit them, from the outset. The extent of the discretion permitted to territorial authorities within the institutional arrangements of the Union both prefigured its founding moment in 1707 and continued to feature in British constitutional discourse thereafter. On occasions it has dominated the political agenda, most notably during the protracted and bitter debate on Irish home rule during the late nineteenth century.

The union bargain struck by the English state with Scotland and Ireland in the course of the eighteenth century was by its very nature an asymmetrical arrangement. It has ensured differential political relations between those countries and with the metropolitan centre as it has, though in much reduced form, for Wales.[10] The uneven quality of territorial relations in the emergent union state indicates that even in the halcyon days of confident, successful British nationhood, the project was a deliberative and self-interested endeavour constructed by political elites in order to fashion political unity out of abiding territorial and cultural diversities. Its outcome was by no means manifest destiny, the natural consequence of mature political development as implied by the unionist narrative. There were, of course, alternative political models available. Federalism was already part of the liberal project for the British Empire, though it found little favour in the lively domestic discourse on constitutional affairs. The classic solution to the challenge of reconciling distinctive, even competing, territorial identities with undivided sovereignty was most influentially expressed by A.V. Dicey in his staunch rebuttal of the federalist principle for organising the governance of the British state.[11]

This doyen of constitutional propriety saw federalism as an 'alien' arrangement undermining parliamentary sovereignty and, as such, depriving 'English institutions of their elasticity, their strength, and their life [for] it weakens the Executive at home and abroad, and lessens the power of the country to resist foreign attack. Thereby imposing on England and Scotland a constitution which they do not want, and which is quite unsuited to the historical traditions and to the genius of Great Britain.' The federal solution was thus discounted even as a solution to the problematic 'Irish Question' for it 'ensures none of the solid benefits to be hoped for from a genuine union with England'.[12]

The influential American model of a federal state has barely figured in mainstream British constitutional thinking about territorial governance. There was never any question in the debate on home rule that the supremacy of the Westminster Parliament, or the primacy accorded to the British executive in the government of the realm, would be surrendered in favour of a federalist separation of powers. This antipathy has persisted, the aspirations of a small but energetic federalist lobby notwithstanding.[13] Contemporary voices regret this residual resistance to constitutional innovation. A properly constructed federal architecture would, as they see it, at least have confronted the abiding problem of territorial imbalance, as between demographically dominant England and the much smaller Celtic nations. To do so, however, would have necessitated tackling the concomitant problem of the lack of a culturally resonant sense of English regionalism.

There has nevertheless always been a discernible if muted federal voice in British constitutional discourse.[14] Though challenged by formidable critics, federalism has continued to find favour amongst those searching for a model of government that, to their mind, takes proper account of the territorial interest in British politics and government, yet who remain unconvinced by 'mere' devolution.[15] The idea was widely aired before the Great War as a solution to Irish nationalist demands for outright independence.[16] It failed, however, to take root in the official mind. Authorities such as Dicey maintained that a British federal polity would lack the essential qualities of mutuality, of a shared sense of national purpose and common identity, the necessary cement binding together any state, let alone a federal state, with aspirations to international stature. As Dicey saw it, for any federal polity to succeed, 'there must exist among the citizens of the confederacy a spirit of genuine loyalty to the Union. The "unitarian" feeling of the people must distinctly predominate over the sentiment in favour of "state rights".'[17]

Of course, political identity is an altogether more ambiguous matter than Dicey – and those who shared his unionist disposition – were prepared to contemplate. The political elite's predilection for the supposed virtues of integration, indeed their conviction that both material and strategic advantages are guaranteed only by a unitary state, was by then deeply lodged in the national mindset. This preference for integration has remained a firm conviction within the British body politic until more recent events challenged this orthodoxy. Even those more amenable to devolving power to territorial polities had, for the most part, resisted a constitutional arrangement likely to fatally compromise that most venerable British talisman, the fount of political virtue, the unwritten Constitution. Those who were charged with the responsibility of reviewing the Constitution avoided needless meddling with traditional verities. The most change that the reform-minded would countenance in this regard was a modicum of devolution. And for the foreseeable future this remains the prevailing opinion.

Devolution has long been the preferred choice of would-be reformers of the British state who, disconcerted by an unduly centralised political architecture, were nevertheless unconvinced by the need for root and branch constitutional surgery. Devolution is defined here as the transfer of some executive competences, a degree of legislative authority – usually with regard to enacting secondary legislation such as statutory instruments – from a higher (national) to intermediate, territorially based political authorities. This horizontal transfer of political authority is not commensurate, however, with the vertical sharing of sovereignty, the *sine qua non* of federalism. In federal polities, the constitution requires divided governance, a formal sharing though not necessarily an equal division of authority between the central (federal) polity and the constituent territorial polities.

The issue was apparently settled, at least as far as the centre was concerned, but it was by no means resolved in the constituent territorial parts of the Union. Indeed, the discourse on the British Constitution ever since the 1707 Act of Union reveals persistent tension between competing ideas about the appropriate architecture of nation-statehood.[18] Problematic national identity, the challenge of managing a plural polity, has been an enduring theme of the British project.[19] It has always been acknowledged that the historical particularities of the United

Kingdom's constituent nationalities require special consideration for their effective political management.[20]

Lord Acton was one Victorian constitutional eminence who did address this issue, prescribing a necessary moral equivalence between those 'different nations [residing] under the same sovereignty'. Acton fully identified the delicacy of the task of ensuring a constitutional balance when he acknowledged that unresponsive unionism equated not with national integration but rather with overbearing centralisation. This 'proper balance', as he saw it, precluded 'the servility which flourishes under the shadow of a single authority, by balancing interests [and] multiplying associations'. Liberty, he maintained, invariably 'provokes diversity, and diversity preserves liberty', so that 'the combination of different nations in one state is as necessary a condition of civilized life as the combination of men in society'.[21] The elusive trick, however, is to enact this liberal doctrine in the fabric of the state.

The architects of the union state did make some special provisions for reflecting its historical diversities. Gladstone went further than most English statesmen in attempting to reconcile awareness of what he called 'local patriotism' within the broad framework of a United Kingdom.[22] Nevertheless, his patronising outlook promised tolerance of persistent territorial differences, though countenanced only within an overarching British framework, and one primarily underpinned by presumptive English cultural hegemony.[23]

The norm here was assimilation rather than the equivalence and thence the mutual reconciliation of different territorial cultures.[24] Even this nominally pluralist outlook did not match the prevailing mood amongst the British political elite. More influential by far was A.V. Dicey's summary dismissal of cultural diversity as a basis for efficient government on the grounds that it undermined parliamentary sovereignty, deprived 'English' institutions and 'weakened the Executive'.[25] This self-regarding account of British history both set the standard for, and indeed became the official narrative of those whose responsibility was the management of national affairs.

DEVOLUTION: AN OVERVIEW

Current devolution represents a significant shift in these historical arrangements. The key organising principle of government and politics from the time the union state was established by the Act of Union with Scotland in 1707 was the supremacy of the parliament at Westminster. A precept aptly described by one leading authority as 'perhaps our only constitutional doctrine'.[26] The consequences of this classic constitutional nostrum, for both the conduct of government and the practice of politics, should not be underestimated – either as a general referent for British political culture, or in more directly political or legal terms. Demands for devolving power from the centre, whether vertically in the form of territorial government, or horizontally as a formal separation of powers between the principal functionaries of the state, seemed until quite recently to be an unwelcome, indeed an unnatural, intrusion on the natural political order. The political establishment – the principal political parties, leading constitutional authorities – and a consensus of academic commentators broadly endorsed this judgement, as did public opinion in the United Kingdom's constituent nations.

As such, devolution was resisted in the development of the British polity by a political elite reluctant to tamper with what they, for the most part, regarded as sacrosanct, the natural because national political order. Opposition to radical constitutional change was sustained not only by habit, by base prejudice, but also by more pragmatic considerations.[27] As a system of government, the Union seemed to work, and to work well. Or at least it did for those whose opinions counted most in national affairs. In this influential constitutional narrative the enduring stability of the British polity, in marked contrast to more turbulent continental politics, was proof positive of a uniquely successful formula for national governance.

These very issues were deliberated at a Speaker's Conference in 1919 whose members were drawn from both Houses of Parliament. The interim settlement of the Irish question took some of the urgency out of the deliberations about devolution, although the Conference did review some key matters relating to home rule in the other parts of the United Kingdom, for instance: territorial arrangements, judicial relations and the competences and fiscal powers of the respective authorities. A decision was reached, however, not to sub-divide England into regional authorities so as to ensure a more equitable balance between the respective territorial polities. There was debate, too, about the authority base for the prospective territorial authorities. The federalist case for their direct election (and therefore for their augmented authority) was lost in the face of an overwhelming preference to avoid undermining the supremacy of Westminster. This was the enduring legacy of these formal deliberations.

The current reform of the state has revisited these issues, and in light of the legacies reviewed above they represent a significant shift in both the architecture and the normative underpinning of the British state. Devolution is an arrangement that, for the most part, is contrary to the conventions and procedures that have shaped the normative discourse and actual practice of British government and politics. It is a remarkable gauge of how far the case for devolution – and for that matter for democracy per se – has recently gained political momentum that few contemporary advocates of constitutional change now seriously question that sub-national governance should draw legitimacy from directly elected territorial assemblies.[28]

This remarkable shift in the terms of the political debate about the structure and modalities of contemporary British government and politics is the central theme of this book. The contributions deal with important substantive aspects of what is a complex and protracted process of political as much as formal constitutional change. In sum, the various authors chart the origins of the union state, map subsequent developments in its relations with the constituent nations and identify the special character of the reformed British polity. A principal theme of this study is to review the emergence and to evaluate the success of political movements whose primary objective has been to challenge and to reform the established framework of the British state. This political architecture was installed during the protracted period of nation building, and formally confirmed by the Acts of Union with Scotland and Ireland in 1707 and 1800, respectively. A second principal objective of this enquiry is to examine and evaluate the detailed consequences for British government and politics of the recent constitutional reforms relating to devolution enacted since 1998.

Each of the contributors to this book examines a particular aspect of the historical process whereby powers and competences previously located in government institutions and political and policy-making procedures at the centre of the union state are devolved to new political institutions in its composite territorial polities. The historical processes that brought about the union state, and the contemporary pressures that have more recently begun to reverse the long-standing centralisation of power, are reviewed in Part One 'A kingdom united'. In Chapter 1, Michael O'Neill examines the historical foundations, the making of the United Kingdom from its constituent and once-sovereign polities. The Union composed of distinct and competing nationalities was always a contested project. The clamour from sub-national political forces to unravel the project, or at least to see enacted constitutional reforms that would permit a significant degree of territorial autonomy or home rule, has accompanied the process of building a unitary British state from the outset. The development and the impact on British politics of this challenge to the logics and norms of central power are reviewed by the same writer in Chapter 2.

The recent and insistent demand for devolution, and the grudging, or at least ambivalent, response to it by the political elite, has significantly transformed British government and politics. The principal focus of discussion in Part Two, 'Re-imagining Britain: the politics of identity', is the impact on political identity in the Union of the current devolution of power to territorial polities in Scotland, Wales and Northern Ireland. Devolution is a considered response to insistent demands from the territorial periphery for rethinking and reassessing traditional perceptions of political identity in the United Kingdom. The gradual process of politicising territorial identity is reviewed by O'Neill in Chapter 3. These developments have prompted a significant revision of the meaning of political and even of cultural identity in these islands, and they may yet have unforeseen consequences for the future practice of British government and politics. Contributors here review the particularities of these identity shifts and appraise their political expressions. In Chapter 4, Antonia Dodds and David Seawright discuss the phenomenon of Scottish nationalism, and, in particular, its principal political expression, the Scottish National Party (SNP). James Hunter in Chapter 5 assesses the contribution of Welsh nationalism through its political agency Plaid Cymru to re-imagining the British state. The process of rethinking centre–periphery relations was begun not in mainland Britain but in Ireland. Rick Wilford in Chapter 6 discusses how events there continue to contribute to the process of reforming the architecture of the British state.

Devolution has major consequences for the British state, for its government, its political institutions and procedures, its policy processes, and not least for its political culture. The consequences of challenges here to familiar procedures and mindsets are discussed in Part Three, 'Reforming the British state'. The reforms proposed and implemented in 1998 by the incoming Labour government represent a watershed in constitutional affairs in Britain. The origins and implications of these reforms are reviewed by O'Neill in Chapter 7. In Chapter 8, David Baker assesses the repercussions of devolution for the British political parties. In Chapter 9, Janice McMillan and Andrew Massey discuss the impact of devolution on the procedures of central government, especially its effect on the conduct both of cabinet government and of business at Westminster.

To an extent, devolution is a response to rising demands by political interests on the geographical periphery of the British polity for a meaningful measure of self-determination. The success of these demands, or even the very fact that they are now part of the political future, is bound to resonate with a majority of English public opinion. In Chapter 10, Christopher Stevens reviews efforts to balance territorial devolution on the margins with a compensating regional government in England. Of course, the momentum for constitutional reform is by no means confined to these islands. Exogenous factors have played an important part in bringing about changes and continue to do so. The extent to which British membership of the European Union has facilitated, or for that matter hindered, the propensity of Britons to alter their concept of statehood is examined by Janet Mather in Chapter 11.

Part Four, 'Reflecting on constitutional change', reviews the overall impact of devolution on the British state. In Chapter 12, Eberhard Bort assesses the record, to date, of the newly devolved institutions in Scotland and Wales. Michael Keating in Chapter 13 looks beyond current reforms and reflects on the prospects for a fully federal polity in Britain. In Chapter 14, Michael O'Neill identifies some of the outstanding problems of the devolution reforms, notably the responses of the 'significant others' in England, and discusses the impact of the present reforms on relations with the European Union. In the concluding chapter, the same writer reviews the critical challenges facing those whose task it is to steer the British state through the choppy and unpredictable waters of the new century. Of particular significance for the future of the British state is the somewhat bewildered, even disappointed reaction of opinion in England to the rise of territorial identity in the other nations. Devolution is both a response to, and an accelerant of, changes already under way in the cultural fabric of British politics.

The cement of Britishness that underpinned the project and which confirmed it in the affections of its constituent peoples over the duration has been loosened by events in the latter decades of the last century. This is a challenge, an opportunity to re-imagine the British project as much as it is a threat to the continuity of the state. The question of identity, or rather of managing multiple identities, is an important enterprise for the future stability of the British polity. It is a task whose outcome may well, over time, bring forth even more radical constitutional reform, perhaps even a quasi-federal constitutional order. The impetus behind recent reforms is by no means confined to domestic British factors. The singular changes that have begun to alter the once-familiar constitutional architecture of the British state are in some measure a response to more ubiquitous international trends. They are a cultural reaction, an attempt to adapt once securely embedded national identities and the nation states that nurtured them in Europe to the dynamic forces of regional integration and beyond that, to the insidious challenges of fast-accelerating globalisation.

NOTES

1. G. Aylmer, The Peculiarities of the British State, *Journal of Historical Sociology* 3 (1990)
2. P. Gartside and M. Hibbert (eds), *British Regionalism 1900–2000* (1989)
3. L.J. Sharpe, The United Kingdom: The Disjointed Meso, in L.J. Sharpe (ed.), *The Rise of Meso Government in Europe* (1993)
4. B. Bradshaw and P. Roberts (eds), *Consciousness and Identity: The Making of Britain, 1533–1707* (1998)
5. W. Blackstone, *Commentaries on the Laws of England* (1870 edition. Book One, chapter 2) p.160
6. V. Bogdanor, *Devolution in the United Kingdom* (2001) p.18
7. J. Bulpitt, *Territory and Power in the UK: An Interpretation* (1983)
8. A.H. Birch, *Nationalism and National Integration* (1989)
9. J. Bradbury, Introduction, in J. Bradbury and J. Mawson (eds), *British Regionalism and Devolution: The Challenge of State Reform and European Integration* (1997)
10. S. Rokkan and D. Urwin, Introduction: Centres and Peripheries in Western Europe, in S. Rokkan and D. Urwin (eds), *The Politics of Territorial Identity. Studies in European Regionalism* (1982)
11. A.V. Dicey, Parliamentary Sovereignty and Federalism, in *Lectures Introductory to the Study of the Law and the Constitution* (2nd edition 1886) pp.128–30
12. A.V. Dicey, Home Rule from an English Point of View, *Contemporary Review* 42 (1882)
13. J. Kendle, The Round Table Movement and 'Home Rule All Round', *Historical Journal* 11 (1968) p.338
14. J. Kendle, *Federal Britain* (1997)
15. J. Pinder, The Federal Idea and the British Liberal Tradition, in A. Bosca (ed.), *The Federal Idea. Vol. 1: The History of Federalism from Enlightenment to 1945* (1991)
16. D. Thornley, *Isaac Butt and Home Rule* (1964) pp.98–9; J. Kendle, *Ireland and the Federal Solution: The Debate over the United Kingdom Constitution, 1870–1921* (1989) ch. 1
17. A.V. Dicey, *England's Case against Home Rule* (1973 Richmond edition) p.178
18. M. Steed, The Core–Periphery Dimension of British Politics, *Political Geography* 5 (1986)
19. D. Urwin, Territorial Structures and Political Developments in the UK, in S. Rokkan and D. Urwin, op. cit. (1982)
20. V. Bogdanor, *Devolution* (1979)
21. Lord Acton, Nationality, in *The History of Freedom and Other Essays* (1909 edition)

22. V. Bogdanor, op. cit. (1979) p.13
23. C. Harvie, Gladstonianism, the Provinces, and Popular Political Culture, in R. Bellamy (ed.), *Victorian Liberalism* (1990)
24. J. Mitchell, Unionism, Assimilation and the Conservatives, in J. Lovenduski and J. Stanyer (eds), *Contemporary Political Studies* (1995)
25. A.V. Dicey, op. cit. (1882)
26. V. Bogdanor, op. cit. (2001) p.1
27. L. Sharpe, op. cit. (1993) p.290
28. See O. Edwards, Who Invented Devolution?, in L. Paterson and D. McCrone (eds), *The Scottish Government Yearbook 1992* (Unit for the Study of Government in Scotland, 1992)

Part One

A KINGDOM UNITED

1 State building and national integration in Britain

Michael O'Neill

FOUNDATIONS

The United Kingdom was not the political outcome of a grand political design to unite the peoples of the British Isles within a common realm. Rather, the British State was a contingent outcome of a cumulative process of political integration over centuries, primarily, though not exclusively, determined by English interests and statecraft. This was not hegemonic statecraft, the plain acknowledgement of superior English power used to justify outright conquest and military subjugation; it was expressed instead through the medium of diplomatic negotiation and embedded in bargains struck between the centre and territorial elites for mutual advantage. Territorial elites were assimilated within the national project, or at least compensated with state patronage and other opportunities for personal preferment. This process of national integration was instigated and implemented without reference to the common people. As such, it was hardly 'the product of a compact, drafted and signed by its constituents', but was rather 'an agglomeration created by the expansion and contraction of territorial power in the course of a thousand years'.[1]

England was the dominant country of the British Isles following the Norman Conquest in 1066, unifying the former Saxon and Viking realms under a system of sound administration, a feudal polity ruled by a ruthless military caste. The process of state building enacted by England's political elite and broadly supported by their territorial counterparts gradually brought under English stewardship the government of the four nations who inhabit the islands of Great Britain and Ireland, promoting England's strategic and economic interests within and beyond the British Isles.[2] The abiding concern of the English state after 1066 was to consolidate territorial security by neutralising the threats from its Celtic purlieus, preferably by bringing these turbulent neighbours under England's indirect influence or direct control. A key motivation here was to safeguard the interests of the culturally dominant and most populous British nation against what the political elite regarded as insidious threats from England's geographic hinterland, threatening political instability and, in later centuries, economic uncertainty. Security was a paramount concern, whether resisting incursions across England's land borders or deterring adjacent territories, especially Ireland, from becoming forward bases for invasion by other European powers.

Political integration was fuelled by dynastic ambition and sustained by a sense of ethnic superiority. It manifested, in turn, the cultural confidence that comes from military ascendancy and unchallenged economic dominance. Economics as much as realpolitik played a part in the making of the United Kingdom. Nor was the process of political integration a wholly one-sided affair, though it certainly privileged English interests above those of the others. The advantages accruing to vested interests in the smaller countries from participating in a common British market and monetary system grew in their appeal as a worldwide economy emerged. Attractive, too, were the opportunities available to non-English political and commercial elites from participating in the expansive English empire, and, for that matter, from having access to both the prestige and the material benefices of lucrative patronage in a larger, more powerful state.

In short, greed and hubris reciprocated by fear and resentment, and sustained by resigned acceptance of political realities, all played a far greater part in forging the union of British nations than any ethereal concern to establish a common-wealth embodying the highest political ideals. Even the more pragmatic objective of reconciling ancient enmities within an overarching British identity was not the principal objective of British political integration. The union state was, and it has remained, a project conferring much the greater advantage on its principal con-stituent. Political and material self-interest was discernible in the political culture of unionism. There was an implied assumption, powerfully disseminated by the usual agents of political socialisation, both official and informal, during the for-mative years of the Union, that the new and overarching British identity mani-fested, in reality, predominantly English cultural values and norms supposedly reflecting that nation's political virtues.

Self-interest, not least amongst the English elite, was a powerful incentive for integration and added strong cement to the Union. But this pragmatic and essen-tially uneven bargain cultivated, as we shall see below, residual resentments. These have persisted ever since, in time sowing seeds of discord that contributed to the Union's unravelling, though these seeds would be a long time germinating. Pique amongst territorial interests over assumed English dominance within the Union sustained the political challenge to the central authorities, giving significant momentum to home rule movements during succeeding centuries in every terri-torial constituent except England. The recent revival of territorial nationalism is merely the latest expression of residual antipathy to the political and cultural bargains that underpinned the union state from the outset.

The challenge to the union state for wholesale re-imagination of the Union began in Ireland during the latter part of the nineteenth century. The contempo-rary home rule movement is again, in large measure, merely the continuance of this visceral antipathy on the territorial margins of British society to the idea of English ascendancy over the Union. In order to understand how this renaissance in territorial identity came to pose a serious challenge to the cultural integrity and the institutional structure of the British state, we must examine the historical roots of territorial identity in these islands. For the principal causes of recent political turbulence lie in the foundations and the dynamics, in the political character, and the structural interactions of the constituent parts of the Union over some three centuries, and indeed in the cultural make-up of the union state.

CONSTITUENTS

England

The Anglo-French aristocracy consolidated England's diverse territorial polities and ethnic groups into a nascent 'English' state after the Norman Conquest of 1066.[3] The defeated Anglo-Saxon realms and the Viking sphere of influence were subsumed within a feudal state dominated by a foreign military caste.[4] There is no academic consensus about precisely when this state ceased to be an alien construct and became repatriated as 'England', eventually becoming the fount of native patriotism. By the thirteenth century, a manifest sense of Englishness was already expressed in a vernacular native language, and with it a growing sense of popular cultural identity took firm hold.[5] An island kingdom surrounded by 'less happy breeds' became rooted in the popular imagination, shaping the cultural fabric of national life.[6]

More significant for ensuring turbulent relations with the other British nations was the fact that England's demographic supremacy and expansive commercial influence exerted a powerful centripetal pull. In time, robust military action and conquest brought about the incorporation of these neighbouring polities, if not quite their acquiescent accommodation within the powerful English state. Cultural assimilation facilitated political integration and by degrees 'the idea of Englishness . . . came to be an integrating one, binding the other parts of the United Kingdom to the centre'. This metropolitan pull impacted, too, on the English regions in as much as 'the heart of England lay in London and the south-east and it is there that power was centralized. England came to be ruled by a strong central government which left little room for provincial loyalties'.[7] The social and cultural consequences of powerful metropolitan influence were quite apparent in the political relations of the islands even before formal changes in political arrangements – colonisation in Ireland, the annexation of Wales, a negotiated union of the two crowns[8] and the subsequent Act of Union with Scotland – established the union state.[9]

The sequence of changes in the political relations between England and the other British nations merely confirmed that country's dominant position, the primacy of English interests, in the islands. Yet this cumulative assimilation in no way obliterated primordial political identity. Indeed, the very asymmetry of intra-British relations sustained a continuing sense of abiding territorial differences. The idea that the smaller British nations were each culturally distinctive in their own right was, in part, a predictable response to English political hegemony and commercial dominance. This mindset both encouraged, and to an extent legitimised, the efforts of territorial opinion formers and political elites to foster a sense of sub-British identity, of belonging to distinctive national communities who defined themselves against the 'significant other' of England. And although Celtic historians and the ideologists of territorial nationalism might contest the point, as sociologists have confirmed, all political identity is in some measure a constructed project – part of a reflexive process of inventing an 'imagined community' rooted in cultural distinctiveness. Accordingly, Celtic nationalism in Britain, manifested as a persistent challenge to the central locus of power in the British state, has, in no small measure, been a response to English hegemony.

Wales

Wales was a principality but never an independent state in the conventional meaning of that term. The English Crown appropriated land there in the thirteenth century and the Principality was annexed by Edward I after the defeat in 1283 of Llewelyn, the last Welsh prince. The process of integrating Wales into the English state was, nevertheless, a protracted one. The vestiges of independent legal, administrative and educational systems were incorporated into the fabric of English public administration only after the accession to the English throne of the native Welsh Tudor dynasty in 1485. It was only during the reign of Henry VIII that this union was formalised. Acts passed by the English Parliament proclaimed Wales to be already 'incorporated, united and annexed to the realm of England' (1536) and thereby permitted Welsh Members to sit at Westminster (1543). The incorporation of 'the Dominion' of Wales into the English state was a political fact long before it was formally acknowledged by the terms of the Wales and Berwick Act (1746).[10]

One notable consequence, indeed a significant vehicle for this process of political annexation and administrative assimilation, was the adoption of English as the official language. The decision of Elizabeth I to permit the translation of religious texts into the vernacular was intended to reinforce the popular appeal of the Protestant faith. But it ensured, too, that language thereafter was the defining essence of residual Welsh identity. The role of language as a conspicuous cultural referent in religious, political and judicial affairs in Wales after so much else that was culturally conspicuous had been lost, ensured that a discernible sense of Welsh national identity survived the incorporation of Wales into the English state. Moreover, political integration took place in a way that deliberately avoided giving offence to territorial sensibilities. For it was characteristic of the developing English state 'to insist upon political unity but to rely upon local interlocutors and the mechanism of indirect rule for the administration of the peripheries'.[11] Local administration and the operation of the justice system thus remained the preserve of territorial dignitaries.

At the same time, the lack of those autonomous national institutions preserved in Scotland after the Act of Union, and the absence, too, of a recent folk memory of independent statehood ensured a different experience of territorial nationality in Wales from that of its Celtic neighbour. It resisted claiming outright independence, or even a significant degree of political autonomy. When Welsh nationalism did eventually emerge as a political movement, it took a different form, manifested in different priorities and preferences, from territorial nationalism in Ireland and Scotland. Welsh nationalism was less viscerally hostile to the political connection with England and even to the underlying idea of Englishness. It was motivated neither by any wish 'to break the British connection; nor, as in Scotland, by a desire to refashion government so as to guarantee her distinctive institutions'. As such, 'Welsh nationalism was concerned less with political independence than with the defence and preservation of a culture and a way of life which seemed under threat'.[12]

In so far as territorial nationalism in Wales had any political resonance, it was far more concerned to secure an equitable share of public goods within the British political context than with securing home rule.[13] The movement gave priority to improving the representation of Welsh interests in the councils of the British state and empire rather than seeking severance of that historical connection.[14] In the view of one leading historian of these events, 'The ideal of Wales was to be recognized as a part of the British political and social structure: the ideal of Ireland was to be severed from it. The object of the one was equality: the aim of the other was exclusion'.[15]

In so far as a residual sense of Welsh national identity survived early political annexation and cultural assimilation by its powerful neighbour, it drew inspiration from still potent cultural symbols. Yet language and distinctive religious affiliation did confirm an abiding sense of a territorial rather than a separate political identity. To the extent that territorial identity here did acquire distinctly nationalist overtones, this was expressed as commitment to non-conformist religious principles: a set of values that, in as much as they had political purchase, were closely associated with the non-metropolitan radicalism of the Welsh Liberal Party, a movement whose ideological preferences favoured land reform and which opposed the privileged position of what adherents regarded as an obtruding established Church. Both of these issues cut across rather than consolidated an exclusive or unambiguous sense of Welsh identity.[16]

The privileged position of the established Church in Welsh life and society was a cause of much resentment in territorial politics throughout the nineteenth century. Nevertheless, the failure of successive Liberal governments to carry legislation to disestablish the Church never remotely mobilised those acutely nationalist sentiments that had resulted from the same party's failure to deliver Irish home rule. There was a marked absence here of the resentment against an alien religion imposed by foreigners – whether Episcopalian prelates foisted by colonial ascendancy or Low Church Presbyterianism imposed by militant plantations – that had nurtured Irish political identity, stimulating in the long run an uncompromising demand for outright separation. Denominational affiliation never acquired anything like the political salience here that it did in Ireland. Rather, religious differences in Wales cut across territorial identity, reducing the issue's political salience. Religious affiliation was much more a cleavage within and between the native population than it was a cultural fault-line demarcating Welsh 'natives' and English 'foreigners'. Consequently, popular and widespread support for home rule in Wales contributed little to the politically potent melding of the religious and national cleavages that sharpened national identity in Ireland.

Over time, national identity did acquire a degree of political salience, but only of modest proportions. Schemes were periodically presented for establishing wholly national institutions. But these were much more administrative than political arrangements. A notable example was the proposal to replace the Local Government Board, the Board of Guardians, Commissioners for Works, and the Welsh Charity Commissioners with a composite Welsh national body. In part, this reform was a response to national sensibilities, but equally one influenced by the contemporary concern with administrative efficiency and thrift. And even this modest reform proposal foundered in the face of competing ideas about Welshness, a conflict rooted as much in cultural differences as in politics per se. Deadlock following on from abiding disagreement about the levels of representation of the respective constituencies, as between the English-speaking and Welsh-speaking counties, ensured the scheme's demise.

There was further if modest success utilising administrative reform to promote national consciousness, notably in public education policy. County councils in Wales were the first in Britain permitted to establish local education authorities (in 1889). The University of Wales was likewise granted a charter in 1893 and a central Welsh Examination Board was empowered in 1896 to supervise the conduct of examinations.[17] Further reforms enabled a Welsh Department of the Board of Education to pursue a more coherent policy for recognition of the Welsh language and literature, both in regard to teacher training and for managing school curricula.

The onset of the collectivist state in the early years of the twentieth century enhanced the by now modest scope for administrative devolution. In common with Ireland and Scotland, Wales acquired (in 1911) a national commission for administering the new National Insurance scheme. In line with developments in Scotland, an Agricultural Commissioner for Wales was appointed (1912), followed by the establishment of a Welsh office of the Board of Agriculture and Fisheries (1919).

The grassroots response to these limited reforms in government confirmed an altogether more temperate nationalist politics. At the very moment when the Union was under challenge from militant and increasingly violent nationalism in Ireland committed at the very minimum to a meaningful degree of home rule in domestic affairs, nationalism in Wales had acquired cultural rather than political resonance. Cymru Fydd (Wales of the Future), a movement committed to advancing Welsh culture, was formed in 1866. And though in the latter decades of the nineteenth century this movement did foster the idea of national identity, its political success was constrained by a marked lack of public support. Rather than embracing the Irish demand for outright independence, Cymru Fydd was content to adopt a low-key approach, preferring the limited objectives of political inclusion and parity with England already adopted by the nascent Scottish nationalist movement. The movement's failure to impose even this modest claim on the agenda of Welsh politics contributed to its eventual demise in 1896.

In marked contrast to the predominantly agrarian politics of Irish nationalism, radical politics on the mainland of Britain was driven by economic modernisation. The acceleration of industrialisation in the late nineteenth century confirmed the prevalence, both in Wales and in Scotland, of class-based rather than territorial politics. Class issues rather than grievances rooted in a radicalised sense of territorial identity became the principal fount of rising political discontent – what was widely perceived on the geographical margins of British society as metropolitan neglect of the economic costs and social consequences of advanced capitalism. The indifference of the national political elite to social deprivation was more readily explained as a structural consequence of the prevailing model of political economy than as the consequence of internal colonialism or territorial subjugation. The 'evils' of industrialisation, viewed through this ideological lens, were not so much caused by English indifference to territorial grievances – and thus to be ameliorated by reactionary or insular nationalism – but rather were seen as ubiquitous social evils. This radical narrative identified injustices to be righted only by implementing the universal moral imperatives of social reform delivered through the enlightened medium of a redistributive socialist society. This shift in ideological priorities away from a party with once-firm social roots in Celtic Britain was a serious blow to the cause of home rule in Wales.[18]

The rise of a new radical movement on the left merely accelerated the long decline of Welsh Liberalism – a movement whose traditional political causes (notably temperance, Church disestablishment and land reform) grew increasingly remote from the germane radical agenda of the emergent Labour movement.[19] This shift in the centre of gravity of national politics contributed much to diminishing the political salience of a territorial cleavage. Labour's provincial origins in late Victorian Britain made it particularly receptive to ideas about democratic devolution from the centre, but supportive too of the old Liberal cause of territorial home rule 'all round'. There was, nevertheless, scant popular support amongst Labour's new social base, either in Wales or in Scotland, for this particular reform option.

The settlement in Ireland in 1920–21 had removed the principal driver for home rule in British politics. In the period after the Great War, class-based industrial politics was the principal cleavage shaping the pattern of party competition, whether at the territorial or the national level of politics. One consequence of this shift was that Labour relinquished its early commitment to devolution, preferring the centralisation of power and national planning as more reliable levers for reversing structural economic decline and redistributing wealth. At a time when Labour's existence as a national party was still precarious, pragmatic considerations – finding a strategy for political survival as much as indulging ideological revision – contributed to refocusing the party's policy priorities. Labour's reliance for maintaining its national base on returning MPs for Welsh and Scottish constituencies did much to sustain the movement's preference for national rather than for an exclusively territorial politics.

Central government made further concessions to territorial interests, more in response to territorial fealty, however, than surrendering to the nationalists' clamour for autonomy. A Welsh advisory council was instituted in 1948 and a Welsh Grand Committee to debate specific Welsh concerns followed, though only in 1960, acquiring full standing committee status in 1969. A Welsh Affairs Select Committee was installed in 1979, albeit as a token, a pale substitute for the devolved assembly lost as a consequence of the 1979 referendum.[20]

Administrative decentralisation begun in the Edwardian era continued apace, establishing by the 1950s seventeen separate administrative units of national government departments. This process did not, however, 'reflect any overall plan of devolution [for] the process of decentralization was entirely pragmatic, and the extent of decentralization differed from department to department'.[21] Furthermore, the dilute quality of this administrative devolution was replicated in parliamentary arrangements, namely brief and infrequent Welsh parliamentary questions and the attenuated meetings of the Welsh Grand Committee. Both of these outcomes reflected the dearth of distinctively Welsh legislation.

Political reform was approached with even greater hesitancy. Overall direction of Welsh affairs, though hardly amounting to effectual coordination, became, after 1951, the nominal responsibility of the home secretary, who took the official title of first minister for Welsh affairs. The minister was formally accountable to Westminster for government policy in Wales and for the annual White Paper, though he lacked either executive powers or the administrative capability of a fully fledged department. After 1957 this superintendence role switched to the minister for housing and local government, who at least enjoyed the advantage over his predecessors of possessing executive competence for several aspects of Welsh affairs.

In response to territorial lobbying for parity with Scotland, the Labour government in 1964 finally fulfilled the pledge of Hugh Gaitskell, the party's previous leader, and upgraded the office of Welsh minister to full Cabinet rank, initially with modest powers.[22] There was by now a marked Welsh presence in central government's key policy committees. But in effect, the modest status of the Welsh Office in the Cabinet pecking order ensured scant influence in major policy battles *vis-à-vis* the big departmental players. Moreover, the absence of a Welsh system of law meant that the Welsh Office was unable to request dedicated Welsh legislation.

Scotland

The Scottish kingdom that emerged as a unitary state from internecine strife during the eighth century brought together under one crown warring tribes and ethnic groups. The proximity of a more populous and powerful neighbour to the south made for tense relations. England periodically exercised a degree of control over Scottish affairs though this provoked resistance and reassertion of Scottish independence. Following the Scots' victory at the Battle of Bannockburn in 1314, the Treaty of Northampton (1328) confirmed nominal independence, though increased trade and commerce accelerated the economic interdependence of the two kingdoms. The succession of the Scottish king, James VI, to the English throne on the death of Elizabeth I unified the two crowns (1603) under the title of Emperor of the whole island of Great Britain. Though not yet a united kingdom, formal unification was only a matter of time. The replacement of monarchical authority by parliamentary government, a process accelerated by the Bill of Rights in 1689, served to confirm uneasy relations. For the most part, Scottish opinion resisted the idea of being ruled by an institution over which it had no direct influence, giving momentum to the idea of a union of the parliaments.[23]

The Act of Union negotiated in 1707 established a permanent union between the two states, with common succession to the unified crown and a single sovereign parliament at Westminster, previously the seat of the English Parliament.[24] In effect, Scotland was incorporated into the English state, hardly a reciprocal bargain. This arrangement was the subject of lively contemporary debate,[25] a discourse continued by scholars and political interests alike over succeeding centuries. The Union was problematical from the start, provoking native resistance and even riotous behaviour. The stationing of English dragoons on the border at Berwick as the Scots Parliament voted (by 109 to 69) to ratify the terms of the Union confirmed not only English unease at the native reception of the Union, but also clear determination, on grounds of national interests, to see it enacted.

The nationalist narrative has made much of this implied threat to territorial integrity and to native interests alike. A more radical narrative, a mix of partisan myth and political expectancy, prefers to see the Union as outright betrayal by a venal native elite, anticipating that the inequitable union bargain might one day be reversed. The native elite is identified by this narrative as one whose vanity and ambition were cultivated, manipulated by imperialist interests intent on absorbing Scotland within a political union for its own selfish ends. Where, in these circumstances, was the constitutional surety for protecting Scottish interests in a parliament dominated by the English political elite? Certainly, there were no constitutional guarantees for the territorial polities in what was merely a treaty arrangement, and indeed, every Article of the Treaty has subsequently been amended, though 'no court has ever struck down legislation emanating from Westminster on the grounds that it breached the Treaty'.[26] As one constitutional expert has observed:

> How, then, could the Scots have held with any confidence that the provisions of the Treaty would be respected by a parliament in which Scots members would be but a small minority? It remains a puzzle how the Scots could believe that such words as 'for ever' and 'in all time' could constrain a sovereign parliament. While from time to time, Scottish judges and commentators have declared that the Treaty is a form of fundamental law, constraining the British parliament, that argument has never been accepted by the courts.[27]

These concerns notwithstanding, the Union was hardly a blind bargain. Nor was it a unilateral arrangement and hardly naked conquest by the stronger partner. The incentive offered to the native political elite – a 'gift' of some £398,085. 10s. otherwise known as 'the equivalent', or compensation for the loss of native customs and excise duties – was widely condemned as bribery. This contemporary account made much of the supposed betrayal by a native landed elite 'bought and sold for English gold'. In fact, many ordinary Scots accepted the Union as a necessary safeguard against the restoration of the Catholic Jacobite monarchy. More favourable accounts of the union bargain emphasised instead a mutual arrangement contracted between equal partners in a joint national enterprise. In this historical narrative the Union represents an exercise in nation state building, a shared endeavour, with mutual opportunities for trade and employment, and, as such, giving rise to common national interests such as better security and enhanced political status in an emergent international order.[28]

The Union opened up commercial opportunities for a native mercantilist class within an expanding British empire as well as employment for the common people. The ignoble collapse of the Scottish colonial project – the Darien scheme – gave added incentive to Scots merchants and traders to seek commercial outlets within England's domains overseas.[29] Public preferment and economic advantage accrued to the elite of a peripheral society, and to a less developed economy through participation in a powerful state, a larger market and an internationally influential monetary and financial system.[30]

These commercial prospects were apparent from the outset, but there were marked differences of outlook on each side. As one commentator has observed: 'While the English came to regard the arrangement as permanent, the Scots continued to see it as conditional upon their getting a good fiscal return on the loss of their sovereignty'.[31] The economic foundations of the Union have remained critical to its success throughout, and especially so for the poorer territorial relations. Once these material benefits grew less, as they did in the twilight years of post-imperial and industrial decline in the latter decades of the twentieth century, popular attachment to the Union amongst the territorial nations declined.

Differences of outlook were expressed in the formal political language used by all sides of this arrangement. English commentaries referred to the 'Act' of Union, whereas Scots' rhetoric preferred the co-equal and provisional terms of a 'Treaty' of Union. At the outset, the Union was for Scots a conditional arrangement whose future depended on receiving due consideration for national sensibilities. It was much less about incorporation, a takeover or even a merger of the smaller state within the larger one, than it was the launch of a distinctive union state.[32] The new constitutional arrangements did, nevertheless, realise a degree of territorial self-determination, and this has remained as an enduring facet of intra-British relations. Although the outcome of the Union was a unitary state, distinctive Scottish institutions did ensure some territorial autonomy.[33]

The evidence points, nevertheless, to one-sided relations. One historian of these events has concluded that, despite the convenient cover of legitimacy confirmed by a negotiated and freely undertaken contract between the two sides, the very fact that the integration process aligned the territorial political dynasties with the English crown ensured that the Union was *de facto* political takeover.[34] It amounted, in effect, to the incorporation of Scotland and Wales into a British state largely dominated by England in everything that matters with regard to national autonomy: politics, economics and the cultural referents of new nationhood.[35]

This asymmetrical bargain did keep alive the idea of future home rule, for it remained as a clear incentive to territorial interests to redefine relations with the British State to better political advantage. The idea of an alternative model of political integration, one that would ensure territorial autonomy but without jeopardising the material benefits of union, has figured in Scottish nationalist rhetoric from the outset.[36] In one famous early narrative of the Union, Fletcher of Saltoun lamented the lack of a 'federal' solution.[37] Although he meant by this term no more than a loose confederal arrangement between small regional centres, it expressed the widespread aspiration to resist English dominance, for maximising national autonomy. These radical ideas had little appeal for those on either side charged with the task of negotiating the Union. Mainstream political opinion north of the border was much less receptive to novel political arrangements regarding 'federalism' in much the same vein as their English counterparts, as merely a fad, a flawed design that would detract from the power available to the new state by weakening its constitutional fabric. Discounted as utopian by mainstream opinion, ideas about reasserting national autonomy did persist within the broad narrative of territorial politics.

In the meantime, the authors of the Act of Union accorded respect to native dignity by permitting autonomous institutions and abiding cultural preferences, sufficient at least to ensure territorial endorsement for the new State of Great Britain. In deference to a long history as an independent kingdom and to the fact of voluntary union of the two ancient crowns in 1603, Scotland's elite negotiated considerably more political autonomy within the British State than was enjoyed by the other sub-nations.[38] Scotland had, for instance, separate legal, local government and education systems, its own banknotes and national press, and its own established Church. A small nation, its geographically concentrated population, broadly common social values (notwithstanding abiding religious differences) and a public education system transmitting vernacular culture contributed to embedding the 'imagined community of fate' that sustains distinctive national identity.[39]

The key institution here was the Scottish Kirk. The Union Treaty was flanked by a separate measure recognising the supremacy of the Presbyterian Church in Scotland. This was a key concession by the English negotiators to Scottish sensibilities about national distinctiveness and cultural autonomy, and a judicious one without which the Treaty would not have ensued.[40] There was in these arrangements an implicit guarantee of autonomy in critical areas of national life. As one commentator has observed: if 'a settlement with England could preserve the Kirk together with other Scottish institutions, then the Scots might be able to co-exist with the English in a unitary state with a common parliament, whilst at the same time maintaining their national identity'.[41] The Treaty (Articles 18 and 19) likewise ensured that Scotland retained its own separate legal system, whilst ensuring a common market and monetary system (Articles 14–25). Even the loss of the national parliament was tempered somewhat by the fact that Scotland's parliament was a relatively new institution, by no means as central at that juncture to the idea of national identity as it subsequently became.

A distinctive Scottish dimension to British government was acknowledged in subsequent administrative changes. A Scottish Office and a secretary were instituted in 1885, a two-way channel of influence and communication representing Scotland at the heart of central government and London's voice north of the border. The secretary became an ex-officio member of the Cabinet in 1892 but only acquired full Cabinet rank in 1926, though demoted from that status during wartime.[42] Despite the Office's relocation from London to Edinburgh in 1939, the secretary acted more as London's viceroy than as Scotland's consul.[43] Although by no means responsible for every central government function, the Scottish Office came, by degrees, to exercise far-reaching competences over key aspects of public policy that in English governance were managed by several important departments, including health, police and judicial affairs, prisons and regional development.

Judicial autonomy required a separate passage of legislation pertaining solely to Scotland, with a Standing Scottish Grand Committee (1907) to steer it through Parliament. A Council of State for Scotland was added to this dedicated machinery during the Second World War, a response to Tom Johnson the then Scottish secretary, who raised the spectre of nationalism in order to enhance Scotland's voice at the centre.[44] The Council consisted of former secretaries and other territorial dignitaries, and was intended to boost the representation of Scotland's interests at the heart of British government. For the most part, however, the Council was poorly attended, largely ignored in the very councils whose deliberations it was designed to influence, and it was discontinued after the war. A Scottish Affairs Select Committee was subsequently affixed to these arrangements in 1979 as part of UK-wide administrative reforms, and rationalised by London, in response to nationalist stirrings, as proof-positive of the special 'Scottish dimension' of British government.

The public policy process gave special consideration to the 'Scottish perspective' through formal representation on relevant Cabinet policy committees. Westminster, too, made special arrangements for Scottish legislation. Bills designated by the Speaker as 'Scottish' bills were considered in one or other of the two Scottish standing committees composed exclusively of Scottish MPs.[45] The accelerated loss of its Scottish seats by the Conservative Party during the 1980s required that party, however, to nominate MPs representing English seats in order to meet its quota on the committee.

The Scottish Grand Committee consisted of Scotland's 72 MPs and was empowered to consider legislation at either the second or third reading stages, or at the report stage in the case of non-contentious bills, though it could not vote. Moreover, a minority of only ten members could block even the discussion of disputed matters. The Select Committee on Scottish Affairs performed effectively as a forum for policy scrutiny, reviewing Scottish Office expenditure, administrative matters and policy. However, none of these committees could pass legislation without the endorsement of the House as a whole.

One notable and adverse consequence of these special arrangements, as far as fostering empathy between the representatives of two countries was concerned, was to marginalise Scottish affairs in the overall conduct of British government, for this arrangement ensured the separation of 'Scottish legislation and administration from non-Scottish MPs most of whom are quite uninterested in it and expected not to interfere'. That said, 'the conventions of the Constitution were bound to limit the extent to which Scotland could be treated as a distinctive unit even within the framework of the union state'.[46]

The distribution of parliamentary seats, too, was favourable to the territorial nations, with Scotland proportionately over-represented (seats to population share) by some 20 per cent. Disbursements from public expenditure were likewise always higher per capita than those for England. In part, this was a response designed to counter accusations of exploitation, and with the post-1945 expansion of public sector and welfare expenditure this arrangement gave Scotland a 20 per cent per capita advantage.[47]

These special arrangements notwithstanding, there was little to show for even a proactive secretaryship promoting Scotland's special interests at the centre. The Johnson regime in the early 1940s did secure increased Treasury investment in Scottish industry and a symbolic victory by persuading the Treasury to prohibit English banks from charging their customers for exchanging Scottish banknotes. Scottish pique was somewhat assuaged too by the palpable economic benefits that accrued from centrally managed wartime production.

These concessions, such as they were, to distinctive territorial interests rooted in Scottish identity seemed to work. Scotland retained the sense, however notional, of being a separate if constituent part of the union state. Moreover, the arrangement appeared to pay off in as much as Scotland secured a higher disbursement from public expenditure than was justified on per capita grounds. This was by no means the complete picture. Even so, the Scottish secretary was hardly a senior figure in the Cabinet hierarchy. Moreover, he was bound by the norms of collegiality and constrained in his demands on the Exchequer by the presence of colleagues representing English interests, or otherwise concerned that the overarching national interest should have priority over narrow territorial interests.[48] The adoption in 1980 of the so-called Barnett formula to adjust public expenditure as between Scotland and England further reduced the Scottish secretary's leverage.

The case is often made that these special institutional arrangements were much less about meaningful territorial autonomy than they were an indicator of growing centralisation in the British State. They contributed little to ensuring accountable government, whether in Scotland or at the centre. The Scottish secretary was only occasionally resident in Edinburgh and whilst there had to attend to party political business as well as to ministerial affairs. As such, his control of administrative minutiae was limited, with responsibility for day-to-day policy implementation left to civil servants. The democracy deficit was further increased because effective supervision over departmental affairs by Westminster was constrained by a lax ministerial grip.[49]

More problematical still was the lack of effective scrutiny by the electorate over Scottish affairs. This mismatch between excessive centralisation and absence of effective leverage over Scottish legislation by its own elected representatives was noted by Lord Kilbrandon, chairman of the Royal Commission on the Constitution established by the Labour government of 1966–70. As Kilbrandon saw the situation: 'It would be hard throughout the familiar world to find a parallel for a country which had its own judicature and legal system, its own executive and administration, but no legislature, its laws being made within another and technically foreign jurisdiction, by an assembly in which it had only a small minority of members, but to which its executive was democratically responsible'.[50]

This situation was less problematical during most of the previous century. For one thing, the party system of Scotland and the fundamental social cleavage that underpinned it had closely mirrored English politics. For another, there was scant popular support for a nationalist movement committed to outright independence. Although two nationalist parties did emerge during the 1930s, merging as the Scottish National Party (SNP) in 1934, the movement's appeal was largely confined to the urban intellectual elite.[51] The impression of a centre–periphery cleavage did instil a radical temper into Scottish politics, but this was primarily expressed as adversarial class-based politics.

Nationalist politics in the form of a political movement capable of mass appeal only took root during the 1960s, a belated response to perceived neglect by the political centre. This mood was compounded by insecurities resulting from the post-1945 challenge to Britain's Great Power status and declining imperial grandeur, reflecting too a much-reduced sense of economic security in a mutable postwar world. Old certainties dissolved, replaced in the United Kingdom's constituent territorial polities by a rising sense of marginality. Declining economic prospects, formerly the solid foundation of the union state bargain, led by degrees to widespread misgivings about the unduly centralised architecture of the state. This, in turn, provided the catalyst for rethinking a Union previously questioned but never seriously challenged by territorial public opinion for two centuries and more, and with dramatic consequences for British politics.[52]

The Conservative Party was the main political casualty of these structural shifts and the cultural changes that accompanied them. Since Labour's emergence as a significant electoral force after 1918 the political balance in the Union had tended to be that of Conservative dominance in English seats, but with Labour polling much better in Scotland – and for that matter in Wales too. Since the 1959 general election, Labour had secured the largest share of Scottish seats, making Conservative governments even more reticent about passing on important legislation to the Scottish committees with their preponderance of Scottish Labour MPs. The Conservatives' steady loss of their Scottish base merely increased this reticence, adding to this democratic deficit. Throughout long periods of Conservative government, Scottish secretaries executed and administered policy for a country whose electorate rejected those policies at successive general elections. The electoral imbalance, and the legitimacy shortfall that was its most serious consequence, worsened during the latter years of the twentieth century, reaching its nadir in the 1997 general election when the Conservatives lost their remaining Scottish seats.

The combination of political change and the seemingly inexorable tendency of the British State to centralise its government in London – though without carrying quite the same conviction with territorial public opinion about the material payoff – threatened the pragmatic bargain on which the union state was founded. And it eroded, too, that commonality of sentiment, those elective affinities that had sustained this arrangement over the duration. Of course, the terms of the founding bargain had altered irrevocably. Acknowledgement of a distinctive Scottish interest manifested by quite separate arrangements for the practice of the law and the rites of the Church was sustainable, more or less, in an age of limited government and the 'night watchman' state. The onset of collectivism in public policy, with expansive public administration and an elaborate welfare system for meeting growing public preferences for social protection and economic security, required altogether new competences, a step increase in the role of the state. This, in turn, brought about policy benchmarking and minimal national norms to ensure uniform provision of public goods throughout the United Kingdom. In the circumstances, the case for some legislative devolution was extirpated by the imperative for conformity of national standards. The political landscape began to shift, paradoxically as Scottish and to a lesser extent Welsh opinion discerned disparities of treatment and formulated quite different territorial needs from those of England. Devolving power from the centre now seemed to offer the best guarantee of proper levels for the provision of public goods.

This, in turn, weakened the cement of Britishness, the long-standing assumption of territorial assimilation to a common nationality. The underlying commonality of purpose that had sustained nation building in Britain was now insufficient for sustaining dependable relations between the Union's constituent parts. The pressure mounted for rethinking, indeed for redesigning the British polity, with new institutional arrangements to give voice to, to take proper account of a reviving sense of territorial interests. Of course, this mood was by no means unprecedented in British politics. The nationalist movements' demands for territorial autonomy merely revisited, albeit in quite different domestic and international circumstances, an issue that has been pivotal in the febrile constitutional debate sparked by Irish home rule during the nineteenth century.

Ireland

Ireland was England's first colony. Conquest by Anglo-Norman armies began in the late twelfth century. The island was only finally brought under the control of the English Crown in 1534, and in 1541 Henry VIII assumed the title King of Ireland. The country was ruled by force from a 'safe zone' centred on Dublin. English Protestant landlords and Scots settlers colonised the land, regarded themselves as 'Britons in Ireland', and imposed their language and customs.[53] Protestant ascendancy was particularly reinforced by Scots immigrants who set up plantations in Ulster during the seventeenth century and who regarded the native Irish as both morally inferior and congenitally disloyal. There were periodic purges from England of the native Catholic nobility, notably after the defeat of the Catholic interest at the Battle of the Boyne (1690). Over time, England moved from a policy of outright oppression to more subtle forms of domination. In the commercial revolution of the seventeenth century this included the assimilation by the emergent native middle class of values and cultural norms imported by 'planters' from the mainland, who used the privileges accruing to the Protestant confession as an inducement to convert from Catholicism.

Irish national identity emerged first amongst sixteenth-century Nonconformists attracted to the idea of a fatherland based not on aristocracy or monarchy but on the radical political idea of a commonwealth of free men. Catholics were disallowed from sitting in the Irish parliament in 1692 and lost the franchise in 1727. This reinforced the sense of separatism from the English state, though the impact of exclusion was lessened somewhat because the Irish parliament was subordinated to Westminster. Nevertheless, in 1782 the Dublin parliament acquired coordinate if limited powers with Westminster and a limited Catholic franchise was restored in 1793. By then, however, exclusion had left its mark on all sides. Protestant patriots, mostly drawn from Dublin's urban middle class, rebelled in 1798. They were influenced by the ideas of radical republicanism disseminated during the American and French revolutions. But they were also disaffected by London's failure to enact Catholic emancipation, to alleviate religious intolerance, discrimination in employment, favouritism in state patronage and repressive penal laws, all directed at Catholics.

The Union of 1800 was in part a response to national rebellion, binding Irish governance more firmly to the English state. Those – for the most part Protestants – who feared the Union would bring about the loss of their ascendancy ironically in light of ubsequent loyalist politics, opposed the Union.

The mutual Acts of Union passed in the Westminster and Dublin parliaments in 1800 both established a parliamentary union and created the United Kingdom of Great Britain and Ireland. But concern to assuage either national or Catholic sensibilities was but a limited objective of these new arrangements. The Union acknowledged a degree of Irish distinctiveness, but without conceding the institutional autonomy enjoyed by the Scots. An Irish administration was established, though with a vice-regal Lord Lieutenant at the head of a government administered by a chief secretary who divided his time between Dublin and London and who sat in the British Cabinet. There was also a separate Irish judiciary.[54]

Failure to deliver emancipation accelerated nationalist support rooted in Catholic grievances. The nationalist and Catholic causes were closely related though not identical movements. The nascent nationalist movement cut its political teeth during the agitation for Catholic emancipation, finally secured in 1829 after a protracted struggle that contributed, in turn, to forging a distinctive national identity. Counter-Reformation Catholics of an ultramontane disposition had rallied to an embryonic nationalist movement centred on the idea of *patria*, a land of 'the true but persecuted' faith. A popular nationalist movement had arisen by the late eighteenth century, though it remained divided about aims and tactics, as Irish nationalism ever has been. On one side were romantics seeking cultural parity for a submerged Gaelic language and culture, but on the other were those altogether more revolutionary elements swayed by the turbulent events and influenced by radical and secular doctrines sweeping Continental Europe. Yet another faction turned its political energies to repealing discrimination against Catholics over land-holding, demanding access to public and political office, and insisting on religious freedom. Some Catholics even supported the Union, believing it to be the best guarantee of their rights and the surest way to secure religious parity.

The Union failed to meet these political expectations and failed, too, to address the serious economic consequences of Ireland's colonial status. The real momentum for a widespread popular nationalist movement came only with the Great Famine of 1845–48 when the potato crop, the staple diet of Ireland's peasantry, failed. This proved to be the critical point, the axis on which Irish history turned thereafter. As one contemporary commentator saw this signal event: 'Society stands dissolved . . . to the past we can never return . . . the potato was our sole and only capital, to live and work on . . . and on it the entire social economy of this country was founded, formed and supported . . . A secure and independent agricultural peasantry is the only base on which a people ever rises or ever can be raised.'[55]

More important still, the widespread impression amongst the majority of opinion in Ireland of English disregard for the immense suffering of the people powerfully reinforced political identity as an exploited and oppressed nation. The use of coercion as an instrument of public order to combat resultant agrarian crime and eventually to counteract widespread political violence directed against British rule, confirmed a wholly different territorial politics in Ireland from that of the other component polities of the British state. Nevertheless, the nationalist movement remained divided throughout the modern period, between moderates who preferred a constitutional solution to the 'Irish Question' and those militants driven to resist English rule by all available means. The consequences of such visceral ideological difference for the politics of home rule and for the tenor of post-independence and post-partition relations between the respective Irish communities north and south, and for their relations with England, are discussed in the following chapters.

NOTES

1. R. Rose, *Understanding the United Kingdom* (London, 1982) p.37
2. J. Wormald, The Creation of Britain: Multiple Kingdoms or Core and Colonies? *Transactions of the Royal Historical Society*, 6th series, 11 (1992)
3. Conrad Russell, Composite Monarchies in Early Modern Europe: The British and Irish examples, in A. Grant and K. Stringer (eds), *Uniting the Kingdom: The Making of British History* (London, 1995) p.146
4. P. Stafford, *Unification and Conquest: A Political History of England in the Tenth and Eleventh Centuries* (1989)
5. H. Loyn, *The Making of the English Nation from the Anglo-Saxons to Edward I* (1991)
6. P. Wormald, Enga Lond: The Making of an Allegiance, *Journal of Historical Sociology* 7 (1994); idem, On Second Thoughts: The Making of England, *History Today* 44 (1994)
7. V. Bogdanor, *Devolution in the United Kingdom* (2001) p.5
8. J. Wormald, The Union of 1603, in R. Mason (ed.), *Scots and Britons: Scottish Political Thought and the Union of 1603* (1994)
9. B. Galloway, *The Union of England and Scotland* (1985)
10. R. Coupland, *Welsh and Scottish Nationalism* (Glasgow, 1954) p.48
11. V. Bogdanor, op. cit. (2001) p.6
12. Ibid., p.7
13. G. Osbourne Morgan, Welsh Nationality, *Contemporary Review*, January 1888
14. K. Morgan, The Welsh in English Politics, 1868–1982, in R. Davies *et al.*, *Welsh Society and Nationhood* (1984) at p.239
15. K. Morgan, *Wales in British Politics* (revised edition 1970) pp.306–7
16. Ibid., p.164
17. R. Coupland, *Welsh and Scottish Nationalism* (Glasgow, 1954) p.199
18. K. Morgan, *Rebirth of a Nation, Wales 1880–1980* (Oxford, 1981) p.376
19. H. Pelling, *Popular Politics and Society in Late Victorian Britain* (London, 1968) pp.112–13
20. G. Drewery (ed.), *The New Select Committees: A Study of the 1979 Reforms* (1985)

21. V. Bogdanor, op. cit. (2001) p.158
22. H. Wilson, *The Labour Government 1964–70: A Personal Record* (1971) p.9
23. J.D. Mackie, *A History of Scotland* (1969) pp.8–9
24. B. Levack, *The Formation of the British State: England, Scotland, and the Union 1603–1707* (1987)
25. K. Brown, *Kingdom or Province? Scotland and the Regal Union, 1603–1715* (1992)
26. V. Bogdanor, op. cit. (2001) p.14
27. Ibid., p.13
28. J. Robertson (ed.), *A Vision for Empire: Political Thought and the British Union of 1707* (1995)
29. R. Cage (ed.), *The Scots Abroad: Labour, Capital, Enterprise, 1750–1914* (1985); A. Calder, *Revolutionary Empire* (1980)
30. G. Pryde (ed.), *The Treaty of Union of Scotland and England* (1950) pp.36–9
31. R. Weight, *Patriots: National Identity in Britain 1940–2000* (2002) p.3; W. Ferguson, *Scotland's Relations with England: A Survey to 1707* (1997) p.234
32. The critical distinction to be made between a union state and a unitary state is discussed by the editors in their Introduction: Centres and Peripheries in Western Europe, in S. Rokkan and D. Urwin (eds), *The Politics of Territorial Identity: Studies in European Regionalism* (London, 1982) p.11
33. R. Finlay, *A Partnership for Good? Scottish Politics and the Union since 1880* (1995)
34. C. Kidd, *Subverting Scotland's Past: Scottish Whig Historians and the Creation of an Anglo-British Identity, 1689–1830* (1993) pp.36–50
35. R. Weight, op. cit. (2002) at p.2
36. W. Scott Dalgleish, Scotland's Version of Home Rule, *Nineteenth Century* (January 1883); W. Mitchell, Scotland and Home Rule, *Scottish Review* 8 (July 1886); W. Wallace, Nationality and Home Rule, Irish and Scottish, *Scottish Review* 12 (July 1888)
37. J. Robertson, Andrew Fletcher's Vision of Union, in R. Mason (ed.), *Scotland and England 1286–1815* (1987) pp.203–5
38. B. Levack, op. cit. (1987)
39. B. Anderson, *Imagined Communities: Reflections on the Origins and Spread of Nationalism* (1983); R. Morris, Scotland, 1830–1914: The Making of a Nation within a Nation, in W. Fraser and R. Morris (eds), *People and Society in Scotland. Vol. II: 1830–1914* (1990)
40. T.C. Smout, The Road to Union, in G. Holmes (ed.), *Britain after the Glorious Revolution* (1969)
41. V. Bogdanor, op. cit. (2001) p.9
42. H.J. Hanham, The Creation of the Scottish Office, *Juridical Review* 10 (1965); idem, The Development of the Scottish Office, in J. Wolfe (ed.), *Government and Nationalism in Scotland* (1969)
43. H.J. Hanham, op. cit. (1965); A. Midwinter, M. Keating and J. Mitchell, *Politics and Public Policy in Scotland* (1991) pp.51–2
44. C. Harvie, Labour and the Scottish Government: The Age of Tom Johnson, *Bulletin of Scottish Politics* 2 (1981)

45. J. Burns, The Scottish Committees of the House of Commons, 1948–59, *Political Studies* 8 (1960); G. Edwards, The Scottish Grand Committee, 1958–70, *Parliamentary Affairs* 25 (1972)

46. V. Bogdanor, op. cit. (2001) p.116

47. For a detailed review of public expenditure figures, see M. Keating and B. Jones (eds), *Regions in the EU* (1985)

48. See the account of the Scottish Office by a former secretary in J.M. Ross, *The Secretary of State for Scotland and the Scottish Office*, Studies in Public Policy, 87 (Centre for Studies in Public Policy, Strathclyde University, 1981)

49. W. Miller, *The End of British Politics? Scots and English Political Behaviour in the Seventies* (Oxford, 1981) p.10

50. Lord Kilbrandon, A Background to Constitutional Reform, Birmingham, cited in V. Bogdanor, op. cit. (2001) p.117

51. R. Finlay, Pressure Group or Political Party? The Nationalist Impact on Scottish Politics, 1928–1945, *Twentieth Century British History* 3 (3) (1992)

52. For an overview of the territorial issue, see P. Madgwick and R. Rose (eds), *The Territorial Dimension in the United Kingdom Politics* (1982)

53. J. Morrill, The British Problem c1534–1707, in B. Bradshaw and J. Morrill (eds), *The British Problem c1534–1707: State Formation in the Atlantic Archipeligo* (London, 1996) at p.10

54. G.C. Bolton, *The Passing of the Irish Act of Union: A Study in Parliamentary Politics* (1966)

55. Cited in L. Fogarty (ed.), *James Fintan Lalor: Patriot and Political Essayist 1807–49* (1918)

2 Challenging the centre: home rule movements

Michael O'Neill

TERRITORIAL RESIDUES

The Union tempered but did not entirely eliminate pre-existing territorial identities. These primordial affinities survived rather than flourished during the process of nation building. In so far as a territorial cleavage persisted in the new polity it was a reaction from the geographical periphery, the cultural margins of the British polity, to perceived English dominance. This mood found expression in various 'core–periphery' issues, notably the Irish Question, Church disestablishment, religious nonconformity, land reform and the temperance issue. The principal core–periphery confrontation here was over Irish home rule, a movement that gathered momentum during the 1870s, the first serious challenge both to the concept of the unitary British state and to the very idea of a United Kingdom.

The Irish situation was, however, exceptional. Throughout the twentieth century territorial affinities lost their resonance in Britain as a primary gauge of political identity. The Labour Party's roots in provincial Britain ensured that during its early years it championed the cause of devolving power away from the metropolitan centre, supporting home rule 'all round'. However, the Irish settlement of 1920–21 removed the principal driver of devolution in British politics. Meanwhile, Labour's steady electoral process after 1918, replacing the Liberals as the principal vehicle for radical politics, established class as the dominant cleavage of British politics, further diminishing the significance of territoriality. Thereafter, for Labour *national* politics meant *class* politics.[1]

Changes in the scale and purpose of government, and the shifts in the social and economic issues that dominated the political agenda after 1918, confirmed this national trajectory. The Labour Party responded to the challenge of mass democratic politics by abandoning its early ideological preference for devolution, embracing centralisation and adopting a hierarchical national party organisation. A unitary state and a centrally managed economy were preferred as the appropriate vehicles for social goals and wealth redistribution, the surest safeguards against retrenchment or the imposition of local differentials in welfare standards and allocating social payments. The determination of the trade union movement, Labour's principal financial backer, to defend the system of national wage bargaining and to avoid competition over wage rates between the economic core and the less favoured periphery to drive down overall wage levels, reinforced this national strategy.

There is a tradition in British radical politics that owes much to Joseph Chamberlain, and subsequently subscribed to even by radical socialists, that interprets territorial nationalism as a chimera, a reactionary cause that severely detracts energy, distracts attention from the forward momentum of a truly progressive politics. This theme has found contemporary expression amongst staunch opponents of devolution in the Labour Party. Critics here regard devolution as mitigating the 'real' interests of working people throughout all parts of the Union, concealing from them the objective truth that politics 'is less about *sovereignty* than about *power*'.[2]

The demarcation between territoriality and class politics was much less clear-cut in practice. The United Kingdom's territorial periphery contained high concentrations of social deprivation and has been disproportionately affected by economic decline. Concern to ensure an appropriate balance between national prosperity and equitable treatment for economic and social interests clustered in less favoured regions fused Labour's class constituency with its territorial base. Territorial *and* class politics were complementary not contending constituencies for a party of the democratic left, though the regional issue was subsumed under the latter, thereby blunting its political impetus. Class vitiated the electoral resonance of territoriality but without entirely eliminating it.[3] After 1945, international economic conditions and competitive pressures impacted negatively on Britain's economy and social order. Growing public disaffection with central government's response to deteriorating economic circumstances sharpened perceptions of relative territorial deprivation, thereby restoring the territorial dimension in British politics.[4]

PATHS TO HOME RULE

Ireland: setting the trend

Compared with nationalist and irredentist movements elsewhere in Europe, the Irish nationalist movement lacked a singular identity rooted either in culture or in ethnicity. Centuries of migration in both directions had facilitated cultural assimilation and this in turn had created a problematic identity, an ambivalence that is still apparent from contemporary attempts to make a lasting settlement between competing versions of Irish identity north and south, and between Ulster's Catholic and Protestant communities. Above all, relations were complicated by the impact of the plantation, ensuring variable definitions of Irish identity. One million or so Ulster Protestants firmly rooted in their own communal identity after some three centuries,[5] but belonging more by birthright now than conquest, complicates Ireland's ethnographic map, ensuring a protracted and tense colonial end-game.[6] The home rule movement highlighted these persistent ambiguities in both religious communities about relations with England.

The debate over home rule and its implications for constitutional practice dominated late Victorian politics. The home rule movement demanded national self-determination, though, apart from the most militant voices, not outright separation. The mainstream nationalist movement concentrated its demands on an Irish parliament elected by a democratic franchise. John Redmond, the movement's moderate leader, defined home rule as powers devolved from the centre:

> The restoration of representative government . . . to mean government with the constitutionally expressed will of a majority of the people, and carried out by a ministry constitutionally responsible to those whom they govern . . . [The] internal affairs of Ireland shall be regulated by an Irish Parliament – that all Imperial affairs and all that relates to the colonies, foreign states and common interests of the Empire, shall continue to be regulated by the Imperial Parliament, as at present constituted. The idea at the bottom of this proposal is the desirability of finding some middle course between separation on the one hand and over centralization on the other.[7]

The third Reform Act (1884) enfranchised the majority of Irish male voters and facilitated the emergence of an Irish party. The 1885 election installed a bloc of 85 Irish nationalists at Westminster who operated with the Liberals in an alliance of mutual convenience. Gladstone's commitment to home rule was a fusion of pragmatism and principle intended to strengthen the Union, governing Ireland by consent rather than coercion.

The Home Rule Bill included in the 1886 parliamentary timetable proposed to modify, but not to rescind, the Act of Union of 1800. Gladstone acknowledged the right to political self-determination within the Union, but he saw this as merely an expression of 'local patriotism', complementing but not competing with the shared and overarching affiliation to the British nation and empire. Walter Bagehot, too, prescribed a liberal rather than a reactionary nationalism, warning against movements mobilised to separate 'alien fragments of old races' from the whole.[8] Self-determination for Bagehot was about accommodating territorial differences within the union state, a convenient safety valve for territorial interests in a highly centralised polity.[9]

A clear distinction should be made here between a permissible local nationality and outright separatist nationalism. This distinction has continued to permeate Britain's territorial nationalist movements. To this extent, acknowledging a right to home rule was more a matter of political strategy than it was about fundamental principles. A strategy devised to conserve or even to reinforce imperial unity rather than to undermine it.[10] There were some convenient models of colonial devolution to point the way here. The arrangements for the government of Canada in the British North America Act (1867) reserved primary powers (defence, foreign affairs, fiscal policy) to the imperial centre, whilst transferring only limited powers of self-government to the territorial polity. This approach became the preferred model for devolution closer to home. An alternative model inspired by American federalism, dispersing powers between the central and territorial authorities, was rejected as alien because disruptive of the 'natural' political order. And, not least, because of official unease about states' rights disputes that had contributed much to the outbreak of bloody civil war in 1861.

The first Irish Home Rule Bill followed this pattern, established the template for future devolution proposals, going further in some respects than contemporary arrangements for colonial self-government. It proposed, for instance, a more extensive allocation of powers to an Irish legislature than was currently enjoyed by colonial legislatures. But in other respects, Irish autonomy was to be more restricted, as with the denial to an Irish parliament of powers over indirect taxation, trade, commerce or military matters – some of the competences already acquired *de facto* by Canada's Dominion Parliament. The abiding concern of opponents, and indeed of some supporters, of limited home rule in the constituent parts of the British state or its dominions further afield, was for containment, of how to hold the line over rising territorial expectations once concessions were made to self-government. For the recipients of devolved powers might well be inclined to test its inchoate boundaries, to extend their designated competences beyond intended limits.

There was some evidence from demands made by more assertive Irish nationalists to support this judgement. Charles Stewart Parnell, for instance, questioned the very idea of the limited devolution on offer in a speech at Cork in 1885. He complained that: 'We cannot, under the British Constitution, ask for more than the restitution of Grattan's Parliament. But no man has the right to fix the boundary to the march of a nation. No man has a right to say to his country, "Thus far shalt thou go and no further," and we have never attempted to fix a *ne plus ultra* to the progress of Ireland's nationhood and we never shall'.[11]

The Liberal Party's solution to the dangers posed by home rule was suitably cautious. It assumed *a priori* that Westminster must retain a veto over the management of even domestic affairs in Ireland. Adverse political consequences might well be anticipated from underwriting continuing British sovereignty by these means, suggesting problematic relations. The British veto was always an option in difficult circumstances, but as with all deterrents it was deemed a matter of last resort, to be used in only the most exceptional circumstances. And once used, there was no sure guarantee as to its likely consequences for future stable relations. The enforcement of such veto powers was also problematical, indicating continuing dependence by requiring external intervention once the devolved police authority had passed into local hands.

The Irish debate highlighted other potential procedural and structural problems in future relations between the territorial authorities and the metropolitan centre. Devolution involves a degree of fiscal autonomy and this issue, too, complicated deliberations over Irish self-government. Gladstone had contemplated ceding control over tariffs and customs duties to an Irish legislature. The majority of his Cabinet, aware that an Irish government might compromise the Liberal preference for free trade by seeking to raise revenue from the imposition of import duties on goods from the mainland, preferred instead to retain this competence at Westminster. In the event, it was agreed that an Irish legislature would exercise control over barely 25 per cent of the country's revenues – a clear indication of the constraints of home rule, but a clear incentive for more militant nationalists to push for full independence.

Defence, too, was a thorny issue for devolution. Ireland's proximity to mainland Britain was bound to make security a delicate matter in post home rule relations. The retention of responsibility by London for Ireland's external security was thinly disguised Imperial self-interest. The demand that Irish taxpayers contribute to the British Treasury compromised Dublin's fiscal, and indeed its political, autonomy. British governments preferred to maintain this 'Imperial Contribution' – amounting to one-fifteenth of all imperial expenditure to cover services such as defence – as a fiscal priority, the first call on the budget of the devolved government. This fixed charge was to be set for thirty years and changed thereafter only by mutual agreement, an arrangement that conjured for nationalists the unacceptable image of a colonial-style levy. It was contested on these grounds by nationalists who insisted that it would leave insufficient revenues for underwriting the future development of domestic policy, and at a time when the anticipated implementation of social policy and welfare provisions was bound to increase domestic fiscal pressures on future Irish administrations.

The subsequent provision in the 1912 Home Rule Bill to meet any future Irish budgetary deficit by means of a subsidy from the British Exchequer proved to be just as contentious for British opinion. And in any event, this would surely have compromised any sense of new-won Irish autonomy in domestic affairs. The circumstances of post-devolution fiscal relations remained the principal objection of Irish nationalists throughout the protracted home rule negotiations. The question of such residual charges on a Dublin government raised serious constitutional and indeed moral issues that go to the heart of devolution, concerning both representation and the responsibility for determining and financing public policy. This issue prefigures a similar concern aired during the recent devolution round. There is also the first indication here of what is now called the West Lothian Question: of how to organise an appropriate level of representation for the territorial authorities at the centre, and of an appropriate balance of power between the respective levels of government in an asymmetrical devolution, that is devolution enacted where the constituent territorial units are disproportionate in terms of their demographics, fiscal resources and political clout.

The critical issues here are those of the proper role, the voting rights and the number of elected representatives from the territorial polities continuing to sit in the UK Parliament post devolution. The most critical of these issues, and consequently the most difficult to resolve, is that of the relations, the balance of political power and the respective competences of the territorial legislatures and central government. Of particular concern here is the role designated for territorial representatives in policy matters pertaining only to English constituencies. Resolving this issue is that much more difficult because there is no comparable devolution to England's regions, a matter further discussed in Chapter 10 and in the concluding remarks in Chapter 14.

The problem of centre–territorial balance has pervaded the debate on devolution from the outset, and it has never been satisfactorily resolved, though its significance for asymmetrical British devolution was quite apparent from the very outset of the home rule debate. Indeed, it was acknowledged to be problematical by William Gladstone, the principal architect of home rule. The 1886 Home Rule Bill identified the predicament facing Irish MPs sitting at Westminster after home rule: how to represent their constituents on those reserved or central competences that remained a charge on Irish taxpayers whilst the House was deliberating on purely English matters. The 1893 Home Rule Bill did finally rule out such exclusive or demarcated legislative domains for Irish MPs at Westminster on the practical grounds of policy complexity.[12] As Gladstone saw it:

> Any proposal to spend money, whether on English, Scottish, or Welsh matters, or on Irish matters, would compete in terms of priorities with any other proposal. The amount of money which accrued to Ireland would remain dependent upon the amount of money which English, Scottish, and Welsh MPs decided to spend upon their own priorities. Therefore, the standard of living of the Irish [and latterly the Scottish] would depend upon decisions made at a forum from which they would have been excluded.[13]

To avoid installing a complex hierarchy of legislative competences, or establishing different classes of membership of the Imperial Parliament, the Liberals settled on a pragmatic solution. An arrangement constructed so as to appease the Irish demand for progress on home rule and to meet the parliamentary Liberal Party's preference to be rid of its reliance on the votes of the Irish party. The proposed 'solution' to the representation dilemma was for reduced Irish representation at Westminster, whilst according these MPs full voting rights. This compromise was subsequently adopted in the 1893 and reiterated in the 1912 Home Rule Bills, and this remains as the untidy answer to this particular devolution dilemma. Only a fully federal arrangement with a second, territorial chamber akin to the American Senate or German Bundesrat can effectively resolve this problem.

The first Home Rule Bill was defeated in the House of Commons by an alliance of Liberal Imperialist and Conservative Members. Further bills were presented at Westminster in 1893 and 1912. The Conservatives remained implacably opposed to the idea of home rule, and Liberal opinion, too, was deeply divided over the issue. Gladstone took a pragmatic view, acknowledging the significance of the territorial dimension in national politics, quite aware that some concession to 'local patriotism', permitting a measure of power-sharing and institutional compromise, was essential for maintaining a stable and strong British state. Some of his contemporaries, however, remained wholly unconvinced. No less a constitutional authority than A.V. Dicey pronounced the idea of home rule to be anathema to the natural course of British political development over the preceding centuries. Dicey regarded such a prospect as a clear threat to the security and prosperity of a kingdom united in prosperity and secure in a world where large states were the powerful players.[14] The political elite, for the most part, preferred Dicey's assessment to Gladstone's. The second Home Rule Bill did pass the Commons but was lost in the House of Lords, whereas the third Home Rule Bill, although defeated in the Lords, was made subject to the provisions of the new Parliament Act that limited the upper House's power of delay to only three parliamentary sessions. This bill did eventually become law in 1914 but it was suspended at the onset of the Great War.

The issue reappeared in the turbulent landscape of postwar British politics. The protracted debate over Irish home rule, as much as any other current mainstream issue, was a critical factor behind the major party realignment that occurred from the latter years of the nineteenth century and in the aftermath of the Great War.

Home rule was primarily a Liberal issue. It was instrumental in the schism that eventually broke the Liberal Party, contributing to its demise as a force in British politics. The issue did much to undermine the long-established Liberal coalition of free traders, Whigs and non-conformists that had dominated Victorian politics.[15] Although it was by no means the only, or indeed the principal, cause of that rift, the issue played a greater role in Liberal politics than it did in the internal affairs of any other party. As such, the issue served as a warning to any would-be radical party committed to far-reaching constitutional change in this essentially cautious political culture. All of the major British political parties have, in some degree, been attached to the idea of the union state, albeit with differing views about how to reconcile territorial discontent with the maintenance of a prosperous, internationally powerful British state. The Conservative Party was instinctively unionist and Labour preferred to identify itself as a class party. As such, devolution has never been an issue exclusively defined in left–right terms, and it continues in this latest phase to be an issue that cuts across more than it polarises national party politics.

Partition

The partition of Ireland implemented in 1920–21 imposed a system of home rule for the twenty-six overwhelmingly Catholic southern counties, whilst establishing a separate Protestant-dominated jurisdiction in the six northern counties. The unionists' demand for partition was underpinned by principled as well as by pragmatic reasoning. Once it was apparent that home rule would happen, unionists maintained that their link with Britain was at least as important for them as home rule was for southern Irish nationalists. Unionist spokesmen had not previously made the case for devolved government within the Union, insisting instead on the status quo, resisting the idea of home rule in any form, including partition.

The unionists' champion Sir Edward Carson argued for the constitutional status quo at Westminster: 'We have never asked to govern any Catholic . . . We are perfectly satisfied that all of them, Protestant and Catholic, should be governed from this parliament [and] we have sought from beginning to end of this controversy to be left alone, and to go hand in hand with Great Britain as one nation with Great Britain'.[16] Carson confidently predicted that an Irish state lacking the ballast of Ulster's industrial prowess and commercial wealth would not be economically viable. The nationalists, too, for entirely opposite reasons, refused to countenance the division of what they regarded as a singular and historical realm.[17]

Partition featured in these deliberations only after 1912, once it had become clear that home rule could only be carried by forcibly incorporating northern Protestants within an Irish state. Thereafter, partition in some form became inevitable, although the British authorities regarded it as merely a temporary arrangement.[18] In the meantime, there were to be separate parliaments and governance in both parts of Ireland. The Government of Ireland Act 1920 was designed to apply to the whole of the island of Ireland. In the event, it applied only in the north after more radical representatives of southern nationalism pressed London for independence rather than devolution.

The 1920 Act, passed without any direct input from Irish representatives after Sinn Féin refused to occupy its seats won in the 1918 general election, contained a provision to end partition by agreement, and eventually to install a parliament for the whole island.[19] In reality, partition promised a much less tidy outcome. Special arrangements were devised to accommodate Ulster's Protestants, resistant to the idea of home rule. After that battle was lost they argued the case for retaining their links with the United Kingdom rather than being governed by Dublin. Devolution was the solution for their particular claims, but complicated demographics determined the political boundaries of the northern enclave.[20]

By the end of the nineteenth century there was a clear majority of Protestant unionists concentrated in the four north-eastern counties of Antrim, Armagh, Down and Londonderry, and with a near-majority in Fermanagh and Tyrone. This ensured Protestant dominance of government in the north-east of Ireland, an outcome that perpetuated in Ulster's fractured politics the deep political–cultural schism that had long fuelled Irish nationalism and unionism alike, ensuring Ulster 'an unresolved conflict of national identities within the context of incompatible national claims'.

The twenty-six southern counties were designated a self-governing state within the Empire, whereas the six northern counties were permitted to secede from this new state – a seemingly pragmatic solution to a predicament rooted in an irreconcilable cultural and religious antipathy. Partition has perpetuated rather than resolved these historical legacies.[21] The 1920–21 settlement created separate governments north and south, the Irish Free State to be a self-governing state though still subject to the British Crown and remaining within the British Empire. Residual loyalty to the Crown was attested by an oath of allegiance and the imperial connection was to be supervised by the office of a British governor-general resident in Dublin. Britain further imposed its writ on the new state by claiming the right to use so-called treaty ports – British naval bases located on Irish soil.

There was no obvious historical logic in a border framed purely for the political convenience of government in London and to obviate the fears of unionists in Ulster, who by now were prepared to accept the border as the lesser of available evils.[22] Unionists, concerned lest historic Ulster – with three counties where nationalist opinion vastly outweighed unionists – might have a nationalist majority, opted for a smaller six-county territory to ensure their ascendancy. Rather, this fundamental rupture was firmly rooted in the colonial past, for as 'a conquered country, Ireland generated a nationalism which sought independence from Britain [and] as a "planted" country, Ireland generated a distinct community which sought to retain the link with Britain . . . The one is a claim based on nationality, the other a claim based on citizenship'.[23]

The 1921 Anglo-Irish Treaty consolidated these *de facto* polities into *de jure* states, though even this arrangement was premised, however vaguely, on some future notion of organising a quasi-federal arrangement. On the British side, the Treaty was primarily about national self-interest, balancing Ireland's resolute demand for nationhood with a continued association with the British Empire. There was scant reference in these arrangements to future reconciliation between these two polities.

A Council of Ireland, with representatives from both north and south, was installed as a device for effecting peaceful transition and a forerunner of the contemporary all-Ireland forum. And whilst this might eventually function as a forum for future reconciliation, it was quite apparent from the outset that the presence of northern unionists in this body was bound to present a serious obstacle to reconciliation, let alone to future reunion.

The all-Ireland Council, included in the arrangement as an incentive to nationalists concerned that the Treaty would consolidate partition of the two parts of Ireland, did briefly raise expectations about incorporating a cross-border, pan-Irish dimension into policy making, except that this arrangement was never endorsed as meaningful by northern unionists and was soon disregarded by London. The circumstances of partition thus left unresolved many of the issues raised during the embittered debate on home rule and likely, sooner or later, to reap a bitter harvest. Partition was merely an instalment in what was clearly an unfinished business.[24]

Irish home rule and its aftermath

Home rule for the southern Irish counties by no means resolved all of the issues raised during the struggle for self-government. British ambivalence about what George Bernard Shaw had called 'John Bull's other island' continued long after the end of the Union of 1800. The Irish Question was always about more than political self-determination. Cultural identity and communal affiliation made for a complicated post-colonial end-game. The claim to democratic rights and national self-determination was accompanied by demands on related cultural issues that proved impossible to resolve. For instance, the matter of cultural respect, the right to use the Gaelic tongue, the prevalence of Anglo-Saxon culture, as well as persistent religious discrimination against Catholics, bolstered the nationalist cause. Conflict over competing ideas about national identity was palpable, yet it was only one, albeit important, facet of an infinitely complicated relationship between native tradition and what was widely perceived by the population at large to be an imposed alien culture. Continuing interaction via trade, migration and even military service, perpetuated ambivalent relations. The bonds binding these nations induced, for instance, some 50,000 citizens of the Republic to serve in Britain's wartime forces, persuading even de Valera's staunchly Republican government to compromise its formal neutrality in favour of its neighbour.[25] The Anglo-Irish *ménage* has retained the sense of being a special relationship regardless of its abiding paradoxes.

In the aftermath of home rule, London remained wary of Irish entanglements, concerned not to foment political violence. There was lukewarm commitment in official circles to Ulster and certainly little support for the unionists' preference to be treated as any other UK region. There was debate, too, about an appropriate model of government to reflect Ulster's special situation. The Protestant community had not demanded devolved governance or even a territorial parliament. On the contrary, their leading spokesman, Sir Edward Carson, had been explicit about retaining the character of the Union, informing Parliament in 1919 that: 'Ulster has never asked for a separate Parliament. Ulster's claim has always been of this simple character: "We have thrived under the Union; we are in sympathy with you, we are part of yourselves. We are prepared to make any sacrifice that you make, and are prepared to bear any burden that is equally put upon us with the other parts of the United Kingdom. In these circumstances, keep us with you."'[26]

The establishment of a parliament at Stormont was principally motivated by concern to avoid criticism that direct rule amounted to continuing domination by London of Ulster's nationalist minority. Once in place, however, Ulster's unionists embraced this parliament as an institutional safeguard, a bulwark against future bad faith by British governments susceptible to Dublin's demand for reunification. Unionism's political representatives used their political power to turn the province into a Protestant enclave in an otherwise hostile island, utilising their monopoly of power to disburse scarce public goods to their own community. The constitutional status of the Province was enhanced in 1949 after the Free State adopted republic status. By the terms of the Ireland Act 1949, the principle of consent was formalised, thereby ensuring that Northern Ireland could cease to be a part of the United Kingdom only by the express consent of its parliamentary representatives at Stormont.

The unionists' preference to reinforce the ties with London has made this an exceptional case of territorial devolution. The Province enjoyed a degree of devolution never seriously contemplated for the mainland territories,[27] at least not until events in Scotland persuaded London to review the fundaments of the unitary British state, creating separate parliaments for both Scotland and Wales. Geographical proximity and London's concern with the security of the Atlantic approaches in the build-up to war in 1939, as much as any sense of residual moral obligation by the centre to the loyalist community, ensured that Ulster was treated as a special case. The Province was not regarded in London with quite the same detachment as far-flung colonial dependencies. For these reasons this novel experiment in devolution hardly offered a suitable model for any future devolution to those parts of the United Kingdom with aspiration to greater autonomy from the centre.[28]

The degree of power devolved to the Stormont executive and parliament was quite exceptional in this centralised and unitary state. The public finance arrangements envisaged in the 1920 Act (designed principally with devolution to the Free State in mind) were also markedly different from those that applied elsewhere in Britain. Although these financial arrangements were subsequently modified for Ulster, to ensure that, in light of its limited (and during the time of economic depression a declining) tax base, its citizens would enjoy the same level of social provision as those that applied in the rest of the United Kingdom. Taxpayers on the mainland continued to subsidise social welfare in Ulster, but with only limited parliamentary scrutiny of budgetary arrangements, and with little direct control over detailed provision – a principle of fiscal autonomy that remains more appropriate to the political logic of federalism than to devolution.[29]

In other areas of public policy, too, such as education provision and housing allocation, considerable discretion was left to Stormont. The inbuilt Protestant majority ensured that government there favoured its loyalist support base. Unease about

London's commitment to the Province persuaded unionists to use their demographic advantage to secure the lion's share of public goods. Accordingly, Ulster's ambiguous political status within the United Kingdom was not settled by partition, in either London or Dublin, let alone for its 'tribal' communities. There was no appetite in the Protestant community for devolved power, and at the outset even some resistance to a development that seemed to betoken a weakening of the constitutional ties with the mainland. The unionists nevertheless accepted Stormont as the symbol of their outright refusal to be excluded from the Union.[30] The minority community, for its part, looked to the paramilitary Irish Republican Army (IRA) or to Republican politicians in Dublin, or to both, as guarantors of their rights and interests with London. What was left after the 1921 settlement of the Irish Question was thereby transmuted into deep sectarian mistrust concentrated within this territorial enclave. Consequently, devolution, at least in this format, became part of the problem rather than an imaginative political solution to reconciling, or at least balancing, Ulster's two competing communal identities.[31]

Meanwhile, central government preferred to shelter behind devolved rule to Stormont. As such, London permitted, even if it did not condone, defective standards in public life that would have scandalised public opinion had they been practised on the mainland.[32] Political arrangements here amounted much more to institutionalised indifference than to an exercise in genuine devolution. It has been estimated, for instance, that Westminster devoted barely two hours a year of its parliamentary timetable to monitoring affairs in the Province.[33] Indifference from mainland public opinion to affairs in Ulster facilitated unionist hegemony and encouraged the practice of discrimination and exclusion that, in turn, fostered disaffection amongst the minority population.[34]

The presence of Ulster MPs at Westminster was balanced by the fact that their seats' allocation was much reduced, in recognition of the fact that the Province had its own assembly. And although these territorial representatives were permitted to vote in matters pertaining to British constituencies, British MPs had no comparable authority in Northern Ireland affairs: a situation made even more complicated by the fact that Ulster's unionist Members at Westminster usually voted with the Conservatives.

There was little initiative from successive British governments to use their residual constitutional powers under the Government of Ireland Act 1920 (section 75) to ensure equity of treatment between the two communities. Discrimination was routinely practised against Catholics in the allocation of public goods, notably in employment, public sector housing and funding for education. Moreover, the boundaries of electoral constituencies were deliberately drawn so as to ensure maximum political advantage to the predominantly Protestant Unionist Party. London preferred to limit its responsibilities to providing fiscal allocations, so as to ensure parity of living standards and welfare provision with those on the mainland, 'although unfortunately, there was no similar commitment to ensure that standards of civil rights should be the same as those in different parts of the country'.[35] This situation was always morally indefensible and over time it became politically untenable, resulting in an unprecedented level of political violence.

The exceptionality of these arrangements was apparent in the constitutional provisions governing relations between Westminster and Stormont. Westminster's pre-eminence went unchallenged by the territorial authorities who retained the right to legislate for Northern Ireland even in those matters transferred to Stormont. Where there was direct conflict between the two jurisdictions, Westminster's writ prevailed. Even so, the practice of devolution ensured considerable territorial autonomy because Westminster was largely reticent about exercising its formal prerogatives in the reserved areas.[36]

In spite of occasional threats of direct intervention in the Province's affairs by the centre, there was no occasion – until 1969 – when Westminster legislated against the wishes of the Northern Ireland government in the area of the transferred competences. To that extent, relations between Westminster and Stormont were more akin to a federal than to a merely devolved arrangement, but without the constitutional safeguards for the rights of minorities usually found in federal polities. Westminster even permitted Stormont in 1922 to rescind the provision in the Westminster Act 1919 for proportional representation for Irish local authorities, and eventually (in 1929) for elections to the Stormont, arrangements designed to ensure fair representation for the minority.[37] These procedural changes were accompanied by a shift in local authority boundaries designed, in effect, to ensure Protestant predominance in local government – an outcome ensured by preventing the fragmentation of the Unionist Party and by limiting the representation of the Northern Ireland Labour Party.

A significant consequence of these arrangements was the consolidation of pro- and anti-Union forces in the Province's politics. The electoral system embedded this singular cleavage as the primary axis of party politics, precluding a politics based on competing class or socio-economic interests. This, in turn, ensured that Ulster's politics, unlike those in the other constituent parts of the United Kingdom, was shaped, and some would say deformed, by visceral intercommunal hostility rather than by the conventional norms and procedures of democratic opposition.[38] A further consequence of such corrosive communal relations was the eventual cessation, after a brief interlude, of constructive cooperation between the nationalist opposition and the Unionist majority at Stormont.[39]

The safeguards enshrined in legislation to ensure fair treatment for the minority community were rarely invoked. The selection of the local judiciary predominantly from amongst Unionist ranks merely confirmed the nationalists in their view that the rule of law was grossly distorted through the prism of Protestant supremacy.[40] The warping of conventional democratic procedure and distortion of liberal norms notwithstanding, in practice it suited London to allow Stormont maximum discretion in the transferred areas. The centre preferred to turn a blind eye to endemic discrimination and sectarian prejudice by public authorities, including the Royal Ulster Constabulary, rather than risk disturbing a veritable hornet's nest. This denial of democratic proprieties reaped a violent response only in the late 1960s when nationalist resentment eventually boiled over.[41]

The social consequences and the political and economic costs of the centre's failure to curb sectarian excesses became clear to see once British governments, under rising pressure from domestic and international opinion, were prompted to exercise unprecedented intervention in the matter of civil rights. After nationalist civil disobedience had provoked a Protestant backlash, the British government pressured the Northern Ireland executive to publicly affirm a commitment: to 'take into the fullest account at all times the views of Her Majesty's Government in the United Kingdom, especially in relation to matters affecting the status of citizens of that part of the United Kingdom and their equal rights and protection under the law'.[42] When arm-twisting failed to produce the desired outcome the only tool left to London was to implement direct rule, a step taken in 1972 by the Conservative government. In response to deteriorating politics, London resorted to desperate measures. A plan devised by the Cabinet Office in 1972 proposed a variant of negotiated ethnic cleansing, repartitioning Ulster, creating a smaller and wholly Protestant three-counties enclave and reassigning both the Catholic population in majority Protestant areas, and majority Catholic areas, to the Republic. This would have required reassigning up to half a million people, in many cases regardless of their consent, and was deemed by government to be politically unfeasible.[43]

The relative ease with which London now imposed its will in policy domains long left to the discretion of the Northern Ireland executive merely highlighted previous reluctance to rein in local power.[44] Leverage from the centre was exerted by policy working parties and through administrative agency, for instance the secondment of a senior Foreign Office official to the Office of the Northern Ireland Prime Minister to 'explain' British policy.[45] Direct rule was hardly democratic governance, with legislation by Orders in Council limiting both parliamentary scrutiny and the opportunity for elected representatives to amend proposals. It likewise failed to accord with the unionists' preference for full integration into the United Kingdom, akin to the status of Scotland or Wales. But this too was politically untenable in light of Ulster's sectarian political culture, the conspicuous nature of its primary political cleavage, and the lack of fit between the territorial party system and that of the mainland.[46] Ulster's elected representatives at Westminster never sat in British governments of whatever political complexion. The communal dynamics driving territorial party competition ensured that Ulster's electorate played no part, either, in making or unmaking a British government, although some of its elected members did support the no confidence motion that unseated the Labour government in 1979.

As one British secretary of state saw the situation, integration 'would have made a bad situation worse. It offered as a permanent solution an approach favoured by only a minority of the Unionists . . . It would have made the position of moderate democratic nationalists impossible, and played into the hands of the terrorists. It would have wrecked any hope of institutionalised co-operation with Dublin.'[47] But direct rule was equally flawed, further underlining the hiatus of history, culture and experience between the Province and the mainland.

The end of Ulster's virtual autonomy was compensated by measures long familiar in other parts of the United Kingdom, for instance increasing parliamentary representation to bring the Province more into line with the ratio of MPs to population elsewhere in the United Kingdom, and by the installation in 1975 of a standing committee for Northern Ireland, subsequently retitled as the Northern Ireland Grand Committee (1994). A Northern Ireland Select Committee was also established in 1994. These belated reforms failed, however, to address a flawed devolution. By the early 1960s, the intrinsic contradictions of a defective devolution ensured its collapse, activating thereafter a search for a new political arrangement acceptable to both of the by now warring communities.

Scotland: cautiously taking the high road

The special arrangements for Scottish government briefly reviewed in Chapter 1 reflected a distinct political identity.[48] The Scottish Home Rule Association (SHRA) founded in 1886 was a by-product of the Liberal Party. The nationalist movement was committed to emulating Irish home rule by means of constitutional change, albeit defined as the achievement of parity with England within the United Kingdom. The movement had a fitful existence, support fluctuating with the tides of political fashion and appealing more to the urban elite and the intelligentsia than to the public at large. Proposals for Scottish home rule were put before the House of Commons on thirteen occasions between 1890 and 1914. Although supported by a majority of Scots MPs, these measures failed to progress even to the committee stage.

The Scottish National Party (SNP), formed in 1934, likewise aspired to home rule, again defined as devolution rather than as outright independence, and with a Scottish parliament as the principal objective. It proved just as difficult to mobilise public opinion around even this modest objective, and the party, disheartened by its failure to make electoral headway, succumbed to internal feuding and eventually, in 1942, to schism. The party's leader, John MacCormick, proposed to jettison the electoral route, replacing it by pressure group tactics, preferring non-partisan lobbying to outright competition with the better resourced major parties. He carried a majority with him into a reformed Scottish Covenant Association, an organisation whose goals mirrored those of the SHRA active during the 1880s.

The party's more radical elements persisted with their aspiration to outright independence. Polling evidence, however, confirmed public support for the SHRA's majority position. The first national poll conducted on the issue of home rule in 1947, despite using an unrefined sampling technique, indicated a distinct if mutable majority for independence. Subsequent polling registered a sharp drop in support to barely 20 per cent. By and large, Scotland's radical instincts at this juncture were channelled through the familiar medium of class rather than territorial politics, with Labour the main beneficiary.

The Scottish National Assembly set up by nationalists organised the signing of a covenant in 1949 calling for home rule but within the framework of the United Kingdom, and to include a Scottish assembly with tax-raising powers and authority for the conduct of domestic policy. The covenant confirmed this minimalist outlook, proclaiming that:

> We the people of Scotland who subscribe to this Engagement, declare our belief that reform in the constitution of our country is necessary to secure good government in accordance with our Scottish traditions and to promote the spiritual and economic welfare of our nation . . . With that end in view we solemnly enter into this Covenant whereby we

pledge ourselves in all loyalty to the Crown and within the framework of the United Kingdom, to do everything in our power to secure for Scotland a Parliament with adequate
legislative authority in Scottish affairs.[49]

The success of the Scottish covenant movement in securing almost 2 million
signatures – an impressive two-thirds of the total electorate – in favour of a national
parliament was in no small measure a direct reaction to the sense of neglected
interests, and confirmed a declining sense of Britishness.[50] Queues formed to sign
the covenant in the principal burghs and cities. The event was notable, 'the first
serious tremor in the body politic of post-war Britain [proving] that Scottish
nationalism was no longer the obsession of a few romantic intellectuals'.[51] It rallied
support in every political party, across all social classes, and was widely endorsed
in the press and by the leaders of Scottish civil society.

The Prime Minister refused to receive a delegation representing the covenant
movement, although the Scottish Secretary did agree to meet with them in Glasgow. The movement's leaders confirmed their modest aspirations by assuring the
minister of their commitment to the Union, merely insisting on parity of status
within the emergent British Commonwealth with the likes of Canada, or indeed
with Northern Ireland,[52] although these petitioners did warn that any lack of a
positive response would provoke further, if unspecified, political action.[53]

The Labour government was preoccupied with national reconstruction through
the medium of central economic planning within the unitary state. After securing
a second term in 1950, the government declared a resolutely unionist position on the
matter of home rule, reiterating the familiar case for a unitary state. It held the view
that Scotland was in no position, economically or otherwise, for self-government,
that it lacked sufficient depth of political ability to send representatives both to
Westminster and to a Scottish assembly. It served notice too that home rule would
require an unspecified reduction in Scottish representation – and by implication
a loss of influence – at Westminster, and likewise warned that inevitable fallouts
over respective centre–territorial competences would undermine good intergovernmental relations. The only palliative here for Scottish feelings was bland affirmation
of continuing regard for Scottish identity and nationhood.[54]

In this less than promising climate, the reaction of the English establishment to the
theft in 1950 by nationalist students of the ancient coronation stone of Scone from
Westminster Abbey merely confirmed the centre's apparent indifference to Scottish
sensibilities, and seemingly with good reason. For although the SNP continued to
make its case at the polls, regardless of Covenant's success the party's electoral support remained no more than modest. The situation did improve, but only slowly, as
the SNP made modest headway during the mid-1950s. Despite building a base in
local government, notably in Glasgow, at the 1966 general election the party secured
barely 5 per cent of the Scottish vote.

The 1960s proved to be a turning point, the decade when nationalism became
a significant force in Scottish politics. Uncertainty about the proper representation
of territorial interests at the centre of government was one significant consequence
of the major economic dislocations that impacted heavily on the United Kingdom

during that decade and thereafter.[55] It became apparent that the postwar revival of the Scottish (and indeed the Welsh) economy was but temporary, a brief respite from the longer-term cycle of economic decline of the interwar years. The fall-off from the late 1950s of the traditional or 'first wave' industries was accelerated by global pressures.

This, in turn, increased the disparity, in both prosperity and employment, between the English and the territorial economies as businesses in the south restructured more rapidly and adapted better to international competitive pressures. The unemployment rate in Scotland and Wales doubled between 1945 and 1959, growing at twice the rate per capita of England. And once opened, that gap has never closed. There was similar imbalance in comparative living standards even for those in employment. These discrepancies were readily seized upon and used by nationalist politicians as evidence of metropolitan indifference, neglect, and even of wilful discrimination.

Economic dislocation fuelled, in turn, political resentment, providing the impetus that turned a once esoteric cause into one with mass appeal, and provoking 'an already sharp sense of cultural uniqueness into a demand for greater autonomy' in the management of territorial affairs.[56] The response of central government to rising dismay in Scotland, and indeed in other parts of the UK's geographical periphery, was typically mundane. It resorted to the palliative conventionally used by central government since the interwar depression, that of disbursing regional aid to facilitate business relocation. It did so in the teeth of strong Treasury resistance and with ideologically inspired objections from a strand of Conservative opinion hostile to the idea of a 'dependency culture', of 'handouts' and the supposedly 'inefficient' use of public resources.

Even Conservative arch-pragmatists such as Harold Macmillan, more sympathetic to a positive role by the state, had initially been reticent about meting out 'exceptional' treatment to some parts of the country. The ethos of the unitary state remained intact, not least because the Macmillan government was concerned not to give credence to the nationalist claim to a 'rightful' territorial differential in public spending. There was concern, too, in a predominantly English party, to avoid English resentment over the inequitable funding of the territorial subsidy to the non-English parts of the Union. As a consequence, public expenditure allocated for economic regeneration, whether in Wales or Scotland, was disbursed under the generic heading of regional aid. The Scottish Development Council became the principal focus for attracting investment, and with some success, for instance by giving official support for regional tourism and for channelling the growing interest in identity and cultural distinctiveness in Britain into support for the heritage industry, one way of countering the claims to political difference in nationalist rhetoric. This was deliberate strategy by central government and designed to contain territorial disaffection.[57] The senior Whitehall official whose task it was to vet official guidebooks was forthright about these underlying motives, asserting that 'nationalism could be contained by encouraging "a reasonable manifestation of patriotism" and that the British could learn something from the way the Soviet Union placated the different nations under its aegis'.[58]

The statistics on regional assistance reflect a nevertheless implicit acknowledgement from the centre that a by now discernible territorial dimension of British politics was becoming a matter for concern. During the 1960s, per capita public spending in Scotland grew to some 22 per cent above the UK average, and was 5 per cent above that level in Wales and 35 per cent in Northern Ireland. This territorial differential was formalised in public policy by the adoption of the Barnett formula. The scale of assistance almost certainly delayed the outbreak of widespread territorial unrest, though it did remind, too, of irksome dependence on the centre. This, in turn, gave credence to nationalist claims that responsibility for this predicament was a direct consequence of Whitehall's mismanagement and Westminster's neglect of discernible Scottish national interests.

Moreover, the politics of regional policy facilitated an approach from the centre aptly described by some as 'divide and rule'. It precluded any notion of a territorial cleavage by requiring that the respective secretaries of state compete for scarce resources in cabinet, in Scotland's case to maintain the differential with Wales. This encouraged the territorial elites to lobby Whitehall in order to maximise their respective budget share, precluding a pan-territorial alliance ranged against central government. Welsh success in securing unprecedented levels of regional assistance by the end of the 1960s vexed Scotland's political establishment.[59] The 1965 decision, for instance, to relocate the Royal Mint to the Rhondda Valley rather than to Cumbernauld illustrated this keen rivalry, as did the decision in 1967 to allow Wales its own economic plan.[60]

By 1974, the SNP had acquired sufficient momentum to present a formidable challenge to both major London-based parties, and especially to the Conservatives, by winning four of its seats in the general election of February 1974, capturing two more from Labour. The nationalists took another four Conservative seats in the October 1974 election, reducing that party's tally in Scotland to 16 seats and barely 25 per cent of the total vote. The margin between Labour's vote share and the SNP's was reduced to merely 6.4 per cent, with the SNP becoming the main opposition to Labour in 35 seats. Between 1959 and 1974 the SNP's share of the Scottish vote grew from just 0.1 per cent to a healthy 30.4 per cent – a trend that confirmed the emergence of a territorially aware electorate and one that was disconcerting for the British parties dependent for maintaining their territorial support bases on the persistence of class-based politics. The emergent nationalist constituency was composed of all social groups, but it was disproportionately drawn from the postwar generation. Only the inbuilt mathematical distortions of the first-past-the-post election system limited the damage inflicted by this shift in attitudes on the established parties of Scottish politics. Indeed, in the October 1974 general election the SNP actually out-polled the Conservatives in its share of the popular vote, and came second to Labour in 42 Scottish seats, including in 35 of Labour's 41 seats. This seismic shift in the electoral landscape was the more dramatic because it was unforeseen. In the 1966 general election, for instance, Labour had secured the party's most convincing victory ever, both in Scotland and Wales, taking 46 of 71 seats and 32 of 36 seats, respectively.

Thereafter, a once-familiar political landscape shifted irretrievably, confirming significant movement in the social base of Scottish politics, and ensuring that an emergent territorial cleavage would now rival class-based identity as a major social and ideological determinant of party competition.[61] The first real indicator of this shift was the SNP's by-election success in 1967 in the once 'safe' Labour constituency of Hamilton, won on a swing from Labour of 16.6 per cent. Although the established parties, and indeed some contemporary psephologists, chose to interpret this success as merely a mid-term protest against the governing party,[62] subsequent events proved otherwise.

There was already some circumstantial evidence to support the view that a shift was under way in the social fabric of Scottish politics. One early indication of a fundamental change in outlook was the extent of the protest against Westminster's tactless decision in 1965 to celebrate the septcentenary of an English parliament as a *British* event. The SNP responded by demanding that all Scots MPs shun an event that was construed as an affront to Scottish national identity. The advice from government to local education authorities throughout Britain to mark this event with a school holiday merely persuaded many Scottish authorities either to ignore the instruction or to celebrate instead the Declaration of Arbroath.

Whether this incident amounts to the singular act of cultural conceit portrayed in nationalist propaganda is debatable, but the unfavourable public reaction should at least have served as a warning to unionists, for it pointed to a significant culture shift, to the onset of a contested rather than a merely compliant attitude to the present state of the Union. It certainly reveals a Scottish mindset that markedly contrasted with the unalloyed support of earlier generations fighting between 1939 and 1945 for the Union's very survival against foreign threat. One commentator has interpreted this event as a signal shift in political culture, in as much as 'the government failed to pass off the story of English democracy as an achievement from which the whole of the island had benefited. That failure highlighted how much Westminster had come to be seen as an English institution with concomitant policies'.[63]

These events assisted the SNP with its strategy of portraying English cultural arrogance and political hegemony as the prevailing norm of relations within the Union. There were clear signs of nationalist pique even before the SNP's spectacular victory in the Hamilton by-election, where its campaign made much of the supposed subjugation of Scottish interests. The editorial writer of the non-partisan *Scotsman* newspaper believed that this outcome indicated 'a loss of faith', not merely in the Labour government but in the Union per se: a verdict rooted, as he saw it, in 'many years of cultural nationalism' and confirming a growing sense of territorial neglect that merely remedial economic measures could no longer deflect.[64] In short, Labour had failed to deliver, or to deliver either sufficiently or soon enough, to reassure a Scottish electorate by now disenchanted and discomfited by policy outputs from the centre.[65]

The nationalist momentum was sustained in part by the normal electoral reflex of a mid-term protest against the incumbent government, but it confirmed, too, the deeper political change begun in the 1960s. The SNP maintained its electoral momentum into the 1970s, an indication of a substantial shift in Scottish political affiliations. The Liberal Party, the usual vehicle for the British protest vote, was largely by-passed in Scotland. As Vernon Bogdanor concludes from an analysis of the performance of these two, by now principal, opposition parties in Scotland:

> It seemed [by the mid-1970s] that the SNP was about to break the constraints of the two-party system in Scotland, something that the Liberals had never succeeded in doing. What might perhaps have originally been a protest vote appeared to be solidifying into something much deeper. It seemed that a new alignment was developing in Scottish politics, something that could be explained only by the powerful sense of Scottish nationality, strongly buttressed by history, which gave to economic and other grievances a shape unmatched in other parts of Britain.[66]

The discovery of oil deposits in the North Sea compounded Labour's growing credibility problem with some Scots voters. In 1972, the SNP launched a timely campaign that laid claim to 'Scotland's oil'.[67] The government countered defensively, emphasising that oil on its own would not solve regional economic and infrastructure deficiencies, calling instead for more domestic investment from Scottish business. But oil was an issue on which the SNP could easily differentiate English self-interest and Scotland's 'right'. Central government's preference for reducing Britain's balance of payments instead of prioritising employment opportunities in some of the country's most economically stricken and socially deprived areas played badly with the Scottish electorate.[68] The appointment of a designated Scottish Office minister to manage affairs relating to 'Scottish' oil was merely belated acknowledgement of SNP success in harnessing this issue in order to mainstream its demand for self-government.

Oil assisted the nationalists' cause in an even more direct way, by giving credence to the once fanciful assertion that Scotland did indeed possess sufficient economic resource to loosen its dependence on England.[69] The quadrupling of international oil prices in the aftermath of the 1973 Yom Kippur War in the Middle East merely strengthened this claim. What followed was a war of statistics, albeit inconclusive, between the SNP and Whitehall. Each side tried to substantiate or refute the economic case for outright independence. Polling evidence indicates that the nationalists had the better of this argument, confirming that the issue of oil revenues reinforced a growing preference, and indeed confidence, amongst the Scottish electorate for greater autonomy from London.[70]

British membership of the European Economic Community (EEC) in 1973 added credibility to this case, with the prospect of a Europe-wide common market and enhanced regional interdependence favouring the Community's smaller states. Membership of an organisation committed to free trade and adhering to the principles of a common market meant, in effect, that in the event of independence England could not threaten, let alone employ, tariffs or any other trade restrictions against Scotland. This issue has since acquired greater salience in the home rule debate as the EC/EU recognised, through the now-fashionable concept of subsidiarity, the rights of its smaller nation states and regions to determine their own policy priorities with Brussels, especially in matters relating to structural policy. In fact, the EU has both developed procedures for enhancing multi-level governance, notably in managing the structural and regional funds, and facilitated direct links between territorial governments and Brussels.

The response from the British parties, that nationalism was merely an aberration, a temporary phenomenon, indicated at the very least a poverty of political imagination. The Liberal Party has traditionally been more receptive than the others to territorial politics. Gladstone's home rule legacy and the party's tenuous support base since 1918 combined to embed a radical disposition consistently favourable to constitutional novelty and democratic empowerment. At the same time, the rise of Celtic nationalism confronted the Liberals with a predicament. On the one hand, the party was quite amenable to the idea of a federal Britain, and indeed from 1950 it had advocated territorial parliaments for both Scotland and Wales.[71] On the other hand, and more problematical for the party, was how to translate the federal principle into the British context, where England is by far the dominant constituent.[72]

England is an historical territorial and cultural entity in its own right, and formerly a state, yet one for the most part lacking any obvious or natural regional identities as the firm base for regional governance. Some 'natural' English regions (most notably in the north-east and south-west) have manifested a nascent sense of regional identity, especially in response to territorial nationalism elsewhere in the country. Most of the other geographical regions, however, remain at best nebulous entities. In these circumstances, the Liberals' preference for federalising Britain has been rather easier to voice as an intellectual exercise, or as a manifesto commitment, than to manifest as workable constitutional arrangements. The issue has been further complicated by its role in the wider debate on party strategy. For the party remains internally divided over how best to maximise its radical third party potential. Some Liberal activists have preferred to make an eclectic national and territorial appeal across all regions and constituent parts of the United Kingdom, as an alternative to narrow class-based politics.[73] Whereas others in the party favour building on its limited but palpable success as the voice of the Celtic periphery.[74]

The Labour Party, too, has faced a similar strategic dilemma, historically the obverse of that described above. Labour began its political life as a non-establishment movement with strong roots both in provincial England and on the Celtic periphery. The Labour Party, not least in Scotland, inherited from its Liberal antecedents a normative commitment to home rule. This has, over time, been overridden by new ideological preferences – an outcome influenced by considerations of electoral success that has determined, in turn, ideological repositioning. The onset of industrial depression after the Great War nurtured in Labour's ranks an orthodox socialist approach to the management of social and economic progress in an industrial society. The Labour Party clung tenaciously to classic socialist nostrums, the ideological conviction that only collectivist preferences delivered by centralised planning within a unitary state could deliver social justice and prosperity for all of the United Kingdom's regions.

This centralist approach to national economic management conformed, too, with the trade union movement's commitment of maintaining national wage standards.

The Labour government of 1945–51 did supplement central planning and resources distribution with some regional measures designed to reduce disparities between the less affluent periphery and the better-off English regions. This conventional socialist exemplar demonstrably failed to deliver anticipated outcomes. So much so, in the view of one commentator, that 'in the late 1960s . . . the centralization of power under Labour was combined not with economic success, but with economic failure, and the politics of class came once again to be complemented by the politics of locality'. In these circumstances, 'Labour was . . . ideologically ill equipped to deal with the revival of nationalism'.[75] By and large, Labour continued to resist the idea of a distinctly territorial role in its economic and structural policies. As such, it was largely unprepared to meet the growing political challenge within its Celtic heartland from a politically mobilised nationalism after the 1960s.

Labour's critique of territorial nationalism shifted focus only after that movement showed little sign of fading. Discounting nationalism at the outset as politically insignificant, as little more than a temporary fad, the party now changed tack, criticising it for undermining Scotland's special position within the British State as embodied in the special arrangements at Westminster and in Whitehall for managing its affairs. Evidence presented by the Scottish Labour Party to the Royal Commission on the Constitution highlighted consternation in official party circles at the supposed threat posed by the 'folly' of devolution to Scotland's future prosperity.[76]

As recently as the February 1974 general election, Labour's manifesto chose to ignore devolution for Scotland, though it did commit to a directly elected assembly for Wales. The SNP's gain of six seats at that election concentrated Labour's collective mind. Within the month, Scottish Labour's rank and file had proposed a directly elected assembly. And although the Scottish Labour executive refused to endorse this proposal, for those very reasons that had been at the heart of traditional Labour thinking on the organisation of state power since the 1930s, party strategists in London took a more pragmatic view. They 'persuaded' the Scottish executive to revisit the issue. A specially convened conference in September 1974 finally endorsed a measure of devolution for Scotland, to be included in the party's manifesto for the October election.[77]

One consequence of these developments was that Labour managed to stem the rising tide of support for the SNP, at least in general elections. Thereafter, Labour maintained a wary commitment to devolution, less from unalloyed political principle than from a pragmatic concern to check the progress of a movement whose demand for outright independence threatened, as Labour strategists saw it, not merely the United Kingdom's constitutional fabric but also the loss of seats in Labour's electoral heartland.

The Conservative Party, too, failed to come to terms with a fast-changing territorial politics. The party's instincts had been fundamentally unionist since its renaissance during the long struggle over Irish home rule, even incorporating the Unionist title into its official name between 1912 and 1965. The Conservatives opposed Scottish home rule whenever the issue was debated at Westminster. There is, however, a counter-tradition amongst Scots Tories who have been long-standing champions of local traditions against the overweening cultural hegemony imposed on Scotland by England's Whig oligarchy. Moreover, past Conservative governments have endorsed institutional and cultural autonomy for Scotland as embodied in the 1707 Act of Union. After all, it was a Conservative government that increased the powers of the Scottish Office, both in 1926 and in 1939, and that in 1951 facilitated a modicum of decentralisation deemed consistent with effective governance at the centre.

A declining electoral base in Scotland after 1955 provided some incentive for Conservative strategists to rekindle the party's appeal there, by adopting a distinctly territorial dimension to its proposals for reforming government organisation in order to combat 'socialist centralism'. These reforms were informed by a familiar Conservative anti-state ideological preference rather than by concern for territorial self-determination per se.[78] Churchill made a direct comparison between rising Scottish nationalism and the centralism imposed by the Attlee government. As he saw it: 'if England became an absolute Socialist state, owning all the means of production, distribution and exchange, ruled only by politicians and officials in their London offices, I personally cannot feel that Scotland would be bound to accept such a dispensation'.[79] It was for these same ideological reasons that the Conservatives, returned to Opposition after 1964, proposed an elected Scottish assembly as a counterweight to excessive state control at their 1968 Scottish Conference.

The Scottish Constitutional Committee appointed by the Conservative leader Edward Heath proposed to balance the fundament of parliamentary sovereignty with a measure of decentralisation. It recommended that a directly elected Scottish assembly or convention be allowed to consider legislation pertaining to Scottish affairs – currently reviewed by the Scottish committees – at the second reading stage. The Speaker of the House of Commons would have the task of defining this 'Scottish' legislation. The third reading and second chamber stages would remain with Westminster, which likewise would retain the prerogative of rescinding decisions made by the Convention. Moreover, the Scottish Office would continue to be accountable to Westminster rather than to the Convention.[80] This arrangement failed nevertheless to resolve the principal objection of contemporary advocates of devolution to what they saw as the democratic deficit at the heart of the current British government: namely, that real power remained at the centre.

The Conservative Party incorporated these modest proposals into its 1970 general election manifesto. On its return to government, however, it simply omitted to legislate on devolution. With Scottish Conservatives deeply hostile to 'constitutional tampering', the Heath government merely opted to reform Scottish local government. In part, this reticence was due to the government awaiting the report of the Royal Commission on the Constitution accredited by their predecessors. In fact, pressing national events overrode territorial matters. A more far-reaching reform of constitutional arrangements was impeded, too, by the incipient crises in international and domestic affairs. Notable here were the negotiations that led to British membership of the EEC, motivated in part by the need to confront abiding structural problems in the British economy, and soon followed by the political fallout from the OPEC (Organisation of the Petroleum Exporting Countries) decision to halt oil production in protest at western governments' support for Israel during the 1973 Yom Kippur War.

The government's deep-seated unionist preference was confirmed by these events. Moreover, the nationalist threat appeared to have peaked. The 1970 general election saw a decline in the nationalists' vote.[81] This assessment was based, however, on a misunderstanding about the role of the territorial dimension in British politics. Whenever national or international issues assume prominence, the territorial electorate tends to suspend provincial concerns. This does not, however, diminish the significance of the territorial factor. The political price of overlooking this crucial point was eventually paid in hard political currency. Meanwhile the nationalist genie had been released in Scottish politics. The nationalist tide had begun to run more strongly in the February 1974 general election, with the SNP taking six seats, five in the northeastern hinterland of the oil industry. The party's eleven seats in the October 1974 election saw it take disproportionately more votes from the Conservatives than from Labour. And though this salutary lesson did briefly revive that party's interest in limited devolution, this was soon set aside, replaced by familiar unionist instincts when Margaret Thatcher was elected party leader in 1976.[82]

Contemporary polling evidence indicates that even non-nationalist voters were increasingly becoming identified more with a Scottish than a British identity, with some 75 per cent of public opinion regularly evincing support for home rule, though not for outright independence. This new territorial momentum was borne along by an abiding sense that the metropolitan centre had failed in its 'holding operation of the previous quarter of a century'.[83]

When the Royal Commission on the Constitution did report in 1973 it added momentum to the strong tide already running for devolution. Although the report did attempt to dispel the facile notion that the Union was the source of every conceivable territorial misfortune, it did, nevertheless, acknowledge a pervasive lack of empathy amongst the majority of English opinion for territorial sensibilities, which in turn ensured hard feelings. This situation, in the words of the report, amounted to nothing less than a stark failure 'to recognize the special character of their separate identity, of which they themselves are keenly conscious and proud'. A situation that 'at the same time . . . implies that the resentment they feel arises only because they are living in the past and getting agitated about something which is no longer important'.[84] A resurgent nationalist movement now directed its reviving political energies to redressing perceived metropolitan neglect.

Wales: the campaign for cultural approval

English domination of domestic affairs in Wales ensured an ambivalent political identity. Enforced annexation and absorption by the English state meant that Wales experienced neither real self-determination nor any autonomous national institutions. Government and administration were conducted from London, thereby reinforcing cultural assimilation. The use of English law precluded either special legislative arrangements or a distinct administrative status. The management of territorial affairs followed the union state model, balancing primary commitment to provincial needs with the maintenance of the overarching national interest. These arrangements permitted special territorial provisions, for instance territorial over-representation at Westminster amounting to 17 per cent based on a seats-to-population ratio.[85]

The dominant narrative of Welsh politics after the great franchise reforms of the late nineteenth century promoted, as in Scotland, a class-based rather than a territorial politics. Indeed, Welsh Labour remained even more firmly wedded to class as the fundament of party competition than its Scottish counterpart. Accordingly, the advocates of constitutional reform limited their demands to modest amendments in the structure of central government. The claim for enhanced status at the centre did eventually gain momentum during the Second World War with a petition to Downing Street endorsed by over one hundred Welsh local authorities. However belated, the demand for a Welsh secretary to complement Scotland's representation in the Cabinet was no more than half-hearted.[86] This was followed by a similar appeal from Welsh MPs approved by the Principality's Churches, trade unions and the press. Significantly, both petitions concentrated on measures designed to strengthen the Union. The campaign was equivocal about the extent of autonomy and hardly bold in claiming nationhood. It amounted to no more than a claim to recognition, for cultural approval within Wales as much as beyond it, and one deliberately couched in the language of reassurance. The words of the latter petition reflect this circumspection:

> The paramount fact is that the Welsh People are a distinct British Nationality and have so regarded themselves from time immemorial . . . We the representatives of Wales in Parliament, pray for this recognition of our nationality . . . The Welsh People, who hope to amplify and make fruitful those special moral qualities which are inherent in their distinctive character claim that their Province shall be henceforth recognized as a National entity and that they, as a people, must be given the opportunity of exhibiting in full nationhood what definitely pertains to their own genius . . . Welsh People, more deeply than at any time in recent history, feel that they are entitled to distinct and separate representation in His Majesty's Cabinet [and that] such recognition of their nationality [would] confer . . . a status both at home and abroad . . . but we are confident that it would still further strengthen the attachment which binds the Welsh People to our fellow Britons of the other Nationalities.[87]

The official response was unexceptional, merely agreeing in 1944 to a Welsh Day in Parliament to review territorial business. The most assertive expression of Welsh identity was mostly confined, at both official and public levels, to cultural matters, in particular to an insistence on official recognition of the native language and to the traditional radical rather than singular nationalist demand for the disestablishment of the Church of Wales.

A nationalist party, Plaid Cymru, had been launched in 1925, though in unpropitious circumstances. As with its Scottish counterpart, it called for a degree of home rule within the Union. The prospects for a more politicised nationalism were, however, hardly auspicious. During its early years, Plaid operated more as a pressure group for a culturally 'threatened' vernacular language, and with only limited success. Persistent lobbying, including direct action, eventually secured parity of recognition for the Welsh language on road signs, official forms and the like. A separate, publicly subsidised, Welsh television channel began broadcasting in 1982.

Lacking either a history of independent statehood or, as in Scotland's case, autonomous institutions as a focus for national revival, the Welsh language was the singular icon of national identity. The success of the Welsh Language Society (Cymdeithas yr Iaith Gymraeg) campaign, begun in 1963 for official recognition of the language, demonstrates the political potency of cultural issues for enhancing national identity.[88] The contrast with cultural politics in Scotland is marked. The role of Gaelic in reviving a popular sense of Scottish identity was largely incidental if not insignificant. By 1961, barely 3 per cent of Scotland's population were native speakers, and most of these in the remotest parts of the country. Welsh nationalism, on the other hand, had little else to call on for rekindling national identity except its language and related cultural referents such as native literature and folk music.

The Welsh language was, nevertheless, in steady decline even in its traditional strongholds in North and West Wales. It was no more than a minority language in the industrial south. Some 90 per cent of the population in 1700 had spoken the language, but by 1851 this figure had already declined to 54 per cent. Despite attempts by the Welsh Board of Education in the early twentieth century to revive the language, native speakers had declined further to barely 23 per cent by 1961, and to a mere 19 per cent by 1991. In the circumstances, playing the language card might have proved to be a divisive rather than an integrative force. As Bogdanor has observed: 'the English-speaking majority could hardly be expected to vote for a party whose main platform was the promotion of a language which they could not speak. If, on the other hand, Plaid Cymru were to underplay the language issue, it might lose its central core of support from those who saw the preservation of the language as the main purpose of self government'.[89]

The nationalist party, in contrast to more extremist groups, assimilated these lessons. Over time, it learned to play this delicate issue to its best advantage, adopting a tolerant and inclusive approach to the language question, though not without experiencing an internal rift that had weakened the party during its early years when simmering resentment in the ranks at what appeared to be the inferior status of non-native speakers had limited the movement's political appeal.[90] Preoccupied with the language issue at the outset, deeply divided over the primacy to be given to language as the principal badge of national identity, a schism opened between traditionalist and modernising factions. The modernisers eventually won the argument and the party has opted latterly for a bilingual policy, changing its name in 1998 to Plaid Cymru – The Party of Wales in order to reflect inclusiveness. Nowadays even non-Welsh speakers feel able to exhibit pride in distinctive cultural attributes. Plaid has also begun to concentrate more on territorial, economic and social issues that unite both language communities.

Progress on the broader political front was rather more modest. Plaid Cymru campaigned for a Welsh parliament in the early 1950s,[91] but alongside the Welsh Labour Party. Labour's support for a measure of devolution in the 1980s reflected, in part, narrow political motives, notably frustration in its ranks over Conservative dominance of the plethora of non-elected bodies running territorial affairs, and concern to make these bodies more politically accountable. Labour preferred reform of local government to any more radical prospectus, proposing an all-Wales tier expressly designed not to govern the country but to better supervise those who did. That such far-reaching reform might stimulate demands for devolution, or at least encourage the nationalists, persuaded some in the Welsh Labour movement to resist reform. More pragmatic party voices, however, warned against underestimating the nationalists' appeal, counselling that 'to ignore the problem of Welsh nationalism would be a short-sighted and perilous course, for it would alienate moderate opinion, increase sympathy for the extremists and risk repeating some of the mistakes made in Ireland and elsewhere'.[92]

Some Labour activists campaigned for limited reform, recommending a Welsh tier for local government, and in 1970 a Labour secretary of state even proposed an indirectly elected assembly, albeit one without legislative or tax-raising powers. Labour's official response to the Conservative government's subsequent proposals for a two-tier Welsh local government system confirmed, however, a residuum of resistance to devolution. Whilst some in the party supported a directly elected territorial assembly, the majority preferred an arrangement operating entirely 'within the legislative decisions of the House of Commons'.[93] Labour at Westminster did propose an elected Welsh Council, albeit one with limited competences and a degree of executive devolution, but with an assembly permitted only to amend secondary legislation. This became the template for the party's subsequent proposals for Welsh devolution in 1978 and again in 1998.

Plaid's impact on events was constrained by its own narrow support base. Plaid has never posed quite the same political threat in industrial and English-speaking Wales that the SNP has for Scottish Labour. The party made slow progress in its early years, confining its serious campaigning to Welsh-speaking areas. The party's rising support during the 1960s was mobilised by the same sense of territorial marginality and resentment at perceived economic neglect by the centre that had boosted support for the SNP. Plaid's vote share between the 1959 and the 1974 general elections increased from 0.2 per cent to 20 per cent. When an electoral breakthrough did occur, with Plaid winning its first Westminster seat in a by-election at Carmarthen in 1966, it came not in the party's cultural heartland but in a former Labour stronghold. The party almost repeated this remarkable feat in 1967, reducing Labour's majority in the Rhondda West by-election to a bare 2,306 and in a seat where only 28 per cent of the electorate were Welsh speakers. At the Caerphilly by-election in 1968, Plaid improved on even that feat, cutting a Labour majority of 21,000 to only 1,874 with a swing of 40 per cent, this time in a constituency with only 12 per cent Welsh speakers.[94]

Plaid failed, however, to build on these promising foundations, or to capitalise on its reasonable showing of 11.5 per cent of the Welsh vote in the 1970 general election. Despite winning two and three seats, respectively, in the two 1974 general elections, it did so with a declining share of the overall Welsh vote. Unlike the situation in Scotland, Plaid lost out to the Liberals as the repository of third party support. Notwithstanding more recent success in local government elections and in the first elections to the Welsh Assembly, the party remains more peripheral in Welsh politics than is its nationalist counterpart in Scotland. Whereas the party has built a modest base in local government, its wider success is limited to a handful of parliamentary and assembly constituencies mostly concentrated in the Welsh-speaking counties.

There is contemporary evidence of manifest as well as merely latent support for a cultural or identity politics, and, on that basis, for extended devolution. A survey on political identity conducted by Strathclyde University indicated that some 69 per cent of respondents now regarded their primary identity to be Welsh rather than British. This figure did not fall below 55 per cent for any particular social group or region of the country, and it matches similar findings on political identity in Scotland.[95] Further polling evidence indicated a marked shift in the proportion of the electorate who now preferred a measure of home rule (up to 59 per cent) and even outright separatism (up to 17.5 per cent). These figures, nevertheless, still lag some way behind the pro-devolution momentum of Scotland's electorate, where 75 per cent now endorse devolution.[96]

Plaid's prospects improved throughout the 1980s, a reflection of the undercurrents of social change and better political organisation. By the 1990s the party had consolidated a constituency in its cultural heartland and was showing signs of widening its popular appeal beyond it, taking full advantage of the Conservatives' steep electoral decline, and even challenging Labour in local government elections in industrial Wales. The limited appeal of Conservatism was further reduced by the impact of the Thatcher revolution. Labour's political dominance in South Wales was undermined, too, by the social consequences of the long-term decline of the primary industries and by diminishing public sector employment. 'Non-competitive' traditional industries were deprived of both state subsidies and public investment. A so-called dependency culture was confronted by successive Conservative governments and gradually replaced by a neo-liberal supply-side strategy for adapting the territorial economy to the rigours of global competitiveness.

The administrative mechanism for structural regeneration was the Welsh Development Agency, whose subsidiary arm, Welsh Development International, set up international offices to attract inward investment. Administrative reform, too, contributed to territorial disaffection, and in ways not anticipated by central government. A centralist reflex, for instance enhancing the powers of the Welsh Office consistent with the Conservatives' unionist instincts and the rapid expansion of a centrally appointed 'quangocracy', all fuelled territorial concern about non-democratic and unrepresentative governance.

The 1974–79 Labour government expanded the authority of the Welsh Office and it acquired greater powers during the Thatcher/Major years, though without commensurate accountability. These powers included responsibility for settling with the Treasury the level of the rate support grant (later the council tax subvention), health service administration, competence in secondary, further and university education, and in agriculture policy. Meanwhile, the Welsh Affairs Committee had no more than a modest watchdog role, constrained as to the scope of its review remit and with an administrative capacity too slight in manpower terms to cope with its formal functions.

The Conservative government in 1995 enacted largely token reforms in response to growing territorial unease: for instance, altering the arrangements for the Welsh Grand Committee to include more regular meetings, and with attendance by Cabinet members including the prime minister to better explain government policy. These changes in procedure did facilitate better-informed deliberations, although declining Conservative representation at Westminster saw party managers allocate Tory MPs from English constituencies to these committees, thereby fuelling concern about the democratic legitimacy of proceedings and the proper representation of Welsh interests at the centre. Local government changes, too, merely added to these concerns, with the establishment in 1991 of new unitary authorities without benefit of an independent commission. Undoubtedly, some of these reforms did contribute to raising the profile of Welsh affairs at Westminster, but the primary intention here was to deflect the territorial demand for devolution.

If this was the intention, these reforms failed to stem territorial unease. Opposition was channelled through the Assembly of Welsh Counties, collaborating with the Convention of Scottish Local Authorities to open a pan-Celtic front to resist overweening, undemocratic and overcentralised governance. But with only limited success, for the government used its majority in 1994 to push an unpopular measure – the Local Government (Wales) Act – through Parliament. The territorial democracy deficit was by now quite apparent, and highlighted during the passage of the bill. Standing Order 86 required that any bill pertaining solely to Wales must include at the committee stage every MP representing a Welsh constituency, a formula that, on the basis of territorial electoral arithmetic, would have ensured the Opposition a majority. The government chose to avoid this outcome by revoking Standing Order 86 in this instance, nominating nine English Conservative members to ensure a majority in committee, an action that confirmed the by now abiding impression in Wales of contempt for territorial opinion.[97]

These events took their toll, encouraging opinion in Wales of the need for an independent territorial voice at the centre. A clear sense that Wales was by now a political as much as a cultural nation infused the debate on territorial affairs, and especially about undemocratic governance, throughout the 1980s. Even staunch unionists began to contemplate a limited devolution. The impact of accelerating European integration, especially after the 1992 Maastricht Treaty introduced subsidiarity, in part to countervail the supremacy of national government in EU policy processes, added momentum to the idea of territorial autonomy in British government. There are distinct similarities here to contemporaneous events in Scotland, important differences notwithstanding.

Multi-level governance in the EU provided out-and-out separatists in Scotland with a convenient political alibi, as well as concrete institutional procedures for effecting exit from the UK, seemingly without economic pain or damage to either its markets or social infrastructure. In Wales, on the other hand, the European dimension is less a vehicle for independence and merely underpins growing national self-confidence for asserting greater autonomy within the Union. Devolution here was seen as feasible because the EU offers wider market opportunities for business and alternative sources of structural funding and regional assistance. The participation in European networks, involvement in regional funding initiatives, even through the conduit of the Welsh Office, and more direct links with Brussels, have all sustained a proactive policy by territorial agencies determined to connect with Europe's regional 'technological tigers'. This has produced agreements on technological collaboration, research and development initiatives, and other exchanges of 'best practice'.[98] The European dimension facilitates greater autonomy from the centre, but this would be far short of outright independence or anything like it.

The cultural payoff from regional interdependence is rather less tangible, though it does foster a more cosmopolitan outlook that sits uncomfortably with an exclusive territorial nationalism. Welsh local authorities through membership of the Assembly of Welsh Counties (AWC) began to network with trans-European organisations, for instance with the Assembly of the European Regions, eventually establishing a Wales European Centre in Brussels against the express wish of the Welsh Office. The AWC likewise proposed a Welsh regional council on the model of revived regionalism throughout Europe. These developments encouraged, over time, widespread support for a far-reaching reappraisal of the country's governance, but they have not, as in Scotland, nurtured any widespread commitment to separatism. Nevertheless, the territorial issue is now firmly at the centre of the political agenda.

A debate on devolution was rekindled in Wales during the 1990s, as it was in Scotland, and for many of the same reasons.[99] A third consecutive election defeat for Labour in 1992 caused the Labour Party in Wales to reflect on the political and economic consequences of a persistent and marked legitimacy deficit: that is, of enduring Conservative dominance at the centre in marked contrast to the territorial balance of power. In these circumstances, devolution was a more serious prospect than it had ever been during the 1970s. A Labour Party commission proposed a directly elected Welsh Assembly with devolved powers in health, education and economic regeneration.[100] There were recommendations, too, for reforming both the undemocratic quango system and the Welsh Development Agency.[101]

These proposals countenanced, however, only a limited devolution, reflecting Welsh Labour's continuing reticence, on the one hand, about any measure likely to improve Plaid's political fortunes, and on the other, concerning anything that weakened its socialist and statist preferences. It was proposed, for instance, to transfer merely limited competences from the centre, to give a Welsh 'cabinet' only a modest executive role, and with the secretary of state operating still as a principal interlocutor for Wales in London. Taken in their wider historical context, these were modest yet significant reforms, for the 1990s did represent a critical juncture in the debate about territorial governance in Wales. The cumulative effect of these events did ensure that devolution not only returned to the territorial political agenda with much firmer popular support, but also figured in the wider debate conducted at the centre about modernising the British polity. There was every indication, as the 1997 general election approached, that a future Labour government would revisit the issue, and the realistic prospect that it would deliver a measure of constitutional reform.

NOTES

1. K. Morgan, *Labour People: Hardie to Kinnock* (1992 edition) p.32
2. V. Bogdanor, *Devolution in the United Kingdom* (2001) pp.52–3
3. P. Jallard, United Kingdom Devolution 1910–14: Political Panacea or Tactical Diversion?, *English Historical Review* 94 (1979)
4. M. Steed, The Core–Periphery Dimension of British Politics, *Political Geography Quarterly* 5 (1986); V. Bogdanor and W. Field, Lessons of History: Core and Periphery in British Electoral Behaviour, 1910–1992, *Electoral Studies* 12 (1993)
5. O. MacDonagh, *States of Mind: A Study of Anglo-Irish Conflict 1780–1980* (1983) pp.19–20
6. A.T.Q. Stewart, *The Ulster Crisis* (1969)
7. John Redmond, Dublin 1898, quoted in G. Morton, *Home Rule and the Irish Question* (1980) pp.87–8
8. W. Bagehot, The Meaning and Value of the Limits of the Principle of Nationalities, *Works*, Vol. viii (1864) p.152
9. B. Harrison, *The Transformation of British Politics 1860–1995* (1996), chapter 3
10. W.E. Gladstone, *Special Aspects of the Irish Question* (1892)
11. Quoted in Paul Bew, *Charles Stewart Parnell* (1980) p.70
12. J. Loughlin, *Gladstone, Home Rule and the Ulster Question, 1882–93* (1986)
13. V. Bogdanor, op. cit. (2001) p.30
14. A.V. Dicey, *England's Case Against Home Rule* (1886)
15. A. Sykes, *The Rise and Fall of British Liberalism* (1997)
16. Sir E. Carson, speech in the House of Commons, 18 May 1920, cited in V. Bogdanor, op. cit. (2001) p.67
17. M. Laffan, *The Partition of Ireland 1911–1925* (1983)
18. R. Fanning, Britain, Ireland and the end of the Union, in R. Blake (ed.), *Ireland After the Union* (1989)
19. N. Mansergh, The Influence of the Past, in D. Watt (ed.), *The Constitution of Northern Ireland: Problems and Prospects* (1981) p.12
20. M. Laffan, op. cit. (1983)
21. R. Armstrong, Ethnicity, the English and Northern Ireland: Comments and Reflections, in D. Keogh and M. Haltzel (eds), *Northern Ireland and the Politics of Reconciliation* (1993)
22. N. Mansergh, *The Government of Northern Ireland: A Study in Devolution* (1936)
23. V. Bogdanor, op. cit. (2001) pp.56–7
24. J. Lee, *Ireland 1912–1985* (1973)
25. F.S. Lyons, *Ireland since the Famine* (1973) pp. 554–8
26. Speech in the House of Commons, 22 December 1919, quoted in V. Bogdanor, op. cit. (2001) p.61
27. N. Mansergh, *The Government of Northern Ireland* (1936)
28. R. Lawrence, *The Government of Northern Ireland: Public Finance and Public Services* (1965) p.181
29. M. Wallace, Home Rule in Northern Ireland: Anomalies of Devolution, *Northern Ireland Legal Quarterly* 18 (1967) p.161

30. S. Bruce, *The Edge of the Union: The Ulster Loyalist Political Vision* (1994)
31. C. Brett, The Lessons of Devolution in Northern Ireland, *Political Quarterly* 41 (1970)
32. Tim Pat Coogan, *The Troubles* (1995) p.360
33. C. Coulter, Direct Rule and the Ulster Middle Classes, in R. English and G. Walker, *Unionism in Modern Ireland* (1996) pp.169–70
34. J. Loughlin, *Ulster Unionism and British National Identity since 1885* (1995) p.173
35. V. Bogdanor, op. cit. (2001) p.68
36. P. Arthur, Devolution as Administrative Convenience, *Parliamentary Affairs* 30 (1977); P. Buckland, Who Governed Northern Ireland? The Royal Assent and the Local Government Bill, 1922, *Irish Jurist* 15 (1980)
37. J. Bardon, *A History of Ulster* (1992) p.499
38. Ibid., p.511
39. C. O'Leary, Northern Ireland, 1921–1929: A Failed Experiment, in D. Kavanagh (ed.), *Electoral Politics* (1992) pp.253–4
40. T. Hadden and P. Hilyard, *Justice in Northern Ireland* (The Cobden Trust, 1973)
41. J. Hewitt, The Roots of Violence: Catholic Grievances and Irish Nationalism during the Civil Rights Period, in P. Roche and B. Barton (eds), *The Northern Ireland Question: Myth and Reality* (1991)
42. The Downing Street Declaration, August 1969
43. *The Times*, 1 January 2003
44. J. Callaghan, *A House Divided: The Dilemma of Northern Ireland* (1973) p.66
45. For a detailed review of direct rule, see Lord Windlesham, Ministers in Ulster: The Machinery of Direct Rule, *Public Administration* 51 (1973)
46. F. Wright, Protestant Ideology and Politics in Ulster, *European Journal of Sociology* 14 (1973)
47. J. Prior, *A Question of Balance* (1986) p.194
48. J. Kellas, Prospects for a New Scottish Political System, *Parliamentary Affairs* 5 (1989)
49. Quoted in J. Brand, *The National Movement in Scotland* (1978) p.246
50. W. Miller, *The End of British Politics? Scots and English Political Behaviour in the Seventies* (1981) p.21
51. R. Weight, *Patriots: National Identity in Britain 1940–2000* (2002) p.130
52. I. Levitt, Britain, the Scottish covenant movement and devolution, 1946–50, *Scottish Affairs* 22 (1998)
53. PRO: CAB129, CP(50) 150, Scottish Affairs, 30 June 1950
54. PRO: CAB129, CP(50) 101, Scottish Affairs, 11 May 1950; and PRO: CAB128, CM(50) 31st Conclusions, Minute 4, 15 May 1950
55. Although, as the impact of the nationalist challenge was assimilated by the party establishments – both territorially and at the centre – their early preference was for more regional discretion rather than for devolution per se. See, for instance, J. Mackintosh, *The Devolution of Power: Local Democracy, Regionalism and Nationalism* (1968); and J. Banks, *Federal Britain? The Case for Regionalism* (1971)
56. R. Weight, op. cit. (2002) p.404
57. PRO: PREM11/4451, Noble to Macmillan, 21 January 1963

58. R. Weight, op. cit. (2002) p.407
59. R. Crossman, *The Diaries of a Cabinet Minister. Vol. 1: Minister of Housing 1964–66* (1975) p.317
60. *Wales: The Way Ahead*, Cmnd 3334 (1967)
61. A Celtic Dawn? *The Times*, 24 November 1967
62. I. Budge and D. Urwin, *Scottish Political Behaviour* (1966)
63. R. Weight, op. cit. (2002) p.410
64. *The Scotsman*, 4 November 1967
65. T. Wilson, Constitutional Implications of Home Rule All Round, *The Times*, 16 November 1967
66. V. Bogdanor, op. cit. (2001) pp.123–4
67. W. Miller, J. Brand and M. Jordan, *Oil and the Scottish Voter* (SSRC, North Sea Oil Panel Occasional Paper No.2, 1980)
68. T. MacKay, *The Political Economy of North Sea Oil* (1975)
69. C. Harvie and S. Maxwell, North Sea Oil and the Scottish National Party, 1970–79, in T. Smout (ed.), *Scotland and the Sea* (1992)
70. W. Miller, B. Sarlvik, I. Crewe and J. Alt, The Connection between SNP Voting and the Demand for Scottish Self-government, *European Journal of Political Research* 5 (1977)
71. HCD, vol. 759 (21 February 1968), cols 432–5; *The Times*, 22 February 1968
72. See the Liberal Party Report *Power to the Provinces* on this issue, and the review in *The Times*, 19 April 1968; D. Steel, Federalism in N. MacCormick (ed.), *The Scottish Debate: Essays in Scottish Nationalism* (1970)
73. K. Young, Orpington and the Liberal Revival, in C. Cook and J. Ramsden (eds), *By-elections in British Politics* (1997)
74. J. Vincent, What Kind of Third Party? *New Society* (26 January 1967)
75. V. Bogdanor, op. cit. (2001) p.168
76. Royal Commission on the Constitution, *Minutes of Evidence, iv* (Edinburgh, 1971), paras 70 and 126
77. For an account of these proceedings see T. Dalyell, *Devolution: The End of Britain?* (1977)
78. W. Ferguson, *Scotland from 1689 to the Present* (1968) p.388
79. Winston Churchill, 14 February 1950, cited in R. Rhodes James (ed.), *Winston S. Churchill: His Complete Speeches, 1897–1963. Vol. viii: 1950–63* (1974) pp.7936–7
80. *Scotland's Government*, The Report of the Scottish Constitutional Committee (Edinburgh, 1970)
81. J. Bochel and D. Denver, The Decline of the SNP: An Alternative View, *Political Studies* 20 (1972)
82. See M. Thatcher, *The Path to Power* (1995) p.322
83. R. Weight, op. cit. (2002) p.555
84. *Royal Commission on the Constitution 1969–1973. Vol.1: Report*, Cmnd 5640 (1973) pp.102–3
85. I. McLean, Are Scotland and Wales over-represented in the House of Commons? *Political Quarterly* 66 (1995)

86. J. Graham Jones, Socialism, Devolution and a Secretary of State for Wales, 1940, *Transactions of the Honourable Society of Cymmrodorion* (1989)

87. PRO: HO45/21644, A Petition from the Welsh Parliamentary Party to the Prime Minister, 28 October 1943

88. A. Butt Philip, *The Welsh Question: Nationalism in Welsh Politics 1945–1970* (1975) p.316

89. V. Bogdanor, op. cit. (2001) p.153

90. A. Butt Philip, op. cit. (1975) p.120

91. J. Graham Jones, The Parliament for Wales Campaign, 1950–56, *Welsh History Review* 16 (1992)

92. PRO: CAB134/2697, DS 2 (68), memorandum by the Secretary of State for Wales, 'Further Constitutional Changes in Wales', 22 February 1968

93. Labour Party Evidence to the Royal Commission on the Constitution (in 1970), cited in J. Osmond, *Creative Conflict: The Politics of Welsh Devolution* (1977) pp.142–3

94. K. Morgan, *Rebirth of a Nation: Wales 1880–1980* (1981) p.387

95. These findings are cited and analysed in A. Butt Philip, op. cit. (1975) pp.125–34

96. R. Weight, op. cit. (2002) p.411

97. J. Osmond, Remaking Wales, in J. Osmond (ed.), *A Parliament for Wales* (1994)

98. B. Jones, in J. Mawson, S. Hall, J. Gibney and S. Bentley (eds), *The English Regional Associations of Local Authorities. The 1995/96 European Work Programme* (School of Public Policy, University of Birmingham) pp.66–7

99. D. Elis Thomas, The Constitution of Wales, in B. Crick (ed.), op. cit. (1991)

100. *Shaping the Vision: A Report on the Powers and Structure of the Welsh Assembly* (Welsh Labour Party, 1995)

101. *Preparing for a New Wales: A Report on the Structure and Working of the Welsh Assembly* (Welsh Labour Party, 1996)

Part Two

RE-IMAGINING BRITAIN: THE POLITICS OF IDENTITY

Politicising territorial identity: theorems of change

Michael O'Neill

STIRRINGS

Constitutional reform became a salient issue in British politics during the 1960s and 1970s. Concern to improve national efficiency and to arrest accelerating economic decline renewed interest in the issue. The Royal Commission on the Constitution, appointed in 1968 by the Labour Government, under the Chairmanship of Lord Kilbrandon, was the principal response to these challenges. The Kilbrandon Report (1973) is a significant juncture in the postwar review of constitutional affairs, although the Commission was never intended when it was appointed to propose far-reaching reform. Neither of the mainstream British political parties had developed a constitutional strategy. There was no initiative, for instance, to synchronise the contemporaneous deliberations of the Kilbrandon Commission, the Redcliffe-Maud Commission to review local government in England, and the Wheatley Commission on Scottish local government.[1]

British politics during the early 1970s was preoccupied by national issues: turbulent industrial relations, fiscal crisis, and prospectively membership of the EC. In opposition and in government alike, Labour's social democratic project gave continued primacy to the state as the primary agency for social change and economic transformation. The Conservative government of 1970 was similarly preoccupied with a national policy agenda that included negotiating EC membership and facing off industrial militancy. It followed its unionist instincts, resisting constitutional changes, settling instead for merely local government reform. In the circumstances, it was hardly surprising that the Kilbrandon Report received little attention in the House of Commons.

Despite the unpropitious circumstances of its launch, the Kilbrandon Report was a signal event.[2] Kilbrandon, a Scots Liberal determined to respond to the rising nationalist challenge, boldly proposed an asymmetrical solution to the problem of administrative and political centralisation by devolving powers to directly elected Scottish and Welsh assemblies, although the report recommended only 'advisory' regional councils for the English regions.[3] These proposals for asymmetrical devolution established the pattern for subsequent constitutional reform.[4]

The majority of the Commission who favoured reform were nevertheless divided over their recommendations. One group preferred to maximise the autonomy of governance for Scotland and Wales within a devolved framework, but not to include the putative English regions.[5] Another group, seeking national coherence, recommended a uniform regional framework for the entire country.[6] A third group took the opposite position and resisted any far-reaching devolution, denying its relevance to Wales though conceding modest legislative devolution for Scotland. A minority Memorandum of Dissent issued by two dissident members, Lord Crowther-Hunt and Professor Alan Peacock, proposed even more far-reaching reform by giving English councils parity of power and esteem with those in Scotland and Wales within a federal framework.[7] Disagreement over the Commission's terms of reference and irreconcilable divisions between its members about appropriate solutions merely reflected widespread national concerns about tinkering with the ethereal mysteries of the British Constitution.

The incoming Labour government of 1974, faced with looming financial crisis, took refuge in the familiar ideological preferences of its centralist project. The prime minister, Harold Wilson, no enthusiast for devolution, shared the conventional wisdom of both the Cabinet and the Parliamentary Labour Party, and regarded the prospect of radical constitutional change with disfavour, as threatening a kind of ratchet effect of unanticipated consequences.[8] The Cabinet's anti-devolutionists wanted to preserve the Union, conveniently seeing this as the best safeguard for territorial interests. They reasoned that acceding to militant demands would merely exacerbate English impatience, perhaps releasing the spectre of English nationalism, with who knew what adverse effects on currently favourable budgetary arrangements for Scotland and Wales. The chair of the Cabinet committee dealing with this issue, Richard Crossman, unequivocally declared that the government had no intention of tinkering with constitutional fundaments that might 'undermine or compromise the sound structure of the United Kingdom just to placate a sudden movement of public opinion'.[9]

James Callaghan, who took over the premiership in 1976, was equally disparaging about devolution. He referred to it as 'parochial nationalism, in conflict with the central power of Cabinet and parliament, as well as with socialist notions of planning'.[10] Events, however, ensured a less dogmatic evaluation of territorial demands as Labour confronted the unpalatable facts of parliamentary arithmetic. When the Labour government did eventually respond to the Kilbrandon proposals, it was motivated not only by a genuine commitment to preserve the Union from volatile centripetal pressures, but also by political self-interest: to deter the growing Scottish National Party (SNP) threat in traditional Labour strongholds.

The October 1974 election gave Labour a majority of only three seats, with the SNP posing a real challenge in Labour's traditional heartland. This sustained a pragmatic concern amongst Labour's strategists in their response to territorial demands. The modalities of parliamentary politics confirmed the salience of devolution, for the party was reliant for a working parliamentary majority on third parties including the nationalists and pro-devolution Liberals. The Parliamentary Liberal Party in 1977 made devolution a condition of entering the Lib–Lab pact designed to sustain the now minority Labour government in office. In the circumstances, devolution for Scotland was unavoidable, and what was offered to Scotland could not reasonably be denied to Wales. The reform of the state was driven, however, more by political self-interest than by principled commitment.[11]

A brief consultative process was followed by the publication of two White Papers: *Democracy and Devolution: Proposals for Scotland and Wales* (Cmnd 5732, 1975) and *Our Changing Democracy: Devolution to Scotland and Wales* (Cmnd 6348, 1975). The eventual decision to combine the reform measures outlined in the proposals for Scotland and Wales within one legislative instrument was a decision that was again determined by the exigencies of parliamentary politics. Labour's parliamentary whips calculated that resistance to devolution from Welsh MPs could be more easily countered if potential rebels were faced with the prospect of denying home rule to Scotland. Welsh anti-devolutionists responded in kind, attaching an amendment – subsequently accepted by the government as an additional clause at the committee stage – requiring public approval by referenda in both countries.[12]

There was resistance, too, from some Scottish MPs concerned lest what they saw as a weakening of the Union would undermine Scotland's social and economic interests at the centre. A particular concern here was the likely consequence for Scottish representation. One notable Labour opponent of devolution, Tam Dalyell, revisited the question first posed by Dicey in 1886 in the context of Irish home rule, and which has come to be known by his constituency name as the West Lothian Question;[13] Namely, how to justify the continuing right of MPs representing the devolved territories to vote on English matters at Westminster, when English MPs have no reciprocal right to vote on devolved matters.

One solution to this constitutional conundrum is to reduce the number of Scottish MPs. Another is to limit the role of Scottish MPs at Westminster. The history of British general elections suggested both procedures threatened Labour's prospects of forming a national government. On three occasions (in 1950, 1964 and 1974), Labour has formed governments without securing a majority of English seats. The fact, too, that by 1974 only two of the previous six Labour governments had secured an overall parliamentary majority, and that of Labour's reliance on its Scottish and Welsh MPs if it was to remain a major national party, could hardly escape the notice of the party's strategists.[14]

The combined devolution bill was lost after an unlikely alliance of Conservatives (under a new leader, Margaret Thatcher, deeply hostile to what she saw as an insidious threat to the very fabric of the Union) and back-bench Labour MPs ideologically resistant to weakening the central state. By now, aware of the significance of the territorial dimension in British politics, the Labour leadership with Liberal support revived the devolution measure as two separate bills for Scotland and Wales. These were passed in the House, but only by using a guillotine motion.

The legislation proposed assemblies for both countries, directly elected by first-past-the-post, and with some legislative competence and executive discretion for Scotland over devolved Scottish Office functions, principally local government, social policy and infrastructural matters. In marked contrast with Scotland's 'cabinet', however, Wales was to have only local-government-style committees to provide 'political direction'.[15] Neither assembly would have fiscal competence; finance was to be provided by bloc grants from the centre. The secretaries of state likewise retained formidable executive powers. Nor was there to be any question of divesting powers from central government in the critical areas of economic or industrial policy, or over energy or agriculture. Westminster's sovereignty was confirmed by retention of the prerogative to legislate on *any* devolved matter, with the judicial committee of the Privy Council arbitrating in any boundary disputes between the two parliamentary jurisdictions.

Resistance to even this modest devolution reveals the Westminster establishment's abiding hostility to far-reaching constitutional reform.[16] Two amendments pressed on the government by opponents of devolution sought additional guarantees for central power. The Ferrers amendment, subsequently incorporated into the Scotland Act 1998 (section 66), provided that in any vote at Westminster on a devolved matter where the parliamentary majority relied on votes of Scottish Members, an Order might be laid before the Commons requiring another vote within the fortnight. A further amendment required that these reforms should have the overwhelming backing of a majority of the electorates in the two countries.

The attempt to redress the inequitable representation of territorial interests at Westminster in the event of devolution illustrates the flaw in asymmetrical devolution in a non-federal polity – a problem that neither the 1978 nor the 1998 legislation has satisfactorily resolved. A potential consequence of the Ferrers amendment was that political pressure on Scottish Labour MPs to withdraw or abstain on a second vote on devolved matters could deny a Labour government a majority. The amendment thus had potentially major consequences for constitutional stability. As one observer has explained this situation: 'There would then be a bifurcated executive, one majority when all MPs were voting and another majority when the Scottish MPs were absent . . . It is not easy to imagine how effective Cabinet government could continue under such circumstances'.[17]

The second amendment was of less dramatic constitutional significance, though it did have more immediate impact on the passage and outcome of the legislation. The Cunningham amendment, proposed by a Scottish Labour MP sitting for an English constituency, required that the proposed legislation must pass a 40 per cent threshold of all registered voters in the subsequent referenda. Even then, the Scotland Bill gave the Scottish secretary some discretion in interpreting the 'popular will', enabling him to 'lay before parliament the draft of an Order in Council providing for its repeal' (Clause 82(82)). This amendment, too, was incorporated into the legislation despite resistance from within the Parliamentary Labour Party.

After a troubled passage, both devolution bills passed the Commons and received the Royal Assent in July 1978. The Cunningham amendment undoubtedly influenced the eventual outcome although it is exaggeration to claim, as one close observer has, that this amendment alone 'doomed Welsh devolution at birth . . . and it made Scottish devolution far more difficult to achieve'.[18] The 40 per cent requirement did prove too steep a hurdle, but the situation was undoubtedly made worse than it might have been by the failure, of both the government and its territorial party establishments, to kindle local enthusiasm for what for them was undeniably unpalatable change. In the event, both devolution campaigns 'turned into a plebiscite on the government's record as a whole during the "winter of discontent", with predictable consequences'.[19]

Neither devolution proposal managed to clear the 40 per cent threshold in the referenda that were held on 1 March 1979. There was an overall majority for devolution in Scotland,[20] but in Wales a margin of almost four to one was opposed, with a majority registered against devolution in every one of Wales's eight counties.[21] An outcome that markedly contrasted with a time in the 1960s when opinion polls in Wales regularly recorded support for devolution running at almost 60 per cent. The referendum figures were as follows:

Scotland

Yes	1,253,502	51.6 per cent of actual turnout, which translates as 32.85 per cent of the electorate
No	1,230,937	48.5 per cent of actual turnout, which translates as 30.78 per cent of the total electorate

Wales

Yes	243,048	20.2 per cent of actual turnout
No	956,330	79.8 per cent of actual turnout

Total turnout	62.9 per cent

The lessons of this defeat can be briefly summarised. The centre had markedly failed to overcome residual hostility within the territorial political establishments to a reform that threatened, as they saw it, to weaken not only the Union but also their own hold on territorial politics. More critical, perhaps, was the failure to convince key territorial elites – notably business and the trade unions, and through them public opinion at large – of the practical benefits of devolving central power. Failure to carry devolution, compounded by widespread public disaffection with the government's handling of industrial relations during the 'winter of discontent' in 1978–79, signally contributed to the downfall of the Labour government in 1979, when SNP Members supported the Conservative Opposition's motion of no confidence. An unholy alliance defeated the proposed reform of the state, with outright separatists and equally staunch unionists combining to outmanoeuvre a government finally persuaded to undertake reform by territorial forces threatening their electoral base. This alliance was founded on merely short-term political convenience, and it had a predictable outcome. The Conservatives' victory in the 1979 general election ensured that, for the foreseeable future, all talk of devolution was discounted. The fact that the Conservatives won eleven seats in Wales, their best performance in the Principality since 1874, merely served to confirm devolution's hiatus at Westminster. The new government led by Margaret Thatcher repealed the two devolution Acts within a month of taking office.

The Thatcher interlude: shoring up the union state

The Thatcher project seemingly put paid to devolution. The new government deprecated territorial identity as merely obsolescent provincialism, a familiar response by Westminster. Devolution was disparaged, too, because it threatened to increase already overblown bureaucracy, a particular preoccupation of the incoming prime minister. Mrs Thatcher has said as much in her political memoirs, averring that devolution 'added a layer of bureaucracy, standing in the way of the reforms that were paying such dividends in England'.[22]

For most of the following decade the discourse of British politics was a class-based narrative, a synthesis of recrudescent British nationalism and a neo-liberal political economy. Conviction politics was riding high and with it an appetite for national hauteur aptly reflected in the Falklands War. There were already signs, too, of an English national backlash against Celtic 'hubris', though mostly confined to the margins of a political establishment more relieved than vexed by the outcome of the devolution moment. The maverick Enoch Powell, amongst others, voiced the irritations of an exasperated and uncomprehending unionism, reminding the nationalists of their vulnerability on the margins of the British Isles, even warning them that: 'If you don't like your geographical position – being away from the dense population markets – get out of it . . . but don't ask people to give you handouts. That's the begging bowl mentality'.[23]

Meanwhile, the new government reverted to the familiar unionist strategy of national assimilation, attempting to reconcile economically marginalised regions with its mission to install an enterprise culture. Thatcherism exalted entrepreneurial norms as much as it excoriated continuing dependence on state-subsidised, state-run industries. Especially so in the coal and steel industries on which the economies of Scotland and Wales were so heavily dependent. The priority was to 'roll back' the state, to reduce 'wasteful' public expenditure, and to liberate the market as the most reliable engine for national growth and prosperity.[24]

These objectives were to be realised not by resorting to deliberative and pluralist politics but rather by reasserting the power of the state over those intermediate agencies or meso levels of governance identified as an insidious threat to the success of the project: and to do so without dismantling the favourable ratio of tax yield to public expenditure enshrined in the Barnett formula.[25] Abrasive leadership from Downing Street merely served to reinforce an impression of indifference, indeed of deep ideological antipathy to territorial autonomy, raising doubts amongst the constituent nations about the benefits of the Union not witnessed since the eighteenth century.[26]

In so far as regional policy figured at all in the neo-liberal armoury for national economic regeneration, it was as no more than a convenient device for improving indicative planning: a means for facilitating inward investment, better land use, more purposive economic development, improved transport reorganisation and rational resource allocation and scale-economies superintended from the centre. Resistance from territorial interests to these structural changes at the periphery was dismissed as merely an irrational reaction to ineluctable modernisation.[27]

The government's response was one of firm resolve, to avoid 'pandering' as their predecessors had done to 'unreasonable' territorial demands. And instead to implement modest reforms in local government and other measures to enhance policy delivery: the better use of national resources, improving services delivery through the medium of agencies, regional offices and quangos appointed by, and above all controlled from, the centre.[28] These arrangements failed, however, to satisfy a rising mood of territorial disenchantment with the unitary state. Even more than this, these reforms bespoke complacency at the centre, a response that confronted head on the once acceptable because pragmatic bargain that underpinned the union state, allowing the constituent territorial nations some degree of self-determination.[29]

Free market logics, too, added much to perceived territorial economic woes. The deregulation of economic and fiscal policy during the Thatcher years accelerated the long-term structural shift in the regional locus of the British economy, confirming the economic advantages accruing to the south-east of England as the primary engine of national economic growth. This showed up in stark relief the relative economic decline of Wales and Scotland. By 1985–86, some £2.4 billion out of a total of £4.7 billion of Scottish manufacturing capital had shifted southwards, with a consequential rise in unemployment from 5.7 per cent in 1979 to 11.1 per cent by 1986.[30]

Regional subsidies formerly used to ameliorate such clear-cut disparities were now severely curtailed, for they represented to the official mind the antithesis of the enterprise culture, embodying an alien socialist creed that merely encouraged dependence. Of course, North Sea oil continued to flow, adding some £62 billion to Treasury receipts, though the tangible benefits of this for Scotland remained, as public opinion saw it, somewhat elusive. In Wales, too, unemployment rose above the national average (from 5.5 per cent in 1979 to 13.2 per cent by 1986) boosted by the severe cutback in the coal industry after the collapse of the 1985 miners' strike – and in this case, without having the palliative of oil to cushion economic decline.

Opposition to the Thatcher project in the territorial polities was galvanised by these developments, though it resided, in the first instance, in a familiar class-based narrative. An ideological exegesis which, in so far as it had a territorial aspect, was based as much on a north–south divide or centre–periphery tension as on relative deprivations rooted in distinctly territorial identities. Labour's ideological crisis and the internal war it set off confirmed the drift away from the territorial issue. The party jettisoned pragmatic devolution in the aftermath of comprehensive electoral defeats in 1979 and again in 1983. These signal events turned the party inwards, launching virtual civil war, a bitter contest for the party's ideological soul.[31]

After Labour's traumatic defeat in 1983, which saw the party barely retain its status as the second British party, a modernising and essentially pragmatic Labour leadership revisited and reviewed the territorial agenda, in the first instance for much the same reasons as the party's belated conversion to the same cause in the mid-1970s. A sharp increase in the nationalist vote in Scotland, in part a rebuff to Labour for its failure to defend the non-English regions against the New Right incubus, threatened Labour's future as a serious political force. The nationalist vote was now much less a reactive protest against the incumbent party and more to do with fundamental political realignment, a response to the SNP's concerted strategy to replace Labour in Scotland as the main opposition to the Conservatives. Events in England did much to precipitate this change. There was a palpable sense of a distinct and growing territorial democracy deficit in the non-English parts of the Union.

Administrative palliatives such as the expansion of Scottish Office competences failed to reassure. By degrees, territorial subjection to radical new-right policies widely regarded by local opinion as punitive was seen as lacking popular legitimacy. Whilst territorial electorates continued to vote overwhelmingly for radical parties, the English majority ensured the return of Conservative governments at Westminster. Whilst the Conservatives lost eleven of their Scottish seats (reduced from 21 to 10) in the 1987 election, and in Wales Conservative representation declined from 14 to 8 seats, in England Margaret Thatcher formed her third administration.[32]

The assumed 'arrogance of power', however, merely accelerated territorial disaffection. The decision to impose the new community charge or 'poll tax' first in Scotland in 1989, a year ahead of England and Wales, was undoubtedly a defining moment in the already deteriorating relations between the government and Scotland. This decision was widely regarded as a mark of Conservatives' disregard, even contempt, for Scotland.[33] But it was also symptomatic of Labour's seeming incapacity to defend Scottish interests. The fact, too, that the Scottish Office was largely sidelined in the policy deliberations that resulted in this unpopular tax was further confirmation of how far Scotland's interests were now marginalised by current institutional arrangements at the centre.[34] A fourth consecutive election defeat for Labour in 1992 galvanised non-English opinion as well as the non-Conservative parties at Westminster on the question of territorial governance.

THE 1980s WATERSHED AND BEYOND

Scotland: the pace accelerates

In the 1979 general election the Conservatives won 22 Scottish seats with 31.4 per cent of the total vote. By 1987, the party's tally was down to only 10 seats and to barely 24 per cent of the total vote. Political disaffection led to a marked rise in public support for devolution. The all-party Campaign for a Scottish Assembly (CSA), a coalition of politicians and representatives from civil society (Churches, trade unions, environmentalists, academia, business, local government and so on), was launched in 1980 precisely to mobilise support for a Scottish parliament. The Conservatives and the SNP refused to join in the Convention for entirely opposite reasons; the former because it was wholly against any measure of devolution, the latter because it wanted nothing less than outright independence.[35]

The Campaign initially had only a limited impact, with modest attendance at CSA rallies.[36] A change in tactics, the decision to establish a Constitutional Steering Committee of 'prominent' Scots, who in turn recommended a convention to make proposals for reforming Scottish government and to include a parliament with real powers, rallied public opinion.[37] The campaign for a constitutional convention was launched in 1989 on the anniversary of the devolution referendum of 1 March 1980. The steering committee produced a Claim of Right for Scotland in 1988, making the case for a Scottish parliament.[38] This amounted to a latterday Declaration of Arbroath and was based on the premise that Scottish sovereignty does not reside at Westminster as the Act of Union maintains but remains with the Scottish people, a nation in its own right.[39] Opinion poll data indicated, however, that a clear majority saw this objective not so much as an end in itself, a loss of confidence in the constitutional order, but rather as a means of resisting alien policies imposed by central government on a people whose ideological preferences differed, by and large, from those of the centre.

The politicisation of Scottish identity was more than merely an expression of material self-interest.[40] Scots voters had few illusions that home rule, let alone outright independence, would somehow resolve the country's manifold problems. Nevertheless, the once firm affiliation to an overarching British identity had been sorely tested by London's perceived neglect, a sentiment that markedly increased during the Thatcher years.[41] Concern with legitimacy shortfall and the democracy deficit, as much as the desire to break the Union, was at the heart of the matter. The Conservatives, by 1987, with only ten Scottish seats and eight in Wales were fast losing their electoral foothold outside of England. The party was facing the prospect of becoming much more an English party than a British party. This, in turn, weakened the sense of mutual and assured benefits that had long sustained the fabric of the Union.[42] In the view of one commentator: 'The more the English revelled in the benefits of Conservative rule, the more the Scots and Welsh saw them as a nation of callous, selfish individuals. In contrast, they saw themselves as peoples with a unique sense of community and compassion, a belief which the nationalist parties encouraged'.[43]

Subsequently, Mrs Thatcher has refuted the accusation that either she or her party abandoned commitment to the Union, replacing it with an exclusively English affiliation. She has maintained instead that traditional Scottish mercantilist values mirrored her own preference for economic self-reliance, though these values of thrift and enterprise had over time become seemingly corrupted by socialist dogma, inculcating instead an unacceptable sense of dependence.[44] She argued this very case before Scottish Conservatives, claiming that: 'Tory values are in tune with everything that is finest in the Scottish character . . . Scottish values are Tory values – and vice versa'.[45] The electorate in Scotland remained unconvinced by this claim, provoking her to write in her memoirs in exculpatory rather than chastened terms about this apparent misconception. She observed that

> Some part of [Conservative] unpopularity must be attributed to the national question on which the Tories are seen as an English party and on which I myself was apparently seen as a quintessential English figure. About the second point I could – and I can – do nothing. I am what I am and I have no intention of wearing tartan camouflage . . . The Tory Party is not, of course, an English party but a Unionist one. If it sometimes seems English to some Scots that is because the Union is inevitably dominated by England by reasons of its greater population. The Scots, being an historic nation with a proud past, will inevitably resent some expressions of this fact from time to time . . . It is understandable that when I come out with these kind of hard truths many Scots should resent it. But it has nothing to do with my being English.[46]

After the 1987 election the government did heed this supposed 'aberration' of Scotland's resolutely collectivist mindset. Ideology rather than pragmatism, the political art of the possible in a heterogeneous polity, drove public policy: the resolute belief that collectivist recidivism was a bad habit, a denial of an inferred native tradition of self-reliance. And it was deemed to be curable only by imposing the market-orientated revolution that had already restructured England's economy.[47] What followed was a concerted drive by central government to privatise transport and the electricity industry, to reform the education and public health services, and to inculcate entrepreneurial habits by reorganising the Scottish Development Agency.[48]

Adopting policies broadly similar to those implemented in Wales, the government dismantled state ownership, relocating some 'public' services – *inter alia* housing administration, higher education, training and development – under an emergent 'quangocracy'.[49] These arrangements were designed 'to take over central and local government functions and delivery programmes thus by-passing what were perceived to be islands of resistance to the Thatcherite agenda in the traditional state bureaucracy'.[50] Of course, some Scottish Conservatives remained sceptical about jettisoning the long-standing unionist tradition of accommodating territorial interests and political culture, reconciling the overarching national interest with a distinctively Scottish identity.[51] But their message went largely unheeded at the centre.

The Major government after 1989 did at least soften the outright confrontation approach to territorial disquiet of its predecessor. Despite pursuing the supply-side revolution in Scotland almost as energetically as its forerunner – including privatisation, market-led reforms, and closure of uneconomic state enterprise – it did so with a more conciliatory political style: a mellowing in tone, if not a change of direction, and one aptly described as a 'compensating unionism'.[52] Prime Minister Major was as hostile to devolution as his predecessor, and in his 1992 general election campaign fastened on the dramatic theme of the Union 'in danger' from Labour's revived and 'ill-considered' devolution proposals.[53] Indeed, by 1995, Labour had firmly repositioned itself within the devolution camp, now advocating English regional government in its proposed constitutional refit. Predictably, Major deprecated the idea, decrying the proposal as 'one of the most dangerous propositions ever put before the British nation'.[54]

Although the Conservatives did adopt a more conciliatory approach to Scotland, and signalled as much during the 1992 general election campaign, by now the political damage was done. Of course, the defence of the Union theme played better with the English electorate than it did with a Scottish electorate deeply attached to the idea of distinctly 'Scottish values' and predominantly voting for those parties it believed represented them. Campaigning unequivocally on an independence ticket, the SNP secured a remarkable 21.4 per cent of the Scottish vote, barely four percentage points behind the Conservatives, though the arithmetic vagaries of first-past-the-post translated this into a mere three seats.[55]

Chastened by this outcome yet resolute in its unionist preference, the second Major government preferred to repeat this blend of modest reform mixed with staunch resistance to home rule.[56] The government pursued the elusive enterprise culture as an antidote to dependence through a Scottish Enterprise Initiative designed to support local business ventures. The 1993 White Paper *Scotland in the Union – A Partnership for Good* (Command 2225) attempted to check the momentum gathering behind devolution, both in the Labour Party and amongst territorial opinion at large. The White Paper emphasised the 'benefits' of the constitutional status quo, highlighting Scotland's 'significant position' in the Union through the medium of the Scottish Office and by its representation at Westminster. The White Paper proposed further changes in the management of Scottish business in Whitehall and at Westminster, measures designed to meet what London still saw as wholly 'misplaced' objections to perceived 'neglect' at the centre of territorial interests.

It was proposed, for instance, to increase the time available, to improve the visibility and to enhance the representation of Scottish interests in Parliament and within the administrative interstices of central government. This goal would be achieved by devolving yet more administrative competences to the Scottish Office, for instance in the fields of industrial support, further and higher education, care in the community, the Scottish Arts Council, and with a watching brief over European Social Fund expenditure. Other recommendations were to increase the powers, the number and the scheduling of meetings of the Scottish Grand Committee and to expand parliamentary scrutiny over Scottish bills so as to provide more opportunities for debate, increasing the opportunity to question the secretary of state.

Arrangements were also made to hold special standing committees on Scottish bills in Scotland, and to make a concerted effort to bring the Scottish Office closer to the people by holding its meetings throughout the country and by setting up information points in the principal urban centres. The Scottish Grand Committee was empowered to hold debates on third as well as second readings of bills. Cabinet ministers, including the prime minister rather than just the Scottish secretary, were to be permitted to attend its meetings, to put motions and to reply to questions, but not to vote.[57] These changes amounted, in effect, to 'the creation of a mini House of Commons for Scotland within the orbit of the UK Parliament'.[58]

These reforms were projected by the government's publicity machine as a significant concession to a distinctive Scottish dimension in government, but short of undermining the union state.[59] Again, cognitive dissonance between centre and periphery ensured that these reforms were regarded by their target audience as rather too little and too late.[60] Election results indicated the extent of this lacuna between the respective mindsets. In the 1994 local government poll the nationalists came second behind Labour. There was evidence of concern at the centre, but no wish to respond to a fast-changing situation with far-reaching constitutional reform. The belated return in 1996 of Scotland's ancient coronation stone was seen then as merely another, and inadequate, palliate, a gimmick that was described by one Scots editorial writer as 'a patronising publicity stunt by a government which can't disentangle myth from reality [for it] speaks volumes for the attitude of Westminster to the Scottish question that they should expect Scotland to be grateful for being awarded this useless lump of sandstone in lieu of self government'.[61]

The 1997 White Paper on the constitution was the Conservative government's final, desperate effort to respond to territorial concerns. But this, too, was viewed as gesture politics, and regarded in much the same sceptical light by its target group. It was a document that was long on declaratory statements reaffirming 'our faith in the

Union', yet deficient on those far-reaching changes in governance now demanded as a minimum response by Scottish political opinion of every ideological compass.[62]

These belated attempts at reform made little impression on Scottish public opinion. A new territorial axis had emerged in British politics, one requiring more than merely constitutional casuistry. The social dynamics shaping the party systems in both Scotland and Wales had been gradually diverging for some two decades from those underpinning the English party system. By the late 1980s, the territorial issue had become a major factor of inter-party (and sometimes of intra-party) competition in Scotland, and to a lesser degree in Wales. The nationalist parties had harnessed this radical momentum to good effect, mobilising public support well beyond their nationalist constituency for a distinctive provincial agenda against the traditional class-based British parties. And this notwithstanding, there were discernible differences over Labour's approach to devolution in the two countries. The political salience of the territorial issue in Scotland, where the SNP posed a greater electoral threat than its counterpart in Wales, persuaded Labour there to build a broad coalition for constitutional change with key elements in Scottish civil society. In Wales, on the other hand, the Labour establishment, or leading elements within its ranks, actually led the debate on territorial reform.

The state of territorial public opinion confirmed this underlying shift in the axis of territorial politics, altogether more receptive now to the idea of devolution as a positive benefit than it had been in the late 1970s. Scottish opinion polls regularly recorded levels of support for devolution running at 75 per cent. The Conservatives' response was predictable: to simply refuse to countenance constitutional change. A new secretary of state, Michael Forsyth, cast in the Thatcherite mould but with Scottish roots, saw devolution as much as outright independence as threatening to the constitutional fabric, undermining the integrity of the Union. He chose instead to confront the nationalist challenge on two fronts. On the economic front, he pursued a distinctly Thatcherite agenda of deregulation, notably in the public sector water industry, attempting to redress Scotland's lagging position in an interdependent global marketplace through accelerated supply-side reforms, in other words fostering infrastructure change to facilitate competitiveness.[63]

On the political front, however, Forsyth resorted to a familiar unionist stratagem, acknowledging distinctive Scottish identity by increasing autonomy for local government, albeit within a still centralised framework. Cumbrous public bodies were divested of their customary competences and these were reallocated to streamlined but wholly unaccountable agencies such as government regional offices and proliferating quangos.[64] It was reform of sorts, but hardly consistent with a growing appetite for territorial democratic self-government. The effects of this reform were quite predictable and less than effective, hardly democratic and in no way convincing to a sceptical territorial opinion.

Opposition perspectives

The opposition parties were better placed to make political capital from unprecedented public disaffection. Labour had long since abandoned its cosmetic approach to devolution, recognising that the nationalist genie had escaped once and for all from the bottle that Thatcherism had apparently consigned it to in 1979, and were aware now that it would hardly be placated without far-reaching constitutional reform. Mere administrative changes had in no way diminished Westminster's control of Scottish affairs. Of course, there was more to this than principled Damascene conversion or conviction politics. Practical politics as much as more principled concerns continued to drive Labour policy. The party's revived interest in devolution in the 1980s had much to do with territorial electoral pressure exerted by the SNP, which in a by-election in 1988 won the once 'safe' Labour seat of Govan, fielding as its candidate a former Labour MP. After a decade of Conservative government, a buoyant SNP was challenging Labour on its home turf. Labour was also facing growing internal dissent support for outright independence from its own constituency activists.[65]

Other strategic considerations, too, played a part in policy shift. As the party most likely to form the next government, Labour strategists anticipated having to respond to Scottish demands for devolution. By the early 1990s, Scottish identity, a previously nebulous, even ambivalent, cultural phenomenon had become firmly politicised.[66] So much so, that the 'awareness of Scottish identity played a key role [and] even though the political element of Scottish feeling was . . . not always prominent, there was a feeling that Scotland did have interests which were not always given their weight'.[67]

The Constitutional Convention launched in 1989 captured this mood shift.[68] In part, this explains why it couched its demand for action in the emotive language of a covenant with the people and referred, amongst other things, to 'the sovereign right of the Scottish people to determine the form of Government best suited to their needs'. Between 1989 and 1992, the Convention, with a Labour majority but without SNP participation, pursued the demand for a devolved parliament in Edinburgh.[69] The all-party proposal that was eventually adopted in 1995 was actually based on the 1978 plan for listing devolved competences rather than those powers to be retained at Westminster. But things had moved on since then. Significantly, Convention literature referred not in the modest nomenclature of 1978 to an assembly but instead to a parliament for Scotland.[70]

The principal outcome of these intra-territorial deliberations was agreement on a Scottish parliament to be elected by the additional member system, a form of proportionality.[71] The Convention even accomplished the remarkable political feat of reconciling the Parliamentary Labour Party to the idea of devolution, and by now as much as a matter of right than as an unavoidable political evil to be accepted as a mere *fait accompli*.[72] There was, too, something of the political deal about this breakthrough. The reforms agreed after Convention's deliberations were reached only after direct intervention by the leaderships of the national opposition parties. This ensured that the proposals became a central plank of Labour and Liberal party policy,[73] though this occurred largely at the price of fudging some of the critical issues for effective management of territorial relations. Rather less attention was given by the Convention to, for instance, resolving the awkward paradoxes of asymmetrical devolution, those very contradictions that had been aired in the constitutional debates during the ill-fated passage of the 1978 legislation – and which, if left unresolved, threatened further political difficulties. Critical issues here were the precise relations between a devolved parliament and the centre, the resolution of conflicts over respective competences, Scottish representation, and the role of Scots MPs at Westminster, all of which remained pending.[74]

Other equally critical constitutional matters remained to be settled from what was, in fact, more an ad hoc inter-party bargain than a considered exercise in constitutional review. Labour resisted, for instance, a Liberal Democrat proposal to abolish the office of secretary of state, the enduring symbol of the unitary state. At this stage, the precise and delicate nature of the territorial link with Westminster and Whitehall was hardly broached, nor was the equally delicate matter of public finance, or the thorny issue of the size and role of Scottish representation at Westminster, and whether these MPs should retain voting rights on issues pertaining only to England. Finance is a problematic matter on several counts. Although discussion in the 1990s did go beyond the 1978 proposal for finance by bloc grant, thus anticipating the nationalists' charge that this would merely be continuing dependence on the centre, the right to raise territorial taxation was as politically controversial as ever. This, in turn, precluded frank and open debate about the merits of the issue. By 1990, there was a consensus amongst pro-devolutionists about combining grant financing with the assignment by the centre of some Scottish income tax revenues, a proportion of VAT, and the Scottish parliament's prerogative to vary income tax within agreed but as yet unspecified limits.

Labour has revisited this delicate issue under Tony Blair's leadership, but for political reasons, concerned to set aside the electorally embarrassing (and in the 1992 election, politically damaging) 'tax and spend' charge levelled by the Conservatives that contributed much to Labour's fourth consecutive election defeat. Labour proposed instead to scale down 'own resources', limiting the income tax levy to a mere three pence in the pound, and reverted to a reliance on a bloc grant as the preferred source of public finance. To ensure minimum political damage, Blair insisted on the inclusion of a second question in the scheduled devolution referendum about the allocation of tax-raising powers.[75]

What is clear from these developments is that Labour's leadership, whether in Scotland or in London, came to realise during the 1980s that it had little choice but to confront devolution head on or suffer the electoral consequences. Politics as much as unalloyed principle made Labour much less circumspect about devolution than was the case in 1978. Labour strategists reflected on the party's historical experience as an occasional rather than a 'natural' party of government. The loss of its once substantial electoral presence in middle-England had confirmed Labour's heavy reliance on its Scottish and Welsh bases. Better then, these party strategists reasoned, to use the next, all too infrequent opportunity of occupying high office, to enact constitutional arrangements that at least dispersed some of the formidable apparatus of central government power to those territorial polities where Labour was by now the usual majority party.

Other factors, too, contributed to this shift of policy. Ideological change, the search for a new social democratic model or 'third way' reinforced the pro-devolution position. 'New' Labour embraced a progressive variant of the 'hollowed out' state realised by Conservative reforms after 1979. Devolution was now seen as entirely consistent with a hybrid liberal–progressive variant of social democracy. New Labour, inured against old-style collectivism and class tribalism as the most suitable base for contemporary radical politics, was equally receptive to new postmodern concerns about identity politics and cultural pluralism, complementing Labour's traditional commitment to community politics and democratic empowerment.

In short, Labour's mission of renewal, the drive to become a modernising force, a radical social democratic party in contemporary guise, put constitutional reform and all manner of related issues firmly at the ideological centre of the New Labour project. Party deliberations, assisted by the think-tank expertise drafted into the party machine, were well apprised of the general trend of reforms under way in western Europe. And although Tony Blair, the new Labour leader, was by no means as instinctively pro-devolution as his predecessor, John Smith, he did nevertheless inherit a radical commitment to devolution as the best way of ensuring the survival of the Union in these difficult times.[76] Above all, his overriding concern was to prioritise constitutional reform, a commitment predictably deprecated by the incumbent prime minister, John Major.[77] Writing in the party's 1997 general election manifesto, Blair sought to legitimise constitutional change as an exercise in ideological revision, to reconcile his unionist predilections with New Labour's preference for democratic pluralism, unequivocally stating that:

> I believe in Britain . . . The United Kingdom is a partnership enriched by distinct national identities and traditions. Scotland has its own systems of education, law and local government. Wales has its language and cultural traditions . . . A sovereign Westminster Parliament will devolve power to Scotland and Wales. The Union will be strengthened and the threat of separatism removed . . . The United Kingdom Parliament is and will remain sovereign in all matters.[78]

This was clear testimony to reform as an exercise in reconciling modernisation with enduring national values, and it became the leitmotif of the Labour government's 1998 proposals for territorial governance.

Wales: imitating the neighbours?

Devolution was always a more equivocal, a less than popular cause in the Principality than in Scotland. Moreover, Plaid was nothing like as threatening as the SNP was to Labour's dominance of territorial politics in Scotland. The outright rejection of the 1978 devolution proposals by the Welsh electorate might have been expected to remove the issue from the territorial political agenda for at least a generation. In fact, the subsequent history of this issue mirrored events in Scotland, with the very same concern evident to redress the democratic deficit *vis-à-vis* the centre that had allowed the imposition of alien political ideas.

Of course, the momentum for home rule in Wales moved at a more leisurely pace, less extensive support indicating continuing ambivalence about political identity. For one thing the Conservatives' assimilation strategy was more successful here, a testament to closer integration with England. The Thatcher reforms, too, had greater success in replacing traditional industries and instilling an enterprise culture.

Economic modernisation, in turn, boosted national self-confidence, though paradoxically this rekindled the debate on self-government.

Significant in this regard was the role of successive Welsh secretaries during the 1980s in mitigating the worst excesses of the Conservatives' neo-liberal reforms, and in securing some important, if largely symbolic, concessions for cultural distinctiveness: notably, a Welsh language Board and a Welsh Development Agency (WDA). The appointment of a 'one nation' Tory, Peter Walker, in 1987 had helped to cushion the Principality from some of the ideological excesses of the Thatcherite agenda. Walker, and his immediate successor David Hunt, had rather more autonomy than was permitted to their Scottish counterparts to preside over a creative mix of public projects and private enterprise. They utilised the WDA in order to generate enterprise, effectively working with the private sector, local government and labour organisations to encourage inward investment. Walker especially backed his corporatist preferences with high levels of public expenditure.[79] Public and private sector partnerships did much to regenerate Cardiff's dilapidated dockland, and urban regeneration resulted from the Valley's initiative. Regional infrastructural initiatives built the second Severn bridge to link Wales via the M4 motorway to the prosperous south-east corridor, improved road access and connected the North Wales counties to markets in England's north-west and Midlands.

These ministers were widely regarded in Wales, even by opposition politicians, as well intentioned, genuinely concerned to redress social exclusion. Energetic engagement on behalf of territorial interests, nevertheless, flattered to deceive. These commendable achievements notwithstanding, there was persistent political friction between territorial representatives still infused with collectivist values and a government driven by unshakeable faith in the market.[80] In the end, acerbic neo-liberalism overcame provincial territorial resistance. The Conservatives' policy agenda found its way past this paternalistic shield, in part through the medium of rapidly multiplying, non-elected quangos – bodies determined to circumvent the Labour-dominated local government establishment.[81] The impact of this on territorial public opinion can be measured by opinion polls that regularly showed that support for devolution was greater by the mid-1980s than at any time since the 1960s.[82]

If the primacy given to the centralist economic orthodoxy was ever in doubt in Wales, the arrival of John Redwood at the Welsh Office settled the matter. A Thatcher zealot, Redwood was appointed by Mrs Thatcher's successor, John Major, ironically a man who was more sensitive to the dangers of ignoring territorial voices. Redwood inflamed an already tense situation. His indifference to local sensibilities took the form of what some saw as merely gratuitous insults, notably outright refusal to sign any official documents written in Welsh, or to implement the reform of the Welsh Grand Committee agreed by his predecessor. Offence caused by this rebuff was merely compounded by an almost vice-regal demeanour in his way of doing business. Nationalist sensibilities were roused, taking deep offence to the point where even the solicitous attentions and civility of Redwood's successor, William Hague, simply failed to allay them.

The appointment of William Hague, another neo-liberal but one of mellower disposition, and who at least tried to learn Welsh, was merely damage limitation.

But the damage had already been done. The Hague tenure did see the return to a familiar, more emollient, Conservative strategy: an amalgam of staunch unionist rhetoric, resistance to far-reaching devolution, but with at least some acquiescence to territorial sensibilities. The long-promised reform of the Welsh Grand Committee was passed in 1995, although the lack of a separate corpus of Welsh law made this a rather paler version of similar reforms in Scotland. There was, for instance, to be no second or third readings of proposed legislation in the Committee, though the peripatetic model was adopted as a territorial concession, with debates and ministerial questions similar to the procedures for Scotland.

The reasons for the Conservatives' historic general election defeat in 1997[83] are many, though amongst the issues contributing to a particularly poor outcome in Scotland and Wales was undoubtedly the party's resistance to far-reaching constitutional change.[84] By now this issue exercised territorial voters as much as the unabated preoccupation with material or lifestyle issues that concerned English voters.[85] For the first time in a British general election not a single Conservative was elected for either a Welsh or a Scottish seat. The Conservatives' manifesto made claim to preventing a dangerous 'unravelling' of the Union's constitutional fabric, 'a constitution that binds our nation together and the institutions that bring us stability'.[86] This hysterical postulation was utterly rejected by the territorial electorates, and in spectacular fashion.[87]

When Labour returned to office in 1997 with a record majority there was widespread support from the territorial electorates for proposed reform of the fabric of the union state. By now, constitutional reform was a legislative priority for the incoming administration. The differential arrangements it proposed for the two territorial polities replicated the familiar asymmetrical pattern of 1978, reflecting apparent differences in circumstances, political aspirations and political identity between the territorial polities.[88] Meanwhile, the situation in Ulster led to an even more novel initiative to break the historical sectarian impasse.

Devolution in Ulster: from protest to power sharing

The outbreak of public protest in the aftermath of the 1960s civil rights movement had obliged central government to confront its responsibilities for public order in the Province. Direct rule was imposed in 1972 in response to rising terrorism, with the effect that 'half a century of the Protestant supremacist state had come to a bloody and chaotic end'.[89] Both communities remained fundamentally divided over the most appropriate response to this crisis, though a majority of both communities preferred peaceful resolution. Extremism flourished on the margins, with support for unprecedented political violence inflated by the massacre of unarmed civilians by British paratroopers in Derry on 'Bloody Sunday' in January 1972. On the Republican side, a revived IRA confronted the Royal Ulster Constabulary (RUC) and subsequently the British Army. In 1972, the worst year of the conflict, some 1,900 bombs were planted, 467 lives were lost and 10,623 people were injured.[90] The two communities became further estranged as intimidation resulted in a variant of ethnic cleansing. Again in 1972, some 7,000 Catholics were forced out of their homes and crossed into the Republic seeking refuge. Protestant householders experienced a similar fate.

With community relations rapidly deteriorating, the Conservative government proposed power sharing. It published a White Paper, *Northern Ireland Constitutional Proposals*, in 1973 that acknowledged the right to self-determination, with an assembly directly elected by proportional representation (single transferable vote, STV) and headed by a power-sharing executive of moderates drawn from both communities. These proposals were implemented in the Northern Ireland Constitution Act 1973.

There was also to be an all-Ireland dimension to these novel arrangements. Following widespread protests after the assembly elections, representatives from all the parties and of the governments in Dublin and London met at Sunningdale in December 1973, setting up a Council of Ireland as a medium for cross-border consultations. The Council was mandated to review common policy areas such as tourism, transport, agriculture and power. This proposal merely exacerbated unionist hostility to the power-sharing experiment, and despite both governments putting their weight behind the scheme by signing an agreement at Sunningdale, the ruling council of the Ulster Unionist Party refused to endorse the arrangement. Dublin tried to reassure unionists that Ulster's political status would not be altered, except by majority consent, although Dublin was unwilling at this juncture to relinquish its claim to sovereignty over the six counties as enshrined in Articles 1 and 2 of the Irish Constitution.[91] This first attempt at power sharing failed after a general strike by Protestant workers in 1974, and direct rule was reintroduced.[92] The pan-Irish dimension was subsequently reconfirmed as part of any settlement by the Hillsborough Agreement (1985).

This was a significant moment in the always fraught relations between the mainland parties and the Unionist majority.[93] In retrospect, as one observer of these problematic relations has remarked:

> The real significance of the Troubles is that they fundamentally changed the British view of Ireland, a process which revealed how much Britishness itself had changed. Until the mid-1960s, Britons regarded Northern Ireland as civilized compatriots under siege from an alien, backward country. By the mid-1970s they were regarded as part of the problem, and by the end of the decade the North was seen as far more backward than the South.[94]

It was quite apparent, as the costs of policing and economic reconstruction soared, and public indifference in England was replaced by uncomprehending anger at wasteful folly and tribal futility, that London must urgently seek an answer to this latest variant of the historic but unresolved Irish Question.[95] The cumulative impact on British public opinion of these dismal failures to move affairs forward in the Province ensured that Ulster was now widely perceived as 'a place apart'.[96] There was particular resentment at the mounting costs to the British taxpayer of subsidising a community obsessed with sectarianism and plagued by political violence. A sentiment reflected in Harold Wilson's acerbic depiction of a Province 'sponging on British democracy'.[97]

A revised Northern Ireland Act in 1982 again included an even more ambitious proposal for an Assembly to be elected by STV, with increased powers of scrutiny over proposed legislation and for making recommendations to the secretary of state.[98] This revised Act permitted a 'rolling devolution' of governance competences if 70 per cent of the Assembly supported this option, a majority requiring the assent of both communities and following approval by the secretary of state. On this occasion, it was the nationalist parties who refused to endorse the proposal, concerned that there was insufficient acknowledgement in the proposal of the all-Ireland dimension. In the event, no single function was devolved from Westminster and the Assembly was dissolved in 1986.

There was clear evidence, nevertheless, by the 1980s of a fundamental and bipartisan shift in official thinking about the governance of Ulster. The Conservative secretary of state in 1990 offered an 'incentive' to nationalists to reduce Britain's military presence in exchange for a terrorist ceasefire, advising unionists to abandon their 'internal exile'. His further announcement, that Britain had neither a 'selfish strategic or economic interest in Northern Ireland', discomfited unionists long used to a status quo that privileged their interests. Realists amongst the unionist community, however, noted and decoded these unmistakable smoke-signals coming from the centre. Resigned, if hardly reconciled, to compromise, they abandoned their implacable resistance to political change. By the late 1990s there were unmistakable signs of movement on the political landscape.[99]

Secret communications between the two governments, and of both with Sinn Féin (the political wing of the paramilitary IRA), eventually launched what became known as the peace process. The joint Anglo-Irish Declaration of intent signed at Downing Street (December 1993) confirmed to most unionists London's determination to resolve the impasse, threatening to leave them dangerously isolated.[100] Under a new leader, David Trimble, moderate unionists reviewed their limited options, agreeing to mediated discussions with London, constitutional nationalists, and even Dublin. Of course, hard-line loyalists saw this as outright betrayal by their leaders and as treachery by London. Meanwhile, paramilitaries from both sides continued with violence. The IRA stepped up its campaign, both in Ulster and on the mainland. Yet something had clearly shifted in a war-ravaged and violence-weary landscape. Levels of civil disorder and the destruction of property that crucially deterred vital inward investment had finally galvanised the mainstream parties into brokering an historic settlement.[101]

Dublin, too, had long since abandoned its ritualistic anti-British posturing, and it worked to bring the Republicans into the peace process by revoking (in January 1994) its broadcasting ban on Sinn Féin. This gesture was eventually reciprocated in London, thus paving the way for the IRA's historic ceasefire. The Combined Loyalist Military Command had little alternative but to follow suit. Close political relations, fostered by the two governments used to working together in the EU, reinforced the appetite on the ground for negotiating an historic bargain. Cooperation was formally sealed in February 1995 in a joint Framework Document that proposed peace talks within a year. The momentum stalled, but only briefly as John Major's weakened Conservative government, relying on Unionist votes for parliamentary survival, delayed the peace process.[102] The incoming Labour government in 1997 built on these firm foundations and relaunched the peace initiative. The IRA immediately responded by reinstating its ceasefire, paving the way for Sinn Féin to join the inter-party talks.[103] The new arrangements agreed in the historic meeting at Stormont in April 1998 completed the new British government's plans for devolution 'all round' in the United Kingdom,[104] though the political dynamic driving the process had quite different causes and resulted in variable institutional outcomes, as befits the variegated history of territorial–central relations in the British polity.

NOTES

1. E. Barendt, The British Constitution: The Kilbrandon Report, *The Round Table* (April 1974)
2. N. Johnson, Editorial: The Royal Commission on the Constitution, *Public Administration* 52 (1974)
3. B. Smith, Confusions in Regionalism, *Political Quarterly* 48 (1977)
4. J. Mackintosh, The Report of the Royal Commission on the Constitution, 1969–73, *Political Quarterly* 45 (1974)
5. Royal Commission on the Constitution, Cmnd 5460 (1973), para. 1123
6. Ibid.
7. Ibid., *Memorandum of Dissent*, Cmnd 5460-I
8. PRO: CAB128/43, CC44 (68), Item 3, 29 October 1968
9. PRO: CAB134/2697, DS 23 (68), Conclusion of the Ministerial Committee on Devolution, 30 May 1968
10. K. Morgan, *Callaghan: A Life* (1997) p.361
11. HCD, 5th series, vol. 870, col. 84, 12 March 1974
12. J. Osmond, *Creative Conflict: The Politics of Welsh Devolution* (1977)
13. T. Dalyell, *Devolution: The End of Britain?* (1977)
14. C. Harvie, *Scotland and Nationalism: Scottish Society and Politics, 1707–1994* (1994) p.191
15. For a detailed assessment and a critique of these proposals, see V. Bogdanor, *Devolution* (1979)
16. V. Bogdanor, The English Constitution and Devolution, *Political Quarterly* 50 (1979)
17. V. Bogdanor, *Devolution in the United Kingdom* (2001) p.186
18. K. Morgan, op. cit. (1997) p.631
19. Ibid. p.677
20. J. Bochel, D. Denver and A. Macartney (eds), *The Referendum Experience: Scotland 1979* (1981)
21. D. Foulkes, B. Jones and R. Wilford (eds), *The Welsh Veto: The Wales Act of 1978 and the Referendum* (1983)
22. M. Thatcher, *The Downing Street Years* (1993) p.619
23. Quoted in C. Harvie, op. cit. (1994) p.183
24. A. Gamble, *The Free Economy and the Strong State* (1988); and D. Kavanagh, *Thatcherism and British Politics: The End of Consensus* (1987)
25. D. Heald, Territorial Public Expenditure in the UK, *Public Administration* 72 (1994)

26. H. Young, *One of Us: A Biography of Margaret Thatcher*, 2nd edition (1991) p.624
27. See J. Cooper, The Scottish Problem: English Conservatism and the Union with Scotland in the Thatcher and Major Eras, in J. Lovenduski and J. Stanyer (eds), *Contemporary Political Studies* (1995)
28. A. Cochrane, The Changing State of Local Government: Restructuring for the 1990s, *Public Administration* 69 (1991)
29. J. Bulpitt, *Territory and Power in the United Kingdom: An Interpretation* (1983)
30. C. Harvie, *Fool's Gold: The Story of North Sea Oil* (1994) p.119
31. See C. Harvie, Thoughts on the Union between Law and Opinion or Dicey's Last Stand, in C. Crouch and D. Marquand (eds), *The New Centralism, Britain Out of Step with Europe?* (1989)
32. C. Harvie, op. cit. (1994) p.119
33. S. Kendrick and D. McCrone, Politics in a Cold Climate: Conservative Decline in Scotland, *Political Studies* 37 (1989)
34. D. Butler, A. Adonis and T. Travers, *Failure in British Government: The Politics of the Poll Tax* (1994) p.195
35. R. Levy, *Scottish Nationalism at the Crossroads* (1989)
36. Jack Brand and J. Mitchell, Home Rule in Scotland, in J. Bradbury and J. Mawson (eds), *British Regionalism and Devolution: The Challenges of State Reform and European Integration* (1997) p.43
37. K. Wright, *The People Say Yes* (1977); J. Mitchell, *Strategies for Self-government* (1996)
38. O.D. Edward, *A Claim of Right for Scotland* (1988)
39. N. MacCormick, The English Constitution, the British State and the Scottish Anomaly, *Scottish Affairs* 14 (1998)
40. R. McCreedie, Scottish Identity and the Constitution, in B. Crick (ed.), *National Identities: The Constitution of the United Kingdom* (1991)
41. A. Marr, *The Battle for Scotland* (1992)
42. R. Johnson, C. Pattie and J. Allsopp, *A Nation Dividing? The Electoral Map of Great Britain, 1979–87* (1988)
43. R. Weight, *Patriots and National Identity in Britain 1940–2000* (2002) p.589
44. T. Smout, Scotland and England: Is Dependency a Symptom or a Cause of Underdevelopment? *Review* 3 (1980)
45. H. Young, op. cit. (1991) p.622
46. M. Thatcher, op. cit. (1993) p.624
47. J. Cooper, in J. Lovenduski and J. Stanyer (eds), op. cit. (1995)
48. K. Aitken, The Economy, in M. Linklater and R. Demiston (eds), *The Anatomy of Scotland* (1992)
49. *The Quango Debate*, special edition of *Parliamentary Affairs*, April 1995
50. J. Bradbury, Conservative Governments, Scotland and Wales: A Perspective on Territorial Management, in J. Bradbury and J. Mawson (eds), op. cit. (1997) p.78
51. J. Mitchell, in J. Lovenduski and J. Stanyer, op. cit. (1995)
52. J. Bradbury, op. cit. (1997)
53. J. Mitchell, Contemporary Unionism, in C. Macdonald (ed.), *Unionist Scotland, 1800–1997* (1998) p.128

54. Cited by J. Mawson, English Regionalism and New Labour, in H. Elcock and M. Keating (eds), *Remaking the Union: Devolution and British Politics in the 1990s* (1998) p.166

55. J. Brand, Scotland and the Politics of Devolution: A Patchy Past and a Hazy Future, *Parliamentary Affairs* 46 (1993)

56. See D. McCrone, Regionalism and Constitutional Change in Scotland, *Regional Studies* 27 (1993); D. Butler and D. Kavanagh, *The British General Election of 1992* (1992)

57. E. Clouston and P. Winter, Tories Counter-attack on Scottish Constitution, *The Guardian,* 1 December 1995; A. Leathley, Battle of Britain Begins over Rival Plans for Scotland, *The Times*, 1 December 1995

58. J. Bradbury, op. cit. (1997) p.83

59. M. Burch and I. Holliday, The Conservative Party and Constitutional Reform: The Case of Devolution, *Parliamentary Affairs* 45 (1992)

60. A. McConnell and R. Pyper, A Committee Again: The First Year of the Revived Select Committee on Scottish Affairs, *Scottish Affairs* 7 (1994)

61. *The Scotsman,* 4 July 1996

62. *Scotland in the Union,* Cmnd 1591 (1997) p.13

63. J. Mitchell, *Conservatives and the Union: A Study of Conservative Party Attitudes to Scotland* (1990)

64. A. Brown, The Context of Change: The Scottish Economy and Public Policy, in A. Brown and J. Fairley (eds), *The Manpower Services Commission in Scotland* (1989)

65. M. Keating and D. Bleiman, *Labour and Scottish Nationalism* (1979)

66. D. McCrone, *Understanding Scotland: The Sociology of a Stateless Society* (1992)

67. J. Brand and J. Mitchell, op. cit. (1997) p.52

68. J. Kellas, Constitutional Options for Scotland, *Parliamentary Affairs* 43 (1990)

69. J.G. Kellas, The Scottish Constitutional Convention, in L. Paterson and D. McCrone (eds), *The Scottish Government Yearbook 1992* (1992)

70. See *Towards Scotland's Parliament* (Scottish Constitutional Convention [hereafter SCC], 1990); *Key Proposals for Scotland's Parliament* (SCC, 1995); *Scotland's Parliament. Scotland's Right* (SCC, 1995); B. Crick and D. Miller, *To Make the Parliament for Scotland a Model for Democracy* (John Wheatley Centre, 1991); J. Kellas, op. cit. (1992)

71. SCC, *Towards Scotland's Parliament* (1990); Scottish Constitutional Commission, *Further Steps Towards a Scheme for Scotland's Parliament* (1994)

72. I. Loveland, Labour and the Constitution: The 'Right' Approach to Reform? *Parliamentary Affairs* 45 (1992)

73. J. Mitchell, *Strategies for Self-government: The Campaigns for a Scottish Parliament* (1996)

74. K. Wright, op. cit. (1997)

75. P. Jones, Labour's Referendum Plan: Sell-out or Act of Faith? *Scottish Affairs* 18 (1997)

76. J. Naughtie, *The Rivals* (2001) pp.174–8

77. Say No to this Doomed Enterprise, *The Times,* 30 August 1997

78. New Labour because Britain Deserves Better. The Labour Party (1997) p.1

79. R. Merfyn Jones, Beyond Identity? The Reconstruction of the Welsh, *Journal of British Studies* 31 (1992) pp.354–5
80. D. Griffiths, *Thatcherism and Territorial Politics: A Welsh Case Study* (1996)
81. Ibid.
82. J. Osmond, *The Divided Kingdom* (1988) p.141
83. O. Edwards, The Strange Death of Unionist Scotland and Wales: An Irish Perspective, *Scottish Affairs* 20 (1997)
84. D. Denver, The 1997 General Election in Scotland: An Analysis of the Results, *Scottish Affairs* 20 (1997)
85. L. Bennie, J. Brand and J. Mitchell, *How Scotland Votes* (1997)
86. Conservative Party, *You Can Only Be Sure With The Conservatives* (1997) p.51
87. D. Butler and D. Kavanagh, *The British General Election of 1997* (1997)
88. J. Osmond, *The Future of Welsh Devolution* (2002)
89. R.F. Forster, *Modern Ireland 1600–1972* p.592
90. Tim Pat Coogan, *The Troubles* (1995) p.151
91. G. Gillespie, The Sunningdale Agreement: Lost Opportunity or an Agreement Too Far? *Irish Political Studies* 13 (1998); K. Kyle, Sunningdale and After: Britain, Ireland and Ulster, *The World Today*, November 1975
92. R. Fisk, *The Point of No Return. The Strike which Broke the British in Ulster* (1975)
93. A. Aughey, *Under Siege: Ulster Unionism and the Anglo-Irish Agreement* (1989)
94. R. Weight, op. cit. (2002) p.530
95. P. Bew and H. Patterson, *The British State and the Ulster Crisis: From Wilson to Thatcher* (1985)
96. D. Murphy, *A Place Apart* (1978)
97. T. Hennessy, *A History of Northern Ireland 1920–1996* (1997) p.229
98. C. O'Leary, S. Elliot and R. Wilford, *The Northern Ireland Assembly 1982–1986: A Constitutional Experiment* (1998)
99. P. Bew and G. Gillespie, *Northern Ireland: A Chronology of the Troubles, 1968–93* (1993)
100. Alan F. Parkinson, *Ulster Loyalism and the British Media* (1998)
101. F. Cochrane, *Unionist Politics and the Politics of Unionism since the Anglo-Irish Agreement* (1997)
102. B. O'Leary, The Conservative Stewardship of Northern Ireland, 1979–97: Sound-bottomed Contradictions or Slow Learning, *Political Studies* XLV (1997)
103. P. Bew and G. Gillespie, *Northern Ireland: A Chronology of the Troubles, 1968–99* (1999)
104. P. Bew and G. Gillespie, *The Northern Ireland Peace Process 1993–96: A Chronology* (1996); J. Ruane and J. Todd, The Belfast Agreement: Conflict, Context, Consequences, in J. Ruane and J. Todd (eds), *After the Good Friday Agreement* (1999)

The politics of identity: Scottish nationalism

Antonia Dodds and David Seawright

INTRODUCTION

The focus of this chapter is on the Scottish National Party (SNP), its relationship with Scottish identity, and an analysis of its electoral support. Its rise in the second half of the twentieth century was the main stimulus to the nationalist movement, and now, in the devolved Scottish Parliament, it is the second largest party and the official Opposition. Out of the four main parties in Scotland it is the only purely Scottish party and the only party committed to Scottish independence. However, the Scottish National Party is not the only agent of Scottish identity, or even of Scottish nationalism, which has, as we shall see below, major implications for the party's strategy and likeliness of electoral success within the new context of devolution.

This chapter begins with an examination of national identity in Scotland. We turn then to a discussion of the SNP's goals and strategies, the internal tensions within the party over the latter, and how the party has responded to the new circumstances of devolution. Next, we look at how national identity and the SNP's location on the conventional left–right political spectrum impact on support for the SNP, which leads on to a psephological exploration of the profile of SNP support, focusing on sex, age, social class and religion. Lastly, we examine the issue of Europe, which not only has a crucial impact on party politics and the emergence of multi-level governance for Scotland, but is now increasingly an important battleground upon which nationalist–unionist manoeuvring is played out.

It is a grievous error to simplistically equate the SNP alone with Scottish identity, or even with Scottish nationalism. A shared sense of Scottish cultural identity has historically been kept alive since the union of 1707 by a range of Scottish institutions including the 'holy trinity' of Church of Scotland, legal and educational systems,[1] and, more recently, by organisations aimed at fostering Scottish culture such as the Saltire Society. Whilst all of these institutions have acted as agents of Scottish identity, they have had varying (or indeed, no) relationships to political nationalism. As Mitchell comments:

> Individuals and bodies without an explicitly political message have also played a part in fostering a sense of Scottish identity. The founders of the Saltire Society included not only political nationalists but also those who were explicitly unionist.[2]

Moreover, all major parties in Scotland have in the past, with varying levels of success, played the 'Scottish card' in relation to Westminster policy for Scotland. This is true even of the Scottish Conservative and Unionist Party, which can be described as the most unionist party in that it was the only one of the four main parties in the twenty or so years before 1997 which did not support some form of legislative autonomy. Since the late nineteenth century, the Liberals and the Tories and then the Tories and Labour, as the alternative parties of Westminster government, have usually in opposition exploited a distinct Scottish discourse and policy agenda in their appeals to the Scottish electorate. Indeed, Mitchell neatly illustrates this when highlighting the claims of the opponents of home rule that it was perfectly possible to be culturally Scottish but politically British.[3] As David McLetchie, leader of the Scottish Conservatives, said on the day of the Parliament's official opening in 1999: 'each and every political party would claim [to act in the best interests of the people of Scotland] . . . for no one party has a monopoly of patriotism in our country'.[4]

The important point to note is that the debate in Scotland is not over the existence of the Scottish nation, or for that matter over issues of Scottish culture. All the political parties assume that the Scottish nation exists and will play the 'Scottish card' to varying degrees – although their readings of Scottishness may vary. As Michael Keating comments: 'nationalism in Scotland has never been the exclusive property of one party, though the SNP represents its clearest expression'.[5] Instead, since the SNP's electoral breakthrough in the last quarter of the twentieth century, the debate has been over the political embodiment of the Scottish nation.

It was the SNP's electoral success which provided the catalyst for the other parties in Scotland, to varying degrees, to become politically Scottish in the sense of pursuing some form of constitutional change. As Table 4.1 shows, the SNP's major electoral success started in the late 1960s and carried on into the early 1970s. SNP success forced the major Westminster parties to question the sufficiency of their existing administrative devolution which was structured through the Scottish Office and the secretary of state for Scotland. No coincidence, as we found in previous chapters, that both the Conservatives (in the Perth Declaration in 1968) and Labour (at the 'Dalintober Street' Conference in August 1974) adopted devolution policies. Whilst Conservative commitment to legislative autonomy was later reversed, Labour's commitment strengthened, eventually resulting, two referenda later, in the establishment of the devolved Scottish Parliament in 1999.

Table 4.1 Percentage share of Scottish National Party vote, 1950–2001

1950	1951	1955	1959	1964	1966	1970	1974 Feb
0.4	0.3	0.5	0.8	2.4	5.0	11.4	21.9

1974 Oct	1979	1983	1987	1992	1997	1999[a]	2001
30.4	17.3	11.8	11.0	21.5	22.1	28.8	20.1

[a] Scottish parliamentary election: percentage share of vote in Scottish constituencies (not including the 'top-up' list vote of the AMS electoral system).

Source: Kellas, J.G., *The Scottish Political System,* 4th edition (Cambridge: Cambridge University Press, 1989); Butler, D. and Kavanagh, D., *The British General Election of 1992, 1997* and *2001* (Basingstoke: Macmillan/Palgrave).

Since the 1997 devolution referendum effectively ended the pre-1997 status quo as an option (namely, Scotland within the Union but without an elected autonomous parliament), the debate has been between the pro-devolution unionists (Labour and the Liberal Democrats, since 1997 joined by the Conservatives) and the pro-independence SNP (with the Scottish Socialist Party and the Scottish Greens). Indeed, although the SNP are widely known simply as 'the Nationalists', political nationalism, understood as the pursuit of some form of autonomy, is not confined to the SNP. Although the parties and pressure groups who supported devolution prior to 1997, particularly Labour, the Liberal Democrats in all their manifestations and the Campaign for a Scottish Assembly, do not use the word 'nationalist' in their political discourse, it is possible to describe the devolution campaigns as nationalist. A striking example of this is found in the Claim of Right, a declaration signed by almost all Labour and Liberal Democrat MPs at the inaugural meeting of the Scottish Constitutional Convention, which explicitly located sovereignty in the Scottish people.[6] This has led to the distinction between 'big N' and 'small n' nationalism, 'big N' referring to the SNP, and 'small n' to a foregrounding of Scotland and Scottishness in general, including the devolution movement.[7]

THE SNP AND NATIONALISM

We turn now to the SNP in particular. What kind of nationalism does the party embody? The first point to note is that the SNP espouses a 'civic' nationalism, based on allegiance to civic institutions and territoriality, rather than an 'ethnic' nationalism based purely on ethnicity and descent.[8] It is an example of what has been called 'neo-nationalism': largely civic, peaceful and pursued via democratic means.[9] Its citizenship policy, for example, is based on residency as well as descent, granting citizenship to all 'whose principal place of residence is in Scotland' as well as 'whose place of birth was in Scotland or either of whose parents was born in Scotland'.[10] Unusually for a nationalist party, the SNP's discourse is characterised by the comparative absence of arguments relating to Scottish ethnicity, language, religion or cultural heritage, as any cursory glance at election campaign literature demonstrates. The SNP repeatedly eschews a potentially exclusive ethnic identity and stresses that it is, 'and must be, the party for all the people of Scotland. We are Scotland's party and we must act accordingly'.[11] The rejection of racism (including that of the anti-English variety) at the policy level, and the creation of ethnic minority groups within the SNP such as 'New Scots for Independence', help to project an inclusive and tolerant nationalism.

Strategies for independence: fundamentalism vs gradualism

The second point to note is that the SNP's fundamental aim is Scottish independence. In this respect it has a 'classical' nationalism, which accords neatly with the famous definition offered by Gellner: 'Nationalism is primarily a political principle, which holds that the political and the national unit should be congruent'.[12]

The SNP desires Scotland's secession from the United Kingdom, so that Scotland would have control not only of health, education and so on, but also, for example, of its own macro-economic and foreign policy. However (and more on this later), since 1988 the SNP has been committed to 'Independence in Europe'[13] – Scotland would become a full member state of the European Union. In addition, it envisages cooperation with the United Kingdom following Scottish secession, through, for example, the Council of the Isles.

Prior to the establishment of the Scottish Parliament, it was SNP policy to see an electoral victory in terms of a majority of the 72 Westminster seats as a sufficient mandate to begin negotiations for independence. However, this has changed and now the SNP proposes to hold a referendum on independence within the first term of an SNP administration in the Scottish Parliament. A referendum would also be held during the first term of office after independence on whether to retain the British monarch as head of state.[14]

There is, however, a long history of divisions within the party regarding the most appropriate route to achieving independence. The 'fundamentalist' wing is content with nothing less than independence, whereas the 'gradualist' wing has always been amenable to adopting a more pragmatic position concerning devolution, viewing it as an acceptable stepping stone along the road to independence. John Swinney, when deputy leader, argued that

> the most effective mechanism of delivering independence comes from building on the powers of the Scottish parliament and using that institution as the means of delivering Scottish independence . . .[15]

The difference is thus (so far) one of strategy rather than of goals.

These tensions are as old as the party itself, and were exacerbated by the failure of the 1979 referendum.[16] Agreeing to campaign for a yes vote in 1979 was a gradualist victory; the failure of the referendum resulted in a backlash which put the fundamentalists in the ascendant.[17] The gradualist wing has been dominant since Alex Salmond's succession to the leadership in 1990, reconfirmed by John Swinney's clear lead over the fundamentalist Alex Neil in the 2000 leadership election after Alex Salmond's resignation. But throughout this period the tensions were still manifest, for example the SNP boycotted the Scottish Constitutional Convention in 1989 and only backed the 'yes–yes' campaign – for a Scottish parliament with tax-raising powers – late in the day after being reassured that the 1997 Scotland Bill did not preclude further constitutional reform for Scotland.[18] Fundamentalists continued to argue that 'we should not dignify devolution by arguing for it'[19] and were highly critical of Salmond's gradualist election strategy for the Scottish Parliament in 1999 which emphasised policies for the devolved parliament more than independence itself, and put independence tenth on the list of election pledges: 'we must not allow Scotland to sleepwalk into thinking that Holyrood is capable of delivering all our nation's expectations'.[20]

Tensions were evident in the run-up to the 2001 general election over the level of support that should be given to full fiscal autonomy for Holyrood.[21] Fiscal autonomy is a double-edged sword: on the one hand, it is postulated that there will be benefits for the party when Scots see that they can control their own taxation and spending. On the other, it may also mean the legitimising of devolution and distracting from the goal of independence. This is not some esoteric debate with discrete relevance for party 'anoraks': it is crucial for the evolving Scottish constitutional settlement and for the future trajectory of party ideology concerning this settlement. As we shall see below when we examine the psephology in more detail, not all SNP voters support independence.

This raises the issue of how devolution has affected the SNP. On the one hand, devolution has been good for the SNP, which is now the official Opposition in Holyrood rather than a fringe party at Westminster. There is a real chance that the party will be in government in Scotland at some point in the next few years. There is also increasing evidence to suggest voter differentiation between Scottish and British elections, with the SNP gaining more support in the Scottish elections. However, devolution also raises questions and tensions over the future of an SNP Holyrood administration – questions which have the capacity to reopen old wounds between the fundamentalist and gradualist strategies. In part this is due to the additional member system (AMS) for the Scottish elections. This both benefits the SNP, in that its vote is geographically spread, which means that under the Westminster first-past-the-post electoral system it wins far fewer seats than its percentage of the vote would represent, and disadvantages it, in that it also makes it unlikely that the SNP (or any other party) could form a majority government on its own. The SNP would most likely have to share power with a unionist party in order to form a governing coalition. And even if the SNP does gain power in Holyrood, a referendum on independence may well not succeed. Now that the SNP is a serious contender for power, it will need to address such an eventuality, but in so doing it could quite easily open up the old sores of fundamentalist–gradualist tensions. The fundamentalists are wary of a 'pragmatist sell-out' whereby the devolution settlement becomes increasingly acceptable, even if the independence message remains implicit in party policy. Conversely, however, different administrations in Edinburgh and London could well test the present structures of devolution to the limit; in this scenario, support for independence could be strengthened.

We turn now from the SNP's strategies to look at the relationship between the SNP and Scottish identity.

NATIONAL IDENTITY AND THE SNP

In the 1950s, as is well documented, the electoral orthodoxy held that class, rather than territory or religion, was *the* key cleavage in explaining British electoral behaviour: 'Class is the basis of British party politics; all else is embellishment and detail.'[22] As late as 1966 it was possible for Ian Budge and Derek Urwin to subtitle their book *Scottish Political Behaviour*, 'a case study in British homogeneity'.[23] The general elections of the early to mid-1950s demonstrated this homogeneous political culture, when such statements as 'to know the swing in Cornwall was to know, within a percentage point or two, the swing in the Highlands'[24] were the accepted orthodoxy, and, as Table 4.1 shows, the SNP obtained less than 1 per cent of the Scottish vote in the 1950s.

It is not our intention here to enter into the highly charged and contested debate[25] concerning the different models of voting behaviour which are posited to explain the rise of the SNP. For our analysis it is sufficient to note the decline of class and the rise of territory as explanations of Scottish (and indeed British) voting behaviour in the postwar period. It may indeed be the case that the 1950s were an aberration, and should not be used as the base with which later voting is compared.[26] Other cleavages, such as religion and, in particular, territory, may have lain dormant, to be reactivated in the late 1960s. Space here does not permit the discussion of whether class dealignment is a cause or effect of such reactivated 'dormant' cleavages and the rise of nationalist parties. Suffice to note at this juncture that both the vote for the SNP and a Scottish national identity did indeed increase in intensity from the 1970s onwards.

We might expect a causal relationship between the rise in national identity and support for the SNP. Scottish identity has certainly increased since the 1970s: as Table 4.2 shows, when respondents are given a 'forced' choice between Scottish or British national identity, around three-quarters of all Scots now choose a Scottish national identity over a British identity, an increase from just over half in 1979.[27] It is intuitive to expect the SNP to do well amongst strongly Scottish identifiers.

However, just as the SNP is not the only carrier of Scottish identity, the rise in Scottish identity found in the electorate since the 1970s cannot simply be attributed to SNP support. Thus, Paterson *et al.* warn: 'while national identity in Scotland does seem part of the taken-for-granted-world, it is not an easy concept to measure. We cannot be sure, for example, that two people who say they are Scottish mean the same thing'[28] – especially when referring to Scotland's constitutional status. Nor can we assume a clear link between national identity, support for the SNP, and support for independence.[29] The relationship is far more complex, as Table 4.3 demonstrates. First we cross-tabulate our 'forced' positions on national identity from the Scottish Election Studies with respondents' preferences on the constitutional question. Although we will have to wait for further evidence from future Scottish Election Studies, it would appear that devolution has so far weakened support for independence, which fell between the 1999 Scottish election and the 2001 general election for both Scottish and British identifiers. More importantly for

Table 4.2 Scottish or British national identity, 1979–2001

Percentage choosing that identity	1979	1992	1997	1999 Holyrood election	2001
Scottish	56	72	72	77	74
British	38	25	24	17	20

Source: Scottish Election Studies, 1979–1999, adapted from Paterson, L. *et al.*, *New Scotland, New Politics?* (Edinburgh: Polygon, 2001), and Scottish Election Study, 2001.

Table 4.3 Constitutional preference by national identity, 1979–2001

Constitutional preferences amongst named identity	1979 %	1992 %	1997 %	1999 Holyrood election %	2001 %
Scottish					
Independence	11	27	32	31	25
Home rule, devolution etc.	66	50	52	58	59
No elected body	23	20	12	6	13
British					
Independence	2	11	10	11	7
Home rule, devolution etc.	58	48	51	62	65
No elected body	40	38	34	24	27

Source: Scottish Election Studies, 1979–99 adapted from Paterson, L. et al., New Scotland, New Politics? (Edinburgh: Polygon, 2001), and Scottish Election Study, 2001.

our analysis, both Scottish and British identifiers still overwhelmingly prefer some form of devolution – in 2001, 59 per cent of Scottish identifiers and 65 per cent of British identifiers chose this option – although it should be noted that support for devolution was already popular amongst both groups even in 1979.

Support for the status quo ante (i.e. that Scotland should not have an elected autonomous legislature) has fallen amongst British identifiers, from 40 per cent in 1979 to 27 per cent in 2001, although this still means that, with devolution a reality, one-quarter of British identifiers still favour the status quo ante. However, support for the status quo ante amongst Scottish identifiers has actually increased since devolution, from 6 per cent in 1999 to 13 per cent in 2001, although this group remains in the minority. This may reflect dissatisfaction with the new Parliament and the spiralling cost of its new building.

Thus, we can see that the majority of Scottish and British identifiers in Scotland opt for devolution, and that crucially having a Scottish identity does not map neatly on to any preference for independence.[30] Moreover, we can see in Table 4.4 that constitutional preference does not map expectantly, let alone neatly, on to party support.

Table 4.4 highlights the relevance of the fundamentalist–gradualist divide for the party's electoral environment, as a substantial number of SNP voters prefer home rule to independence. In 2001, 42 per cent of SNP voters preferred a devolved Scottish Parliament to the party's main goal of independence. The high level of support for home rule found in 1979 (55 per cent) may simply reflect the reality of Scottish politics in the wake of a recently lost referendum on devolution. But even in the 1999 Scottish elections, 39 per cent of SNP voters, a similar level to that found throughout the 1990s, preferred home rule to independence. To further complicate the picture, in the first two elections of the 1990s nearly one-quarter of Labour supporters preferred independence to their party's policy of devolution, although this number has declined since the establishment of the Parliament, to

Table 4.4 Constitutional preferences of Labour/SNP voters

Election	Labour voters for independence %	SNP voters for home rule %
1979	5	55
1992	20	38
1997	23	35
1999	18	39
2001	13	42

Source: Scottish Election Studies, 1979–2001.

just 13 per cent at the 2001 general election. This data demonstrates the complexity of contemporary Scottish political identity.

The comparison with Labour here is also important not only because its hegemonic electoral hold on Scotland is only seriously challenged by the SNP but also because the SNP utilises a similar left-of-centre discourse. In the past two decades the SNP has increasingly used the language and ideals of social democracy.[31] It is thus salutary to examine this important component of the SNP's 'nationalist ideology': a contiguous jostling with Labour's ideological position on the left–right spectrum, as the SNP competes for votes in Labour's heartland.

THE LEFT–RIGHT SPECTRUM

The SNP may nowadays unequivocally promote itself as a party of the left but this has not always been the case. For a considerable period, the party was far more reticent on such divisive class-based policy. At first it viewed itself as an umbrella party which could unite all those who supported independence, regardless of their ideological background. Independence was the magic formula and it would have to be obtained first before conventional socio-economic policies could even be considered.

> Whereas in the past it regarded itself as an 'umbrella party', uniting different political interests for the achievement of a single aim, then to disperse, it now sees itself as a future government of Scotland. The SNP intends to continue as a party after independence because it believes that it has an approach to politics that is different from that of any other party in the Scottish context.[32]

However, the claim that it had an approach different from that of any other party in the context of day-to-day Scottish politics merely allowed the Tories and Labour an attack from both left and right flanks, the Conservatives stressing SNP socialism and the Labour Party famously describing the SNP as 'Tartan Tories'.

The SNP had ideologically mixed origins, formed as it was in 1934 from the merger of the National Party of Scotland (NPS) and the Scottish Party. The NPS was itself formed from earlier groups whose membership overlapped with that of the early Labour and Independent Labour parties, and inclined more towards radical social and economic policies.[33] However, the Scottish Party's formative roots were distinctly unionist, as it drew a large part of its membership from the Cathcart Divisional Unionist Association in Glasgow,[34] also attracting leading Tories. The Scottish Party very much favoured Scottish participation in a strong British Empire. The introduction into the nationalist movement of this right-wing element was not to the liking of many socialist members and caused the defection of radicals in the branches.[35]

From the 1970s, the SNP began to adopt a more conventional ideological stance, towards the left of the spectrum, although there is some confusion over precisely when the party declared itself as unequivocally left wing,[36] and as late as 1979 the fundamentalist victor who beat Margo MacDonald for vice-chair had 'right wing views'.[37] The transition to a more left-wing agenda was underpinned by certain factions within the party. The '79 group (including the young Alex Salmond) argued that the SNP should adopt a more socialist position, based on the assumption that the SNP needed to have a winning strategy and that the majority of the Scots vote was on the left. Although members of the '79 group were expelled, their expulsion nonetheless marked the party's swing to a more defined position. The SNP has also been anti-nuclear since 1961, with repeated calls for nuclear disarmament and the closing of the nuclear submarine base in Scotland. Continued Conservative victories at Westminster throughout the 1980s no doubt aided this leftward swing and a pact was concluded with Plaid Cymru in 1986 in which both parties stated they would not enter an alliance with the Conservatives.

Importantly, the Scots electorate was aware of this new defined position on the left. A question in the 1979 and 1997 Scottish Election Studies asked the respondents if they would place the SNP closer to the Conservative Party or the Labour Party. In 1979, 22 per cent of Scots thought the SNP was closer to the Tories and 47 per cent to Labour. By 1997, however, the number of Scots believing the SNP closer to the Tories had more than halved, from 22 per cent to 10 per cent, but those viewing the party as closer to Labour had increased by nearly one-third to 62 per cent. No doubt then, that in the eyes of the Scots electorate, the SNP was now firmly a party of the left, which meant an increasing competition with Labour but on similar electoral ground.

With the emergence and success of New Labour, one SNP strategy was to appeal to the supposedly traditional social democracy of the Scots, advocating policies to the left of New Labour. For example, during the campaign for the 1999 Scottish parliamentary elections the SNP proposed to increase income tax by one penny – the 'Penny for Scotland' campaign. Although polls showed support for increased taxation to fund better public services, the policy was widely seen as an opportunistic response to Gordon Brown's reduction of income tax. Commentators cited such 'social democracy too far' as alienating not only the business community and the middle class but also the working class in Labour heartlands as the reason the SNP did not do as well in the election as it had hoped.[38] Notably, the campaign was dropped for the 2001 UK general election, and Swinney announced in September 2002 that it would not be policy for the 2003 Scottish elections either.

We should note, however, that the electoral ground upon which the parties compete for this left-wing Scots vote has become increasingly congested. The SNP needs to find a way of distinguishing itself from Labour but not so that it loses votes from voters positioned slightly to the SNP's right. And of course the party, like Labour, must also consider the serious threat in urban constituencies from the new Scottish Socialist Party, which also advocates independence and is positioned far more to the left. As a potential party of government, the SNP now needs to find the optimum position on the left–right spectrum to harness the votes that it needs to win office, and in the early 2000s it has begun to sound far more like New Labour. Policies for the 2003 Scottish elections include the commitment not to use the Parliament's tax-raising powers, and it has also dropped its commitment to lifting the ceiling on National Insurance contributions. However, like New Labour before the 1997 general election, it is keen to project itself as a competent future party of government and is now assiduously courting the business community, with the reduction of business rates being a flagship policy for the 2003 Scottish election[39] – a policy which the party shares with the Scottish Conservative Party, not Labour.

However, in order to become the party of government, the SNP first has to defeat its main rivals, Labour. With this in mind, we now take a psephological look at the profile of the SNP voter in relation to that of Labour, because it is from the Labour vote that the SNP most needs to win new support.

A PROFILE OF SNP SUPPORT

Sex

In September 2002 the SNP unveiled a 'softer' colour shade of 'heather' to supplement the traditional black and yellow in order to attract the female vote.

> In the beginning was the SNP leader's tie, then there was his shirt, and now the entire party's colour scheme has followed suit. John Swinney has reinvented his party colours based on his own lilac-hued wardrobe and the hillsides of his Perthshire constituency. Party chiefs have decided that the SNP needs a softer, less macho scheme to attract women voters, who have traditionally been dubious about voting for the Nationalists.[40]

This traditional female dubiousness was clearly shown in the 1979 election (Table 4.5), where we find a nine-point gap in voting between men and women. Although this 'macho divide' in SNP support did attenuate in the 1990s – down to an average of 5 points, and then down to 3 in 2001 – no such problematic trend was manifest in Labour support in Scotland. Indeed, in 1992 and 1999 more women than men voted for Labour (see the figures in parentheses in Table 4.5). Interestingly, in the 1990s, New Labour also flirted with the colour purple, in the seemingly successful hope of attracting more of the female electorate who had traditionally been more supportive of the Conservatives in Britain.[41] However, it should be noted that the SNP itself does have a history of high-profile female parliamentarians, including Winnie Ewing, Margo MacDonald and Roseanna Cunningham. Moreover, in the first elections to the Scottish Parliament they were second only to Labour in terms of sex parity: women comprised 43 per cent of the new SNP MSPs.

Table 4.5 Social characteristics of Scottish National Party voters, 1979–2001 (figures for Labour in parentheses)

	1979 %	1992 %	1997 %	1999 %	2001 %
Sex					
Male	29 (33)	22 (29)	17 (41)	23 (28)	21 (54)
Female	20 (32)	18 (34)	13 (40)	17 (30)	18 (49)
Age					
18–24	17 (11)	15 (10)	8 (9)	6 (6)	4 (5)
25–34	29 (18)	23 (19)	21 (23)	22 (15)	13 (16)
35–44	19 (20)	23 (20)	16 (17)	20 (17)	18 (20)
45–54	13 (15)	21 (15)	24 (16)	24 (15)	28 (14)
55–64	13 (19)	11 (16)	17 (15)	12 (16)	16 (13)
65+	9 (16)	6 (18)	15 (21)	17 (31)	20 (32)
Social class					
Salariat	n/a	20 (22)	12 (25)	21 (25)	19 (45)
Working class	n/a	23 (39)	17 (52)	22 (36)	19 (62)
Self-assigned class					
Middle class	25 (19)	12 (12)	13 (28)	18 (20)	20 (26)
Working class	23 (47)	23 (44)	16 (46)	21 (34)	21 (64)

Source: Scottish Election Studies, 1979–2001.

Future Scottish election surveys will no doubt enlighten us as to the success or otherwise of such political communication strategies as 'lucky purple heather', as well as showing whether having high numbers of female parliamentarians, and placing greater emphasis upon policies which are seen as more in touch with women's concerns, such as health, education and law and order, make a difference to patterns of electoral support.

Age

If social class was becoming less salient as regards voting behaviour by the 1970s, we may expect younger voters to be attracted to a new party. Scarcity and security being less of a concern may lead the young towards post-materialist values[42] and away from the 'old class parties', with nationalist parties such as the SNP benefiting from such trends. The evidence in Table 4.5 suggests that this was indeed the case in 1979 and 1992. In both elections the SNP has a larger share of the under-34s vote than does Labour, 46 compared with 29 per cent in 1979 and 38 against 29 per cent in 1992. However, in the two UK elections of 1997 and 2001, Labour won out in this under-34 category, although the SNP maintained its lead in this category at the 1999 Scottish election. However, we should note that as we move through the 1990s the relationship between age and vote becomes similar as the younger vote tails off, with both parties' support found more amongst the older age cohorts. The decline in younger voters supporting the SNP may reflect the greater institutionalisation of the SNP in the Scottish political system, as we do see the retention of that previously young age group into the 35–44 group category at later elections.

Social class

The next two variables to be examined from Table 4.5, as correlates of vote, have specific relevance for the left–right divide and the SNP's ability to mount an effective challenge to Labour on this ideological spectrum. After all, intuitively we would expect those at the lower end of the socio-economic scale to be more attracted to the redistributive message inherent in such social democratic appeals than the voters from the wealthier classes. But, even at the time when the SNP was positioning itself as a left-wing party, Webb could claim that 'the nationalist movement has drawn members exactly proportionally from all classes'.[43] In reality, all parties draw members disproportionately from the middle class, but it is instructive to see whether the SNP draws votes from across the class spectrum, or, as it moved to the left, more from the working class.

Brand *et al.*[44] found the SNP and Labour vote to be similar in 1992 as the SNP moved to the left, but what of longer-term trends? If we examine the objective class position[45] first, we see that the SNP drew only 3 per cent more votes in the working class category in 1992 than in the salariat, whereas Labour drew 17 points more in the working class than in the salariat. As expected, the SNP's working class vote does indeed strengthen slightly at the 1997 general election, up to 5 points over the salariat, but in 1999 the difference is only 1 point, and in 2001 the two are exactly the same. Given that our two social groups come from either end of the socio-economic class schema, we may in 2001, with some elasticity, claim that the SNP has drawn support exactly proportionally from all classes. Unfortunately, the 1979 Election Study did not have the Goldthorpe categories with which a comparison could be made, but when examining 'social grade' from the 1979 election we see that 35 per cent of the 'higher managerial class' voted SNP and only 10 per cent Labour, whereas 33 per cent of the skilled manual grade voted SNP but 38 per cent Labour. Such trends strongly suggest that the SNP, even after a decade or so of social democratic rhetoric, is not unequivocally a working class party in terms of electoral support. When analysing SNP voting we find more symmetry of support from both the lower and higher ends of the social economic scale, rather than the disproportionate support from the working class that we would expect to find.

Further evidence from the subjective class position of voters in Table 4.5 adds weight to the hypothesis that there is symmetry of class support for the SNP. This 'self-assigned' category shows how respondents feel about their class position irrespective of the objective reality. Indeed, if the Scots are an electorate imbued with a social democratic value system, then they may be more prone to choose a working class identity. But, more importantly, a party that seeks to challenge Labour on the left of the socio-economic ideological spectrum should be seen to be prospering in this category of working class identifiers. However, the data in this category mirrors that of the objective class position above. In 1992, the SNP had an

11-point lead in 'assigned' working class votes over middle class ones, but in later elections the gap becomes negligible, especially relative to Labour's strong performance in the working class category. In fact, we find 2 per cent more support for the SNP from the middle class in 1979, but again, after nearly two decades of a distinctly left-wing agenda, there is no discernible benefit to the SNP in attracting working-class support; in 2001 we see that the party attracts an almost identical level of support from both class positions.

Religion

The final variable to be analysed in our profile of SNP support is religion. The received wisdom in contemporary academic circles is to discount the importance of religion as a social cleavage, but in one crucial respect the religious cleavage in Scotland has retained much of its influence on Scottish electoral behaviour,[46] namely in the predilection of Catholics to vote Labour. This is of relevance to the future electoral prospects of the SNP *vis-à-vis* its attempt to woo votes away from Labour.

Table 4.6 shows the relationship between religion and vote in Scotland between 1979 and 1997. It is clear that Catholics as a group overwhelmingly support Labour; this support by Catholics for a left-wing party is in stark contrast to the support given to Christian right-of-centre parties on the Continent. There are two historical explanations for this. Firstly, many Scottish Catholics were originally Irish immigrants who entered the labour market on the lowest rung of the ladder, consequently supporting the party that offered the most attractive policies to the working class, which at the time was Labour. Secondly, the prewar SNP and some of its precursors[47] (as well as many other institutions in Scottish society) were sometimes hostile to Catholicism, whether explicitly or implicitly, although the postwar SNP, especially in the 1990s, has been very careful to present itself as an inclusive, non-sectarian party. Moreover, in the past, Scottish Catholics were wary of the SNP's goal of independence, as an independent Scotland would be overwhelmingly Protestant. More recently, however, it has been equally generally held that this Catholic perception of mistrust had evaporated somewhat at the most recent elections.[48] Paradoxically, the evidence in Table 4.6 would seem to offer partial support for both of these two contradictory claims, that there is still Catholic mistrust of the SNP and that the relationship between Catholics and Labour 'seems to be weakening with time and as such may make it easier for the SNP to eat into Labour's voting base'.[49]

There is no doubt that there is still a very strong Catholic alignment with Labour. Over the five elections presented in Table 4.6, Labour obtained, on average, 75 per cent of the Catholic vote, whereas the SNP has enjoyed higher levels of support from Protestants and from those of no religion.[50] However, with our above paradox in mind, we see that patterns of Catholic support for the SNP have gone in waves, rising from a trough of 8 per cent in 1979 to a crest of 20 per cent in 1992, falling to 10 per cent in 1997 before rising again to 23 per cent in 1999, and falling back in 2001 to 8 per cent, the 1979 level. So far as there has been any religious dealignment in recent years it has been in a crumbling of the traditional Catholic caution towards the SNP at the 1992 and 1997 elections. However, unfortunately

Table 4.6 Religion and vote in Scotland, 1979–2001

	Protestant %	Roman Catholic %	None %
1979			
Conservative	45	12	27
Labour	27	77	46
Liberal	11	3	8
SNP	17	8	19
1992			
Conservative	35	7	19
Labour	31	65	39
Liberal	12	8	12
SNP	22	20	30
1997			
Conservative	19	5	9
Labour	45	81	55
Liberal	15	4	13
SNP	21	10	23
1999			
Conservative	22	1	11
Labour	36	70	41
Liberal	15	6	13
SNP	27	23	34
2001			
Conservative	26	10	5
Labour	42	82	54
Liberal	16	0	15
SNP	16	8	25

Source: Scottish Election Studies, 1979–2001.

for the SNP, Catholic circumspection towards it is still evident at the 1979, 1997 and 2001 elections. This undulating wave model of denominational vote for the SNP does not exactly follow the rise and fall of the performance of the party at each election. It is noteworthy, too, that between 1979 and 1999, both the Catholic vote and the vote of those with no religion have followed a similarly undulating pattern, whereas the Protestant vote is more stable.

Recently the SNP has been proactive in courting the Catholic vote. For example, on the sensitive question of education it has vigorously defended Catholic schools, arguing that their contribution to 'the diversity and richness of the Scottish educational scene' should be fully realised.[51] Nevertheless, in an increasingly secular society[52] the SNP has not as yet mounted a substantial threat to Labour regarding either the secular or the Catholic vote. Indeed, at the 2001 election, the Protestant SNP vote fell in a similar way to its Catholic and secular counterparts. Future election surveys will further elucidate this pattern of support, and demonstrate whether the SNP's courting of the Catholic vote translates into electoral support.

INDEPENDENCE IN EUROPE

If trends in national identity or in social and economic cleavages do not appear to be moving in a direction which is discernibly favourable to the SNP, then what of other flagship policies? One such policy, since its adoption by the party at the 1988 Conference, was a more enthusiastic engagement with European integration. However, one constant in over forty years of debate on the extent and character of this supranational entity, is the refusal of the electorate to elevate Europe into a first-order election issue. The EU as a political project is simply not an issue which resonates with the majority of the electorate. It does, however, have the capacity to vex elites, including political parties.[53] It is worth noting that the timing of the SNP's change in direction on the issue of Europe occurred during the 1980s, following more or less on the heels of the Labour Party's similar conversion.

Is it a contradiction in terms for a nationalist party committed to Scottish sovereignty and secession from the United Kingdom to pursue membership of such a supranational entity as the EU? In the 1960s and 1970s the SNP thought so. The party was hostile to the idea of joining the European Economic Community (EEC) and campaigned vigorously for withdrawal at the 1975 referendum. Billy Wolfe, the SNP chairman at this time, could equate the 'centralism' of the Common Market with that of the 'English Parties'; it was seen as 'the logical continuation of their centralist thinking which has been so damaging to Scotland's people and Scotland's economy'.[54]

Several factors influenced the SNP's conversion to Europe. The first was the result of the 1975 referendum, which stunned the party. It was duly noted that only Shetland and the Western Isles voted for withdrawal, with the most heavily populated regions voting to remain within the EEC. Secondly, the breakaway Scottish Labour Party, led by Jim Sillars, supported Scottish membership of the EEC. This was to be the precursor of the 'Independence in Europe' policy, advocated just as strongly by Sillars on joining the '79 group in 1980.[55] Thirdly was the experiences of Winnie Ewing, SNP MEP from 1975, who became convinced of the benefits of Scottish participation in Europe. Thus, throughout the early to mid-1980s both the left and right of the party moved to a more enthusiastic position concerning Europe – particularly as the Tories and the English voters seemed to be going in the opposite direction – to the extent that by the 1990s the party, like Labour, was extremely positive about European membership. However, Labour and the SNP have very different views on Scotland's place in Europe, Labour arguing that Scotland will benefit more from Europe by remaining a part of the United Kingdom, and the SNP arguing that greater benefits will arise if Scotland is a full member state.

By the time the Maastricht Bill proceeded through Parliament in the early 1990s, both the SNP and Labour were very much in favour of European union. However, with the Conservatives needing every vote they could muster for Maastricht to proceed, Labour indulged in partisan warfare in the hope of ousting the Conservatives from office. But in 1993 the SNP accepted an arrangement from Ian Lang, the Conservative secretary of state for Scotland, whereby in return for SNP support on Maastricht, Scotland would receive between six and eight seats on the

Committee of the Regions. Not only did this course of action cause problems within the party but it also provoked loud and sustained criticism from Labour and its supporters in the media. Although both parties were now very much Europhile, the issue of Europe rapidly became one more issue over which battles concerning Scotland's constitutional position could be played out.

There is, evidently, a nationalist–'unionist' divide over Europe, bearing in mind, however, that not all unionist parties hold similar views on Europe – there is a substantial difference between Conservative and Labour policy on Europe. By 'unionist', we are focusing here on Labour. Even so, the debate on Europe is not polarised simply between the unionist Labour position that Scotland is best served in Europe via UK membership versus the SNP argument that Scotland would be best served as an independent member state. Devolution in Scotland has opened up new channels of influence and opportunity for Scotland in Europe, and the current (Labour) first minister, Jack McConnell, is extremely active in promoting Scotland in networks of other European 'constitutional regions'. An agreement was signed in May 2002 with Catalonia, to strengthen relations between the two nations. Moreover, the constitutional regions, including Scotland, are pushing for more involvement in European decision making in the context of the current Convention on the Future on Europe. Thus there is a potential trajectory here of a unionist administration pushing for increased Scottish participation in Europe, albeit stopping short of assuming full member state status.

We turn now to the issue of how Europe plays out domestically, within the Scottish Parliament. The divide between Labour and SNP is evident in the respective positions taken by SNP and Labour MSPs outlined in Table 4.7. Such data neatly illustrates the extent to which both parties are now engaged in 'trench warfare' on this issue.[56]

Table 4.7 draws upon a survey of MSPs undertaken in 2001.[57] The extent of both parties' enthusiasm for Europe is evident from statement 4.7.1, where we find four-fifths of each party willing to endorse a quasi-propaganda role for the Scottish Parliament promoting European issues in Scotland. However, no such consensus is evident on any statement concerning Scotland's constitutional position *vis-à-vis* European integration; here our nationalist–unionist 'trench warfare' comes to the fore, with party positions polarised opposites. The SNP is near unanimous in preferring Brussels to Westminster (4.7.4), and unanimous in its distrust of UK ministers in European negotiations (4.7.3) and the present financial relationships between Westminster and Edinburgh regarding EU funding (4.7.2). Interestingly, four-fifths of SNP MSPs believe that full tax-raising powers for Holyrood would help in regard to EU funding opportunities (4.7.5), underpinned by the view from 90 per cent of its MSPs that the German Länder, Catalonia and the Basque country have more influence than Scotland in the EU (4.7.6). On these issues, an overwhelming number of Labour MSPs take a diametrically opposed, unionist position.

The final two statements (4.7.7) and (4.7.8) are instructive for delineating the extent of future nationalist–unionist battles over Europe. Nearly three-quarters of Labour MSPs believe that Scotland has no automatic right to become an independent nation in the EU (4.7.8), and the two groups of MSPs have diametrically

Table 4.7 SNP and Labour MSPs' views on Europe

	Strongly agree	Neither agree nor disagree	Strongly disagree
4.7.1 The Scottish Parliament should act to promote European issues in Scotland.			
SNP	82%	16%	0%
Labour	83%	7%	11%
4.7.2 The financial relationships established between Westminster and the Scottish Parliament prevent Scotland from taking full advantage of EU funds.			
SNP	100%	0%	0%
Labour	8%	4%	89%
4.7.3 UK Ministers cannot adequately represent Scottish interests in European negotiations.			
SNP	100%	0%	0%
Labour	7%	4%	89%
4.7.4 The EU is a better forum for advancing Scottish interests than Westminster.			
SNP	85%	15%	0%
Labour	4%	25%	71%
4.7.5 Full tax-raising powers for the Scottish Parliament would allow Scotland to take greater advantage of EU funding opportunities.			
SNP	80%	15%	5%
Labour	7%	18%	75%
4.7.6 Scotland lacks the influence in Europe enjoyed by other regions such as the German Länder, Catalonia and the Basque country.			
SNP	90%	10%	0%
Labour	11%	18%	71%
4.7.7 After the Nice Treaty Scotland enjoys greater influence in the EU through UK representation than it would as an independent nation.			
SNP	0%	0%	100%
Labour	89%	11%	0%
4.7.8 Because of the possibility of other states' objections, an independent Scotland would have no automatic right to EU membership.			
SNP	10%	5%	85%
Labour	72%	21%	7%

Source: ESRC funded survey R000223242, Mapping Scottish and Welsh Parliamentarians' Attitudes to European Integration, 2001.

opposite views on the Treaty of Nice (4.7.7). This issue is extremely important, given the SNP view that, 'clearly, after Nice, Scotland will have significantly greater influence in the European Union as an independent nation than as part of the United Kingdom'.[58] But Labour was quick to imply that Nice was in fact a 'nasty blow for the SNP'.[59] The Labour MP Douglas Alexander, who is seen as a close confidant of Chancellor Gordon Brown, put the case that Nice was an enhancement of British power at the expense of the influence of smaller countries:

'Against this new background, the nationalists' claim that Scotland's interests will be best served by "Independence in Europe" sound ever less credible'.[60]

Europe, then, for the foreseeable future, is an important battleground for the SNP, one on which it sees the possibility of its aspirations being realised. But there will be problems distinguishing its pro-European position from that of Labour, particularly if a Scottish electorate is not as enthusiastic on further integration as the SNP is. For example, opinion polls in Scotland show that levels of reserve about the euro are similar to those found in England, and increasingly we are finding strange bedfellows on both sides of the euro debate, with the SNP's former architect of 'Independence in Europe', Jim Sillars, joining the campaign against the euro. This suggests that 'Independence in Europe' may not garner more support amongst the electorate than 'Devolution in Europe'.

FUTURE PROSPECTS

The SNP has been the major fuel of the nationalist movement. It has been extremely influential in the politicisation of Scottish identity, and devolution is due in no small part to electoral pressure brought to bear by the SNP. However, the SNP is not the only agent of national identity, or even of political nationalism, in Scotland. National identity is disseminated widely, and it is possible to see a 'small n' nationalism in the unionist parties which supported devolution. The paradox of Scottish nationalism is that whilst there is a widespread sense of national identity, which has strengthened over the past twenty years, this national identity does not map neatly on to party support or constitutional preference. Whilst the SNP has been the main initial motor of change, it may not be able to benefit electorally – because it is competing with Labour for the same vote.

This poses a major problem for the SNP: how to challenge Labour's electoral hegemony? We have seen that the SNP cannot readily convert the voters' feelings of national identity into votes for the party. It faces similar problems with its position on the left–right ideological spectrum and also regarding class structure, sex, religion and even in some respects Europe. In all these respects, the SNP could look like an imitation of the very party that it needs to defeat: Labour. The fundamental difference between the SNP and Labour remains independence, but even this may lose much of its resonance within a world of increasing multi-level governance, in both the United Kingdom and the EU, especially with a Labour/Liberal Democrat administration in Scotland being proactive about Scottish involvement in Europe.

Devolution presents the SNP with new challenges and opportunities. On the one hand it has been advantageous, giving the party a far higher profile and increasing its chances of government. But devolution also heightens the party's fundamentalist and gradualist strategies, and the fundamentalists are always on guard against a sell-out by those less committed to complete withdrawal from the United Kingdom. Their circumspection is warranted in that 42 per cent of SNP voters give 'home rule' and not independence as their first preference (Table 4.4). Pursuing policies such as fiscal autonomy is, as we have seen, a double-edged sword, as it may underpin as much as undermine the case for devolution.

Finally, the future of the Scottish national movement as a whole is not dependent only on the SNP. The rise of the SNP in the 1970s was the initial impetus for Labour adopting devolution as a policy, but devolution itself was not achieved until it was supported by a broader coalition, namely the devolution movement of the 1980s and 1990s, which included the Labour Party itself. Similarly, it is likely that the SNP will continue to set the agenda for future constitutional change, but it is quite possible that the Scottish Parliament will accrue further powers even without the SNP in government, once a broad coalition has formed around the desirability of further powers. The debate on fiscal autonomy is already wider than the SNP: many recent opinion polls have shown that there is more support for increasing the Parliament's powers than there is for independence, and various other interest groups as well as a few individual Conservative MSPs have also come out in favour of this. Nor are the SNP any longer the sole vehicle of independence: the 2003 elections saw the pro-independence Scottish Socialist Party and the Scottish Green Party gain six and seven seats respectively. The likelihood of increased powers for the Parliament, and the potential discussed above for greater Scottish involvement in Europe, could represent a 'third way' for Scottish nationalism, between the two poles of the new unionist status quo and the SNP option of independence in Europe. In the future, as in the past, Scottish nationalism is likely to be a broader and much messier phenomenon than simply support for the SNP. The 'settled will of the Scottish people' may in fact be far from settled. Whatever happens over the coming years, the continuing debates around Scotland's constitutional status are sure to continue to provoke considerable interest, both within Scotland and further afield.

NOTES

1. Numerous writers stress this, including Paterson, Lindsay, *The Autonomy of Modern Scotland* (Edinburgh: Edinburgh University Press, 1994); Keating, Michael, *Nations Against the State: The New Politics of Nationalism in Quebec, Catalonia and Scotland* (Basingstoke: Palgrave, 2001) p.134; Webb, Keith, *The Growth of Nationalism in Scotland* (Harmondsworth: Penguin, 1978)
2. Mitchell, James, *Strategies for Self-government: The Campaigns for a Scottish Parliament* (Edinburgh: Polygon, 1996) p.28
3. Ibid. p.26
4. Speech by David McLetchie in Parliament Hall, 1 July 1999, Scottish Parliament website www.scottish.parliament.uk
5. Keating, op. cit. (2001) p.180
6. Scottish Constitutional Convention, 'A Claim of Right for Scotland', 30 March 1989, in *Towards Scotland's Parliament* (Edinburgh: SCC, 1990)
7. Nairn, Tom, Upper and Lower Cases, *London Review of Books* (24 August 1995) pp.14–18
8. See Smith, Anthony D., *National Identity* (London: Penguin, 1991) for an examination of such ideal types of nationalism.
9. Other examples include Catalonia and Quebec. On neo-nationalism, see especially Keating, op. cit. (2000); MacInnes, J. and D. McCrone (eds) Stateless Nations

in the 21st Century, *Scottish Affairs* Special Issue (2001); and McCrone, D., *The Sociology of Nationalism: Tomorrow's Ancestors* (Routledge: London, 1998) ch. 7

10. SNP, *A Constitution for a Free Scotland* (Edinburgh, 2002) p.7

11. Salmond, Alex, MP, National Convener, speech to National Conference, 26 September 1997

12. Gellner, Ernest, *Nations and Nationalism* (Oxford: Blackwell, 1983) p.1

13. Mitchell, op. cit. (1996) p.233

14. SNP, op. cit. (2002)

15. Quoted in *The Scotsman*, 24 September 1999

16. Mitchell, James, Factions, Tendencies and Consensus in the Scottish National Party in the 1980s, in Brown, Alice and Parry, Richard (eds), *Scottish Government Yearbook 1990* (Edinburgh, 1990)

17. Mitchell, op. cit. (1996) pp.216–24

18. McEwen, Nicola, The Scottish National Party after Devolution: Progress and Prospects, in Hassan, Gerry and Warhurst, Chris (eds), *Tomorrow's Scotland* (London: Lawrence & Wishart, 2002) pp.57–8

19. Iain Blackford, then SNP party treasurer, Go South to Create a New Scotland, *The Scotsman*, 24 September 1999

20. Margaret Ewing, Convener of the SNP's parliamentary group, at the 1999 Party Conference, quoted in *The Scotsman*, 24 September 1999

21. Fiscal autonomy would mean that rather than being funded from Westminster by the block grant, the Scottish Parliament would raise all its own taxes and transfer a certain amount down to Westminster to pay for retained powers such as defence.

22. Pultzer, Peter G., *Political Representation and Elections in Britain* (London: George Allen & Unwin, 1967) p.98. Lipset and Rokkan's 'freezing hypothesis' – that the cleavages in society in the 1960s reflected those of the 1920s when adult male suffrage became a reality – was generally accepted for the whole of Britain (Lipset, Seymour Martin and Rokkan, Stein (eds), *Party Systems and Voter Alignments* (New York: Free Press, 1967))

23. Budge, Ian and Urwin, Derek, *Scottish Political Behaviour: A Case Study in British Homogeneity* (London: Longman, 1966)

24. Crewe, Ivor, Great Britain, in Crewe, Ivor and Denver, David (eds), *Electoral Change in Western Democracies* (London: Croom Helm, 1985) p.103

25. For example see Denver, David and Hands, Gordon (eds), *Issues and Controversies in British Electoral Behaviour* (London: Harvester Wheatsheaf, 1992)

26. For example see Bogdanor, Vernon and Field, William H., Lessons of History: Core and Periphery in British Electoral Behaviour, 1910–92, *Electoral Studies* 12 (1993) pp.203–24

27. In the British/Scottish Election Studies, respondents have to choose between either Scottish or British national identity. This could be seen as a rather blunt instrument, but this trend towards a more exclusive Scottish identity has been mirrored in most contemporary surveys, even when the choice is not so stark. For example, the Moreno scale surveys allow a graded choice varying from

exclusively Scottish, through equally Scottish and British, to exclusively British (Paterson *et al.* (2001) pp.102–3), and here too the trend has seen Scots prioritise their Scottishness above or at the expense of Britishness.

28. Paterson, Lindsay, Brown, Alice, Curtice, John, Hinds, Kerstin, McCrone, David, Park, Alison, Sproston, Kerry and Surridge, Paula, *New Scotland, New Politics?* (Edinburgh: Polygon, 2001) p.102

29. For example, see Brown, Alice, McCrone, David and Paterson, Lindsay, *Politics and Society in Scotland*, 2nd edition (Basingstoke: Macmillan, 1998); Bond, Ross, Squaring the Circles: Demonstrating and Explaining the Political 'Non-Alignment' of Scottish National Identity, *Scottish Affairs* 32 (2000), pp.15–35; McCrone, David, *Understanding Scotland: The Sociology of a Stateless Nation*, 2nd edition (London: Routledge, 2001); Bond, Ross and Rosie, Michael, National Identities in Post-devolution Scotland, *Scottish Affairs* 40 (2002), pp.34–53; McCrone, David and Paterson, Lindsay, The Conundrum of Scottish Independence, *Scottish Affairs* 40 (2002) pp.54–75

30. However, we should note that periodically the number of Scots choosing the independence option increases in polls which pose the future event of a referendum. For example, in January 2000 an ICM poll found that 47 per cent would vote for independence, 43 per cent against with 9 per cent don't knows (http://www.icmresearch.co.uk/reviews/polls-archive.htm).

31. There is a (contested) view that social democracy is an intrinsic part of Scottish identity, and hence the SNP (and Labour) can utilise social democratic values in a nationalist manner, rather than appealing to ethnic or cultural markers. See, for example, George Reid ('Oh to be in Britain?', Donaldson Lecture 1995, http://www.snp.org.uk (accessed July 2000)) who portrays social democracy as a bond between Scotland's many constituent groups. For an academic analysis see: Hamilton, Paul, The Scottish National Paradox: The Scottish National Party's Lack of Ethnic Character, *Canadian Review of Studies in Nationalism* XXVI (1 sol. 2) (1999) pp.17–36, and Henderson, Ailsa, Political Constructions of National Identity in Scotland and Quebec, *Scottish Affairs* 29 (Autumn 1999) pp.121–38. David Seawright, *An Important Matter of Principle: The Decline of the Scottish Conservative and Unionist Party* (Aldershot: Ashgate, 1999), dates this increasing movement to the left from the 1960s to early 1970s.

32. Webb, op. cit. (1978) p.140

33. Mitchell, op. cit. (1996) pp.180–7

34. Between 1912 and 1965 the Conservative Party in Scotland was known as the Scottish Unionist Party after its formal merger with the Liberal Unionists.

35. On the Tory membership and leadership of the Scottish Party, and its effects on the SNP, see Webb, op. cit. (1978) p. 74, Mitchell, op. cit. (1996) p.189. On the early SNP, see Finlay, Richard, *Independent and Free: Scottish Politics and the Origins of the Scottish National Party 1918–1945* (Edinburgh: John Donald, 1994)

36. Mitchell quotes Kellas, in the 1970 British Nuffield Election Study, as describing the SNP as 'something of a social democratic party', although it was the '1974 February manifesto [that] made explicit reference to the programme of social democracy' (Mitchell, op. cit. (1996) p.207). However, Brand cites the

1982 SNP diary as first explicit self-description of the SNP as 'a moderate, left-of-centre party' (Brand, Jack, Scotland, in Michael Watson (ed.), *Contemporary Minority Nationalism* (London: Routledge, 1990) p.27)

37. Mitchell, op. cit. (1996) p.225

38. Kerevan, George, From 'Old' to 'New' SNP, in Hassan, Gerry and Warhurst, Chris, *A Different Future* (Edinburgh: Centre for Scottish Public Policy, 1999)

39. For example, see *Scotland on Sunday*, 5 January 2003, and *The Guardian*, 14 January 2003

40. SNP Shows True Colours to Attract Women Voters, *Scotland on Sunday*, 22 September 2002

41. Ibid.

42. Inglehart, Ronald, The Silent Revolution in Europe, *American Political Science Review* LXVII (1971) pp.991–1017

43. Webb, op.cit. (1977), p.50

44. Brand, Jack, Mitchell, James and Surridge, Paula, Social Constituency and Ideological Profile: Scottish Nationalism in the 1990s, *Political Studies* XLII (1994), pp.616–29

45. A good introduction to the different socio-economic groups and schema used for such analyses can be found in Paterson *et al.*, op. cit. (2001) pp.168–82. In Table 4.5 we use the top and bottom classes from the five-class Goldthorpe schema which is derived from OPCS Standard Occupational Classification combined with employment status, 1. Salariat (professional and managerial); 2. Routine non-manual workers (office and sales); 3. Petty bourgeoisie (the self-employed, including farmers, with and without employees); 4. Manual foremen and supervisors; 5. Working class (skilled, semi-skilled and unskilled manual workers, personal service and agricultural workers).

46. See also Seawright, David, A Confessional Cleavage Resurrected? The Denominational Vote in Britain, in Broughton, David and ten Napel, Hans-Martien (eds), *Religion and Mass Electoral Behaviour in Europe* (London: Routledge, 2000), for an examination of the continuing relevance of the denominational vote.

47. Some elements of the Scottish Party, one of several early nationalist parties which merged in 1934 to form the SNP, brought to the early SNP not only a desire to strengthen the unity of Britain and the empire, but also 'a strong element of anti-Catholic bigotry and Irish racism was also evident'. Mitchell, op. cit. (1996) p.181

48. Mitchell, James, The 1992 Election in Scotland in Context, *Parliamentary Affairs* 45 (1992) p.624

49. Brand, Jack, Mitchell, James and Surridge, Paula, Will Scotland Come to the Aid of the Party?, in Heath, Anthony, Jowell, Roger and Curtice, John, with Taylor, Bridget, *Labour's Last Chance? The 1992 Election and Beyond* (Aldershot: Dartmouth, 1994) p.227

50. In all surveys, religion is the denomination to which the respondent feels they belong rather than an indication of religious observance. To all intents and purposes these 'Protestant' figures are overwhelmingly Presbyterian and most Protestants in Scotland would identify with the Church of Scotland.

51. SNP manifesto, *We Stand for Scotland* (2001)

52. In 1979, 29 per cent of the survey did not belong to a religion but this secular group jumps dramatically to 44 per cent in 2001.

53. For example, see Baker, David and Seawright, David, *Britain For and Against Europe* (Oxford: OUP, 1998), and Franklin, Mark and Wleizen, Christopher, The Responsive Public: Issue Salience, Policy Change, and Preferences for European Unification, *Journal of Theoretical Politics* 9 (1997) pp.347–63

54. Mitchell, James, Member State or Euro-Region? The SNP, Plaid Cymru, and Europe, in Baker and Seawright, op. cit. (1998)

55. See Mitchell, op. cit. (1998) for an excellent overview of SNP policy regarding Europe.

56. Ibid., p.124.

57. The ESRC funded survey (R000223242) elicited Likert-type responses from attitudinal statements on European integration from MSPs and Assembly Members (Wales), and was conducted between March and June 2001 by David Baker, Andrew Gamble, Nick Randall and David Seawright. A postal survey was mailed to all members of both institutions, with an overall response rate of 52 per cent for the Scottish Parliament and 55 per cent for the National Assembly for Wales. In addition, around 30 in-depth interviews were conducted with members of the four main parties in Scotland and Wales.

58. SNP manifesto, *We Stand for Scotland* (2001)

59. Alexander, Douglas, How Nice was a Nasty Blow for the SNP, *The Scotsman*, 26 December 2000

60. Ibid.

5 The politics of identity: Wales

James Hunter

INTRODUCTION

The institutionalisation of nationhood within the political infrastructure of a territory should in theory enable political parties with a clearly identifiable nationalist ideology to reap the rewards of the reawakening of national sentiment brought about by the establishment of new forms of democratic representation. The scale of this 'institutional' boost to nationalism may be further enhanced if the electoral system adopted for the new democratic forum directly encourages the second-order voting patterns[1] necessary for minority parties to secure levels of support that will disrupt traditional political fault lines. However, instrumentalist conceptions of nationalism suggest that majority elite stakeholders[2] will also employ discourses surrounding national identity as a mechanism for competing over the distribution of economic resources and political power.[3] More specifically, the institutional and policy context created by majority elite stakeholders in response to minority nationalism may provide an arena in which demands for greater autonomy or self-government can be directly challenged.[4]

The aim of this chapter is to examine the extent to which the instigation of devolved government in Wales has provided a forum for the emergence of an instrumental politics of identity that is evoked by state building as well as minority nationalist parties. The central premise of the argument advanced here is that the devolution-inspired reconfiguration of the political environment potentially creates a form of cognitive order that serves to restrict rather than enhance the future advancement of minority nationalism. In order to explore the idea of devolution as an 'anti-minority nationalism' mechanism, the concept of territorial communities is developed. The nature of the discourses surrounding identity espoused by elite stakeholders, it is argued, is determined by the cognitive order of a territorial community – which in turn is determined by the characteristics of, and degree of homogeneity within, the indigenous population of the community, its status as a primary or secondary political arena, the institutional and policy framework operating within it, and finally the nature and extent of the links it has with other territorial communities. This cognitive order also serves to confer 'insider' and 'outsider' status upon the authors of specific discourses within the territorial community, which ultimately influences and determines their ability to advance specific political objectives. Whilst instrumental conceptions of nationalism as a conduit for competition over political power between elite stakeholders feature strongly within the conceptual framework developed here, the concept of the cognitive order within territorial communities draws upon the ideas contained within the policy communities and networks literature conventionally employed to analyse the operation of the policy process.

The analysis of the nature and implications of the reconfiguration of the cognitive order within post-devolution Wales is undertaken in a series of stages. Firstly, a brief overview of the central arguments contained within the idea of policy communities and networks is provided in order to identify the constituent elements of the cognitive order of communities. Secondly, the nature and location of territorial communities, and the basis of the link between them, are outlined. The status of territorial communities, and the populations that reside within them, however, is unlikely to be equal. The basis of this inequality is then explored in terms of the definition of different territorial communities as primary or secondary arenas within the state. The primary or secondary status of a territorial community is likely to determine not only the nature of its links with other territorial communities but also the degree of demands for greater autonomy or secession amongst its population. The third stage of the analysis is then concerned with examining the alternative forms of cognitive order based upon different discourses surrounding identity advanced by the competing elite stakeholders operating within the territorial community. Minority nationalist parties, it is suggested, will espouse a conception of identity that emphasises the uniqueness of the experiences and values of the population residing within the territorial community in order to enhance the legitimacy of their demands for self-determination. In response, majority elite stakeholders will seek to employ a number of alternative strategies designed to demonstrate the extent of, and need for, maintaining common links between the territorial community seeking greater freedom and the other constituent elements of the state. Finally, having outlined the conceptual framework in an abstract form, the concept of territorial communities and the cognitive orders that they bring forth is applied to pre- and post-devolution Wales.

COGNITIVE ORDER, TERRITORIAL COMMUNITIES, NATIONALIST DISCOURSES AND THE BEHAVIOUR OF ELITE STAKEHOLDERS

Prior to outlining the conceptual framework in more detail, it is necessary to define certain terms, identify the scope of the framework and to establish the presence of certain caveats that may limit the application of the idea of territorial communities to the analysis of nationalism within other political contexts.

1. Firstly, the aim here is not to generate a universally applicable descriptive or prescriptive framework for analysing nationalism and responses to nationalism, but to develop an analytical tool that can aid the analysis of developments within pre- and post-devolution Wales. Therefore, the type of state architecture incorporated within the framework relates solely to multiple territory-based states in which there are clearly identifiable majority and minority cultures and populations.

2. Secondly, the framework does not seek to promote the primary importance of elite groups (and hence instrumental explanations of nationalism) above other structural and non-structural factors in understanding nationalism. Whilst the framework buys into the concept that relevant stakeholders may be able to evoke specific forms of cultural symbolism, it is assumed that the nature and interrelated manifestation of these factors provides them with a pervading presence that is above and beyond the entire control of the elite stakeholders.

3. Finally, the framework developed here is one that primarily concerns the internal structures, workings and regions of the state. In this context, the types of nationalist discourse incorporated within the analysis relate solely to those initiated by majority and minority elite stakeholders within the confines of the state itself.

Policy communities, policy networks and the components of the cognitive order of communities

The concept of policy communities and policy networks emerged in British political science in response to identified weaknesses in pluralist explanations of the operation of the policy process, and the emergence of sub-government as a result of segmentation and sectorisation within the institutions and activities of the state.[5] More specifically, the emergence within Britain of a consensus style of policy making that is characterised by the prominence of clientilism between groups and government departments, the development of exchange relationships, bargaining over rather than the imposition of policy decisions, and the institutionalisation of compromise was denoted.[6] In this context it is argued that policy decisions, and the control of the policy agenda, are determined by the existence of policy communities operating outside of, and beyond, the formal institutionalised structures of government.

Policy communities are multiple interlocking and overlapping phenomena that function through the existence of policy networks that facilitate the interaction of different stakeholders and the exchange of information and resources. They are also characterised by a 'cognitive' order concerning the nature of policy problems and the responses required to these policy issues, ideological and institutional structures, fixed and closed agendas, stability and the presence of insider and outsider groups.[7] The accepted cognitive order of a policy community is designed to promote internal solidarity amongst its members and to prevent stakeholders promoting alternative agendas that might threaten the status of the policy community and its constituents from gaining access to key decision-makers. Specific policy stakeholders may be members of a number of policy communities that are linked together by professional, intergovernmental, produce- or issue-based policy networks – and their status as insiders or outsiders may change depending upon the specific policy community that is under scrutiny. The characteristics of policy communities, their cognitive order and the insider/outsider status of the stakeholders contained within or outside their confines, it is argued, strongly reflects the nature of territorial communities and the alternative discourses surrounding identity promulgated by the competing elite stakeholders residing within them.

The concept of territorial communities

Territorial communities are spatial political entities that exist on the basis of either official recognition within the constitutional, institutional or policy infrastructure of states/multi-state collectives (for example the European Union), or adherence to their existence by groups or populations residing within them. Territorial communities may thus be constructed on the basis of either single sources of identity (i.e. they exist as a result of either official recognition or self-generation by their indigenous populations), or multiple sources of identity (i.e. they exist as a result of both official recognition and self-generation by their indigenous populations).

Territorial communities will exist in multiple forms within and beyond state boundaries, and operate at different spatial scales. Their boundaries may be concentric, interlocking or overlapping. They may be conceived or constituted on the basis of local population settlements, regions within states, entire states or multi-state entities. The link between geographical and territorial community boundaries, however, is not an automatic one. The relationship between territorial communities will be based upon, and maintained through, the application of a number of alternative mechanisms. In extreme circumstances where the link between two territorial communities has been enforced, and is subsequently contested by the population of the 'occupied' community, the connection may be maintained by the imposition of military occupation, martial law or the exercise of economic sanctions. Where historical instability in the link between territorial communities has been replaced by a settled contemporary relationship, territorial communities may be connected to one another through constitutional arrangements that are underpinned by the operation of common economic, political, institutional, legal or policy frameworks.

Acceptance of the existence of territorial communities by populations residing within and outside them is dependent upon a number of factors. Firstly, the extent to which the criteria employed to define the territorial community act as an including or excluding mechanism. If the characteristic operating as the linchpin of the territorial community is not a homogeneous entity amongst the internal population, then the existence of the territorial community, or the criteria upon which it is constructed, is likely to be contested. For example, a territorial community whose population is multi-ethnic may find it harder to maintain a stable existence where the presence or status of the different ethnic groups is unequal than would a territorial community whose ethnic characteristics are homogeneous. This situation is equally true in circumstances where the social, cultural or religious attributes of the indigenous population are not uniform.

Secondly, since individuals are likely to be members of multiple territorial communities, the balance of personal allegiances may determine the strength and stability of these territorial communities. If individuals disproportionately identify with one territorial community over another, the strength and continued existence of the lesser-supported territorial community may be in question. Thirdly, territorial communities will enjoy greater long-term stability where they are constructed on the basis of single sources of identity, or where the multiple sources of identity reinforce rather than introduce conflict between the respective community boundaries.

Fourthly, the socio-economic and political conditions existing within a territorial community may threaten its stability. The topographical character, natural resource base, and location in relation to central economic markets may combine with the socio-economic characteristics of the indigenous population to afford territorial communities with distinct advantages or disadvantages. The uneven economic and social development that is likely to arise within, and between, different territorial communities will result in the existence of differing levels of quality of life and equality of opportunity. If the internal stratification of the population within territorial communities is based upon criteria such as social class or patronage, this may further add to the resentment felt by sections of the indigenous population towards certain groups existing within and outside the specific territorial community. Even where uneven socio-economic conditions and unjust social stratification are tolerated by members of a territorial community, a sense of imbalance in the value accorded to them as citizens by the state may be sufficient to undermine the community's stability.

Finally, the extent to which the existence of one territorial community poses a threat to the status, or continued existence, of another territorial community is crucial. Even where the threat emanating from the existence of a territorial community is neither direct nor explicit, the actual or perceived threat to the self-interests of either elite stakeholders or populations residing within other territorial communities may be sufficient to challenge its continued existence.

Primary/secondary arenas and the status of territorial communities

A further factor determining the status and stability of territorial communities is the extent to which they act as primary or secondary arenas within which political institutions, activity and competition are located. Primary arenas may be thought of as the political spheres within a state in which primary economic and political powers, institutions and stakeholders reside, and they are normally to be found within the central infrastructure of the state. The location of primary executive decision making, legislative powers and constitutional authority locates political power within these primary arenas, and provides them with a formalised status within the architecture of the state. Thus territorial communities that operate as the embodiment of the state as a whole may be conceived of as primary arenas or primary territorial communities.

In stark contrast, secondary arenas are much weaker political spheres that are usually the product of a decision by the central state to devolve administration to a regional or local level. They are characterised by limited political powers and government functions, and populated by stakeholder organisations whose existence and rationale are constructed on the basis of regional or local identity.

Territorial communities operating at a sub-state level within a centralised political framework will conventionally be allocated the status of a secondary arena. Even within states whose architecture incorporates high levels of decentralised power or federal structures, the concentration of power within primary arenas provides them with an institutionalised level of authority, and control over key economic and political resources, that awards them significant political advantages over secondary arenas.

The secondary status of a territorial community will act as both a catalyst and a focal point for minority nationalist demands for greater autonomy or secession. The potential for such demands to emerge within a secondary territorial community will be multiplied if an overseeing primary territorial community (a) attempts to impose an alien political, social or cultural cognitive order upon the population of the secondary territorial community; (b) enforces this imposition through the allocation of elite positions within the political and social infrastructure of the secondary territorial community to individuals or groups drawn from populations and cultures outside its confines; and (c) fails to address the socio-economic inequalities arising out of either the peripheral location of the secondary territorial community in relation to the economic epicentre of the state or its low status within the architecture of the state and the ensuing impact this has upon its position in terms of policy priorities and the redistribution of resources.[8]

Nationalist discourse and elite stakeholder behaviour within primary and secondary territorial communities

In the face of this imbalance between the status and power of primary and secondary territorial communities, the initiation of change in the relationship between the territorial community and the wider state may be more forthcoming through the pursuit of reform from within as opposed to petitioning majority elite stakeholders residing within the institutions of the central state. Self-generating internal change may be best achieved if a democratic mandate for reform of the status of the territorial community can be demonstrated to exist amongst its indigenous population. Whilst minority elite stakeholders can attempt to evoke normative arguments concerning either the ideological legitimacy of the retention of centralised power by the state, or the morality of the mechanisms by which 'their' territorial community was originally incorporated into the wider state, this is a strategy which in itself is unlikely to be sufficiently persuasive in the eyes of elite majority stakeholders. Only in circumstances where there is a clear democratic mandate, and an ideological transformation in the overarching value system or conception of ideal forms of government amongst the elite majority stakeholders takes place, is change likely to be sanctioned by the state. In order to achieve the desired democratic mandate for change, minority elite stakeholders need to persuade the population within the territorial community to give voice to their dissatisfaction at the existing status quo by registering high levels of support for minority nationalist parties and other political movements that are seeking change. The best strategy open to minority elite stakeholders in seeking to mobilise the population and galvanise support for minority nationalism will be to evoke a discourse surrounding nationhood and national identity.[9]

The literature on nationalism unsurprisingly abounds with multifarious and competing arguments concerning constructs of national identity and nationalism. There is strong disagreement about the nature of nationalism, and the cause of its emergence, amongst primordialists (nationalism is based upon an understanding of nations as primordial given entities), modernists (nationalism is the product of both the characteristics and consequences of modernity), and ethno-symbolists (nationalism is shaped by premodern ethnic and cultural ties).[10] However, whether nationalism is the product of factors such as uneven economic development,[11] the existence of internal colonies,[12] invented traditions,[13] or imagined communities,[14] it is unanimously seen as a vehicle for creating group solidarity amongst the disparate elements of minority ethnic or cultural groups. Nationalism is chosen as a 'call to arms' by those minority elite stakeholders seeking to kick-start opposition to dominant groups and forces because it has the potential to appeal to a wide range of groups in society and to transcend ties based upon social class or race.[15]

The extent to which nationalism may engender solidarity, however, depends upon the basis of the construct of national identity employed by minority elite stakeholders. Unless the disparate groups that nationalist movements seek to unite identify with the construct of national identity that they espouse, group solidarity is unlikely to be forthcoming. For example, national identity premised on the basis of ethnicity can achieve solidarity only in situations in which ethnicity is a homogeneous entity within the territorial community. In circumstances in which ethnicity is not homogeneous, the definition of national identity on the basis of ethnicity may prove to be a divisive mechanism rather than one that engenders solidarity. Minority elite stakeholders therefore need to exercise caution in the form of national identity that they evoke. The adoption of the wrong manifestation of nationhood within a specific context may prove to be an instrument of division, and cause splits between members of the population of the region that minority nationalist movements are seeking to 'liberate'.

Discourses surrounding nationalism and national identity have conventionally been seen as initially the preserve of minority groups.[16] Indeed, the identification of nationalism as belonging exclusively to minority groups seeking to overthrow the existing order is seen as the basis of frequent attempts by majority elite stakeholders to define nationalism as inherently bad[17] – and often results in a paranoid response amongst these groups when nationalism appears to be rearing its ugly head within the attitudes and behaviour of majority populations. Despite the existence of a status and power imbalance between primary and secondary territorial communities, and the power that control of the primary territorial community affords majority elite stakeholders, they too will engage in discourses concerning national identity – especially in the wake of the emergence of significant levels of political support for minority nationalist movements. This form of nationalist rhetoric has been defined as official or state nationalism, and its primary function is to act as a mechanism for state building.[18]

Since official nationalism seeks to operate as a mechanism for inclusion rather than exclusion, it is likely to be based upon a construct of national identity that is significantly different in nature from that advanced by minority elite stakeholders. The linchpin around which minority nationalist movements are constructed is the uniqueness of the values and experiences of the minority groups that they seek to represent. Whether this uniqueness is constructed on the basis of distinctive ethnic, cultural or territorial characteristics, the legitimacy of the claims of minority groups for greater political autonomy rests upon the recognition of each group's unique status. The necessity of attaining a level of autonomy that enables the creation of different institutional structures that can facilitate the pursuit of different political and policy responses within a territorial community is therefore premised upon demonstrating the existence of differences between majority and minority populations. Minority nationalism is therefore often based upon constructs of national identity that are firmly embedded in traditional conceptions of the characteristics of nationhood that reside within different territorial communities.[19]

In contrast, the interests of majority elite stakeholders (and the preservation of the union between territorial communities) have traditionally been viewed as best served by the development of a form of national identity that emphasises the degree of commonality in the values and experiences shared by both majority and minority groups inhabiting different territorial communities. However, values and experiences are not necessarily nation or nation state specific, and in themselves may constitute weak mechanisms through which to emphasise group solidarity. Official nationalisms may therefore employ a strategy of constructing state identity on the basis of alternative mechanisms such as citizenship.[20] The allocation of the status of citizenship is conventionally thought of as bestowing certain individuals with specific rights that will be enforced and upheld by the state to which they have sought to demonstrate an allegiance. However, the practice of state agencies both explicitly and implicitly pursuing the creation of 'model' citizens suggests an attempt to instil within individuals certain fundamental principles and values. The application of citizenship tests, for example, in which immigrants seeking to enter a state are required to demonstrate acceptance of specific core values, emphasises the idea that citizenship also incorporates the recognition of a common set of fundamental beliefs which are enshrined within the nature and operation of the state, and which the citizens of that state are expected to uphold. The use of citizenship as a construct of national identity is not, however, without problems since strong evidence exists to suggest that the context inhabited by different individuals within different regions of the state may cause the adoption and recognition of very different notions of citizenship and nationality.[21] However, the point here is not to propose the existence of an alternative to ethnic or culturally based constructs of national identity that is superior, but merely to demonstrate that forms of official nationalism employed by majority elite stakeholders will be different in nature from those espoused by minority groups.

The second strand of the tripartite response of majority elite stakeholders to minority nationalism may be to attempt to underpin the use of official nationalism through the institution of common frameworks of governance and policy outputs that serve to emphasise the need for the adoption of common policy responses to common problems. Even where significant material differences exist between majority and minority groups, common frameworks of governance and policy responses will be promoted by majority elite stakeholders as being the best mechanism for advancing the achievement of minimum standards, and greater equality of opportunity, that might start to address such differences. Within this situation, pluralism in the institutional structures and policy frameworks of the state may exist, but it is likely to take the form of the exercise of discretion by policy stakeholders within the implementation of policy rather than the nature of policy programmes and outputs themselves.

The final element of the response of majority elite stakeholders to minority nationalism may be to recognise the existence of the uniqueness of minority groups, but only in the context of the cultural distinctiveness of their customs or language. Within the territorial community inhabited by minority groups, the central state may pursue policies that directly facilitate the promotion and use of cultural symbols. This may be an effective strategy for majority elite stakeholders to pursue since it enables them both to appear to be receptive to the needs of minority populations and to enforce notions held within the wider populations of the state that the needs of minority populations are merely culture-based and confined to the boundaries of specific territorial communities.

Changes in nationalist discourse and elite stakeholder behaviour following the introduction of devolved government

The central premise of instrumental explanations of nationalism which emphasise the importance of government policies and the wider political context in shaping official and minority nationalist discourses suggests that the introduction of devolved government within a territorial community may reconfigure the contours of political debate and alter the behaviour of majority elite stakeholders. The instigation of devolved government with secondary (or in some cases limited primary) legislative powers within this territorial community will result in the creation of a formalised arena within which internal political activity and discourse take place. The strategy utilised by majority elite stakeholders of employing common frameworks of governance no longer applies to the same extent within a devolved state since the creation of devolved government explicitly implies the emergence of policy outputs within a territorial community that diverge significantly from those pursued elsewhere within the state. The formalisation of a territorial community, and the institutionalisation of a nationalist dimension within its political infrastructure which is likely to enhance support for minority nationalist groups, means that the strategy of simply utilising official nationalist discourses as a mechanism for unifying majority and minority populations may no longer work.

Forced to directly participate within the formalised political arena of the territorial community, the attitude of majority elite stakeholders to a hitherto avoided direct engagement with discourses concerning national identity may change. The best mechanism for nullifying the potential growth in support for minority nationalism may be to seek to capture ownership of national identity within the territorial community. However, whereas the strategy employed within the context of a wholly centralised state was to develop a construction of identity that emphasises commonality between the populations of different territorial communities, majority elite stakeholders may seek to reinvent national identity in a form that acts as an instrument of inclusion amongst the diverse populations or cultures within the territorial community. Whilst the politics of identity therefore becomes internalised within the territorial community, an identity discourse that promotes greater inclusion may break the connections amongst a uniqueness-based conception of identity, support for minority nationalism, and demands for greater autonomy within, or the secession of, the territorial community. Minority elite stakeholders may seek to respond to this threat by attempting their own redefinition of national identity. However, the conception of national identity based upon ethnicity or cultural symbolism may be so firmly entrenched in the mindset of the population that the promotion of new forms of national identity may be harder for minority elite stakeholders to achieve than for the majority elite stakeholders who previously have not been directly associated with promoting discourses of national identity.

In addition to seeking to gain the upper hand in the politics of identity through the reinvention of national identity, majority elite stakeholders may seek to capture control of the devolved institutions within the territorial community in order to pursue a programme of policy reforms that addresses the inequalities and problems experienced by the population of the territorial community as a result of its peripheral and secondary economic and political status. As with the transformations in strategies surrounding the promotion of official nationalism, majority elite stakeholders will switch from utilising common policy frameworks to instigating a raft of policy initiatives that deliver distinctive and territorial-community-specific outcomes. In conjunction with their ability to promote themselves as the architects of devolution, the provision of distinctive policy programmes that address the needs of the population of the territorial community may shatter the notion promoted by minority nationalist groups that only minority nationalism can act as a conduit for initiating the political and policy reforms necessary to transform the status of the territorial community and the circumstances of the people residing within it.

It is of course possible that minority elite stakeholders may capture control of devolved government within the territorial community, and therefore be the primary political beneficiaries of any policy dividends that subsequently emerge. However, there is one further advantage that majority elite stakeholders possess over their minority nationalist adversaries in this context. Whilst minority nationalist parties may gain representation within primary state legislatures, the restriction of their candidature within the confines of the territorial community ensures that they will operate as a minor player within the primary territorial community of the state. Control of devolved institutions of government which possess only secondary legislative powers, and a corresponding lack of control over the primary legislature, may therefore restrict the ability of minority elite stakeholders to deliver distinctive and community-specific policies because of the strong policy steer emanating from majority elite stakeholders within the central state.

It is thus the ability of majority elite stakeholders to capture the institutions of government within both the territorial community and the wider state, and hence to deliver distinctive policy programmes, that raises the potential for devolved government to pose a direct threat to levels of support for minority nationalism. A new inclusive style of cognitive order within the territorial community will come into existence in which insider status will be bestowed upon the institutions, policies and discourses created by majority elite stakeholders. If ownership of the policy and political dividends arising from devolution flows the way of majority elite stakeholders, then their status as outsiders who previously perpetuated an 'alien' political and social culture may be transformed into that of insiders. In contrast, the hitherto insider status enjoyed by minority elite stakeholders within their own territorial community may be transformed to outsider. Their rhetoric of emphasising the need for further reform of the status of the territorial community, alternative policy programmes and culture-based constructs of national identity will be deemed obsolete and unnecessary in the context of a majority-stakeholder-inspired cognitive order that is capable of meeting the unique needs of the territorial community.

TERRITORIAL COMMUNITIES, COGNITIVE ORDERS AND THE POLITICS OF IDENTITY IN POST-DEVOLUTION WALES

The chapter now turns to the application of the ideas incorporated within the conceptual framework in order to evaluate political, institutional and policy developments within post-devolution Wales. The focus here concerns the extent to which a minority nationalism-threatening cognitive order has emerged, and this is analysed on the basis of whether certain criteria implicitly set out within the conceptual framework have been fulfilled. Initially, the status of Wales as a political arena, and its nature as a territorial community, are considered in order to explore the politics of identity within Wales and to provide a backdrop to the conclusions that are developed concerning the emergence of an anti-minority nationalism cognitive order four years into the operation of the devolution project in Wales.

Wales as a secondary political arena and the politics of identity

There is little doubt throughout even its modern history that Wales has been ascribed the status of a secondary arena within the institutional and political architecture of the state. The Welsh Office and a secretary of state within the Cabinet did not come into existence until 1964. Operating as little more than a decentralised administration with no democratic mandate, and dependent upon the delegation of responsibilities by other Whitehall ministries, the Welsh Office had been constrained prior to devolution by the policy priorities of central government and the financial settlement it received from the Treasury via the Barnett formula. In addition, the policy outputs of the Welsh Office during this period, it is claimed, were characterised by a lack of strategy and coherence.[22] The phenomena of the 'quangocracy' and appointment of a succession of 'English outsiders' as secretaries of state that were visited on the Welsh political landscape during the Thatcher/Major administrations did little to deter the perception of Wales as a secondary political arena. In socio-economic terms, the Welsh population has long endured circumstances associated within regions that are peripheral to the economic and political epicentres of the state. Even four years after the establishment of the Assembly, Wales continues to have lower average levels of gross domestic product per head, economic activity, employment rates, average weekly household income and educational attainment compared with many regions of the United Kingdom.[23]

Unsurprisingly, the status of Wales as a secondary political arena possessing a system of governance that was widely perceived as unable to address the needs of communities in Wales provoked considerable demands for political reform. However, in the context of the politics of identity, these did not exclusively emanate from minority nationalist movements and parties within Wales. The prevailing status of Wales in terms of its relationship within the institutional and political architecture of the central state had equally worked against the political interests of the Labour Party in Wales. The implementation of policy programmes during eighteen years of Conservative rule at Westminster for which there was no democratic mandate in Wales, and which the Labour Party was powerless to withhold despite its domination at the ballot box in general and local elections within Wales, transformed opinion within Welsh Labour concerning the need for constitutional reform. The anti-devolution tendencies of the party that had predominated at the time of the abortive devolution referendum in 1979 gave way to demands for the instigation of an institutional bulwark against a politically hostile central government.[24] In addition, the hegemonic status of Labour within both general and local elections, and the ensuing lack of effective political competition in large parts of Wales, had come to be recognised as a partial cause of the democratic deficit that afflicted the Welsh polity.[25] Under the leadership of Ron Davies, Welsh Labour became the primary driving force behind the emergence of devolution onto the political agenda, and the subsequent form and structure of government adopted within the new Assembly.[26]

The consequence of the arrival of devolved government in Wales, in conjunction with the abandonment by Plaid Cymru of the pursuit of independence in favour of seeking self-government for Wales within the context of full nation status membership of the European Union, has arguably altered the rhetoric and internalised the location of the politics of identity in Wales. Devolution has failed to address many of the 'old order' tensions between the respective primary and secondary political arenas of Westminster and Cardiff Bay, and the establishment of the Richards Commission in 2002 to examine the need for the Assembly to acquire primary legislative powers is testament to the existence of unresolved issues. However, whilst these factors still stimulate demands for further constitutional reforms, the formalisation and institutionalisation of the political infrastructure in Wales have ensured that the politics of identity is now driven as much by the competition between political parties within Wales as it is by the relationship between primary and secondary political arenas. Although a range of surveys examining national identity since 1979 has shown a majority selecting Welsh over British identity when forced to do so, the Welsh Assembly Election Survey in 1999 revealed that a conception of identity in which they conceived of themselves as equally Welsh and British was the preferred choice of a majority of respondents.[27] National identity is still important in determining support for minority nationalism in Wales,[28] but the competing conceptions of Welsh and British identity are now acted out more explicitly within the confines of Wales as a territorial community rather than within the context of internal relations between Wales and the British state.

Wales as a territorial community

Although Wales has long been recognised as a nation on the basis of clearly defined geographical boundaries and a distinct framework of laws, language and customs,[29] it is a country and a people whose history has been characterised through the ages by constant reinvention and adaptation to social, economic and political developments.[30] Despite the recognition of its external boundaries, the history of Wales as a country and nation has been symbolised by deep internal social and geographical divisions which still shape much of the discourse surrounding competing conceptions of Welsh identity.[31] Within the context of the devolution project, for example, these have materialised in the existence of a geographical divide across the regions of Wales over Labour's devolution proposals in the 1997 referendum,[32] or the perception amongst certain inhabitants of North Wales that the location of the Assembly in Cardiff Bay institutionalises a significant and long-standing political and economic bias in favour of South Wales.[33]

Whilst echoing socio-economic, political and cultural developments that predate the forces of modernity, contemporary Wales is best understood as consisting of three separate (but not geographically homogeneous) territorial communities. These have emerged and adapted as a result of the economic prosperity and decline, industrialisation, urbanisation, immigration and rural depopulation that have characterised different periods of history in Wales since the eighteenth century.[34] They have been shaped by the interaction of social class, culture, language, religion, politics and geography, and whilst the extent of their boundaries has fluctuated over time, their existence and impact upon Welsh life and competing conceptions of Welsh identity have remained relatively intact. Although empirically unsustainable, it is perhaps an apposite truism that the existence of England as the dominant driving force within the primary territorial community of the United Kingdom is the one catalyst that often unites many of the disparate elements of Wales.

'Welsh-speaking Wales', which covers North-West, Mid and parts of West Wales, is defined by the prevalence of rural communities whose primary concerns are those of the preservation of their language, culture, and the impact of (primarily English) immigration upon their way of life and cultural and social sustainability. 'Industrial Wales', which was hewn by the forces of industrialisation, urbanisation and the inwards migration of labour from the Midlands and south-west of England during the Industrial Revolution, covers South Wales from the Gwent Valleys to the environs immediately beyond Swansea, and parts of North-East Wales that border on Merseyside and Cheshire. With the 'halcyon' days of 'King Coal' and extensive steel production soon to fade into distant memory, the concerns of the communities occupying these regions of Wales surround the consequences of the decline of traditional heavy industry, and the extent to which the economic and social restructuring necessary to sustain their existence can materialise. Finally, 'Anglo-Wales' is the territorial community that covers the border areas of Monmouthshire and Powys, the Vale of Glamorgan and South Pembrokeshire. It is the Wales whose inhabitants and culture most explicitly bear the hallmarks of anglicisation and whose identity is ostensibly British rather than Welsh.[35]

The existence of multiple territorial communities has unsurprisingly manifested itself in the form of a distinctive political geography that further embeds the politics of identity into the Welsh psyche.[36] Whilst the political boundaries of these territorial communities have ebbed and flowed, the concentration of support for individual political parties within specific regions has remained a constant within Welsh politics. Labour has traditionally enjoyed a hegemonic position within industrial Wales, which prior to devolution has only seen short-lived and non-status-threatening incursions by Plaid Cymru and the Conservatives. Welsh-speaking Wales, which was the bedrock of the Liberalism that dominated nineteenth-century Wales, has in terms of Westminster and European elections since the 1980s and 1990s, respectively, become the preserve of Plaid Cymru. The border areas of Anglo-Wales covering Montgomeryshire and Brecknock conversely are the last bastions of Welsh Liberalism – and whilst modern Wales could not by any stretch of the imagination be defined as a happy hunting ground for the Conservative Party,[37] it has managed to secure, in different periods, representation in Monmouthshire and the coastal fringes of South, South-West and North Wales. Thus despite the dominance of the Welsh political landscape by the Labour Party throughout its history, and the pretensions signified by the adoption of Plaid Cymru in 1998 of a bilingual suffix, no political party has been able to lay claim to the title of 'The Party of Wales'.

Devolution in Wales: a new cognitive order?

Evidence relating to the extent to which the criteria for the establishment of an anti-minority nationalism cognitive order have been satisfied in the wake of the introduction of devolved government in Wales is summarised in Table 5.1. On the basis of this evidence it is argued that, despite its status as the architect of devolution and the position of power that it has enjoyed throughout the life of the Assembly, Welsh Labour has not been able to deliver a devolution settlement that fully evokes an anti-minority nationalist cognitive order. In fact, despite the relaunching of the devolution project following Rhodri Morgan's accession to the position of first minister in February 2000, and the sense of strategic purpose that has come to a much greater extent to characterise the operation of the Assembly,

Table 5.1 Overview of evidence for the emergence of an anti-minority nationalism cognitive order arising from the instigation of devolved government in Wales

Criteria for the emergence of an anti-minority nationalism cognitive order	Extent to which criteria met	Evidence
Majority elite stakeholder engaged in rhetoric surrounding the politics of identity	Moderate	• 'Welsh values are synonymous with Labour values' • Emphasis placed upon branding of the Labour Party in Wales as Welsh Labour • 'Clear red water between Welsh and New Labour'
Minority elite stakeholder engaged in rhetoric that is non-inclusive or perceived to be non-inclusive	Moderate	• Strong association between Plaid Cymru and cultural forms of national identity, e.g. Welsh language • Plaid Cymru perceived as party of Welsh-speaking communities • Plaid Cymru perceived also as party of working class in Wales thus enabling party potentially to appeal to working-class 'socialist' vote in 'Industrial Wales'[a]
Characteristics of territorial community evokes politics of identity	Strong	• Clear evidence of status of Wales as a secondary political arena • Existence of multiple territorial communities within Wales. Three Wales model: Welsh-speaking Wales, Industrial Wales and Anglo-Wales • Distinctive political geography with support for all main political parties predominantly locked into single territorial communities[b]
Majority elite stakeholder holds political control over central state and devolved legislatures	Strong/moderate	• Labour Party in power in Westminster since 1997 • Welsh Labour largest group in Welsh Assembly following the first elections in May 1999 (with 28 Assembly Members) – in control throughout the first four years of the Assembly either as minority administration or dominant partner in coalition administration (with Liberal Democrats) • In 2003, Labour increased control of Assembly by returning 30 Assembly Members
Absence of second-order voting patterns that are likely to challenge traditional political fault lines	Moderate/weak	• Strong support for Plaid Cymru in first Assembly elections (1999) and European elections (1994/1999) – extension of Plaid Cymru vote beyond Welsh-speaking heartlands in 1999 Assembly elections – capture of Labour citadels within South Wales • Support for Plaid Cymru in second Assembly elections falls away – Labour regains South Wales strongholds lost to Plaid Cymru in 1999 and makes inroads in Welsh-speaking heartlands
Powers of devolved institution enable controlling political group to deliver distinctive policy outputs within the territorial community	Moderate	• Primary function of Assembly is to provide strategic steer to spending decisions concerning the allocation of the block grant received by the secretary of state for Wales from the Treasury via the Barnett formula • Secondary legislative powers afford Assembly considerable discretion over the implementation of state-wide policy programmes within Wales[c]

Table 5.1 (Continued)

		• Debacle over matching funding for Objective One status during 2000, and continual dissatisfaction with Barnett formula emphasises retention of central policy steer within Westminster[d]
		• Lack of overall Labour majority enabled Plaid Cymru and Liberal Democrats to have input to strategic policy plans developed by the Welsh Assembly, and hence the ability to claim part of the distinctive policy dividend for themselves[e]
Distinctive policy outputs afford political dividends to majority elite stakeholders in control of devolved institution	Moderate/weak	• According to Welsh Labour: existence of policy outputs unique to Wales: free prescriptions for under-25s, mass testing scrapped within primary schools, reintroduction of student grants[f]
		• According to Plaid Cymru: widening of poverty gap between Wales and other parts of the United Kingdom since Labour came to power in 1997[g]
		• Perception of voters that the Assembly has made no difference to circumstances in Wales, especially in the areas of health and education[h]
		• Primary instigator for policy change still perceived to be Westminster Parliament[i]

[a] R. Wyn Jones and D. Trystan, *A 'Quiet Earthquake': The First National Elections to the National Assembly for Wales*, Working Paper No. 85 (Oxford: Centre for Research into Elections and Social Trends, 2001)

[b] D. Balsom, P. Madgwick and D. Van Mechelen, The Political Consequences of Welsh Identity, *Ethnic and Racial Studies* 7 (1984) pp.160–81

[c] M. Marinetto, The Settlement and Process of Devolution: Territorial Politics and Governance under the Welsh Assembly, *Political Studies* 49 (2001) pp.306–22

[d] J. Osmond (ed.), *Devolution: 'A Dynamic Settled Process?' Monitoring the National Assembly for Wales July–December 1999* (Cardiff: Institute of Welsh Affairs, 1999)

[e] J. Osmond (ed.), *Coalition Politics Comes to Wales: Monitoring the National Assembly for Wales September–December 2000* (Cardiff: Institute of Welsh Affairs, 2000)

[f] Welsh Labour Party, *Working Together for Wales: Welsh Labour's Manifesto 2003* (Cardiff: Welsh Labour Party, 2003)

[g] Plaid Cymru, *The Party of Wales: Manifesto 2003* (Cardiff: Plaid Cymru, 2003)

[h] Electoral Commission, *Wales Votes?* (Cardiff: Electoral Commission, 2002)

[i] Ibid.

there is little sign that Welsh Labour will see off the long-term threat of minority nationalism with any great ease.

In the first Assembly elections in 1999, the 'natural order' of politics in modern Wales did not come to pass. Breaking free from the sporadic and localised electoral fortunes that had characterised its political history up until this point, Plaid Cymru caused a 'quiet earthquake' in Welsh politics by securing 28.4 per cent of the constituency vote and 30.1 per cent of the regional vote.[38] More importantly, nationalist support surged out from the boundaries of Y Fro Gymraeg,[39] and Plaid Cymru captured the much-prized Labour strongholds of Llanelli in the west, and Islwyn and the Rhondda in the south. Clear evidence of second-order-style voting both within the constituency and regional ballots called into question the continued relevance of the 'three Wales' model[40] that had gained wide acceptance within contemporary political analyses of the electoral fortunes of political parties within Wales.

Four years later, the aftermath of the outcome of the 1999 elections in conjunction with internal criticism of the party for failing sufficiently to target the 'threat' of minority nationalism,[41] materialised in an explicit rhetoric concerning the politics of identity. In the run-up to the 2003 Assembly elections, Labour portrayed the future of the devolution project as a stark choice between the 'separatism' of Plaid Cymru and the continued improvement in public services in Wales brought about by the Labour administration in Cardiff Bay.[42] Under Morgan's leadership, the Labour Party has been overtly branded as Welsh Labour, attempts have been made to signify that Welsh values are synonymous with Labour values,[43] and the retention of core socialist values within the Labour administration in Cardiff Bay has been signalled by the existence of 'clear red water' between Welsh Labour and New Labour.[44] In terms of the outcome of the 2003 Assembly elections, it might be suggested that the 'Welshification' of Labour's rhetoric produced the required political dividends. The old political order in Wales was restored with the return of 'Industrial Wales' en bloc to Welsh Labour, and the party made inroads to the Welsh-speaking heartlands with the capture of Conwy. Evidence of second-order-style voting diminished, and the three Wales model appeared to have re-established itself after a temporary sojourn in 1999.

However, political control is only one of the central planks of the achievement of an anti-minority nationalist cognitive order. The conceptual framework suggested that the emergence of a policy dividend following the creation of devolved government might provide majority elite stakeholders with a significant weapon in their fight against minority nationalism. It is the case that after the first four years of the Assembly's operation, Welsh Labour was able to demonstrate that despite the absence of primary legislative and tax-raising powers, the devolution project could deliver distinctive and unique policy outputs in Wales. However, the evidence from the Welsh Assembly Election Survey in 2001[45] suggests that the majority of the electorate believe that the Assembly has, in policy terms, had no impact upon their lives – and that change to their personal circumstances is more likely to emanate from Westminster than from Cardiff Bay. In addition, it might be suggested that the need for New Labour to demonstrate the success of devolution as part of its modernising governance agenda has facilitated the emergence of distinctive policy outputs within Wales (and Scotland). Whilst Downing Street has been happy to endorse policy divergence within Wales in policy areas that are not seen as constituting cornerstones of the Labour government's policy platform, the evoking of the 'Welsh Labour not New Labour' rhetoric might not be so readily tolerated if it were employed to signal opposition to a central plank of New Labour reforms (for example the establishment of foundation hospitals). Devolution in Wales has also existed only in the context of symmetry in political control within Cardiff Bay and Westminster. The establishment of a central government whose political persuasion was of a different colour from that residing within the Welsh Assembly might significantly reduce the potential for distinctive policy outputs within Wales. In this context, therefore, it is questionable whether any long-term policy dividend that might be employed as an effective instrumental device in competition for control of the Assembly actually exists.

One mechanism for enabling the Welsh Assembly to make a genuine policy impact upon communities within Wales is the extension of the institution's current powers. Welsh Labour has acknowledged that it will give careful consideration to the findings of the Richards Commission, and would not automatically rule out supporting any extension to the powers of the Assembly.[46] Plaid Cymru has explicitly linked the need for reform of the Assembly's powers to the delivery of policy programmes that address the specific policy needs of Welsh communities.[47] In the context of apparent support for enhancing the jurisdiction of the Assembly by majority as well as minority elite stakeholders, the type of rhetoric employed by Welsh Labour concerning the separatist and constitutional reform obsessions of Plaid Cymru in the run-up to the Assembly elections in May 2003[48] may be difficult to sustain and drive home in the minds of the electorate. Evidence of the retention of the old order in the relationship between the primary/secondary territorial communities of the central state and Wales concerning disputes between Cardiff Bay and Westminster over, for example, the financial settlement provided by the Barnett formula also arguably weakens the ability of state-building parties to disparage the 'extension of powers' based rhetoric employed by minority nationalists.

Finally, and perhaps the most telling problem for Welsh Labour, is that a new cognitive order surrounding the instigation of devolved government will not emerge unless the Welsh people take the Assembly to their hearts. In the 1997 devolution referendum, the 'Yes' campaign secured victory by a margin of only 6,721 out of a possible 280,500 votes. Turnout was only 50.1 per cent, effectively rendering the new institution support from the equivalent of only 22.5 per cent of the Welsh electorate. Whilst it might be argued that in casting their ballots the electorate was voting for an unknown institutional and policy outcome, a turnout of only 45.9 per cent for the first Assembly elections in 1999 revealed that the legitimacy crisis had not improved. In 2003, turnout in the second Assembly elections collapsed across Wales to just 38 per cent. In this context, whilst support for the Assembly has declined since the 1999 elections, the potential for achieving real policy dividends via the acquisition of primary legislative powers for a Welsh parliament seems remote. Extending the powers of the Assembly will require securing a further mandate from the Welsh electorate, and it is a mandate which on the basis of current evidence they are unlikely to grant.

CONCLUSION

The analysis presented here has demonstrated that the concepts of territorial communities and primary/secondary political arenas are useful mechanisms for understanding both the nature of minority nationalism and the responses to surges in support for nationalism by majority elite stakeholders. The explicitly Welsh rhetoric adopted by the Labour Party was in direct response to the incursion of support for Plaid Cymru into 'Industrial Wales' in 1999, and was ultimately successful in repelling nationalist attempts to retain a significant element of the working-class vote within the Labour heartlands in the 2003 elections. Arguably, Labour has demonstrated a greater ability to undertake the type of rapid political learning that the instigation of new political infrastructures and systems require than the nationalists. The successful participation within a political institution whose focus is distinctively Welsh is crucial for a political movement whose *raison d'être* is encapsulated within the very essence of devolved government. However, for Plaid Cymru the Assembly represents an unresolved conundrum. Keen to be seen to support the first formalised stage of a series of stepping stones towards self-government, Plaid Cymru openly endorsed the Assembly at the outset despite the Assembly's limited powers and structural flaws. Following the emergence of the Labour–Liberal Democrat coalition in 2000, and a more oppositionist stance by the party under Ieuan Wyn Jones, Plaid Cymru has been cast as the official Opposition within an institution which it is desperately keen to see succeed. In the context of the retrenchment of nationalist support within its traditional heartlands in 2003, and the casting of Plaid Cymru as a stakeholder existing outside the current devolution settlement, the second Assembly elections might be seen as constituting a similar wake-up call to that received by Labour in 1999.

However, the discourse of identity adopted by Welsh Labour is an electoral discourse that arguably still emanates from the old order within Welsh politics. The advent of devolution was designed to conjure up a new form of inclusive elite politics. To an extent, the strategy of Ron Davies in achieving cross-party participation in the 'Yes' campaign for the 1997 devolution referendum, and in membership of the National Advisory Group that contributed to the design of the internal architecture of the Assembly, augured well for a genuinely fresh approach to politics in Wales. Developments subsequently, however, have witnessed a return to the traditionally entrenched position of both majority and minority elite stakeholders. This regressive step which does not appear to have had a positive impact upon support for devolution in Wales, might be reversed if the Assembly were seen as a catalyst for the development of a new politics of identity. If the competing stakeholders in Welsh politics wish truly to claim the mantle of a 'Party of Wales' that unifies the disparate Welsh territorial communities, it is perhaps through a politics of identity that is of a modern socially progressive European form, and one that does not pander to the cultural/ideologically based constructs that have acted as divisive mechanisms in the past, that a truly new cognitive order will emerge.

NOTES

1. The concept of second-order elections suggests that voting patterns are governed by the primacy attached to specific elections by the electorate, and the perception by the electorate of the secondary importance of non-primary legislature elections (e.g. European, regional or local) may result in a departure from traditional voting patterns (see K. Reif and H. Schmitt, Nine Second

Order Elections: A Conceptual Framework for the Analysis of European Election Results, *European Journal of Political Research* 8 (1980) pp.3–44

2. Within this chapter the term 'majority elite stakeholder' is employed to refer to elite groups representing dominant socio-economic or cultural populations – the term 'minority elite stakeholder' relates to populations who are in a minority on the basis of their socio-economic or cultural characteristics.

3. P. Brass, Elite Groups, Symbol Manipulation and Ethnic Identity among the Muslims of South Asia, in D. Taylor and M. Yapp (eds), *Political Identity in South Asia* (London: Curzon Press, 1979)

4. P. Brass, *Ethnicity and Nationalism: Theory and Comparison* (Newbury Park, CA: Sage, 1991)

5. J. Richardson and A. Jordan, *Governing Under Pressure: The Policy Process in a Post-Parliamentary Democracy* (Oxford: Martin Robertson, 1979)

6. A. Jordan and J. Richardson, The British Policy Style of the Logic of Negotiation, in J. Richardson (ed.), *Policy Styles in Western Europe* (London: Allen & Unwin, 1982)

7. R. Rhodes, Policy Networks: A British Perspective, *Journal of Theoretical Politics* 2(3) (1990)

8. M. Hechter, *Internal Colonialism: The Celtic Fringe in British National Development, 1536–1966* (London: Routledge & Kegan Paul, 1975)

9. U. Ozkirimli, *Theories of Nationalism: A Critical Introduction* (Basingstoke: Macmillan, 2000)

10. Ibid.

11. T. Nairn, *The Break-up of Britain: Crisis and Neonationalism*, 2nd edition (London: Verso, 1981)

12. M. Hechter, op. cit. (1975)

13. E. Hobsbawm, *Nations and Nationalism since 1780: Programme, Myth, Reality* (Cambridge: Cambridge University Press, 1990)

14. B. Anderson, *Imagined Communities: Reflections on the Origins and Spread of Nationalism*, 2nd edition (London: Verso, 1991)

15. M. Hroch, *Social Preconditions of National Revival in Europe: A Comparative Analysis of the Social Composition of Patriotic Groups among the Smaller European Nations* (Cambridge: Cambridge University Press, 1985)

16. T. Nairn, op. cit. (1981)

17. U. Ozkirimli, op. cit. (2000)

18. J. Kellas, *The Politics of Nationalism and Ethnicity* (New York: St Martin's Press, 1991)

19. A. Smith, *Nationalism and Modernism* (London: Routledge, 1998)

20. D. McCrone, Who Do You Say You Are? Making Sense of National Identities in Modern Britain, *Ethnicities* 2 (2002) pp.301–20

21. D. McCrone and R. Kiely, Nationalism and Citizenship, *Sociology* 34 (2000) pp.19–34

22. L. McAllister, The Road to Cardiff Bay: The Process of Establishing the National Assembly for Wales, *Parliamentary Affairs*, 52 (1999) pp.634–48

23. Office for National Statistics, *Regional Trends*, vol. 37 (London: HMSO, 2003)

24. M. Laffin and A. Thomas, Designing the National Assembly for Wales, *Parliamentary Affairs* 53 (2000) pp.557–76

25. A. Thomas, The Welsh Assembly Debate: 1979 Re-visited?, *Public Money and Management* (April 1995)

26. L. McAllister, Changing the Political Landscape? The Wider Implications of Recent Elections in Wales, *The Political Quarterly* 71 (2000) pp.211–22

27. L. Patterson, Is Britain Disintegrating? Changing Views of 'Britain' after Devolution, *Regional and Federal Studies* 12 (2002) pp.21–42

28. R. Andersen, *National Identity and Independence Attitudes: Minority Nationalism in Scotland and Wales*, Working Paper No. 86 (Oxford: Centre for Research into Elections and Social Trends, 2001)

29. J. Davies, *A History of Wales* (Harmondsworth: Penguin, 1994)

30. G. Williams, *When Was Wales?* (Harmondsworth: Penguin, 1991)

31. P. Jenkins, *A History of Modern Wales 1536–1990* (London: Longman, 1992)

32. The outcome of the 1997 referendum revealed a distinctive east (no) – west (yes) geographical division in support for the devolution project across Wales which strongly echoed the territorial boundaries of Pura Wallia and Marchia Wallia that had existed within medieval Wales.

33. Electoral Commission, *Wales Votes? Public Attitudes towards Assembly Elections* (Cardiff: Electoral Commission, 2002)

34. K.O. Morgan, *Rebirth of a Nation: Wales 1880–1980* (Oxford and Cardiff: Clarendon Press/University of Wales Press, 1981).

35. D. Balsom, The Three Wales Model, in J. Osmond (ed.), *The National Question Again: Welsh Political Identity in the 1980s* (Llandysul: Gomer, 1985)

36. D. Balsom, P. Madgwick and D. Van Mechelen, The Political Consequences of Welsh Identity, *Ethnic and Racial Studies* 7 (1984) pp.160–81

37. After the 2001 general election, the Conservative Party was removed from the face of Welsh politics. In the 1999 Assembly elections it won only a single constituency (Monmouth), and returned only nine Assembly Members in total (largely on the basis of its regional share of the vote).

38. The National Assembly for Wales is elected using a variant of an additional member system. Forty of the 60 Assembly Members (AMs) are elected on the basis of first-past-the-post votes polled within constituencies whose boundaries are coterminous with existing Westminster constituencies. The remaining 20 AMs are selected on the basis of regional top-up party lists (with four candidates being elected within each of the five European parliamentary regions in Wales).

39. Y Fro Gymraeg (or the Welsh Heartlands) is the area of Mid and North-west Wales which is characterised by predominantly Welsh-speaking communities.

40. D. Balsom, op. cit. (1985)

41. L. McAllister, op. cit. (2000)

42. Welsh Labour Party, *Working Together for Wales: Welsh Labour's Manifesto 2003* (Cardiff: Welsh Labour Party, 2003)

43. Speech by Rhodri Morgan at the Labour Party Conference, Blackpool, 2 October 2002

44. Speech by Rhodri Morgan to the National Centre for Public Policy, Swansea, 11 December 2002
45. Electoral Commission, op. cit. (2002)
46. Welsh Labour Party, op. cit. (2003)
47. Plaid Cymru, op. cit. (2003)
48. Welsh Labour Party, op. cit. (2003)

6 Northern Ireland: resolving an ancient quarrel?

Rick Wilford

INTRODUCTION

The 1998 Belfast Agreement[1] has been described, aptly, by David Trimble as 'a master-piece of constructive ambiguity'.[2] Its constructiveness lay in knitting together the three 'strands' of interlocking and mutually interdependent political institutions – those within Northern Ireland, those between north and south and those linking the island of Ireland with Great Britain.[3] Its ambiguity resided in the formal recognition of Northern Ireland's conditional constitutional future by both the United Kingdom and Ireland – and this remains the (terrible) beauty of the Agreement. By entrusting the status of Northern Ireland to its electorate, the Agreement's eight signatories[4] – and the British and Irish governments – seemed to offer something for almost everyone. The mutually exclusive futures of, on the one hand, the unification of the island and the retention of the Union on the other, were both made available and biddable.[5] Devolution within the United Kingdom is, from these alternative perspectives, simul-taneously an end state and an interim arrangement.

The Agreement's constitutional ambivalence is underwritten by its entrenchment of the 'consent principle',[6] thereby subjecting Northern Ireland's constitutional status henceforth to the (potentially recurring) test of popular sovereignty. In that key respect, the Agreement cannot be represented as a final settlement – hence the inter-rogative title of this chapter. Effectively, Northern Ireland's constitutional status seems cast more in aspic than marble. The decision to apply the test, by way of a referendum or 'border poll', is a matter for the secretary of state alone. S/he is empowered to call a referendum 'if at any time it appears likely to him [*sic*] that a majority of those vot-ing would express a wish that Northern Ireland should cease to be part of the United Kingdom and form part of a united Ireland'.[7] The sole motive for holding such a poll is, thus, one in favour of constitutional change, thereby underlining Northern Ire-land's status as a fluid rather than a steady state(let). Such immanent fluidity appears more consistent with Gerry Adams' portrayal of the Agreement as a transitional phase in the project to unite the island of Ireland than David Trimble's claim, voiced during the 1998 referendum campaign, that it secured Northern Ireland's place in the Union.

Mr Trimble explicitly acknowledged the conditionality of its status on being re-elected (unopposed) as leader of the Ulster Unionist Party (UUP) in March 2002. In his acceptance speech he urged the then secretary of state, Dr John Reid, to hold a referendum on the same day as the second Assembly election, then scheduled for 1 May 2003. The outcome would, in the UUP leader's view, 'put the issue to bed for another generation' and 'copper-fasten' the Union.[8] Mr Trimble's reasoning was that a high turnout by unionists, allied to a small proportion of pro-Union Catholics (and others), would yield a comfortable majority in favour of retaining the link to the UK.[9]

This calculation is, no doubt, a sound one, at least for the foreseeable future. Yet, if the result is a foregone conclusion – namely a healthy pro-Union majority – there would be no reason for the secretary of state to arrange a referendum. However, the significant narrowing of the demographic gap between Protestants and Catholics that was anticipated would be revealed by the results of the 2001 census, encouraged nationalist and, especially, republican politicians to believe that pressure would mount for constitutional change. But, whilst the census results published on 19 December 2002 did show a closing of the demographic gap, it was not on the scale forecast by, for instance, Mitchel McLaughlin, Northern chairman of Sinn Féin.[10] The results showed that Protestants constituted 53.1 per cent of the population, Catholics 43.8 per cent, whilst 2.7 per cent stated that they belonged to no religious community and a further 0.4 per cent that they belonged to some other religious community. (In the 1991 census just over 50 per cent were from the Protestant community and slightly more than 38 per cent from the Catholic community, but 12 per cent did not state their religious affiliation. This latter proportion was then recalculated and redistributed to yield a 58 per cent Protestant and 42 per cent Catholic balance.) Thus, whilst the gap had narrowed it was insufficient to generate the perception that support for unification was likely to grow to a challenging level in the short or medium term. But, of course, the extent of such a challenge arises only if one accepts the questionable proposition that an exact fit obtains between Catholic religious identity and political support for Irish unification.

Whilst demographic pressure has eased as a dynamic for constitutional change – and with it prospective demands for serial, septennial referenda as provided by the Northern Ireland Act 1998 – should Sinn Féin emerge as the leading nationalist party at the next Assembly election[11] the demands are unlikely to recede entirely. This would reinforce the inherent uncertainty of unionists about their own future, albeit that the current Irish government is at best lukewarm about an early referendum. If at some future point there were to be a secessionist majority in Northern Ireland, bolstered by the necessary pro-unification majority in the south, this would be but the prelude to protracted negotiations about the terms of unification – a debate yet to be fully joined.

In the shorter run, if the perception within the unionist electoral 'bloc' is that Sinn Féin (SF) is likely to consolidate its electoral lead established in 2001 over the Social Democratic and Labour Party (SDLP), unionist voters may be more inclined to assign their first preferences[12] to anti-Agreement candidates, chiefly the Democratic Unionist Party (DUP). Such a choice, if exercised, should not, though, be construed as an anti-devolution vote. Rather, it would demonstrate that, without complete and verifiable decommissioning, a declaration that 'the war is over' and the disbandment of the IRA,[13] the further prospect of Sinn Féin ministers in the devolved administration – including, perhaps, as deputy first minister – would be generally unacceptable to the unionist electorate. Indeed, if the DUP were to eclipse the UUP, and SF were to be the leading nationalist party, then the Assembly and the Executive Committee could be stopped in their tracks. In such a context, devolution in Northern Ireland could, to controvert the hapless Ron Davies' much-quoted remark, become an event rather than a process. Such an electoral outcome would likely trigger the early, formal review of the Agreement's implementation, scheduled to take place four years after the transfer of powers (i.e. towards the end of 2003), and firm up the resolve of the DUP amongst others to attempt to renegotiate a new Agreement.

The DUP's likely preference for a form of administrative devolution[14] – effected through a system of committees enjoying primary legislative powers but minus an executive – would receive short shrift from nationalists and republicans, and both the Irish and British governments.[15] Whilst such a reduced model of chopped-up rather than joined-up government may not be ruled out by at least a section of the UUP – minus, presumably, David Trimble at its helm – the immediate outcome would be the maintenance of direct rule. Short of the exclusion of Sinn Féin from a newly formed executive – unless, that is, there is an unambiguous and transparent statement from the IRA concerning its embrace of exclusively democratic politics and an equally palpable process of decommissioning – there seems no feasible alternative to the current status quo.

There are many ifs and buts in the above scenario – and Northern Ireland retains the capacity to surprise even the most jaundiced of observers. The achievement of the Agreement was in itself an arresting development, as well as a close-run thing. At the subsequent referendum in May 1998, however, the Agreement, whilst legitimised by the overwhelming majority of nationalists in Northern Ireland, was endorsed only by a narrow majority of unionists.[16] A month later, at the Assembly elections, the electorate returned an overwhelming majority of ostensibly pro-Agreement candidates (80 out of a total of 108 members).[17] Yet, anti-Agreement unionist parties secured a fractionally larger share of first preference votes than their pro-Agreement unionist rivals and in that formal sense could be said to have won the contest within their electoral bloc.[18] Moreover, a number of the UUP's successful candidates were known publicly to have voted against the Agreement at the referendum, which meant that the majority of two (30–28) held by ostensibly pro-Agreement unionists over their unionist opponents was at least shaky and, at worst, inherently unstable.[19] The outcome of the Assembly election within the dysfunctional unionist 'family' helped dispel the brief moment of mild optimism that had followed in the wake of Good Friday 1998. In disclosing the delicate balance of unionist opinion, the results narrowed – but not entirely dimmed – the prospect that Northern Ireland had embarked on a new, inclusive political trajectory.

FALTERING IMPLEMENTATION

If the process of reaching the Agreement was itself tortuous, that of implementing it was to prove no less difficult. Whilst the 'shadow'[20] Assembly met for the first time on 1 July 1998 to elect the first and deputy first ministers designate, choose the presiding officer (speaker), and establish a jointly chaired (UUP/SDLP) committee to draft its standing orders, there was a great deal of unfinished business to contend with. Two 'wicked' issues in particular had yet to be resolved: the decommissioning of paramilitary weapons and the reform of the RUC, the latter delegated to the Independent Commission headed by Chris Patten, the former to the Independent International Commission on Decommissioning (IICD), led by General John De Chastelain.[21]

More immediately, the four parties eligible for the nascent Executive Committee or cabinet – UUP, SDLP, DUP and SF – embarked upon negotiations over the shape and size of the new administration (but not the allocation of portfolios[22]) and the number and functions of cross-border bodies.[23] In effect a bargain was struck, in essence between the UUP and the SDLP. The negotiations took almost six months[24] and yielded a confected agreement: a dozen north–south bodies and ten new government departments, plus the Office of First and Deputy First Ministers (OFMDFM) with a complement of twelve ministers, including the first and deputy first ministers.[25]

The contrived,[26] rather than carefully designed, devolved administration within Northern Ireland owed little to administrative rationality and much to political bargaining – or, to employ a less pejorative phrase, political accommodation. Such accommodation sat comfortably with the consociational[27] philosophy animating the Agreement, which realised the creation of a power-sharing executive, the application of proportionality rules within the proposed government and the legislature, and provision for both segmental autonomy and a mutual veto over 'key' decisions.[28] But the Agreement also included confederal arrangements, via the north–south and east–west axes included in, respectively, Strands Two and Three: hence its characterisation as 'consociationalism-plus'.[29]

The intricacy of the Agreement's three-stranded architecture, allied to new equality and human rights regimes, reform of both the police and the criminal justice systems, the release of prisoners on licence, a policy for victims and, perhaps above all, the decommissioning of paramilitary weapons, loyalist and republican alike, did signal the birth of a new Northern Ireland. But it was a troubled delivery, and one that has required intensive post-natal care. Senator George Mitchell, who had acted as the political midwife of the talks process leading to the Agreement, having earlier devised a set of Principles[30] that had facilitated the talks themselves, was re-enlisted in the late summer of 1999 to try to resolve the impasse over weapons decommissioning and thereby pave the way to the transfer of devolved powers.

Senator Mitchell's reappearance to nurse the ailing Agreement followed the attempt by the British and Irish Governments to lend assisted birth to devolution, akin to a forceps delivery, such that Northern Ireland could enjoy its transferred powers concurrent with Scotland and Wales.[31] This attempt proved abortive. The refusal by the UUP to engage in the nomination of an Executive on 15 July 1999 – because there had been no tangible movement on decommissioning by the IRA – rendered the exercise futile. Whilst both the SDLP and SF went through the ritual of nominating ministers (and the DUP refused to do so), the nominations were invalid because the composition of the potential cabinet was not consistent with the principle of inclusivity that lay at the Agreement's heart.[32] In turn the UUP's absence from the proceedings occasioned the resignation of the SDLP's deputy first minister designate, Seamus Mallon, adding to the fraughtness of the context for the Mitchell Review.

Intended to be a short, intensive process, the Review was to take ten weeks between September and November 1999. Its duration signalled the depth of the outstanding problems, but, as with the talks leading to the Agreement, its outcome demonstrated the apparent suppleness of the leading pro-Agreement parties, especially the (majority of) Ulster Unionists and Sinn Féin. On 18 November, Senator Mitchell set out the choreographed sequence that would lead to actual rather than virtual devolution. The steps were based upon a set of principles agreed by the pro-Agreement parties the previous June following negotiations hosted by Tony Blair and Bertie Ahern that were intended to trigger devolution on 15 July. In order, these were that devolution should take effect, the Executive Committee should meet and paramilitary organisations should appoint their interlocutors to the IICD 'all on the same day and in that order'.[33] This sequence proved sufficient to enable David Trimble to carry a majority of his party's governing body, the Ulster Unionist Council (UUC), in support of the UUP's entry into the devolved Executive where they would hold four of its twelve seats following the application of the d'Hondt rule. The UUC's endorsement was, however, a conditional one. To assuage those within the Council who doubted the wisdom of 'jumping first' into the Executive, that is prior to an act of IRA decommissioning, Mr Trimble made it known that he had lodged a post-dated resignation letter with the UUC's president which would take effect should the decommissioning process fail to begin. There was uncertainty about the date on which his resignation and that of his three fellow ministers would occur, but it would be no later than 12 February 2000 when the UUC was to reconvene to review progress on the decommissioning issue.

Thus, twenty months after Good Friday 1998, and the subsequent referendum and elections, the stage was set to formally transfer powers to Northern Ireland. On 30 November 1999, the then secretary of state, Peter Mandelson, moved the Order in the House of Commons to devolve powers to the new administration: 'After a quarter of a century,' he remarked, 'the curtain is finally coming down on Direct Rule.'[34] It was, perhaps, a vainglorious assertion, and certainly lacked perspicacity. Seventy-two days later, following the receipt of two reports[35] from the IICD indicating that there had been no substantive progress on IRA decommissioning, Mr Mandelson unilaterally suspended devolution so as to prevent the resignation of the UUP's four ministers. It was an inauspicious start to the devolution enterprise and because of its unilateral nature certainly strained relations between the UK and Irish governments. And, as events were to show, suspension did not prevent further crises in the outworking of the new arrangements.

Between 2 December 1999 – devolution day – and July 2002 the devolved institutions experienced arrested development. During this two-and-a-half-year period, the three strands operated concurrently for sixteen months, and for four months (from mid-February to the end of May 2000) had been suspended in their entirety. At the end of October 2000, the continued absence of IRA decommissioning had occasioned David Trimble's refusal to sanction the attendance of SF ministers at both sectoral and plenary meetings of the North–South Ministerial Council, prompting SF's retaliatory boycott of the British–Irish Council. The former act led to the courts, only one instance of post-Agreement litigation[36] involving the outworking of devolution, and the latter was resolved only following Mr Trimble's abandonment of his unilateral veto which itself occurred in the wake of the first act of IRA decommissioning.[37] Indeed, the UUP leader had resigned as first minister on 1 July 2001, enforcing a six-week period during which the devolved administration functioned with a caretaker acting first minister (Sir Reg Empey, UUP) and an acting deputy first minister (Seamus Mallon, SDLP).[38] At the expiry of the six weeks, the legislation required a fresh election for the first and deputy first ministers. In the absence of decommissioning, however, no UUP candidate was prepared to stand, and Dr Reid used his power to suspend devolution for 24 hours for a further six weeks, and was to employ the same device at the end of that period. It was not until early November 2001 following confirmation that an unspecified number of IRA weapons had been put beyond use, that Mr Trimble sought re-election alongside Mark Durkan[39] (SDLP) on the joint ticket of first and deputy first ministers.[40] This, however, proved to be no easy matter because of the rules governing the election.

'Key' decisions as defined in the Agreement require cross-community consent. There are two tests of such consent: parallel consent and a weighted majority.[41] However, in the case of the election of the first and deputy first ministers, one such key decision, only the first – and stiffer – of these tests applies. Following the withdrawal of the UUP whip from Peter Weir – he had voted against the Agreement at the 1998 referendum – who subsequently sat alongside DUP members on the Assembly benches,[42] the balance of pro- and anti-Agreement unionists in the chamber was exact, with 29 members each. However, one other UUP member, Pauline Armitage, was also disaffected, believing that the one act of IRA decommissioning was just that – an act, in both senses – and thereby insufficient to justify the return of Mr Trimble to office. In the event, both she and Mr Weir voted against the joint ticket.[43] Despite the redesignation of one of the Women's Coalition's MLAs as a 'unionist' immediately prior to the vote,[44] the action of Mrs Armitage and Mr Weir ensured that the joint ticket was not endorsed by a sufficient number of unionists, despite the fact that over 70 per cent of all MLAs present and voting supported the Trimble/Durkan candidacy. It was not until three members[45] of the pro-Agreement Alliance Party agreed to redesignate, temporarily, as unionists when the Assembly reconvened that Mr Trimble was reinstated and Mr Durkan elected.

This episode was revealing. Not only did it confirm the unrest in the UUP's Assembly group it also displayed the readiness of both the Women's Coalition and, rather more grudgingly, Alliance to redesignate to sustain devolution. It also demonstrated that there were sufficient pro-Agreement unionists in the chamber to engineer the required changes to standing orders.[46] However, the decision by the Secretary of State not to impose a third 24-hour suspension following the failed attempt to elect Messrs Trimble and Durkan on 2 November (the six-week period expired on the following day) prompted a legal challenge by the DUP. In its view, the second election held on 6 November was invalid because it occurred beyond the time allowed for the vote to be taken and that, as such, the Secretary of State should have dissolved the Assembly and made the necessary arrangements for an early election. The DUP lost the case in the Belfast courts, and thereafter, in the person of Peter Robinson, appealed to the House of Lords. On 25 July 2002, the appeal was dismissed by three of the five Law Lords. Had the DUP's appeal succeeded, not only would the election of first and deputy first ministers have been invalidated, but all legislation passed by the Assembly since 6 November 2001 and accorded Royal Assent would be null and void. In that situation the choice confronting the Secretary of State would have been stark: either to pave the way to an early election, at which the likely beneficiaries would be the DUP and SF, or legislate with retrospective effect to legitimise the Assembly's endorsement of the Trimble/Durkan partnership.

The election episode also disclosed the preparedness of the UK government – without, on these occasions, demurral from the Irish government – to act, to say the least, in an inventive way to maintain what Peter Mandelson had once described as 'the only show in town'. This succession of crises in the unfolding of devolution has meant that only faltering progress has been achieved in 'making a difference'[47] to the lives of the plain people of Northern Ireland.

In such a fragile context, statesmanship elides with brinkmanship and statecraft with crisis management. What is compelling, however, is that no Northern Ireland pro-Agreement political leader wishes to teeter over the brink and be perceived to have undone, single-handedly, the hard-crafted bargain reached on 10 April 1998. Hence, for instance, David Trimble's insistence at the meeting with the UK and Irish prime ministers in early July 2002 that the onus lay with Tony Blair to resolve the issue of IRA decommissioning by instigating sanctions against Sinn Féin, up to the exclusion of its ministers from office. This demand was lent even more urgency by allegations over republican responsibility for the break-in at Castlereagh police barracks and the activities of the 'Colombian Three' in FARC-controlled territory[48] that had eclipsed the significance of the second act of IRA decommissioning which occurred in April 2002. Nevertheless, there is a marked reluctance on the part of Mr Trimble, or indeed any other pro-Agreement leader, to be labelled as *the* politician who must bear responsibility for toppling the devolved institutions. This, however, is not a sufficient basis to ensure their continuance – at least, not in their present, inclusive form. Hence the attempt in early March 2003 by the UK and Irish governments to achieve a new, agreed basis for the full implementation of the Agreement at Hillsborough Castle. The terms of this new agreed basis are discussed below but, as a preamble, we can note the troubled unfolding of the Agreement and its fitful survival up to the suspension of October 2002.

ASSESSING DEVOLUTION

The Executive Committee

Mere survival is perhaps too low a threshold by which to assess the achievement of devolution thus far, although it cannot yet be said to have flourished. That is especially the case in relation to the Assembly and its developing relationship with the Executive. First, a word about the latter – and I do intend to focus on the Strand One institutions, rather than encompass fully all three institutional expressions of the Agreement.

There are structural flaws in the design of the Agreement that have their roots in what Horowitz has styled its maximalism and its inclusiveness.[49] Immediately prior to the initial phase of devolution which began on 2 December 1999, the four Executive parties-in-waiting had each nominated their own ministers through the d'Hondt mechanism, a process of departmental allocation akin to the plucking of political straws. The automaticity of the nominating process meant, amongst other things, that the co-equal first and deputy first ministers could exercise no powers of ministerial patronage, save for the appointment of junior ministers.[50] The occasion proved to be an event of high political drama, not least because SF members had agreed not only to take their seats in what was an effectively partitionist legislature but also to share in the governing of part of the United Kingdom, albeit in a consociational and confederal framework.[51] One unforeseen[52] outcome of the lottery of d'Hondt was that SF opted to take the health and education portfolios, thereby placing their nominees in charge of the two largest spending departments. In particular, the nomination of Martin McGuinness as education minister provoked spasms of outrage in unionist and loyalist communities. Whilst it was not unanticipated that he would be one of the party's two ministers, the presence in government of the former second-in-command of the IRA in Londonderry where he would assume responsibility for the education of primary and secondary schoolchildren, made the shock of the new even more abrupt.

What was especially pertinent about the nomination process was that the Northern Ireland Act (1998) implementing the Agreement vested executive powers in each of the ministers rather than the Executive Committee as a whole.[53] This rendered the convention of collective 'cabinet' responsibility to be more of an aspiration than a standard operating procedure. The vesting of authority in individual ministers was not, however, inconsistent with the adoption of the PR STV (proportional representation with single transferable vote) electoral system that rewards solidarity within electoral voting blocs and discourages 'vote-pooling' between rival ethnic parties.[54] The intention of the Agreement to be inclusive meant that each prospective governing party needed to maximise its first preferences (and transfers) so as to ensure its place around the Executive Committee table. This meant that there were no incentives for pro-Agreement voters to cross ethnic lines and vote for other pro-Agreement candidates drawn from the relevant 'other' community.[55] Given the stipulation in the Agreement that there were to be up to ten departments, in addition to OFMDFM, there was every incentive to pile up first preferences and transfers *within* competing ethnic blocs.[56] As with previous electoral contests, this rendered the 'first order'[57] Assembly election a dual party competition: that between the UUP and anti-Agreement unionist parties, notably the DUP, on the one hand, and between the SDLP and SF on the other. In Northern Ireland where the unionist electorate was sharply riven, the risk to party leaders – particularly David Trimble – of appearing to be moderate to the point of encouraging voters to exchange vote transfers to pro-Agreement ethnic rivals, was immense. In such circumstances, as Horowitz states, 'compromise is not likely to be rewarded by the electorate'.[58]

In the context of not only a divided society but also a bifurcated unionist electorate, this logic of electoral choice, compounded by d'Hondt, precluded the possibility of a pre-electoral 'coalition' between or amongst the contending parties. It meant that each nominee to the political top table was parachuted into a post-electoral 'coalition', albeit a voluntary one in the sense that there was/is no compulsion on eligible parties to exercise their ministerial options. For different reasons, both the DUP and SF could, in theory, have chosen to go into opposition in the Assembly, the former on the grounds of its unstinting antipathy to the presence of republicans in government, the latter on the basis of the Agreement's perpetuation of partition and the continuing British presence in Northern Ireland. However, political logic dictated that neither would opt for this alternative: instead, each chose to nominate two ministers as enabled by d'Hondt, making it in effect an involuntary coalition arrangement, although the DUP refused to 'sit in an Executive polluted by the representatives of terror'.[59] Following the restoration of devolution at the end of May 2000, the DUP also undertook to rotate its ministers. The first two incumbents, Peter Robinson and Nigel Dodds, were replaced by Gregory Campbell and Maurice Morrow, respectively, in July 2000, the party reverting to the original pairing in November 2001. The DUP's decision to rotate its ministers threatened to disrupt the operation of the Executive even more and was to lead to another round of post-Agreement litigation.

The maximal and inclusive nature of Executive formation, and the vesting of authority in individual ministers, also meant that the latter, indeed all MLAs, owed their primary allegiance to their respective electoral blocs rather than the Executive Committee. To perhaps overstate the negative case, there was – and is – little to prevent ministers from acting as minor barons within their own departmental fiefdoms. As one anti-Agreement minister put it, rather approvingly: 'there is nothing they [i.e. other ministers] can do to get me out of my departmental bunker'.[60] Their roles are assured through electoral mandates and their tenure relies almost entirely upon the support of the relevant party group within the Assembly. I say 'almost' because it is the case that a motion of no confidence can be tabled in any one minister or party holding Executive office, but it has to be carried on the basis of cross-community support.[61] To date, there have been motions of no confidence in both David Trimble and Martin McGuinness and a series of votes seeking to exclude the Sinn Féin ministers from office, but none has succeeded, precisely because of the absence of bi-communal support. Even if a vote of no confidence in an individual minister were to be carried, the portfolio would remain in the hands of the same party for the life of the relevant Assembly.

There is, however, some 'glue' holding the Executive together, not least the requirements that each of the ministers affirms the ministerial pledge of office, and agrees to both the draft Programme for Government (PfG) and annual draft budgets. (These requirements conform to the unanimity rule that is one of the characteristics of a consociational democracy.) In addition, the Executive

Committee agreed to set aside certain moneys during the budgetary cycle for Executive Programme Funds (EPFs), which are allocated to the departments in pursuit of a set of agreed thematic policy objectives following a competitive bidding process.[62]

Such glue as these obligations and decisions provide has not, though, proved to have the same adhesive effect on all Executive parties. Sinn Féin and the DUP have each sought to amend annual budgets during debates on the floor of the Assembly, whilst the DUP has also moved amendments to successive PfGs, thereby making an apparent mockery of agreed decisions within the Executive. This is a structural flaw in Northern Ireland's mode of Executive formation enabling governing parties to behave as both government and opposition, if they so choose. The fact, too, that the DUP's two ministers do not attend Executive meetings also places a strain on the aspiration to achieve 'joined-up' government, a strategy only partially accomplished through the device of EPFs which the then finance minister defined as 'an antidote to Departmentalism'.[63]

In Northern Ireland's model of devolution, there is little resembling either the cabinet *system* in Whitehall, with its infrastructure of both standing and ad hoc ministerial and official committees, or the structures that have been put in place in post-devolution Scotland and Wales.[64] Whilst the DUP ministers do meet and otherwise communicate with both their UUP and SDLP counterparts, they have no direct communication with the Sinn Féin ministers. Additionally, the DUP boycotts both Strand Two and Strand Three institutions, notably the North–South Ministerial Council (NSMC) and the British–Irish Council (BIC), enforcing the Executive Committee to utilise the proxy arrangements provided by the Agreement. The readiness of the pro-Agreement parties not only to make such alternative arrangements but also to facilitate Executive business by other means has kept devolution alive. For instance, the ten pro-Agreement ministers have permitted officials from the DUP's two departments to brief them in the stead of their ministers and have conducted what Mark Durkan has described as 'government by correspondence course'[65] with the DUP's ministers themselves. However, the DUP's studied behaviour has not escaped sanction.

Following the restoration of devolution at the end of May 2000, the DUP announced that it would resume its ministerial roles, but on a rotational basis.[66] The party stated that this strategy would allow its ministers 'to uncover and reveal what is going on at the heart of Government'. It continued, 'We shall not hesitate to be whistle-blowers – exposing each of Trimble's further concessions to Sinn Féin/IRA.'[67] More worryingly for the other members of the Executive, the press release also stated that the rotating ministers would act only in a 'holding capacity', implying a threat of serial disruption to Executive business. Further, it stated that none of the ministers 'will be regarded as being bound in any way by any Ministerial Code of Conduct or any notion of collective responsibility' – a strategy that would be sustained up to the 2001 general election.[68] The other ministers could not allow the announcement to pass unnoticed and issued their own response. This included: the assumption of responsibility for transport matters, part of the brief of the DUP's regional development minister, at the BIC by the first and deputy first ministers; the refusal to nominate DUP ministers to the Joint Ministerial Committee to discuss wider UK policy areas alongside representatives of both the UK government and the devolved administrations; and, 'pending the receipt of satisfactory assurances about the confidentiality and integrity of Executive Committee business', that neither of the DUP's ministers would receive Executive papers 'as a matter of course'.[69]

The latter sanction led the DUP to seek a judicial review which found for the Executive.[70] A subsequent ruling in the High Court declared, however, that the First and Deputy First Ministers had acted unlawfully in withholding papers dealing with free public transport for the elderly, formal responsibility for which lay with the Department for Regional Development.[71] The issue of free fares for pensioners also revealed the absence of collective responsibility. On the one hand the DUP claimed proprietorship of the policy whilst, on the other, so too did the Executive Committee: this parental squabble over policy paternity further underlined the absence of ministerial cohesion.

Such chronic internal strains and continuing organisational difficulties, punctuated by acute crises brought about by David Trimble's threatened or actual resignation, have thus far at least been managed, but not resolved. Moreover, in the post-Agreement period, community relations have deteriorated and the level of support within the unionist population for the Agreement itself has declined significantly.[72]

Diverging popular attitudes

Whilst there was a period when both the nationalist and unionist populations tended to converge around the proposition that each had gained from the implementation of the Agreement, this mood of 'win–win' has more recently been transformed into one of 'win–lose', with unionists believing that they are the losers.[73] Unionists perceive post-devolution Northern Ireland to have become a 'cold place' for them, a view articulated by the progressive and frequent use of the term 'concessions' to describe the UK government's perceived stance towards republicans. Whilst it remains the case that a majority of Protestants (79 per cent) wish to sustain the union with Britain and that a majority of Catholics (59 per cent) aspire to unify with the Republic of Ireland, the 2001 Northern Ireland Life and Times survey disclosed a healthy level of support (47 per cent) amongst Protestants for not just devolution, but 'devolution-plus': that is, an Assembly modelled along Scottish lines with both legislative and tax-varying powers, an option also supported by one in seven Catholics.[74]

The same survey also revealed that two-thirds of all respondents supported the proposition that the existing Assembly should exert most influence over the way Northern Ireland is run, including 61 per cent of Protestants and 74 per cent of Catholics. Amongst party supporters, more than half of DUP voters endorsed this option, as did 72 per cent of their UUP counterparts – but it was SDLP and SF voters who accorded the Assembly the greatest levels of support, at 77 per cent and 80 per cent respectively. Given that both Protestant unionist support for the

Agreement has declined significantly and that Catholic nationalist support for a united Ireland has remained buoyant, their endorsement of the Assembly's increasing influence and, in the case of Protestants, of enhanced devolution, seems somewhat paradoxical. How can this be explained? The answer lies in the fact that it is not paradoxical, but eminently rational from each perspective.

Protestant support for the development of devolution can be understood as a form of anticipatory self-defence. Suspicious of the UK government's long-term strategy and alienated by its perceived appeasement of republicanism,[75] an enhanced model of devolution, without republicans in government, is attractive to them. It would provide the means and the opportunity to encourage broadening support amongst the Catholic population for the retention of the constitutional status quo by making Northern Ireland a more stable, plural, inclusive, just and equal society. And, of course, it would be underpinned by the guarantee of the consent principle. Whilst Catholics are less enamoured of a more muscular Assembly, their higher level of support for its influence over Northern Ireland affairs is also explicable. It does not preclude unification, offers the prospect of loosening the ties with Britain, of promoting greater self-confidence amongst all sections of the community and of creating the context within which nationalists and republicans, by their actions, can eliminate unionists' apprehensions about an all-Ireland state. In short, it offers the opportunity for their political leaders to act as persuaders for Irish unity, whether in muted or strident tones. Although the pace of demographic change has slowed, the narrowing of the Protestant:Catholic population differential does indicate a secular trend approximating towards communal balance. Albeit a slowly changing demographic context, the direction of change suggests that nationalist and republican politicians may need only to be patient in their attempts to persuade a relatively small proportion of their Protestant and 'other' neighbours to carry a referendum in favour of constitutional change.

In effect, each community wants the other's political rationale for devolution, whether in its current or enhanced form, to fail and its own to succeed. For pro-Agreement unionists, devolution is a terminus; for nationalists and republicans – and anti-Agreement unionists – it is perceived as a staging post to a united Ireland. The co-existence of these mutually exclusive ambitions means that each pro-Agreement party has a considerable investment in the effective and efficient operation of the devolved institutions, especially the legislative Assembly since it is the leading agency through which mutual trust and confidence can be built. Indeed, even the anti-Agreement unionists have been reluctant to subvert the Executive and Assembly.[76]

The Assembly

Anti-Agreement unionists are not opposed to devolution per se, but rather its inclusivity, the institutionalised character of cross-border relations – dismissed by them as mere 'north–southery' – and, *inter alia*, the reform of the RUC to which they were utterly opposed. The DUP in particular has had to finesse its unremitting opposition to the Agreement. It has assumed its ministerial roles and participated fully and, for the most part, constructively in the Assembly's committees whilst at the same time maintaining its campaign to expose the 'treacherous' UUP leadership and thereby emerge electorally as the leading unionist party. As several statements from the DUP have put it, their goal is to 'punish the pro-Agreement parties, not to punish the people'.[77]

To stave off the allegation that they would act as wreckers within government, the DUP has been at pains to demonstrate the competence of its ministers. For instance, on the occasion of the first ministerial rotation, Peter Robinson, one of the outgoing duo, insisted that 'the two new DUP Ministers would carry out the functions and responsibilities of their Departments with total professionalism and dedication', adding, 'and would prove to be head and shoulders above other Ministers'.[78] The DUP's determination to be seen to be working responsibly within its own departments has lessened the risk of administrative implosion. A combination of inventiveness, improvisation and the occasional turning of a blind eye, has enabled both the Executive and the Assembly to function. Yet, it would be misleading to suggest that devolution has flourished in the sense that its policy outcomes to date have made a substantive difference to the lives of the population.

Besides the constraints created by the stuttering co-existence of the three institutional strands, the absence of regional government since 1972[79] had created not only a democratic deficit but also a policy deficit. Under direct rule the political parties were preoccupied with constitutional and security issues, and had little opportunity, or inclination, to devote their energies towards developing an expansive and coherent platform of 'bread and butter' policies. When devolution appeared to be imminent, all parties, especially those who were to assume a governing role, had to embark on a steep learning curve in order to prepare themselves for office and to contemplate how a four-party coalition of unlikely ideological bedfellows might operate. For the UUP in general, and David Trimble in particular, this was a delicate matter. In addition to his external unionist critics, he also had to contend with a divided party, including a number of critical MLAs within his Assembly group. This, potentially, was even more delicate because the relationship between the Assembly and the Executive as delineated by the Agreement is akin to a partnership.

In many respects the Assembly is a conventional legislature, performing the normal range of parliamentary functions, not least through the activities of its standing and statutory committees. The latter are of particular interest and significance. They are charged to scrutinise their associated departments, assist in the development of departmental policy, and to initiate legislation, the latter a considerable and significant power to vest in legislative committees. The memberships of the statutory committees (each is eleven-strong) are constituted along proportional lines, reflecting in broad terms the relative party strengths in the chamber.[80] Thus, as with the Executive, the committee structure of the Assembly embodies consociational principles that are reinforced by the stipulation in the Agreement that the chairs of the statutory committees should not be drawn from the same party as that of the relevant minister over whom the committees have oversight. In effect, this is another expression of power sharing, and places particular stress on the working relationships between ministers and the committees, not least their chairs.

To work effectively, which requires consensus or at least accommodation, the partnership model has to apply not only between the committees and the departments, but also within and between committees. The proportionality of the statutory committees means, however, that each is dominated by MLAs drawn from the four Executive-forming parties who, in total, account for 90 of the Assembly's 108 seats. This marginalises the non-Executive parties, whether pro- or anti-Agreement, and, in relation to key decisions that require cross-community consent, renders irrelevant in the division lobbies those who designate as 'other'. In effect, the requirement that all Assembly members cast themselves as either 'unionist', 'nationalist' or 'other' helps to entrench a sense of over-identification, especially amongst those members who fall into the first two categories, that is all but seven of the Assembly's MLAs.[81] Designation reinforces the primary and exclusive identity of each Executive party bloc and provides no incentives for their members to do other than represent their discrete communities and support unequivocally 'their' respective ministers. The premium on party loyalty thus elides with communal loyalty and in that respect, the UUP aside, the whips of the governing parties have had an easy time of it.

As in more 'orthodox' parliamentary democracies, the nexus between ministers and their party bloc(s) is close. However, Northern Ireland's devolved system of governance is anything but orthodox. There is no formal Opposition in the sense of an alternative government in waiting that can rise up and turf the incumbent rascals out – if rascals they be. All other things being equal, should there be a second Assembly election the same four parties that constitute the current Executive will form the next, thereby perpetuating the lack of an Opposition. This does not mean that there is no opposition as such; indeed, in some procedural respects the statutory committees perform oppositional functions.

For instance, each statutory committee takes the committee stage of all primary legislation and can agree amendments to be tabled at subsequent stages in the legislative process.[82] Additionally, when a minister opens a debate, makes a statement or moves the second stage of a bill, the convention is that the chair of the relevant committee will reply and the deputy chair wind up on its behalf. The statutory committees are also routinely consulted during the development of departmental (and, via the EPFs) interdepartmental policies, the PfGs, and departmental bids during the annual budget cycles. Thus, although much of their energy is directed towards their associated departments, including – like Westminster's select committees – the scrutiny of their policy, administration and expenditure, there has been growing evidence of a committee *system* within the Assembly. For instance, the Finance and Personnel Committee, chaired by Francie Molloy (SF), coordinates the responses of all other statutory committees to their respective department's budgetary and EPF bids and tables proposed changes to the process of budgetary scrutiny following consultation with its sister committees. On occasion, two committees have sat jointly to take evidence from witnesses at hearings, and each committee routinely informs others where proposed legislation or policy cuts across the relevant departmental responsibilities. In addition, an informal chairperson's liaison committee has been established, serviced by the Assembly's

Committee Office, whose purpose is to discuss procedural and other matters of common interest – although, because it has no statutory basis, the DUP's two statutory committee chairs[83] do not participate in its proceedings.

The statutory committees also embark upon their own freely chosen inquiries into aspects of their department's responsibilities and issue reports at their conclusion all of which, unlike Westminster's select committee reports, are debated on the floor of the chamber. Similarly, the committees produce written reports following the committee stage of a primary bill that form the basis for subsequent debate. In these respects, the committees are routinely integrated into, indeed are an indispensable part of, the business of the Assembly. And, given the growth of correspondence and cooperation between and amongst committees, one can suggest that there is more evidence of joined-up scrutiny within the legislature than joined-up government within the Executive.

Inter-party relations within the committees are, for the most part, businesslike and even cordial.[84] However, the committees can be criticised for both their lack of transparency and their sedentary character. Research has disclosed that an alarming proportion of committee meetings are held in private,[85] whilst MLAs have proven reluctant to move beyond the precincts of Stormont's Parliament Buildings to take evidence. Unlike Scotland, for instance, where MSPs have held plenary sessions in both Glasgow and Aberdeen, and committees regularly move about the country, in Northern Ireland all roads have tended to lead to Stormont.

To no small extent, the reluctance of MLAs to adopt a semi-peripatetic existence is explained by the high incidence of dual, or even triple, mandates. More than half of Assembly members are also local councillors, twelve are also MPs, including one – Ian Paisley – who is also an MEP, two are peers, whilst five members hold three elected offices.[86] Such a workload inevitably impairs the extent to which many members can dedicate themselves to the work of the Assembly, the remit of which is considerable. Given the ineligibility of the ministers, including the two junior ministers, to sit on committees, the boycott of them by four anti-Agreement members[87] and the fact that both Gerry Adams (SF) and Lord Kilclooney – John Taylor – of the UUP have declined a committee role, means that there are 87 MLAs available to fill a total of 183 committee places. This entails that a number of members have at least dual committee memberships. Twenty MLAs sit on just one committee, leaving 67 to cover the remaining 163 places. Two members – John Dallatt (SDLP) and Roy Beggs Jr (UUP) – each sit on four committees, 19 on three and 46 on two.

The provision for 108 members[88] in the Assembly may appear generous, especially when considered alongside Northern Ireland's 18 Westminster MPs, 582 local councillors, 3 MEPs and over 2,000 places on non-departmental public bodies. However, the scope and volume of business, the dual mandate problem, plus, it has to be said, the low calibre of many members, has not enabled the Assembly to flourish – nor indeed to make a difference, in two senses.

Firstly, the 2001 Northern Ireland Life and Times survey referred to earlier disclosed that a plurality of respondents (44 per cent) believed that the Assembly made no difference to the ability of people to have a say in the way Northern

Ireland is governed, a view adopted by half of all Protestants. Equally, 48 per cent of the total sample believed more generally that devolution had made no difference to the way the UK as a whole is governed, including 43 per cent of Catholics and 48 per cent of Protestants. In relation to public services, especially health, education and the economy, most thought that they had deteriorated post-devolution, whilst a plurality (44 per cent) considered that the Assembly had not proven to be good value for money (35 per cent think it has), although Catholics (44 per cent) were more likely to hold a positive view than Protestants (25 per cent).[89]

Respondents were also asked whether they thought members worked together to help solve Northern Ireland's problems. Overall, more than half said either 'not very much' or 'not at all', whilst 43 per cent said they cooperate either a great deal (6 per cent) or 'a fair amount' (37 per cent). Again, a communal division is evident. A majority of Catholics (55 per cent), compared with 39 per cent of Protestants, gave a positive response, whereas 59 per cent of Protestants opted for the more negative responses. The overall judgement of the population about the performance of the Assembly was, however, rather downbeat, though Catholics were more favourably disposed to its workings. That pluralities tend to believe both that devolution has made little or no difference to the way Northern Ireland is governed, and that the voice of the man and woman in the street is no louder or stronger as a consequence of the transfer of powers is something of an indictment. Few, though, believe that the new arrangements have led to *less* of a voice for ordinary people or that devolution has weakened the union with Britain. Nevertheless, the perception that devolution has had a limited impact means that at best it has been only a qualified success.

The second sense in which devolution can be said not to have made a difference is in terms of the evolving relationship between the Executive and the Assembly. As noted earlier, whilst the Agreement delineated a partnership between them, in practice the relationship has become a patron–client one. As at Westminster, Executive dominance has prevailed. Whilst committees enjoy the power to initiate legislation, none has yet done so.[90] The Executive has thus far been the fount of all primary legislation, much of which has been prompted by the need to achieve parity with British legislation, notably in the field of social security. 'Home-grown' legislation has been in relatively short supply, although some two dozen Executive bills were readied for the 2002–03 session.[91] Whatever the provenance of bills, the legislative role of the committees, their scrutiny of both departmental budgetary bids and the draft PfGs, and their consultative role in the development of departmental policy strategies, taken together have meant that the bulk of their activities has been structured by the Executive's agenda. This means that, like Westminster, the Assembly is Executive-dominated: that particular mould has not been broken by devolution.

Just as there has been no statutory committee bill as yet, there is no corpus of private members' legislation either.[92] In part this has been because of a lack of administrative support. It has only been since April 2002[93] that the financial and personnel resources have been put in place to assist MLAs in drafting legislation, but there was no concerted demand from the Assembly[94] to press for these resources. This is indicative of the pliancy of MLAs, notably those in the Executive-forming parties. Their reluctance to do other than back 'their' ministers has bridled the considerable opportunities that the committees have to exert influence and autonomy. On two occasions, statutory committees have produced reports critical of ministers, but when these have come to the floor of the chamber, MLAs from the same parties as those of the relevant ministers have abandoned the relevant committee and voted along party lines.[95] Members have, in short, turned out to be party animals rather than committee creatures. This disposition to back ministers rather than committees, whilst explicable, is nonetheless disappointing. In that respect, MLAs have proven to be less independent-minded than their counterparts in Edinburgh and Cardiff and even, perhaps, those sitting at Westminster.

CONCLUSION

As mentioned earlier, the remarkable thing about the Agreement is that it was reached in the first place. That its implementation has proven to be fitful and difficult is no surprise. Unlike in Scotland where the path to devolution was paved by lengthy discussions under the aegis of the Constitutional Convention, and Wales where an Advisory Group assisted in the devolution process, politicians in Northern Ireland were pitchforked into a context of perpetual negotiation and renegotiation because there were wicked issues left unresolved. Given four rounds of suspension and the associated hiatuses in relation to the North–South Ministerial Council and the British–Irish Council, one might assume that little or nothing of substance has been achieved thus far. This, though, would be too negative a conclusion to draw.

The Executive's Programmes for Government (PfGs), which are reviewed on an annual basis, have proven to be ambitious sets of actions and targets aligned with its five priorities for government.[96] The first PfG outlined 256 actions to be taken in support of the priorities, and contained detailed public service agreements for each department, including 236 targets that reflected the outcomes each department intended to deliver. In terms of tangible policy achievements, there was much to report. For instance, free public transport for the elderly, free nursing – though not personal – care for the same cohort, a new package of measures for victims of the conflict, the reduction of fuel poverty, new domestic energy efficiency schemes, almost 500 new community care packages, the implementation of the enhanced New Deal for those aged 25 and over, the abolition of further education fees for full-time students enrolled in vocational courses, and over 100 new summer literacy and numeracy schemes intended to improve the performance of underachieving primary schools. In addition, there has been increased spending on roads, rail safety and public transport and financial assistance for new gas pipelines thereby broadening access to a cheaper energy source for both domestic and commercial users. There is more to come, including new strategies for public health, regional development and regional transportation. This, of course, does not place the Executive beyond criticism – far from it. If anything, the range of targets may have proven to be too ambitious in terms of raising popular expectations, albeit that at the outset of devolution the electorate's anticipation of an improvement in public services erred on the side of caution.[97]

The rather measured view that devolution would make a positive difference in policy terms and that public services would become more expensive with the transfer of powers suggests the electorate was prepared to pay more for service delivery. In the run-up to, and during the initial phase of, devolution, 57 per cent of all respondents – including 68 per cent of Catholics and 49 per cent of Protestants – believed that public services would become more efficient when placed in the hands of local politicians. A similar proportion also believed that they would become more expensive, a view held by 55 per cent of Catholics and 56 per cent of Protestants.[98] What is interesting about those results is that there was overall majority support (57 per cent) for an increase to the revenue-raising powers of the devolved administration – akin to those enjoyed but not as yet exercised in Scotland – especially amongst Catholics.[99]

The issue of financing devolution in Northern Ireland is a vexed one and, moreover, has tended to unite the parties. There are few means available to the Executive to raise finance, which are restricted largely to the income from the district and regional rates. Northern Ireland's heavy reliance on a block grant calculated by the population-based Barnett formula, tightly administered by the UK Treasury, has caused widespread antipathy in the Assembly and the Executive, provoking a condition of 'irritable Barnett syndrome' amongst members. Support for a needs-based formula is a popular alternative amongst the parties, even though such a change could have negative consequences for Northern Ireland relative to, for instance, the English regions.[100] Prior to the suspension of October 2002, and as a hedge against the shortfall in income, the Executive embarked on a review of rating policy that included within its scope the option of introducing water charges. In the event, it was the team of direct rule ministers that took the decision to change the basis on which the rates are calculated, switching from a system based on rental value to one based on market value that will undoubtedly increase the yield available to the Executive. In addition, the direct rule ministers also decided in principle to introduce water charges, although they are to consult further on whether they should be levied on a flat-rate basis or via a metering system. Either way, the Executive will benefit from an increased revenue source. Finally, the Executive was actively exploring ways of developing public–private partnerships and various private finance initiatives[101] to improve Northern Ireland's infrastructure, but these, like the introduction of water charges, are proving to be highly controversial.

In the shorter run, the Executive was aided by the unveiling in early May 2002 of the Reinvestment and Reform Initiative (RRI) by the Prime Minister and the Chancellor of the Exchequer during a flying visit to Belfast. This enables the Executive to borrow £125 million in the period up to March 2004, repayable to the Treasury from existing regional rate income, and releases a further £75 million accruing from end-of-year flexibility moneys and underspend by Northern Ireland departments. The Initiative also introduced a new borrowing facility, effective from the beginning of the 2003–04 financial year, intended to lever in low-cost borrowing to address the historical lack of investment in infrastructure. In December 2002, Ian Pearson, the direct rule minister with responsibility for the finance portfolio, announced a proposal for a £2 billion infrastructure spending programme, as the first phase of investment under the aegis of the RRI. It represented, he said, 'a major turning point for Northern Ireland's public services'[102] – a point underlined by the accompanying announcement that the estimated £3 billion infrastructure deficit of the water service would be funded by the introduction of charging.[103]

Against a background of political uncertainty, chronic bouts of intercommunal violence and a leaching away of Protestant support for the Agreement, much has been accomplished and, prior to the most recent suspension, the Executive, whilst internally divided, was planning for the medium to longer term so as to 'make a difference'. The Assembly has functioned to some effect and results from the 2002 Life and Times Survey released in the midst of the post-October suspension indicate that the public was bemoaning its loss.[104] Asked whether the Assembly had achieved a lot, a little or nothing at all, overall 77 per cent said it had achieved either a lot (26 per cent) or a little (51 per cent), whilst just 18 per cent believed it had achieved nothing. Protestants, at 25 per cent, were much more likely to take the latter view than Catholics (10 per cent), and at 70 per cent were less likely to say that it had achieved a lot or a little than Catholics, 86 per cent of whom adopted the more upbeat view of its achievements. A rather sharper communal divide was apparent in responses to the matter of how well or badly the Assembly and the Executive had performed in the day-to-day running of Northern Ireland. More than half of Catholics (56 per cent) thought the institutions had done a good job, compared with just 29 per cent of Protestants, most of whom (50 per cent) emerged as fence-sitters, believing they had done neither a good nor a bad job, a view shared by one-third of Catholics. However, only 15 per cent of Protestants believed that MLAs and ministers had performed badly – a perhaps surprisingly low proportion – as compared with 6 per cent of Catholics. But the most revealing finding was that a plurality of Protestants (42 per cent) said that they would be either quite disappointed (28 per cent) or very disappointed (14 per cent) if the Assembly were to be suspended 'for a number of years', and only 14 per cent that they would be quite pleased (8 per cent) or very pleased (6 per cent) if that were the case, whilst 37 per cent adopted the more neutral stance by stating that they would be neither pleased nor disappointed. By comparison, two-thirds of Catholics (67 per cent) said they would be either quite (27 per cent) or very (40 per cent) disappointed by this outcome, 21 per cent would be neither pleased nor disappointed and just 6 per cent that they would be either quite or very pleased, 1 per cent and 5 per cent, respectively. These findings suggest that an indefinite suspension is not the preferred future and lend encouragement to the attempts to restore devolution following the efforts of both governments in early March 2003, the fruits of which were due to be published a month later.

At the time of writing, the outcome of the post-suspension negotiations is still awaited. Aspects of the 'joint declaration' prepared by the UK and Irish governments, whilst as yet unpublished, have seeped out into the public domain and give some sense and shape to the commitments that London is prepared to fulfil in order to restore devolution. These include a timetable to 'demilitarise' Northern Ireland, reforms to the criminal justice system, the devolution of policing powers, a bill of rights, equality legislation and, short of a general amnesty, measures to deal with republican paramilitary 'on the run' suspects. In addition, the package also includes a proposal to introduce sanctions against those deemed to be in breach of a commitment to exclusively peaceful and democratic means of resolving the wider conflict, administered by an independent panel consisting of representatives from the two governments and the American administration. Indeed, the decision of President Bush to visit Northern Ireland for a war summit with Tony Blair shortly before the blueprint was due to be published enabled him to lend his support to the proposals during brief meetings with pro-Agreement politicians. However, such high-level diplomacy failed to achieve the desired effect.

The sticking point is the reluctance of the IRA to state unequivocally that the 'long war' is, in effect, over and that it will decommission and disband. Its initial unpublished response to the joint declaration was, it appears, a less than constructive exercise in ambiguity. Despite a further clarification from the IRA, again unpublished, the Anglo-Irish blueprint for the full implementation of the Agreement remains under wraps. As such, the prospect for a symmetrical and reciprocal process of, to use Tony Blair's phrase, 'acts of completion' to occur in the short run seems to be receding. Amongst other things, failure to resolve the current impasse jeopardises the planned Assembly election rescheduled to 29 May 2003. With no reciprocity from the republican movement designed to permit closure on the outstanding matters, there may be little to be gained from holding the election. If it is postponed, this would serve to underline that, far from being resolved, the 'ancient quarrel' can as yet only be managed. In turn, this would entail that direct rule remains in place for the foreseeable future.

NOTES

1. *The Agreement: Agreement Reached in the Multi-Party Negotiations* (UK Government, n.d.)
2. David Trimble, BBC Radio Ulster, 13 April 1998
3. The interlocking and mutually interdependent character of the institutions does, however, seem to have been belied by events following the suspension of devolution in October 2002. Whilst the Executive and the Assembly were placed in, at least, cool storage the British and Irish governments agreed a new treaty that enabled strand two's North–South Ministerial Council (NSMC) to continue to function in the post-suspension period. The treaty, agreed between the two governments on 19 November 2002, led to the tabling of the British–Irish Agreement Bill in the *Dáil*, which was rushed through the Irish Parliament on 26 November. Its purpose was to amend the British–Irish Agreement Act 1999 to enable the decisions of the NSMC in relation to the six all-island Implementation Bodies to be taken by the British and Irish Governments together during the suspension

period. It was presented by the Irish Government as a temporary, purely remedial measure, designed to provide care and maintenance for the bodies and to protect the jobs of the 700 or so officials engaged in their work and which would cease to be operative if and when devolution was restored. Unionist politicians, whether pro- or anti-Agreement, were outraged by what they perceived as a back-room deal by the two governments, the outcome of which was at odds with the ostensible interleaving of the Belfast Agreement's institutions. David Trimble accused the Northern Ireland Office (NIO) of 'dirty tricks' (UUP *Press Release*, 9 December 2002), while his party colleague and fellow MLA, Esmond Birnie, detected a risk of 'joint authority by the back door' as a consequence of the new legislation (UUP *Press Release*, 28 November 2002). In addition, the British–Irish Council (BIC), one of the strand three institutions, has also continued to meet in the post-suspension period with NIO ministers in attendance. According to private sources, the procedural guidance agreed by the two governments with the devolved administrations does not prevent the Council from continuing to operate in such a circumstance. Moreover, because the BIC – unlike the NSMC – is a consultative, rather than an executive, body, no fresh legislation was required to enable its continued activity.

4. They were: the Ulster Unionist Party, Social Democratic and Labour Party, Sinn Féin, Alliance Party, Progressive Unionist Party, Women's Coalition, Ulster Democratic Party, and Labour. The latter two failed to get any of their candidates elected to the Assembly.

5. There are other theoretical futures, including independence, joint authority and, in the event of the failure of the Agreement, the reversion to direct rule *sine die*. Thus far, there have been four periods of direct rule post-devolution. One was lengthy, between 11 February and 30 May 2000; another is lengthier, beginning on 14 October 2002 and is still in place at the time of writing (April 2003). The remaining two periods of suspension/direct rule lasted just 24 hours each: the first on 11 August 2001, the second on 21 September 2001. For a contemporary record of these events see the quarterly monitoring reports on the 'Nations and Regions' page of the Constitution Unit's website, www.constitution-unit/ monitoring. For a rehearsal of alternative futures see Paul Mitchell, Futures, in Paul Mitchell and Rick Wilford (eds), *Politics in Northern Ireland* (Boulder, CO: Westview Press, 1999), pp.265–84

6. See Roger Mac Ginty *et al.* (2001), Consenting Adults: Northern Ireland's Constitutional Future, *Government and Opposition* 36 (4), pp.472–92

7. Northern Ireland Act 1998, Schedule 1

8. Speech to the UUP's annual general meeting, Belfast, 9 March 2002

9. The 2001 Northern Ireland Life and Times (NILT) survey showed that 79 per cent of Protestants, 15 per cent of Catholics and 46 per cent of those professing 'no religion' state that Northern Ireland should remain part of the United Kingdom. This, however, is likely to have underreported the level of Protestant support for the Union – and perhaps overreported Catholic support – in the fevered context of a referendum. All NILT survey results are available at www.ark.ac.uk

10. In a BBC interview two days before the census results were disclosed Mr McLaughlin forecast that the proportion of Protestants would fall below 50 per cent. Against the background of this predicted scenario he stated: 'It is understandable that unionists are nervous and unsure about the future given the demographic trend, but refusal to accept change will not prevent it.' BBC News Online, 17 December 2002

11. Following 30 hours of talks among the pro-Agreement parties and the UK and Irish governments at Hillsborough Castle over 3–5 March 2003, Tony Blair announced that the scheduled election would be put back until 29 May. Any agreed basis paving the way towards the election – and a post-poll resumption of devolution – remains to be published at the time of writing. It was due to come into the public domain on 10 April 2003, but was delayed because of a lack of clarity on the part of the IRA about its future intentions in regard to disarmament, disbandment and a declaration that its war is over. The bill providing for the postponement of the election was enacted on 20 March 2003 after its guillotined passage through the UK Parliament.

12. All local and regional elections in Northern Ireland employ the single transferable vote method of proportional representation. For a discussion of the electoral systems employed in Northern Ireland throughout its existence, see Paul Mitchell and Gordon Gillespie, The Electoral Systems, in Mitchell and Wilford (eds), op. cit. (1999) pp.66–90. At the 2001 general election, SF won 4 seats, with a 21.7 per cent vote share, compared to the SDLP's retention of its three seats on a 21 per cent vote share. At the local government elections held on the same day (7 June), SF secured 21 per cent of first preferences compared to the SDLP's 19 per cent, although the latter won 117 council seats and the former 108 seats. These were the first elections at which SF had overtaken the SDLP.

13. This trio of demands was an indispensable part of the 'acts of completion' equation set out by Tony Blair during his speech delivered in Belfast on 17 October 2002. Reciprocally, he undertook to implement the 'normalisation' of Northern Ireland – what republicans refer to as 'demilitarisation' – and to protect the devolved institutions against what he termed 'arbitrary interruption and interference', including the withdrawal of the UK government's unilateral power to suspend devolution. For the text of Mr Blair's speech, see www.nio.gov.uk

14. This was the preferred initial position of the UUP during the talks leading to the 1998 Agreement. It proved to be unacceptable to both the SDLP and SF then, and will find few friends if it is put back on the table by the DUP in a post-election context.

15. At Prime Minister's Questions immediately following the Hillsborough talks, Tony Blair made it clear that the 1998 Agreement remained the only template for the future. Asked about his hopes for progress in Northern Ireland he stated: '[T]here is no way in which the agreement [sic] is going to be renegotiated: it is either implemented or we do not have the peaceful future in Northern Ireland that we all want to see'. HC Debs, 5 March 2003, col. 811

16. Exit polls for *RTE* and the *Sunday Times* reported, respectively, that 52 per cent and 55 per cent of Protestants had voted yes to the Agreement, whilst more than 9 out of 10 Catholics had done so.

17. On the pro-Agreement side, the results in terms of seats won at the election were UUP 28, SDLP 24, SF 18, Alliance 6, PUP 2, Women's Coalition 2. Ranged on the anti-Agreement side were the DUP 20, UKUP 5, Independent Unionists 3. The latter subsequently formed the United Unionist Assembly Party. Four members of the UKUP were to split away and form the Northern Ireland Unionist Party, one of whom – Roger Hutchinson – was later expelled following his decision, against party policy, to serve within the Assembly's committee system. After a spell as an Independent, he joined the DUP with effect from January 2001.

18. Even discounting the first preference votes cast for anti-Agreement UUP candidates, the successful anti-Agreement parties and Independents secured 23.9 per cent of all first preference votes, while pro-Agreement unionists achieved 23.8 per cent. See Paul Mitchell, Transcending an Ethnic Party System? The Impact of Consociational Governance on Electoral Dynamics and the Party System, in Rick Wilford (ed.), *Aspects of the Belfast Agreement* (Oxford: Oxford University Press, 2001), pp.28–48

19. Among the UUP's successful candidates, Peter Weir, Roy Beggs Jr and Pauline Armitage had each voted no at the referendum. At face value, though, the predominantly pro-Agreement UUP had 28 seats, supplemented by the Progressive Unionist Party's two MLAs.

20. The shadow Assembly met between 1 July 1998 and 1 December 1999. During this period each of its publications carried the prefix 'New'. With the formal transfer of devolved powers the prefix was dropped.

21. The reform of the criminal justice system was also delegated to an independent body.

22. The allocation of departments was the outcome of the triggering of the d'Hondt mechanism on 29 November 1999. For an explanation of d'Hondt, see Rick Wilford, Epilogue, in Mitchell and Wilford (eds), op.cit. (1999) p.314

23. The inter-party negotiations yielded 12 cross-border bodies. Six of these would cooperate through existing bodies in each separate jurisdiction on the following matters: transport, agriculture, education, health, environment and tourism. Cooperation on the six remaining matters was to be effected through new 'implementation bodies' operating on a cross-border or all-island basis. These were inland waterways, food safety, trade and business development, special EU programmes, language, and aquaculture and marine matters. The North–South Ministerial Council met in transitional form at Parliament Buildings, Belfast on 1 December 1999. The inaugural plenary meeting of the Council took place in Armagh, Northern Ireland, on 13 December 1999, and occurred without any street protests.

24. The outcomes of the negotiations were announced in Parliament Buildings by the first and deputy first ministers (designate) on 15 December 1998.

25. The eleven departments, and their initial ministers, were Office of the First and Deputy First Ministers (David Trimble, UUP and Seamus Mallon, SDLP); Agriculture and Rural Development (Brid Rodgers, SDLP); Culture, Arts and Leisure (Michael McGimpsey, UUP); Education (Martin McGuinness, SF); Enterprise, Trade and Investment (Sir Reg Empey, UUP); Environment (Sam Foster, UUP); Finance and Personnel (Mark Durkan, SDLP); Health, Personal Social Services and Public Safety (Bairbre de Brún, SF); Higher and Further Education, Training and Employment (Sean Farren, SDLP); Regional Development (Peter Robinson, DUP); and Social Development (Nigel Dodds, DUP). The ministerial 'team' was later complemented by the appointment of two junior ministers to OFMDFM: Dermot Nesbitt (UUP) and Denis Haughey (SDLP). Nesbitt later became environment minister, following the retirement of Sam Foster, and was replaced by James Leslie (UUP). Upon his election as deputy first minister in November 2002, Mark Durkan was replaced as finance minister by Sean Farren who, in turn, was succeeded by Carmel Hanna (SDLP) at what had been renamed as the Department for Employment and Learning in July 2001. The DUP has rotated its ministers twice during the life of the Assembly, in July 2000 and November 2001. Between those dates Gregory Campbell took over from Peter Robinson and Maurice Morrow from Nigel Dodds. The latter pair resumed their original briefs in November 2001.

26. During the negotiations, the UUP (and the non-participating DUP) had favoured the creation of a total of seven departments and the SDLP ten, plus the Office of First and Deputy First Ministers. The UUP wanted to limit the number and functions of the cross-border bodies to the 12 areas of north–south cooperation indicated, but not prescribed, by the Agreement, whilst the SDLP (and SF) wanted to create a much more extensive network of organisations. The outcome was a classic compromise. The UUP acceded to ten departments, plus OFMDFM, in return for the SDLP's agreement to a dozen cross-border bodies. The outline of the devolved administration was unveiled in December 1998, but it was not until the following February that the final allocation of functions to all departments was finally approved by the Assembly. A great deal of tidying up of the functions occurred over the two-month period, leaving some departments, including Finance and Personnel and especially the Office of First and Deputy First Ministers with a somewhat untidy sprawl of responsibilities.

27. See Arend Lijphart, *The Politics of Accommodation: Pluralism and Democracy in the Netherlands* (Berkeley/Los Angeles, CA: University of California Press, 1968); Arend Lijphart, Consociational Democracy, *World Politics*, 21 (1969), pp.207–25; and Arend Lijphart, *Democracy in Plural Societies: A Comparative Exploration* (London: Yale University Press, 1977).

28. Key decisions require cross-community consent and include the election of the Assembly's speaker and its three deputy speakers; the election of the first and deputy first ministers, budget allocations to the departments and Assembly standing orders. The Executive's first Programme for Government (PfG) was also subjected to a cross-community vote because it, too, was

assumed to be a key decision. However, this requirement was abandoned in December 2001. Following the vote on the first PfG, the Finance and Personnel Department approached the Assembly's Business Office querying the requirement for a cross-community vote on the ground that the Programmes do not raise or allocate moneys from the Consolidated Fund. The advice of the Business Office, based on a fresh reading of section 63.3 of the Northern Ireland Act 1998, was that since the Programmes are no more – and no less – than a statement of the Executive's aims and objectives, they could be endorsed by a simple majority. Only pre-designated key decisions, or those deemed as such by way of a 'Petition of Concern' requiring the signatures of 30 MLAs, are subject to cross-community voting. All other votes are decided by the simple majority rule.

29. See Brendan O'Leary, The Character of the 1998 Agreement, in Wilford (ed.), op. cit. (2001) pp.49–83; and Wilford, Epilogue, in Mitchell and Wilford (eds), op. cit. (1999) pp.285–303

30. The Principles provided the substance of the Mitchell Report of January 1996, the outcome of the three-man Mitchell Commission, established to gauge the prospects for decommissioning. (The other members were Harri Holkeri, former Finnish prime minister, and General John De Chastelain, the Canadian chief of staff and former ambassador to the United States.) The Report noted that those in possession of illegal arms were committed to disarmament, but not prior to the projected all-party talks. However, it indicated that the parties should consider that some decommissioning take place *during* the talks process. The Principles themselves included that all those involved in negotiations must affirm their commitment to democratic and exclusively peaceful means of resolving political issues and to the total disarmament of all paramilitary organisations; that such disarmament must be verified by an independent commission; that all parties must themselves renounce force or the threat of force, or the same by others, in order to influence the course or the outcome of negotiations; that they agree to abide by the terms of the agreement reached in the negotiations and to use only democratic and peaceful means in seeking to alter any aspect of that outcome with which they may disagree; and that they urge the ending of of all punishment beatings and killings and take effective steps to prevent such actions. See Paul Bew and Gordon Gillespie (1999) *Northern Ireland: A Chronology of the Troubles, 1968–1969* (Dublin: Gill & Macmillan) pp.318–19

31. *The Way Forward: A Joint Statement by the British and Irish Governments*, Belfast, 2 July 1999

32. The inclusive character of the Agreement was bolstered on the morning of 15 July, when the then secretary of state, Dr Mo Mowlam, issued a note to the initial presiding officer (speaker). The note introduced an additional standing order to the effect that any Executive (designate) must include at least three self-designated 'unionists' and three self-designated 'nationalists'. For a contestation of this decision by Dr Mowlam, see O'Leary, op. cit. (2001) p.81

33. For the full text of Senator Mitchell's statement see the *Irish Times*, 18 November 1999

34. HC Debs, 30 November 1999, col. 253

35. The first of the IICD's reports was scheduled to be published on 31 January 2000 but, owing to its gloomy tone, it was held over to be published alongside the second report *after* suspension on 11 February 2000. For the full texts of the reports see the *Irish Times*, 12 February 2000

36. Various parties have had recourse to the courts post-devolution including the UUP, DUP and Sinn Féin. In addition, a campaign group seeking to prevent the closure of the Jubilee Maternity Hospital by the health minister – Bairbre de Brún (SF) – sought and eventually won a judicial review into its closure.

37. The first act of decommissioning by the Provisional IRA took place in October 2001 and the second in April 2002, both witnessed and verified by the IICD. Prior to these acts, in May 2000 the PIRA had agreed as part of a 'confidence building measure' that two international arms inspectors could examine an unspecified number of its arms dumps. The two inspectors, named by the British and Irish governments in May 2000, were former Finnish president Martti Ahtisaari and ex-ANC secretary-general Cyril Ramaphosa. By the time of the first act of decommissioning, they had carried out at least three inspections, though no details were made public as to the location or nature of the *matériel* involved.

38. During this interregnum, Seamus Mallon dubbed himself, rather wryly, as DFMIABN: Deputy First Minister In All But Name.

39. Seamus Mallon decided to stand down as deputy first minister (and deputy leader of the SDLP) on the grounds of advancing years in the autumn of 2001.

40. In the midst of this phase and prior to the first act of IRA decommissioning the crisis deepened when, following failed attempts by both the UUP and the DUP to exclude the Sinn Féin ministers from office for a period of 12 months, the five remaining unionist ministers also resigned.

41. Parallel consent requires an overall majority of members present and voting, including a majority of both those designated as unionists and as nationalists. The weighted majority test requires 60 per cent of those present and voting, including at least 40 per cent of both unionist and nationalist members.

42. Subsequently Mr Weir became a member of the DUP with effect from 30 April 2002.

43. Mrs Armitage was suspended from the UUP for her action and continued to sit as an Independent Unionist until the suspension on 14 October 2002.

44. Monica McWilliams redesignated as a nationalist and Jane Morrice as a unionist.

45. David Ford and Eileen Bell, respectively the leader and deputy leader of Alliance, plus Mr Ford's predecessor as party leader, Sean Neeson.

46. The original standing orders enabled parties and individual members to change their designation once during the life of an Assembly, provided they gave 30 days' written notice of the proposed change to the Speaker. However, the amendments to standing orders allowed MLAs to indicate a change of designation with immediate effect, and to revert to their original designation

on the same basis. Thus, the three Alliance members who redesignated as unionists for the purpose of the second vote reclaimed their 'other' status in the wake of the Trimble/Durkan election. The two NIWC members, McWilliams and Morrice, did not redesignate as 'other' until the start of the Assembly's 2002–03 session.

47. 'Making a Difference' is the subtitle of the Executive's Programmes for Government.

48. In August 2001 three Irish republicans – Niall Connolly, Martin McCauley and Jim Monaghan – were arrested by the Colombian security forces whilst leaving an area of the country controlled by the Marxist guerrilla group FARC. They were charged with travelling on false passports and, more seriously, with training FARC members in the making of bombs. Mr Monaghan is a former member of Sinn Féin's executive committee, whilst Mr Connolly was Sinn Féin's representative in Cuba. All three deny the charges. At a US Congressional hearing in April 2002, the House of Representatives' International Relations Committee heard claims that as many as 15 IRA members had visited Colombia since the late 1980s. In the wake of 11 September 2001, the allegations against the three republicans carried enormous impact in Washington and it was probably no coincidence that the first act of IRA decommissioning occurred in October 2001.

    Suspicions about the activities of republicans were further stoked when, in March 2002 – on the night of St Patrick's Day – the headquarters of the Police Service for Northern Ireland at Castlereagh in Belfast were broken into. Three men not only gained entry to the complex, but penetrated into the offices of Special Branch, overpowered the officer on duty and removed batches of files, many of which were highly sensitive. The police have alleged that the IRA perpetrated the break-in, allegations refuted utterly by Sinn Féin who have made the counter-claim that British intelligence agencies were responsible and that their purpose is to subvert the peace process. Two enquiries, one by the PSNI and another headed by Sir John Chilcot, a former senior civil servant with considerable experience of Northern Ireland, were set up, neither of which has as yet reported.

49. Donald Horowitz, The Northern Ireland Agreement: Clear, Consociational and Risky, in John McGarry (ed.), *Northern Ireland and the Divided World: Post-Agreement Northern Ireland in Comparative Perspective* (Oxford: Oxford University Press, 2001) pp.89–108

50. Only two junior ministerial positions were created in the Assembly's first term, both within OFMDFM: Dermot Nesbitt (UUP) and Denis Haughey (SDLP). Mr Nesbitt was later made environment minister, and his role was taken by party colleague James Leslie.

51. The Sinn Féin team took little part in Strand One negotiations, focusing instead on the 'external' aspects of the Agreement, especially in relation to Strand Two and to a lesser extent those in Strand Three.

52. There was no prior agreement among the Executive parties about the distribution of ministerial portfolios. Beyond the shared understanding between the

UUP and the SDLP over their respective first choice of departments, each of the four parties embarked on something of a ministerial mystery tour. Private information.

53. Section 23(1) of the 1998 Act reaffirms Westminster's sovereignty by stating that executive power remains vested in the monarch. Section 23(2) states that in relation to transferred, i.e. devolved, matters the royal prerogative is exercisable by any minister/department.

54. See Donald Horowitz, Constitutional Design: Proposals versus Processes, in Andrew Reynolds (ed.), *The Architecture of Democracy: Constitutional Design, Conflict Management and Democracy* (Oxford: Oxford University Press, 2002), pp.15–36

55. See Paul Mitchell, op. cit. (2001)

56. The deal struck between the UUP and SDLP in December 1999 over the number of both devolved departments and north–south bodies meant that there would be parity of ministerial numbers, if not esteem, around the Executive Committee table: six unionists and six nationalists, albeit that the DUP's two ministers refused to participate in its meetings.

57. On first- and second-order elections see Christopher Anderson and Daniel Ward, Barometer Elections in Comparative Perspective, *Electoral Studies* 15 (4) (1996), pp.447–60; and Karlheinz Reif and Hermann Schmitt, Nine Second-order Elections: A Conceptual Framework for the Analysis of European Election Results, *European Journal of Political Research* 8 (1980), pp.3–44

58. Horowitz in Reynolds (ed.), op. cit. (2002) p.25. Note too that in 1998 whilst there was a UK government-backed 'Yes' campaign, there was no all-party, cross-community pro-Agreement campaign leading up to the referendum. Instead, each of the parties sought to mobilise their own electoral blocs.

59. Peter Robinson, DUP Press Statement, 5 March 2001

60. Interview with author.

61. The necessary procedural device whereby a no confidence motion or one seeking the exclusion of a party from the Executive can be tabled is a 'petition of concern'. This requires the endorsement of 30 MLAs. Such a motion is subject to the two tests of cross-community support, i.e. either parallel consent or a weighted majority.

62. The five cross-cutting themes covered by the EPFs are 'Social Inclusion/Community Regeneration', 'New Directions', 'Infrastructure and Capital Renewal', 'Service Modernisation' and 'Children'.

63. Mark Durkan, *Official Report*, 11 December 2001. The use of the EPFs to promote joined-up government has not been a conspicuous success. The first round of bidding for the funds was almost entirely mono-departmental.

64. The Executive Committee established its first sub-committees in 2002. One was to oversee the region-wide review of public administration that is intended to streamline Northern Ireland's overgoverned polity. The terms of reference for the review – which exclude the devolved institutions – were published in February 2002 and the review itself was launched in June 2002. The second sub-committee was established following the unveiling of the Reinvestment

and Reform Initiative by both the UK's prime minister and Chancellor of the Exchequer in Belfast in May 2002. This Initiative, negotiated by the first and deputy first ministers and the finance minister (Sean Farren, SDLP) and the UK Treasury, created a new loan facility for the devolved administration earmarked to tackle Northern Ireland's infrastructure deficit. For further details on the Initiative and the review of public administration see www.ofmdfm.gov.uk

65. *Official Report*, 26 November 2001

66. The decision to rotate the two departments among an unspecified number of its MLAs is alleged to have been a compromise amongst the DUP's leadership. Some wanted the two incumbents simply to resume their ministerial positions, others for the party to withdraw from the Executive and take up the role of official Opposition in the chamber, and yet others to withdraw from both the Executive and the Assembly. Private information. The press release announcing the decision to rotate ministers stated that there would be 'a series of short-term Ministerial appointments replacing resigning Ministers with others at regular intervals' (31 May 2000).

67. DUP Press Release, *Fundamental Review*, Part 3, 31 May 2000

68. *Loc. cit.* The time-limited nature of these actions implied that there would be no further ministerial rotation in the period after the general election of June 2001. However, the DUP engaged in a second rotation the following November.

69. Executive Committee Press Release, 8 June 2000

70. See Executive Committee Press Release, 30 March 2001

71. DUP Press Release, 17 January 2002

72. The 2001 *NILT* survey showed that the level of unionist support for the Agreement had fallen to 34 per cent. See www.ark.ac.uk. In October 2002, immediately following suspension, a poll for BBC Northern Ireland's *Hearts and Minds* programme confirmed the low level of support among unionists. Asked how they would vote if a referendum were held 'today', just 32.9 per cent said they would vote yes, compared with 82 per cent of nationalist voters. Moreover, 58 per cent of unionists said they were not prepared to support power sharing with either the SDLP or SF. See http://news.bbc.co.uk/1/hi/northern_ireland/2335861.stm

73. Since 1998 successive *NILT* surveys show that the proportion of the population believing that the Agreement has been of equal benefit to unionists and nationalists has fallen from 55 per cent to 31 per cent. In the 2001 survey, a plurality of respondents (41 per cent) believed that nationalists had been the greatest beneficiaries, whilst just 3 per cent thought that unionists had reaped either major or minor benefits from the implementation of the Agreement. Catholic respondents, whilst more likely than Protestants to state that there have been equal gains for both communities, also believed that they have benefited most from the Agreement. Ibid.

74. Ibid. See also Roger Mac Ginty, *Fortnight*, July 2002. Given the alternative option of enhanced devolution, Catholic support for Irish unification falls by 10 per cent, to 49 per cent.

75. See Henry Patterson, From Insulation to Appeasement: The Major and Blair Governments Reconsidered, in Wilford (ed.), op. cit. (2001) pp.166–83

76. On 5 June 2000, at the first post-suspension session of the reconvened Assembly MLAs were required to approve the Appropriation Bill (2000) by means of an accelerated passage procedure in order to release expenditure to the devolved departments. There was a need for the urgent approval of the Bill, else there would be no moneys available to the Administration from mid-August (the Assembly was scheduled to break for the summer recess on 7 July) which would have brought the departments to a grinding halt. The accelerated passage procedure provides that there be no committee stage for the relevant Bill but in order for it to be adopted there must be unanimity in the chamber. Any anti-Agreement member or party could have frustrated this procedure simply by objecting during the course of the debate. None chose to do so. Had there been an objection, as the Speaker later observed (*Official Report*, 4 July 2000, p.26) 'the Bill would not have been able to pass before the end of the session'. David Trimble did not miss the opportunity to score a significant point off the DUP. Speaking during a debate on a DUP motion – which he opposed – to exclude Sinn Féin from the Executive, he observed: 'If the DUP really wanted to stop the Assembly it could have done so. There was a moment a few weeks ago when we had before us the matter of the accelerated procedure for the Appropriation Bill. If that had been objected to, the Northern Ireland Administration, the Assembly and all associated bodies could have been brought to a complete halt by just one person saying one word: "No"' (*Official Report*, ibid., p.25)

77. See, for instance, DUP Press Release, 27 July 2000

78. Ibid.

79. That is with the exception of the 1973–74 power-sharing administration which survived for just five months. The 1982–86 Assembly had no executive powers. See Rick Wilford, Regional Assemblies and Parliament, in Mitchell and Wilford (eds), op. cit. (1999) pp.117–41; and Cornelius O'Leary *et al.*, *The Northern Ireland Assembly 1982–1986: A Constitutional Experiment* (London: Hurst, 1988).

80. In addition there are six standing committees, five of which are smaller in size than the statutory committees, each of which has 11 members. These are the Audit, Business, Procedure, Public Accounts and Standards and Privileges Committees. The sixth is the 17-strong Committee of the Centre that monitors the Office of First and Deputy First Ministers. The Assembly also has authority to establish ad hoc committees which are created from time to time largely to scrutinise draft legislation emanating from within the Northern Ireland Office (NIO). Under the terms of the Agreement, the NIO, in the person of the Secretary of State, retains authority for 'excepted' and 'reserved' matters, i.e. those not devolved to Northern Ireland. See Brigid Hadfield, Seeing It Through? The Multifaceted Implementation of the Belfast Agreement, in R. Wilford (ed.), op. cit. (2001), pp.84–106. There have been nine ad hoc committees in the post-devolution period: see the committee page of the Assembly website www.ni.assembly.gov.uk

81. The seven 'others' comprised five Alliance members and the two members of the Women's Coalition. There was a sixth Alliance member elected to the Assembly in 1998, John (Lord) Alderdice, but he accepted the invitation of the then secretary of state, Dr Mowlam, to act as interim presiding officer (later speaker). Lord Alderdice was not confirmed in the office of Speaker by means of a cross-community vote during the Assembly's first term and has announced that he will not stand for re-election to the Assembly for a second term.

82. The legislative process is distinctive and comprises the following: First Stage, Second Stage, Committee Stage, Consideration Stage Concluded, Further Consideration Stage, Final Stage and Royal Assent. See the 'Legislation' page of the Assembly's website www.ni.assembly.gov.uk

83. Rev. Ian Paisley (Agriculture and Rural Development) and Rev. William McCrea (Environment).

84. See Rick Wilford and Robin Wilson, *A Democratic Design? The Political Style of the Northern Ireland Assembly* (London: The Constitution Unit, 2001)

85. Liz Fawcett, Political Communication and Devolution in Northern Ireland, ESRC Conference paper, Belfast, 2000

86. See the debate 'One Elected Office', moved by Jane Morrice (WC), *Official Report*, 28 May 2002

87. The three NIUP members – Cedric Wilson, Paddy Roche and Norman Boyd – and Robert McCartney (the sole UKUP MLA) do not participate in any committee. One UUP member, Duncan Shipley-Dalton, was removed by the party whip from the statutory Enterprise, Trade and Investment Committee because of poor attendance. The volume of committee work is considerable and, in part for that reason, in the autumn of 2001 the Assembly agreed changes to its standing orders reducing the quorum for meetings and enabling committees to establish sub-committees.

88. There are six Assembly members for each of Northern Ireland's 18 Westminster constituencies.

89. In the financial year 1998–99, no budget was set for the Assembly, though £10m was spent. In 1999–2000 the budget was established at £36m, although actual expenditure was just £16m because of the period of suspension. The following year the budget was set at £37m, but again the Assembly was suspended leading to actual expenditure of £24m. In 2001–02 the budget increased to £39m. See *First Report of the Northern Ireland Assembly Commission* (NIA 102/01), 2002

90. Prior to the 2002 summer recess, the Agriculture and Rural Development Committee indicated that it was considering a committee bill to introduce an early retirement scheme for farmers and a young entrant scheme into the agriculture industry. See *Committee Minute*, 17 May 2002. Further, in the period leading up to the fourth suspension (14 October 2002), the standing standards and privileges committee was preparing a bill leading to the creation of the Assembly's commissioner for standards.

91. See Assembly legislation page of the Assembly's website, www.niassembly.gov.uk

92. Jane Morrice (WC) did table a private members' bill, but it was superseded by the decision of OFMDFM to legislate in the same area, namely the establishment of a Children's Commissioner for Northern Ireland. Ms Morrice's bill has not proceeded beyond its first stage on 30 April 2001.

93. See the answer to a written question from David Ford (Alliance), *Written Answers Booklet*, 26 April 2002, AQW 2784/01, 77. The drafting resources had been put in place on 1 April 2002 following agreement by the Assembly Commission, which is chaired by the Speaker.

94. See Procedure Committee, First Report 2001–2002 Session, *Review of the Legislative Process in the Northern Ireland Assembly*, 1/01r, 16 January 2002. The Committee put back the consideration of committee and private members' legislation. Following the provision of resources to enable private members' bills to be tabled, there were four such bills in the legislative wings at the time of suspension. One of these was a proposal to designate all horses as agricultural animals: dubbed, by some, the 'let horses be cows' bill.

95. The two committees were Health, Personal Social Services and Public Safety and Higher and Further Education, Training and Employment, now redesignated as Employment and Learning. In the former case, the committee had voted in favour of a site in south Belfast for the city's new maternity hospital, whereas the minister, Bairbre de Brún (SF) had decided in favour of west Belfast, her own constituency. In the latter case, the higher education committee had put down a motion to implement its recommendations in relation to a reformed system of student finance, whereas the then minister, Sean Farren (SDLP) had put down an amendment requiring him to 'take note' of the recommendations. The committee's SDLP members fell into party line when the vote was taken.

96. The five PfG priorities are: 'Growing as a Community'; 'Working for a Healthier People'; 'Investing in Education and Skills'; 'Securing a Competitive Economy'; and 'Developing North/South, East/West and International Relations'. The Executive's report on the first PfG was published on 1 July 2002 and debated in the Assembly on the same day.

97. See Rick Wilford *et al.*, A Triumph of Hope over Experience? Attitudes Towards and Knowledge of Northern Ireland's Devolved Institutions, *Regional and Federal Studies* (2003). The figures in the text are derived from the 1999–2000 NILT survey.

98. Ibid.

99. Sixty-eight per cent of Catholic respondents supported a tax-varying power for the Assembly, compared with 49 per cent of Protestants. Ibid.

100. Assembly debates concerning the annual budgetary process are peppered with criticisms of the Barnett formula from all parties. Any change to a need-based formula is unlikely to occur in advance of the implementation of English regional government. For a sane discussion of the formula see David Bell and Alex Christie, Finance – The Barnett Formula: Nobody's Child?, in Alan Trench (ed.), *The State of the Nations 2001: The Second Year of Devolution in the United Kingdom* (Thorverton: Imprint Academic, 2001) pp.135–51

101. *Review of Opportunities for Public Private Partnerships in Northern Ireland*, Northern Ireland Executive, May 2002

102. Northern Ireland Information Service, 11 December 2002

103. When the RRI was unveiled, the UK government also announced the transfer of a number of security facilities/bases to the Executive for the purpose of redevelopment. These included the Maze – site of the 'H-blocks' – and Crumlin Road prisons, and British army barracks in Belfast, Londonderry and Magherafelt. The latter measure was emblematic of the hoped-for vision of a new beginning for Northern Ireland that was embodied within the 1998 Agreement. As the accompanying press statement put it: 'sites which symbolise the period of conflict can become the engine for economic and social regeneration'. Northern Ireland Executive Press Release, 2 May 2002. 'For sale' signs have now appeared on a number of these sites.

104. See Lizanne Dowds, Public Attitudes and Identity, *February 2003 Monitoring Report* (2003), available at the 'Nations and Regions' page of the Constitution Unit's website www.constitution-unit/monitoring

Part Three

REFORMING THE BRITISH STATE

Reforming the British state: the 1998 watershed

Michael O'Neill

DEVOLUTION REVISITED

Reform of what was widely seen as an outmoded constitution was central to the New Labour project, though the party was careful to reaffirm the integrity of the Union. The 1998 reform of territorial governance was expressly designed to confirm continued commitment by the centre to the very idea of a union state whilst accommodating the territorial preference for home rule. The proposed reforms hardly measured up to the aspirations of Scotland's Claim of Right, which Scotland's Labour MPs, including the designated first minister, had subscribed to. The Claim had insisted that sovereignty in Scotland resides with its people, whereas the new legislation expressly maintained that sovereignty ultimately and irrevocably remained in the Union, albeit devolved in some degree, but in no way divested from central government or its institutions.

The new prime minister was less instinctively pro-devolution than his two predecessors as party leader. For one thing, their political roots were firmly in territorial politics, whereas Blair, though a born Scot, was moulded more by his experience of English education and legal training. Moreover, he was especially concerned to maximise Labour's appeal with the voters of middle England, who had once been the Conservatives' exclusive electoral preserve. There was concern, too, in New Labour's ranks not to alienate regional opinion in England. This much was apparent from the official response to mounting expectations for devolution in Wales, and especially in Scotland. Once again, referenda were held in both countries in order to validate devolution, but also to pre-empt anticipated opposition from Labour's rank and file.

On this occasion, however, and in marked contrast to 1978, the referenda were to be conducted before the legislation was presented in Parliament. Scotland's electors (but not those in Wales) were asked two questions: whether or not they endorsed a territorial parliament, and whether this institution should have any (though as yet unspecified) tax-raising powers. This politically sensitive question was carefully couched, referring quite deliberately to 'tax-varying powers' – a form of words deliberately used in the event that radical devolutionists might subsequently seek to expand this competence beyond what central government had originally intended. The fiscal question was included by a government concerned to pre-empt public disaffection, to counter Labour's reputation as a spendthrift party with both the electorate of middle England and moderate Scots voters alike.

LEGITIMISING CONSTITUTIONAL REFORM

The proposed devolution was to be both asymmetrical and cooperative. Asymmetry, rather than inconsistency – a familiar virtue of Britain's unwritten and flexible constitution – is the paramount characteristic of these latest reforms, with Scotland and Northern Ireland enjoying rather more self-government than Wales. Cooperative, in as much as devolution does not follow the classic federalist doctrine of slicing sovereignty in agreed policy domains, but instead accommodates the United Kingdom's constituent territorial nations to the idea of a hierarchy of shared competences with central government. The precise allocations of authority between the respective tiers or layers of government, though formally iterated in the legislation, will be settled by practice, as it is in any multi-level polity.

Both Acts were approved in referenda held in September 1998. In Scotland there was a ringing endorsement on a turnout of 60.4 per cent. On the first question asked in the referendum, 'I agree/do not agree that there should be a Scottish Parliament', the result was:

Agree: 1,775,045 (74.3 per cent)
Disagree: 614,000 (25.7 per cent)

On the second question, 'I agree/do not agree that a Scottish Parliament should have tax-varying powers', the result was:

Agree: 1,512,889 (63.5 per cent)
Disagree: 870,263 (36.5 per cent)

With their embedded sense of nationality, and regardless of ideology, social class, religious affiliation or geographical location, Scottish voters in the 1998 referendum exhibited much less circumspection about devolution than those of Wales. They endorsed the proposal by a majority of three to one (74.3 to 25.7 per cent in favour, with 63.5 to 36.5 per cent in favour of the new parliament's tax-raising powers), and from a much higher turnout (60.4 per cent). A figure that far exceeded the slender 33:32 per cent margin in favour in 1979. All 32 voting regions endorsed the parliament, with only two regions, Dumfries and Galloway and Orkney, voting marginally against tax-raising powers.

As a proportion of those entitled to vote, these figures look rather less impressive: 44.7 per cent in favour of a parliament but only 38.1 per cent favouring powers over taxation. The pro-devolution figure represented a swing of 23 per cent in favour of devolution since 1979, compared to a pro-devolution swing in Wales of 30 per cent. More alarming for the centre was the fact that some 50 per cent of Scots indicated to pollsters a preference for outright independence, with the largest proportion of those preferring autonomy concentrated in the 18–34 age-cohort, and with a majority of Scots anticipating this dramatic outcome within fifteen years.[1] Nevertheless, support for the Scottish National Party (SNP), the one party offering this option, declined to 28.8 per cent during the elections for the Scottish Parliament, a figure lower than the support recorded for the party in its halcyon year of 1974. This figure reveals continued public reticence about endorsing a separatist agenda once that opportunity actually beckoned. This indicates the electorate's abiding pragmatism where financial obligations are concerned. The preference to have one's cake and to consume it prevailed over wilder flights of political fancy that could be safely indulged when devolution was still a remote prospect.

Economics was the key to such reticence. The pro-Union parties forced an admission from the SNP of the likely start-up costs of independence, calculated by one source as at least £16 billion, and thus requiring tax rates of something like 38 pence in the pound, even assuming the unlikely prospect that England would relinquish rights over most of the 'Scottish' oil reserves.[2] In these circumstances, the considered view of one commentator, that on balance 'for most Scots, the Parliament was a symbol of their nationality rather than the start of a new polity which they stood to gain from materially', is a reasonable one.[3]

Although the choices facing Wales were much less momentous or disruptive of normal politics, devolution there was endorsed by only the barest of margins (559,419 votes or 50.1 per cent to 552,698 votes or 49.9 per cent), and that on a relatively low turnout of 51.3 per cent. In effect, devolution passed by fewer than seven thousand votes in 1,112,117. This was hardly ringing endorsement and was revealing of persistent doubts about even a restricted home rule. This was evidence, too, of a still problematic Welsh identity. The figures confirm a marked differential in public opinion about the appeal of a distinctly Welsh polity. The long-held assumption that home rule is more appealing to the Welsh-speaking regions than it is in English-speaking Wales was apparent from the referendum returns. In fact, the picture was altogether more mixed. Despite the distorting effect of a low turnout there is a positive correlation in the voting figures between strong cultural identity and firm support for home rule. Areas with a higher proportion of English-born voters remained cautious about devolution, and there is a clear division, too, between east and west Wales, reflecting a correspondence between resistance to constitutional change and cultural-cum-geographical proximity to England.[4]

On the basis of these results, the Scotland Bill and the Government of Wales Bill were put before the House of Commons in 1997. The fact that the principle of devolution had already been endorsed in referenda, and that many of the specific features contained in the enabling legislation were widely known and referred to in the referendum campaigns, pre-empted the parliamentary debacle that had accompanied the passage of the 1978 legislation. The timing of these bills, immediately after the election of a new government, ensured a degree of legitimacy for these changes that was manifestly lacking in 1978. It also served to lessen Parliament's appetite for subjecting the legislation to the rigorous scrutiny it had exercised over the previous legislation. And though these proposals were received rather more critically by the Upper House, the fact that the government had clearly signalled devolution as a policy priority for its first term weakened their Lordships' resolve to obstruct its passage.

THE SCOTLAND AND WALES ACTS 1998

The reforms proposed in the Scotland Act and the Government of Wales Act of 1998 reiterated most of the 1978 proposals, extending them so as to reflect increased public support for constitutional change. The Scottish Parliament now has modest revenue-raising powers and the first-past-the-post electoral system of the 1978 proposals is replaced by a form of proportionality. The commitment in the 1974 White Paper not to reduce Scottish representation at Westminster has likewise been revised, not least as a sop to concerns expressed by some English MPs. More recently, a government White Paper (2002) has raised the prospect of devolution for England. At the time of writing, the outcome remains uncertain. On balance, it is difficult to demur from the judgement of one commentator that 'it is the similarities and not the differences which are remarkable when comparing the legislation of 1978 with that of 1998'. Consequently, decisions made hastily and in response to immediate political pressures in the 1970s have come 'fundamentally to determine the shape of devolution in the 1990s'.[5] The principal features of these devolution arrangements are described in the following sections.

Asymmetry

The latest reform in the political architecture of the unitary state goes some way beyond the 1978 proposals, though it echoes many of the features of the earlier legislation and indeed repeats many of its drawbacks. The arrangements are again asymmetrical, with different governance for Scotland and Wales to reflect what are still deemed to be quite different requirements and aspirations of two distinct territorial polities. The outcome is a variegated, even untidy, constitutional arrangement. Whilst the debate on devolution in Scotland made reference to nationhood,[6] the language employed in Wales referred merely to an exalted regional status.[7]

Scotland, and for that matter Northern Ireland too under the terms of the Stormont Agreement, enjoy greater self-government (similar to Bavaria's semi-autonomous status within Germany's cooperative federalism) than does Wales (which enjoys rather more self-government than a French regional council, though less than any Spanish *comunidade autonomas*). The English regions are currently denied any devolved status, though the Labour government has, as noted above, revisited this issue in its second term.

Political rhetoric in Scotland refers to home rule as restoring an 'ancient right', a claim now enshrined in a parliament with wider powers than those of the Welsh Assembly. An altogether more ambivalent political identity in Wales has been satisfied, at least for the time being, with enhanced regional status: in the words of a *Financial Times* commentary in July 1997, 'bringing Whitehall to Wales and making it more accessible'.[8] A former Welsh secretary referred to an 'all but inseparable' status in relation to England, betokening the lack of clear political identity and perhaps of the self-confidence which has sustained Scottish or Irish nationalism. This historical proximity finds expression in special arrangements for Wales. The Report of the Royal Commission on the Constitution promised parity with Scotland in responding to rising awareness of national identity[9] but this promise was not met in either the 1978 or the 1998 reforms.

The principal distinction between the two variants of devolution is legislative devolution for Scotland but only executive devolution for Wales. The Welsh Assembly is denied the prerogative to pass primary legislation and may only enact secondary legislation, that is those orders, regulations and rules that give detailed substance to the basic precepts or framework of primary legislation. Westminster retains the competence for primary legislation. A degree of power is conferred on the Welsh National Assembly whereby ministerial functions previously exercised at the centre may be transferred (section 22 Government of Wales Act 1998) by Order in Council to the Assembly, confirmed by a resolution of both Houses of Parliament.

The main focus here is the transfer of powers from the secretary of state for Wales, though additional transfer Orders permit the subsequent delegation of executive functions from other ministers with regard to affairs in Wales. Another source of power for the Assembly is the acquisition of functions directly bestowed by a particular Act of primary legislation (sections 27 and 28 Government of Wales Act 1998) which allows for amendments of primary legislation by secondary legislation. Here, too, there is scope for further primary legislation that directly increases the Assembly's powers. There is at least an implied promise of ongoing review, the intention to monitor the process with a view to further incremental devolution, should circumstances merit it. Future legislation emanating from Westminster may – though there is no guarantee of this – move the process in Wales closer to the Scottish model. The conferring of a tax-varying power, however, perhaps the surest measure of autonomy from Westminster, will require dedicated primary legislation.

There is, of course, real substance, a meaningful degree of power even in this otherwise subordinate role, though it is of a different order and degree from that enjoyed by the Scottish Parliament. The distinction is clearly stated thus: 'Legislative devolution involves a *transfer* of powers, executive devolution involves a *division* of powers at present united in the hands of ministers as well as a transfer of powers.'[10] As such, Welsh devolution is somewhat diminished, at least for the time being. Central government does, however, have discretion when drafting the primary legislation, to determine the basic framework of a particular Act, whilst leaving determination of much of the detail to the Assembly. This does not alter the fact that such self-determination remains at the behest of Westminster. In some ways this distinction mirrors the customary relations between central and local government, but that this is the preferred model for Welsh devolution surely diminishes the significance of, and indeed curbs the aspirations for self-determination.

The problem of limited self-determination has political consequences that may or may not cause future difficulties in relations between the centre and the Principality. More certain are the difficulties implied by this form of executive devolution for current administrative and political relations, as between the centre and Wales. The problem here stems from the horizontal ethos of executive devolution, problems previously not encountered in British government. Establishing a mutually acceptable balance of power between Westminster and what is, even in this reduced form, a territorial level of government, presents a serious challenge to drafters of future legislation in as much as:

> Primary legislation for Wales will have to be drawn up more loosely than primary legislation for England, so as to give scope to the Assembly, without giving too great a discretion to ministers in charge of English departments. This means that future statutes will have to be framed differently for England and Wales. For if they were to be framed similarly, either they would be very loosely drawn both for England and Wales, in which case the Assembly would have considerable scope but English ministers would be given too wide a discretion; or, alternatively, if the legislative framework were drawn up equally tightly for England and Wales, the Welsh Assembly would find its powers over secondary legislation did not amount to very much.[11]

Proper demarcation of the boundaries between primary and secondary legislation is imperative for effective law making in any devolved or federal polity, and this is a priority yet to be properly addressed in the case of Welsh devolution. Moreover, new cooperative habits between the territorial level and the centre, as anticipated at the outset in the Report of the Royal Commission on the Constitution, are just as indispensable for smooth functioning of even this modest devolution.[12] This is by no means easy to ensure in a state whose fundamental operational principles, as well as the instincts and experience of its politicians and administrators, have been historically determined by the norms, and framed according to the procedures, of a unitary state. New arrangements – and dare one say proper 'constitutional guarantees' – are required that clearly demarcate these new boundaries, determining the definitive compass of jurisdiction as between central, territorial, and indeed local government. Federal polities address these boundary issues as a matter of constitutional propriety, embedding multi-level government within a formal, binding but (usually) flexible constitutional framework where disputes over demarcations are anticipated but adjudicated by a constitutional court. The devolution system that operates in Wales is altogether more ad hoc. And therein lies its potential danger.

Consultations between the secretary of state and the Assembly about the Welsh executive's proposed programme are required by the legislation (section 31 Government of Wales Act 1998), but only at the secretary of state's discretion and not on every specific of legislation. Dialogue will be that much more difficult where the political composition of the executive differs from that of the government at Westminster. Impasse may well ensue, so it is important to settle appropriate rules of demarcation whilst relations between Cardiff and London are 'normal' rather than tense or antagonistic. The closest approximation in the present arrangements to this sensible requirement is the rather vague provision for non-statutory, non-judicially enforceable concordats intended to facilitate a climate of cooperation between Cardiff and London. The Joint Ministerial Committee (JMC) consisting of ministers of all four governments likewise plays its part in ensuring smooth intergovernmental relations.

Few observers doubt that there is a marked advantage for Wales in these new arrangements. Whether or not London involves the Welsh executive in the pre-drafting stage of legislation, the Assembly 'will . . . yield more detailed scrutiny, openness, and public participation in the making of secondary legislation than occurs at Westminster'. Moreover, 'it will be possible to amend secondary legislation for Wales in the Assembly, while at Westminster, by contrast, secondary legislation must either be accepted or rejected and no amendment is possible'.[13]

On the face of it, home rule in Wales is less about maximising territorial autonomy than ensuring that Welsh interests are voiced on their own terms after years of unremitting centralisation by the Welsh Office and a plethora of non-elected quangos – estimated by 1997 at some 120. Nevertheless, this is surely not the constitutional end state of devolution as the union state adjusts to the exigencies of contemporary politics. For it is in the very nature of such asymmetrical arrangements that they invite the less autonomous territorial polities in an uneven constitutional framework to 'catch up' with the pacesetters, as circumstances change and aspirations burgeon. Scotland's greater devolution is certainly invidious to committed Welsh nationalists, offering a clear incentive to emulate their neighbour by demanding parity of status as and when territorial public opinion feels ready to close the gap. Plaid Cymru has already raised the issue of constitutional parity.[14]

An asymmetrical architecture is difficult to manage in a polity used to singular and uniform governance, but it is by no means the weak arrangement that some critics aver. There is strength in flexibility as much as there is jeopardy in clinging to an unduly rigid formula in any state embarked on reform. Any constitutional arrangement where there is power sharing between discrete levels of governance depends on both constant vigilance by the central authorities and mutual goodwill to sustain the bargain. This balanced formula will surely be the acid test for Welsh devolution.

Cooperative intergovernmentalism

Overlap or concurrence between the respective levels of government, rather than their outright separation, sometimes occurs, or is even formally designated, in federal systems of the concurrent variety. It is, however, an unavoidable outcome of British devolution.[15] Westminster both retains an interest in those policy areas devolved to the territorial governments, and continues to hold *de jure* power to act (subject to political constraints and an appropriate legal norm) in every area of public policy.[16] There is nothing untoward in this. It is a regular feature of governance in non-unitary states, though potential for political frictions requires skilful political management to avoid provoking serious administrative gridlock and debilitating political crisis.

There are several reasons for anticipating continuing overlap between territorial and central government competences, though rather more so in Wales than in Scotland. The overarching responsibility of central government is for national policy; and with public policy made for England bound to impinge, even in devolved matters, on that of the territorial governments, this responsibility is one likely source of conflict. There is further scope for contested jurisdiction in Scotland because of the extent of its legislative autonomy and even the quite modest fiscal competence; and in Wales, paradoxically, because of the closer fusion of the Assembly's authority and that of Westminster, underpinned by a common legal base. The 1998 Act shares responsibility for *all* legislation between Westminster and the Welsh Assembly: Westminster passing primary legislation, the Assembly providing the secondary legislation. A less febrile nationalism and the more remote prospect of a nationalist administration in Cardiff suggest rather better prospects here for resolving any disputes.

As originally conceived, and indeed following the precedent of the 1978 legislation, there was no provision in the 1998 legislation for formal procedures to involve the territorial administrations in ministerial deliberations at the centre dealing with reserved policy areas that directly impinge on devolved matters. The government, wisely, has revised these arrangements, proposing instead a system of Joint Ministerial Committees serviced by officials and a joint secretariat, albeit with only consultative status.[17] A Joint Ministerial Committee that includes the prime minister, the territorial secretaries of state, and senior executive members from Scotland, Wales and Northern Ireland and meeting in a plenary session is the principal forum for coordinating territorial and central government. The JMC also has various specialised functional formats, for the knowledge economy, for Europe, for poverty and for health. The delicate matter of intergovernmental relations in regard to external relations and EU policy are covered by a Memorandum of Understanding[18] and by concordats negotiated in October 1999 between the UK government and the devolved authorities.[19] This is a modest provision though it does confirm the centre's acknowledgement of the requirement for constructive dialogue with the territorial executives. There will, over time, undoubtedly be increasing pressure from the territorial polities to enlarge their access to the policy-making process at the centre.

The actual balance of power between central government and the territorial authorities will depend as much on events, on how these arrangements actually work out in practice, as on constitutional formalities. Westminster not only retains an interest in those policy areas devolved to the territorial governments but also continues to exercise *de jure* power, subject to the usual exigencies of politics. Public policy decided at Westminster for England in the devolved matters is bound to impact on the arrangements in these same areas in Scotland and Wales. This is a normal outcome of intergovernmental relations in other devolved and even in quasi- or fully fledged federal systems. The requirement, too, for central government to transpose EU policy directives and regulations into national law, as well as similar obligations under international treaties, likewise promises awkward intergovernmental relations. The territorial governments' limited fiscal autonomy means that even their devolved policies cannot vary significantly from those devised by central government for England. The fact, too, that Scottish and Welsh civil servants remain ultimately answerable to the UK civil service further confirms the central government's dominant role in national policy.[20]

British devolution clearly does not conform to the neat separation of powers usually found in federalism. Rather than ceding outright authority, central government instead accommodates territorial interests, agreeing to share its competences in a restricted number of legislative and administrative matters. Boundary disputes are certain to arise in those areas of concurrent or overlapping power. Again, there is nothing untoward in this, though a culture of common-sense intergovernmental cooperation is indispensable if conflicts over interpretation are to be contained, let alone resolved.

A balance has to be struck, eschewing outright dominance from the centre but avoiding constant and debilitating tension between the respective tiers of government threatening the policy process with gridlock. Federal systems resolve this problematic issue by incorporating the territorial dimension into the very architecture of the state, ensconced as a territorially based second chamber of parliament. There is a democratic bonus from this solution. On the one hand, there is direct territorial representation at the centre that redresses a clear democracy deficit; on the other, it allows additional parliamentary scrutiny, shedding light on to the delicate process of balancing territorial–central relations, ensuring public accountability and proper scrutiny, thereby avoiding murky insider dealing and the closeted bargains of less formal arrangements. The recent debate on reform of the House of Lords was, as some commentators have appropriately observed, a squandered opportunity in this regard. It presented an opportunity to democratise the process of resolving intergovernmental differences, making more transparent those necessary trade-offs between the national and the territorial interests, and a way too of incorporating an emergent territorial dimension in British politics within the nation's evolving constitutional architecture.[21]

Multiple checks and balances are incorporated into these new arrangements, as befits an experimental devolution of power from a central government more used to exercising legislative and executive discretion without regard to sub-national authorities, and equally unsure about the consequences for political stability and executive effectiveness. This was intended as a clear deterrent to any territorial interest minded to push the boundaries of political/legislative/executive discretion beyond those intended by the centre. Veto power is implied here, though it is clearly exercised with territorial sensibilities in mind, and only as a last resort should gridlock or worse ensue, for there is always the prospect in a devolved polity that extremist nationalists, dissatisfied with what they perceive to be insufficient territorial discretion, will challenge the existing boundaries of power – a familiar imbroglio in historic federal systems, from the United States and Canada to India and Belgium.

The new UK polity is not, of course, a federal system, and will not become one for the remotely foreseeable future. Nevertheless, the same systemic tensions between the respective tiers of government can be anticipated from devolution. Presiding officers, first ministers, executive office holders, law officers, the Judicial Committee of the Privy Council and ultimately – and not least and perhaps decisively – the secretaries of state acting with the full weight of cabinet behind them, determine the exercise of the legislative capacities of the devolved assemblies.

Those bent on provoking political crisis in intergovernmental relations will only be effectively marginalised, however, if there is a workable consensus both at the centre and within the territorial polities alike about making devolution work. The unionist parties at both levels, too, must accommodate to the new politics, embracing a common purpose over and above their differences on policy and even about ideology if they are to deflect public cynicism or to counter wrecking tactics from militant nationalists.

Bold predictions about the eventual balance of power, or about the temper of relations between central and territorial governments, are bound to be wide of the mark. Politics is contingent, driven by events. What is clear so far, however, is that the United Kingdom is embarking on the new and potentially volatile politics now familiar in every European polity with devolution or federal arrangements. Outcomes will depend on the capacity of elites at each level of governance to construct mutually acceptable procedures, to develop norms and to adopt habits of behaviour that make cooperation rather than conflict the prevailing standard of intergovernmental relations. In effect, there is a new political culture to be learned by all sides.[22]

Institutions

The legislation established a four-year fixed-term parliament for Scotland with 129 seats: 73 members, to be elected by first-past-the-post for the present Westminster constituencies, with a further 56 members, 7 elected from each of eight regional lists based on the current Euro-constituencies according to the additional member 'top-up' principle, to ensure that regional representation is as proportional as possible to the total share of the vote for each party. Likewise in Wales, a 60-member Assembly is elected by the same hybrid system: 40 members elected directly from Westminster constituencies and 20 from regional lists controlled by the national party machines. Although the Scottish Parliament has a fixed four-year term, it may be dissolved and an interim election held if two-thirds of SMPs vote to so do, or if it fails after a 28-day period to nominate a first minister.

Executives are appointed by the first ministers (leaders of the principal parties) of each legislature, with electoral proportionality making coalition government the most likely outcome. The inaugural elections of both bodies produced a formal coalition in Scotland and an informal inter-party arrangement in Wales. In both cases the nationalist parties were excluded from government. Ultimate responsibility for framing election rules and procedures remains with Westminster, unlike the situation in federal systems where discretion in these matters is usually conferred on the territorial governments.

The adoption of a proportionality system was the result of Labour's cooperation with the Liberal Democrats in the Scottish Constitutional Convention. One reason highlighted by political analysts for the failure of the Scotland Act 1978 to secure adequate public support in the 1979 referendum was the fear that the first-past-the-post electoral system preferred in that legislation would result in non-representative government: in effect that, 'in a four-party system, Labour, representing just the central belt of Scotland, might gain an overall majority on just 35 per cent of the vote; or alternatively, that the SNP might gain an overall majority on just over 35 per cent of the vote and use that majority to claim that the Scottish people had given a mandate to independence [whereas] under proportional representation ... the SNP would need to win 50 per cent of the vote to claim a mandate'.[23]

Accepting the principle of proportionality was an important concession, although Labour's strategists refused to concede the Liberal Democrat preference for the single transferable vote (STV) system. One consequence of STV is intense and usually protracted post-election inter-party bargaining over policy programmes. As such, this system is apt to exacerbate intra-party squabbles or worse in a party where ideological rectitude is the norm. The additional member system, on the other hand, tends to encourage a more balanced slate of candidates, not least facilitating the selection of more women candidates. As Bogdanor sees it: 'whereas under a single-member constituency system it is the *presence* of a candidate who deviates from the male norm which is noticed, in a party-list system, it is the *absence* of a female candidate, the failure to balance the ticket, that would be noticed and made the subject of adverse comment'.[24]

The additional member system has other democratic and representational virtues. It facilitates voter choice as between party candidates, thereby sending clear signals to party leaders about grassroot preferences with regard to coalition outcomes, though there is no guarantee that such hints will be acted on. The adoption here of closed rather than open lists does, however, limit voter choice, with electors unable to place candidates from the same party in preference order. Party leaderships thereby retain considerable leverage over the composition of these elected chambers. Critics of this arrangement see both a lost opportunity for citizen empowerment and a serious impediment to effective devolution. As Bogdanor assesses the potential for adverse consequences:

> Much of the work of the Scottish Parliament and the Welsh Assembly will involve nego- tiations between different branches of the Labour Party machine in London, Edinburgh, and Cardiff. Members of the Scottish Parliament and the Welsh Assembly might, as a result of the electoral system, be a little too eager to support a party leadership so that they can be renominated to a high position on the party list. Thus the electoral system will tend to the strengthening of the devolved executives at the expense of the legislatures. The additional-member system, especially when accompanied by a closed list, operates against the values of devolution and democratic accountability which require the trans- ference of power away from Westminster to Edinburgh and Cardiff. It could easily lead to the recentralization of power through party machines.[25]

Comparisons with Scotland that highlight a devolution differential are repug- nant to committed nationalists in Wales, though implicit in this disparity is the assumption of quite different historical experiences. The secretary of state who piloted the Wales Bill referred to that country's 'all but inseparable' status *vis-à-vis* England, implying an accompanying lack of political self-confidence that makes for what one commentator has described as 'a kinder, more gentle nationalism' in Wales.[26] Scotland's parliament was perceived, even by Scots of a unionist disposition, as 'righting an ancient wrong', whereas public support for Welsh devolution is altogether more ambivalent. There is still an abiding sense that political self-determination is much less the point of Welsh devolution than ensuing better democratic scrutiny of powers exercised by the Welsh Office and an excess of non-elected quangos.[27]

Constitutional limits are built into the arrangements for both countries that confirm the intention of enacting 'merely' devolution, a loosening of the bonds between centre and periphery, rather than a quasi-federal shift in the locus of power and authority in the British state. The rooted principle of Westminster supremacy, the inalienable sovereignty of Parliament, is confirmed in the legislation. Responsibility for framing the rules and procedures of elections remains with Westminster, a markedly different arrangement to the degree of autonomy enjoyed in these same matters by constituent polities in federalism. There is, nevertheless, a significant shift in emphasis in what was once a rigidly centralised unitary state. For the first time since it was formerly a separate state, Scotland's Executive and Parliament has regained a direct link with the Crown, albeit one now appropriate to the norms and procedures of a constitutional monarchy. Scottish legislation does not now pass to the secretary of state for assent, except in cases where such legislation might be deemed to be in conflict with the wider national interest (section 35 Scotland Act 1998).

Making governments

The direct link between territorial government and the Crown is most evident in the procedures for confirming a new Scottish government in office. The presiding officer of the Scottish Parliament fulfils the sovereign's constitutional duties, recommending the appointment of the Parliament's designated first minister (section 46(4) Scotland Act 1998) and determining when the criteria for dissolution are met (section 3). Making and indeed sustaining governments in office will be an altogether more complicated business in light of the impact of a proportional election system on the Parliament's political make-up.[28] One consequence of proportional representation systems is the presence of a larger number of parties, thereby complicating the selection of both a first minister who requires the confidence of the House, and the actual party make-up of the governing coalition. There is the additional consideration, too, that coalitions are potentially volatile, apt to splinter in comparison with governments formed by one party.[29]

The prospect, should these circumstances arise, for political manipulation or undue exercise of political discretion for personal or party advantage by the incumbent first minister is considerably reduced by the adoption of a four-year fixed-term Parliament, and by vesting the authority for dissolution in the presiding officer. This is the case, too, even in the exceptional situation anticipated in the Scotland Act 1998, whereby two-thirds of the Parliament votes for a pre-term dissolution, or where the Parliament – presumably politically deadlocked – fails to designate a first minister within the 28-day deadline. In both instances, the task of advising the monarch falls to the presiding officer and not, as at Westminster, to the incumbent prime minister. The two-thirds rule, too, is designed to enhance the power of the Parliament at the expense of ministerial discretion, for in the proportionality system now in use in Scotland, such a majority is unlikely. The prospect of a first minister manipulating his or her own parliamentary colleagues in order to engineer a dissolution under the 28-day rule is rather more feasible, though a sophisticated and increasingly sceptical electorate might, in these circumstances, be expected to wreak an appropriate revenge at the ensuing election.

The Welsh Assembly is elected for a fixed term but there is no provision in the enabling legislation for early dissolution. Proportionality in the electoral system offers the same prospects as in Scotland for political deadlock during the course of a parliamentary term, but without the same convenient mechanism for resolving it. Despite being the principal party both at Westminster and in the territorial assemblies, Labour has been required by the exigencies of proportional representation to form coalitions in the latter with the Liberal Democrats based on jointly negotiated programmes.[30]

Legislative competences

Whilst the principle of legislative devolution is enshrined in both 1998 Acts, the legislation does reveal abiding tension over central government's ultimate sovereignty, with potential, even in this limited self-determination, for contested authority – and more so in Scotland due to the more extensive range of devolved powers. The two territorial legislatures do nevertheless exercise jurisdiction over some aspects of public policy previously reserved to Westminster. The constraints imposed on the exercise of their power by the legislative bodies' respective officers are made explicit in the legislation. Telling, too, is the fact that the Scotland Act lists the reserved functions rather than the devolved ones, as was the case in the 1978 legislation. As such, Scotland's Parliament has altogether more extensive scope for self-government than has the Welsh Assembly. In either case there is devolution of competences previously exercised on behalf of both countries by Westminster, albeit with significant variation.

The Scotland Act sought to limit the potential for future disputation over contested jurisdictions by avoiding a definitive list of devolved powers such that might tempt nationalists, looking for a symbolic fight with London, to challenge unduly rigid boundaries. The preferred approach here is to emphasise continuity of governance, confirming primacy of the union state in the crucial aspects of 'high politics' by reiterating Westminster's reserve powers. The Scotland Act thus lists the 'exceptions' to outright devolution, outlining those aspects of legislative competence reserved to Westminster.

These functions are the meat of government in any modern state. They are listed as follows: constitutional matters and matters pertaining to the Crown; nationality, immigration and asylum policy; extradition; civil service affairs; the conduct and rules relating to national elections and the local government franchise; currency and financial services; taxation (though Scotland's parliament has the right to levy an additional top-up income tax of up to three pence in the pound), macro-economic management and fiscal and monetary policy other than local taxation and expenditure; competition policy, markets and import/export regulations; company regulation (to avoid unduly distorting Britain's internal market in goods, services and manpower); employment policy, health and safety, and industrial relations; abortion; broadcasting; telecommunications and the Post Office; energy policy, with modest exceptions; social security; security matters and emergency powers.

Included in this last is defence and foreign affairs, though Scots ministers do sit alongside UK ministers in European councils where matters pertinent to devolved competences are discussed, and with a bargaining position agreed in advance of formal negotiations, following the procedure in federal states, as in the relations between the German Länder and the Belgian territorial governments[31] and their respective national ministers. It must be noted, however, that under British devolution this right is not formally entrenched in statute but rather is enshrined in the aforementioned Memorandum of Understanding.[32]

Those matters not expressly reserved to Westminster are within the competence of the Scottish Executive and Parliament. The devolved matters include: health; education (schools and universities); local government; law and order/criminal justice matters; transport; housing; fisheries; food standards; trade and exports; sport and the arts; forestry. The Scotland Act (section 28) expressly limits the Parliament's role to legislating only within its own areas of competence. However, the Parliament's legislative prerogatives are further constrained. Westminster may usurp the Parliament's role in the non-reserved competences should it see fit to do so, for subsection 7 of section 28 of the Act states: 'This section does not affect the power of the Parliament of the United Kingdom to make laws for Scotland'.

The legislation reinforced this precept by expressly limiting the exercise of the Scottish Parliament's legislative powers to domestic affairs. Furthermore, Edinburgh may exercise its domestic powers only in matters that do not impinge on Westminster's responsibility, and not in ways deleterious to the overall British public interest (section 35(1)(b) Scotland Act 1998). There is a budget of some £14 billion per annum available for the Parliament/Executive to spend in these areas as it sees fit. Most of this funding for domestic initiatives comes from a block grant. There are, nevertheless, bound to be contested areas, as between the respective parliamentary jurisdictions, which promise some difficult situations ahead.

A more circumscribed devolution of legislative competence to the Welsh Assembly, and a smaller annual budget allocation of some £7 billion, makes for less problematical relations between central and territorial government. In marked contrast to the Scotland Act, the Government of Wales Act specifies (Schedule 2) devolved rather than reserved functions. The Welsh Assembly has competences in the following policy domains: economic development; agriculture; forestry; fisheries and food; industry and training; health, housing and local government; water; environment; town and country planning; transportation and roads; tourism, recreation and sport; social services; the arts, culture and the Welsh language. Westminster retains responsibility for enacting primary legislation in *all* other aspects of public policy, as well as responsibility for the same designated areas of 'high policy' as in Scotland, with UK ministers retaining competence over EU matters/negotiations; taxation and macro-economic management; fiscal policy and the maintenance of a British common market; broadcasting; and social security. There is no designated formal role in British external policy for the Welsh Executive. The Welsh Assembly is precluded, too, from introducing primary legislation and is restricted to secondary legislation, with the prospect of Westminster overruling the Assembly by insisting on primary legislation for any matter it deems to be politically significant.[33]

The distinction between the arrangements for Scotland and Wales confirms the preference for asymmetrical devolution in the home rule agenda from its beginnings in the later nineteenth century. The key distinction between the two operational models is that the Welsh Assembly has executive but not the primary legislative functions enjoyed by the Scottish Parliament. It has the modest power to make subordinate legislation in some matters that were previously the prerogative of central government ministers, for the most part those of the secretary of state for Wales. The closest these arrangements come to a legislative capacity is the power given to the Assembly (section 27 Government of Wales Act 1998) to take over the functions of the health authorities, and likewise those given under section 28 to Welsh nominated bodies.

Representation

The issue of representation, and especially the number and role of Scottish MPs sitting on committees and voting at Westminster on legislation pertaining to English matters was first raised in the Kilbrandon Report on the Constitution, which observed:

> We have ... noted the thorny problem of the representation of Scotland and Wales at Westminster if they alone were to have legislative assemblies of their own; the difficulties are not, however, in the view of most of us so great as to make legislative devolution to Scotland and Wales impracticable unless it is extended to England.[34]

The key issue here is the political, indeed the constitutional, imbalance of an asymmetrical devolution in a unitary state. The matter of uneven representation figured in the parliamentary debates on the Labour government's initial devolution proposals during the late 1970s.[35] This issue has since become known colloquially as the West Lothian Question after it was raised by Tam Dalyell, Member for that Scottish constituency. Dalyell questioned the political fairness, post-devolution, of permitting Scottish MPs to continue to sit at Westminster and to vote on legislation pertaining to English affairs when English MPs have no reciprocal right to a voice in Scottish domestic affairs. The same concern applies to the justness or otherwise of appointing to a ministerial or cabinet post a Member sitting for a Scottish constituency whose functions include policy pertaining to English affairs.

The problem is resolvable either by abandoning devolution altogether, as Dalyell preferred, or by enacting even more far-reaching constitutional reform. One solution is to adopt a fully federal constitution with symmetrical representation for each territorial polity, as in the American, German, or more recently Belgian polities. Another solution is to adopt a comprehensive and regionally balanced system of devolution in the United Kingdom that includes regional assemblies for England with powers commensurate with those of the new territorial polities. Both solutions would amount to a level of constitutional reform that the English political establishment and public opinion seem to be resistant to, at least for the time being.[36] The solution presented to correct this imbalance – a standing committee on regional affairs to review specifically English affairs, offered when devolution seemed imminent in the 1970s – was a stop-gap measure, a typically ad hoc response to an altogether more complicated constitutional problem.[37]

A third, and compromise, solution is to reduce the number of Scottish seats at Westminster and/or to reduce the role of Scots Members in reviewing and voting on 'English' matters. This was first mooted during the debates on Irish home rule in the late nineteenth century, but implementing such a procedure and, not least, deciding where to vest authority for deciding exclusion or what constitutes a solely 'English' matter, was never satisfactorily resolved. The withdrawal of voting rights from the governing party at Westminster, where that number is greater than the government's overall majority, would raise the controversial matter of what constitutes a mandate to govern. And it would more than likely provoke a constitutional crisis.

The response of some English opinion to this problematic – the wholesale exclusion of Scottish Members – is misplaced, a response *in extremis* with so many reserved matters relating to Scottish well-being, to its security and prosperity, remaining as Westminster's prerogative. Whereas, barring Scottish Members from participating in parliamentary business when solely English matters are discussed, though less drastic, remains equally problematical because much 'English' legislation is bound to impinge on what happens to legislative proposals in Edinburgh. The problem is now, as it were, on the table, though the political delicacy surrounding such a symbolic issue precludes an easy solution.[38]

The only response to this sensitive issue in the recent legislation is the modest quantitative rather than qualitative reduction in Scottish representation, revising the original bargain on territorial representation as a palliative to a territorially uneven Union. The pro rata over-representation of the Scottish electorate was a direct outcome of the political trade-off by which Scotland was assimilated into a Union demographically dominated by England. The idea here was institutionalised reassurance for the minority population, for 'since the whole country was being incorporated into a larger, there was special reason to ensure its interests could not be ignored or belittled . . . There was also concern about unfair discrimination against the interests of a minority with a long prior history of conflict with the new majority'.[39]

The case for compensatory representation persists in contemporary constitutional deliberations, and indeed was so identified by Kilbrandon, though this Report did recommend reducing non-English representation at Westminster in the event of devolution.[40] In fact, as McLean has pointed out in a recent study, myth tends to obscure hard facts. Scotland has in fact been over-represented at Westminster only since 1922.[41] After the 1998 devolution, both Scotland and Wales have retained their Westminster representation in the same numbers, though change is imminent in Scotland. The Scotland Act 1998 (section 86) alters the provision of the

Parliamentary Constituencies Act 1986 guaranteeing Scotland *no fewer* than 71 Westminster constituencies. The Act also directs the boundary commissioner for Scotland at the next review of parliamentary boundaries to employ the same electoral quota as that used in England. This will result in a reduction of Scottish representation at Westminster from 72 to 59 seats. Wales is exempted from this reduction on the grounds that Westminster retains responsibility for Welsh primary legislation. These are critical issues regarding the matter of balanced representation as between Westminster and the territorial assemblies. The prevailing view is that this important constitutional issue is no nearer resolution than it was when devolution was first mooted.[42]

Executive styles

Devolution establishes cabinet-style government in both Scotland and Wales, directed by 'first ministers'. Differences in both scope and functions again mark this as asymmetrical devolution. It is here that the devolved power resides, albeit subject to checks and balances both constitutional and political. Scotland is governed in devolved matters by an Executive appointed by the first minister, and including two law officers: the Lord Advocate and the Scottish Solicitor-General. First ministers are appointed by the monarch, as are UK prime ministers, though only with the approval of assembly/parliamentary members democratically sanctioned by a working majority. Office-holders wield considerable patronage and power, not least in the appointment of executive members, though unlike British prime ministers this prerogative is circumscribed by their need to consult with both the presiding officers over legislative and associated matters and, rather less formally but no less significantly, with other party leaders on whom they might depend for a working majority. Coalition governments will make for a more mutable politics than those at Westminster, perhaps even facilitating a degree of legislative independence largely unknown in the modern House of Commons.

Scotland provides the benchmark for the current devolution, a measure of both how much, and indeed how little, power has actually shifted from central government. Scotland's first minister is invested with the constitutional trappings of power: a territorial prime minister in all but name, appointed by the Queen in common with his British counterpart as the leader of the major party in the Parliament. As keeper of the Scottish seal, the symbol of legitimate power in the realm, he embodies the supreme executive authority previously vested in the office of the Scottish secretary.

As with its legislative competences, the Welsh executive is the weaker of the two territorial institutions. The Government of Wales Act 1998 enjoins the Assembly to elect a first secretary as well as committees proportionate in their composition to the respective strengths of the parties in the Assembly. The Assembly must also approve an Executive Committee of the First Secretary and Assembly secretaries, appointed by the first secretary and operating, in effect, as a cabinet. Less authority by far is vested in the Welsh chief executive than in his Scottish counterpart, though both offices are formally appointed by the monarch after 'election' by an absolute majority of the Assembly. The first secretary has considerable formal power and informal prestige and enjoys extensive patronage, including appointment of Executive members. Unlike the British prime minister however, this elective prerogative is circumscribed by the requirement to consult on legislative proposals with the Assembly's presiding officer and, should elections result in a hung parliament, by the political imperative to bargain with the other party leaders.

A constitutional innovation that reflects concern about the increased likelihood – and consequences for stable governance – of coalition government is the appointment by both elected chambers of a presiding officer, a role akin to but not identical with that of the Speaker in the House of Commons. The office combines the functions of speaker on internal parliamentary procedures with those of a non-party political interlocutor or arbitrator in some European parliamentary regimes – a key figure who holds the ring between the parties, or between the territorial and central governments, in the event of a breakdown in relations. The prospect of coalition government, much increased by proportional representation, clearly enhances this role.

Presiding officers have a symbolic function, embodying the parliaments' democratic legitimacy. As such, they officially oversee the appointment of a first minister, either after an election or by designating a substitute to act in his or her stead should the incumbent resign or be otherwise proved incapable of carrying out their duties. Presiding officers are responsible, too, for facilitating smooth intergovernmental relations, ensuring that acts of parliament do not incur central government's wrath by offering a political and constitutional challenge to Westminster or are otherwise acting beyond their powers. They take the chair at plenary sessions or when the parliament and assembly exercise their prerogative to hear expert evidence on matters within their competence. An important prerogative of this office is to propose a suitable date for a general election if the parliaments have voted to hold one, and of notifying the monarch of this fact.

The interaction of these three offices is both novel and complicated, its eventual political chemistry difficult to predict with any degree of certainty. Only time and experience will mark out clear boundaries and embed the norms of mutually acceptable operation, for although the legislation formally demarcates the respective competences of devolution, as one observer has aptly noted, 'such constitutional plans cannot take any regard for the intangible at the heart of government: politics itself'.[43]

Centre–periphery relations

Although their functions are not specified by either Act of Parliament, secretaries of state with British cabinet rank continue, at least for the time being, to be the principal intercalaries between London and the territorial executives. As such, they embody the very idea of the Union's continuing policy interests and convey this message from the centre to each territorial government. To that extent they constrain the latter's discretion, ensuring direct intervention by the centre in territorial affairs by 'representing Scottish interests in reserved areas' and by embodying the Union's duty to promote an overarching British national interest.[44]

By closely working with the first ministers and the presiding officers, secretaries of state facilitate intergovernmental relations, promoting, at least in principle, a cooperative rather than a tense association. The objective here is to avoid policy impasse, or at least to reduce its impact should it arise. Beyond this still important role, the Scottish secretary has forfeited his direct executive functions, a situation that has prompted some commentators to conjecture that the future of the office is uncertain and indicating a far from settled arrangement between the centre and the territorial governments. The 1998 Act does, nevertheless, provide for a residuum of influence.

Although the secretaries of state exercise no overt veto power, in contrast to the 1978 bill, sovereignty clearly does still reside at Westminster. The definitive statement here is Clause 33 (Scotland Act 1998) which allows the secretary of state to rescind any proposed legislation deemed to be constitutionally improper. Direct intervention in territorial governance is permitted should central government consider that proposed territorial legislation strays into those areas of Scots private law subject to Westminster's prerogative, to challenge its reserved powers, or to otherwise contradict UK obligations under international treaty. In this regard, section 35 of the Scotland Act empowers the secretary of state to prohibit the Scottish Parliament's presiding officer from sending any bill for Royal Assent that he presumes to be in conflict with obligations under international law and protocols, as determined by the British government.

A key clause of the Scotland Act in this regard (Clause 27) leaves no doubt about the real seat of legitimate authority. Despite a significant shift towards territorial self-government, empowering the Parliament to 'make laws, to be known as acts of the Scottish parliament', Westminster's right to make Scotland's laws is in no way abrogated, even in devolved matters.[45] As such, the secretary of state's ruling is definitive, though such direct interventions may be subject to challenges in the courts, in both politically controversial and jurisdictional grey areas, for the legislation also specifies, in the spirit of devolution, that the centre must show 'reasonable grounds' for its actions *vis-à-vis* the territories, not least where these interventions are contested by the elected territorial representatives.

Welsh arrangements mirror those for Scotland, though as things stand, with rather less uncertainty as to the constitutional outcome. The Welsh secretary, too, remains in the Cabinet for the time being, representing the Principality's interests at the centre and, rather more to the point here, Westminster's policy preferences in Wales. The difference in legislative capacity between the elected bodies of Scotland and Wales makes for a significant difference in the capacity and power of the respective secretaries of state. The Welsh secretary has responsibility for primary legislation, with its implementation the task of the Assembly.[46]

In both cases, however, this member of the British Cabinet stands uneasily between territorial and national governments, and is likely to be regarded in the former as the voice of the centre, a shadow without real substance and perhaps even as an obstacle to territorial will. Moreover, when the political complexion of territorial and national governments differs, as one day it surely will, this cabinet member may perhaps become a focal point for territorial resistance to the centre and a source of real political tension between territorial and central governments, for in both countries this office remains as a patent symbol of London's intentions, embodying the Union's constitutional supremacy. All of this confirms a far from settled status. A change in the official title is widely mooted, perhaps, as the Constitutional Unit has recommended, with an amalgamated secretaryship heading a new Whitehall department for constitutional affairs.[47]

The Joint Ministerial Committee (JMC) has been the principal forum for resolving any substantive differences between central government and the territorial authorities. Although this procedure was not mentioned in the 1997 White Papers on devolution to Scotland and Wales, it was subsequently included in the devolution machinery in response to apprehensions about adequate provision for intergovernmental liaison. Almost an afterthought, 'the JMC has grown to become the central piece of political machinery in underpinning the devolution settlement'.[48] The government regarded this institution, however, as one of last resort in case of serious policy imbroglio or political impasse, and this is still the prevailing view. In the words of the Memorandum:

> The UK Government and the devolved administrations believe that most contact between them should be carried out on a bilateral or multilateral basis, between departments which deal on a day to day basis with the issues at stake. Nevertheless, some central co-ordination is needed. Therefore the administrations agree to participate in a Joint Ministerial Committee (JMC) consisting of ministers of the UK Government, Scottish ministers, members of the Cabinet of the national assembly for Wales and ministers in the Northern Ireland Executive Committee.[49]

The evidence to date points to largely untroubled intergovernmental cooperation, with only occasional meetings of the JMC, called more often than not to meet the political requirements of central government,[50] though there have been rather more frequent meetings of the specific JMC that coordinates intergovernmental responses to EU-related policy matters.[51]

Contested jurisdiction and conciliation procedures

Devolution will test inchoate boundaries between the respective jurisdictions, and has potential for causing political friction even where authority formally resides with the territorial polity or the centre,[52] or where new legislative competences subsequently arise that are neither expressly nor clearly allocated to either legislative domain. Energy policy, for instance, remains a UK prerogative that impinges on the symbolic and still politically sensitive matter of 'Scotland's' oil. Likewise, nuclear energy with its perceived risks and environmental impact has the potential to cause a clash between central and territorial governments. If the experience of devolved and federal governments elsewhere is any yardstick, there is every reason to expect that disputation will be an occasional if not a regular feature of devolved politics. Common sense and mutual goodwill at both the central and territorial levels are indispensable for resolving deadlock, but only formal consultation procedures can provide a reliable forum for conciliation.

There are provisions in the Scotland Act 1998 for policing the boundaries of devolved competences to ensure that the territorial parliament does observe its 'proper' limits. For instance, the presiding officer is required to see that all legislation conforms to the *de jure* rules with regard to competences. This injunction does not, however, resolve the issue of contested jurisdiction in the event that the officer and a majority of the Parliament hold different views from those of central government about the legitimate scope of proposed legislation. The presiding officer is also required to submit bills for Royal Assent, but only after a four-week period, to enable the Law Officers to refer the measure, or any part thereof, to the Judicial Committee of the Privy Council for legal scrutiny to determine legislative competence. This arrangement, too, has obvious shortcomings.

To all intents, the Judicial Committee of the Privy Council, in its capacity as the court of last resort, performs the judicial review functions of a constitutional court that are familiar in federal polities. The principal drawback of this procedure, however, is that it compromises the sense of neutrality indispensable for legitimate and effective arbitration, for this arrangement is too closely identified with the former constitutional order. The facts that there is a majority of English judges on the committee and that its presiding officer, the Lord Chancellor, is a member of the Cabinet hardly inspire confidence in neutral constitutional arbitration.[53] If boundary disputes do become a frequent occurrence, a more impartial adjudicative mechanism will be required, one more patently detached from the centre. The Law Lords sitting at Westminster are precluded from acting in this constitutional capacity precisely because their impartiality is compromised by their membership of the second chamber of the UK Parliament.

The present arrangement – a system of abstract rather than concrete judicial review – is equally problematical, for it 'puts the courts and the Judicial Committee of the Privy Council in the position of deciding a question of *vires* in the abstract rather than in the context of a concrete case, without which there may be an incomplete understanding of the facts'. Accordingly, 'any opinion is bound to be in large part hypothetical, since it would be given before the Act had come into operation and without any real evidence as to the effect of the legislation'.[54]

The common law tradition with its reliance on ad hoc judicial review is even less appropriate for formal adjudication of power sharing between authorities in a system of multi-level governance. As Richard Cornes has astutely observed: 'cases will inevitably arise in which there are a range of issues, with devolution matters intermingled with other areas of law. The proposed bifurcation at the apex of the UK court system may lead to a division and a lack of coherence in the case law'.[55] The courts figure, too, in the provision for post-assent judicial review that allows a legal challenge to any legislative Act before the ordinary courts, and ultimately before the Judicial Committee of the Privy Council. Arrangements for Wales mirror those described above, the courts, with the Judicial Committee of the Privy Council as the final arbiter, having the power to review the Assembly's exercise of appropriate competence.

Other adjudication and conciliation procedures similar to those adopted in federal or quasi-federal systems will be required if the present arrangements falter.

Such procedures include intergovernmental conferences and heads of government, ministerial or senior officials' meetings, which may be instigated either as a regular channel of communication facilitating cooperation or as summits called to resolve particular crises and concordats and intergovernmental agreements[56] negotiated between the devolved institutions and central government departments and agencies.[57]

The 1998 Acts sought to deter any regional political interest minded to push the boundaries of its legislative/executive discretion beyond what is consistent with the putative national interest. This much implies a central veto power, though if such an interdict is ever exercised it will almost certainly be as a last resort and applied with due regard to regional sensibilities. Otherwise political crisis beckons. This is by no means a remote prospect, for the possibility does exist in these arrangements for ultra-nationalists, dissatisfied with 'constrained' devolution, to challenge still nebulous constitutional boundaries, especially so in Scotland where separatism has greater resonance.

Those bent on constitutional mayhem will be marginalised only if public opinion in general is comfortable with the present arrangements, and this is a situation that in turn depends less on formal vetoes exercised by the centre and much more on instilling common sense into intergovernmental relations. Balance is required between, on the one hand, satisfying valid demands for a meaningful exercise of self-government and, on the other, sustaining an abiding sense of a shared endeavour and common purpose. The equivalent must be found and embedded of what is widely understood elsewhere as a 'federalist culture': those habits of mutual tolerance and cooperation between levels of government indispensable to stable and effective power-sharing arrangements.[58]

Goodwill is a necessary but by no means sufficient resource for carrying this off. Experience elsewhere suggests that durable power-sharing arrangements depend, too, on embodying effective conciliation procedures in specific institutions. There is rather less guidance on this crucial matter in the legislation than there ought to be for ensuring stable intergovernmental relations. Clearly, further constitutional reform beckons, and especially so if intergovernmental relations become fraught with tension. In this, as in other matters, devolution presents a continuing challenge to the fitful art of British constitutional reform. But the prospects for calibrating the relations between the prospective authorities are by no means unpropitious. Nor will the occasional outbreak of intergovernmental friction remotely imply the impending break-up of the United Kingdom. On the contrary, the experience of federal and federalising polities elsewhere is that political tension between respective authorities can be a creative as much as a subversive force, encouraging the search for positive solutions to what might in more static polities seem crisis politics. The politically sensitive matter of delimiting and respecting the new bounds of legislative competences as between the parliaments is a matter that will surely be further tested as events unfold. But the situation requires the setting of judicial precedents appropriate to circumstances not particularly suitable for effecting manageable compromises, or for avoiding divisive and even destabilising zero-sum outcomes. This is a daunting challenge for British devolution, as it is for any polity based on power sharing between different levels of government.

Financial arrangements

A measure of financial autonomy is indispensable for meaningful devolution, whether revenue comes via direct fiscal transfers from the centre (as in Germany) or from fully fledged tax-raising powers (as in Canada and the United States). These are, of course, all examples of mature, fully federal systems with an entrenched culture of power sharing not yet remotely realised in Britain. The history of the financial arrangements for UK local government confirms wholly different norms about fiscal relations as between the central and subsidiary levels of government, reflecting the centre's marked reluctance to relinquish firm control over the public purse. Following the usual practice of unitary states, central government assumes responsibility for maintaining fiscal equilibrium, for balancing the books, and for cultivating a reputation for fiscal probity both with domestic taxpayers and in the international markets.

The excessive centralisation of decisions about financial disbursements was pointedly criticised in the Report of the Royal Commission on the Constitution, but without avail.[59] Whitehall's determination to maintain close control of the public purse has actually increased over recent decades. This will, in turn, make for strained post-devolution relations, and the future tenor of financial relations will certainly become a critical determinant of a smooth or otherwise problematic devolution.

Even so, fiscal relations are far from passive or one-sided in any intragovernmental arrangement. Sub-national government will always direct its political energies to the acquisition of adequate revenue, for the most part from the centre, in order to fund local services provision. This, in turn, tends to make for tense relations with central government. The Conservative government, for instance, introduced rate capping in the 1980s precisely to curb 'spendthrift' Labour councils that threatened its national goal of reduced public expenditure, and the incoming Labour government in 1997 barely relaxed these constraints. The same government was just as much exercised by the prospect of future non-Labour administrations in Edinburgh and Cardiff acquiring tax-raising powers to fund social expenditure programmes in the devolved areas that would pose a threat to national financial prudence.

The fiscal arrangements of the union state did acknowledge what might be called the 'territorial dividend', a level of fiscal support from the centre for Wales, Scotland and Northern Ireland disproportionate to their share of public expenditure, and calculated solely on the basis of population. This differential was based on acknowledgement by the centre of specific patterns of territorial economic development and similar variations in the distribution of social exclusion. This calculus reflected a concept of territorial 'need' broadly subscribed to after 1945 by both major political parties, and indeed by the Treasury.[60]

Despite a marked shift in the ideological firmament of British politics during the 1980s, both major parties continued to broadly endorse this system for allocating public expenditure, though by now for quite different reasons. The Labour Party remains wedded, by and large, to its social democratic commitment to universal standards of social provision throughout Britain, whereas the Conservatives' recent flirtation with neo-liberal ideas of political economy has persuaded them of the need for both stronger financial discipline and retrenchment of public expenditure. These latter objectives are more likely to be delivered if central government retains a firm handle on fiscal mechanisms. The advocates of neo-liberal ideas saw British territorial government outside of England as led by a profligate, welfare-dependent socialist establishment, and as bastions of obsolescent social democracy.

The formula for disbursing public moneys to the territorial authorities remains, in its principal rationale under devolution, what it was before 1998. The Barnett formula was the fiscal device negotiated in 1978 as a prelude to the earlier devolution proposal, and based, in turn, on a long-standing fiscal compensatory mechanism for the three non-English constituents of the Union. The Barnett formula calculates public expenditure levels (both increases and reductions) for Scotland, Wales and England to take proper account of territorial needs. The idea behind the formula was to introduce a more or less objective calculus so as to minimise a politically delicate, or otherwise unseemly, annual round of wrangling over respective territorial funding levels. The formula has been modified as to its emphasis though not its outcome, from an internal fiscal mechanism to one that regulates the transfer of public moneys between different tiers of government.[61] On the face of it, the revised formula looks to be an appropriate mechanism for devolution, a variant of fiscal federalism designed for an objectively negotiated disbursement of public moneys from the centre to the territorial authorities.[62] Whether this is still the most appropriate or flexible fiscal formula for current devolution is, however, questionable.

The allocation system works as follows. Resources are dispensed from central revenues after lobbying and negotiation between regional representatives and central government, on the basis of a calculus of social need. The formula was premised on the idea that fiscal requirements in Wales and Scotland are determined according to the concept of need. This concept reflected the poorer communications, dispersed populations, greater levels of social exclusion as manifested by key social indicators such as higher concentrations of public housing and welfare needs, and lower health standards in the 'other' constituent nations than in England. Any alteration here automatically triggers a change, whether an increase or decrease, for the other territories. Realists, however, were always aware that this formula was also a compensatory device, and as such one devised to bolster territorial support for the Union.

Rather than these 'needs' being assessed according to territorial criteria per se, as they tend to be in federal or even in federalising polities, the formula was calculated as territorial block grants according to an agreed ratio calculated on the basis of population. The levels of territorial public expenditure are measured against the benchmark of public expenditure levels for England. This ratio was initially 85:10:5. The revised ratios are now 85.7:9.14:5.16. Wales duly received 5.88 per cent, subsequently revised to 6.02 per cent, with Northern Ireland's share rising to 2.87 per cent. When Northern Ireland was included in the formula its ratio came out at 2.75. Scotland received a fixed proportion, assessed at 11.76 per cent of any increase/decrease in public expenditure, and reduced in 1992 to 10.66 per cent to reflect population reduction on the basis of evidence gathered in the 1991 census.

That politics as much as any objective definition of 'need' was a prominent motive for this compensation mechanism was quite apparent from the very inequity built into the arrangement. Scotland, for instance, where nationalism was always deemed to be a threat to the Union's political equilibrium, was allotted more public expenditure per capita under Barnett than Wales, though by any objective assessment of need Wales was the poorer country. This inbuilt subsidy, and all that it entails for a union state dominated by England, is now vulnerable to demands for recalculation, especially so in the case of Scotland as a direct consequence of the inclusion in the 1998 legislation of a tax-raising power that was expressly precluded from the 1978 scheme. Moreover, change in the ratio of block grants will now be rather easier to negotiate after the government addressed the charge of inflexibility, introducing annual revisions to reflect changing circumstances, though only after full consultations with the territorial authorities.[63]

Other sources of friction over financial relations beckon. Policy preferences in the territorial administrations that differ markedly from those of central government, especially where higher levels of disbursements occur, increase the prospects for political backlash in England. Moreover, 'the more expenditure patterns come to differ from those in England, the more arbitrary the formula may appear, and the more incentive there will be for the devolved administrations to press for alterations in the formula on the ground that the different pattern of expenditure justifies more money. Thus, the formula approach seems to contradict the very purpose of devolution.'[64]

Some commentators have pointed out that it is more consistent with the spirit of devolution to permit territorial governments, now directly accountable for these decisions to their territorial electorates, greater scope to raise their own revenue directly from territorial taxation. Further, this revenue base could be supplemented by allocating each territorial government a proportion of reserved central government revenues and with some transfer of central moneys calculated on the equalisation of the provision of services principle. Another possible solution, and one consistent not just with fiscal federalism but also with the coordinate arrangements associated with federal political culture, would be an arrangement whereby Scotland purchases or 'buys into' central services, making a pro rata payment to the centre for the armed services, diplomatic representation and so on. That these novel fiscal options were never seriously contemplated let alone adopted in the recent devolution arrangements says much about the residual centralism of British government and reflects an official mindset that is still absorbed by the idea of consolidated central government.[65]

Change there has been, however, and certainly with more to follow. The Report of the Commission on the Constitution anticipated problems with the block grant system of financing devolution, recommending instead 'a more flexible system which, whilst retaining the block grant idea, would include a fairly sensitive measurement of marginal needs, probably every year'.[66] The Treasury, too, in anticipation of devolution, undertook a needs assessment survey in the mid-1970s that indicated rather different ratios required for convergence, but the Barnett formula was never adjusted to take account of them.[67] The formula was left intact for political reasons, to avoid the political ructions of reducing the size of the Scottish ratio consequent on declining population. Devolution will, however, make English public opinion rather more sensitive, less tolerant of its comparative disadvantage, putting this discretionary formula and the convergence reasoning that drives it under even greater political scrutiny.

There is no guarantee, certainly nothing in law, to prevent a shift in these block allocations that penalises the devolved authorities. Politics may induce due caution from the centre in these matters but it may just as easily work to the disadvantage of the new authorities, with many English MPs critical of a ratio of public expenditure to population that gives Scotland and Wales a 20 per cent advantage over England. The demand from English interests for a more equitable public expenditure ratio may worsen the climate of relations. English taxpayers may already be much less receptive to a public expenditure ratio that facilitates a 25 per cent per capita spend in Scotland over England once 'justified' as the necessary price to be paid for the unionist principle of equitable provision of state services throughout the realm. It seems likely that eventually – and perhaps sooner rather than later should the Scottish Parliament use its tax-raising power – the House of Commons select committee on the Treasury will review the current territorial arrangements for public expenditure, and this notwithstanding the Chancellor Gordon Brown's assertion that the Treasury alone has the prerogative to alter these territorial expenditure ratios.

There is certainly a rational case made, beyond mere rancour or envy, for reassessing expenditure allocations in the light of changing demographics. However, this matter cannot easily be separated from politics, and with the government promising greater openness about expenditure allocations under devolution there is increased scope for discord between the putative winners and losers. On one side of the argument there are many English MPs from all parties, and even some senior ministers, who support a thoroughgoing review of the Barnett arrangement. On the other side are the separatists, and even those who are content with a degree of territorial autonomy, who will readily seize on any reduction of central funding as a calculated act of political spite. For its part, nationalist opinion rejects as patronising and as plain falsehood the very suggestion of an English net subsidy to Scotland, citing distorted Treasury statistics and making the counter-claim that Scotland more than pays its way.[68] Friction may result, too, from central government taking devolution to what some there might see as its logical conclusion. For instance, the Board of Trade has already challenged the privileged status of the Development Agencies in Wales and Scotland, one of the few devolved economic functions, insisting that their bids to attract inward investment must conform to Treasury guidelines. It has demanded a 'level playing field' for English regions faced with similar levels of unemployment and economic hardship and social exclusion.

The devolution debate has certainly highlighted the stark issue of comparative advantage and disadvantage in public expenditure, giving some poorer English regions cause to complain about what they perceive to be relative deprivation. As one commentator sees this situation: 'In the eighteen years prior to 1979, Scotland and Wales seemed to have gained considerably in terms of relative public expenditure per head. The formula was intended to help secure territorial justice by preventing further relative gains on the part of Scotland and Wales, and indeed by producing convergence in levels of funding per head.'[69] This is clearly not the perception in some parts of England, and for the formula to work as intended requires balancing two equally volatile values: on one side, the rate of growth of English public expenditure, and on the other the stability of UK population relativity. A falling population in Scotland has precluded convergence in levels of public funding.

The secretaries of state remain the principal paymasters of the devolved administrations, disbursing a block grant from funds agreed between territorial executives/parliaments and London. This arrangement confirms London as still holding the purse strings, thereby wielding a crucial veto on territorial spending projections. This, too, might become a source of future friction between the centre and the territorial governments. Lobbying by both secretaries of state during the Cabinet's annual fiscal round looks set to continue as standard practice, and there is scope for the territorial executives/parliaments to canvass their special needs. The determination of British ministers to defend their departmental interests from Treasury retrenchment in the reserved policy areas and against mobilised territorial interests again makes for an uncertain fiscal future.

Less transparent is the mechanism for distributing funds. The annual deal negotiated between the Welsh and Scottish secretaries and the rest of the Cabinet remains an opaque procedure. Devolution elsewhere tends to be more transparent with regard to fiscal matters than appears to be the case in the United Kingdom. For instance, a formula for direct and clearly recorded fiscal transfers from the centre operates in Germany, and there is altogether more scope in constitutional law for publicly accounted local tax raising in Canada, the United States and Belgium. The question of fiscal discretion is central to the very idea of democratic and accountable governance. The fiscal arrangements accompanying devolution 'divorce the power to raise money from the power to spend it. That these two powers should be in the same hands has long been thought of as a fundamental tenet of responsible government . . . In Scotland and Wales, with the responsibilities separated, the danger will always be that the Scottish and Welsh executives claim credit for improvements in services while blaming their problems on the parsimony of London.'[70] The potential in these arrangements for political turmoil is moderated somewhat by the fact that Labour is the principal governing party both at Westminster and in the territorial executives. When this situation alters we might anticipate greater political turbulence.[71]

The same implied threat attends the question of territorial taxation. The legislation is explicit about territorial tax-raising competence. A tax-varying power of up to three pence in the pound in the basic rate of income tax is permitted to Scotland, incorporating the suggestion made by the Scottish Convention, though this prerogative is denied to Wales. It is frequently pointed out that, lacking any degree of revenue-raising power, the Welsh Assembly is even more disadvantaged than a parish council. The top-up provision even for Scotland accounts for only a very modest amount of revenue, thereby ensuring that, to all intents, the Scottish Parliament and Executive will continue to rely for public finance on the centre. It is far from clear how Westminster would react should this power be used.

Additional sources of potential revenue are available both to the Scottish Parliament and to the Welsh National Assembly. The two territorial bodies may keep back for their own purposes central funds allocated to local government. The block funds allocated to the devolved bodies include the revenue support grants intended for local government. In the case of Scotland, this amounts to over £5 billion, approximating to some 40 per cent of the central allocation. Restoring to local authorities the right to levy the uniform business rate might persuade the territorial authorities to reduce the amount they allocate to the local tier, increasing territorial revenue but also promoting friction between territorial governments and their local authorities. For this would then require local authorities to make up the shortfall in order to protect services by enacting politically unpopular increases in the rate of the council tax or the non-domestic rate. As local government is a devolved matter, it is entirely at the discretion of the territorial authorities whether, or indeed how much of, this grant they pass on. The Scotland Act requires, and indeed political common sense suggests, that these fiscal decisions compel proper consultation with the local authorities.

There are even more contentious constraints on fiscal discretion, for central government remains responsible for ensuring macro-economic discipline. In the event of inflation in territorial public expenditure threatening national fiscal targets, jeopardising the overall management of the UK economy (indisputably a reserved matter), there is little doubt that London will intervene directly. The White Paper *Scotland's Government* promised, or more to the point threatened, as much, clearly stating that: 'Should self-financed expenditure start to rise steeply . . . if growth relative to England were excessive and were such as to threaten targets of the United Kingdom economy . . . it would be open to the United Kingdom government to take the excess into account in considering the level of their support for expenditure in Scotland.'[72]

The arrangements reviewed above have each contributed to an unprecedented shift in the locus of political power, though it is only the passage of time – and with it accommodation to these new procedures, indeed widespread adjustment to new political norms – that will determine the success or otherwise of devolution. The same conditional conclusion equally applies to complementary changes in the government of Northern Ireland and the quest to ensure that 'normal' democratic politics are properly embedded there. The general view of devolution some four years into these new arrangements for governance is that the British state and polity, its various stakeholders at every level, have adjusted well to unprecedented changes, without any real tribulations let alone crises, though, as reviewed below, the situation in Ulster continues to give cause for concern. As one leading commentator sees it:

There have been no disasters, no major rows between governments, no public standoffs of the kind which many had feared. There have of course been disagreements, but these have mostly been dealt with behind the scenes. The formal machinery for resolving disputes has yet to be tested: the joint ministerial committee has not been convened in dispute resolution mode, and the mood in Whitehall is one of quiet satisfaction at a job well done.[73]

This is a remarkable outcome to unprecedented constitutional change, but it can only be an interim verdict. It is one, too, that is the direct outcome of fortuitous circumstances unlikely to be a permanent feature of the new British politics. New Labour's electoral dominance, its hold on politics both at the centre and in the two principal territorial polities, together with the Labour government's loosening of the public purse strings in those policy domains with particular appeal to Scottish and Welsh voters, all help to explain becalmed devolution. What will happen to this relative quietude once Labour's electoral fortunes decline is another matter entirely. It is only when political strains test the process *in extremis* that the pliancy of the new arrangements, the efficacy of the conciliation procedures and the resilience of the public mood at every level to find a way through impasse, will be properly tested. As Robert Hazell has aptly observed: 'And when these things happen, and when the devolved governments become more self-confident and more self-conscious of their own powers, then we can say that the devolved governments will have come of age.'[74]

NORTHERN IRELAND: RESOLVING AN ANCIENT QUARREL?

The Stormont Agreement (April 1998) made between the warring factions in Northern Ireland, sponsored by the governments in Dublin and London and mediated by Washington, promised new beginnings in a society riven by sectarianism and ravaged by civil war. The accord established a Northern Ireland Assembly (108 members) elected by STV from six constituencies and exercising both legislative and executive authority for wide-ranging competences devolved from the Northern Ireland Office to six Northern Ireland government departments. Power sharing, to ensure equitable access by all citizens to civil and social rights and the benefices of public policy regardless of religious affiliation, is the crux of this arrangement.[75] It provides for devolved non-sectarian government in Northern Ireland, and installs cross-border bodies that bring an all-Ireland dimension into the management of public policy.

The Executive is constituted on the same power-sharing principle. Unlike the 1973 procedure, a first and deputy first minister elected jointly by the Assembly, and thereby possessed of authority firmly based on cross-community support, preside together over the Executive. Candidates for ministerial office make a pledge of office affirming commitment to peaceful and democratic politics, abjuring discrimination in the exercise of their public office. In effect, the principle of parity of esteem now replaces institutionalised sectarianism as the basis of self-government. This marks a remarkable shift in the foundations of governance, measured against the benchmark of tradition here. Decisional procedures, too, have a consociational logic previously unheard of in this deeply divided society. They rely on qualified majority voting so that critical decisions (for instance, election of the chief ministers and the Assembly chair, as well as budget allocations, and setting up Standing Orders) are inclusive of both communities.[76] There is provision, too, for operating similarly 'weighted' votes on other matters, should Assembly members petition for them.

Government resides in a multi-party, inter-community power-sharing Executive of twelve ministers, so constituted as to be 'inclusive' of interests on both sides. The administration is headed by a first and a deputy first minister, one from each community and with commensurate status and co-equal powers. In contrast to the 1973 proposal, the Executive is not the creature of the secretary of state; nor, as in the 1982 proposal, is it dependent on the Assembly – or at least, not in quite the same way. At its inaugural meeting after a Provincial general election, Assembly members must register a declaration of their political identity.

The special majorities arrangement is a classic *proportz* mechanism similar to those used in other culturally divided or socially pillarised (*verzuillen*) societies: a requirement for passing measures, either by *parallel consent* – an Assembly majority of all members voting but also requiring a majority of both communities – or by *weighted* majority requiring 60 per cent of the Assembly members present at a vote, with a minimum 40 per cent of representatives of the two communities both present and voting. Decisions are reached by one of these two majoritarian formulae requiring support from both communities as designated in that initial declaration of political identity.

This is devolution in the same asymmetrical spirit as the devolution now refashioning relations between the centre and the United Kingdom's other territorial polities, although the outcome of a wholly different politics. The new Assembly has devolved competences in finance, human resources, economic development, social services and the environment, though unlike the new Scottish Parliament it has no tax-raising powers. The means for resolving any dispute over the legitimate exercise or definition of these devolved powers is the same as in the other devolved arrangements: ministerial reference of the disputed matter for adjudication to the Judicial Committee of the Privy Council. There is provision, too, for increasing the devolved competences – to include police and justice affairs, always a politically delicate matter in such a deeply divided community – should local opinion concur, and subject to formal agreement with London.

Remarkable, too, are the arrangements in the Agreement for mitigating political divisions enshrined in the 1921 Treaty. Cross-border bodies will enhance the 'Irish dimension' of public policy making on both sides of the border. A North–South Ministerial Council is designed to cement cooperation between authorities in 'both' Irelands that are already promoted by European integration. A British–Irish Council (or Council of the Isles) will, likewise, encourage mutuality as an antidote to separatist tendencies in mainland Britain. Participation in this 'islands forum' by every territorial component of Great Britain – Ulster, Wales, Scotland, the UK and Irish governments, and eventually too the English regions and lesser islands, the Channel Islands and Isle of Man – is designed to enhance mutuality and a willingness to foster common regional interests.[77]

These devolved arrangements were the subject of historic twin referenda, held concurrently in both parts of Ireland. Ulster's voters were asked whether they favoured power sharing, and the Republic's electorate whether they would authorise changes to the 1947 Constitution (Articles 2 and 3), relinquishing Dublin's territorial claims to sovereignty over the six counties. Some 94.39 per cent endorsed the changes[78] in the Republic, whilst in Ulster the vote was 71 per cent to 29 per cent in favour in an electorate where Protestants still outnumber Catholics by some 58 to 42 per cent. The results of the Assembly elections that followed within the month provided rather more conclusive evidence of change, both of the old sectarian fault-lines and in the prospects for an entirely new politics. The combined tally of seats won by the mainstream pro-Agreement parties (52 of 108), with those of like-minded parties (the Alliance, the Progressive Unionist Party, the Women's Coalition and Sinn Féin), ensured a working majority for power sharing (80 seats) in line with the parallel majority principle. Anti-Agreement parties – the Democratic Unionist Party, UK Unionists and independent unionists – won only 28 seats.

Nevertheless, some Ulster Unionist Party members continue to resist their party's official line, and the potential for reversing the present balance of power remained only a vote of confidence away. Sinn Féin, too, has been no more reliable as a 'partner for peace', stubbornly resisting meaningful and transparent decommissioning of its armoury, although the movement's unprecedented apology to victims of Republican terrorism did indicate surer foundations, both for communal reconciliation and for democratic stability. Nevertheless, some four years on, political normality is by no means either restored or assured. A complicated parliamentary arithmetic, and the prospect of legislative ambushes from militants in the Assembly less amenable to compromise, continue to threaten the Province with an uncertain future.[79]

The partition of Ireland persists in these new arrangements, as do abiding communal differences within the Province. Nevertheless, these momentous developments do at least indicate greater willingness amongst those of moderate disposition to address, and perhaps finally to resolve, an ancient quarrel that has long blighted Irish politics and social development. A majority on both sides now recognise the right of Ulster's people to determine their own political future by the democratic principle of consent.[80] After the Northern Ireland parliament was first suspended in 1972 the guarantee included in the Ireland Act 1949, to the effect that Northern Ireland would not be excluded from the United Kingdom without the consent of its parliament, was reformulated. Accordingly, the Northern Ireland Constitution Act 1973 recognised the consent principle through the democratic medium of 'the majority of the people of Northern Ireland voting in a poll', to be held periodically.[81] A constitutional guarantee in the 1998 Stormont Agreement now allows for periodic plebiscites every seven years or so to determine whether or not there is majority support for reunion with the Republic. Institutionalised sectarianism in Ulster is now set aside in favour of power sharing and non-discriminatory access to public goods, although the present impasse over arms decommissioning and occasional outbursts of political violence serve to underline the scale of the challenge to be faced if the recent peace is to become permanent.

The Belfast Agreement has not conclusively settled the 'Irish Question', but in one way it has at least normalised the debate about – if not quite the practice of – political relations between this semi-detached Province and the rest of the United Kingdom. Above all, it has relocated a unique and once problematic issue firmly within the mainstream debate about the structure of territorial governance in these islands. There is a curious kind of historical déjà vu about this novel arrangement. As one leading authority on British constitutional affairs has observed:

> The Agreement has a double significance for the government of the United Kingdom since it proposes not only a solution to the Irish problem, but also a recognition of the process of devolution to the non-English parts of the United Kingdom. It offers, in essence, a return to the original Gladstonian conception of Home Rule in a form suited to modern conditions . . . a chance of realising the underlying theme of Gladstonian thinking – recognition both of the various and distinctive national identities within these islands, but also of the close and complex links between them.[82]

Whether this is indeed a genuine opportunity for peace or merely a brief interlude in an otherwise intractable struggle is difficult to say at present. The historic bargain of 1998 is by no means a secure one, with periodic outbreaks of political turbulence and occasional violence. From one perspective, there seem to be some ominous signs. The Republicans have postponed rather than abandoned their historical goal of reunifying Ireland. Less gloomy is the fact of Sinn Féin's condemnation of continuing violence by Republican splinter groups that seems to confirm that organisation's commitment to the peace process. Four years and more after the Stormont Agreement was signed, and despite periodic stalling in the peace process, it has so far managed to resist the efforts of diehard opponents to reverse it. Militant Protestants have likewise resisted the formal peace process, and paramilitary action, albeit on the fringes, means that Ulster has not yet seen an end to sectarian violence. Further communal strife may yet be triggered, and by any number of catalysts, in this still deeply divided and endemically mistrustful society.

Matters have deteriorated somewhat since the heady days of 1998, and at the time of writing these singular and historic arrangements are in temporary if indeterminate abeyance. Communal trust on both sides remains as tenuous as ever, with the pro-Agreement Unionists threatening to permanently collapse the process in the face of what they see, or choose to see, as Republican duplicity or worse. London has temporarily suspended the Executive, reintroducing direct rule from the centre. Optimists prefer to see this as inevitable wobble during a protracted period of inter-communal accommodation, whilst a wholly new devolution takes time to become assimilated by its prospective stakeholders on all sides, used to rather more partisan arrangements. Only time will tell whether the arrangement will stick, though prosperity and indeed wider currency for post-material values will have a significant influence on the outcome. Devolution and power sharing may well be the propitious answer to the problematic 'Irish Question', though more sceptical voices still see in these events an insidious and corrosive mistrust, an ominous lack of empathy for shared objectives without which devolution is mere chimera and, as such, wholly unworkable.

The logistics of power sharing between parties with so little in common certainly adds its own pressures. Coalition politics may be an art best practised in less polarised polities, but it is required here more than ever if reconciliation is to endure and devolution is to work for the common good.[83] There is, however, amidst the gloom that is normal reaction to these dismal politics, some limited cause for optimism. The recent novelty of living without fear of endemic violence in the streets has already brought its own rich rewards; and that has been coupled with material incentives – inward investment, infrastructure development and jobs – capable of defusing the corrosive resentment that fuels sectarianism. The peace process is still in its infancy and those who are its tribunes in both camps must strive resolutely to isolate the extremists, to avoid the witch-hunts and recriminations that have dogged 'peace and reconciliation' initiatives in other fractured societies. A majority on both sides is at least aware, however grudgingly, that the Province had to make this historic choice between peaceful co-existence and the abyss.[84] The coming decades will be critical for determining the future trajectory of politics in this much-troubled province.

Constitutional engineering is at the heart of this project, as it is of less agonised but no less novel experiments with devolution elsewhere in the United Kingdom. The belief is now more widely shared than ever before that the provident management of public affairs by moderate people of mutual good faith holds the key to balancing what might otherwise become a culturally exclusive politics with zero-sum outcomes. The model adopted here mirrors, in some important respects, the devolution arrangements for Scotland, though these are tailored here to meet Ulster's special territorial requirements, where deep-rooted communities still contest the very meaning of 'Irish identity' and continue to dispute amongst themselves the nature of the preferred link with the Union.[85] A recent commentary has summarised the prospect for these new political arrangements as follows:

> Northern Ireland will above all be a test case for bi-nationalism. On the one hand it may see the reconstruction of 'Britishness'. The reformed Ulster Unionist Party may build a more inclusive conception of British identity and break decisively from the Orange supremacism of the past – an identification that the British of Great Britain no longer understand or care for. On the other hand the new institutions unequivocally endorse the equality and parity of esteem of both national and political traditions in Northern Ireland and the island of Ireland as a whole. If they work, they will accommodate both equality and diversity in a pattern that may yet find imitators at home and abroad.[86]

This summation is both a measure of the scale of the task facing this divided society, but it is no less a testament to how far it has travelled, and in a relatively short time, towards political normality.

NOTES

1. Evidence cited in S. Heffer, *Nor Shall My Sword: The Reinvention of England* (1999) p.1
2. These calculations were made by the Centre for Economic and Business Research and published in *Scotland on Sunday*, 25 April 1999
3. R. Weight, *Patriots: National Identity in Britain 1940–2000* (2002) p.699
4. J. Osmond, *Welsh Politics in the New Millennium* (1999)
5. V. Bogdanor, *Devolution in the United Kingdom* (2001) p.179

6. *Scotland's Parliament*, Cmnd 3658 (1997)

7. *A Voice for Wales*, Cmnd 3718 (1997)

8. *Financial Times*, 23 July 1997

9. Cmnd 5460 (1973) para. 1100

10. V. Bogdanor, op. cit. (2001) pp.255–6

11. Ibid., pp.259–60

12. Cmnd 5460 (1973) para. 282

13. V. Bogdanor, op. cit. (2001) pp.262–3

14. Plaid Cymru, *Towards Full National Status: Stages on the Journey* (2000)

15. See R. Cornes, Intergovernmental Relations in a Devolved UK: Making Devolution Work, in R. Hazell (ed.), *Constitutional Futures: A History of the Next Ten Years* (1999)

16. R. Hazell, Intergovernmental Relations: Whitehall Rules OK?, in R. Hazell (ed.), *The State and the Nations: The First Year of Devolution in the United Kingdom* (2000)

17. HLD, vol. 592, col. 1488, 28 July 1998

18. *Memorandum of Understanding and Supplementary Agreements on the Joint Committee*, Cmnd 4444 (1999)

19. J. Poirier, The Functions of Post-devolution Concordats in a Comparative Perspective, *Public Law* (Spring 2001)

20. R. Parry and A. Jones, The Transition from the Scottish Office to the Scottish Executive, *Public Policy and Administration* 15 (2000)

21. R. Russel, The Territorial Role of the Upper House, *Journal of Legislation Studies* (2001)

22. R. Hazell, Introduction: The First Year of Devolution, in R. Hazell (ed.), op. cit. (2000) pp.9–12

23. V. Bogdanor, op. cit. (2001) p.220

24. Ibid., pp.223–4

25. Ibid., pp.226–7

26. Jonathan Freedland, *The Guardian*, 8 September 1997

27. *The Guardian*, 23 July 1997

28. G. Leicester, Scotland, in R. Hazell, op. cit. (2000) at pp.16–23

29. Ibid., pp.25–6

30. See, for instance, *Putting Wales First: A Partnership for the People of Wales. The First Partnership Agreement of the National Assembly of Wales*, 6 October 2000; see also J. Osmond, *Coalition Politics Comes to Wales: Monitoring the National Assembly, September to December 2000* (2001)

31. B. Kerremans, Determining a European policy in a Multi-level Setting: The Case of Specialized Co-ordination in Belgium, *Regional and Federal Studies* 10 (2000)

32. R. Hazell, op. cit. (2000) at pp.171–5

33. J. Osmond, A Constitutional Convention by Other Means, in R. Hazell (ed.), op. cit. (2000) pp.55–8

34. Cmnd 5460 (1973) para. 1111

35. House of Commons Debates, 5th series, vol. 936, col. 316, 26 July 1977

36. J. Kendle, Conclusion to *Federal Britain – A History* (1997)

37. R. Borthwick, When the Short Cut may be a Blind Alley: The Standing Committee on Regional Affairs, *Parliamentary Affairs* 38 (1978)
38. See *The Procedural Consequences of Devolution*, Procedure Committee Fourth Report of Session 1998–99, HCD 185, 19 May 1999, especially at para. 27
39. N. MacCormick, The English Constitution, the British State and the Scottish Assembly, *Scottish Affairs: Understanding Constitutional Change* (1998) p.131
40. Cmnd 5460 (1973) para. 815
41. I. McLean, The Representation of Scotland and Wales in the House of Commons, *Political Quarterly* 66 (1995)
42. R. Cowley and M. Stuart, Parliament: A Few Headaches and a Dose of Modernisation, *Parliamentary Affairs* 54 (2001)
43. *The Scotsman*, 19 December 1997
44. *Scotland's Parliament*, Cmnd 3658 (1997) para. 4.12
45. *The Scotsman*, 19 December 1997; A. Page and A. Batey, Scotland's Other Parliament: Westminster Legislation about Devolved Matters in Scotland since Devolution, *Public Law* (2002)
46. M. Laffin, A. Thomas and A. Webb, Intergovernmental Relations after Devolution: The National Assembly for Wales, *Political Quarterly* 71 (2000); see also, *Memorandum of Understanding between the United Kingdom Government, Scottish Ministers, the Cabinet of the National Assembly for Wales and the Northern Ireland Executive*, Cmnd 4806 (2000)
47. R. Hazell and B. Morris, Machinery of Government: Whitehall, in R. Hazell (ed.), op. cit. (1999) p.137
48. *Memorandum of Understanding*, Cmnd 4444 (1999) p.1
49. Ibid., p.7 para. 22
50. R. Hazell, Introduction: The Dynamism of Devolution in the Third Year, in R. Hazell, *The State of the Nations 2003* (2003) p.7
51. S. Bulmer, M. Burch, C. Carter and A. Scott, *European Policy-making under Devolution: Britain's New Multi-level Governance* (European Policy Research Unit working paper 1/01, Department of Government, Manchester, 2001)
52. L. Hunter, *Managing Conflict after Devolution: A Toolkit for Civil Servants* (Constitution Unit UCL and Governance of Scotland Forum, Edinburgh, 2001)
53. A. O'Neill, Judicial Politics and the Judicial Committee of the Privy Council, *Modern Law Review* 64 (2001)
54. V. Bogdanor, op. cit. (2001) p.206
55. R. Cornes, op. cit. (1999)
56. J. Poirier, op. cit. (2001)
57. R. Rawlings, Concordats of the Constitution, *Law Quarterly Review* 116 (2000)
58. See M. O'Neill, Belgium: Language, Ethnicity and Nationality, *Parliamentary Affairs* 53 (2000)
59. Cmnd 5460 (1973) para. 659
60. A. Midwinter, Territorial Resource Allocation in the UK: A Rejoinder on Needs Assessment, *Regional Studies* 36 (2002)

61. D. Heald and N. Geaughan, The Fiscal Arrangements for Devolution, in J. McCarthy and D. Newlands (eds), *Devolution in the United Kingdom* (1999)

62. J. Kellas, The Scottish and Welsh Offices as Territorial Managers, *Regional and Federal Studies* 8 (1998) p.96

63. HCD, 6th series, vol. 302, Written Answers, col. 513 9

64. V. Bogdanor, op. cit. (2001) p.251

65. I. McLean, A Fiscal Constitution for the UK, in S. Chen and T. Wright (eds), *The English Question* (2000)

66. Cmnd 5460 (1973) para. 7.27

67. HM Treasury, *Needs Assessment Study Report* (1979)

68. A. Midwinter, Why Replacing Barnett would be a Mistake, *New Economy* 7 (2000)

69. V. Bogdanor, op. cit. (2001) p.244

70. Ibid., pp.241–2

71. D. Heald and A. McLeod, Beyond Barnett? Financing Devolution, in J. Adams and P. Robinson (eds), *Devolution in Practice: Public Policy Differences in the United Kingdom* (London: Institute for Public Policy Research, 2002)

72. Cmnd 3658 (1997) para. 7.27

73. R. Hazell, Conclusion, op. cit. (2003) p.300

74. Ibid., p.301

75. *The Belfast Agreement*, Command 3883, para. 1(v), 1(vi)

76. B. O'Leary, *The British–Irish Agreement: Power-sharing Plus* (London: The Constitution Unit, 1998); and R. Wilford and R. Wilson, *A Democratic Design? The Political Style of the Northern Ireland Assembly* (London: The Constitution Unit, 2001)

77. *The British–Irish Council: Nordic Lessons for the Council of the Isles* (London: The Constitution Unit, 1998)

78. M. O'Neill, 'Appointment with History': The Referenda on the Stormont Peace Agreement, May 1998, *West European Politics* 22 (1999)

79. R. Wilford and R. Wilson, A 'Bare Knuckle Ride': Northern Ireland, in R. Hazell (ed.), op. cit. (2000) pp.112–15

80. *The Belfast Agreement*, Command 3883, para. 1(v), 1(vi); R. McGinty and R. Wilford, Consenting Adults: The Principle of Consent and Northern Ireland's Constitutional Future, *Government and Opposition* (2002)

81. Section 1 The Northern Ireland Constitution Act (1973)

82. V. Bogdanor, op. cit. (2001) at p.109

83. R. Wilson and R. Wilford, Northern Ireland: End Game, in A. Trench (ed.), *The State of the Nations 2001: The Second Year of Devolution in the United Kingdom* (2001) at p.104

84. J. Murray Brown, Past Tense, Future Hopeful, *Financial Times*, 25 May 1998

85. R. Wilford and R. Wilson, *A Democratic Design*, op. cit. (2001)

86. R. Hazell and B. O'Leary, A Rolling Programme of Devolution: Slippery Slope or Safeguard of the Union? in R. Hazell (ed.), op. cit. (1999)

8 Intra-party relationships of British state-wide political parties within the developing territorial agenda

David Baker

Constitutionally, devolution is a mere delegation of power from a superior political body to an inferior. Politically, however, devolution places a powerful weapon in the hands of the Scots and the Welsh; and, just as one cannot be sure that a weapon will always be used only for the specified purposes for which it may have been intended, so also one cannot predict the use which the Scots and the Welsh will make of devolution. (Vernon Bogdanor, *Devolution*, 1999)

This is a politics of one-party dominance, old boy networks and cronyism . . . Changing Scotland involves more than a few policy initiatives and endless bouts of consultation: it involves developing a vision, values and narrative of what devolution is meant to be. A radical devolution would challenge vested interests in Scotland – in the quangos, local government and business. It would offer leadership and take risks. (Gerry Hassan, *The Guardian*, 8 November 2001)

INTRODUCTION

The focus of this chapter is on the internal politics and intra-party relations of the British 'state-wide'[1] parties caused by the emergent territorial agenda, with particular attention paid to how these parties have responded (or not, as the case may be) to the fact of devolution since 1997. The chapter reviews the prospects for a new type of internal party politics created since devolution and looks in particular at the likelihood of an erosion of the dominance of the familiar centralised party organisations, of tensions between national and territorial parties, and of possible frictions between the political centre and the sub-national peripheries.

In his classic study *British Political Parties*, researched in the 1950s, Robert McKenzie was dismissive of the policy-making role of the regional branches of the Conservative and Labour parties, viewing them as principally local administrative structures under the policy direction of central party organisations, and until recently this remained the conventional wisdom of British political science. But radical constitutional adjustments, such as devolution, although in essence 'structural' in character, have traditionally been seen leading to spillover effects in elite political culture and electoral behaviour which open the way for a 'new politics'. However, as McAllister has wisely pointed out: 'significant changes in governance initiated through devolution do not naturally and inevitably instigate alterations in the way parties, politicians or the electorate behave'.[2]

The study of political parties has centred on a number of influential models of party organisation – 'mass', 'catch-all', 'professional-electoral' and 'cartel' parties, and their sub-categories of 'business-firm' and 'democratic cadre' parties.[3] All suggest that sophisticated and complex populist mass parties are capable of continually adapting to meet new challenges in their socio-political and institutional environments. In particular, the cartel party model of Katz and Mair suggests that parties are able to manipulate their environment and defend themselves against pressures for change, with party organisational structures developing in a dialectical process, as parties continually adapt to the changing contours of the political and institutional systems in which they are embedded.[4]

If true, this ability to adapt has never been more essential for the UK political parties than in the present rapidly evolving contexts of devolution, decentralisation, multi-level governance, elected mayors, new electoral systems and changing intra- and inter-party relationships. As a result, the homogeneity and discipline of British state-wide political parties appears problematical as never before, and as devolution develops, the structure and interrelationship of such parties and their regional offshoots may well be radically altered. The extent to which non-nationalist offshoot parties in Wales, Scotland and the EU are insisting on greater autonomy in Wales, Scotland and Brussels, is clearly an issue. In one sense we have been here before, as there has been a tension between the European parliamentary wings of national parties and their state-based host parties across Europe – most particularly in the United Kingdom.[5]

Whether British state-wide parties have ceded new freedoms to their devolved counterparts in Scotland and Wales, or have retained traditional controls, is a litmus test of the devolution settlement in practice. Thus, as McGarvey rightly suggests, 'new research [on Scottish politics] must also examine the role of the national UK parties and their own internal psychological and organisational responses to devolution . . . The role of political parties as a potential inhibiting factor in the devolution process is crucial'.[6]

In addition, knowledge of the extent to which power in the offshoot parties is still largely located amongst traditional elites, or shared more widely with other local elements, would indicate whether devolution has brought about a more participatory and open 'new politics' as envisaged and sought by the pro-devolution lobby. If the latter scenario proves correct, Tony Blair's well-documented (and largely successful) attempts to tighten central control over his party may yet be undermined by the more decentralised, pluralistic and fragmented party system developing at the 'periphery' of the British state. Post-devolution Scotland and Wales have already witnessed early evidence of distinctive patterns of politics emerging, with the nationalist parties providing the main opposition to Labour rather than the Conservatives or Liberal Democrats and coalition government being the norm. It therefore appears that an opportunity exists to break the mould, or at least loosen the grip, of monolithic, Westminster-based, state-wide parties and to reflect a more diverse multi-level 'new' politics, based on localised and structurally confederalised parties.

Experience (for instance Mrs Thatcher's shareholding and 'property owning democracy' privatisations) tells us that political parties can influence social change as well as alter the political institutions and electoral arrangements under which they operate, and are not, therefore, helpless victims of their given environment. And in line with this, Blair's tinkering with the constitution for pragmatic and electoral reasons, is leading to some interesting outcomes – although not necessarily those anticipated or sought.[7]

The adoption of various mixed PR (proportional representation) systems for elections to the Scottish Parliament, the Welsh and Northern Ireland Assemblies, and the London mayoral and European Parliament contests, means that Westminster's first-past-the-post system is now the exception to the rule. Should this system migrate to the Westminster parliament, the ramifications would represent a considerable leap in the dark for the main parties and involve two possible scenarios according to Sanders. One is largely 'benign' with the emergence of a range of new parties representing ethnic and religious cleavages and/or urban/rural ones, while the basic state-wide British identity will remain as the bedrock of party politics, with state-wide parties retaining their 'inclusive, national appeal', while minority interests are enhanced. In the 'malign' scenario, a range of exclusive 'identity' parties would merge to focus on whites-only English nationalism, Islamic and Asian fundamentalism and Afro-Caribbean separatism, thus politicising the ethnic and religious cleavage of Britain's multi-cultural society and opening the way to dangerously right-wing and ultra-nationalist impulses.[8]

The practice of devolved government is already starting to promise uncertain outcomes for UK state-wide parties, creating minority rule in Wales and coalition government in Scotland (now also in Wales), and the PR voting system also gave incentives to disillusioned minorities to break away (at least in regional elections) and openly support nationalist parties. This fragmentation of the electorate and old party systems has seen other parties gaining representation at the expense of Conservative and Labour in both Scottish Parliament and Welsh Assembly elections and also in the London Assembly and European Parliament ballots. All is not well at Westminster either, with successive 'landslide' election victories for New Labour gained on proportions and numbers of votes that would have embarrassed party leaders only a generation before.[9] Yet state-wide parties continue to remain the core organs of democratic choice and elite recruitment across mainland UK.

In their work on the determinants of partisan alignment, Lipset and Rokkan[10] identified three major 'cleavages' which traditionally divide modern western societies and produce group alignments and coalitions expressed, at one level, as political parties. Two of those factors – religion and social class – are in agreed long-term decline.[11] This is in good part due to an increasingly 'dealigned' electorate, voting on the basis of contemporary and instrumental issues, rather than the old party-based 'partisan alignments', a process partly caused by creeping embourgeoisement of society and the associated spread of individualistic values. In the case of Scotland and Wales, however, dealignment appears also to have reflected Lipset and Rokkan's third cleavage, namely core–periphery divisions, as all parties have made, or been forced to make, increasingly direct appeals around issues of national identity.[12]

This is a considerable change from the uniformity and homogeneity of the party and electoral systems from the 1950s through to the early 1980s where, typically, three-quarters of all Scottish and Welsh seats were within 2 per cent of the national median swing between the two leading parties.[13] In this context, the major parties were truly state-wide, contesting elections across the whole of the United Kingdom on more or less the same ticket. And in spite of the emergence of the Scottish National Party (SNP) as a force in Scotland, the majority of votes remained cast for 'British' issues. Moreover, with no significant division around core–periphery cleavages, state-wide parties had no need (or wish) to mobilise support around such issues.[14]

However, once the SNP succeeded in placing constitutional change on the agenda of Scottish electoral politics in the early 1970s, the other 'Scottish' parties were compelled to respond, basing their appeals partly along lines of national identity. Fragmentation of the electorate thereafter increased, and in both the 1992 and 1997 general election campaigns the 'constitutional card' was played by all parties in Scotland and Wales and again in the elections for the Scottish Parliament and Welsh Assembly held under PR, where Labour and the Liberal Democrats variously campaigned for watered-down versions of home rule, and the Conservatives campaigned on a traditional unionist platform – at great electoral cost. The message from the electorate was simple: only those parties able to portray themselves as 'Scottish' could prosper in Scotland after 1991. Nor was there any doubt as to the fact that this counted in the minds of electors, as Table 8.1 demonstrates.

The greatest loser was the Conservative Party which, after a hundred years of unparalleled success as a party of consummate state-wide statecraft,[15] appeared to be losing its remaining toe-hold in the sub-regions as voters in Scotland and Wales shifted their identification with class and party towards 'consumer' calculation and regional (including anti-English) identities.[16]

However, there is a complex relationship between regional identity and issue voting at work, as the 1997 referendum on devolution in Scotland demonstrated, with relatively high levels of instrumental voting for anticipated benefits in welfare and the local political economy, rather than brute nationalist sentiment.[17] Nevertheless, the rise in regional identity has been associated with increased support for regional parties at the ballot box, but the full implications of this remain unclear and under-researched.[18]

Devolution has clearly raised the profiles of the SNP and Plaid Cymru, a factor enhanced by the chosen PR electoral systems which have reinforced the impact of

Table 8.1 The institution with most influence over the way Scotland is run

	1999	2000	Should have[a]
Scottish Parliament	41	13	72
UK government at Westminster	39	66	13
Local councils in Scotland	8	10	10
European Union	4	4	1

Source: Scottish Social Attitudes, 1999 and 2000 ([a]data based on 2000 survey), and David McCrone, Scottish Civic Forum, http://www.civicforum.org.uk/projects/auditproject/audit_report_appendix_four.htm

regional identity on the electoral preferences of the new regional identifiers. In response, all the state-wide parties have tried hard to distance their regional hybrid parties from the national parties in order to attract votes. So far, the state-wide parties have not been particularly successful, as regional identities continue to benefit the SNP and Plaid Cymru disproportionately. The strategy now is to develop sufficient regional 'brand differentiation' to reclaim votes from the SNP and Plaid, by adopting relatively minor variations on national manifestos – but these differences are becoming more marked.

On most issues, a large degree of overlap exists between voters' attitudes and motivations across mainland Britain. The main difference is that both the Scots and the Welsh are slightly (and perhaps increasingly) to the left of the English – a fact reflected in the social welfare and education legislation passed by the Scottish Parliament in its first term. In most respects, though, English, Welsh and Scottish electors still share similar views. This, in turn, implies that the competition amongst parties for their votes will not be completely different across the United Kingdom (Northern Ireland excepted). As a result, nationalist parties such as the SNP and Plaid Cymru must continue to create a broad policy base that appeals beyond regional identifiers in order to succeed. But devolution has already played a significant role in changing the voting intentions of some, since 'loyal' state-wide Labour and Tory voters in both Wales and Scotland have been willing to switch votes directly to Plaid and the SNP, calculating that their interests in Wales and Scotland will be better protected by the nationalist parties. These moves render this phenomenon much more than simply a vague and temporary protest vote against the 'English'-based parties.[19]

CHANGING STATE-WIDE LABOUR PARTY ORGANISATION

Under old Labour, intra-party democracy rested on bargaining between the leadership, Conference, the National Executive Committee (NEC) and the unions, a particularly slow and cumbersome form of decision making and insider horse-trading.[20] After 1992, Tony Blair campaigned to 'democratise' the party, and in 1996 the draft election manifesto was approved by balloting individual party members. The Annual Conference was by-passed and a plebiscitary style of leadership was instigated in which the framework was set and policies decided by the leader group, and party members offered a simple yes/no vote. Thus, Blair and his inner coterie paradoxically achieved greater autonomy and centralised power through this process of 'democratisation'.[21]

This process has since been reinforced by Blair's exceptionally high personal ratings and the party's two landslide election victories in 1997 and 2001. Blair also strengthened his press office and created a Strategic Communications Unit and an Intelligence and Research Unit in 10 Downing Street, employing groups of advisers to deal bilaterally with individual cabinet ministers and their officials. The emphasis on 'on-message' loyalty amongst MPs was reinforced by a new 'code of conduct' which included penalties for openly criticising the leadership.

But the intra-party spillover of the devolution process in Scotland and Wales threatened to disrupt this smooth centralisation of power. The party list system of proportional representation was used to reward loyalists and punish dissenters in selection for parliamentary and Assembly elections in Scotland, Wales and also in the European elections.[22] In Scotland, a number of sitting MPs and activists failed to be selected as Labour candidates or to rank high enough on the party list to be elected to the Scottish Parliament. In Wales, the leadership intervened to support Alun Michael over Rhodri Morgan in the contest to choose the leader of the Welsh Labour Party; it intervened again in favour of Frank Dobson over Ken Livingstone in the run-up to the London mayoral election in May 2000.

Thus, Blair has repeatedly used the votes of members over those of more critical activists to achieve his top-down and centralising ends. Some authorities have characterised this as a Napoleonic style of government.[23] New Labour's 'modernisation' has also 'professionalised' the party, changing it from an activist-orientated party of traditional social democratic doctrine and ethos, to an aggressive vote-maximising party of the centre-right.[24]

CHANGING CONSERVATIVE AND LIBERAL DEMOCRAT STATE-WIDE PARTY ORGANISATION

In the aftermath of the catastrophic 1997 election defeat, William Hague made radical changes to the Conservative Party's structure, creating for the first time a single mass party by merging the Parliamentary Party with the National Union (and its formerly autonomous constituency associations) and also the party bureaucracy in Central Office. The newly created mass membership was also given a direct say in the ballot electing the party leader, ending the MPs' monopoly. This allowed the party leader the same plebiscitarian ability to appeal directly to the party members in a ballot as Blair enjoyed and was used for the first time in 1998 to approve the new constitution and endorse Hague's tough line on staying out of the single European currency for the foreseeable future.

The Liberal Democrats inherited the highly decentralised federal organisation from the old Liberals and little has changed in this structure in recent years. In both Scotland and Wales they operate a fairly autonomous form of institutional organisation, with state-wide issues fed down from Westminster. By UK standards the Liberal Democrats are a relatively democratic party internally. Their federal structure has allowed the creation and maintenance of distinct parties in England, Scotland and Wales within an overall federal structure, but it has not guaranteed their identification with the political cultures of either Scotland or Wales, hence the offshoot Liberal Democrat parties' post-devolution struggles to be identified as sufficiently Scottish or Welsh.[25]

THE DISCIPLINES OF THE 'NEW POLITICS'

Originally associated with the rise of environmentalism and later regionalism and globalisation,[26] 'new politics' was a term frequently employed by political commentators to describe elements of Blair's first administration. Today, devolution is seen as a testbed for new politics in the United Kingdom.[27] Three elements of devolution have become associated with the creation of the new politics: the creation of new institutions, of new processes/procedures, and of a new political culture.[28]

The most comprehensive study of the new politics in Scotland was based on the results of a survey of candidates in the 1999 Scottish Parliament elections, alongside comparator surveys of candidates in Scottish local government elections and of the whole Scottish electorate, all undertaken at the time of these elections. Of special interest is the discussion of the possible emergence of a 'new' type of politician – more likely to be female, and not necessarily politically experienced, who would emerge with fresh ideas, unencumbered by the old politics.[29]

In 1999, 37 per cent of all members of the new Scottish Parliament were women and Scottish Labour's balance of the sexes was perfect, with 28 men and 28 women, largely the result of twinning constituencies (only 18 per cent UK MPs were women in 1997). Although ministerial positions did not reflect this sex profile, the input into the Scottish Parliament by women remains potentially considerable and provides an important example of the scope for a new politics emerging from the devolution process.[30] Nevertheless, a considerable degree of continuity exists with the old politics. Most new MSPs were career politicians from within their parties who had already been election candidates; in many cases they were former elected representatives, usually at the local level. They were also overwhelmingly middle class and university-educated. Twenty-three of the 56 also emerged from local government backgrounds: 15 were former council leaders (10 on the Labour benches). Labour MSPs were also the youngest, with an average age of 43 years (Westminster Labour MPs average 49 years).

As Hassan has clearly demonstrated, Scottish Labour remains a party of 'many paradoxes' with its own identity, history, culture and politics.[31] Thus, whilst its degree of autonomy may have been formally and informally circumscribed, the need to fight and win votes in Scotland against the SNP, combined with the useful distance from London (and not just in miles), has led to a distinctively Scottish identity which emerges in the widely held belief that Scottish Labour is the national party of Scotland. During the long Thatcher/Major years, Scottish Labour occupied the mantle of a quasi-establishment party, merging elements of the local state and civil society by dominating Scottish local government at all levels and using this platform to wage a defensive guerrilla war against the 'Tartan Tory' Scottish Office. As Hassan asserts, this one-party dominance allowed Scottish Labour's values and goals to become those of the local state and wider civil society. But he argues that, whilst in the process the party became bureaucratised and dominated by pragmatic (largely male) career politicians, this was never a New Labour marketised and incentivised pragmatism, since old Labour was never defeated electorally in Scotland.[32]

To take just one example of continuity with the old practices, ethnic minority members remain conspicuous by their absence amongst both candidates and MSPs. Continuity was also reflected in the occupants of the first Scottish Executive (nine Scottish Labour ministers, plus two Liberal Democrats), a pattern reproduced at junior ministerial levels. Together they comprised a mixture of experienced politicians with a Westminster and/or local government background (the so-called

Big Mac group), Henry McLeish, ex-Westminster, Jack McConnell and Tom McCabe ex-leaders of Stirling and South Lanarkshire Councils, and a smaller group with no experience of elected politics, including Wendy Alexander and Susan Deacon. Those tensions which emerged in the Executive did not follow an old/New Labour fault-line, but instead rested on disputes over implementing the new politics, as opposed to continuity with the old Scottish Labour 'socialist' and establishment culture of Edinburgh and Glasgow.[33] With the new politics of national identity complementing rather than supplanting old identities, it is clear that local allegiances, class and even religion remain necessary elements in understanding post-devolution Scottish politicians.

Assessment of the social backgrounds and career paths of MSPs relative to their counterparts at Westminster and wider Scottish society has revealed that, aside from the degree of male/female balance, Scottish representatives at Westminster were actually *more* representative of the Scottish population than their MSP colleagues. Traditional career paths were less important to them and Scottish MPs were more representative of ethnicity and the working class in Scotland than their MSP colleagues. Thus, as Bennie *et al.* have suggested, it appears that traditional Scottish political culture is set to linger on long after devolution.[34]

CHANGING PARTY ORGANISATION IN SCOTLAND: THE CLARK MODEL

Robert Michels was deeply pessimistic towards all forms of intra-party democracy which in his model always falls prey to a small oligarchic elite, a belief central to a number of influential models, including catch-all and electoral-professional parties.[35] In contradistinction to this, a valuable recent study of post-devolution Scottish politics has usefully adapted the notion of 'stratarchy' to explain the focus of power in Scotland's post-devolutionary parties.[36] The concept of party organisational 'stratarchy' posits that, under normal circumstances, no single elite can dominate a party. Rather, a plurality of relatively autonomous elites exists throughout its organisational structures, making the success of the party dependent on their support and cooperation. These elites include the voluntary organisations within the party in which ordinary members participate, with their own distinctive goal structures, campaigning to realise the common goals of the party.[37]

The model posits that local leaders are often better able to judge the political and electoral situation on the ground than the core party elite, creating an accommodation between different elites and 'downward deference' from the leadership to the party at large.[38] In short, in order to be successful, the beliefs and wishes of middle-ranking party strata must be taken into account by party leaders and compromises must be made on both sides to avoid a breakdown of this system of mutual dependence. In essence a pluralist model of intra-party relations, stratarchy exists whenever power is dispersed between various party strata. The key to this model is understanding the importance of *informal* influence and accepted mutual dependence between the core and periphery of party organisations.

Applying this to the post-devolution Scottish Labour Party (SLP), Clark questions the degree of influence the policy consultation process engaged in in Scotland gave to the lower echelons of the party in the crucial post-1998 Scottish Policy Forum. In spite of the local policy forums which took place amongst the Scottish leadership, 50 Constituency Labour Parties and various other branches and affiliate organisations, ministers and representatives of the Scottish Executive Committee appear to have dominated the process of drafting the policy documents, thereby undermining wider participation and debate.[39]

The Scottish parliamentary elections raised a number of issues about New Labour in Scotland. Firstly, the pre-selection process for candidates for the first Scottish parliamentary elections saw the party institute a central system for approving candidates to go on to a selection panel. The metropolitan party's centrally approved panel of candidates and 'twinning' of constituencies (ostensibly to achieve parity of the sexes) were also employed in the selection process. Applicants were then interviewed by a selections board appointed by the Scottish Executive Committee. In a repeat of the national party's actions before 1997, a number of nationalist-left candidates were not selected, in particular Dennis Canavan and two other sitting left-wing MPs, leading to allegations of fixing from London.

A survey of those selected through this process revealed that 27 per cent thought the panel process was undemocratic, as did 24 per cent of panel non-candidates (the 167 Labour applicants approved for the list by the panel but unsuccessful in the later round). Three-quarters of both groups felt the list selection process was undemocratic. In additon, whilst only 22 per cent of candidates thought the leadership had unduly influenced constituency selection, this figure climbed to 74 per cent over list selection. Furthermore, 25 per cent believed that the interview process had been neither fair nor democratic. Criticisms were also made of the board that selected candidates for regional lists, suggesting that the leadership placed its favoured candidates at the top of lists. A considerable majority felt this was both undemocratic and unfair. In addition, some constituencies openly accused London of using the 'twinning' process to prevent other locally preferred nationalist-left candidates from being selected.[40] Thus, Scottish Labour's selection processes have, it appears, reinforced its essentially clientist-oligarchic nature, with power residing primarily in the Scottish leadership in close association with London.[41] Nevertheless, Clark suggests that devolved Scottish Labour has displayed at least some stratarchic elements, by formally incorporating ordinary party members and their representatives into the policy process.

Hassan's study of the political sociology of Scottish Labour sees it as operating very much as a party within a party. The process of winning all Scottish elections since 1959 and achieving local dominance during the 1980s and 1990s underlined this sense of difference (even superiority) in relation to the Westminster party, opening up different strategies and self-images. In recent years this tendency has been reinforced by bitter electoral battles with the Scottish National Party and further fuelled by a belief that New Labour's marketised ethos and pseudo-communitarian doctrines were superfluous in the Scottish context. Another consequence was that the Scottish party managed the shift to a multi-party system far better than its English parent.[42]

Devolution also forced the party to devise a formal procedure to elect a Scottish leader, in the process revealing tensions between Holyrood and Westminster. Donald Dewar was elected Labour's first leader in September 1998 with a 99.8 per cent vote, and Henry McLeish – also London's candidate – became its second in October 2000, narrowly defeating the local candidate Jack McConnell by 44 votes to 36. McConnell was later elected Scottish Labour (Party) leader without an open contest after gaining 97.3 per cent of a mini electoral college vote.

The shift of policy-making power from the Scottish Annual Conference to the new Scottish Policy Forum also allowed greater centralisation and management of relations within the party in Scotland. This trend was further reinforced by the creation of the Scottish Parliament, where ministers, their advisers and parliamentary assistants, now shape most of the agenda and debates of the Forum.[43] Consequently, any emergent 'new politics' in the executive policy-making process appears to remain something of a pious hope, since Holyrood's top-down processes have been reinforced by experienced parliamentarians in the Scottish Executive facing a back-bench Labour group largely made up of relative political novices.

Hassan argues that this has given rise to an internal party political culture which is, at times, even less consultative than that of the Westminster party. Labour MSPs have often found themselves cut out of policy-making decisions by ministers on the Scottish Executive. Discussions have often been curtailed and there remains no formal channel for proper consultation between the Executive and main body of MSPs, all the more surprising given that this occurs within a much more intimate system than Westminster. As a result, and mirroring Westminster, a group of senior back-bench MSPs rapidly emerged, employing 'informal channels' in order to exert policy-making influence on the Executive, again mirroring Westminster.[44]

WESTMINSTER: A CONTINUING ROLE IN SCOTTISH LABOUR POLITICS

Unsurprisingly, Westminster has traditionally offered the main channel of political advancement of the Scottish Labour establishment, and past recruitment patterns of Scottish Labour reflected this state-wide ambition and career focus. The numbers of Scottish Labour MPs at Westminster has followed an ever-rising trend, peaking at 56 in 1997, and Blair's cabinets have contained a disproportionate number of Scottish ministers, most notably Lord Irvine, Robin Cook and Gordon Brown. Cutting this political umbilical is proving very problematic, with the initial intake of MSPs coming from Scottish local politics and the most ambitious Scottish Labour politicians still jostling for Westminster seats.

Devolution has also raised intra-party tensions over how MPs and MSPs work together over constituency matters. The different and yet overlapping political directions and priorities of Labour at Holyrood and Westminster have surfaced in concerns raised by some at Westminster about the calibre of Holyrood Labour MSPs. Some even fear that the national electorate could vote on the profligate and radical record of Labour MSPs.[45]

The hidden hand of the state-wide party was also in evidence during the election of a successor to the first minister and Scottish Labour leader Donald Dewar in October 2000. The victor, Henry McLeish (a Westminster MP since 1987), represented the Scottish state-wide Labour establishment, whereas the loser, Jack McConnell, ex-leader of Stirling Council, embraced a pro-autonomy, new politics agenda. After McLeish's dramatic fall from grace over alleged financial irregularities, the seemingly uncontested election of Jack McConnell in November 2001 was proceeded by the 'secret' withdrawal of another candidate, Wendy Alexander (new to politics and a 'new politics' moderniser, supported by Gordon Brown), apparently because Charles Clark, the English party chairman, intervened to ensure that the election would be held under one member, one vote procedures, so killing off her chances. Thus, as Hassan points out, the party 'missed both a historic opportunity to begin the process of democratising itself and the chance to hold a wider debate about the role and direction of the Labour-led Scottish Executive, which the party has so far not had'.[46]

Westminster's role in Scottish politics is, however, likely to change significantly in 2005 when the number of Scottish seats in the House of Commons falls to 59, causing sitting MPs to compete for one of the reduced number of safe seats. (There has been some controversy about reducing the number of MSPs at Holyrood too.) Devolution has also hollowed out Scottish Labour local government organisations, with a noticeable decline in the prominence and ability of councillors and organisers. This has been brought about by the more charismatic and experienced council leaders becoming MSPs, leaving behind them the bureaucratic party politicians. In that sense the focus of Scottish Labour has changed and the Parliament is the more important locus of ambition and power, with major long-term implications for Scottish Labour's internal ethos.

This change was reflected during the 1999 election campaign where there was a London-supported attempt to formally 'rebrand' the local party 'Scottish New Labour' with corporate colours and slogans. However, at the local level, most candidates fought an essentially 'old Labour' campaign, avoiding the agenda, symbols and priorities of New Labour. A survey of 52 of Labour's 73 constituency candidates found that just 17 per cent used the phrase 'New Labour' and 10 per cent 'Scottish New Labour' in their election materials, whilst 86 per cent used the more traditional 'Labour' and 58 per cent 'Scottish Labour'.[47] Hassan is one of the foremost critics of this continuation of old SLP culture:

> We . . . need to understand the strange creature that is Scottish Labour. It is different from the other parties in Scotland, and Labour elsewhere in the UK (but has similarities with Welsh Labour). The Scottish party has run Scotland, and large parts of it in particular, for so long that it sees no conflict between its interests and that of the state. Scottish Labour's organisational backbone is provided by a series of networks and financial arrangements between the party, unions, councils and the private sector.[48]

Nevertheless, the pattern of Scottish and UK politics looks unlikely to maintain such continuities, especially if Labour's present dominance in Scotland comes under threat and a non-Labour led administration becomes a distinct prospect. How Scottish Labour reacts to such a situation, and interacts with other parties, will play a crucial role in defining future intra-party relations.

SCOTTISH TORIES

The Conservatives have not performed well in the post-devolution Scottish environment. In particular, they remain electorally becalmed as the fourth party in Scotland with no meaningful influence on the direction of the devolved political system. Nor are the signs of a revival promising. In the wider tradition of the state-wide party, ordinary members of the Scottish Conservatives have little formal influence within the policy process of the Scottish Conservative Party (SCP). Scottish Conference decisions have only advisory status for the leadership. Prior to devolution, the secretary of state for Scotland was responsible for coordinating the writing of the Scottish manifesto, in consultation with the Scottish chairman and president. The Scottish Executive Committee was also assisted by advisory groups for different policy areas, all in consultation with government ministers, leaving the veto power in the hands of the state-wide party leadership. The current Tory Scottish leader, McLetchie, has been allowed to develop some policies tailored to Scottish conditions. This accounts for the Tories' endorsement of the abolition of student tuition fees and their support for free care for the elderly. Although the party's relatively poor showing in the 2001 general election appeared to weaken McLetchie's position to the point that the Tories' Scottish policy emphases throughout the first half of 2002 seemed to be being led by Iain Duncan Smith, subsequently the national leader's poor performances meant that the Scottish party was able to emphasise its own distinctive approach to policy. This marks a return to the Scottish party's traditional moderate unionism.[49]

Constituency parties have traditionally wielded power within the SCP. Traditionally, local activists were allowed to choose constituency candidates from a central shortlist, and as early as 1992 constituency associations had one member, one vote (OMOV) ballots for candidate selection. As a result, the nature of the Scottish party was at least partly decided at local level. These devolved arrangements were also adopted for the 1999 Scottish Parliament elections.[50]

But the central party acted decisively in candidate selection procedures in the run-up to these elections, where list rankings were adjudicated by an elite group from Smith Square, including the chair and deputy chair of the party. As a result, one-quarter of Conservative candidates polled afterwards considered leadership influence over list selection was too great, and 38 per cent thought that list selection had been to some extent undemocratic. Nevertheless, 97 per cent thought constituency selection was either quite, or very, democratic, whilst 62 per cent thought the same of list selection.[51] This controversy over candidate selection continued into 2003 with the Scottish parliamentary elections approaching and some unsuccessful aspirants claiming that they were being denied the right to challenge sitting MSPs for list seats, despite an earlier commitment by McLetchie to allow open competition for such placings. If true, this suggests that London still supervised the Scottish Conservative and Unionist Party's (SCUP's) recruitment agenda.[52]

However, the candidate selection procedures were changed at a special party conference/meeting in June 2002 where it was decided by 182 to 64 that instead of having only hustings meetings to select candidates, a system of OMOV postal ballots would be introduced for Constituency Party members to have their say. This was initially resisted by Central Office and a public debate on the issue was avoided at their May Conference. However, this appears to be a fairly significant democratising move for the Scottish party, and one which to some degree undermines the ability of London to supervise its recruitment agenda. Essentially, then, the Scottish party remains dependent upon the London leadership's goodwill for its freedom of manoeuvre and reaction to specifically Scottish circumstances. Mrs Thatcher caused huge problems for the Scottish party with the early imposition of the Community Charge in Scotland and subsequently John Major's principled opposition to devolution unleashed similar difficulties. And whilst Hague allowed the Scottish leadership policy-making room to manoeuvre during the first phase of devolution, Iain Duncan Smith is widely acknowledged to have reduced McLetchie's independence, partly because of the failure to revive the Tory vote in Scotland in the 2001 election and partly because the SCP's policies were seen as too left of centre for national party officials. However, Conservative policy remains in flux, with some signs of policy formation ebbing back towards the Scottish party and their moderate brand of unionism.

SCOTTISH LIBERAL DEMOCRATS

James Mitchell suggests that devolution has been very positive for the Scottish Liberal Democrats (SLD).[53] It has clearly boosted their political profile as part of a power-sharing parliamentary executive, and reinforced the importance of their decentralised systems of policy making.[54] Equally, however, they have had their problems, not least keeping their identity in coalition with Labour. On balance, though, it appears that devolution has done them some good, particularly since they have been able to claim that they have implemented 80 per cent of their 1999 manifesto. The party's grassroots and decentralised participatory policy-making process is inherently democratic across all levels and branches of the party. And whilst the state-wide party takes precedence on issues such as foreign policy, defence and budgetary matters, there is reciprocal Scottish representation on all Liberal Democrat federal policy-making bodies. Nevertheless, the Scottish Policy Committee (SPC) clearly remains the dominant player in formulating and promoting SLD policy. Thus, as with other regional offshoots of state-wide parties, Conference is largely confined to accepting, modifying or rejecting policy, seldom actually formulating it. However, in the state-wide Liberal Democrat tradition, Scottish Conferences are more robust than their Labour or Conservative equivalents, querying and even rejecting party policy on local issues such as candidate sex balance, taxation and environmental protection.[55]

Relative to its two state-wide offshoot rivals the SLDs also operate a more democratic set of candidate selection procedures. Of the 200 aspirants standing in 1999, only 15 per cent failed to be selected. Constituency parties shortlisted candidates and held hustings based on the OMOV system and list selection was similarly decentralised, with the main disagreement arising over the necessity of achieving balance of the sexes – a proposal rejected by Conference on general fairness grounds. Indeed, when polled afterwards, every candidate thought constituency selection had been democratic, whilst 95 per cent thought list selection had also been fair and open. Ninety-one per cent of constituency candidates and 85 per cent of list candidates also approved of the leadership's levels of influence in the process.[56]

Power within the party appears, in Clark's terms, 'stratarchically' organised, with no section of the party's various internal power blocs dominant, since not only is a process of accommodation necessary between formally empowered sections of the party, but the leadership in practice exercises a 'downward deference' to lower party strata, which is the result both of the party's participatory ethos and of its relatively high dependence on its membership for support over fundraising and volunteer election activities.

Although the Scottish Liberal Democrats claim notable policy successes, there is little doubt that the reality of jointly holding office with Scottish Labour since 1999 has had the effect of holding back some of the SLD's more radical policy proposals and reinforcing the power of senior parliamentarians. However, as the 2003 Scottish parliamentary election approached, pressures grew for the party to distance itself from Labour, particularly since Labour's initial enthusiasm for proportional representation in local government seemed to be dimming. On the other hand, the Liberal Democrats were also keen to run on their record in office, which has seen a number of popular policies in education and social welfare partly instigated and then steered through into Scottish law with their support.

THE STATE-WIDE PARTIES IN WALES

As in Scotland, opportunities have clearly been opened up in post-devolution Wales for new relationships to develop between the state-wide parties and their Welsh sub-parties. Welsh devolution has at least the potential to provide a catalyst towards the development of new forms of party politics, creating genuine shifts in the patterns of regional inter- and intra-party politics.

It is salutary to recall that the SLP's electoral dominance has never been as strong as its Welsh equivalent. The SLP has never secured a majority of the Scottish vote, whereas the Welsh Labour Party (WLP) has won over 50 per cent of the vote in eight out of sixteen postwar elections (although only once since 1974).[57] As in Scotland this, coupled with fierce competition with Welsh nationalism, has tended to create a self-confident, confrontational, male-dominated, ideologically left-of-centre, and South Wales based elite.

Following the creation of the National Assembly, with 60 elected Assembly Members (AMs) in May 1999, many commentators hoped for a new, less confrontational and 'modern' form of politics to emerge. And in contrast to Scotland, a seismic change did appear to be under way, as the two sets of elections held in Wales in 1999 saw an electoral upheaval with implications for both state-wide and linked regional parties. The first Assembly elections saw Welsh voters abandoning the local Labour Party in considerable numbers, and crossing directly to Plaid Cymru which, for the first time, transcended its traditional electoral heartlands in the north and west of the country. Neither the Conservatives, already wiped out in the election of May 1997, nor the Liberal Democrats made any significant headway either – a pattern repeated in the elections to the European Parliament a month later. What emerged from this initial sifting process was a minority Labour administration, cutting bilateral deals with whichever party or parties would support separate parts of its legislative programme.[58]

One of the major causes of this local desertion by New Labour state-wide supporters was that Welsh voters and politicians believed that Welsh Labour was a puppet of the state-wide party. A poll conducted for Harlech Television days before the elections showed that nearly two-thirds of those questioned believed this to be the case.[59] Labour also proceeded to further undermine Welsh public opinion's belief in the independence of the Welsh Labour Party through the London-imposed candidature of Alun Michael as the Welsh party leader. Much of the powerful and sustained local opposition to his candidature rested largely on the belief that he was a Blairite candidate parachuted in from London.

As in Scotland, the proportional representation system awarded extra candidate selection power to party elites, at both Cardiff and Westminster. In fact, the additional member system (AMS) gives precedence to the non-proportional voting method, with only one-third of Assembly Members elected by the fully proportional method. Regional list candidates also found it difficult to exert individual influence over their large constituencies. Finally, there was little chance of candidates from outside the main parties being elected to the relatively small number of seats in the 'open' part of the ballot because of the sheer quantity of votes necessary to meet the d'Hondt formula for redistribution of votes.[60]

Also as in Scotland, the nomination and selection of candidates lies at the heart of the internal power structure of all Welsh parties, influencing the ideological ethos and future direction of the local parties and making it a highly contentious arena. From the outset, many local politicians of all parties were determined that their parties should attempt to choose candidates who faithfully reflected the wider Welsh population, with sex, ethnicity and disability key areas for improvement. Welsh political parties, even more than their Westminster counterparts, were traditionally top-down, male-dominated and adversarial. The fact that the first Assembly executive contained five women out of nine members appeared to have delivered part of this remit, but old-style Welsh politics remained much in evidence in the 'new democracy'.

As in Scotland, candidate selection in the immediate pre- and post-devolution eras proved a constant source of tension in relations between Westminster and Welsh Labour. An approved list of Labour's Assembly candidates was published in August 1998 after a rigorous interview procedure. Almost immediately, a further set of names was added after threats of appeal were made by several omitted from the original list, ostensibly because of their refusal to stay 'on message' on the limited devolution package being offered, and their continued demands for greater internal devolution from the state-wide party.

As far as the balance sheet is concerned, after four years in devolved government, the process of political and administrative devolution in Wales has yet to be matched with an internal devolution of authority and control to the Welsh party. The party's policy-making framework remains resolutely under the control of the state-wide hierarchy, handicapping it from developing distinctive policies which reflect the priorities of Wales, rather than the United Kingdom as a whole.

This has also allowed Plaid Cymru to plausibly occupy the electoral territory of 'the party of Wales', which accounts for the movement of voter preferences between Labour and Plaid. But in the run-up to the 2003 Assembly elections there were clear signs of a change under electoral pressures. It is becoming clear that both the Scottish and Welsh Labour parties now operate electorally well to the left of their state-wide host parties. Reflecting this, Labour's leader Rhodri Morgan sought to place 'clear red water' between Cardiff and London by fielding a Welsh Labour manifesto which included the abolition of prescription charges, free homecare for the elderly, free admission to swimming pools for children and the elderly, free breakfasts for primary school pupils and no top-up fees for Welsh universities.[61]

This same process has led to the marginalisation of the other two major state-wide parties in Wales. Like Labour, both have failed to create a credible and positive Welsh identity for their regional parties. And both have also suffered further from the voters' identification of Plaid Cymru as Labour's main challenger. In addition, despite the Liberal Democrats' independent Welsh structures, they possess no high-profile Welsh leaders who can compete with those from other parties, so that once Labour had rejected a coalition, the depth of the Welsh Liberal Democrats' problems became clear: finishing fourth to the Conservatives (who had no Westminster seats in Wales), they were marginalised within the new Assembly.

CONCLUSION

This brief survey study of post-devolution intra-party relationships in the three state-wide political parties underlines the truth of Ron Davies's opinion that devolution needs to be seen more as a dynamic 'process' than as a static 'event' – and the important point is that this process has hardly begun. It would be unrealistic to expect significant changes to occur during the immediate transitional period from the old system to the new, especially in parties which already had well-developed regionalised offshoots with a degree of local identity and self-government but still linked to powerful state-wide party elites. In short, one needs to be cautious and to stress the dynamic nature of all this in a continually changing environment.

Prior to devolution, Peter Lynch plausibly argued that 'the new devolved institutions of government will not merely alter centre–regional relations between Westminster/Whitehall and Scottish and Welsh parliaments, but they will also alter existing centre–regional relations within political parties in a number of ways'.[62] And Sanders is clearly correct to suggest that 'regional identity will continue to exert significant effects on voters' party preferences'.[63] Because of this, the future direction of Scottish and Welsh politics for the three state-wide parties depends, in good part, on the success or failure of the regional branch parties to differentiate themselves in both image and policy terms from their 'English' Labour, Conservative and Liberal Democrat host parties.

Clark claims that Scottish Labour and Liberal Democrats can now be seen as largely autonomous, in the case of Scottish Labour a recent development begun by McLeish (with his anxiety not to be seen as London's 'poodle' and consequent shift of emphasis on to such issues as free care for the elderly), but in essence coinciding with McConnell's accession to the Scottish leadership.[64] The degree of autonomy enjoyed by Scottish Conservatives has always varied according to the tolerance and whim of the national party leadership. Anecdotal evidence suggests that the party's continuing poor performance in the 2001 general election and the general drift rightwards in the 'English' party is eroding the SCP's policy-making and candidate selection autonomy. Also, as Clark points out, since the state-wide parties have retained ultimate control of party finances, their Scottish and Welsh offshoots remain circumscribed in deciding on appointments and in crucial elements of electoral strategy.[65] However, recent fundraising difficulties have left British Labour unwilling to fund the 2003 Scottish election campaign, with clear implications for the independence of Scottish Labour in the future.[66]

The answers to all these questions will not become apparent until long after the dust on the 2003 elections has settled, and new and more detailed empirical research has been carried out into the Scottish and Welsh offshoot parties. But it is surely not unreasonable to suggest that the dynamic nature of devolution will see further intra-party organisational evolution and adaptation in the second period of Scottish and Welsh devolved government. Moreover, in this process the success, or failure, of the state-wide parties in their head-to-head competitions with the local nationalist parties will be crucial. What is almost certain is that, under such electoral pressures and out of self-interest, both the Scottish and Welsh client parties will continue (for a variety of reasons) to seek greater organisational and policy-making autonomy from their host parties. And this will not cease until, as Sanders suggests, the devolution process 'stabilises', either through full independence or through a general acceptance that the devolution process need develop no further.[67]

NOTES

The author would like to express his special appreciation to Alastair Clark for reading and commenting in detail on an earlier draft of this chapter.

1. The term 'state-wide' will be employed to describe the Westminster-based Labour, Conservative and Liberal Democratic parties, to distinguish them both from their regional offshoots (Scottish Labour etc.) and from the regional nationalist parties (Plaid Cymru, the Scottish National Party etc.).
2. L. McAllister, Changing the Landscape? The Wider Political Lessons from Recent Election in Wales, *Political Quarterly* 71(2) (2000) p.591
3. O. Kirchheimer, The Transformation of the Western European Party Systems, in J. LaPalombara and M. Weiner (eds), *Political Parties and Political Development* (Princeton, NJ: Princeton University Press, 1966); A. Panebianco, *Political Parties: Organisation and Power* (Cambridge: Cambridge University Press, 1988); R. Katz and P. Mair, Changing Models of Party Organisation and Party Democracy: The Emergence of the Cartel Party, *Party Politics* 1(1) (1995) pp.5–28; J. Hopkin and C. Paolucci, The Business Firm Model of Party Organisation: Cases from Spain and Italy, *European Journal of Political Research* 35(1999) pp.307–39; A. Krouwel, The Catch-all Party in Western Europe 1945–1990: A Study in Arrested Development (PhD thesis, Vrije Universiteit Amsterdam, 1999).

4. R.S. Katz and P. Mair, op. cit. (1995)

5. P.J. Pappamikail, Britain Viewed from Europe, in D. Baker and D. Seawright (eds), *Britain For and Against Europe: British Politics and the Question of European Integration* (Oxford: Clarendon Press, 1998); P. Mair, The Limited Impact of Europe on National Party Systems, *West European Politics* 23(4) (2000) pp.27–51

6. N. McGarvey, New Scottish Politics, New Texts Required, *British Journal of Politics and International Relations*, 3(3) (2001) pp.431–2

7. S. Driver and L. Martell, *Blair's Britain, 2002* (London: Palgrave, 2002), pp.179–81

8. D. Sanders, Electoral Competition in Contemporary Britain, in C. Hay (ed.), *British Politics Today* (Cambridge: Polity Press, 2002) p.93

9. A. Geddes and J. Tonge (eds), *Labour's Landslide* (Manchester: Manchester University Press, 1997)

10. S.M. Lipset and J. Rokkan, *Party Systems and Voter Alignments: Cross National Perspectives* (London: Macmillan, 1967)

11. D. Seawright and J. Curtice, The Decline of Scottish Conservative and Unionist Party: Religion, Ideology or Economics?, *Contemporary Record* 9(2) (1995)

12. A. Brown, D. McCrone, L. Paterson and P. Surridge, The Scottish Electorate and the Scottish Parliament, *Scottish Affairs*, Special Issue: Understanding Constitutional Change (1998)

13. I. Crewe, Great Britain, in I. Crewe and D. Denver (eds), *Electoral Change in Western Democracies: Patterns and Sources of Electoral Volatility* (London: Croom Helm, 1985) pp.101–4

14. I. McAllister and R. Rose, *Voters Begin to Choose: From Closed Class to Open Elections in Britain* (London, 1985)

15. J. Bulpitt, The Discipline of the New Democracy: Mrs Thatcher's Domestic Statecraft, *Political Studies* 34(1) (1986)

16. D. Sanders, op. cit. (2002) p.86

17. P. Surridge *et al.*, op. cit. (1998)

18. D. Sanders, op. cit. (2002). See also the excellent special issue of *Party Politics*, 'Party Democracy and Direct Democracy' (5(3), 1999) edited by Susan Scarrow, for several important articles on the theory and evolving practice of intra-party democracy in Europe and North America. The volume promotes the belief that neither direct democracy nor intra-party democracy automatically undermines the importance of parties as is sometimes suggested in the literature.

19. Ibid., 2002, pp.98–9

20. L. Minkin, *The Labour Party Conference* (London: Allan Lane, 1978)

21. R. Heffernan and J. Stanyer, The Enhancement of Leadership Power: The Labour Party and the Impact of Political Communication, in C. Pattie *et al.* (eds), *British Elections and Parties Year Book*, Vol. 7 (London: Cassell, 1998)

22. D. Baker, D. Wring and D. Seawright, Panelism in Action: The Outcomes of Labour's New Selection Methods for the 1999 European Elections, *Political Quarterly* 71(2) (2000)

23. D. Kavanagh and A. Seldon, *The Powers behind the Prime Minister* (London: HarperCollins, 1999); P. Hennessy, *The Blair Centre: A Question of Command and Control* (London: Public Management Foundation, 1999)

24. H.M. Drucker, *Doctrine and Ethos in the Labour Party* (London: George Allen & Unwin, 1979); A. Panebianco, op. cit. (1988)

25. P. Lynch, Third Party Politics in a Four Party System: The Liberal Democrats in Scotland, *Scottish Affairs* 22 (1998); idem, Partnership, Pluralism and Party Identity: The Liberal Democrats after Devolution, in G. Hassan and C. Warhurst (eds), *Tomorrow's Scotland* (London: Lawrence & Wishart, 2002)

26. See R. Inglehart, *The Silent Revolution: Changing Values and Political Styles Among Western Publics* (Princeton, NJ: Princeton UP, 1977); idem, Values, Ideology and Cognitive Mobilization in New Social Movements, in R.J. Dalton and M. Kuechler (eds), *Challenging the Political Order* (Cambridge: Polity Press, 1990); C. Offe, New Social Movements: Changing Boundaries of the Political, *Social Research* 52 (1985) pp.817–69

27. S. Fielding, A New Politics?, in P. Dunleavy *et al.* (eds), *Developments in British Politics* (Basingstoke: Palgrave, 2002) pp.10–28

28. J. Mitchell, New Parliament, New Politics in Scotland?, *Parliamentary Affairs* (2000)

29. J. Bennie *et al.*, Harbingers of New Politics? The Characteristics and Attitudes of Candidates in the Scottish Parliament Elections 1999, in J. Tonge *et al.* (eds), *British Elections and Parties Review*, Vol. 11 (London: Cass, 2001)

30. A. Brown, Taking Their Place in the New House: Women and the Scottish Parliament, *Scottish Affairs* 28 (1999) p.48

31. G. Hassan (2002) A Case Study of Scottish Labour: Devolution and the Politics of Multi-level Governance, *Political Quarterly* 73(2) (2002)

32. Ibid.

33. Ibid.

34. J. Bennie *et al.*, *How Scotland Votes: Scottish Parties and Elections* (Manchester: Manchester University Press, 1997) pp.11–13; J. Bennie, op. cit. (2001) p.20

35. R. Michels, *Political Parties: A Sociological Study of the Oligarchical Tendencies of Modern Democracy* (New York: Dover Publications, 1959); J. Brand, *British Parliamentary Parties: Policy and Power* (Oxford: Clarendon Press, 1992)

36. A. Clark, The Location of Power in Scotland's Post-devolution Political Parties: An Exploratory Analysis, paper presented at the PSA Annual Conference, University of Aberdeen, 5–7 April 2002

37. S.J. Eldersveld, *Political Parties: A Behavioural Analysis* (Chicago: Rand McNally, 1964); J. May, Opinion Structure of Political Parties: The Special Law of Curvilinear Disparity, *Political Studies* 21(2) (1973)

38. A. Clark, op. cit. (2002) p.4

39. Ibid. (2002) pp.4–5; P. Seyd, New Parties/New Politics? A Case Study of the British Labour Party, *Party Politics* 5(3) (1999) pp.392–4; G. Hassan, The Paradoxes of Scottish Labour: Devolution, Change and Conservatism, in Hassan and Warhurst (eds), op. cit. (2002) p.32

40. J. Bradbury, J. Mitchell, L. Bennie and D. Denver, Candidate Selection, Devolution and Modernisation: The Selection of Labour Party Candidates for the 1999 Scottish Parliament and Welsh Assembly Elections, in P. Cowley, D. Denver, A. Russell and L. Harrison (eds), *British Elections and Parties Review*, vol. 10 (London: Frank Cass, 2000) pp.156–61 and 166.

41. See R. Levy, Nationalist Parties in Scotland and Wales, in L. Robins, H. Blackmore and R. Pyper (eds), *Britain's Changing Party System* (London: 1994) p.156

42. G. Hassan, A Case Study of Scottish Labour (2002) p.145

43. Ibid., p.148

44. Ibid., pp.150–2

45. T. Brown, Responsibility without Power, *New Statesman*, 12 June 2000

46. G. Hassan, The Paradoxes of Scottish Labour (2002) p.52

47. Ibid., pp.153–4

48. G. Hassan, Scotland the Brave, *The Guardian*, 22 March 2001

49. L. Bennie and A. Clark, Scotland's Post-devolution Party System, paper presented to EPOP Annual Conference, University of Salford, 13–15 September 2002; B. Agasoster, Party Cohesion and Local Agendas: A Study of Variations in Local Campaign Strategies in Scotland, PhD thesis, University of Aberdeen (2001) p.136

50. J. Bradbury *et al.*, op. cit. (2000) pp.2–3 and 12

51. Ibid., pp.20–1

52. D. Fraser, McLetchie Accused of Sitting MSP 'Stitch-Up', *Sunday Herald*, 12 August 2001; D. Seawright, The Lesser Spotted Tory, in Hassan and Warhurst (eds), op. cit. (2002)

53. J. Mitchell, Political Parties, in *Nations and Regions: The Dynamics of Devolution Quarterly Report* (The Constitution Unit, February 2002) p.43

54. Whilst the regional party in Scotland has its own constitution and the organisational structure of the party mirrors the national Liberal Democrat power and policy-making structures, best represented as 'a balance of power between five elements: the party leader, the parliamentary party, the Federal Policy Committee (FPC) and its policy working groups, the Federal Conference Committee (FCC) and the Federal Conference'. D. Brack, Liberal Democrat Policy, in D. MacIver (ed.), *The Liberal Democrats* (Hemel Hempstead: Harvester Wheatsheaf/Prentice Hall, 1996) p.97

55. P. Lynch, op. cit. (1998); idem, *Scottish Government and Politics: An Introduction* (Edinburgh University Press, 2001)

56. J. Bradbury *et al.*, op. cit. (2001) p.95; B. Agasoster, op. cit. (2001) p.134

57. G. Hassan, A Case Study of Scottish Labour (2002) p.145

58. L. McAllister, Changing the Landscape? The Wider Political Lessons from Recent Election in Wales, *Political Quarterly* 71(2) (2000)

59. Ibid., p.213

60. L. McAllister, The New Politics in Wales: Rhetoric or Reality?, *Parliamentary Affairs* 53(3) (2000) p.593

61. *The Guardian*, 12 April 2003

62. P. Lynch, Regional Party Organisations and Territorial Politics in Britain, Political Studies Association Data Bank (1997), p.559, available at http://www.psa.ac.uk/cps/1997/lync.pdf

63. D. Sanders, op. cit. (2002) pp.90–1

64. A. Clark, op. cit. (2002) p.13

65. Ibid.

66. B. Brady and J. Allardyce, Scottish Labour Faces £1m Election Bill, *Scotland on Sunday*, 17 March 2002

67. D. Sanders, op. cit. (2002) pp.90–1

BIBLIOGRAPHY

Agasoster, B. (2001). Party Cohesion and Local Agendas: A Study of Variations in Local Campaign Strategies in Scotland, PhD thesis, University of Aberdeen.

Allardyce, J., and MacLeod, M. (2002) Time to Grasp the Thistle, *Scotland on Sunday*, 03 March 2002.

Baker, D. and Seawright, D. (eds) (1998) *Britain For and Against Europe: British Politics and the Question of European Integration* (Oxford: Clarendon Press).

Baker, D., Wring, D. and Seawright, D. (2000) Panelism in Action: The Outcomes of Labour's New Selection Methods for the 1999 European Elections, *Political Quarterly* 71(2).

Bennie, L. and Clark, A. (2002) Scotland's Post-devolution Party System, paper presented to EPOP Annual Conference, University of Salford, 13–15 September.

Bennie, L., Brand, J. and Mitchell, J. (1997) *How Scotland Votes: Scottish Parties and Elections* (Manchester: Manchester University Press).

Bennie, L. *et al.* (2001) Harbingers of New Politics? The Characteristics and Attitudes of Candidates in the Scottish Parliament Elections 1999, in J. Tonge *et al.* (eds), *British Elections and Parties Review*, Vol. 11 (London: Frank Cass).

Bogdanor, V. (1999) *Devolution* (Oxford: Oxford University Press).

Brack, D. (1996) Liberal Democrat Policy, in D. MacIver (ed.), *The Liberal Democrats* (Hemel Hempstead: Harvester Wheatsheaf/Prentice Hall).

Bradbury, J., *et al.* (2000) Candidate Selection, Devolutions and Modernization: The Selection of Labour Party Candidates for the 1999 Scottish Parliament and Welsh Assembly Elections, in P. Cowley *et al.* (eds), *British Elections and Parties Review*, Vol. 10 (London: Frank Cass).

Bradbury, J., Mitchell, J., Bennie, L. and Denver, D. *et al.* (2001) Innovation in British Party Candidate Selection: The Role of Government Decentralisation and Government Reform', ECPR Joint Sessions, Grenoble, 6–11 April 2001.

Brady, B. and Allardyce, J. (2002) Scottish Labour Faces £1m Election Bill, *Scotland on Sunday*, 17 March 2002.

Brand, J. (1992) *British Parliamentary Parties: Policy and Power* (Oxford: Clarendon Press).

Brown, A. (1999) Taking Their Place in the New House: Women and the Scottish Parliament, *Scottish Affairs* 28.

Brown, A., McCrone, D., Paterson, L. and Surridge, P. (1998) The Scottish Electorate and the Scottish Parliament, *Scottish Affairs*, Special Issue: Understanding constitutional change.

Brown, T. (2000) Responsibility without Power, *New Statesman*, 12 June 2000.

Bulpitt, J. (1986) The Discipline of the New Democracy: Mrs Thatcher's Domestic Statecraft, *Political Studies* 34(1).

Clark, A. (2002) The Location of Power in Scotland's Post-Devolution Political Parties: An Exploratory Analysis, paper presented at the PSA Annual Conference, University of Aberdeen, 5–7 April.

Crewe, I. (1985) Great Britain, in I. Crewe and D. Denver (eds), *Electoral Change in Western Democracies Patterns and Sources of Electoral Volatility* (London: Croom Helm)

Curtice, J. (2001) Public Attitudes, in *Nations and Regions: The Dynamics of Devolution Quarterly Report* (The Constitution Unit, November).

Curtice, J. (2002) *New Scotland, New Society? Are Social and Political Ties Fragmenting?* (Edinburgh: Polygon).

Dalton, R.J. and Wattenberg, M.P. (eds) (2000) *Parties Without Partisans: Political Change in Advanced Industrial Democracies* (Oxford: Oxford University Press).

Deacon, R. (1998) The Hidden Federal Party: The Policy Process of the Welsh Liberal Democrats, *Regional Studies* 32(5).

Driver, S. and Martell, L (2002) *Blair's Britain, 2002* (London: Palgrave).

Duverger, M. (1964) *Political Parties: Their Organization and Activity in the Modern State. 3rd edition*, (London: Methuen).

Eldersveld, S.J. (1964) *Political Parties: A Behavioural Analysis* (Chicago: Rand McNally).

Epstein L.D. (1967) *Political Parties in Western Democracies* (London: Praeger).

Farquharson, K. (2002) Revealed: Blair's Bid to Bar Rebels from Holyrood, *Sunday Times*, 3 February 2002.

Fraser, D. (2001) McLetchie Accused of Sitting MSP 'Stitch-up', *Sunday Herald*, 12 August 2001.

Hassan, G. (2001) Scotland the Brave, *The Guardian*, 22 March.

Hassan, G. (2001) Just Another Layer of Politicians, *The Guardian*, 8 November.

Hassan, G. (2002) A Case Study of Scottish Labour: Devolution and the Politics of Multi-level Governance, *Political Quarterly* 73(2).

Hay, C. (1999) *The Political Economy of New Labour: Labouring under False Pretences* (Manchester: Manchester University Press).

Hay, C (ed.) (2002) *British Politics Today* (Cambridge, Polity Press).

Heffernan, R. and Stanyer, J. (1998) The Enhancement of Leadership Power: The Labour Party and the Impact of Political Communication, in C. Pattie *et al.* (eds), *British Elections and Parties Year Book*, Vol. 7 (London: Cassell).

Hennessy, P. (1999) The Blair Centre: A Question of Command and Control (London: Public Management Foundation).

Ingle, S. (1996) Party Organisation, in D. MacIver (ed.), *The Liberal Democrats* (Hemel Hempstead: Harvester Wheatsheaf).

Katz, R.S. and Mair, P. (1995) Changing Models of Party Organization and Party Democracy: The Emergence of the Cartel Party, *Party Politics* 1(1).

Kavanagh, D. (1985) Power in British Political Parties: Iron Law or Special Pleading?, *West European Politics* 8(3) pp.5–21.

Kavanagh, D. (1998) Power in the Parties, *West European Politics* 21, pp.28–43.

Kavanagh, D. and Seldon, A. (1999) *The Powers behind the Prime Minister* (London: HarperCollins).

Kelly, R.N. (1989) *Conservative Party Conferences: The Hidden System* (Manchester: Manchester University Press).

Kirchheimer, O. (1966) The Transformation of the Western European Party Systems, in J. LaPalombara and M. Weiner (eds), *Political Parties and Political Development* (Princeton, NJ: Princeton University Press).

Lees-Marshment, J. and Quayle, S. (2001) Empowering the Members or Marketing the Party? The Conservative Reforms of 1998, *The Political Quarterly* 72(2).

Levy, R. (1994) Nationalist Parties in Scotland and Wales, in L. Robins, H. Blackmore and R. Pyper (eds), *Britain's Changing Party System* (London: Leicester University Press).

Lynch, P. (1997) Regional Party Organisations and Territorial Politics in Britain, Political Studies Assocation Data Bank, available at http://www.psa.ac.uk/cps 1997/lync.pdf

Lynch, P. (1998) Third Party Politics in a Four Party System: The Liberal Democrats in Scotland, *Scottish Affairs* 22.

Lynch, P. (2001) *Scottish Government and Politics: An Introduction* (Edinburgh: Edinburgh University Press).

Lynch, P. (2002) Partnership, Pluralism and Party Identity: The Liberal Democrats after Devolution, in G. Hassan and C. Warhurst (eds), *Tomorrow's Scotland* (London: Lawrence & Wishart).

McAllister, I. and Rose, R. (1985) *Voters begin to Chose: From Closed Class to Open Elections in Britain* (London).

McAllister, L. (2000) The New Politics in Wales: Rhetoric or Reality?, *Parliamentary Affairs* 53(3).

McAllister, L. (2000) Changing the Landscape? The Wider Political Lessons from Recent Elections in Wales, *Political Quarterly*, 71(2).

McGarvey, N. (2001) New Scottish Politics, New Texts Required, *British Journal of Politics and International Relations* 3(3).

McGarvey, N. (2001) Political Parties, in *Nations and Regions: The Dynamics of Devolution Quarterly Report* (The Constitution Unit, August).

MacIver, D. (1996) Political Strategy, in D. MacIver (ed.), *The Liberal Democrats* (Hemel Hempstead: Harvester Wheatsheaf).

McKenzie, R. (1963) *British Political Parties*. 2nd edition (London: Heinemann).

McLean, I. (1997) The Semi-detached Election: Scotland, in A. King *et al.* (eds), *New Labour Triumphs: Britain at the Polls* (London: Chatham House).

Mair, P. (2000) The Limited Impact of Europe on National Party Systems, *West European Politics* 23(4), pp.27–51.

May, J.D. (1973) Opinion Structure of Political Parties: The Special Law of Curvilinear Disparity, *Political Studies* 21(2).

Michels, R. (1959) *Political Parties: A Sociological Study of the Oligarchical Tendencies of Modern Democracy* (New York: Dover Publications).

Minkin, L. (1978) *The Labour Party Conference* (London: Allan Lane).

Mitchell, J. (2000) New Parliament, New Politics in Scotland?, *Parliamentary Affairs*.

Mitchell, J. (2001) The Study of Scottish Politics Post-devolution: New Evidence, New Analysis and New Methods?, *West European Politics* 24(4).

Mitchell, J. (2002) Political Parties, in *Nations and Regions: The Dynamics of Devolution Quarterly Report* (The Constitution Unit, February).

Neumann, S. (1956) Toward a Comparative Study of Political Parties, in S. Neumann (ed.), *Modern Political Parties: Approaches to Comparative Politics* (Chicago: University of Chicago Press).

Norris, P. (1997) Anatomy of a Labour Landslide, in P. Norris and N. Gavin (eds), *Britain Votes 1997* (Oxford: Oxford University Press).

Offe, C. (1985) New Social Movements: Changing Boundaries of the Political, *Social Research*, 52, pp.817–69.

Panebianco, A. *Political Parties: Organisation and Power* (Cambridge: Cambridge University Press).

Riddell, P. (1993) *Honest Opportunism: The Rise of the Career Politician*. (London: Hamish Hamilton).

Sanders, D. (2002) Electoral Competition in Contemporary Britain, in C. Hay (ed.), *British Politics Today* (Cambridge: Polity Press).

Scarrow, S.E. Does Local Party Organisation Make a Difference? Political Parties and Local Government Elections in Germany, *German Politics* 2(3).

Scarrow, S.E. (1999) Party Democracy and Direct Democracy, special issue of *Party Politics* 5(3).

Seawright, D. (2002) The Lesser Spotted Tory, in G. Hassan and C. Warhurst (eds) *Tomorrow's Scotland* (London: Lawrence & Wishart).

Seawright, D. and Curtice, J. (1995) The Decline of Scottish Conservative and Unionist Party: Religion, Ideology or Economics?, *Contemporary Record* 9(2).

Seyd, P. (1995) New Parties/New Politics? A Case Study of the British Labour Party, *Party Politics* 5(3).

Shephard, M. (1999) Is It Really Devolution? Scottish Devolution and Blair's Clones, paper presented to the American Political Science Association Conference, Atlanta, September.

Shephard, M., McGarvey, N. and Cavanagh, M. (2001) New Scottish Parliament, New Scottish Parlimentarians, *Journal of Legislative Studies* 7(2).

Smith, C.F. and Gray, P. (2000) The Scottish Parliament: (Re-)Shaping, in D. Tanner, C. Williams and D. Hopkins (eds), *The Labour Party in Wales 1900–2000* (Cardiff, University of Wales Press).

Surridge, P. *et al.* (1998) The Scottish Electorate and the Scottish Parliament, in *Understanding Constitutional Change: Scottish Affairs* (Edinburgh).

Webb, P. (2000) *The Modern British Party System* (London: Sage).

Central government and devolution

Janice McMillan and Andrew Massey

INTRODUCTION

The process of devolution necessarily impacts on the operation and management of central government. It is understandable that much time and effort, on the part of politicians and academics alike, is invested in consideration of the impact of the newly created administrations on the process of governing. There is a related impact on the centre, however, that must not be overlooked if the full story of devolution is to be told.

This chapter will address the major changes to central government resulting from the devolution settlements. Given the asymmetrical form of devolution in the United Kingdom there is the possibility that the impact of devolution on the centre may in turn help define further developments in the devolved administrations. Even in devolution, then, it may be argued that the centre is pervasive.

The chapter has three main sections. First, the major changes in structures and procedures at Westminster are considered. The second section looks at the civil service outside Whitehall and how devolution has impacted on each of the constituent nations. The final section considers the view from Whitehall and how devolution has impacted on central departments.

NEW STRUCTURES AND PROCEDURES

The impact of devolution on the centre in terms of structures and procedures has been relatively limited. There were many guidance papers produced to ease the transition to devolution but, to date, 'situations of conflict have not arisen and the more formal aspects of the inter-governmental arrangements have not needed to be invoked'.[1] There is clear, if occasionally over-detailed, guidance in the Memoranda of Understanding drawn up by the Lord Chancellor's Department to guide relations between Whitehall and devolved administrations, as amended in later 'concordats'.[2]

In many respects the pre-devolution situation at Westminster continued after the establishment of the devolved administrations. The sum is mainly of addition not subtraction. As currently structured, devolution may not pose as great a threat to the power of the centre and the unitary state as first thought, yet clearly great difficulties lie ahead, not least of which is the switch of allegiance of those officials working in Scotland and Wales, to the devolved administrations, yet nominally employed by central government departments and paid out of national taxation.[3] In the same way that the centre sees the Home Civil Service as an integrator, so the centre itself has attempted to remain an integrating force as structural reforms to ensure coordination between the devolved administrations are located within the governmental machine. Administrative devolution (rather than political devolution) in this respect does not provide an obvious clear path for reform, and the varying forces will take many years to play out. The organic change, which is an inherent feature of the reform processes, is often unpredictable and the best that observers can do is to give a snapshot of the current situation. There will be a plethora of structural changes as the impact of devolution raises the pressures and tensions within the machinery of government and this works through the system. A further complicating factor of the impact of devolution on the centre is that, as in most reform processes, the natural concomitant is a welter of unintended consequences, and it is these unforeseeable changes that can have their most important influence in the years to come.

The initial formal changes to structure and operation at the centre concern the desire to retain power at UK government level. As part of the devolution settlements the new administrations were tied into relations with the central departments through a series of concordat agreements. The legal standing of these concordats has not been tested to date. But when combined with the impact of Europeanisation, devolution has conspired to transform British central government (politically if not so obviously administratively), hollowing out the state into a differentiated polity where the writ of Whitehall is constrained and the desire of the constituent nations to obey a central authority is itself limited.[4] To use a computing analogy, although the hardware looks broadly similar in style and structure, the software has changed. As a result, the whole system, although superficially changed only minimally, has now to behave in ways compatible with the new operating system. When combined with the application of other fundamental changes, such as the Human Rights Act 1998 and parliamentary reform, that have also reconfigured the software of governance, we may observe a step change in the machinery of government. One of the effects is an increased role for the judiciary in overseeing the process and activity of Whitehall and the executive; as in most federal systems based on codified constitutions, the judiciary is called upon to arbitrate. It is no coincidence that it is the Lord Chancellor's Department that has taken the lead in structuring the relationship between London and the devolved countries. It is injecting unelected and democratically unaccountable judges into the day-to-day policy process. It may be that judicial reform will be the result of judicial review of the executive.

It is surprising, therefore, to find that there are so few new structures devoted to coordinating the new quasi-federal United Kingdom, situated within the context of a federalising Europe. Perhaps the most notable of the few new integrating structures is the Joint Ministerial Committee (JMC). The JMC is composed of the prime minister (who chairs it), the deputy prime minister, secretary of state for Scotland, secretary of state for Northern Ireland, secretary of state for Wales, Scottish first minister, Scottish deputy first minister, Northern Ireland Assembly first minister, Northern Ireland Assembly deputy first minister, Welsh first minister and Welsh Assembly deputy first minister. There is provision for other ministers to be invited as and when necessary.

The terms of reference of the JMC are

> to consider non-devolved matters which impinge on devolved responsibilities, and devolved matters which impinge on non-devolved responsibilities; where the UK Government and the devolved administrations so agree, to consider devolved matters if it is beneficial to discuss their respective treatment in the different parts of the United Kingdom; to keep the arrangements for liaison between the UK Government and the three devolved administrations under review; and to consider disputes between the administrations.[5]

There are also Joint Ministerial Committees on the European Union; the knowledge economy; poverty and health. These in practice represent sub-committees. The composition of these sub-JMCs naturally varies according to the issue. The central government minister who holds the respective portfolio chairs them. The sub-JMCs necessarily have a larger membership than the JMC and average around 15 members drawn from central government and the devolved administrations.

The JMC, however, is not a widely known phenomenon and its first meeting went almost unnoticed by politicians and practitioners alike. This led one civil servant to comment: 'the first meeting of the Joint Ministerial Committee was an extraordinary constitutional event which nobody remarked on'.[6] This may be tempered, however, by another observation by the same senior civil servant that 'we have a knack of taking decisions under anaesthetic, and it hasn't worn off yet'.[7] It may be argued, then, that it is not that those at the centre want little to be known about the JMC meetings (in an attempt to use them as a political and management tool), but rather that the JMC has little day-to-day relevance for even senior civil servants.

Although there has been little influence on the committee structure in Westminster, this may not always be the case. Recent research questions the long-term viability of the territorial ministries in a devolved polity. Hazell forwards the argument that the continuation of the three territorial ministries beyond a five- to ten-year period would signal a failure of the devolution project. He acknowledges that Northern Ireland provides a specific set of political and cultural problems that require a separate ministry for the foreseeable future, but that the Scottish and Welsh secretaryships should be merged into a single post – a secretary of state for the Union. The holder of this post would then be able to take a broader view of issues affecting the Union and devolved administrations.[8] In a sense, cabinet committees have begun to be structured to recognise this change. As late as 2002, there was still a Cabinet Committee on Devolution, known as the Ministerial Committee on Devolution Policy (DP). It comprised the:

Lord Chancellor (chair)
Deputy prime minister and secretary of state for the environment, transport and the regions
Secretary of state for foreign and commonwealth affairs
Secretary of state for the home department
Secretary of state for education and employment
President of the Council and Leader of the House of Commons
Secretary of state for Scotland
Secretary of state for health

Parliamentary secretary, Treasury and chief whip
Secretary of state for culture, media and sport
Secretary of state for Northern Ireland
Secretary of state for Wales
Secretary of state for social security
Minister of agriculture, fisheries and food
Lord Privy Seal, Leader of the House of Lords and minister for women
Secretary of state for trade and industry
Chief secretary, Treasury
Captain of the Gentleman at Arms
Attorney-General
Advocate-General for Scotland
Minister of state, Cabinet Office

Other Ministers are invited for items in which they have departmental interest. It had as its terms of reference, 'to consider policy and other issues arising from the Government's policies for devolution to Scotland, Wales and Northern Ireland and the regions of England and to promote and oversee progress of the relevant legislation through Parliament and its subsequent implementation'.[9] By early 2003, however, this committee had been superseded by the Ministerial Committee on the Nations and Regions (CNR), which is composed of the:

Deputy prime minister and first secretary of state (chairman)
President of the Council and Leader of the House of Commons
Lord Chancellor
Secretary of state for the home department
Secretary of state for environment, food and rural affairs
Secretary of state for transport
Secretary of state for health
Secretary of state for Northern Ireland
Secretary of state for Wales
Secretary of state for work and pensions
Secretary of state for Scotland
Lord Privy Seal and Leader of the House of Lords
Secretary of state for trade and industry
Secretary of state for education and skills
Secretary of state for culture, media and sport
Parliamentary secretary, Treasury and chief whip
Minister without portfolio
Chief secretary, Treasury
Attorney-General
Advocate-General
Minister of state, Office of the Deputy Prime Minister

The foreign secretary and the secretary of state for defence receive papers. It has as its terms of reference, 'to consider policy and other issues arising from devolution to Scotland, Wales and Northern Ireland; and to develop policy on the English regions'.[10]

With the new emphasis on the development of devolution to the English regions, the impact of John Prescott as champion for the English regions was becoming more important to the policy process. The White Paper *Your Region, Your Choice*, where a policy for establishing regional assemblies and a more integrated approach to Whitehall policies through the Government Offices of the Regions was set out, was also coordinated through this committee and its sub-committees, often replicated at departmental level by officials.[11] The need for full territorial input from the devolved countries, via their secretaries of state, appears in UK-wide cabinet committees as well. Examples include the Ministerial Committee on Domestic Affairs (DA), which comprises the:

Deputy prime minister and first secretary of state (chairman)
Chancellor of the Exchequer
President of the Council and Leader of the House of Commons
Lord Chancellor
Secretary of state for the home department
Secretary of state for environment, food and rural affairs
Secretary of state for transport
Secretary of state for health
Secretary of state for Northern Ireland
Secretary of state for Wales
Secretary of state for defence
Secretary of state for work and pensions
Secretary of state for Scotland
Lord Privy Seal and Leader of the House of Lords
Secretary of state for trade and industry
Secretary of state for education and skills
Secretary of state for culture, media and sport
Parliamentary Secretary, Treasury and chief whip
Minister without portfolio
Chief secretary, Treasury
Attorney-General
Minister for the Cabinet Office and Chancellor of the Duchy of Lancaster
Minister of state, Office of the Deputy Prime Minister

Its terms of reference are 'to consider issues relating to the Government's broader domestic policies, ensuring the work of its sub-committees contributes to achieving the Government's overall agenda'.[12]

Another interesting example of this kind of UK-wide domestic committee is the Ministerial Sub-Committee on Energy Policy (DA(N)), which comprises the:

Deputy prime minister and first secretary of state (chairman)
Secretary of state for environment, food and rural affairs
Secretary of state for transport

Secretary of state for Wales

Secretary of state for department of trade and industry

Chief secretary, Treasury

Minister for the Cabinet Office and Chancellor of the Duchy of Lancaster

Minister of state, Office of the Deputy Prime Minister

Minister of state, Foreign and Commonwealth Office

Minister of state, Department of Trade and Industry

Parliamentary under-secretary of state, Scotland Office

Parliamentary under-secretary of state, Department of the Environment, Food and Rural Affairs

The chief scientific adviser is invited to attend. It considers 'the principles and objectives which should underlie Great Britain's energy strategy; to oversee the Performance and Innovation Unit's energy policy study; and to report as necessary to the Committee on Domestic Affairs'.[13]

At UK Cabinet level there is no mechanism for coordinating with the devolved administrations beyond those measures outlined above, that is a range of concordats and ad hoc structures. Representatives of the Scottish Parliament or Welsh Assembly do not sit on the ministerial committees as of right or even at the invitation of UK ministers. Coordination takes place through the offices of the secretaries of state and the Whitehall ministries. Thus although some critics of the devolved settlement who wish to see greater autonomy taken by the constituent countries have criticised the lack of independence, another way of viewing the arrangement is that it has evolved into a quasi-federal structure. London's officials and politicians may not issue instructions, but must now negotiate with Edinburgh and Cardiff; as such, Scotland and Wales are served through the JMC as well as their secretaries of state and a host of networks. Government has given way to governance and intergovernmental diplomacy.[14] The work of the cabinet committees as policy-coordinating and delivery oversight bodies requires skill in these fields. It is England that lacks a unified body or representative individual here.

The survival of the Westminster territorial forums is closely linked to the fate of the secretaryships. If the secretary of state posts are merged or otherwise reformed then the sum of addition may turn to subtraction. Subtraction is also likely to be influenced by the level of devolution granted. The Scottish committees will find it harder to survive given a more advanced devolution settlement: they will have to look for work to do. The more bounded devolution granted Wales may have the unintended consequence of strengthening Welsh forums as a way of integrating and coordinating the interests of the central and devolved administrations.[15]

The sum of Westminster representation may be brought back into balance if formal English forums are created. To date, and perhaps somewhat surprisingly however, calls for an English locus in Westminster have been rather muted. Whether this is because the current levels of representation are sufficient or that the 'English Question' does not vex MPs, remains to be seen.[16] It has been argued elsewhere that this is a sleeping giant. The patent unfairness of the devolution settlement from the English perspective is yet to play out. It is obvious that:

> In population and economic power, England dominates the UK. Yet, although English MPs may no longer legislate on Scottish issues, Scottish MPs in Westminster may continue to legislate on English matters. There is also an inflated number of Scottish and Welsh MPs because they have much smaller constituencies than their English counterparts. Furthermore, Scottish MPs may vote on taxation affecting English citizens and how much of that money will be used in Scotland, but English taxpayers and their representatives may not have a say on how that money is used. This is a fundamental inequity and represents taxation without representation. It may be that these issues will only be settled by a Scotland and England independent of each other within a federal European Union.[17]

The 'West Lothian Question' has not been answered, indeed it has first been ignored and then any questioner who has dared to raise it has been treated as if they had uttered a profanity during Holy Communion.

Whatever the political issues and potential problems, at the level of departments and their constituent parts, it may be argued that, overall, the new system of intergovernmental relations has been successful. This is of course due in great part to the compatibility between London administratively and the devolved administrations. There are also 'political' maintenance factors at play. Firstly, the civil service as an integrating mechanism and, secondly, through finance, the centre still tugs at the purse strings, and without true fiscal freedom intergovernmental relations are a necessary concern of the devolved administrations. True devolution, with Scotland, Wales and Northern Ireland gaining substantial tax-raising powers but losing most of their considerable subsidies from the taxpayers of London and south-east England, would of necessity change this.

DEVOLUTION AND THE CIVIL SERVICE

The role and operation of the national civil service has taken on new importance post devolution. The civil service has long been considered the glue of the British state, the constant amongst repeated waves of organisational and public service reform. In the devolution settlements of Scotland and Wales the civil service was clearly cast in the role of integrator in an increasingly dis-United Kingdom through its reserved status. Indeed, as Rhodes *et al.* suggest, 'the civil service is an excellent vehicle for exploring broader themes in the territorial governance of the UK. The current Labour government and many senior interests in the civil service remain strongly attached to maintaining a unified civil service in the UK, even though elements in the devolved administrations of Scotland and Wales favour separate civil services, along the lines of that of Northern Ireland'.[18]

It is somewhat surprising then that relatively little attention was given to the role, powers and structure of the civil service in the devolution settlements and even less consideration given to the operation of the new administrative structures. As Parry argues, 'the maintenance of the Home Civil Service including

Scottish and Welsh officials was one of the checks and balances of the devolution settlement, designed to prevent any drift towards conflict and isolation'.[19] Perhaps, then, as forwarding any operational rules would raise the civil service as a devolution issue, the centre was willing to leave the civil service off this particular reform agenda. The issue then arises of how much of a change devolution has elicited on this element of central government and how far the civil service remains an integrator.

Scotland

Parry argues that 'the gesture signified by the creation of a British government department is frequently more important than the substance of administrative change. The process is essentially that of the attachment of political symbolism to pre-existing agencies and staff.'[20] It may be argued that, for the Scottish civil service, devolution provided more symbolism than substance. Although devolution involved the transfer of Scottish Office civil servants to the new administration, very little changed.

This continuation perhaps tells us more of the pre-devolution system of administration in Scotland than it does the extent of differentiation brought about by devolution. Within the Scottish polity, the civil service represents 'a bureaucracy derived from, and knowledgeable of, its people and their special needs . . . [This] has given the Scottish Office in recent years an overall sense of direction lacking in much of Whitehall, and certainly in any region of England'.[21]

This sense of direction was strengthened by several operational features of the civil service. The Home Civil Service in Scotland fell into two broad categories: those that worked in the Scottish Office departments and agencies and those that worked for central departments. The latter far outweighed the former in numerical terms but this supremacy was not carried through in the daily power games of politics. Scottish Office civil servants were generally more senior and had a career history more firmly based in the Scottish experience. They soon came to dominate. Dominance was furthered by recent operational history, for, as Brown *et al.* argue, the twentieth century overall was the era of the technocratic state in Scotland. In this the politics that mattered was administrative politics.[22] Brown *et al.* further argue that

> The experts in the civil service shared a culture with similar experts in pressure groups, trade unions or employers' organisations. This common professional outlook was more important in shaping the character of legislation – and, through that, of social development – than the rather amateurish activities of MPs or even of ministers . . . [so] by the middle of the twentieth century Scotland had as much autonomy as could reasonably be hoped for, because it had its own indigenous bureaucracy in the Scottish Office and the other branches of the bureaucratic state.[23]

Devolution, then, formalised a situation in territorial politics that was already well developed. Indeed, this is also the case in other recent public service reform programmes. For example, the agencification of the civil service had only a slight structural and managerial impact as the civil service was already operating along such lines. Devolution did, however, bring some changes to civil service operation in Scotland.

Perhaps it was the relatively strong position of the civil service that made the transition to devolution so smooth. Devolution was greeted with the feeling that 'devolution must work', this sentiment born as much from a wish to maintain position as from any great desire for further decentralisation. Initially, then, devolution brought for the civil service a desire to cooperate with the Executive.[24] Such 'collegial attitudes are likely to dissipate as politicians strive to show that Scottish government is distinctive and effective and as they become more dominant in the policy process'.[25]

For the civil service the most immediate and obvious change in working relationships involved the closeness of Scottish ministers and changes in the parliamentary system. Civil servants now have ministers on their doorstep, and even for those not directly reporting to them the ministers' presence looms large. This has led, at least perceptually, to a feeling of tighter scrutiny of civil service input in the policy process.[26] There is now also an opposition close at hand duplicating the scrutiny function. Further, concerns that the civil service may become more politicised in order to maintain its power base in the new set-up echo concerns long held by senior Whitehall mandarins for the pre-devolution civil service.

Devolution is viewed here as a process. The impact of devolution on the organisation and management of the civil service in Scotland is a continuing and evolving process. The decentralisation evident before devolution and that afterwards is countered by the continuation of the unified service. Even in post-devolution Scotland, the pull of the centre is strong. The civil service is in this respect an integrating mechanism. For example, for senior civil servants, experience of working in Whitehall still provides a useful stepping-stone to further promotion. As noted earlier, relations between the new Executive and the central departments are set out in a series of concordats. The concordat between the Scottish Executive and the Cabinet Office makes it clear that inter-administration mobility is to be promoted. It is the intention that there will be no separate Scottish civil service. In practice, however, the dual allegiance of Scottish civil servants working in Scotland has been heavily weighted in favour of Edinburgh and away from London.

The influence of the centre can be most clearly seen in human resources issues as 'a significant indicator of the level of regionalisation and differentiation is the variation in recruitment and selection, pay and conditions and equal opportunities'.[27] Initially, devolution made little difference to the role of the centre in organisation and management of the civil service. That has begun to change. The Management Code (the framework within which all civil servants work) still reigns supreme but it has been amended to take into account the realities of political and administrative devolution. For example, *Amendment Circulation 43, Civil Service Management Code: Revision of Section 4.1 Annex A: The Civil Service Code*, states that:

> The purpose of this amendment to the Civil Service Code is to reflect the change in the practical arrangements that will be brought about as a result of devolution. The majority

of the proposed amendments reflect the different accountability arrangements that will apply as a result of the new arrangements for Scotland and Wales (paragraphs 1–5 and 9). The purpose of the amendments in paragraphs 10 and 13 is to clarify the duties of responsibility and confidentiality. The amendments in paragraphs 11 and 12 recognise the fact that conventional 'Departments' will no longer exist under the new arrangements in Scotland and Wales.[28]

There is, and always has been, a degree of differentiation, but this is still within parameters set by the centre. It may be argued, therefore, that 'Scotland travels its own route but the end destination is often the same and, in the case of the civil service (as a reserved power) often prescribed'.[29] It is likely this will no longer remain the situation as devolution evolves.

Looking at pay and conditions as an example, the prescriptive nature of the old route map can be seen. For conditions of service, powers were already delegated to the secretary of state for Scotland. After devolution the powers remained the same and continue to be structured by the complexities and realities of the local context of the Management Code. For pay there is supposedly no constraint on what the new Scottish administration can pay staff outside the senior civil service. In practice, however, differentiation from the centre is constrained not only by the Management Code but also by the government's general policy stance on public service remuneration.

For the centre, devolution has highlighted the role of the civil service as integrator. Currently the civil service has two contradictory pressures working on it. Firstly, the process of devolution augments differentiation. Secondly, the government's modernisation agenda serves as a deliberate centralising force.[30] The influence of these pressures means that there is no clear developmental path for the civil service under devolution. Hazell and Morris argue that the civil service in Scotland may pull away from the centre to become a separate service because 'the conventions of a permanent, anonymous and apolitical service operating in a confidential relationship with whichever government is in power have themselves been the products of a particular constitutional arrangement. The more the arrangement is altered, the more the conventions themselves come under stress'.[31] A second possibility is that the current level of regionalness remains buoyed by the desire to achieve joined-up government. Thirdly, and a possible unintended consequence of joined-up government, is that the civil service links with other services to become part of a unified public service in Scotland.[32] Such predictions are, of course, more or less likely depending on the political make-up of the devolved administrations and the future changes at Westminster and Brussels.

Wales

Although there is evidence in the devolved administrations of 'authenticity of the devolutionary spirit', this was tempered in Wales by a concern for the quality of local politician that was likely to emerge.[33] Thus in Wales there is a stronger feeling of belonging to a unified service serving Wales than of a distinct Welsh civil service. This reaction to devolution is an outcome of the administrative history of

Wales in which nationalism has never enjoyed the levels of support experienced in Scotland or Ireland/Northern Ireland. In administrative terms, of the three smaller countries of the UK, Wales has been historically the most closely integrated into England, partly reflecting the nature of Wales's forcible incorporation into the Union by the Tudors.[34] In legal terms, for example, there is no provision for the separate arrangements seen in Scotland and Northern Ireland. Certainly, unlike Scotland and Northern Ireland, the extent to which Welsh difference has been manifest in institutional terms has been altogether more limited.

The history of the civil service in Wales shows a strong commitment to the benefits of unity. Parry[35] summarises those benefits as, firstly, allowing officials in the devolved administrations to function within a tried and tested constitutional framework. Secondly, it reduces the likelihood of operational barriers appearing between devolved and non-devolved parts of the service. Over time, then, unionist politicians and Whitehall's civil servants have favoured the benefits of a unified civil service. Division of authority was avoided in the belief that the situation in Wales was not distinct enough to warrant special treatment and that by challenging the strength of the United Kingdom the strength of Wales was challenged. Wales took its position in the world from its position in the United Kingdom.[36]

The distinctiveness of the Welsh position has therefore never been a major administrative imperative for decentralisation. The Welsh Office has provided a bulwark to separatist calls, and even with criticism of its work in more recent history the separatist tendency remained far smaller than that witnessed in Scotland, for example. The Welsh Office and successive secretaries of state have, however, helped to create a culture through which Wales could express its differentiation from the centre. The administration has become reflective of that culture through the view that the civil service is serving Wales but is not a wholly Welsh institution.

The Government of Wales Act 1998, which followed the 1997 referendum vote in favour of devolution, gave political and institutional form and substance for the first time to Welsh nationalism. In 1999, devolution introduced a new system of governance for Wales that provided concrete recognition for Cymru. Under the devolved arrangements for Wales, a new National Assembly for Wales has assumed responsibility for all but a handful of Welsh Office functions. Although it does not have primary legislative powers, the Assembly's ability 'to adapt statutory provision to suit particular Welsh conditions' is indicative of its 'not insignificant powers, for they effectively allow the Assembly to adjust policy provision for the Welsh context'.[37] Virtually all the Welsh Office's staff (numbering some two thousand) were transferred to the National Assembly for Wales once the Transfer Order was completed, 'thus establishing a "Welsh arm" to the unified British civil service'.[38] Little coverage has been afforded to the minutiae of administrative management in the 1998 Act, though it is a sensitive issue. Now, rather than acting under the power of the Welsh secretary, Welsh civil servants 'will act under the authority of the Assembly acting corporately'.[39] The complexity of the devolution arrangements means that 'the workings of the National Assembly will be far more intermeshed with Whitehall than will be the case with the new institutions in Scotland and Northern Ireland'.[40] Certainly, there 'seems to be agreement that a unified civil service will be difficult to maintain within the new institutional context, again reinforcing the theme of devolution as a process not an event'.[41]

For the Welsh civil service, devolution brought several changes in their working relationships. Firstly, and similar to their Scottish counterparts, the closeness of ministers means that there is a new directness in dealings. There is also a similar wish to please. The relationships have also been changed for those ministers. The opposition is more closely organised and honed on local issues. Secondly, the power games played out between politicians and civil servants are now more likely to end up in an honourable draw. Certainly, the breadth and depth of responsibilities of the pre-devolution Welsh Office meant that civil servants held the traditional role of expert. Initial indications suggest that politicians, and especially ministers, may become as expert as the work of the new administration rolls out. There is a 'professionalisation of politics' occurring. This is clearly aided by a growth in scrutiny and accountability through informal mechanisms.[42]

Beyond the confines of institutional boundaries, relationships are also changing. Policy networks are reconfiguring in membership and in orientation towards the new locus. As these moves play out, the relative power of network members will change and it is expected that the voluntary sector will become a key actor in many policy networks. The elevation of voluntary interests, however, may be as much an outcome of general central government policy for public services than an outcome of devolution processes.

In human resources issues, Wales differs from Scotland in that devolution brought more control of the civil service to the principality. Although not particularly considered in the legislation that established the National Assembly, concern for the administration of the new system was addressed in supporting documentation. For example, the *Memorandum of Understanding and Supplementary Agreements between the United Kingdom Government, Scottish Ministers and the Cabinet of the National Assembly for Wales* notes that the 'Minister for the Civil Service has, however, delegated to the National Assembly for Wales the responsibility for a wide range of terms and conditions of service for staff of the National Assembly for Wales'.[43] The responsibilities devolved, however, do not surpass those already devolved in Scotland, and the civil service remains part of a unified service maintained by the centralising codes, concordats and Orders in Council.

There is evidence, however, that within Wales there are drives to make the civil service a Welsh civil service. The Assembly members in particular have been pushing for Wales to be given a greater degree of devolution akin to that in Scotland. The perception of civil servants that they are clearly home civil servants who just happen to administer Welsh affairs is beginning to break down. Indeed, there have been clashes between senior civil servants and Assembly members on the degree of freedom that Wales does hold to determine its own affairs beyond the grasp of the centre. The coalition partners in the first term went as far as to state: 'We will review the existing structures and workings of Assembly officials to ensure they are in tune with the reality of political devolution. We seek to move towards an increasingly independent and Welsh-based civil service – investigating ways of introducing an assembly "fast-track" programme to attract and retain high quality staff'.[44] A clearer challenge to the unified civil service it would be hard to find and as Parry notes, 'Wales continues to offer the most interesting arena for civil service reform in the UK'.[45]

Northern Ireland

Northern Ireland provides a unique example in the study of the impact of devolution on the civil service. As Rhodes *et al.* argue, 'there is one part of the UK in which the notion of a national unitary civil service is undermined completely. In Northern Ireland, the operations of the Home Civil Service are accompanied by those of the Northern Ireland Civil Service'.[46] Northern Ireland has also had experience of devolved government in the period 1921–72 before the current experiment with devolution-plus 1999 to date (with the exception of temporary suspensions).

In this first period of devolution the Northern Ireland Civil Service (NICS) was created to administer the transferred or devolved powers from staff previously working in British government departments in Dublin. NICS is therefore based on, but separate to, the Home Civil Service. 'NICS has always had its own head, civil service commission (to deal with recruitment and promotion) and internal grading system'.[47]

Transfer to direct rule brought with it the creation of the Northern Ireland Office (NIO) and with that a gentle steer towards Westminster and Whitehall practices. Whilst there has never been any strong drive to bring NICS formally under Whitehall control as part of a unified Home Civil Service, the practicalities of structures, policies and importantly public management reforms have had the result of tying the two administrations closely together.[48] The civil service has almost by default taken on an integrating role similar to that seen in the other devolved administrations. Further, NICS became an 'administration awaiting devolution' in the same way that the Scottish Office civil servants dominated the pre-devolution Scottish polity.[49] In this sense, the second phase of devolution was eased into practice.

Under the 1999 model of devolution, the Northern Ireland Assembly and Northern Ireland Executive were added to the institutional make-up of governance. Departmentally, six became ten through a reconfiguration of responsibilities, and certainly more than any other devolved administration Northern Ireland became enmeshed in an almost bewildering plethora of coordinating and integrating governmental mechanisms and institutions. It would not be difficult to argue that Northern Ireland is overgoverned in terms of the number of formal inputs. As well as the JMC mentioned above, Northern Ireland is now part of a North–South Ministerial Council, an East–West Forum and other cross-border and cross-administration implementation networks.[50] Carmichael styles the new configuration of Northern Ireland governance 'devolution-plus'.[51]

For the civil service devolution has meant a new array of masters. The pre-devolution versions of the NIO and Northern Ireland secretaryship continue but with reduced portfolios. However, as Hazell notes above, there is a likelihood of longevity here that does not exist in Scotland or Wales because the delicate balancing act that is the peace process requires a strong central government presence in the equation. In similar moves to the other devolved administrations, NICS now administers work in the Northern Ireland differentiated polity. The impact on the day-to-day operation of the civil service is similar to that noted above, in that the political presence is more direct with a close working relationship growing between ministers and the civil service. The power of the Assembly committees means that policy-making initiatives can come from other than the minister. The networking skills of NICS are being put to the test. Also it is not difficult to see that the pressures toward politicisation of the civil service are likely to broaden and deepen in this governmental system.

The multiple and varied pressures on the civil service of Northern Ireland provide a valuable insight into the impact of devolution on central government. It is not easy or indeed always applicable to compare NICS with civil services in the other constituent nations. However, the centralising and decentralising pressures on the civil service are no clearer seen than here. NICS remains a separate entity and, as noted, to date there have been no serious proposals to bring NICS under the wing of the Home Civil Service.[52] There is evidence, however, that NICS is undergoing the same reforming drive that the Home Civil Service has seen over the past few years. Global pressures are just that and recent reforms of NICS closely mirror those being followed in the Home Civil Service as part of New Labour's modernisation agenda.

Whether differentiation is desirable is a continuing question for the United Kingdom's civil services. Recent evidence, from the operation of NICS in relationships with the new devolved structures, suggests that separate civil services may not be the nightmare the centre fears so much. Parry argues that 'there is no evidence that working relationships on policy matters with other UK administrations are impeded by the separate NICS'.[53] On the personnel side, the separate NICS does cause some problems in the interface with the Home Civil Service, since NICS posts are not normally accessible to home civil servants in Northern Ireland, including those working for the Northern Ireland Office. The lesson from Northern Ireland is that a separate civil service has proved an entirely workable part of inter-institutional relations, but that it may result in some loss of flexibility in personnel movement, and a lesser involvement in wider UK developments in public sector management. Perhaps the real question then is not the desirability of separate UK civil services but whether the centre fears the independence it seeks to bestow.[54]

England

Of the constituent nations, England alone is without a territorial ministry. This curiosity begs the question, is there an English civil service? Further, it raises questions regarding how devolution to Scotland, Wales and Northern Ireland has impacted on civil service representation in England and whether civil servants in England are similarly regarded as a unifying force by the centre.

Without a territorial ministry there is no clear locus for civil servants to promote the English case. It is generally held, however, that the closest approximation to an English civil service constitutes civil servants working in the government offices for the regions (GOs). The then Departments of Trade and Industry, Education, Employment, and Environment and Transport established GOs in April 1994. The initial commitment to the GOs came in the Conservative Party's 1992 election manifesto where there was a felt need to strengthen central government's influence in the English regions.[55] This need was fuelled, among other things, by the concerns of those at the centre that there was a lack of organisation in, and information on, the English regions as distinct entities. It is clear then even from the outset that the GOs were to be viewed as instruments of central government policy in the regions and they were not playing the tune of the regions at the centre. The GOs are therefore examples of decentralisation of bureaucratic authority and do not fit the model of devolution as seen in Scotland, Wales and Northern Ireland.[56]

The regional dimension of English governance was strengthened with establishment of the regional development agencies (RDAs). These RDAs are a response to calls for a more regional emphasis on development policy to counteract the worst excesses of inequality of investment. In particular, RDAs were strongly supported by MPs with northern constituencies.[57] RDAs are at the hub of New Labour's regional policy and were first considered around the same time that the Conservatives were formulating ideas for the GOs. For New Labour, RDAs would provide the blueprint for fully democratic regional government. The White Paper *Your Region, Your Choice*,[58] noted above, set out the government's plans for new structures and the reasons behind English regional devolution, and is discussed in more detail in Chapter 10 of this book.

The question of democracy provided for New Labour the major criticism of GOs. The GOs were clearly not designed for democratic representation and, with the planned reform agenda for the other constituent nations, New Labour saw RDAs as providing for the English regions a little decentralised power. Although there was no wish to provide devolution, the RDAs do have the developmental capacity should there be the need in the future.[59]

As the representative element of regional governance, it is easy to see how the RDAs could render GOs almost impotent. However, it can be argued that as an unintended consequence, RDAs have given a new life to GOs as watchdogs and potential go-betweens between local, regional and central government. This potential development is forwarded by Rhodes *et al.* through the contention that

> the continued development of GOs is linked with that of RDAs in order to: develop the process of administrative and political decentralisation within the unitary polity of England; provide an administrative coherence to the cross-cutting policies of central departments such as that identified by various taskforces and to coordinate those and other policies with the sub-national governments and agencies in England; engage in the kind of intergovernmental diplomacy inherent to systems of governance characterized by a hollowing out of the core executive.[60]

It is clear from the above that the GOs, although being representative of an English civil service, are by no means a traditional regional civil service like that represented in Northern Ireland or even those in Scotland and Wales. Yet even this example of a regional civil service demonstrates the tensions of British government: how to devolve and decentralise within the framework of a unitary state. Recent events in the devolved power-sharing institutions in the constituent nations show that 'hands-off' is the hardest lesson for central government to learn.[61]

There are similarities between the GOs and the civil services in Scotland, Wales and Northern Ireland in their relationships with the centre. After devolution the similarities are fewer and arguably less marked, and perhaps the most likely match for the GOs is the devolution units of Whitehall departments. As Hazell and Morris argue, the GOs are 'simultaneously looking outward . . . and inward to the central co-ordinating mechanism in Whitehall itself'.[62]

The GOs are clearly viewed as an integrating mechanism and, with the establishment of RDAs and the degree of English devolution extended, this role can only grow more important. Rhodes *et al.* consider that GOs have several roles to perform in English governance. The link to the civil service as an integrator is clear:

> to develop the original co-ordination functions for which they were originally established and extend them to include central government departments and agencies, the RDA, local authorities, Non-Departmental Public Bodies operating in the region and important private sector organisations involved in the delivery of public services; to monitor and audit the delivery of central government policies and intervene when and where appropriate using a range of fiscal and executive powers to encourage compliance with national strategies, as defined by the national government; to use their privileged position straddling the national and regional arenas, to act as neutral brokers between the different actors involved in the policy networks at regional level, as well as to facilitate their access to supranational (EU) level on relevant issues.[63]

Development post devolution may also see the GO framework extended to public service organisations beyond the limits of the civil service.

THE VIEW FROM WHITEHALL

The devolution project also impacts on those home civil servants who have to interact with the new administrations. It is argued that, in Whitehall, change to accommodate the new governance of devolution has been slow. Ministers have failed to give leadership on how devolution is likely to impact on central departments with the Treasury being the only department up to speed on changes in relationships.[64] However, there is the danger of damning Whitehall as an elitist fiefdom; Whitehall reactions may only be a reflection of the extent of the impact of devolution on day-to-day business to date. Civil servants cannot react to what they do not know. A high degree of professionalism in the civil service means that there are unlikely to be formal changes directing all interactions with the devolved administrations. Too prescriptive an approach and problems will appear in the detail of the working out of how to make devolution work. So far (with some exceptions in education policy and social policy), there has not been the major rush of differentiation in policy that may require a response from Whitehall. The still unified nature of the civil service is important here – if you are as one then there are no false enemies.

However, it is possible to contend that Whitehall has reacted to the process of devolution. Most central departments now have liaison units for interactions with the devolved administrations. On a less formal note, civil service culture is such that there are close links across boundaries in order to maintain parity; for example, information sharing allows the civil service to act almost effortlessly in maintaining the whole through promotion of best practice. Time will tell how far the civil service remains an integrating mechanism.

CONCLUSIONS

The process of devolution is an exciting one. In the case of Britain the experiment is even more interesting because there are contradictory tensions at play. The devolution project may sometimes give the impression that perhaps the centre is trying 'to give', but not too much, in fear that extending devolution will threaten Britain as a unitary state. It may be the case that the time of the unitary state has already passed into history. The Westminster model on which it is based was always more of a model, indeed a rough guide, than a reality. Devolution also brings questions of capacity: capacity to function as a viable entity. For example, in granting a degree of political devolution to the regions of England, do you open up calls for further strengthening of regions within the already devolved administrations? If that is the case, to what extent may the UK government tax wealthy regions and disburse that wealth to poorer regions?

The impact of devolution on the centre is often overlooked. There are, however, always costs in that direction. Not least of these are diverging policy agendas that make overall strategy more difficult to deliver. The devolution project in the United Kingdom has highlighted the need for integrating mechanisms to maintain the whole, and the civil service has been cast as star in that role. So far, the civil service has resisted pressures to form into territorially separate services. For the civil service there are clear counter-trends that they must engage with – the desire of the devolved administrations to be in step with Westminster whilst at the same time exercising the right to diverge. Civil servants have to cope with the desires and ambitions of their political masters as well as develop their own skills to cope with the new political and organisational geography of governance. The civil service is at the heart of the devolution project, trying to juggle the calls on their loyalty, knowledge and expertise. So far this juggling act has been successful, but as devolution unfolds then the tensions apparent may make the civil service's role as integrator harder to fulfil. The centre must not overlook the difficulties that may arise if the glue that is the civil service starts to crack. Such consideration by the centre, however, will necessitate a re-evaluation of trust. At the heart of the new administrative reality the ability to barter, bargain and negotiate hard may be the most valuable personal commodities officials can bring to their service.

NOTES

1. R. Parry, *The Home Civil Service after Devolution: The Devolution Policy Papers* (Devolution and Constitutional Change Programme: ESRC, 2002)
2. Lord Chancellor's Department, *Memorandum of Understanding and Supplementary Agreements between the United Kingdom Government, Scottish Ministers and the Cabinet of the National Assembly for Wales*, Cm 4444 (London: HMSO, 1999); Lord Chancellor's Department, *LCD and the Scottish Executive: Concordat between the Scottish Executive and the Lord Chancellor's Department* (London: HMSO, 2000)
3. R.A.W. Rhodes, P. Carmichael, J. McMillan and A. Massey, *Decentralising the Civil Service: From Unitary State to Differentiated Polity in the United Kingdom* (Buckingham: Open University Press, 2003) pp.70–127
4. Ibid., pp.151–67
5. Joint Secretariat, JMC Committee Composition and Terms of Reference
6. Rhodes *et al.*, op. cit. (2003)
7. Ibid.
8. R. Hazell, *Three into One Won't Go: The Future of Territorial Secretaries of State* (London: Constitution Unit, 2001)
9. www.cabinet-office.gov.uk/cabsec/2002/cabcom/dp.htm
10. www.cabinet-office.gov.uk/cabsec/2003/cabcom/da.htm
11. Office of the Deputy Prime Minister, *Your Region, Your Choice: Revitalising the English Regions* (London: HMSO, 2002)
12. www.cabinet-office.gov.uk/cabsec/2003/cabcom/da.htm
13. Ibid.
14. Rhodes *et al.*, op. cit. (2003) pp.151–67
15. Constitution Unit, The Impact of Devolution on Westminster, Nations and Regions, briefing paper (2003)
16. Ibid.
17. A. Massey, *The State of Britain: A Guide to the UK Public Sector* (London: CIPFA, 2002) pp.22–3
18. Rhodes *et al.*, op. cit. (2003) p.3
19. Parry, op. cit. (2002)
20. R. Parry, The Centralisation of the Scottish Office: An Administrative History, paper presented to the Political Studies Association Conference, April 1982, p.2
21. J. Kellas, *The Scottish Political System* (Cambridge: Cambridge University Press, 1984) pp.79–80
22. A. Brown, D. McCrone and L. Paterson, *Politics and Society in Scotland* (Basingstoke: Macmillan, 1998)
23. Ibid., p.55
24. Rhodes *et al.*, op. cit. (2003) p.153

25. Ibid., p.153
26. Ibid.
27. Ibid., p.82
28. Cabinet Office, May 1999
29. Rhodes *et al.*, op. cit. (2003) p.84
30. Parry, op. cit. (2002)
31. R. Hazell and B. Morris, Growing Apart, *Public Service Magazine* (May 1999) p.19
32. C. Ryan, Growing Apart, *Public Service Magazine* (May 1999)
33. Parry, op. cit. (2002) p.1
34. Rhodes *et al.*, op. cit. (2003) pp.100–27
35. Parry, op. cit. (2002)
36. Rhodes *et al.*, op. cit. (2003)
37. L. McAllister, The Road to Cardiff Bay: The Process of Establishing the National Assembly for Wales, *Parliamentary Affairs* 52(4) (1999) pp.632–48
38. Ibid., p.643
39. J. Osmond, *Adrift but Afloat: The Civil Service and the National Assembly* (Cardiff: Institute for Welsh Affairs, 1999) p.7
40. Ibid., p.8
41. McAllister, op. cit. (1999) p.643
42. Rhodes *et al.*, op. cit. (2003)
43. Cabinet Office (1999) paragraph 13
44. Osmond, 2000, at p.13, as quoted in Rhodes *et al.*, op. cit. (2003) pp.100–27
45. Parry, op. cit. (2002) p.2
46. Rhodes *et al.*, op. cit. (2003)
47. Ibid., at p.37
48. Ibid.
49. Ibid.
50. Ibid.
51. P. Carmichael, Territorial Management in the 'New Britain': Towards Devolution Plus in Northern Ireland?, *Regional and Federal Studies* 9(3) (1999) pp.130–56
52. Rhodes *et al.*, op. cit. (2003)
53. Parry, op. cit. (2002) p.4
54. Rhodes *et al.*, op. cit. (2003)
55. K. Spencer and J. Mawson, Government Offices and Policy Co-ordination in the English Regions, *Local Governance* 24(2) (1998) pp.3–11; J. McMillan and A. Massey, A Regional Future for the UK Civil Service? The Government offices for the English regions and the Civil Service in Scotland, *Public Money and Management* 21(2) (2001) pp.25–31
56. McMillan and Massey, op. cit. (2001)
57. Rhodes *et al.*, op. cit. (2003)
58. McMillan and Massey, op. cit. (2001); Office of the Deputy Prime Minister (2002)
59. Rhodes *et al.*, op. cit. (2003)
60. Ibid., p.138

61. R.A.W. Rhodes, New Labour's Civil Service: Summing-up Joining-up, paper presented to the British Council New Public Management Series, Palazzo Chigi, Rome, 5 October 1999; Rhodes *et al.*, op. cit. (2003)
62. Hazell and Morris, op. cit. (1999) p.19
63. Rhodes *et al.*, op. cit. (2003) p.148
64. H. MacDonnell, Westminster Fails to Adapt to Devolution, *The Scotsman*, 22 July 2002

English regional government

Christopher Stevens

INTRODUCTION

In December 1991, Joyce Quinn, the MP for Gateshead East, initiated a Parliamentary debate on the need for regional government in England. She moved:

> That this House deplores the excessive centralisation of government in the United Kingdom since 1979 and the failure to decentralise and devolve power . . .; notes that this is in direct contrast to the general trend towards decentralisation evidence [*sic*] elsewhere in Europe . . .; expresses alarm at the regional divisions which continue to characterise the United Kingdom economy; and considers the creation of a regional tier of government in the English regions as well as national devolution to Scotland and Wales is now vital to the United Kingdom's future economic and political well-being.[1]

This motion contains in essence the argument for English regional government. Regional government is promoted as essential to any modernisation project, as democratically desirable, and as a mechanism for giving focus to regional diversity. Most of all, it is seen as economically efficient. Indeed, arguments relating to democracy are often less about any intrinsic democratic value and more about the ways in which democracy – here meaning regional choice rather than any developed notion of participation – can drive forward economic success.

By 1997, both the Liberal Democrat and the Labour Party had adopted regional government as party policy. The former outlined its policy in a document in 1993. It proposed devolution to the nations and regions, underpinned by a federal constitution.[2] The Labour Party's regional policy was developed over fifteen years. John Prescott advocated directly elected regional chambers in the 1982 document *Alternative Regional Strategy*, and this was reiterated in the 1991 policy statement *Devolution and Democracy*. The phased approach that both these documents advocated was taken up by Jack Straw, whose 1995 consultation paper, *A Choice for England*, became the basis of the September 1996 policy statement, *A New Voice for England's Regions*. These proposals advocated a two-phase policy. The first phase involved establishing accepted boundaries,[3] the setting up of voluntary, non-elected chambers in each region, with strategic responsibility for European funding, economic development, land use and transport planning,[4] and extensive consultation.[5] The second phase, the move to elected assemblies, would take place only after the voluntary chambers had been 'given time to establish themselves properly over a reasonable period of time',[6] and a 'predominantly unitary system of local government' had been created.[7] Rather than the centre creating a comprehensive system of regional government from above, Labour intended regions to be allowed to opt out altogether and only those that could overcome what Labour calls its 'triple safeguards on regional assemblies' – approval of the region's voluntary chamber, approval of Parliament and a regional referendum – could move forward.[8] Meanwhile, in July 1995, John Prescott established a Regional Policy Commission, chaired by Bruce Millan. Its report, published in May 1996, advocated the establishment of regional development agencies (RDAs) 'separate from the regional chambers, but responsible to the chambers and acting as their executive arm in the area of economic development'.[9]

The election of the Labour Party in 1997 was followed by the introduction of phase one of this policy, under the coordination of John Prescott, deputy prime minister and secretary of state at the Department of the Environment, Transport and the Regions (DETR), 1997–2001. There were, however, two significant diversions from the blueprint. Firstly, RDAs were appointed by and accountable to ministers.[10] Secondly, there was no legislation introducing voluntary chambers. Richard Caborn, the Minister for Regions, Regeneration and Planning, announced that there was too little parliamentary time available.[11] Robert Hazell's view was that this 'was nonsense: the real reason was a failure of collective political will'.[12] However, another reason might be suggested. The RDA legislation did, as will be seen, prompt the creation of regional chambers to scrutinise RDA work, a process encouraged by the government. The indirect procedure adopted allowed the government to delay judgements about the precise composition of the chambers.

The Cabinet remained divided. There were concerns about the creation of a powerful regional tier, and worries about the attitude of business, which 'did not want the dead hand of local government too near the new RDAs'.[13] The RDAs policy was seen widely as a victory for the Home Secretary, Jack Straw, perceived as a regional government sceptic. Government enthusiasm for regions was rekindled prior to the 2001 election, especially after Gordon Brown's intervention to suggest that greater engagement at the regional level was needed. Although the subsequent government rearrangement saw responsibility for the regions divided between the new Office of the Deputy Prime Minister and the reconstituted DETR, this did not have the negative effect that might have been anticipated. The White Paper *Your Region, Your Choice*, which outlined stage two of the policy, was published in May 2002. A month later, John Prescott indicated that it was the intention of the government to 'have a referendum in at least one region during the 2001 Parliament'.[14] This will presumably be in the north-east of England, where the demand is most deeply entrenched. Whether supporters of change can get over the hurdles put in front of them remains to be seen.

There is an assumption that Labour Party plans will create an asymmetrical system of devolved power. Part of this is correct. The United Kingdom will have an asymmetrical system with respect to Scotland, Wales and England. However, within England, the system will be multi-speed, but not asymmetrical, excepting the possibility that some regions will opt out permanently. Regions with elected chambers will find that their chambers have the same range of powers.

What will these elected chambers do? In an important contribution to the debate, Mark Sandford and Paul McQuail have outlined and costed three possible

Table 10.1 McQuail and Sandford's indicative models of regional government

Type	Function	Budget for each chamber
Strategic/coordination	Strategic coordination and democratic accountability	Approx. £20m
Strategic-executive	Additional responsibilities and resources to allow significant choices[a]	£1.1bn – £2.5bn depending on size of region
Welsh model	Range of functions comparable to those of Welsh Assembly	£6bn – £14bn depending on size of region

[a] Source here is G. Marquand and J. Tomaney, *Democratising England* (London: Regional Policy Forum, 2000).

models of regional government.[15] These are outlined in Table 10.1. Perhaps unsurprisingly, it is the strategic/coordination model that is outlined in the White Paper. Accordingly, chambers will be small, between 25 and 35, depending on the size of the region.[16] Two-thirds will be elected on a constituency basis. The remainder will be appointed from party lists through the additional member system.[17] Chambers will have responsibility for regional strategies for economic development, skills and employment, spatial planning, sustainable development, transport, waste, housing, health improvement, culture and tourism and biodiversity. Funding will be through a block grant, allowing some freedom over the setting of priorities, and a small precept on the rates.[18] There are those in the regions for whom the comparatively small scale of the enterprise is not a problem. They believe that once regional government is set up, it will have its own momentum, and the transfer of additional powers will be unavoidable. In this they can look at the way in which the Welsh Assembly's bid for legislative powers has followed on from its first period of office.[19] However, they are unlikely to be proven right. The weakness of regionalism within England and the centralist tenor of sub-centre government, from which the Blair government has not deviated, make such an eventuality extremely unlikely.

Proponents of regional government face one major obstacle. The English regions do not show any strong regional identity. In an important work, Michael Keating divides regions into three groups. The first are regions that comprise 'historic nationalities', in which he includes Scotland and Wales, and areas with distinct linguistic or historical identity, but without national pretensions. This group has strong regional identity. The second group comprises regions whose institutions have acquired 'political space and an effective system of action'. The third group comprises administrative regions without a common sense of identity and other regional attributes. This group has the weakest regional identity. It is in this group that Keating includes the English regions.[20] English regions have been driven by a process of regionalisation, rather than the cultural and historical regionalism of the first group; and that regionalisation is not sufficiently embedded to produce the embryonic regionalism of the second group. In this formulation, categories one and two may create popular consent for regional government, but the third is not likely to do so without central government intervention. In a series of important contributions to the debate,[21] John Tomaney has detailed the development of both what he calls 'official regionalism', the growth of governmental apparatus, and 'civic regionalism', the engagement of elites and others at the regional level, the implication being that such activity has begun to move some English regions into Keating's second group. It is the contention of this chapter that whereas it is possible to observe both official and civic *regionalisation* in England, this is not strong enough to create *regionalism*.

THE ECONOMICS OF REGIONAL GOVERNMENT

The issue of whether regional government is able to deliver economic gains is a central one. The argument has three interlinked strands to it. The first of these concentrates on the capacity of regional government to direct funding into an area by attracting inward business investment. This may not be an effective argument for regional government at all. Firstly, there is no reason to believe that an elected chamber will be any more effective in garnering resources than an appointed one. It may be that business will find the latter more conducive to investment strategies. Secondly, this strategy offers no mechanism for increasing national prosperity. If regional government is partial, such apparatus might benefit those with it at the expense of those without it; but a level playing field would cancel this out. If the RDA structure is as effective as elected chambers in this respect, that level playing field already exists.

The second strand stresses the economic advantages of improved coordination of regional economic strategies and the advantages regional government has in fashioning these strategies, and the institutions on which their delivery depends, to meet diverse regional needs. Democracy becomes not just an end in itself, but an essential mechanism in articulating diversity and in creating patterns of cooperation and partnership. However, whilst there is sufficient evidence to suggest 'that institutional capacity – the extent and form of regional organisations – plays an important role within the economic development trajectory of a region',[22] the work of Harding *et al.* suggests that such institutional capacity can be created as effectively by appointed governmental machinery, such as RDAs, as by elected ones.[23] As Barter notes: 'there is no clear evidence regarding what regional government could add to the economic development agenda'.[24] The evidence to the contrary comes from European studies which link economic success to regional autonomy such as those for Italy and Spain.[25] However, there are inevitably other factors involved in European successes, and, as Barter concludes, 'there has been no comprehensive study of transferability of international lessons to the English context'.[26] It may be that patterns of cooperation and partnership can never be replicated at regional level in England for domestic institutional reasons, especially as the centre is more likely to constrain the regions in the United Kingdom than in Italy and Spain. Alternatively, it might be that appointed administration is in theory quite capable of delivering such strategies, but will not do so in the English context unless an elected dimension is added.

The third strand assumes that such institutional capacity will deliver a regional policy. As *A Choice for England* argues: 'England is handicapped by a serious regional imbalance . . . In order to correct this imbalance Britain needs an economic strategy which is geared to the particular needs of its regions. This can only be developed by those regions themselves'.[27] The notion that the development of regional institutional capacity will affect regional imbalances is taken for granted rather than theorised and it is almost certainly wishful thinking. There is every likelihood that regional government will enable prosperous regions to increase their wealth at the expense of the poorer ones. As Harvie points out, the growth of regionalism in Europe is driven, in part, by the 'particularism of the affluent',[28] what might be termed autarchic regionalism.[29] European success stories may be the result of the capacity of potentially wealthy regions to opt out of the constraints of national policy. Moreover, any region-centred regional policy would require a considerably greater devolution of power than that currently proposed. Even then, key economic controls would continue to reside with the Treasury.

REGIONAL GOVERNMENT AND REGIONAL GOVERNANCE

Interest in modernising sub-centre government in the 1960s led to the adumbration of the range of activity already taking place at regional level, exemplified in the 1968 book by John Macintosh entitled *The Devolution of Power*. A later mapping, edited by Brian Hogwood and Michael Keating, was happy to refer to the developing regional tier as 'regional government'.[30] By the end of the 1990s this formulation had changed. The restructuring of sub-centre government, so that policy was both formulated within and implemented by networks of public, private and voluntary bodies, changed the way political scientists viewed the activities of the state. The term 'government', better reserved for formal institutions underpinned by electoral accountability, became inadequate as a means for describing this process. At the same time, those studying international politics, such as James Rosenau, began to use the term 'governance' as 'a more encompassing phenomenon than government [which] embraces governmental institutions, but . . . also subsumes informal, non-governmental mechanisms'.[31]

The result of this development was a shift in terminology from 'regional government' to 'regional governance' to describe the blossoming tier of regional administration in England. However, there is a paradox within this analysis. Leaving aside the issue of democratic accountability, the essence of 'government' is territorial integrity. Thus, sub-centre 'government' is allocated a precise area of territory and given *de jure* jurisdiction over delegations of administrative (or much more rarely, legislative) authority. Such authority is multi-purpose and integrative, even where limited by the centre. Governance is, in contrast, the effect of policy making by a wide range of governmental and non-governmental institutions and organisations, whether directed specifically at a territorial area or affecting it from without. It utilises a variety of governmental and non-governmental bodies with varying jurisdictions, and it is predominantly multiple-body, each often single-purpose. When Hogwood and Keating produced their book in 1982, the regional institutions they surveyed were largely the by-product of the operation of the central state and its public corporations. They were single-purpose and were not integrated. There were some attempts to manage government activity at regional level, but these remained tentative and fragmented. Moreover, as Hogwood and Lindley showed, regional boundaries were ad hoc and varied.[32] In 1982, then, regional administration had all the hallmarks of governance.

By the end of the 1990s, this had changed considerably. It is worth devoting some time to considering five developments. The first of these is the creation of a network of Government Offices for the Regions in April 1994.[33] Prior to 1994, government departments and agencies operated regional offices, but their activities were neither integrated nor compatible in scope, nor necessarily operating on the same regional boundaries. The complexity of these arrangements is demonstrated by the study of the West Midlands by Keating and Rhodes. They concluded that there was 'no consistent definition of the region and no consistent concept of regional government [sic]. Instead there [was] a variety of bodies covering different areas, with different functions and covering different areas'.[34] The Major government brought together within the same regional boundaries the regional offices of the DTI, Employment, Environment and Transport under a regional director, 'as a single point of contact for local authorities, businesses and local communities'.[35] By 2002, this had expanded to involve up to eight government departments,[36] most integrated within the regional office, but some co-locating with external reporting structures.[37] This increased role for the government offices (GOs) has been due to a number of factors. Some of these are a consequence of the increased commitment of the Blair government to the regional tier and the policy focus of New Labour. Cross-cutting policy initiatives on social inclusion, urban regeneration and neighbourhood renewal led to further administrative integration; whilst a report by the Performance and Innovation Unit led to the establishment of a Regional Co-ordination Unit as a headquarters for the GO network in 2000.[38] This gave the GOs an increased presence at the centre in a way which proselytised for further integration. Other causes are more to do with the successful workings of the GOs themselves. As government departments increased their collaboration with the GO network, they have embraced further the regional dimension. Thus, some areas of activity have moved from co-location to integration.[39]

The second development is the converse of the first. By 1992, there was national coverage of English regional associations (ERAs) and regional planning conferences (RPCs), bringing together representatives of local authorities in each region.[40] The majority of these concentrated on disseminating regional planning guidance. However, some looked more like prototype chambers. The North of England Assembly began to press for recognition (and funding) as such in 1995.[41] Labour Party policy for the 1997 election promised 'voluntary' regional chambers, based on the ERAs, whose secretariats they would adopt, but with arrangements for a role for business organisations, trade unions and voluntary associations.[42] As noted above, rather than use legislation to set up these chambers, the government used encouragement. The December 1997 White Paper *Building Partnerships for Prosperity* offered voluntary regional assemblies the opportunity to monitor and scrutinise the work of the proposed RDAs. It also insisted that there should be a political, sexual and ethnic balance and that local economic and social partners should sit in the assemblies alongside representatives of local government,[43] which the government's *Guidance on Voluntary Regional Chambers*, issued in August 1998, set at 'no less than 30% of the chamber'.[44] Section 8 of the subsequent Regional Development Agencies Act 1998 empowered the secretary of state to designate bodies as regional chambers and give them a statutory responsibility to monitor and scrutinise the work of the RDAs. As a result, chambers of varying sizes and compositions were set up in all eight regions, the largest with 117 members, and the smallest with 36. All but Yorkshire and Humberside call themselves assemblies, not chambers. The creation of chambers has been an undoubted success, and the significant variation between them does reflect both local differences and the differing state of debate in each region, which makes the government's decision not to legislate for them a wise one, even if it was taken inadvertently. The 2002 White Paper was able to trumpet their successes.[45] As Tomaney points out, citing the 1999 Environment, Transport and Regions Select Committee Report on RDAs, progress was 'remarkable', especially so 'in areas such as the South West, the East of England and the East Midlands, which had little tradition of partnership working at regional level'.[46]

The third development was the creation of regional development agencies, which formally came about on 1 April 1999, bringing together a host of preceding regional business-led quangos. Tomaney[47] notes the interdepartmental conflict that surrounded their establishment, which meant they 'began with a smaller range of powers than had been anticipated',[48] and the small and constrained nature of their budgets, a consequence of the resistance by government departments to financial devolution to non-governmental departments.[49] However, RDAs are significant in the evolution of regional governance. They were devised to formalise business involvement in each region, which had formerly been fragmented, and to give it strategic impetus through a small board of twelve or thirteen, of which one-third comprises local councillors, reflective of size of authority, geographical spread and political balance (a seeming mathematical impossibility), but not acting as 'delegates of their own authorities'.[50] This would enable them 'to promote sustainable economic development and social and physical regeneration and to co-ordinate the work of regional and local partners in areas, such as training, investment, regeneration and business support'.[51] The RDAs are intended to be 'ultimately accountable to Ministers' but are 'responsive to the communities which they serve'.[52] The RDAs in five regions are simply called development agencies, as in the North West Development Agency. Three have gone for catchier titles: One North East, Yorkshire Forward, Advantage West Midlands.

The fourth development is the apparent agreement over regional boundaries.[53] These are based on the original GO areas, with one minor adjustment. In 1994, a separate GO had been created for Merseyside, an echo of the Heseltine involvement there in the early 1980s, which had led to the creation of development corporations. The Merseyside Office was merged with GONW in early 1998 to create nine standard regions, including London. This brought the North-West into line with the ERA region. In the south there was a second discrepancy as the RPC for the South-East, SERPLAN, covered London as well. The disbanding of this in April 2001 ended that discrepancy. Thereafter, GO, chamber, planning and RDA boundaries coincided.

The final development concerns the creation of regional-level networks. An interview with a senior officer in 2002 in one region where there has been little tradition of this kind of activity elicited the unprompted response that few would have dreamt that the GO, RDA and chamber would have operated so well together two or three years previously. Of course, caveats can be entered here. This may be being exaggerated, or cooperation may result from the capture of the network by a dominant coalition of groups which is able to exclude more divisive issues. Nor does cooperation mean that the transition to elected regional assemblies will be particularly smooth. As the same interviewee reported, the strength of cooperation meant that few wanted to disrupt that through moving to an elected chamber. The personnel in the chamber and the RDA are drawn largely from the same regional elite. Election might be perceived as a threat to their achievements. It will also introduce political parties into a body constructed to exclude such political dynamics. Nevertheless, in terms of the evolution of regional governance, this cooperation is significant. There have been a number of concordats signed between chambers, GOs and RDAs, starting with that for Yorkshire and Humberside, which went on to sign a concordat with the regional TUC.[54] Most regions have followed suit, some with the regional local government association included, and the results can be found on chamber websites. The depth and breadth of cooperation can be seen from two detailed regional profiles, one of the West Midlands by Ayres and Pearce, which contrasts nicely with the study of the same area by Rhodes and Keating, and one by Tomaney and Humphrey for the North-East.[55] Alongside such arrangements we have Tomaney's civic regionalism. This is embodied in the growth of organisations operating at regional level that seek to create a regional identity and to shift opinion in favour of elected chambers. Following both the Scottish and the Welsh experiences,[56] the formal apparatus has tended to be called constitutional conventions. These are mapped in Tomaney.[57]

Taken together, these five developments amount to a significant change in the ways in which regional governance functions. Thus, the Labour government of 1997–2001 saw a decisive shift from regional governance to what might be termed 'integrated regional governance'.[58] A schema for this development is set out in Table 10.2.

Following its election in 1981, the Mitterrand government in France moved swiftly to legislate for regional assemblies, building on the regionalisation that had deep roots dating back to 1959–60,[59] and artfully delaying the first elections until regional support for the reforms could be constructed.[60] Whether deliberately or not, the Blair government intends to follow a similar strategy, allowing regionalisation to embed and trying to build up regional support for the reforms. However, there are vital differences. Firstly, regionalisation has a much longer

Table 10.2 Typology of regional government/governance

Regional governance	• Ad hoc boundaries • Ad hoc machinery, both governmental and non-governmental, either directed specifically at a territorial area or affecting it from without • No regional assembly
Integrated regional governance	• Agreed boundaries • Shift from non-governmental to governmental machinery • Extensive delegated administration centred on the region • Assembly, if any, appointed by the centre or by local authorities
Regional government	• Agreed boundaries • Governmental institutions • Wide-ranging administrative (or legislative) autonomy, (usually) entrenched by law/constitution • Directly elected assembly

Source: Stevens, C. and Wright, A. (2002) Regionalism, Regionalisation and Regional Government, *Teaching Public Administration*, xxii(1), p.4.

pedigree in France and has been the locus of regional planning. The United Kingdom went through a similar if less wholehearted process in the 1960s, but these developments were largely undone by the Thatcher governments. Secondly, there is greater commitment to localities and regions by the French political elite. Thirdly, and perhaps most critically, the Mitterrand government legislated immediately for regional government. In contrast, the Blair strategy is gradualist and an open-ended process.

This is the paradox at the heart of current Labour proposals. If these proposals are designed to succeed – and it may be the case that they are merely designed to balance the pro and anti forces – it will be because regionalisation, together with the strong commitment of regional elites, has produced sufficient regionalism to produce consent for regional government. Perhaps this need happen in only one region. Thereafter, economic success there will cascade regionalism to other regions. In other words, rather than regionalism produce regionalisation, regionalisation is expected to produce regionalism, and that regionalism is expected to produce regional assemblies. This may work. The work of John Tomaney, who is both a much-published academic commentator on regional government and an activist for a North-East assembly, emphasises the extent to which the administrative apparatus now clustered at regional level has created regionalism. This may be the case for the North-East and one or two other areas, such as the North-West, where regionalisation meets a willing audience. Only time will tell. However, it is more likely that this misses out a vital ingredient. Not only is the weak regionalism thus fashioned unlikely to produce consent for regional government in a polity in which such matters excite little passion, but elected regional government is a vital component of any attempt to strengthen regionalism. Elected regional government offers, to quote Keating once more, 'political space and an effective system of action', and its linkage with resource allocation within the region has the capacity to inspire regional loyalty. The Labour Party may have to create elected assemblies first, if it is to succeed in creating public consent for regional government.

DEMOCRACY AND THE STRATEGIC LEVEL

Despite its reputation to the contrary, the United Kingdom does not have a developed democratic tradition. The monarchic conceit that the United Kingdom is a unitary state in which sovereignty lies with the Crown in Parliament rather than with the people, continues to dominate the political landscape.[61] It is at odds with competing pluralist views of the UK state, which see political life as a federation of interests and associations, in which sovereignty is fragmented and exercised at other levels as well as the central state. The vocabulary of participation sits uneasily within the current British system, and the notion of subsidiarity, the idea that policy should be formulated at the appropriate level within the polity, is almost wholly absent. Democracy is seen primarily as a means of electing a government and recalling it every four or five years. In contrast, any real accumulation of policy-making power at the sub-centre level is seen as conflicting with parliamentary sovereignty. This has been exacerbated by a set of political dynamics which has often juxtaposed a Conservative centre with a Labour sub-centre. In consequence, little space is left for autonomous sub-centre government. This offers one context for understanding the debate over regional government. Supporters argue that it has the capacity to restructure the English polity to embrace regional diversity and to recognise the fragmented nature of sovereignty. One problem here is the apparent lack of demand for such differentiation evidenced by England's weak regionalism. Moreover, even if demand exists, it is difficult to see how the strategic/coordination model currently proposed could meet such an ambition. This invites a discussion about the nature of the strategic level.

The most thoroughgoing postwar analyses of sub-centre government remain the work of two Royal Commissions. The Redcliffe-Maud Commission sat from 1966 to 1969. Its majority report proposed eight indirectly elected provinces, whilst a minority report by Derek Senior proposed five appointed ones. Both allotted mainly coordinating functions to these bodies. The Kilbrandon Commission sat from 1969 to 1973. Two of its members recommended directly elected regional assemblies with executive powers. The majority supported indirectly elected, non-executive bodies. One member wished to see full devolution to local authorities.[62] The starting point for both Redcliffe-Maud and Senior was that local government had two distinct types of function. The first was the provision of personal services, which required closeness to the community. The second was strategic which needed some scale. The majority report argued that, with the exception of three geographical areas, it had found a scale that could provide both through unitary authorities. Senior kept to two tiers, except for four areas, and proposed that 35 city regions carry out the strategic function. The Conservative Party's Local

Government Act of 1972 followed neither recommendation, but it did accept the initial analysis, creating a two-tier system of local governance, with counties offering a strategic level of activity and districts providing personal services.

Thatcherite restructuring in the 1980s had no place for the strategic level. Prosperity was perceived as dependent on positioning business interests and businesspeople at the heart of the policy process. Democracy was seen as an obstacle to that relationship. In consequence, the strategic increasingly became the preserve of appointed bodies at conurbation and regional level. The Major government sought to institutionalise this development, setting up the Banham Commission in 1992 as a means of moving to a system of unitary authorities. Whereas the Redcliffe-Maud Commission had intended a series of strong unitary authorities with strategic capacity, the Thatcher/Major reforms sought to create a local 'enabling state' as a provider of personal services, rather than a strategic actor. The agenda here was not to create a single tier, but to abolish the strategic tier.[63]

In consequence, a strong argument has developed that a democratic deficit has developed around the strategic activities of the appointed Tory state. This is clustered at both the local and the regional level (although, since 1997, the Labour Party has sought to move it to the latter), creating an arena of networked organisations. Policy decision emerges as a consequence of activity within this network rather than through Parliament, and policy coordination is a by-product of interorganisational power bargaining rather than a strategic activity. Moreover, the appointed state is characterised not by pluralism but by embryonic neo-corporatism, in which some bodies are privileged over others. This has squeezed democratic involvement to the periphery of the policy-making process. Neither Parliament nor local authorities can be effective instruments of accountability here. Regional government, it is argued, will reassert democracy and accountability into this process and create the capacity for better policy coordination.

On regional government, New Labour is characteristically ambiguous in respect to its Tory heritage. Three examples of this will suffice. Firstly, the White Paper suggests that 'Representatives of stakeholders and other unelected people with experience or expertise should be able to participate in all aspects of an assembly's work which do not directly involve decisions being taken'.[64] This might involve giving stakeholders voting rights as co-opted members of the chamber's scrutiny apparatus.[65] Secondly, the relationship of chambers within the regional network remains ambiguous. *A Choice for England* suggested that chambers were to work closely with GOs and the appointed state during phase one of the policy.[66] Only in the process of moving to phase two was there to be consideration 'as to whether there were functions currently exercised by [GOs] and quangos which could more appropriately be transferred to elected regional assemblies, or where responsibility might be shared with the assemblies'.[67] This relationship remains ambiguous in the White Paper. Regional government is to play a key role in a range of strategic activities, but its precise engagement with the existing institutions remains unclear. Powers and functions are to be transferred from the GOs. However, at the same time, the government is strengthening the latter.[68] RDAs will continue to exist, and although the elected chamber will be given the role of electing its chair and the board, half of the board must comprise those with current or recent experience of running a business, the chamber must consult government on board appointments, and government can interfere if it thinks that RDA policies are not in line with national needs or are detrimental to another region.[69] The result of this will probably be that policy is made as the result of complex bargaining between the chamber, the GO and the RDAs. It will be interesting to see whether this stipulation allows a region without a chamber to lobby government to ensure that it is not disadvantaged when trying to seek inward investment in competition with a region with a chamber. Thirdly, the Labour White Paper reflects the philosophy of the enabling state when it argues that local government 'will *continue* to focus on local service delivery and community leadership'.[70]

There is another respect in which Labour, and surprisingly Liberals as well, have fallen in with the Conservative analysis. The notion that it is unacceptable to have three sub-centre tiers of government – region, county and district[71] – has almost completely dominated the debate. Concerned in opposition to nullify the Conservative allegation that it was creating unnecessary bureaucracy, the Labour Party insisted in 1995 that regional government be based on a *predominantly* unitary system of local government. By 2002 it had moved further, insisting that a unitary system in a region *must* precede regional government. Any region that becomes a candidate for a referendum will be referred to the Boundary Commission for England, which will be charged to make the necessary changes, which will need Parliamentary approval.[72] This has created sub-centre battle lines. Labour's *A Choice for England* asserted that, 'as shire counties could not generally co-exist with a system of elected regional assemblies [the] creation of the latter would therefore need to coincide with the abolition of the former'.[73] The Conservative Party, in contrast, has pledged to maintain and re-empower the county council, seen as a mainstay of Toryism.[74]

This begs the question of where the strategic function should be properly located. Gerry Stoker has revisited Senior, suggesting a return to the city region principle. Thus, he argues that, 'if the missing link in our structure of government is defined in terms of a strategic, joined-up capacity', large-scale administrative regions are not the answer.[75] He concludes: 'City regions integrate the democratic and economic arguments for regional government and may provide a stronger focus of identity and a more meaningful politics in many areas of the country'.[76] The point about city regions is that they seek to redesign the county-level tier to take into account the demographic changes that came about as the result of industrialisation. In terms of scale, they are not unlike counties. The reasoning behind the Conservative reform of 1972–74 was similar to that of Senior, excepting that it kept to the historical divisions whenever possible. However, it did seek to break with these by creating six metropolitan counties to cover the Manchester, Liverpool, Leeds/Bradford, Sheffield, Birmingham and Newcastle conurbations, and three new shire counties, quasi-metropolitan in character – Avon, Cleveland and Humberside – to cover the Bristol, Teesside and Hull conurbations, respectively. It is difficult to see how regional government will replace the strategic gap left by the abolition of these in the 1980s and 1990s. The case of Teesside offers a good example. A directly elected chamber for the North-East might advantage the Teesside conurbation through mediation of governmental centralism and through regional management of some key policy areas. However, joined-up strategic management will still be needed at conurbation level. The White Paper does make provision for such eventualities, suggesting that regions might create sub-regional apparatus.[77] The effect may be that there will be a significant layer of devolved strategic management within each region. Given that the new regions will probably not absorb much of the current appointed state, that devolved tier will continue to be part of a network of public, private and voluntary bodies at county/conurbation level. The issue, then, is which of these two strategic layers is best given a democratic basis. The regional level has some attractions. It will be more effective than county government in its capacity to bargain with the centre, and it is the locus of the apparatus of economic development. In contrast, directly elected counties, or city regions, coupled with indirectly elected bodies to coordinate their work at regional level might create much less of a democratic deficit.

CONCLUSION

Will English regional government happen in the near future? The answer must be a qualified no. The first hurdle that reformers must cross is to secure government agreement for a referendum. As Nick Raynsford, minister for the regions, recently spelt out, the government will be cautious in allowing a referendum. The decision will be taken only after wide consultation with stakeholders, and it will be a matter 'for Ministers' *judgement*'.[78] The strength of Tomaney's 'civic regionalism' may unite enough interests behind reform in the North-East to clear the way for unitary local government and a referendum there; and there is no reason to suppose any great mobilisation of opinion against a yes vote. The North-West might follow. Thereafter, even then there are serious obstacles. It is hard to see regions such as East England and the South-West agreeing on a unitary tier of authorities or a referendum. Nor will Tories willingly give up a county council power base for a set of regional chambers in which they do not believe. So there is unlikely to be a comprehensive regional tier in the near future. Other regions might go either way. Supporters may hope that regions will begin to look enviously on those with elected chambers, and recognise its economic benefits, resulting in a spillover effect. The evidence here is not encouraging. The appointed state, together with the more advanced existing base of the South and Midlands, may have no difficulty in maintaining and even widening the economic gulf with the North. Even where referendums are successfully held, reform still needs to achieve parliamentary approval, which will need the support of the government. The government has not yet spelled out how it will treat a referendum that produces a small majority and/or a very low turnout. However, it cannot be taken for granted that the government will move in response, especially if reform elsewhere looks very remote.

Firstly, there is a central ambiguity at the core of the New Labour project. The government is unclear whether it is at heart an heir to a social democratic tradition that emphasises the collective over the individual, or to the neo-liberalism of Thatcherism, which endowed individual 'business' leaders with an innate ability to act in the national interest, which it simultaneously denied to elected representatives other than those in the elite of national government. This ambiguity was carefully balanced during phase one of the reform. Voluntary chambers were given the guiding hand of economic partners, whilst business-led RDAs, buttressed by local authority board members, were there to oversee regional investment. The White Paper shifted this balance towards the elected principle, underpinning social democracy. However, the shift is not absolute. RDAs, albeit with chamber-appointed leadership, will still be there to represent business interests. As the White Paper insisted, the presence of business leaders on RDA boards will ensure 'that business will be at the heart of the decision-making process for regional economic development'.[79] The tension between the perceived business imperative of regeneration and the civic regionalism emerging amongst some regional political elites may yet persuade the Blair government to pull back from reform. The decisive move against by the Confederation of British Industry[80] cannot have helped. Secondly, the debate over regional government within Cabinet has still not been resolved. Although supporters are temporarily in the ascendant, that position cannot be taken for granted, especially as the bulk of the reform will come after the next general election (2004 or 2005), with consequent changes in the top offices of state. The hands of the antis will be strengthened if referendums in the North-East and perhaps the North-West look like the only ones likely to succeed. Finally, if the argument of this chapter has been accepted, the dynamic that should drive the change from regionalisation to weak regional assemblies is not there.

If regional government does come about, what will it look like? It will certainly have strategic capacity rather than executive authority, and it is unlikely to acquire the latter through incremental changes. More important, it is hard to see the proposed chambers embodying a central characteristic of government – control of the governmental apparatus in the region. Given the nature of New Labour's regional policy, chambers are more likely to find themselves acting as part of a regional network, comprising in addition GOs and RDAs, and having to negotiate strategy through this. It is the contention of this chapter that, as currently planned, this may leave elected regional chambers looking more like a component in an integrated system of regional governance than regional government per se. There is a catch-22 situation here. Ambitions for a national system of regional chambers depend on spillover, as the benefits of established chambers become apparent to those without them. Minimal regional government in one or two regions, which adds, or is allowed to add, nothing economically to a region, is unlikely to generate demand for elected chambers in other regions. The absence of spillover will encourage the government to minimise regional government and force it to intervene to maintain inward investment in areas without chambers. Regional government may be with us by 2010, but it is likely to be both partial and minimal.

NOTES

1. Hansard, 6 December 1991, col. 512
2. Liberal Democrat Party, *Here We Stand: Liberal Democrat Policies for Modernising Britain's Democracy*, Federal Paper 6 (London: Liberal Democrat Publications, 1993) pp.32–6. Despite this rhetoric, the proposals were similar to Labour ones. The working group that compiled the proposals was chaired by Andrew Adonis, soon to be one of Blair's advisers.
3. Labour Party, *A Choice for England: A Consultation Paper on Labour's Plans for English Regional Government* (July 1995) p.18
4. Ibid., p.2
5. Ibid., p.20
6. Ibid., p.19
7. Ibid., p.3
8. Ibid., p.21
9. Regional Policy Commission, *Renewing the Regions: Strategies for Regional Economic Development* (Sheffield: Sheffield Hallam Publications, 1996) p.33
10. R. Hazell, Regional Government in England: Three Policies in Search of a Strategy, in Selina Chen and Tony Wright, *The English Question* (London: Fabian Society, 2000) pp.32–3
11. E. Wood, *Regional Government in England*, House of Commons Research Paper 98–009 (13 January 1998) p.12
12. Hazell, Regional Government in England, p.33
13. Ibid.
14. Office of the Deputy Prime Minister, *DPM Speech to the LGA Annual Conference, 3 July 2002* (2002)
15. M. Sandford and P. McQuail, *Unexplored Territory: Elected Assemblies in England* (London: UCL, Constitution Unit, 2001) pp.72–85; P. McQuail and M. Sandford, Elected Regional Government: The Issues, in J. Tomaney and J. Mawson (eds), *England: The State of the Regions* (Bristol: Policy Press, 2002) pp.178–80
16. *Your Region, Your Choice: Revitalising the English Regions*, Cm 5511 (London: The Stationery Office, 2002) p.53
17. Ibid., Annex G
18. Ibid., pp.34–43
19. On Wales, see J. Osmond, In Search of Stability: Coalition Politics in the Second Year of the National Assembly for Wales, in A. Trench (ed.), *The State of the Nations 2001: The Second Year of Devolution in the United Kingdom* (London: Imprint Academic, 2001)
20. M. Keating, *The New Regionalism in Western Europe: Territorial Restructuring and Political Change* (London: Edward Elgar, 1998) p.110. Some may differ with Keating over the location of Wales in the first category rather than in the second.
21. See below, passim.
22. W.R. Barter, *Regional Government in England: A Preliminary Review of Literature and Research Findings* (London: The Stationery Office, 2000) p.18

23. A. Harding, R. Evans, M. Parkinson and P. Garside, *Regional Government in England: An Economic Solution?* (Bristol: Policy Press, 1996); R. Evans and A. Harding, Regionalism, Regional Institutions and Economic Development, *Policy and Politics* 25(1) (1997) pp.19–30

24. Barter, *Regional Government*, p.18

25. R. Nanetti, *Growth and Territorial Politics: The Italian Model of Social Capitalism* (London: Pinter, 1988); A. Rodríguez-Pose, Growth and Institutional Change: The Influence of the Spanish Regionalisation Process on Economic Performance, *Environment and Planning C: Government and Policy* 14 (1996) pp.71–87

26. Ibid., p.38

27. Labour Party, *Choice for England*, p.11

28. C. Harvie, *The Rise of Regional Europe* (London: Routledge, 1994) p.5

29. C. Stevens and A. Wright, Regionalism, Regionalisation and Regional Government, *Teaching Public Administration*, xxii(1) (2002) pp.4–7

30. B.W. Hogwood and M. Keating (eds), *Regional Government in England* (Oxford: Clarendon Press, 1982)

31. J.N. Rosenau, Governance, Order, and Change in World Politics, in J.N. Rosenau and E.-O. Czempiel (eds), *Governance Without Government: Order and Change in World Politics* (Cambridge: Cambridge University Press, 1992) p.4

32. B.W. Hogwood and P.D. Lindley, Variations in Regional Boundaries, in Hogwood and Keating, *Regional Government in England*, pp.21–49

33. The terminology for these has changed from Integrated Regional Offices (IROs) to Government Offices for the Regions (GORs) to simply Government Offices (GOs).

34. M. Keating and M. Rhodes, The Status of Regional Government: An Analysis of the West Midlands, in Hogwood and Keating, *Regional Government in England*, p.72

35. Department of the Environment *News Release*, 731 (4 November 1993); The Constitution Unit, *Regional Government in England* (London: UCL, 1996) pp.39–48; J. Mawson and K. Spencer, The Government Offices for the English Regions: Towards Regional Governance?, *Policy and Politics* 25(1) (1997) pp.71–84; J. Mawson and K. Spencer, The Origins and Operation of the Government Offices for the English Regions, in J. Bradbury and J. Mawson (eds), *British Regionalism and Devolution: The Challenges of State Reform and European Integration* (London: Jessica Kingsley Publishers, 1997); K. Spencer and J. Mawson, Government Offices and Policy Co-ordination in the English Regions, *Local Governance* 24(2) (1998) pp.101–9

36. (i) Home Office, (ii) Culture, Media and Sport, (iii) Environment, Food and Rural Affairs, (iv) Education and Skills, (v) Trade and Industry, (vi) Transport, (vii) Work and Pensions, (viii) Health.

37. See Office of the Deputy Prime Minister, *Introducing the Government Offices* (London: The Stationery Office, 2002), and the websites of the Regional Co-ordination Unit and the various regional offices.

38. See Cabinet Office, *Reaching Out: The Role of Central Government at Regional and Local Level*, Performance and Innovation Unit (London: The Stationery Office, 2000)

39. Interview.

40. Alan Harding *et al.*, *Regional Government in England*, p.84

41. North of England Assembly of Local Authorities, *Regional Government Consultation Paper* (August 1995)

42. Labour Party, *Choice for England*, p.2

43. Crown, *Building Partnerships for Prosperity: Sustainable Growth, Competitiveness and Employment in the English Regions*, DETR, Cm 3814 (London: The Stationery Office, 1997) pp.52–3

44. Department of Environment, Transport and the Regions, *Guidance on Voluntary Regional Chambers*, press release, 11 August 1998

45. *Your Region, Your Choice*, p.24

46. J. Tomaney, The Regional Governance of England, in R. Hazell (ed.), *The State of the Nations: The First Year of Devolution in the United Kingdom* (London: Imprint Academic, 2000) p.129; The House of Commons, *Regional Development Agencies: Report of the Environment, Transport and Regions Select Committee*, HC 232–1 (London: The Stationery Office, 1999), para.30

47. Ibid., pp.124–8

48. Ibid., p.124

49. Ibid., pp.125–7

50. *Building Partnerships for Prosperity*, p.50

51. Ibid., p.9

52. Ibid., p.49

53. The White Paper does not close the door on boundary adjustment, pointing out for example that were it to adjust the GO regions to meet national needs, the chamber regions would be required to follow suit (*Your Region, Your Choice*, p.49).

54. Tomaney, Regional Governance, p.131

55. S. Ayres and G. Pearce, *Who Governs the West Midlands? An Audit of Government Institutions and Structures* (Aston Business School, March 2002); J. Tomaney and L. Humphrey, *Regional Government in North East England: A Study for the North-East Assembly* (Newcastle: Centre for Urban and Regional Studies, University of Newcastle, 2001)

56. As John Osmond writes on Wales, 'Looking back on the National Assembly's first year, it is hard not to conclude that what took place was in effect, a Welsh alternative to the Scottish Convention – a Welsh Convention by other means.' (Osmond, 2000, p.76)

57. J. Tomaney, New Labour and the Evolution of Regionalism in England, in Tomaney and Mawson, *England: The State of the Regions*.

58. Stevens and Wright, Regionalism, Regionalisation and Regional Government

59. J-C. Douence, The Evolution of the 1982 Regional Reforms: An Overview, *Regional Politics and Policy* 4(3) (1994) p.17

60. V.A. Schmidt, *Democratizing France: The Political and Administrative History of Decentralization* (Cambridge: Cambridge University Press, 1990) p.107

61. The Scottish Claim of Right disputes this, asserting that sovereignty in Scotland lies with the Scottish people, on the grounds that the union of the two states could not deprive the Scottish people of this right. Unionists find this particularly worrying both because it underlines the right of Scots to opt for a non-unionist destiny and because unionists are intrinsic monarchists for whom the Union is a manifestation of the Crown in Parliament.

62. *Royal Commission on the Constitution, 1969–1973*, Cmnd 5460 (London: HMSO, 1973), vol. 1, p.353

63. C. Stevens, The Attempted Re-organization of Local Government, 1992–1995 (forthcoming)

64. *Your Region, Your Choice*, p.52

65. Ibid., p.54

66. Labour Party, *Choice for England*, 1995, pp.18–19

67. Ibid., p.20

68. *Your Region, Your Choice*, pp.28–30

69. Ibid., p.38

70. Ibid., p.34; emphasis added

71. Alongside the partial parish council structure; but that too is under pressure.

72. *Your Region, Your Choice*, pp.60–1

73. Labour Party, *Choice for England*, p.16. There is a troubling contradiction in Labour policy, here. The White Paper stresses that regional government will entail devolution from the centre and not the transfer upwards of local authority functions (*Your Region, Your Choice*, p.34). This is clearly impossible.

74. Conservative Party, *Time for Common Sense*, Election Manifesto (London: Conservative Party, 2001) p.23

75. G. Stoker, Is Regional Government the Answer to the English Question?, in S. Chen and T. Wright (eds), *The English Question*, pp.72–3

76. Ibid., p.75

77. *Your Region, Your Choice*, p.49

78. Office of the Deputy Prime Minister, *Speech by Nick Raynsford to the Campaign for the English Regions Conference, Newcastle, 31 July 2002* (2002); original emphasis

79. *Your Region, Your Choice*, p.38

80. CBI position statement, 14 October 2002: 'We are unable to support the White Paper. We have therefore urged the Government to abandon these flawed plans and to work on other means of improving governance and economic improvement in the regions'.

The impact of European integration

Janet Mather

INTRODUCTION

This chapter examines the impact of European integration on devolution in the United Kingdom. It begins by pointing out that the United Kingdom lacks the essential attributes of a classic unitary state, primarily because, given its uncodified constitution, it has within it sufficient flexibility to change both its constitutional arrangements and its policy-making practices. In particular, it is pointed out, the UK has made a number of those adaptations in response to the demands of and opportunities provided by the European Union. One of these adaptations, it is suggested, is devolution itself. The chapter then looks at how the devolved bodies have reacted to their new position *vis-à-vis* the EU. It examines the way in which they have organised themselves internally and how they have adapted to operating at the supranational level, in terms of both their formal and informal activities within the EU. It is noted that whilst both the Scottish and the Welsh bodies have become active, there is a difference between them. One of these differences is that Scotland has begun to form alliances with other regions and countries of the EU. In other words, it is beginning to assume the behaviour of a state in its interactions. Wales's chosen forums for participation are European inter-institutional associations, indicating that Wales has accepted its status as a region (despite its objections to the term) of the United Kingdom. In both cases, devolution has enabled them to participate at the supranational level of governance.

The chapter argues that if the EU has helped establish *multi*-level governance, evidence is most likely to be found by looking at the implementation of its regional policy. The administration of the structural funds, partially by-passing the national level of government, has given influence and authority to the United Kingdom's sub-national governmental levels. Particularly since 1994, the focus has been upon involving non-governmental participants in the form of the 'social partners' – representatives of employers, labour and 'other interests'. Yet, it is acknowledged, multi-level participation is not the same as multi-level governance.[1] Central government in the United Kingdom can, for its own purposes, encourage the *involvement* of sub-national actors and non-governmental interests, but this does not mean that it need confer *powers* upon them, or that it has done so.

However, another potential effect of the EU's policy upon the devolved institutions needs to be considered. It has encouraged the United Kingdom, the unitary state, to 'devolve' – to develop regionally elected tiers of governance. This was partly to capitalise upon the distribution of EU funds, but it was also partly because the particular utility of a unitary state itself is challenged when the United

Kingdom, 'at the heart of Europe', finds itself one amongst fifteen member states most of which have discovered other means of effective governance. Evidence of shifting attitudes, it is argued, can be found by examining the continued efforts made by the New Labour government to devolve power to the *English* regions. The final section of the chapter looks at the apparent impact of the EU in this area, by noting the government's own arguments for regional devolution as presented in the 2002 White Paper *Your Region, Your Choice: Revitalising the English Regions*.[2]

The chapter suggests, then, that the impact of the EU upon devolution in the United Kingdom is multi-faceted. It coalesces into a blend of economic and political factors, resulting in changing practices and changing dynamics between central and sub-national actors. Whatever the cause, however, it is noted that the outcome demonstrates again the flexibility of the 'classic unitary state'.

A CLASSIC UNITARY STATE?

Of the fifteen member states of the EU, Britain is regarded as being one of those that most closely matches the model of a classic unitary state. Various aspects of UK governance lend legitimacy to this judgement. Firstly, the UK has no written constitution that could guarantee the powers of a sub-national level of government. There is therefore no horizontal separation of powers. Secondly, the UK's constitutional practice has resulted in a doubtful vertical separation of powers amongst the executive, legislature and judiciary. This fuzziness used to be epitomised in the person of the Lord Chancellor, who was simultaneously a member of all three, but more importantly it is made explicit by the facts that members of the Cabinet are invariably[3] drawn from the Houses of Parliament, and that Cabinet ministers retain their positions as members of Parliament. Thirdly, the single member simple plurality (first-past-the-post) electoral system helps to provide a majority party in the House of Commons. The powers of patronage of the prime minister mean that the executive is therefore usually in a position to claim loyalty from the majority of the legislature – strengthening not only a unitary government but also the unitary nature of the state. For example, Margaret Thatcher was effectively able to abolish the Greater London Council and the six metropolitan county councils by calling upon her simple majority in the House of Commons.

However, it is important to note that there is no such thing as a classic unitary state amongst modern western liberal democracies. Both the principle of liberalism, which implies limited governmental *practices*, and the principle of democracy, which involves a means of limiting governmental *powers*, prevent a liberal democratic state from developing the degree of centralised authority that a classic unitary state would require. In addition, there are few countries in the western world that consist of a homogeneous polity, and the United Kingdom is not one of them. The United Kingdom has a multi-nationality, multi-cultural population, whose loyalty to the centre state depends upon the state's leaders taking account of their needs and preferences. This is more than just a quibble in the context of the impact of European integration. A state that really operated effectively only from the centre, and which consisted either of a homogenised polity or a homogeneous public would not have been able to continue as a member of the EU for almost thirty years, and certainly not from 1986[4] with the adoption of the Single Market programme. In reality, the United Kingdom, overtly reluctantly, but in practice cooperatively, has accepted its position as part of a supranational organisation, and has changed its practices, and thus its policy processes, accordingly. For example, in 1987 during Margaret Thatcher's term of office, the government created Her Majesty's Inspectorate of Pollution – a unified inspectorate of pollution – in response to the EU's environmental agenda as laid out in the Single European Act (SEA). The establishment of this agency in turn meant a change in the form of interaction within the governmental bureaucracy and between bureaucracy and interest groups.

Despite its centralising characteristics, then, the UK polity has been open to adjustments, if not always to radical changes, in its constitutional arrangements and its policy processes when they were needed. One reason for this is the well-known 'flexibility' available to a state without a codified constitution. Modifications can develop incrementally and almost unnoticeably, as circumstances require, and there is no need for the media spotlight, with potential for intense debate and uncertainty, that results from procedures laid down for changes in written constitutions.[5] However, constitutional 'flexibility' is not the only reason, nor even the best one. Ironically, probably the best reason is one of the factors that give the United Kingdom its reputation for being a centralised state. Where radical change is needed, and where the need coincides with the presence of a prime minister who is prepared to grasp the nettle, it may be accomplished relatively easily. Given a loyal House of Commons, and a cooperative House of Lords, councils may be abolished, or sub-national parliaments created, on the back of prime ministerial determination.

So far as the EU is concerned, there has been a succession of prime ministers, from both political parties, who have been sufficiently pragmatic to make necessary 'adjustments' to enable the United Kingdom to meet the requirements of membership of a supranational polity. Edward Heath, Conservative prime minister from 1970 to 1974, took the United Kingdom into the European Communities; Harold Wilson, his Labour successor, held the first ever referendum – over the heads of his cabinet and parliamentary colleagues – to endorse the nation's membership. Margaret Thatcher put her name to the SEA, and enabled the United Kingdom to measure up to its main requirements by accepting the requirement for almost 300 modifications to existing trading practices. John Major took the first, and possibly the most significant, step towards modern regionalisation when he established ten integrated regional governmental offices throughout England, which were needed to enable the United Kingdom to benefit from the EU's structural funds. Tony Blair, Major's Labour successor, made the political map of the United Kingdom *appear* to conform to a devolved, rather than a unitary, state of the EU.

Of course, this summary of events does not do justice to the number or extent of adjustments that have been made to the United Kingdom's constitutional arrangements or institutional practices. Simply by joining the Communities, the United Kingdom accepted the primacy of EC law over laws passed by its own parliament.[6] The question of diminished sovereignty, in as much as it is a realistic question to ask in a globalised world, has since generated much animated discussion, all of which *starts* from the assumption that the United Kingdom's powers of self-determination have shrunk. In this context, then, a consideration of multi-level governance, and its impact upon the United Kingdom's policy processes, also begins with the observations, first, that the United Kingdom does not have *single-level* (or state-centric) governance, and, secondly, that this situation results from conscious decision making on the part of its leaders.

UK DEVOLUTION AND THE EUROPEAN UNION

It may be argued that the government elected in 1997, led by Tony Blair, drew strength from its fellow EU governments when devolving governance to the non-English British nations.[7] Most other EU states, as the government's 2002 White Paper[8] points out, have some form of regional governance. It is also possible that other EU states' experience of devolution has demonstrated that the sovereign state need not fear it.[9] Whether or not the government needed reassurance from the EU, between 1998 and 1999 Scotland was granted its own parliament; Wales and Northern Ireland[10] their own assemblies, and London, alone within England at the time, gained a mayor and elected assembly. The rest of England was given regional development agencies (RDAs) accountable to central government,[11] with non-elected regional chambers (later assemblies).[12] (RDAs are already common in central and eastern Europe, and their establishment is a prerequisite for EU applicant states.)

The government initiated devolution, not federalism, so that the UK Parliament retains the constitutional power to claw back its gift. It was also ambiguous about the extent to which some powers or responsibilities were being devolved. One example of this, as Bogdanor points out,[13] was the question of the part played in practice in negotiations with the EU by the devolved Scottish Parliament, which was left in the air in the government's White Paper on Scotland.

Bogdanor[14] notes, for example, that the Scottish Executive was to have full responsibility for implementing EU directives on agriculture and fisheries, but its rights of representation on the Council of Ministers, where policy is formulated, depended upon it accepting the government's ground rules. The Welsh Assembly similarly has responsibility for implementing EU directives, but no guaranteed rights of consultation. In any case, representatives at this level have to speak collectively for the United Kingdom – that is, they voice views as determined by central government, acting as the agent of the sovereign Parliament, rather than on behalf of their sub-national body.[15] The EU requires one, rather than three, UK voices on the Council of Ministers and, as Bulmer *et al.* comment, 'Devolution may not increase the range of policy options on matters where the EU requires member state-wide solutions.'[16]

Bogdanor, writing before the institution of the new bodies, speculated that their position *vis-à-vis* the EU could actually be weakened, since, whilst their representatives have no automatic right of representation at either Cabinet or Council meetings, devolution has meant that Scottish and Welsh secretaries of state have reduced roles at both.[17] However, he pointed out that secretaries of state were infrequent attendees at the Council in any case, so he suggested that the Scottish and Welsh bodies might gain as pressure groups more than they lost by the disappearance of their former 'champions'.

Since the new institutions have been operating for a relatively short time, it is hard to estimate their importance as actors within public policy involving the EU. However, the EU has provided opportunities for devolved bodies seeking status and autonomy,[18] and, if the Scottish Parliament and Welsh Assembly may be taken as examples, they have responded with enthusiasm to the challenge. At any rate, they have both undertaken a significant amount of activity in both the United Kingdom and the EU.

Devolved governments and their EU structures

Both the Scottish Parliament and Welsh Assembly have structured their institutions to respond to EU matters. Surprisingly, however, there is no one minister from the Scottish Executive with responsibility for European matters. It is shared between the deputy first minister, who is responsible for external relations, especially development and implementation of links with Europe, and the minister for finance and public services, who is responsible for the administration of European structural funds. The External Relations Division of the Scottish Executive Secretariat supports the Scottish Executive in its dealings with the EU. In Brussels, the Scottish Executive European Union Office acts in an advisory capacity to the Executive.

There is a European Committee of the Scottish Parliament, which is currently convened by Irene Oldfather, the Scottish Parliament's representative on the EU's Committee of the Regions (CoR). The European Committee visited Brussels on two occasions during the first three years of the Scottish Parliament (the conveners of other parliamentary committees also visited Brussels) to discuss topics of concern to Scotland with representatives of EU institutions – particularly the Commission, UKRep and the European Parliament. It has also used its status to begin a dialogue with its social partners in business, the voluntary sector, the educational establishment and other institutions.

The structure of the Welsh Assembly[19] has also responded to its role within the EU. It has instituted a European and External Affairs Directorate, which is one of the four divisions of its Economic Development Department. Amongst other responsibilities, the European Directorate is concerned with EU regional and competition policy and takes care of the Brussels Office of the National Assembly for Wales. The Welsh Assembly also has a European and External Affairs Committee, which attempts to ensure that the Assembly as a whole adopts a consistent approach to the EU. The Committee also considers the impact of the EU's institutions on Welsh interests, and all Welsh representatives at the EU level, nominated or elected, have a standing invitation to attend its twice-yearly meetings.

Devolved governments in Brussels

The establishment of lobbying offices in Brussels is regarded as being one of the more obvious manifestations of the multi-level governance thesis – that is the notion that decision-making is conducted by means of interaction amongst participating levels of government.[20] This is because it enables sub-national actors to enlarge their roles, and also to make use of the opportunities offered by proximity to interact with EU-based institutions, including the Commission, the Committee of Permanent Representatives (Coreper), and the Parliament (when it is there). Both the Scottish Parliament and the Welsh Assembly have formalised their presence in the EU. In 1999, the Scottish Executive's Europe and External Affairs department opened an office in Brussels – Scotland House – which is geographically close to the EU's institutions there. The premises are shared with Scotland Europa, an umbrella body established in 1992 representing various public, private and voluntary interests. The Scottish Executive EU Office has a wide-ranging remit. It acts as the interface between Scotland and the EU, gathering and exchanging information between Scottish governmental and non-governmental bodies and the EU's institutions, attempting to influence EU policy, and, by its presence and its activities, trying to raise Scotland's profile in the EU. It also, in common with other UK offices in Brussels, interacts with the United Kingdom's permanent representation to the EU – UKRep – on devolved matters, and on non-devolved matters that have an impact upon Scotland.

The Welsh Assembly has adopted a similar path, but on a smaller scale. A Brussels office was established in 2000. Its role is similar to that of Scotland House, although it has only a small permanent staff of three. However, the Welsh Assembly seconds officers to the Commission and to UKRep.

Devolved governments and EU institutions

Ministers from the devolved governments have attended meetings of the Council of Ministers. From May 1999 to May 2000, the Scottish Executive EU Office recorded that it had attended 11, two of which were informal, but officials from the office had also attended 75 Council working groups.[21] The minister for rural affairs, Sarah Boyak, minister for environment and transport, had attended an Environment Council; Ross Finnie had attended Agricultural Council meetings, and the deputy minister, Rhona Brankin and her predecessor, John Home Robertson, had attended Fisheries Council meetings. Working relationships have also been set up with Scottish members of the European Parliament (MEPs), and with Scottish members of the CoR. The European Parliament (EP) has received delegations from Scottish MSPs and Scottish civil servants. The EP's calendar of activities for 2001 lists three visits from MSPs and two from civil servants, whilst a meeting was held between the Committee on Petitions of the European Parliament and the corresponding Committee of the Scottish Parliament in Edinburgh in June 2001.[22]

Welsh ministers also attend meetings of the Council of Ministers, even, on occasion, leading for the United Kingdom.[23] The Assembly's first minister, Rhodri Morgan, commented that he thought that ministers had achieved a much higher level of attendance at the Council of Ministers than he thought would be possible in its first two years.[24] There is also evidence of Welsh ministers meeting UKRep, the European Commission and the CoR. Welsh MEPs have standing invitations to the meetings of the Committee of European Affairs, along with Welsh representatives on the European Economic and Social Committee, the CoR, the European Commission Representation in Wales and the Head of the Assembly's office in Brussels.[25]

Following devolution, Scotland and Wales have been able to nominate their own direct representatives to the CoR,[26] whilst the Greater London Authority (GLA) and existing English regional assemblies propose one representative and one alternate member each through the Local Government Association (LGA). The LGA makes proposals for the remaining English seats.[27] The Scottish Executive provides the joint secretariat for the UK delegation whilst supporting its own members.

Devolved governments working in the EU

Both Scotland and Wales have made full use of their status as regions to form relationships with their opposite numbers within the EU, and, on occasions, with candidate countries. An early example of the Scottish Parliament's European activities was the inauguration of a forum of the chairs of the United Kingdom's European committees, involving the Scottish Parliament, the Welsh and Northern Ireland Assemblies and the Houses of Commons and Lords. The first meeting of the European Chairs – UK Group (EC-UK) took place in Strathclyde in November 2000. Since then, it has met every six months in each region in turn.

Most Scottish initiatives in relation to forming relationships with other EU states and regions seem to have been individualistic. To date, the Scottish Regional Committee has emphasised the forming of links with the Swedish Parliament and with other EU regions such as Saxony-Anhalt (Germany); the Flemish Parliament, the Basque region, Bavaria and Catalonia. Wales, on the other hand, has emphasised its involvement with groups within the EU. For example, it notes its attendance at the Conference of Presidents of Regions with Legislative Powers and the Annual General Assembly of the Conference of Peripheral and Maritime Regions. It has also accepted an invitation from the president of the Emilia-Romagna region of Italy[28] to join a network looking at the implications of the Commission White Paper on governance for regional tier governments.

The impression is that whilst the Scottish Parliament views itself as an embryonic state, forming alliances with other states or potential states, the Welsh Assembly envisages its future as that of a devolved region in the EU (although its newsletter reminded its readers that 'regional' was an EU term; its own term was 'national'[29]).

Powers or influence?

It has been shown that both Scottish and Welsh devolved institutions are actively engaged with EU institutions and with other EU states and regions. This does not prove that either has gained power, nor can it be ascertained from this how much influence they have. Scottish or Welsh ministers may attend Council of Ministers meetings, and even lead for the United Kingdom, but there is no way of estimating how independent or influential their contribution has been. Council meetings are usually held *in camera*, and the informal pre-meeting negotiations are always private, whilst the tendency of ministers to try to reach agreement hides both the presence and the absence of dissenting views. For example, in December 2000, the Fisheries Council, in which Rhona Brankin MSP represented the United Kingdom,[30] took a decision to raise the total allowed catch of cod and haddock in the west of Scotland from the levels proposed by the European Commission.[31] This decision was clearly in the short-term interests of Scotland, but there is no way of estimating the effectiveness or otherwise of Ms Brankin's presence.

Nevertheless, there is some evidence that both devolved institutions have gained status within the EU since their inauguration as units of governance. The Scottish Parliament has managed to establish a tradition of receiving visits from ambassadors of countries due to assume the EU presidency, whilst the Belgian ambassador visited the Welsh Assembly on the eve of Belgium taking on the EU's presidency in 2001. This implies that both devolved institutions have gained something of a foothold as players on the European scene.

The real test of the impact of devolution, however, is based upon its impact within the United Kingdom, to determine whether recently devolved institutions play a significant part in implementing EU policies. The area chosen for this examination is the application of the EU's structural funds. Not only is this an area that directly concerns all regions of the United Kingdom, but also the participation of sub-national units of government is actually required by the EU.[32] For this reason, structural policy is frequently selected by proponents of the multi-level governance theory as a test case for the thesis. Indications of increasing autonomy on the part of sub-national working within a system of multi-level governance should be found within this area.

MULTI-LEVEL GOVERNANCE AND THE POLICY PROCESS

It has been argued that the determination of public policy in the twenty-first century is defined by a number of levels of governance. The argument that proponents of this theory make is not that national state actors are now marginalised, but rather that they are no longer the only important decision-makers. Multi-level governance theorists do not only believe that the EU has changed the policy process by taking on more powers, they think also that the interaction amongst players at supra-, national and sub-national levels of governance – resulting from the way in which the EU operates – has led to a movement away from the previous state-centric model of policy making.

Marks *et al.*[33] isolate three main strands to the multi-level governance argument. Firstly, they point out that decision-making competences are not monopolised by national actors, but rather that they are shared by actors operating at a number of different levels. This means that supranational institutions have independent influences that are not only derived from their role as agents of the state executive. Institutions such as the European Commission, the European Court of Justice, and the European Parliament take on a 'European' identity of their own, rather than being composed of groups of competing interests derived from each member state. Thus, it is necessary to analyse the role played by European-level actors when looking at policy making that has a European dimension. In the case of the United Kingdom, it is shown below that, in relation to the structural funds, devolution has affected the dynamics of the interaction between the EU level, national level and sub-national levels of government.

Secondly, Marks *et al.* point out that collective decision making amongst national state representatives means a loss of control for each individual state executive. Decisions requiring unanimity tend only to concern 'big issues' such as areas of further integration. Once a policy area is decided as being a matter of common concern, the decisions made within that policy area, even where they affect the internal affairs of an individual state, are made in accordance with qualified majority voting. In relation to agriculture and fisheries, this is clearly demonstrated. However, in relation to the EU's structural funds, whilst important decisions are made at the supranational, rather than the national, level, they do not entirely follow the pattern prescribed by the multi-level governance thesis. The criteria for allocating the funds to member states for 2000–06 were decided by the Berlin European Council in 1999.[34] The Commission then determined the distribution of funds on the basis of these criteria.

Thirdly, Marks *et al.* note that political arenas are not contained just within member states. Sub-national actors, from sub-national government or non-governmental areas (groups), operate themselves within the supranational, as well as the national, arena by interrelating directly with the EU's supranational institutions. Such activities would be assisted, of course, by physically locating in Brussels. Whilst the central state is an important actor in these interrelations, it is not the only one, although the relative importance of sub-national institutions depends upon the scale of autonomy granted to them by the centre state. The thesis also accepts that the degree of multi-level governance varies amongst policy areas, and that it is particularly relevant in relation to structural funds.[35]

Public policy analysts argue that policy making (like devolution[36]) is a process rather than an event. This means that public policy passes through a number of stages, each of which helps to shape the policy. The simplest model, defined by Jordan and Richardson in 1987,[37] includes agenda-setting, solution-finding, decision-making, implementation and evaluative stages. Looking at each of these stages in relation to EU's policy areas, there is *prima facie* evidence for the relevance of the multi-level governance theory. For example, the agenda for regional policy was set at the EU level primarily as an offshoot of the Single Market programme (see below). The EU's structural funds were devised, in negotiation with member states, to resolve the question of regional imbalances, although, in the context of the decision-making stage, the amount the EU contributes to the structural funds was decided upon by means of hard bargaining within the Council.[38] The 1999 Council decision, in fact, has been said to mark a movement *away* from the multi-level governance thesis, towards giving more control to central governments.[39]

However, Marks *et al.* think that the implementation stage shows multi-level governance at its most prominent. The Commission is the supranational body charged with executing the implementation of decisions, but national governments are the bodies responsible for implementation. These responsibilities are shared. National governments monitor the executive powers of the Commission, but this is conducted in conjunction with sub-national governments and non-governmental institutions. The Commission in practice has a more than executive interest over implementation and this brings it into close contact with sub-national governments and groups. Again this applies particularly to the structural funds, where Behrens and Smyrl allege that the Commission has the 'institutional advantage' over central governments.[40]

Marks *et al.* list their reasons for emphasising the importance of the implementation stage. Firstly, they point out that although the Commission is responsible for delivering administrative regulations, it does this in cooperation with national governments and also, especially in technical matters, with sub-national officials or representatives of groups. Secondly, apart from the formulating of regulations, implementation automatically requires regular contacts amongst the different levels of government. These can be formalised or voluntary. The participants in these kinds of contacts are selected by central government, but we can assume that governmental control over their input is limited to some extent. In the UK case, the delivery of the EU's structural funds involves, as shown below, a number of bodies below the national level. Thirdly, Marks *et al.* refer to the direct involvement of the Commission in day-to-day implementation. This is particularly noticeable in the administration of the EU's structural funds. In this policy area, as shown below, the Commission has direct involvement with sub-state authorities. This could lead to a decline in the power of the centre state – both in directing the EU's policies in this area and in directing its own policies towards its regions.

UK DEVOLUTION AND THE EU'S STRUCTURAL FUNDS

The structural funds

Structural funds have existed since 1975, but they were developed and formalised from 1987 in the report of the then Commission president, Jacques Delors, *Making a Success of the Single Act*, which strengthened the basis from which funds could be distributed[41] and committed the Community to doubling the resources available to it. From 1987 also, it has been the EU, rather than the member states, that decided which regions should benefit. Specific geographical areas in the EU are eligible for assistance through regional programmes and structural funds based on criteria determined by the EU.[42] The development of the funds was formulated to iron out the economic discrepancies and social imbalances among the EU's regions. There were two main reasons for the EU assuming this role. Firstly, for economic reasons, the EU wanted to assist in maximising the benefits of the internal market, following the implementation of the SEA,[43] by increasing the overall financial basis of the Community.[44] Secondly, for political reasons, the EU wanted to help persuade individual states to accept other EU policies by using the funds as bargaining counters.[45] The programmes are seen as cornerstones of EU policy, but member states have always shown themselves keen to retain control of the funds. For example, the Commission's attempt to draw up a map of EC regions was over-ruled by the Council. Confusions arose also in the early days of administering the funds because there was no definition of a region. Some were defined politically, for example the German Länder; others were based upon national planning decisions, for example the United Kingdom.[46]

Over one-third of the EU's budget[47] is devoted to regional policies. Structural funds, to be allocated directly to the EU's regions, social funds, community initia-tives[48] and cohesion funds[49] target the poorest regions. The resources available for commitment from the funds for the period 2000–06 are €213 billion at 1999 prices (about £154 billion). The United Kingdom has been allocated 8.52 per cent of the total.[50] It should be pointed out that this is a relatively small amount of the overall spending directed at the United Kingdom's regions.

The EU has laid down three primary Objectives to be met.[51] Objective 1 is designed to promote the development and structural adjustment of regions whose development is lagging behind. Objective 1 is allocated 69.7 per cent of the struc-tural funds (that is, a total of €135.9 billion[52]) including 4.3 per cent for transitional support. Merseyside, South Yorkshire, Cornwall and the Isles of Scilly, and West Wales and the Valleys are included as Objective 1 areas.[53] Objective 2 supports the economic and social conversion of areas facing structural difficulties. It is allocated 11.5 per cent of the structural funds (that is, a total of €22.5 billion[54]) including 1.4 per cent for transitional support. Many regions in the United Kingdom, particu-larly Yorkshire, the north-west, north-east and the West Midlands of England, the north-east, north-west and south of Scotland and east Wales, are recipients of Objective 2 funds. Objective 3 supports the adaptation and modernisation of policies and systems of education, training and employment. It is allocated 12.3 per cent of the structural funds (that is, a total of €24.05 billion[55]). In the United Kingdom, there are currently programmes benefiting east Wales and the parts of England and Scotland not in receipt of funds for Objectives 1 and 2. A number of other objectives, such as the Rural Development Plan for Wales, and four community initiatives – Leader+,[56] Urban II,[57] Interreg IIIa[58] and Equal[59] – are also directed by and partly financed by the EU.

The significance of this in relation to devolution is the part that the regional and non-governmental levels play in deciding how the funds should be spent. Since 1988, it has been the regional level, along with national governments and, from 1994, in conjunction with the 'social partners' (representatives of industry and rep-resentatives of labour) who have to submit regional development plans to the Commission. They must detail proposed arrangements for spending Community structural funds. This is said to have had the effect of stimulating political mobilisation around programmes and spending projects. However, the 1999 Berlin European Council was concerned about how the funds were to be administered and managed:

> The administration of the Structural Funds should be substantially simplified by giving practical effect to decentralising decision-making and striking the right balance between simplification and flexibility so as to ensure that funds are disbursed quickly and effectively. To achieve this, responsibilities of Member States, their partners and the Commission will be clarified, bureaucracy reduced and monitoring, evaluation and control strengthened, thereby ensuring improved and sound financial management.[60]

It decided that central governments should have a greater role in the mid-term review process and that they should continue to select sub-national partners.[61]

The outcome of the decisions made in Berlin has been a streamlining of the administration of the funds. Whilst the member states individually propose their development programmes,[62] involving 'actors in economic and social affairs', the Commission negotiates and approves programmes, and allocates funding. The approved document becomes the Community support framework (where a Commission decision is needed to implement the programme) or single programming document (where it is not) for each region. Implementation, including the awarding of tenders, is also conducted by the member states, but with the involvement of the regions. Together they have the responsibility of managing, selecting, controlling and assessing programmes. The Commission helps evaluate the programmes, and commits and pays out approved expenditure, if its evaluation is satisfactory. It also checks the control systems established.[63]

It is important to note, however, that the Commission lays emphasis upon 'decentralisation' and 'subsidiarity', along with 'transparency', so far as the implementation of the 2000–06 programme is concerned. One of the criteria for successful implementation is the involvement of interested parties. The Commission's Regional Policy website, following the guidance set by the Berlin European Council, makes it clear that:

> Partnership and decentralisation (the corollary of the former) are the basic principles underlying a new approach to structural policy, which is more in line with the need for a new form of governance, in place of traditional management, to conceive and implement the programmes in question.[64]

The concepts of subsidiarity (literally meaning taking decisions at the lowest *possible* level) is a recurrent theme in EU governance, intended initially to popularise it, and also to reassure the more centralist of its member states that the EU did not intend to encroach upon their jurisdictions any more than it had to when developing and implementing its policies.[65] However, whilst this state-centric[66] concept of subsidiarity could achieve this effect *de jure*, implementing it has, as the above suggests, enabled the Commission to bring about a *de facto* decentralisation well beyond the boundaries of the nation state, by requiring the input of sub-national actors, which has been formalised in the 2000–06 programme. In the field of regional policy, it does this alongside a corresponding determination to ensure the predominance of the supranational priorities. Thus, the Commission, in its role as paymaster, ensures that programmes comply with Community policies on, for example, the environment, equal opportunities and state aids.[67]

Sutcliffe[68] concludes that whilst the determination of the 2000–06 structural fund administration has given an enhanced role to member states, primarily because of the reduced funding and number of objectives, it has not necessarily done so at the expense of the other levels of governance. The Commission and sub-national partners still have a substantial role to play, although, Sutcliffe notes, the extent of sub-national participation varies from state to state.[69] John and Ward point out that the United Kingdom is one of the few states of the EU that lacks *local* politicians with *national* standing.[70] In this case, before devolution, it was likely that links between the EU and the locality would be solely responsible for legitimising the participation of the sub-national actor. However, devolution itself potentially enhances the national standing of sub-national actors, and in time a Jack McConnell or a Rhodri Morgan may play an influential part on the national stage as the spokesperson of the devolved parliament.

Implementing the structural funds in the United Kingdom

There is, as shown above, a general agreement amongst academics that the multi-level governance thesis is most likely to apply in the field of the structural funds, and that the most likely stage in the policy process where it will apply is in the implementation. It was also noted that the relevance of the thesis depends in part upon the degree of autonomy afforded by central government to sub-national levels. Hence, the way in which structural funds are implemented in the United Kingdom may help to ascertain how far down the road of independence devolution has carried the regions.

In 1988, the UK government resisted the Commission's influence over determining where and how the structural funds were to be spent.[71] Although this point was conceded, and although sub-national actors were given a heightened role at the same time, the UK central government kept most of its control in regard to implementation, thereby frustrating the Commission's attempt to empower sub-national actors through its partnership principle.[72] From 1993, government offices (GOs), staffed by civil servants, had the responsibility of approaching and organising suitable partners as required by the EU. In addition, the government reduced the amount of funding that could be allocated by sub-national agencies by launching Regional Challenge competitions that would 'top-slice' the amount available within each region. Programme monitoring committees (PMCs) were largely controlled by central government through the GOs, particularly in England, although where relations between the GO and the locality were good, the GO could be seen to be supporting the locality, rather than central government.[73]

The 2000–06 programme, however, followed devolution affecting all regions of the United Kingdom. The main impact that this had upon the implementation of the funds concerned the passing of the role of managing authority from the governmental department[74] to the Scottish Executive and Welsh Assembly.[75] These changes meant that, in Scotland and Wales, the unit of devolved government put forward draft proposals for the funds. The new managing authorities became responsible for approving individual schemes for spending them and were therefore accountable for both policy and overall administration. In the future also, Scottish and Welsh ministers would deal directly with the European Commission.

It should be pointed out that the ways in which the structural funds have been implemented in the United Kingdom have always varied. For example, Scotland has a longer tradition of partnership working than other UK regions, and before devolution it had created independent secretariats to service structural fund PMCs, to avoid the centralising effects experienced by other regions who used secretariats provided by central government regional offices. The Welsh experience prior to devolution, according to Bache,[76] was an unhappy one; McAllister[77] notes that public policy before devolution had been conducted by civil servants operating within the constraints of Whitehall.

Scotland

Scotland has been allocated structural funds of €1.693 billion (£1.094 billion) by the EU for the 2000–06 period.[78] Proposals were put forward and provisionally approved by the European Commission in December 1999, and the draft SPD (single programming document), prepared by representatives of business, employees, education and the voluntary sector, was submitted to the Commission, following consultation with both partners and the European Committee of the Scottish Parliament, in May 2000. It was approved without undue comment. The first round of specific schemes was approved by the deputy minister of finance and public services, Peter Peacock MSP. By the end of 2001, all five programmes covering Scotland were in position.

In relation to implementing the structural funds, a steering committee was formed in November 1999 chaired by Lex Gold, the director of the Scottish Chambers of Commerce. Its role was to determine the model for administering the structural funds, particularly how the roles and responsibilities for the new programmes should be divided between the levels of governance. The result was the establishment of a complex system of managing bodies. There is a PMC (which is a statutory requirement of the EU Structural Funds Regulations and which includes a representative of the European Commission), whose primary role is to determine which projects should be recommended for funding. Beneath this, there is a programme management committee and a joint management board for each programme. All of these comprise representatives of partner organisations, and, for the first time, this included elected members of local government. This is one indication of increased local involvement, since although there was no reason why elected councillors should not have been appointees previously, in practice only the north-west region of England included local councillors before devolution. Each programme management committee has advisory groups covering each priority, to provide technical support and advice. There is also a horizontal themes policy group whose role is to assist in coordinating cross-cutting themes. All of these comprise representatives of the partner organisations. Evaluation of the programmes is coordinated by the Scottish European Structural Funds Forum, which is intended to link into UK- and EU- level evaluation groups.

Wales[79]

A draft SPD was completed in October 1999. It was criticised by the Commission on the grounds that it was too vague and showed little evidence of private sector involvement. The Commission also thought that it concentrated unnecessarily upon small and medium enterprise (SME) growth. A revised draft was approved in June 2000, although there were still some outstanding concerns. A Wales European Taskforce, set up by the former secretary of state for Wales in September 1998, considered management issues that would be raised by the 2000–06 programme. It included representatives from national and local government, the Welsh Development Agency, and the business and employees community. However, the Taskforce was abolished by the Welsh Assembly's director of economic affairs in September 1999, leaving an impression, according to McAllister, that the Assembly wanted to stamp its own authority over the management of the structural funds.[80] A Shadow Monitoring Committee, with representatives from regional, non-governmental, national and EU levels, was established in its place in March 2000, to be succeeded by a programme monitoring committee when programmes became operational. The Wales European Funding Office (WEFO) is responsible for the day-to-day administration and payments for the schemes. It is also expected to assist partners in developing new schemes. However, political management of the structural funds is conducted by the Assembly's Economic Development Committee, rather than by its European Affairs Committee. McAllister suggests that this could mean either that the Assembly's approach to economic management is holistic or that its committees are engaging in turf wars. The effect has been that the first secretary, Rhodri Morgan, who chairs the Economic Development Committee, has a heavy workload, since he is also the chair of the monitoring committee.

England

Outside London, where the mayor and Greater London Authority are the designated managing authority, fewer changes between the implementation of the 1994–99 and the 2000–06 structural fund programmes can be seen within the English regions. The Department of Trade and Industry is now the managing authority[81] and there is so far no formal role for the unelected English regional assemblies except as consultees. However, the establishment of regional development agencies (RDAs) in 1999 has meant that whilst the regional government offices (GOs) remain the primary administrators, the RDAs are regarded as being the primary coordinators and representatives of partners' views, which they are expected to channel through to the GOs. RDAs, however, are potential project applicants and match funders in their own right. They are also responsible for evaluating and recommending adjustments to the programmes. In England, as in Scotland and Wales, the partnership theme has been significant. Partners are involved in every level of the programme from drawing up the SPD to membership of the programme monitoring committee and other working groups. They are also involved in day-to-day administration and evaluation of the programmes' effectiveness.

Assessment

It was shown above that the EU's emphasis in the latest round of structural fund distribution has been upon the involvement of a multi-layered polity. Paying the piper, in this instance, appears to have had the greatest impact upon the tune that has resulted. Scottish, Welsh and English implementation of the funds has given more formal representation to a greater number of governmental levels and groups than was previously required. However, it is not so clear that this has changed the reality of programme management. In practice, given the nature of the purpose of the structural funds, involvement of interested parties was essential. The Scottish Executive and Welsh Assembly have gained the power (or responsibility) to manage the funds, but, with the exception of the Scottish deter-mination to involve local councillors more closely, this has not resulted in many changes in implementation.

Nevertheless, devolution in combination with the EU's competence in relation to the structural funds has had the impact of increasing the authority of the devolved institutions. They can now be seen, without rival, to be 'making a differ-ence' to their areas, as their ministers announce that they have approved funding for cherished projects. This, in addition to their enhanced capacity to operate on the European level, has meant that both Scottish and Welsh devolved bodies have become something more than semi-detached units of the United Kingdom's central government.

MOVING FORWARD: THE EU, INTERDEPENDENCE AND UK DEVOLUTION

As other member states' experiences have encouraged semi-autonomy for Scotland and Wales, their experiences have continued to open the agenda for *English* regions. The government appears to be responding to this agenda. In 2002, it issued a White Paper, *Your Region, Your Choice: Revitalising the English Regions*, which promotes the idea of forming *elected* regional assemblies 'where people wish to have them'.[82] The intention is that, following referenda (the North-East is held to be the likeliest of the English regions to initiate a referendum), assemblies elected by means of the additional member system will be instituted, although the White Paper assumes that not all regions will want to go forward on this basis. The government hopes to have in place the enabling legislation soon enough that the first assemblies can begin their operations during the current parliament.[83]

The White Paper makes several references to the EU. It points out that 'England now includes virtually the only regions within the European Union which don't have the choice of some form of democratic regional governance'.[84] It proposes that the new assemblies should take over the role currently undertaken by the regional GOs in relation to the EU's structural funds.[85] This would give elected persons more involvement with the implementation of the structural funds, which, the government believes, have 'heavily influenced' the relationship between the regions and the EU, providing 'one of the most visible signs . . . of the benefits of EU membership'.[86]

Significantly, the White Paper admits that 'there are important relationships to be built and maintained at regional [as well as national] level' and that 'influence within the EU begins well before the process of formal negotiations between member states and operates through many more channels than the formal EU and intergovernmental processes'.[87] The White Paper relates this adjustment in governmental approaches to the European Commission's White Paper *Reforming European Governance*,[88] commenting that the Commission contribution welcomed the input of sub-national government, with the acknowledgement that 'the principal responsibility for involving the regional and local level in EU policy would remain with national administrations'.[89]

The above indicates that the impact of the EU has helped to set the agenda for English devolution. However, the government's White Paper claims that the main purpose of the proposals is to increase the 'unquantifiable' benefits of additional democratic accountability,[90] and it covers many other aspects of regional governance in England. It may be, then, that the impact of the EU in this respect can be regarded as marginal.

This may not be the end of the story, however. It is noticeable that the government, in the 2002 White Paper, is not at present inclined to enable much more than 'participation' even in relation to the implementation of EU funds. When commenting upon the desirability of involving sub-national actors in 'less formal discussions with the institutions of the EU', it took reassurance from the Commission's White Paper that national governments should retain 'principal responsibility' for sub-national government's interaction with the EU.[91] However, the Commission is concerned to strengthen this interaction, and has put forward suggestions as to how it may accomplish this. For example, it proposes to involve sub-national government at the agenda-setting stage by establishing 'a more systematic dialogue with representatives of regional and local governments through national and European associations at an early stage in shaping policy'.[92] The Commission intends to remove some of the initiative from national government by establishing and publishing its own minimum standards for consultation on EU policy. It has already given some evidence that it intends to put this into practice, as shown above. The Commission also gave notice that it would move beyond these minimum standards where it thought it desirable, in the interests of openness and 'representativity'.[93] It appears, then, that despite the government's rhetoric in the White Paper, there are other supranational players in the field of involving sub-national and non-governmental actors. The White Paper may, despite itself, facilitate their involvement, at least in England, if it does lead to elected regional assemblies.

CONCLUSION

The investigation of the impact of the integrating EU upon devolution in the United Kingdom has looked at a number of aspects of the new relationships that are forming by and within the devolved units of UK governance. The investigation has focused upon relationships at supra- and sub-national levels, although it should not be forgotten that as Scotland's and Wales's representatives speak for themselves at EU level, this changes the dynamic of their relationship with actors at the national level – as they become more akin to equals who may demand, rather than subordinates who may only request.

The EU fits into the situation in a number of ways. It has helped to initiate devolution; it has assisted in making devolution *de facto*, by accepting regional participants as legitimate partners; and it has provided Scottish and Welsh devolved bodies with opportunities to become actors within the EU in their own right, rather than as adjuncts to the UK government.

None of these developments is much more than a trend at present. The United Kingdom is still the member state of the EU, and it is a devolved state, not a federal one. Scotland and Wales are just regions. The Commission needs the participation of sub-national actors; but even more than this it needs to keep the goodwill of national governments. It cannot, and would not, empower those below. Scotland may receive presidential ambassadors and form a relationship with a small member state, but assuming some of the trappings of a state does not make it one.

Nevertheless, there is no sign either that the trends are shifting direction. On the contrary, the United Kingdom is preparing to devolve further still, according to the 2002 White Paper, encouraged by the example of its fellow EU states and reassured by the EU's implicit promise to leave member states in the driving seat so far as their sub-national units are concerned. The EU's, or more strictly the Commission's, assurance, may have less value than the UK government believes. As shown above, the Commission is intending a more comprehensive system of communication with sub-national governance. Therefore, whilst there is no prospect that the EU will lead to further *de jure* devolution, the *de facto* outcomes may actually threaten any state that attempts to remain a unitary one.

NOTES

1. I. Bache, The Extended Gatekeeper: Central Government and the Implementation of EC Regional Policy in the UK, *Journal of European Public Policy* 6(1) (1999) p.42
2. DTLR, *Your Region, Your Choice: Revitalising the English Regions*, Cm 5511 (London: Department of Transport, Local Government and the Regions, 2002)
3. They do not have to be, but on only a few occasions has a prime minister appointed a cabinet minister who was not a member of the House of Commons or House of Lords. In each case, the new minister quickly became a member of one or the other.

4. The rigidity resulting from such exclusiveness would have precluded the United Kingdom's full participation in the internal market, given the number of non-tariff barriers to trade that needed to be removed.

5. Membership of the EU has afforded this opportunity to a number of its states, noticeably Denmark, France and Ireland, when treaty ratification was required or wanted.

6. Pilkington, in *Britain in the European Union today* (2001), points out that the government accepted 43 volumes of EC legislation, constituting over 2,900 regulations and 410 directives, just by joining the EC in 1972. The volume of legislation – the *acquis communautaire* – has, of course, increased immensely since.

7. M. Marinetto, The Settlement and Process of Devolution: Territorial Politics and Governance under the Welsh Assembly, *Political Studies* 49(2) (2001) p.308

8. DTLR, op. cit. (2002) p.10

9. J. Mather, *The EU and British Democracy: Towards Convergence* (Basingstoke: Macmillan, 2000) p.201

10. Suspended in 2002

11. Except that the London Development Agency is responsible to the mayor and Greater London Authority.

12. See J. Mather, Labour and the English Regions: Centralised Devolution?, *Contemporary British History* 14(3) (2000) for a description of the current position of the English regions.

13. V. Bogdanor, *Devolution in the United Kingdom* (Oxford: Oxford University Press, 2001) p.280

14. Ibid., p.281

15. Ibid., p.280

16. S. Bulmer, M. Burch, C. Carter, P. Hogwood and A. Scott, European Policy-making under Devolution: Britain's New Multi-level Governance (University of Manchester, European Policy Research Unit, paper no 1.01, 2001)

17. Bogdanor, op. cit. (2001) p.282

18. Marinetto, op. cit. (2001) p.307

19. The Welsh Assembly has a cabinet and a committee structure.

20. J. Sutcliffe, The 1999 Reform of the Structural Fund Regulations: Multi-level Governance or Renationalization?, *Journal of European Public Policy* 7(2) (2001) p.292

21. http://www.scotland.gov.United Kingdom/euoffice/shr2000.asp

22. http://www.europarl.eu.int/natparl/calendar/byevent/default_en.htm

23. Welsh Assembly newsletter, November/December 2000

24. Welsh Assembly newsletter, June/July 2001

25. http://www.wales.gov.United Kingdom/subieurope/content/comms-e.htm

26. Members of the Committee of the Regions are appointed by the Council of Ministers, acting on proposals from member states' governments.

27. There are 24 United Kingdom members and 24 alternate (substitute) members on the Committee of the Regions.

28. This is not a designated 'Special Region' in Italy.

29. Welsh Assembly newsletter, September/October 2001

30. As well as Elliot Morley, parliamentary secretary for fisheries and food, and Brid Rodgers, minister for agriculture and rural development of the Northern Ireland Assembly.

31. Council of the European Union, 14518/00 (Presse 479) 2320th Council meeting: Fisheries – Brussels, 14 and 15 December 2000

32. Structural policy has also been considered to be at the cutting edge of multi-level governance by multi-level governance theorists (Bache, op. cit. (1999) p.35)

33. G. Marks, L. Hooghe and K. Blank, European Integration from the 1980s: State-centric v. Multilevel Governance, *Journal of Common Market Studies* 34(3) (1996) pp.341–78

34. The European Council decided that: 'In accordance with the Commission's proposals, the allocation of resources to Member States for Objectives 1 and 2 will be based, using transparent procedures, on the following objective criteria: eligible population, regional prosperity, national prosperity and the severity of structural problems, especially the level of unemployment. An appropriate balance will be struck between regional and national prosperity. For Objective 3, the breakdown by Member State shall be based principally on the eligible population, the employment situation and the severity of the problems, such as social exclusion, education and training levels and participation of women in the labour market, with a relative weighting as outlined by the Commission'. (*Conclusions of the Presidency.* European Council, 24 and 25 March, Berlin, 1999)

35. Sutcliffe, op. cit. (2000) p.292

36. Ron Davies, cited by Bulmer *et al.,* op. cit. (2001) p.8

37. A.G. Jordan and J.J. Richardson, *British Politics and the Policy Process* (London: Unwin Hyman, 1987)

38. The Council also decides the basis of distribution of the structural funds in accordance with the EU's Objectives, again with the input of both supra-national (Commission and EP) and national (Council) actors. The Council decides upon the budget; acting on a proposal from the Commission, negotiated with the Parliament. (http://europa.eu.int/comm/regional_policy/intro/regions7_en.htm)

39. Sutcliffe, op. cit. (2000) p.291

40. P. Behrens and M. Smyrl, A Conflict of Rationalities: EU Regional Policy and the Single Market, *Journal of European Public Policy* 6(3) (1999) p.421

41. Politically, legitimacy to the development of structural expenditure was achieved by the inclusion of a title on 'economic and social cohesion' and a statement to the effect that the internal market required the strengthening of economic and social cohesion that could be assisted by means of the structural funds. The Act contained a further statement that the ERDF was intended to redress principal regional imbalances, and its Article 130d instructed the Commission to submit proposals leading to the increased efficiency of the structural funds.

42. S.S. Andersen and K.A. Eliassen, *The European Union: How Democratic is it?* (London: Sage, 1996) p.89

43. The most significant part of the Act was to give flesh to the Commission White Paper *Completing the Internal Market*, which indicated the number of measures needed to effect this. To this end, the SEA included provisions for qualified majority voting in these areas, to avoid individual states impeding the process.

44. Behrens and Smyrl, op. cit. (1999) p.420

45. C. Archer, *The European Union: Structure and Process* (London: Continuum, 2000)

46. Ibid.

47. The main contributors are: the European Regional Development Fund (ERDF) (amounting to 49 per cent of the total); the European Social Fund (ESF) (comprising 29.9 per cent of the total); the European Agricultural Guidance and Guarantee Fund (EAGGF) (17.7 per cent of the total) and the Financial Instrument for Fisheries Guidance (FIFG) (2.9 per cent of the total).

48. Since 2000, there are three Community initiatives, which collectively amount to 5 per cent of the total structural fund allocation: (1) INTERREG (cross-border, transnational and interregional cooperation – with particular emphasis on cross-border activities, in particular in the perspective of enlargement); (2) Equal (transnational cooperation to combat all forms of discrimination and inequalities in the labour market – with particular emphasis upon the social and vocational integration of asylum seekers); and (3) Leader (rural development).

49. Cohesion funds are provided to the cohesion states: Spain, Portugal, Greece and Ireland. They are intended to contribute to projects in the fields of environment and transport infrastructure. The idea was to prepare these states for European Monetary Union and closer political union contained in the Treaty.

50. The Council of the European Communities, Council Regulation (EC) laying down general provisions on the Structural Funds, 1998

51. This was narrowed down from seven Objectives in the 1994–99 period, in accordance with Council Regulation (EC) 'laying down general provisions on the Structural Funds 1998', and as agreed by the Berlin European Council 1999.

52. It is funded from the ERDF, ESF, EAGGF Guidance Section and FIFG.

53. The Highlands and Islands and Northern Ireland are currently included, but they are being phased out.

54. It is funded from ERDF, ESF and FIFG; with support from EAGGF to rural development.

55. It is funded from ESF.

56. Leader+ stimulates rural economies via support to local, innovative projects. It is funded from EAGGF.

57. Urban II assists schemes for economic and social revitalisation in depressed urban areas. It is funded from ERDF.

58. Interreg IIIa assists internal and external border areas of the EU to overcome the special development problems arising from their relative isolation. It is funded from ERDF.

59. Equal enables the development and dissemination of new ways of delivering employment policies in order to combat all forms of discrimination and inequality felt in connection with the labour market. It is funded from ESF.

60. The Berlin European Council also reduced the overall amount available from the sum recommended by the Commission (Sutcliffe, op. cit. (2000) p.303)

61. Ibid., p.305

62. It should be pointed out that they are also partly responsible for funding programmes. The EU normally provides no more than 50 per cent of the total costs, although in Objective 1 areas, this can rise to 75 per cent.

63. http://europa.eu.int/comm/regional_policy/country/partners/index_en.htm

64. Ibid.

65. See the *Conclusions of the Presidency* at the 1992 Edinburgh Summit.

66. Mather, op. cit. (2000) citing P. Spicker, Concepts of Subsidiarity in the European Community, *Current Politics and Economics in Europe* V, (2/3) (1996) pp. 163–75

67. http://europa.eu.int/comm/regional_policy/intro/regions5_en.htm

68. Sutcliffe, op. cit. (2000) p.305

69. Ibid.

70. P. John and H. Ward, Political Manipulation in a Majoritarian Democracy, *The British Journal of Politics and International Relations* 3(3) (2001) p.318

71. Sutcliffe, op. cit. (2000) p.295

72. Bache, op. cit. (1999) p.35

73. Ibid., p.37

74. Formerly the Department of the Environment, Transport and the Regions. The managing authority for the structural funds in England is now the Department of Trade and Industry since the government restructuring of 2002.

75. The National Assembly has established an agency – the Welsh European Funding Office (WEFO) – which has delegated authority for the programmes.

76. Bache, op. cit. (1999) p.36

77. L. McAllister, Devolution and the New Context for Public Policy-making: Lessons from the EU Structural Funds in Wales, *Public Policy and Administration* 15(2) (2000) p.39

78. Scottish European Committee, *Report of the Inquiry into European Structural Funds and their Implementation in Scotland*, 6th Report (2000)

79. Much of this material was derived from McAllister, op. cit. (2000). See pp.44–52 of that article for a fuller account.

80. McAllister, op. cit. (2000) p.46

81. Since the departmental restructuring of 2001.

82. *Your Region, Your Choice*, op. cit. p.9

83. Ibid., p.67

84. Ibid., p.10. See also p.33

85. Ibid., p.39

86. Ibid., p.61

87. Ibid., p.60

88. Commission of the European Communities, Brussels, *European Governance*, Com (2001) 428 Final (25 July 2001)

89. Ibid. The White Paper actually pointed out that 'there needs to be a *stronger interaction* with regional and local governments and civil society. Member

States bear the principal responsibility for achieving this'. The United Kingdom government's interpretation omitted the words italicised by the author.

90. *Your Region, Your Choice*, op. cit. p.47
91. Ibid., p.60
92. *European Governance*, op. cit.
93. Ibid.

BIBLIOGRAPHY

Andersen, S. S. and Eliassen, K. A. (1996): *The European Union: How Democratic Is It?* (London: Sage).

Archer, C. (2000) *The European Union: Structure and Process* (London. Continuum).

Bache, I. (1999) The Extended Gatekeeper: Central Government and the Implementation of EC Regional policy in the United Kingdom, *Journal of European Public Policy* 6(1).

Behrens, P. and Smyrl, M. (1999) A Conflict of Rationalities: EU Regional Policy and the Single Market, *Journal of European Public Policy* 6(3).

Bogdanor, V. (2001) *Devolution in the United Kingdom* (Oxford: Oxford University Press).

Bulmer, S., Burch, M., Carter, C., Hogwood, P. and Scott, A. (2001) European Policy-making under Devolution: Britain's New Multi-level Governance (University of Manchester, European Policy Research Unit, paper no. 1.01).

Commission of the European Communities Brussels (2001) *European Governance*, Com (2001) 428 Final.

Council of the European Union (2000) 14518/00 (Presse 479) 2320th Council meeting: Fisheries – Brussels, 14 and 15 December.

DTLR (2002) *Your Region, Your Choice: Revitalising the English Regions*, Cm 5511 (London: Department of Transport, Local Government and the Regions).

John, P. and Ward, H. (2001) Political Manipulation in a Majoritarian Democracy, *The British Journal of Politics and International Relations* 3(3).

Jordan, A. G. and Richardson, J. J. (1987) *British Politics and the Policy Process* (London: Unwin Hyman).

Marinetto, M. (2001) The Settlement and Process of Devolution: Territorial Politics and Governance under the Welsh Assembly, *Political Studies* 49(2).

Marks, G., Hooghe, L. and Blank, K. (1996) European Integration from the 1980s: State-centric v. Multilevel Governance, *Journal of Common Market Studies* 34(3).

Mather, J. (2000) *The EU and British Democracy: Towards Convergence* (Basingstoke: Macmillan).

Mather, J. (2000) Labour and the English Regions: Centralised Devolution?, *Contemporary British History* 14(3).

McAllister, L. (2000) Devolution and the New Context for Public Policy-making: Lessons from the EU structural funds in Wales, *Public Policy and Administration* 15(2).

Pilkington, C. (2001) *Britain in the European Union Today* (Manchester: Manchester University Press).

Spicker, P. (1996) Concepts of Subsidiarity in the European Community, *Current Politics and Economics in Europe* V (2/3).

Sutcliffe, J. (2000) The 1999 Reform of the Structural Fund Regulations: Multi-level Governance or Renationalization?, *Journal of European Public Policy* 7(2).

Welsh Assembly newsletter, November/December 2000.

Welsh Assembly newsletter, June/July 2001.

Welsh Assembly newsletter, September/October 2001.

Part Four

REFLECTING ON CONSTITUTIONAL CHANGE

12 The new institutions: an interim assessment

Eberhard Bort

> When we ask how this new institution is getting on with its much older neighbours, we cannot possibly expect a satisfactory answer after just a few years. (Lindsay Paterson)[1]

> I confess that I expected greater tension between Edinburgh and London than has proved to be the case. (Brian Taylor)[2]

INTRODUCTION

For 'mainland Britain', the devolution package approved by referenda in Scotland and Wales in September 1997 which led to the establishment of the Scottish Parliament and the National Assembly for Wales in May 1999 was the biggest constitutional change since 1707 – the Union of parliaments of Scotland and England. Together with the Belfast Agreement of April 1998, the Wales and Scotland Acts of the same year created the legal framework for the assemblies in Northern Ireland and Wales and the parliament in Scotland, along with their respective 'governments'. The Belfast Agreement also created the British–Irish Council involving the United Kingdom, the devolved UK territories, the Crown dependencies and the Republic of Ireland.

What is the verdict on these new institutions after their first term? Have expectations been fulfilled, or is there a widespread sense of frustration and disillusionment? Bearing in mind Lindsay Paterson's caveat quoted above, this chapter tries to assess what are still very young and developing institutions, focusing mainly on Scotland (but with the occasional glance at the other devolved territories).

Even before the new institutions were established, a number of 'doomsday scenarios' had emerged:

1. Devolution as provided by the Blair government would never be allowed to settle down, as the 'sovereign' parliament – Westminster – would persistently rule into the devolved areas and, more importantly, overrule any devious route taken by the devolved chambers. This would result in permanent friction and undermine the authority of the new institutions and their acceptance. It would also not allow them to develop their own profile and routine.

2. The new electoral systems would create no overall majorities in the devolved chambers and thus lead to either unstable minority governments or power-sharing coalitions. Both run against the grain of British experience and 'cannot work'. For the Scottish Executive, the demise was predicted within months as the coalition partners (Labour and the Liberal Democrats) would not be able to

bridge the gulf between their respective positions, for example *vis-à-vis* the abolition of university tuition fees.

3. The fiscal and budgetary arrangements – the Barnett formula – would create an English backlash and would, again, paralyse the working of devolution.

It would be too easy to just point out that none of these gloomy predictions has come true. But one of the astonishing facts of devolution is to what degree the new institutions have embedded themselves in the public consciousness. Hardly anyone questions their existence.

Yet, there do remain questions about the performance of the institutions themselves, about intergovernmental relations, the relationship between executives and parliaments/assemblies, the role of the secretaries of state, the pace and direction devolution is taking in England, the transformation of the National Assembly for Wales 'from Corporate Body to Virtual Parliament',[3] the future of power-sharing devolution in Northern Ireland, the role of the British–Irish Council, and the relationship of the devolved territories with an enlarged and reformed European Union and its institutions.

PERFORMANCE

In its report of December 1998, the Consultative Steering Group laid down four key principles for the operation of the future Scottish Parliament:

1. Power sharing: between the Scottish people, the legislators and the Executive.
2. Accountability: of the Executive to the Parliament, and of Executive and Parliament to the Scottish people.
3. Access and participation: an open, accessible Parliament enabling a participative approach to policy making and the legislative process.
4. Equal opportunities: balance of the sexes and equal opportunities for all in the Parliament's operation and appointments.[4]

These principles, widely endorsed by the supporters of the Constitutional Convention as well as by all political parties in Scotland, have guided the establishment and early years of the Parliament.[5]

The principle of power sharing, between Parliament and Executive and, even more importantly, between the Parliament and the people, is the most distinctive feature of the Scottish Parliament. The new electoral system secures that the Parliament broadly reflects the votes cast by the people of Scotland in electing their Parliament. The Parliament's accessibility and accountability demand an optimum transparency in its operations. Although this has, arguably, not been fully achieved,[6] the system seems much more open than Westminster.

The 'failure' of the 1979 referendum had shown the deep divisions within Scotland.[7] These were impressively bridged by the Scottish rejection of Margaret Thatcher and most things she stood for – the 'unwilling and unwitting midwife' of the Scottish Parliament[8] – but, as has been pointed out after the 1997 referendum, 'the geography of relative support and scepticism remained unaltered'.[9]

It was therefore clear from the outset that the Parliament, now based on a much higher level of support across Scotland, would need to reflect the whole population of Scotland in all its geographic, demographic and ethnic diversity. That is why it is deemed important that the Scottish Parliament should retain its 129 MSPs, even if and when the number of Scottish MPs is reduced from its present 72 to around 59.[10] The size and make-up of the Parliament are an attempt to reflect this varied geography and demography of Scotland, to offer opportunities for the increasingly diverse ethnic base and, in particular, to maximise the participation of women in the Parliament. Scotland's legislature has been praised internationally for its early commitment to family-friendly working practices and for the high number of women MSPs – at over 37 per cent (39.5 per cent after 2003 elections), amongst the top five in the world.[11]

No one denies that the Scottish Parliament had a problematic start. Petty debates about seating order in the chamber, 'selfish' issues like MSPs' pay and holidays, and the awarding of medals to themselves – just for having been at the opening of the Parliament – did scratch the reputation of the fledgling institution. More seriously, questions of privileged access to Scottish Executive were raised ('Lobbygate');[12] a storm broke loose over the Executive's declared intention of repealing section 28(2A) on the teaching of homosexuality in Scotland's schools, including a private referendum sponsored by bus tycoon Brian Souter; and, by the summer of 2000, the Executive found itself embroiled in the collapse of the exam system supervised by the Scottish Qualification Authority (SQA).

The political commentator Iain Macwhirter detected 'a tidal wave of disillusion . . . at the succession of disasters that have marred devolution's infancy' and 'a meltdown of public confidence' as Donald Dewar's administration 'staggers from crisis to crisis'.[13] In October 2000, Donald Dewar died. His successor, Henry McLeish, was, arguably, just finding his feet in the autumn of 2001, when he was engulfed in an affair about office sublets from his time as a Westminster MP, and had to resign. Jack McConnell became the third first minister in under three years of the Parliament's existence.

It is astonishing to look at the legislative record of the Parliament, considering the permanent 'excitement' which prevented any settling down into a working routine. And indeed, the record of the Executive and the Parliament is all but dismal. By the end of its first year in office, eight bills had been passed (all of them introduced by the Executive), eleven bills were in progress (amongst them the first private members' bills). Already, this compared favourably with the one or two Scottish bills Westminster found time to pass per year. In September, Donald Dewar announced a programme of eight new bills (on housing, domestic abuse, regulation of care, protection of rape victims from cross-examination, water services, salmon conservation, European Convention on Human Rights legislation, and graduate endowments) to be introduced in the second year of the Scottish Parliament.[14] This was, even before officially made public, branded as 'uninspiring and unambitious'. Yet, it was a social programme which would affect the lives of ordinary Scots: 'A lot of it might be bread-and-butter fare but that is surely what government is about, and it is something the Executive is finally getting on with'.[15]

For any observer, it became abundantly clear that public debate in Scotland was nearly completely refocusing from Westminster to Holyrood. What a difference from pre-devolution days when the only opportunity to debate Scottish affairs in Parliament was Scottish Question Time at Westminster, when, seven times a year for 45 minutes, the 72 Scottish MPs could try to put a question before the secretary of state for Scotland. Now – and in addition to that – 129 MSPs were sitting for two days a week in the Scottish Parliament, and in public meetings of the parliamentary committees, debating Scottish policies. Instead of a dozen journalists covering Scottish politics from Westminster, there were now 150 accredited to the Parliament, and the press gallery was usually well attended with reporters who picked up every word spoken in the chamber.

A degree of disillusion was perhaps inevitable, as parliaments – even 'sovereign' ones – cannot change political, social or economic structures over night. This sense of disappointment has been reinforced by the diverse blunders of, foremost, the Executive. Acknowledging that the perceived performance of these bodies is often confused, Macwhirter put things, only a week after his deeply pessimistic intervention, into a more differentiated perspective:

> MSPs are only too aware of how dangerous the confusion in the public mind between the parliament and Executive has been. The dismal performance of the latter has blackened the reputation of the former. But they're no longer prepared for this confusion to remain. In future we are going to see a much more assertive parliament.[16]

Two years on, the Parliament seemed indeed much more assertive. The number of bills which had been passed had mounted to twenty-eight. More importantly, there had been no repeat of the SQA debacle – a feather in the cap of education minister Jack McConnell, but even more so for the Education Committee of the Parliament, which had rigorously investigated the scandal and made the necessary recommendations enabling the minister to avoid an embarrassing re-run. Another victory for Parliament and Executive was the implementation of the Sutherland Report on free personal care for the elderly which was eventually implemented in July 2002. Criticised by the opposition, the £27 million rescue package for Scottish fisheries was a remarkable devolved response to an existential crisis, as was the rapidity of putting a £10 million package together for the victims of foot-and-mouth disease, in farming and tourism.

The implementation of the (Gavin) McCrone report on schools and teachers' pay was beginning to make a difference for Scottish education, as was the abolition of up-front university tuition fees. Then finance minister Angus MacKay, impressive in his presentation of the funding of free care for the elderly – 'as part of the state's duty' rather than a 'burden . . . slowly being shifted onto the individual'[17] – also struck a first matchstick to light the long-announced 'bonfire of the quangos'. Restructuring quangos (for example merging the three existing water authorities into one Scotland-wide body), freedom of information, and care for the elderly were among the eighteen Executive bills Henry McLeish introduced for the legislative year 2001–02 at the beginning of September. Others included the replacement of poindings and warrant sales promoted by Socialist Tommy Sheridan MSP, the continuation of land reform, mental health and local government. The latter, to the disappointment of the Liberal Democrats, did not contain the introduction of proportional representation for local council elections (to be held in May 2003 together with the Scottish Parliament elections). Deputy First Minister Jim Wallace's Freedom of Information (Scotland) Bill, criticised as being still too secretive, was way ahead of Home Secretary Jack Straw's effort at the UK level in giving access to Executive information.

By the beginning of 2003, 45 bills had received Royal Assent. Eight of these bills were non-Executive bills. In January, the landmark Land Reform Bill passed its third stage, and a very busy few months brought the tally up to 62 bills – of which 50 were Executive bills, 8 were members' bills, 3 were Committee bills and 1 was a private bill[18] – before the Parliament's dissolution at the end of March. In addition, over 2,000 pieces of secondary legislation have passed Holyrood.

The view in the press reflected the respect the Parliament had won.[19] In the light of these figures, it is understandable that Sir David Steel, the Parliament's presiding officer, spoke of the impact of the Scottish Parliament in terms of a 'seismic shift'.[20]

PUBLIC OPINION

Is the public disillusioned? Have they lost confidence in the new institutions? The social and political surveys of the past few years paint a different and more differentiated picture.[21] Table 12.1 looks at constitutional preferences since 1999, and shows that the current system of devolution, an elected parliament with powers of taxation, is still the preferred option. Those wishing to turn the clock back to pre-devolutionary days number only one in ten of those surveyed.

Much has also been made of the putative English backlash to devolution in Scotland (and Wales), but once again there is little evidence for such claims. Taking the different surveys in England and Scotland at their proximate years (1999 and 2000, respectively), we find virtual agreement north and south of the border as regards the preferred outcome for Scotland. Neither the people of Scotland nor those of England want, at present, full independence for Scotland or to return to the situation of no elected parliament (Table 12.2).

Table 12.1 Constitutional preferences, 1999–2002 (%)

	1999	2000	2001	2002
Independent from UK and EU	10	11	9	11
Independent from UK within EU	18	19	18	18
Elected parliament with taxation powers	50	47	54	43
Elected parliament without taxation powers	8	8	6	8
No elected parliament	10	12	9	12
base	*1,482*	*1,663*	*1,605*	*1,665*

Source: Scottish Social Attitudes surveys, 1999–2002.

Table 12.2 Constitutional preferences in England and Scotland

	English respondents 1999 %	Scottish respondents 2000 %
Scotland should be:		
Independent from UK and EU	8	11
Independent from UK within EU	16	19
Parliament with taxation powers	44	47
Parliament: no taxation powers	10	8
No elected parliament	13	12

Source: for English respondents, British Social Attitudes, 1999; for Scottish respondents, Scottish Social Attitudes, 2000.

There has, though, been some tailing off from the high levels of optimism at the time of the opening of the Parliament. The percentage agreeing that it would give (or has given) people more say in Scotland's governance has halved, as has the percentage believing it would improve educational standards. But then, we need to note that the earlier data reflected expectations; as devolution progressed, real assessment entered the picture. And the modal positions in both cases are to the effect that it has made no difference either way, rather than that it has made matters worse (Table 12.3).

That 'realism' has set in is also reflected in the trends shown in Table 12.4. Most people locate the more influential level of government at Westminster. Yet, whilst two-thirds think Westminster *is* more influential, fully 72 per cent think that Holyrood *ought* to be more influential, suggesting that the Scottish electorate is more than capable of distinguishing between reality and aspiration.

This is confirmed by Table 12.5 which supports the view that there is a consistent differential on the question as to which level of government people in Scotland trust to look after the country's interests. Even though there has been a falling away in support for both institutions, almost three times as many people in Scotland trust the Scottish Parliament over the UK government to represent Scotland's interests.

Finally, from Table 12.6, it appears that discontent with the Scottish Parliament takes the form of thinking that it should have more powers rather than fewer (the question was not asked in the 2002 survey).

Table 12.3 Democratic effectiveness and the Scottish Parliament, 1999–2002

% agreeing that Scottish Parliament will/has:	1999	2000	2001	2002
Give ordinary people more say in how Scotland is governed	64	44	38	31
Increase standard of education in Scotland	56	43	27	25
Improve Scotland's economy	43	36	43	n/a
Improve NHS in Scotland	49	n/a	45	n/a

Source: Scottish Social Attitudes surveys, 1999–2002.

Table 12.4 Institution with most influence over the way Scotland is run, 1999–2002 (%)

	1999	2000	2001	2002
Scottish Parliament	41	13	15	13
UK government at Westminster	39	66	66	66

Source: Scottish Social Attitudes surveys, 1999–2002.

Table 12.5 Trust in Scottish Parliament or UK government to represent Scotland's interests, 1999–2002 (%)

	1999	2000	2001	2002
Scottish Parliament	81	53	65	53
UK government	32	18	22	20

Source: Scottish Social Attitudes surveys, 1999–2002.

Table 12.6 'The Scottish Parliament should be given more powers', 1999–2001 (%)

	1999	2000	2001
Agree strongly	14	23	20
Agree	42	43	48
Neither	20	15	14
Disagree	18	12	12
Disagree strongly	4	5	4

Source: Scottish Social Attitudes surveys, 1999–2001.

Taken together, it is difficult to sustain the view that the electorate is disillusioned. They may be critical of its practitioners and their practices, but the Scottish Parliament scores much higher than the UK Parliament, and there is very little demand to turn the clock back. Murray Ritchie summed up public opinion on the Parliament:

> Of course they might not cheer it as enthusiastically now, but don't run off with the idea that the parliament is a failure, as its enemies claim, or that the Scots would ever have second thoughts about the whole home rule project. All the evidence shows that, if you ran a poll tomorrow asking if Scotland wanted a return to the old way, the answer would be a deafening NO.[22]

NEW POLITICS?

Much-trumpeted before the first Scottish elections, has the 'new politics' – non-confrontational, consensus-orientated – arrived in Scotland? Some indicators cast doubt on that. The focus on the weekly confrontation in Parliament at 'hamster wars', as Question Time has been termed after Donald Dewar and Alex Salmond left the field for the likes of John Swinney, Henry McLeish and Jack McConnell, is regularly billed as the 'highlight of the week'.[23] The impression conveyed is not all that far from Westminster's 'confrontational politics'. There is also growing dissatisfaction among back-benchers that the party-controlled 'bureau' and the rigid time constraints for debates seriously disadvantage them.

The view changes if one looks at the place where most of the parliamentary work is actually being conducted: the committees. In the monocameral Scottish Parliament, the main function of the committees is scrutiny and revision of legislation. But the committees – 'the real success story ... the engine room of a new politics'[24] – have six important functions:[25]

1. to consider and report on the policy and administration of the Scottish Administration;
2. to conduct inquiries into such matters or issues as the Parliament may require;
3. to scrutinise primary and secondary legislation and proposed EU legislation;
4. to initiate legislation;
5. to scrutinise financial proposals and administration of the Scottish Executive, and
6. to scrutinise procedures relating to the Parliament with recommendations.

It is important that the committees can generate bills, or adopt private members' bills, and thus initiate legislation. It makes them a proactive force in legislation. It is therefore not surprising that committee work takes up substantial parliamentary time.[26] The Parliament, in 2001, already adapted its committee structure to ensure that MSPs have the ability to participate fully in the important and time-consuming consultative, legislative and scrutinising role of the committees.

Here, in the committees one can see at work what might be called 'new politics' – the working together of MSPs who seem fully concentrated on the matter in hand rather than their party line. By the beginning of 2003, over 1,600 committee meetings had taken place, 50 of them outside Edinburgh,[27] creating a sense of parliamentary presence beyond the Central Belt. The committees are, thus, an essential link between the Parliament and civil society, reassuring the electorate that the Parliament is working in partnership with them and for their interests. The Parliament's powerful committee structure and impressive number of cross-party groups emphasise the involvement of civil society in its work, offering and facilitating contact and dialogue between the legislature and the people it represents.

To take but one example: the Public Petitions Committee under the convenership of John McAllion MSP which, by early 2003, had received over 600 submissions, has proved its value as a vital link between the Parliament and the citizens. Peter Lynch and Steven Birrell have argued that 'public petitions have provided some level of "connectivity" between citizens and public institutions, through linking individuals and organisations into the parliamentary process in a meaningful way'.[28] It is also important to note that Scotland is pioneering the use of information and communication technologies to provide interactive networks for citizens and experiment with e-democracy.[29]

But it is not just the busy schedule of the Parliament and its committees, it is also the fact that the Parliament has repeatedly asserted itself during its first four years – be it by defeating the Executive over fisheries or the closure of fire stations, or by correcting the exams fiasco through diligent committee inquiry. Unfortunately, all too often the Parliament is blamed for policies and administrative problems in the Executive's responsibility, stemming from a confusion over the distinction between Parliament and Executive.[30]

WALES, ENGLAND AND NORTHERN IRELAND

Whilst Henry McLeish got himself into a bit of a 'stushie' when he tried to rebrand the Executive as a 'government', and backed down, the Welsh seemed to have no big qualms about the same move. The National Assembly established, in March 2002, clear blue water between the Assembly and the government, dividing staff and functions. This went beyond symbolic change as it marked the move from a corporate assembly towards a parliament and an accountable government – an important revision of the Government of Wales Act 1998.

As in Scotland, the committee structure is seen as central to the operation of the Assembly, but not all of them seem to have solved the tensions between their scrutinising and policy-making roles, and not all of them have broken new ground and left behind the adversarial patterns of Westminster politics. The latter seems to have been reinforced since the formation of the coalition government in 2000 as, since then, there has been a much clearer government agenda to be implemented.

As in Scotland, and on the basis of a strikingly similar election result in 1999, the parties have to come to terms with the new situation. The Labour Party's problems, according to Gerald Taylor, 'have been about creating an identifiably "Welsh" policy base, in the sense of one clearly originating from within the Welsh party and the Assembly, rather than emanating from Millbank in London'.[31] Plaid Cymru, like the Scottish National Party for the first time a fully fledged parliamentary party, and likewise having changed their leadership (from Dafydd Wigley to Ieuan Wyn Jones), seems still to have difficulties in making the transition from London to Cardiff, from an 'aspirational to an implementing party',[32] highlighted by the troubled water it found itself in after raising the issue of immigration and its threat to the Welsh language. It was, apparently, easier to present a united Welsh front in Westminster than to make policy in the cultural minefield of Wales. The Conservatives and the Liberal Democrats, too, have had leadership problems – Rod Richards was replaced by Nick Bourne, and the Lib Dem leader Mike German had to 'temporarily stand down' from his cabinet post as deputy first minister in July 2001.

Whilst the Liberal Democrats are ardent advocates of a federal Britain, the Welsh Conservatives show tentative signs of conversion to devolution. As in Scotland, the Tories have profited from an electoral system they did (and do) not want and an assembly they resisted to the last ditch. Since the formation of the partnership government, they have been able to position themselves more clearly as an opposition party.

What seems to be a common phenomenon between Scotland and Wales is the turn of focus away from purely constitutional questions towards policy delivery. But constitutional issues are never far below the surface. In light of its experience over the first two years, there has been an Assembly Review of Procedure. More far-reaching is the provision in the Partnership Agreement of an independent commission – the Richard Commission – which is expected to report in late 2003/early 2004. The coalition in favour of increasing the powers of the Assembly is nigh-universal in Wales, extending from the Lib–Lab coalition to the nationalist opposition and to most outside commentators and experts. The Commission's proposals will, to a degree, be influenced by the type of government formed after the 1 May 2003 elections – coalition or not – but it is widely expected that it will make the case for extending the powers of the Assembly, clarifying its competences and giving it primary legislative responsibilities and thus to move substantially beyond the confines of the Government of Wales Act 1998.

As Morgan and Mungham pointed out, the Welsh devolution arrangements have highlighted the complexity of relationships between the Assembly and local government, UK government, and Europe.[33] What we see evolving in Wales is perhaps more akin to regional tiers of governance elsewhere in Europe than the Scottish example. It is definitely more directly applicable to the English regions.

England has only belatedly joined the devolution bandwagon. Whilst, apart from the establishment of the Greater London Authority in 2000, little appears to have been going on in England on the ground, at the constitutional level, institutional developments with constitutional implications have gathered pace. In 1998, Labour created regional development agencies across the English regions – consisting of local authorities and other regional stakeholders – and thus set up the political and administrative structures from which 'regional chambers' would emerge. Following Whitehall reorganisation in 2002 and the creation of the Office of Deputy Prime Minister with responsibility for regional government, English regionalism is back on the agenda. In May 2002, the UK government published a White Paper on English regional government,[34] with Deputy Prime Minister John Prescott's new office responsible for delivering it.

English regionalism, long characterised as 'the dog that didn't bark',[35] seems to stir at last. The White Paper led to the publication of a bill on referenda for the English regions in November 2002, and the first referendums expected for 2004[36] are in the North-East, the North-West and Yorkshire/Humberside. From a Scottish or Welsh perspective, there may be a temptation to dismiss many of the English regions as artificial constructs, largely devoid of identity and thus unworthy of distinct political representation, but this line of thinking should be qualified in two important respects. Firstly, we know that desire for self-government in Scotland primarily related to political expectations, rather than having been driven by sentiments of national identity.[37] Secondly, experience from other countries has shown that devolution can work even in 'artificial' regions, as in some of the federal Länder of Germany, or in Spain.

Whilst Scotland, Wales and England offer examples of what Henry McLeish once termed the 'evolution of devolution', Northern Ireland is, unsurprisingly, a different story. The quarrelling over IRA decommissioning of weapons has led to no less than four suspensions of the Northern Ireland Assembly since it was first elected in 1998, on the basis of the Belfast (Good Friday) Agreement.[38] Whilst in business, the Assembly and the power-sharing Executive worked in a remarkably 'normal' way, managing to pass 29 pieces of legislation since December 1999. Indeed, one of the hopes for a peaceful future in Northern Ireland is the fact that all parties seem to have enjoyed the exercise of power under devolution, rather than being at remote control from London.

INSTITUTIONAL DEFICIENCIES

The latter part of the first session of the Scottish Parliament saw a process of review and retrospective assessment of the procedures and practice of the institution, comparing them to the principles and goals set out in the initial documents of devolution. The Procedures Committee published, in March 2003, a detailed report into whether the Parliament has lived up to its founding principles. The five-volume report[39] makes 135 recommendations on issues including the need for: a less pressurised legislative process; full openness in the legislative process; greater transparency in the committee process and the work of the Parliamentary Corporate Body, Bureau and Conveners' group; civil service reform and greater scrutiny of quangos.

From Ron Davies and Rhodri Morgan in Wales to Donald Dewar, Henry McLeish, Angus MacKay and Jack McConnell – they all promised a 'bonfire of the quangos'.[40] Indeed, there were some tentative moves, such as the concentration of the various water boards in Scotland into Scottish Water which came into effect on 1 April 2002, but, generally speaking, the bonfire has not exactly set the heather ablaze.[41] Particularly under fire is Scottish Enterprise, seen by many critics as inefficient and thus at least partly responsible for Scotland's laggard economy.[42]

There are tensions between devolved governments working with, and relying on, a UK civil service, apart from the adaptation process of closer proximity of the civil service to Executive and Parliament under devolution. Chief civil servants being cited before Parliament committees to be questioned and scrutinised was a new experience, and the civil service is still coming to terms with the new dispensation.

The Parliament has commissioned research on the work of the committees and the cross-party groups to compare the practice which has emerged during the first session, particularly in terms of public participation in the scrutinising, consultative and policy-making process. There is a minority debate about the need of a second chamber, whilst the majority of observers attest the committees that they are doing a thorough job in scrutinising and revising legislation.

The way the Scottish Parliament disappears during dissolution – whilst the National Assembly (like local councils) carries on until the day before the election – has attracted criticism.[43] And the electoral system – the additional member system (AMS) – is still not fully accepted, particularly in its closed list element. The Liberal Democrats, the Scottish National Party and some members of the Labour Party would like to move on to the single transferable vote (which, in their view, would maintain a greater connection between representative and represented). Others, such as the Tories and some in the Labour Party, still favour the Westminster model of first-past-the-post, despite the fact that in a six-party system this would lead to serious distortions of the voters' will.

But these perceived deficiencies, which will have to be addressed in the second session of the Parliament, are not questioning the very existence of the new institutions. Of course, the Scottish National Party, the Socialist Party and the Greens remain, at core, independence parties. They would, if coming to power, ask for a mandate (by referendum) to transform the present institutions into bodies of an independent country.

INHERENT INSTABILITY OR SETTLEMENT?

Is devolution the 'settled will' of the people? Is it a stable settlement? As mentioned initially, constitutional change in the United Kingdom is paramount. But it is not following any apparent grand design. It is pragmatic – on a 'give the people what they want' basis: a 'consocietal' Assembly for Northern Ireland,[44] a Parliament for Scotland, a National Assembly for Wales, an elected mayor for London, optional devolution for the English regions. Initial, half-hearted, and stalled reform of the House of Lords, and electoral reform has turned the United Kingdom into a laboratory, experimenting with a variety of electoral systems (first-past-the-post for Westminster; additional member/proportional representation (PR) for Scotland and Wales; single transferable vote (STV) for the Northern Ireland Assembly; and a pure PR list system for the European Parliament elections).

Clearly 'a process not an event',[45] we have seen that a majority of Scots want the powers of the Scottish Parliament extended.[46] Whether devolution will lead to some form of independence eventually, is hotly debated. A whole spate of books – from left and right – published in the past few years have all commented on the alleged demise – imminent or already fact – of the United Kingdom.[47]

Independence for the constituent parts of the United Kingdom would be the only clear-cut, 'neat' solution – a straightforward federal structure is hardly imaginable, considering the disproportionate size of England (48 million people), compared with the relatively small populations of Wales (2.8 million), Scotland (5 million) and Northern Ireland (1.6 million), let alone the unequal distribution of economic power. Any federal structure involving England would be asymmetrical for that reason. Yet, a federal structure involving the English regions, rather than England, would also be asymmetrical because it would mix regions with nations.[48] Brian Taylor concludes: 'The federal solution which works in the United States and Germany – where no single state is completely dominant – would not easily translate to the UK, where one constituent nation has the vast majority of the population and the firmly established UK capital'.[49]

Further new institutions, triggered off by the Northern Irish peace process, and based on the Belfast (Good Friday) Agreement of 1998, further complicate the constitutional picture. North–south institutions mean that a devolved part of the United Kingdom (Northern Ireland) shares institutional responsibilities with a sovereign state (the Republic of Ireland). The British–Irish Intergovernmental Conference exercises joint authority over a devolved part of the United Kingdom (Northern Ireland); and the British–Irish Council (of the Isles) brings together devolved territories of the United Kingdom (Northern Ireland, Scotland, Wales), the sovereign governments of the United Kingdom and of the Republic of Ireland, as well as the Crown dependencies of the Isle of Man and the Channel Isles (which are part neither of the UK nor of the European Union).[50]

What is the future of the institution of the secretaries of state (for Scotland, Wales, Northern Ireland)? Would they already be abolished, or amalgamated into a cabinet office of the devolved territories, had the Belfast institutions been continuously operating? Or will this happen alongside devolution in England?

Quite apart from debates about fiscal autonomy for Scotland,[51] what would happen if elections in the UK and in Scotland produced different political outcomes? Would the conventions of partnership and cooperation established through the concordats signed in the autumn of 1999 between Whitehall and Edinburgh departments prevail? Would Wales's progress towards a parliament with legislative power and English devolution make the constitutional pattern of the UK more sustainable?

It could yet become a problem that there is no thought-through blueprint for devolution. Three paradoxes are clearly evident in the New Labour reform project:

1. Media policy is a reserved matter. But there is no effort to make the 'nation speak to nation'. One could be forgiven for harbouring hopes that the devolution project in itself would be deemed so interesting that it would generate a greater flux of reporting and critical assessments across and between the devolved territories. Yet, night after night, the BBC presenters relegate us to our own neck of the devolved wood when they hand us over to their 'news teams across the UK'. Thus, those in Scotland learn little about the state of play in Wales, and vice versa. Of Northern Ireland we hear only in the context framed by 'Troubles' reportage; little does trickle through about the 'normality' of the Northern Ireland Assembly.

2. A UK reform government that wants to strengthen the Union and counteract 'separatist' tendencies would need to tie in the devolved institutions with UK governance. The House of Lords could provide this tie-in, if it evolved into a second chamber with regional representation. During the recent controversy about House of Lords reform, the concentration was fully on the ratio of elected members – hardly a thought was given to this regional dimension.

3. It would make sense to give the devolved territories a say in European governance, as that would go a long way to taking the wind out of 'independence in Europe' aspirations. Being part of a strong EU member state and having access to the European institutions and decision-making processes could weigh more in terms of influence and participation than being a small 'independent' state.

There is no sign that the UK government plans to address these paradoxes. Day by day, the media reinforce the potential of drifting apart and thus 'sleepwalking into the break-up of Britain'. Regional representation in a reformed House of Lords could also help overcome the dichotomy of elected and appointed members: with successive English regions electing their own assemblies, the proportion of regionally elected members could grow and the ratio of appointed members be reduced.

In Europe, the UK government strongly advocates a 'Europe of nation states',[52] seemingly unaware that this hands a perfect argument for independence to nationalist parties in Scotland and Wales.

DEVOLUTION AND EUROPE

With devolution in the UK, Scotland has been put firmly on the political map of Europe. Together with similarly powered 'regions',[53] Scotland's Parliament and Executive are making their case for an input of the 'third level' into a multi-level system of European governance. Is there room at the top for Scotland and the 'constitutional regions' of Europe? The answer to this question may play a significant role in determining Scotland's future: either as an integrated part of both the UK and Europe, or as an 'independent' state in the EU.

Despite the fact that the Scotland Act 1998 defines foreign relations and 'Europe' as a reserved matter, i.e. firmly within the responsibility of the ('sovereign') Westminster Parliament, both the Scottish Executive (with external relations as a ministerial portfolio) and the Parliament have engaged in EU affairs. After all, about three-quarters of legislation emanating from the EU is being implemented at regional or local level.[54] The committee structure of the Scottish Parliament includes a European Committee.[55] Since March 2003, its new name – European and External Relations Committee – reflects the growing remit of the Committee even beyond the EU:

1. proposals for European Communities legislation;
2. the implementation of European Communities legislation;
3. any European Communities or European Union issue;
4. the development and implementation of the Scottish Administration's links with countries and territories outside Scotland, the European Communities (and their institutions) and other international organisations; and
5. coordination of the international activities of the Scottish Administration.

Of particular importance for Scotland are fisheries, agriculture policies and structural funds. But the Committee has also taken an active role in dealing with issues such as EU enlargement and internal EU reform. And it played an active part in establishing institutional links across and beyond the EU between the Scottish Parliament and other assemblies and parliaments.

In April 2002, the European Committee agreed to conduct an inquiry into Scotland's representation in the EU. Its report was published at the end of November 2002, detailing a plethora of organisations and individuals representing Scotland in the EU. Scotland at present has eight representatives (four full and four alternate members) in the Committee of the Regions (CoR), established as a consultative body of the EU in the Maastricht Treaty of 1991, and inaugurated in 1994. Apart from the fact that the CoR is merely consultative, there is the great diversity of regions and localities represented in it.[56] In a previous report,[57] the Committee had come out in favour of an increased role for CoR in EC/EU decision making, including access to the European courts.[58] In addition to the many representations Scotland already has in the EU (Executive, social partners, and so on), the final recommendation is that the Scottish Parliament acquire a distinct presence of its own in Brussels.

Both the European and External Relations Committee and the Scottish Executive have been active in building new 'regional' links between Scotland and other 'constitutional regions' in the EU and small states inside and outside of the present EU. One of the first steps the devolved Executive took in 1999 was the establishment of Scotland House in Brussels, a public–private clearing house both representing Scottish interests in Brussels and gathering and disseminating information about European initiatives and pre-legislative processes.[59] In December 2000, after an initial phase of information gathering and 'learning to walk', the then minister with responsibility for Europe, Jack McConnell, announced a 'step change' in Scotland's engagement with Europe.[60]

The first visible sign of that step change came when First Minister Henry McLeish signed, on 28 May 2001, the Flanders Declaration, a document expressing the intent of seven self-governing 'constitutional' regions in the EU to coordinate their approach to the 2004 Intergovernmental Conference and Berlin summit, where the input of sub-member-state legislatures into the system of European governance will be on the agenda.

On 2 May 2002, the Scottish Executive signed a protocol of cooperation with the government of Catalonia, which was substantiated in November 2002 in an action plan signed by Deputy First Minister Jim Wallace and Catalan prime minister Artur Mas at the Palau de la Generalitat in Barcelona. The range of cooperation envisaged reaches from e-government through financial and economic interchanges, education and training, combating of drug abuse, culture, sport, the environment, to food and agriculture, youth and employment.[61]

From the beginning, in September 2000, Wales has – like Scotland – been part of a network of European 'constitutional' regions which, in May 2001, formulated the Flanders Declaration. In view of the 2004 Intergovernmental Conference, Wales joined Bavaria, Catalonia, Flanders, North Rhine-Westphalia, Salzburg, Scotland and Wallonia arguing for a stronger role of self-governing regions in Europe: 'I am convinced', wrote Rhodri Morgan, 'that regions with legislative power have a vital part to play in bringing the work of the EU closer to its citizens'.[62] Clearly, the First Minister is linking the debate about European governance and subsidiarity with the demand for an increase in the Assembly's powers.

Scotland and the United Kingdom's other devolved administrations and other European regional governments have come together to discuss matters of mutual interest and to maximise their influence within the EU in the 'Regleg' group of Regions with Legislative Powers. The Scottish Executive and the Welsh Assembly play an active role in this group and, once devolution is restored, the Northern Ireland Executive would be likely to do so too.

During a Regleg conference in Tuscany on 15 November 2002, Jack McConnell met Claudio Martini, the president of the regional government of Tuscany, and signed another cooperation agreement, taking forward cooperation with Tuscany, as part of the Executive strategy of developing links with regional governments.[63] In February 2003, Enterprise Minister Iain Gray signed a third regional partnership agreement, this time with North Rhine-Westphalia, focusing on biotechnology and 'green' technology, but also on EU policies of common interest such as structural aid and the discussions on the Future of Europe.[64] In addition, the Executive has, over the past four years, established friendly contacts and exchange with the Czech Republic, the Baltic states and Scotland's Scandinavian neighbours across the North Sea.

The Scottish Parliament and the European Committee have reinforced and complemented these 'regional' links. According to the most update report of the European Committee, recent initiatives within the United Kingdom and across the EU include:

1. The establishment of the EC–UK group (European Chairs – United Kingdom), a grouping of the European Committees of the devolved assemblies and parliaments and Westminster which has met on four occasions so far, discussing common interests.
2. Working on an agreement with the European Affairs Committee in the German State Parliament of Saxony-Anhalt with a view on closer inter-regional cooperation, particularly in the area of regional development funds.[65]

On 7 September 2002, after a series of successful video conferences, the Network of Regional Parliamentary European Committees (Norpec) was established at its first meeting in Edinburgh, a nascent network including, at present, the Scottish, Catalan and Flemish Parliaments' European Committees. They agreed to expand the network's activities, and to broaden its membership to other committees of similarly powered 'regional' parliaments in the EU.[66]

The Laeken Summit in December 2001 established the 105-member Convention on the Future of Europe[67] under the presidency of former French president Valéry Giscard d'Estaing. It had its inaugural session in Brussels on 28 February 2002. The Convention's remit is to look into four major areas:

1. A better division and definition of 'competence' in the EU: clarifying and defining where the EU should act, where member states should act, and where they should act together.
2. How to simplify the way in which EU policies and legislation are implemented.
3. Democracy, transparency and efficiency in the EU.
4. The drafting of a constitution for European citizens.

Its task was, in other words, to formulate solutions in order to ensure the effectiveness of an expanding Union in a globalised world. But it was also about reconnecting the citizens of Europe with the institutions of the EU, about enhancing the democratic legitimacy and the transparency of the Union and its institutions. It has been working on a European constitution and is expected to report in June 2003. Its results will, to a large extent, determine the success of the subsequent Intergovernmental Conference.

The Scottish Executive has contributed in three ways to the Convention's deliberations:

1. First Minister Jack McConnell delivered a speech to the European Policy Centre in Brussels on 6 June 2002, entitled 'The Future of Europe Debate: A Scottish Perspective'.[68]

2. In Florence, on 14 November 2002, the Executive signed a Declaration by 40 Regions with Legislative Power on the Future of Europe.

3. Through the work of the Committee of the Regions (CoR), including the adoption of a CoR Opinion prepared by the first minister: 'More Democracy, Transparency and Efficiency in the EU'.[69]

At the beginning of February 2003, a paper entitled 'Europe and the Regions' was submitted to the European Convention by the UK minister of Europe, Peter Hain, in his capacity as the UK government's representative on the EU Convention. This was a joint submission on behalf of the Scottish Executive, the Northern Ireland Office, the Welsh Assembly government and the UK government. It concurs with the Scottish Parliament's demand for full institutional status of 'a new' Committee of the Regions, perhaps under a new name,[70] but emphasises the EU as a 'Union of Member States, each responsible for its own internal constitutional arrangements'.[71] It urged greater pre-legislative scrutiny, more contact between the Commission and regional administrations and a more formal involvement of devolved parliaments and assemblies in the United Kingdom's internal procedures under the proposed 'early warning system' to monitor subsidiarity.[72]

On 16 September 2002, the European Committee had invited the general public to a full-day event in the Scottish Parliament Debating Chamber. Over 120 delegates met and had their say on the future of Europe. Along with the contributions the Committee received on its interactive internet forum, the views expressed at this 'Scottish Parliament Convention on the Future of Europe' were incorporated into the Committee's December 2002 report.

The Parliament's position goes further than the Executive's. It advocates a twenty-first century EU as a 'Union of its nations, regions and its people'.[73] Not surprisingly, it holds that the founding principles of the Scottish Parliament should be 'used as a template for a new European union': power sharing between citizens, legislators and executive; accountability (EU executive accountable to European Parliament; Parliament and Executive accountable to the EU's citizens); an accessible, open and responsive EU with a participative approach to the development, consideration and scrutiny of policy and legislation; and equal opportunities.[74]

It demands a 'new relationship between the Commission and the "regions"' which would see 'constitutional regions' acquire the status of 'partners of the Union', as an 'integral part of the EU's structures', 'recognised as such in the Treaties and working procedures'. It also calls for the creation of a regional affairs council involving ministers from the regions with legislative powers and working alongside the Council of Ministers. Crucially, it wants 'direct access' for the legislative regions and the CoR to the European Court of Justice[75] (whilst the Scottish Executive, even having signed up to that demand in the Flanders Declaration, has repeatedly stated 'that it not fully endorse the calls for the right of access to the ECJ').[76]

Despite the fact that the 74 self-governing regions in the EU represent 56.3 per cent of the EU's population,[77] and that excluding them from European governance would run counter to the remit of reconnecting citizens, Giscard d'Estaing's first draft of a European constitution did not explicitly mention the regions.[78] Neither did the cornerstone speeches on the future of Europe by German foreign minister Joschka Fischer[79] and French president Jacques Chirac[80] in Berlin or Tony Blair in Warsaw.[81] This was particularly puzzling in Joschka Fischer's case; had the German Greens not been champions of a 'patchwork Europe', a 'Europe of the Regions'? At the beginning of the twenty-first century we find ourselves a long way from the rhetoric of a 'Europe of the Regions' as demanded, by, amongst others, the German Länder until the early 1990s.[82]

The German Länder managed, during the ratification of the Maastricht and Amsterdam treaties, to secure participation and veto rights within the constitutional framework of the Federal Republic through their role in the second chamber, the *Bundesrat*.[83] There is no equivalent for Scotland. Lacking a written constitution, and given the wording of the Scotland Act 1998, Scotland's influence in European affairs on the UK level depends on goodwill and convention.

That is one of the major differences between the early deliberations of the Constitutional Convention and the terms of devolution as laid down in the Scotland Act. Whilst its 1990 document demands the 'statutory entitlement for Scotland's Parliament and/or Executive to be represented in UK Ministerial delegations to the Council of Ministers',[84] this was, in its final document, watered down to representation 'in UK Ministerial delegations to the Council of Ministers where appropriate'.[85] In the White Paper of 1997, the definition was clear: 'Relations with Europe are the responsibility of the United Kingdom Parliament and Government.' And: 'The Scottish Parliament will have an important role in those aspects of European Union business which affect devolved areas'.[86] The Scotland Act confirms this 'subsidiary position for the Scottish Parliament in Europe'.[87]

In 1999, a concordat was agreed between Whitehall and the Scottish Executive outlining cooperation and partnership in this section. Up to now, with a Labour-led government in power both in London and in Edinburgh, this seems to have worked, despite criticisms concerning the handling of the Scottish fishing crisis. But the litmus test would come if different parties formed governments in Scotland and the United Kingdom.

If reconnecting citizens with the policy-making institutions of the EU is a priority of the Convention and the next Intergovernmental Conference, then the accommodation of regional aspirations towards gaining their share in the EU's policy making must not be ignored, otherwise a majority of EU citizens could feel, at least partially, disenfranchised.

There are, basically, three routes or scenarios by which this can be achieved:

1. By giving self-governing regions direct access to the decision-making institutions of the EU, either by transforming the Committee of the Regions or by creating a Council of the Regions which would tie in the 'constitutional regions' to the governance of the EU, in an integrated multi-level governance system.
2. By giving self-governing regions a share in European policy making on the member state level, in an EU which, then, would in all likelihood be retaining a greater

degree of intergovernmentality, because the regions' participation in policy making would be largely restricted to the member states' governance.

3. By transforming legislative regions into member states of a more or less integrated or intergovernmental EU.

In Scotland's case, these options will be amongst the factors which will determine whether devolution will turn into a settlement or whether the political road map will lead towards independence and the 'break-up of Britain'.[88]

Clearly, the European Committee and the majority of the Scottish Parliament are pushing for the first scenario, with the second as a potential fall-back option. The Scottish Executive seems to favour a mix of the first two scenarios, with a preference for the second, arguing that being part of an influential big member state might become even more important for Scotland in view of EU enlargement. At present, so the argument goes, Scotland enjoys the best of both worlds. It may participate in the formulation of European policies at the UK level, but is also free to increase its foothold in Europe and to forge strategic partnerships in Europe in order to increase its direct influence (as long as these endeavours do not run counter to UK European policies).

It is noteworthy at this point that multi-level governance must mean shared responsibility and full integration between the different levels of governance – supranational, member state, region and local. It is, as Amanda Sloat has pointed out, one of the weaknesses of the multi-level governance discourse that it fails to acknowledge the extent to which member states' governments will continue to control access to the EU's political theatre, playing a 'gatekeeper' role. Multi-level governance must not confuse *influence* with *participation*.[89]

Whilst it supports any strengthening of Scotland's profile in Europe, the Scottish National Party's policy aims at an independent Scotland as part of the EU, and thus clearly pursues route three. Whether this would mean a nineteenth-century-type of nation state, or a state within an integrated, federal EU, is not clear. There are conflicting tendencies within the party.[90] The majority SNP position is that an election victory of the party would trigger a consultative referendum on 'independence in Europe'. If the referendum were won, this would be seen as a mandate for negotiations with the UK government. An independent Scotland would then seek a close association with the other parts of the United Kingdom and Ireland, but be a 'sovereign' EU member state.

The next few years will be pivotal for Scotland. There is the question of internal reform of the EU and the debate about an EU constitution. If a satisfactory, participative role for self-governing regions in European governance could be found, this would support the devolution side of the argument. If such a scenario were absent, and at the same time a dozen new member states were to join the EU as 'independent' states, most of which are smaller than Scotland, then that would add ammunition to the arsenal of the independence camp.

If constitutional change in the United Kingdom progressed, creating regional assemblies in England,[91] that would certainly stabilise devolution and reduce some of the glaring asymmetries in the political geography of the United Kingdom.

Moreover, if House of Lords reform would create a second chamber with regional representation,[92] a quasi-federal United Kingdom could well fit into a quasi-federal EU.

But if these developments were stalled, and at the same time – as looks likely – the Convention and the IGC took the stance that accommodating regional participation in European policy making was to happen strictly within the boundaries and constitutions of member states, whilst at the same time the new EU members planted their flag at Brussels and took their seats in the EU institutions, then the SNP would have a persuasive case to argue, with a view of gaining popular backing for its independence plans in the 2007 Scottish Parliament election.

In the absence of real perspectives of direct access to the European institutions, the question could be, as Noreen Burrows has put it, less about Scotland in Europe than about 'Scotland in the UK in Europe'.[93] Best of both worlds, as the promoters of devolution argue, or double blockage, as the nationalists contend? Will Scotland have a guaranteed say in the formulation of the UK position in European policy making? Will there be room at the top in Europe for Scotland as a 'constitutional region'? The answer to these questions will, perhaps more than any inherent doubt about the devolved institutions themselves, play a decisive part in determining whether or not the 'break-up of Britain' is on the cards.

NOTES

1. Lindsay Paterson, Civic Democracy, in Gerry Hassan and Chris Warhurst, *Anatomy of the New Scotland: Power, Influence and Change* (Edinburgh: Mainstream, 2002) p.56
2. Brian Taylor, *Scotland's Parliament: Triumph and Disaster* (Edinburgh: Edinburgh University Press, 2002) p.319
3. John Osmond, From Corporate Body to Virtual Parliament: The Metamorphosis of the National Assembly for Wales, in Robert Hazell (ed.), *The State of the Nations: The Third Year of Devolution in the United Kingdom* (Exeter: Imprint Academic, 2003) pp.13–47
4. Consultative Steering Group, *Shaping Scotland's Parliament* (Edinburgh: The Stationery Office, 1998) p.3
5. See Alice Brown, Designing the Scottish Parliament, *Parliamentary Affairs* 53(3) (2000) p.549
6. See Philip Schlesinger, David Miller and William Dinan, *Open Scotland? Journalists, Spin Doctors and Lobbyists* (Edinburgh: Polygon, 2001) ch.12, pp.226–44
7. John Bochel, David Denver and Allan Macartney, *The Referendum Experience: Scotland 1979* (Aberdeen: Aberdeen University Press, 1981) p.141
8. Kenyon Wright, *The People Say Yes: The Making of Scotland's Parliament* (Glendaruel: Argyll Publishing, 1997) p.140
9. Charles Pattie, David Denver, James Mitchell and Hugh Bochel, The 1997 Scottish Referendum: An Analysis of the Results, *Scottish Affairs* 22 (Winter 1998) p.9
10. See Eberhard Bort, The Numbers Game – 129 and the Scottish Parliament: Does Size Matter?, *Scottish Affairs* 39 (Spring 2002) pp.1–14

11. Peter Lynch, *Scottish Government and Politics* (Edinburgh: Edinburgh University Press, 2001) p.52
12. See Philip Schlesinger *et al.*, op. cit. (2001)
13. *The Sunday Herald*, 3 September 2000
14. Iain Martin in *The Scotsman*, 17 August 2000
15. *The Herald* (leader), 15 September 2000
16. *The Sunday Herald*, 10 September 2000
17. James Cusick in *The Sunday Herald*, 5 August 2001
18. Scottish Parliament, *Summaries of Bills Passed by the Scottish Parliament in the First Session*, SP Paper 846 (Edinburgh: The Stationery Office, 2003)
19. See Mark Nicholson, 'Pretendy parliament' shaking off detractors, *Financial Times*, 25 February 2003
20. Sir David Steel MSP, State of the Nations Annual Lecture, given at Edinburgh on 29 January 2003
21. See David McCrone, Peeblin' Wi' Stanes: Assessing the Scottish Parliament, 1999–2003, www.institute-of-governance.org/onlinepub/mccrone/assessingscotparl.htm
22. Murray Ritchie, How Has the Parliament Performed?, *The Herald*, 27 March 2003
23. In Scottish Television's programme *This Week in Politics*, every Thursday.
24. Mark Irvine, Triumph of Consensus, Not Combat, *New Statesman*, 5 June 2000
25. Consultative Steering Group (CSG), *Shaping Scotland's Parliament* (Edinburgh: HMSO, 1998) p.26
26. Mike Watson, *Year Zero: An Inside View of the Scottish Parliament* (Edinburgh: Polygon, 2001) p.165
27. Fewer than initially anticipated, but financial constraints apparently did not allow for a greater spread of sessions across the country.
28. Peter Lynch and Steven Birrell, Linking Parliament to the People: The Public Petitions Process of the Scottish Parliament, *Scottish Affairs* 37 (Autumn 2001) p.17
29. See Neal Ascherson, Designing Virtual Citizens: Some Scottish Experiments with Electronic Democracy, *Scottish Affairs* 43 (May 2003); also Eberhard Bort, Scotland: On the Road to eDemocracy?, *Upgrade* ('e-Government: Public Administration for a New Century'), IV(2) (April 2003)
30. The latest example is the reportage in the Edinburgh *Evening News* about the cost of Executive ministers' limousines, where an attack on the Executive was turned into a generalisation about MSPs in general, as if every one of the 129 were driven around at taxpayers' cost by a chauffeur.
31. Gerald Taylor, Mediating between Levels of Government: The Role of the Political Parties, in J. Barry Jones and John Osmond (eds), *Building a Civic Culture: Institutional Change, Policy Development and Political Dynamics in the National Assembly of Wales* (Cardiff: Institute of Welsh Affairs/The Welsh Governance Centre, 2002) p.202
32. Ibid.
33. Kevin Morgan and Geoff Mungham, *Redesigning Democracy: The Making of the Welsh Assembly* (Bridgend: Seren Books, 2000)

34. *Your Region, Your Choice* (London: The Stationery Office, 2002)
35. Christopher Harvie, English Regionalism: The Dog that Never Barked, in Bernard Crick (ed.), *National Identities: The Constitution of the United Kingdom* (Oxford: Blackwell, 1991)
36. See John Tomaney and John Mawson (eds), *England: The State of the Regions* (Bristol: Policy Press, 2002)
37. Alice Brown, David McCrone, Lindsay Paterson and Paula Surridge, *The Scottish Electorate: The 1997 General Election and Beyond* (Basingstoke: Palgrave, 1999) p.137
38. Eberhard Bort, The 1998 Belfast Agreement: Peace for a 'Troubled' Region?, in Eberhard Bort and Neil Evans (eds), *Networking Europe: Essays on Regionalism and Social Democracy* (Liverpool: Liverpool University Press, 2000) pp.429–61
39. Scottish Parliament Procedures Committee, 3rd Report 2003, *The Founding Principles of the Scottish Parliament: The Application of Access and Participation, Equal Opportunities, Accountability and Power Sharing in the Work of the Parliament*, SP Papers 818 (Edinburgh: The Stationery Office, 2003)
40. Quangos Must Go Says Minister, BBC News Online, 21 June 2001; Executive to 'Get Tough' on Quangos, BBC News Online, 9 February 2000
41. Assembly 'Breaking' Quango Promise, BBC News Online, 2 October 2001
42. Paul Rogerson, Scottish Enterprise Under Fire, *The Herald*, 16 April 2003
43. See Eberhard Bort, There are No Members of the Scottish Parliament: Mind the Gap?, *Scottish Affairs* 43 (May 2003)
44. Brendan O'Leary, The 1998 British–Irish Agreement: Power-sharing Plus, *Scottish Affairs* 26 (Winter 1999) pp.14–35
45. 'Ron Davies, *Devolution: A Process Not an Event* (Cardiff: Institute of Welsh Affairs, 1999)
46. See Paula Surridge Society and Democracy: The New Scotland, in Lindsay Paterson, Alice Brown, John Curtice, Kerstin Hinds, David McCrone, Alison Park, Kerry Sproston and Paula Surridge, *New Scotland, New Politics?* (Edinburgh: Edinburgh University Press, 2002) p.136
47. See, for example, Tom Nairn, *After Britain: New Labour and the Return of Scotland* (London: Granta, 2000); Andrew Marr, *The Day Britain Died* (London: Profile, 2000); John Redwood, *The Death of Britain?* (Basingstoke: Palgrave, 1999); Simon Heffer, *Nor Shall My Sword: The Reinvention of England* (London: Weidenfeld & Nicolson, 1999); Peter Hitchens, *The Abolition of Britain* (London: Quartet, 1999)
48. See Archie Brown, Asymmetrical Devolution: The Scottish Case, in *Political Quarterly* 69 (3) (1998) pp.215–23; see also Michael Keating, What's Wrong with Asymmetrical Government?, in *Regional and Federal Studies* 8 (1) (1998) pp.195–218
49. Brian Taylor, *The Scottish Parliament* (Edinburgh: Edinburgh University Press, 1999) p.257
50. See Gerry Hassan and Robin Wilson, *The British–Irish Council as a Multi-form Organisation* (Edinburgh: Centre for Scottish Public Policy, 1999)
51. See David Heald (ed.), *Scottish Affairs* (special issue: Fiscal Autonomy), 41 (Autumn 2002)

52. See Rory Watson, Britain to Push for EU Shaped by Nation States, *The Times*, 16 April 2003

53. 'Regional' is not a preferred term in the Scottish political discourse, as Scotland is a nation; yet, in European discourse, 'region' seems to fit the bill for a self-governing, legislative or 'constitutional' sub-state territory.

54. Scottish Parliament European Committee, 5th Report 2002, *An Inquiry into Scotland's Representation in the European Union* (21 November 2002) p.13

55. Under the convenership of Irene Oldfather MSP (Labour), it has the following eight members: Sarah Boyack (Lab), Colin Campbell (SNP), Dennis Canavan (Ind), Helen Eadie (Lab), John Home Robertson (Deputy Convener, Lab), Lloyd Quinan (SNP), Nora Radcliffe (Lib Dem) and Ben Wallace (Con), plus two substitute members: Winnie Ewing (SNP) and Tavish Scott (Lib Dem).

56. The range of the present 222 members reaches from 18 million strong North Rhine-Westphalia to the smallest of Greek local councils – the 74 self-governing regions are far outnumbered by local authorities.

57. Scottish Parliament European Committee, 9th Report 2001, *Report on the Governance of the European Union and the Future of Europe: What Role for Scotland? Vol. 1: Main Report* (11 December 2001)

58. Ibid., p.28

59. See Peter Lynch, *Scottish Government and Politics* (Edinburgh: Edinburgh University Press, 2001) pp.159–61

60. Jack McConnell, Tide Turns for Europe, *Scotland on Sunday*, 3 December 2000

61. www.scotland.gov.uk/pages/news/2002/11/p_SEJD141.aspx

62. Quoted in John Osmond, Constitution Building on the Hoof, in J. Barry Jones and John Osmond (eds), *Building a Civic Culture*, op. cit. (2002) p.65

63. www.scotland.gov.uk/pages/news/weekly/000255.aspx

64. www.scotland.gov.uk/pages/news/2003/02/SEet272.aspx

65. Scottish Parliament European Committee, 5th Report 2002, p.7

66. Ibid., p.19

67. The Convention comprises representatives from each of the national governments and parliaments, the European Commission, the European Parliament, the 13 candidate countries, and from non-governmental organisations and academia. Former French president Valéry Giscard d'Estaing is the chairman, flanked by two former prime ministers – Giuliano Amato of Italy and Belgium's Jean-Luc Dehaene – as his deputies.

68. www.scotland.gov.uk/about/FCSD/ExtRel1/00014768/page1239857280. aspx

69. www.scotland.gov.uk/pages/news/2003/01/p_SEjd200a.aspx

70. Names mentioned are 'Congress of European Regions', 'Convention of European Regions' or 'European Assembly of Regions'. Scottish Parliament European Committee Briefing Paper, *Executive Response to the Committee's Future of Europe Report* (19 February 2003) p.7

71. Ibid., p.4

72. Scottish Parliament European Committee, *Convener's Report: Annex A – Meeting with Rt Hon Peter Hain MP* (20 February 2002) p.2

73. Scottish Parliament European Committee, 6th Report, p.10

74. Ibid., p.11
75. Ibid., pp.11–12
76. Scottish Parliament European Committee Briefing Paper, *Executive Response to the Committee's Future of Europe Report* (19 February 2003) p.3
77. The Role of Regions with Legislative Power in the EU, contribution from Mr Kimmo Kiljunen MP (Finland) and 14 other signatories to the European Convention, 4 and 7 October 2002, CONV 321/02 Annex, p.2
78. Stephen Castle, 'We, the people of Europe . . .': The document that will shape our futures, *The Independent*, 7 February 2003
79. Joschka Fischer, From Confederacy to Federation: Thoughts on the finality of European integration, speech by Joschka Fischer at the Humboldt University in Berlin, 12 May 2000, www.europa-digital.de/aktuell/dossier/reden/fischer.shtml
80. Jacques Chirac, Notre Europe, www.elysee.fr/cgi-bin/auracom/aurweb/search/file?aur_file = discours/2000/RFA0006D.html
81. Tony Blair's Warsaw speech, A Superpower, But Not a Superstate. See *The Guardian*, 7 October 2000. Full text: www.scotlandeuropa.com/DOWNLOAD/SPEECH%20PM.doc
82. See Alfred Geisel, The Future of Europe: Federalism – Regionalism – Centralism, in Eberhard Bort and Neil Evans (eds), *Networking Europe: Essays on Regionalism and Social Democracy* (Liverpool: Liverpool University Press, 2000) pp.39–52
83. See Roland Sturm, *Föderalismus in Deutschland* (Berlin: Landeszentrale für politische Bildungsarbeit, 2001) pp.117–37
84. Constitutional Convention, *Towards Scotland's Parliament* (Edinburgh, November 1990)
85. Constitutional Convention, *Scotland's Parliament, Scotland's Right* (Edinburgh, November 1995) p.16
86. UK government White Paper, *Scotland's Parliament* (The Scottish Office, 1997)
87. Brian Taylor, op. cit. (1999) p.272
88. See Tom Nairn's seminal *The Break-up of Britain* (London: New Left Books, 1977)
89. See Amanda Sloat, *Scotland in Europe* (Frankfurt: Peter Lang, 2002) especially ch.2
90. See Jo Eric Murkens with Peter Jones and Michael Keating, *Scottish Independence: A Practical Guide* (Edinburgh: Edinburgh University Press, 2002) pp.1–3
91. The first regional assemblies are expected to be elected perhaps as early as 2005 or 2006, but not all regions in England favour self-government. See John Tomaney and Peter Hetherington, England Arisen?, in Robert Hazell (ed.), *The State of the Nations 2003: The Third Year of Devolution in the United Kingdom*, (Exeter: Imprint Academic, 2003) pp.49–77
92. Reintroduced by Jack Cunningham MP into a debate dominated by the dispute concerning the ratio between elected and nominated members in a reformed House of Lords. See Ben Russell, Plan for Regions to Elect Upper House, *The Independent*, 7 February 2003
93. Noreen Burrows, Relations with the European Union, in Gerry Hassan and Chris Warhurst (eds), *The New Scottish Politics: The First Year of the Scottish Parliament and Beyond* (Edinburgh: HMSO, 2000) p.125

The United Kingdom as a post-sovereign polity

Michael Keating

STATE AND NATION IN THE UNITED KINGDOM

Devolution to the constituent nations and regions is not a new idea in the United Kingdom. It was William Ewart Gladstone's response to the problem of accommodating national diversity and parliamentary authority in an era of mass industrial society and emerging democracy. Every home rule proposal since Gladstone's plan of 1886 has essentially built on this basis.[1] Political opposition, however, delayed home rule 'all round' for over one hundred years, and it finally came about in a radically different environment, not that of the British Empire but that of European integration and a globalisation which, unlike the globalisation of Gladstone's era, was no longer subject to British hegemony. Whilst governments in the period 1886–1997 were, with some brief exceptions, unwilling to concede political power to the constituent nations, the United Kingdom, unlike most of its continental neighbours, did not engage in a process of cultural assimilation or institutional standardisation. Rather they cultivated the national identities of the non-English parts of the realm, consciously fostering a multinational conception that is reflected in the very name of the state. From 1885–86, the date of the failure of the first Irish home rule effort, administrative decentralisation was progressively extended to Scotland and, from 1965, to Wales. Northern Ireland, after 1922, was entrusted to a local hegemony organised around the Ulster Unionist Party. Recognition of the nations was given in symbolically important areas such as the army and the monarchy. Around the institutions of administrative decentralisation there formed an array of interest groups and forms of political accommodation, so that the distinct civil societies of the smaller nations were strengthened rather than weakened. Even within the Westminster Parliament, the Scottish MPs were able to create a *chasse guardée*, a field into which other parliamentarians did not stray.[2]

As a result, there survived within Scotland, Ireland and to some extent Wales, a concept of the United Kingdom as a political union rather than a unitary state.[3] In a union, the component parts of the state maintain their own identities and many of their traditional institutions and rights within the new united polity. A union, however, is different from a federation, in which there are legislatures at two levels, and a constitutionally entrenched division of powers: a solution expressly rejected by the framers of the Acts of Union in 1707 and 1801. This, it must be emphasised, was not merely a doctrine for nationalists and home rulers. Unionism itself, especially in its conservative forms, was predicated on the idea of a union of nations and is very different from the jacobinism of Continental Europe with its emphasis on assimilation. It is precisely this recognition of the power of nations and nationalism that has led unionists historically to oppose home rule, since they fear that self-governing nations would necessarily challenge the absolute supremacy of the Westminster Parliament.[4] Indeed, unionists have usually been more prepared to countenance secession than the concession of self-government within the Union. Labour unionists were rather more assimilationist, emphasising common class interests, but within the Labour movement there also survived a strong home rule tradition emphasising the rights of the smaller nations, even if this did increasingly conflict with Labour's commitment to uniform standards of social provision and centralised economic management.[5]

These two factors, the European and global context of devolution and the survival of the unionist rather than assimilationist tradition, ensured that devolution in the United Kingdom is more then mere decentralisation within a unitary state. It also represents an adjustment in the relationships amongst self-determining peoples. This further means that predictions from the other side, that it is the prelude to dissolution of the United Kingdom into independent nation states,[6] are also not obviously valid. Indeed, considerable confusion and argument remains about the nature of the settlement of 1997–98 and its constitutional implications.

What we might call the Westminster view is contained within the devolution Acts for Scotland, Wales and Northern Ireland, which make clear that the absolute sovereignty of the central Parliament is unabridged: Westminster may make laws in devolved matters, amend the devolution Acts and even abolish the devolved institutions themselves. Government representatives repeatedly reassured their audiences during the devolution process that this was so, as Gladstone did in an earlier era. Indeed, Gladstone was able to use Dicey's doctrine that parliamentary sovereignty cannot be alienated or abridged against Dicey's own complaint that Irish Home Rule would do just that.[7] Devolution, in this view, is a rather conservative measure, an effort to readjust and secure the old constitution in new conditions. The absence of overtly federal features such as a second chamber representing the nations and regions, and the failure to codify the constitution and provide a special mechanism for changing it, reinforce this interpretation.

Against this, the dominant interpretation in Scotland, at least outside the ranks of the Labour Party, is that there has been a fundamental change in the terms of the Union which cannot be challenged unilaterally by Westminster. This rests on two pillars. The first is that the Scottish Parliament is the legatee of an element of sovereignty that was never surrendered in the Union of 1707. There is some legal basis for this in the famous judgment of the Court of Session in 1953 in *MacCormick vs. the Lord Advocate*, when Lord Justice Cooper ruled that, the principle of absolute parliamentary sovereignty never having been established in Scotland, the new parliament of Great Britain could not have inherited it in 1707. Considered for many years as little more than an interesting intellectual curiosity, this doctrine has been revived in the new conditions.[8] Indeed, Scottish Nationalist MSP Winifred Ewing took the opportunity of her being given first word at the opening of the Scottish Parliament in 1999 to announce that the parliament had been reconvened. The second pillar is the referendum of 1997, seen as an act of self-determination by the Scottish people. Already in the 1980s, the Scottish Constitutional Convention had framed its demand for devolution as a claim of self-determination, noting that this right had never been surrendered, so bringing together the arguments about historical right and present will.[9] To this extent, unionists who feared that home rule would produce bodies claiming inherent rights to national self-determination are correct; whether this will lead to secession is another matter.

The Good Friday Agreement in Northern Ireland modifies parliamentary sovereignty in another way. Not only does it give the people of Northern Ireland, alone amongst the peoples of the United Kingdom, the legal right and means to leave the state, but it also gives another state a say in the affairs of the United Kingdom. More than an internal rearrangement of the state, it includes an international treaty, although the degree to which this is binding was called into question when London temporarily suspended the Northern Ireland Assembly without the consent of Dublin.

The same uncertainties and ambiguities are found in a consideration of the role of the European Union and the European Convention for the Protection of Human Rights (which is part of the Council of Europe machinery). In the 1970s, there was a strong tendency for both political leaders and the public in the peripheral nations of the United Kingdom to oppose European integration, on the ground that it was a threat to their future dreams of national sovereignty and was even more remote than London. During the 1980s, this changed, and nationalist parties came to favour European integration as a way of loosening ties with the centre.[10] Home rulers also began to think about how their project could link into the developing European polity. As a result, the devolution settlements incorporate the European dimension directly. Laws of the Scottish Parliament and the Northern Ireland Assembly and secondary legislation of the National Assembly for Wales can be struck down by the courts if they are found to conflict with EU laws, as is the case with laws of the Westminster Parliament. In addition, Scottish, Northern Irish and Welsh Acts can be struck down if they violate the European Convention for the Protection of Human Rights, whereas in the case of Westminster laws, the courts can only draw Parliament's attention to the problem. The result is that Scotland and Northern Ireland are incorporated into European systems of law rather directly, without any need for intervention on the part of Westminster. Again, the Westminster doctrine is that this applies only because and so long as Westminster allows it. The reality is that a distinct legal practice is developing in the non-English parts of the United Kingdom, which is becoming part of the unwritten constitution and which undermines the idea of unfettered parliamentary sovereignty.

THE UNITED KINGDOM AS AN ASYMMETRICAL FEDERATION

Given the reality that power has been dispersed amongst the nations and regions, it might be argued that the United Kingdom would best be understood as an emerging federation, on the same lines as Belgium or Spain. Federal thought does have a long history in the United Kingdom, and although it was more often imposed on colonial possessions becoming independent than adopted at home, it has featured in the debate on devolution. There does appear to be a logic in the basic principles of federalism, providing for a sphere of separate powers at two levels of government and for a sphere of shared powers. Federalism also typically balances separate legislatures at the two levels with a second chamber of the federal parliament representing the federated units, so binding them into the state. Fiscal federalism similarly provides for each level to raise its own taxes and also for a mechanism to redistribute resources so that the richer regions will help the poorer ones.

The United Kingdom has some of these elements. Despite the continuing rhetoric about absolute parliamentary sovereignty, there is a constitutional division of powers, although in Wales this applies only to administrative and not legislative competences. Yet the United Kingdom lacks other key elements that might make it a federation. Not all parts of the state have their own legislatures, with the Westminster Parliament doubling up as the legislature for England. Taxation is almost entirely monopolised by the centre, which also decides on the formula for distributing resources. Despite a great deal of discussion, the House of Lords has not yet been reformed to make it the chamber of territorial representation.

There are, in any case, serious problems with a federal solution for the United Kingdom, of which the greatest is the dominant position of England. England is several times larger in population and wealth than all the other nations together and would seriously unbalance any federal arrangement. It would dominate in power and resources not only the other national parliaments but also the federal parliament of the United Kingdom. Regional government for England might in many ways help the cause of decentralisation, democratisation and balanced development, but it would not solve the problem of federal imbalance unless the regions were to have the same powers as the Scottish Parliament, something for which there is almost no demand. Formal federalisation has also been resisted in London, as it has in Spain, since it would bind the central state itself to a constraining constitutional formula. Losing some control at the periphery is one thing, but federalism would lead to a loss of control across the state as a whole.

The United Kingdom can therefore be considered not to be federal but to have some federal features. Even as a quasi-federation it has some distinct features, the most pronounced of which is its asymmetry. It has often been argued that asymmetrical federations are inherently unstable and multinational federations even more so.[11] There will, it is said, be endless competition over powers, with weaker entities seeking to match the stronger ones and constant battles over resources. Governments representing nations rather than mere regions will take upon themselves the role of representing the entire range of citizen concerns and claim absolute sovereignty, with the result that the federal state will disintegrate. On the other side, it is argued that where the underlying social and political realities are asymmetrical, then an asymmetrical constitution is the only answer; an effort to impose a uniform solution will merely undermine national unity by weakening the state needlessly or frustrate the minorities by denying them their aspirations to self-government.

More specific objections to asymmetry focus on powers, representation and citizen rights. It may be argued that the Scots, Welsh and Northern Irish are gaining an advantage over the English by having the right to govern themselves and that Scotland has an advantage over Wales in having more powers. The answer to this, provided in the Spanish constitution and in emerging British practice, is to let nations and regions have self-government if they want it but not to force them where they do not want it. In the Spanish case, this resulted in the rapid spread of self-government from the historical nationalities to all the regions. In the United Kingdom, Scottish and Welsh devolution has helped stimulate the demand for regional government in England, but only within limits. English regions are concerned to equip themselves with the powers for economic and social development rather than with self-determination in a broader sense, so it is fitting that the powers they are given should respond to their demands and not to a template made in Scotland or Wales.

A more serious objection is encapsulated in the famous West Lothian Question posed in the 1970s by anti-devolution Scottish Labour MP Tam Dalyell. The question, which had also preoccupied Gladstone in the nineteenth century, was whether MPs representing the devolved territories at Westminster should be allowed to vote on matters affecting England alone, when the corresponding matters within their own nations were handled by the devolved assemblies. Dalyell framed the question in an alliterative manner by asking why he could vote on matters in Liverpool but not Linlithgow, Birmingham but not Bathgate.[12] There does seem to be a real issue of principle here, although it has failed to become a political issue in the years since devolution, possibly because Labour has enjoyed a majority in England as well as in Scotland and Wales, so that English measures have rarely been voted through on the basis of Scottish votes. Surveys of opinion show that, when the anomaly is pointed out to them, voters in both England and Scotland think that it is wrong for Scottish MPs to vote on English matters but it is not something that comes spontaneously to mind.

There are two answers to the West Lothian Question. One, which is normally given in Scotland, is that it is up to the English to demand their own national parliament or regional assemblies but that if they choose to use the Westminster Parliament as their domestic legislature then they do not have a right to throw out the Scottish, Welsh and Northern Irish Members. In this way, the problem is turned back upon England. The other answer, more commonly given in England, is to exclude the Members from the other nations from voting on English matters where the matter in question is devolved to their own territories. Objections to this are firstly that it is impossible to distinguish purely English matters; secondly that it would create two classes of MP; and thirdly that governments, used to commanding a majority in parliament, could find themselves with majorities on some matters and not on others, so creating instability. The answer in turn would surely have to be a further round of constitutional reform. The devolution legislation does not contain any list of purely English matters since it regards Westminster as competent over everything whilst *allowing* the devolved bodies to deal with matters not expressly reserved to the UK level. Public expenditure decisions, for example, are made on the basis of functional allocations to English departments, which then form the basis for block grants to Scotland, Wales and Northern Ireland. Most legislation, however, has a clear geographical remit and there will be need in due course for a more transparent system for allocating expenditure amongst the nations (see below). The objection about there being two classes of MP, similarly, is an effort to retain the unity of the UK Parliament as though devolution had not happened. Scotland's over-representation in Parliament, whilst historically largely accidental, was defended as a compensation for the lack of home rule and as necessary to cope with the volume of Scottish legislation. Under the devolution legislation, the number of Scottish MPs is being reduced. Changing their role would be merely a further logical consequence of devolution. The final objection, that governments with a UK majority might not have one on purely English matters, also points to the need for further constitutional change, away from the assumption that governments will have disciplined one-party majorities. It might mean that governments in England, like those in Scotland and Wales, would need to seek support outside the ranks of the leading party, through coalitions or pacts with other parties. To expect the Westminster parliament to function as though devolution had not happened is a very conservative way of addressing constitutional reform.

Devolution has also left considerable asymmetries in public expenditure amongst the various parts of the United Kingdom. This is due less to conscious planning than to the incremental effects of historical decisions, in particular the relative decline in the populations of Scotland, Wales and Northern Ireland compared with England, and the failure of public expenditure levels to adjust. Indeed, the presence in the Cabinet of secretaries of state from the territories meant that they were able to defend relatively generous financial settlements, although the existence and scale of these advantages are subject to much argument. Since the 1970s, expenditure for Scotland, Wales and later Northern Ireland has been governed by the Barnett formula, which allocates increases or decreases in expenditure levels on English services to the territories on the basis of population. The idea is that per capita expenditure levels should gradually converge as the share allocated by population overtakes the historical base levels. For a variety of reasons, including fears of nationalism, this did not happen through the 1980s and 1990s but it does appear that, following devolution, the formula is being applied more strictly. In that case, the present advantage enjoyed by Scotland, Wales and Northern Ireland, and their enthusiasm for the formula, will diminish.

Already interests in London and the English regions have been attacking the Barnett formula in the mistaken belief that it is responsible for the territories' advantage – rather than for the gradual erosion of that advantage. In this respect, devolution is making the United Kingdom rather more symmetrical, although allocating expenditure on an equal per capita basis throughout the country irrespective of need is hardly a rational formula. It is likely, therefore, that the issue will be revisited and that some form of fiscal federalism will be introduced, balancing the raising of taxes locally with a system of equalisation to ensure fairness.

A final issue in asymmetry is the possibility of citizens enjoying different levels of basic rights depending on which part of the country they live in. This may be a criticism of devolution but it cannot count in favour of the pre-devolution regime where such inequalities already existed, notably between Northern Ireland and the rest of the United Kingdom. As part of the devolution settlement, however, the European Convention for the Protection of Human Rights has been incorporated into the constitutions of Scotland, Wales and Northern Ireland, ensuring a greater security for basic rights than existed before. There is still, however, one possibility for asymmetry. The Convention has been incorporated into UK and English law subject to the principle of the sovereignty of Parliament, which can decline to provide a remedy for breaches of rights, and can suspend application of the Convention when it is inconvenient, as it has indeed done. In the devolved territories, however, its application is direct, so that it could be the case that an identical law could be pushed through in England and struck down in Scotland. In this case, however, it is not devolution that has created the anomaly but the UK Parliament's refusal to accept the implications of its own constitutional reform programme.

SOVEREIGNTY AND POST-SOVEREIGNTY

To understand the implications of devolution, however, we must take the process outside the narrow framework of UK constitutional reform and the Westminster model, and place it in the broader context of changes in the very meaning of statehood and sovereignty. In traditional political thought, sovereignty has usually been seen as inseparable from the state as an all-encompassing agency of regulation and the ultimate source of legitimate authority. It is a unitary principle which cannot be divided or shared. This, as we have seen, is the essence of the Westminster doctrine. Yet, in recent years the transformation of the state has raised questions about the extent and nature of its authority, and consequently about the doctrine of sovereignty itself. These challenges have come at three levels.

The first stems from the apparent divorce of functional systems of regulation from the formal institutions of the state as the state sheds power upwards to global and transnational systems; downwards to regional and local systems of regulation; and outwards to the market and civil society. The state is apparently being hollowed out, losing power and authority and sparking off debates about the end of sovereignty[13] or changing patterns of sovereignty.[14] These arguments have not been resolved and often the participants seem to be talking past each other. Some people insist that the fact that states have lost power or are now interdependent rather than independent is irrelevant. They are still sovereign in legal terms and can, if they choose, exercise all their powers. Yet, if the state is losing power but retaining formal sovereignty, the latter risks ending up as a stranded concept, of little use in practical analysis. Sovereignty then becomes an empty shell, a formal principle with no substantive value.

The second level of challenge has come from groups unwilling to accept the claims of state sovereignty and insisting on their own rights as peoples, or on the importance of universal principles or transnational civil obligations that override the principle of sovereignty. In many parts of Europe, parties representing stateless nations have abandoned dreams of statehood (where they ever had them) and instead are focusing on the multiple ways in which a nation can be represented and act.[15] Demands from Catalans, Basques, Scots and Welsh are undermining the mystique of the sovereign and all-powerful nation state and introducing a more pluralistic way of thinking about political authority.

The third level of challenge has come from a recognition of legal pluralism and the possibility of normative orders beyond the state, through international law, transnational regimes and most specifically the emergence of a European order including the EU and the European Convention for the Protection of Human Rights. There is endless debate on whether the EU is merely an association of states or a supranational order, but a growing body of legal scholars see it as a legal order in its own right alongside the states if not in opposition to them.[16] Embedded as they are in these new forms of overarching authority, states themselves are losing important parts of their sovereignty.

So instead of seeing sovereignty as a unitary principle rooted in the state as the fount of all authority, we can see it as dispersed and shared in complex ways and across several layers of government. This way of thinking is rather alien to state elites and certainly violates the British principle of parliamentary sovereignty, but is consistent with historical traditions in the stateless nations. Precisely because nations such as Scotland or Catalonia were historically weak and threatened by more powerful neighbours, they developed doctrines about shared sovereignty and international order, seeking on occasion to play their powerful neighbours off against each other. They may thus be better placed than the former great powers to adapt to a European and international order in which power and sovereignty are dispersed and shared, and politics is a matter of negotiation and accommodation.

All of this remains controversial and there is a lack of clarity about the new understandings of authority, but it can be argued that we are moving into a new era of post-sovereignty. By this it is not meant that sovereignty has disappeared but that it has been transformed and its old meanings lost. Instead of being a unitary principle associated with the state, it has become plural and dispersed. It is consistent with this understanding of sovereignty to say that the EU, the Westminster Parliament and the Scottish Parliament all partake of sovereignty, although none of them monopolises it.

THE UNITED KINGDOM AS A POST-SOVEREIGN STATE

These trends are widely visible in the modern world, but the United Kingdom provides a particularly interesting example because of its explicitly multinational character, the devolution of power to the constituent nations, and the co-existence of devolution with European integration. It is a puzzle because the United Kingdom has never had a codified, written constitution above the ordinary law of the land, relying on the principle of parliamentary sovereignty to answer the question as to where ultimate authority lay. Once this principle is itself called into doubt, the question becomes extremely difficult to answer. There are, as we have seen, competing doctrines, and there is often a difference between doctrine and practice. So even those who insist that Westminster sovereignty is intact despite devolution will admit that if it were to abolish the Scottish Parliament unilaterally this would be so contentious politically as to provoke a constitutional crisis and possibly the secession of Scotland. The whole basis of the British constitution is indeed based on convention and we can expect firm conventions to develop that Westminster does not interfere in Scottish devolved affairs. Breaking the convention would thus be a serious matter, just as the failure of the House of Lords to observe conventional limitations provoked a constitutional crisis in 1910. We could also argue by extension that if Westminster were to overrule the Scottish Parliament on a devolved matter, this would violate the convention established in 1999 that Westminster would legislate on devolved matters only at the request of Scotland or following a failure to meet European or international obligations. Indeed, in an analogous matter, the Supreme Court of Canada ruled in 1998 that the federal power to disallow provincial legislation no longer existed since it had not been used for so long and a binding convention had developed to the effect that it would not. It could also be argued that if a future UK government were to withdraw from the EU, this would not be binding on Scotland, Wales or Northern Ireland, since membership of the EU is part of their constitutional settlement and could not be changed without their consent.

The United Kingdom thus qualifies as a post-sovereign polity in which authority has been dispersed in complex ways within and beyond the state, although constitutional thought in London has yet to come to terms with it. Devolution has been described as a process not an event, and there is a widespread expectation that it will develop over time, although less agreement on what direction this will take. Much will depend on the process of European integration with which it is now so linked. We can identify three broad schools of thought here, as in other plurinational European states. The first, which is the official view of the Scottish National Party (SNP), is that the European framework permits Scotland to become an independent state, since Europe will take care of difficult matters such as trade and the currency and, although the SNP is ambivalent about this, defence. The second position, associated with the Labour Party, is that Scotland, Wales and the regions of England will be accommodated within a reformed but united UK state which will have a single presence in the world. Sovereignty will remain with the Westminster Parliament but the nations and regions will be able to act autonomously within their devolved spheres and cooperate under the benign leadership of London. Northern Ireland is a matter apart. The third position is the post-sovereigntist one, associated with Plaid Cymru and with nationalists in Catalonia and Flanders, with some Basques, and even with a sector of the SNP. These argue that the meaning of sovereignty has been so changed in the modern world that independence no longer makes sense as a short-term strategy. Instead, nationalists should promote ever more self-government within the state and in broader European arenas, gradually building the nation and strengthening it. What matters here are the powers in the hands of the nation and the ability to project the nation in the new networks of decision making. Some, such as the Catalan party Esquerra Republicana de Catalunya, see independence as a long-term goal within a Europe of the Peoples, after the existing states have faded away under the influence of Europe on one hand and devolution on the other. The larger Catalan party, Convergència i Unió, are more reluctant to commit themselves to a long-term goal, arguing that we will know the future of Catalonia only when we know the future of Europe. Northern Ireland's Social Democratic and Labour Party (SDLP) sees great hope in Europe as it gradually erodes borders, brings the two parts of Ireland together and makes partition ever more irrelevant. Ulster Unionists have been much more wary, emphasising the sovereignty of the United Kingdom, as have Sinn Féin, with its demand for a sovereign and united Ireland. Yet the Good Friday Agreement, with its sharing of sovereignty, its provisions for change and its link into Europe, is a classic example of a post-sovereign regime, to which all the parties in Northern Ireland, with the exception of Ian Paisley's Democratic Unionists, have given their consent.

It is sometimes argued that, whatever leaders and intellectuals may think, ordinary voters are tied to the traditional nation state formula.[17] Yet such evidence as we have from public opinion suggests that it is very open to new forms of authority and does not make a sharp distinction amongst the categories of devolution, federalism and independence in Europe.[18] Polls since 1999 have shown overwhelming acceptance of devolution in Scotland and even in Wales, where the 'yes' side won such a marginal victory in the referendum. People would in general like to see more powers given to their devolved assemblies, especially in the taxation and spending area, but otherwise see the new settlement as an acceptable balance.[19] Yet there are some intriguing results which suggest the electors would like to keep their options open. A series of polls in Scotland between 1998 and 2001 showed support for independence at around 25 per cent when measured against the options of devolution or a return to centralised government. Yet when the same pollsters asked how people would vote in a referendum on Scottish independence, around half of respondents consistently reported that they would vote for independence. Similar apparent contradictions are visible in opinion polls in Catalonia, Quebec and the Basque Country.[20] Even in Northern Ireland, polls in recent years have shown much less intransigence about the question of unification than has usually been assumed, and a willingness to experiment with new formulas. It is tempting to say that the electors are confused, but a more likely interpretation is that they refuse to make the clear distinctions between independence and more autonomy that the classic theory of sovereignty would require. This is confirmed in evidence that people in the stateless nations of Europe are able to adopt multiple political identities, with the nation, the state and even with Europe. It does appear, then, that the politics of post-sovereignty have an appeal both to political leaders and to the general public.

PRESSURES AND STRAINS

Devolution does not provide a definitive constitutional settlement for the United Kingdom and, as we have seen, voters see it as an evolving arrangement. Certain of the pressures that might lead to further adjustments can already be identified.

One is demographic change in Northern Ireland, with the Catholic population gaining a majority. This would not necessarily lead immediately to Irish unity, since it is by no means clear that all Catholics are nationalists, but it could lead at least to a nationalist-led government in the Province, with the Protestants taking advantage of the minority rights provisions built into the Good Friday Agreement. Protestants could also take more interest in the kind of shared sovereignty and dual identity mechanisms of the Agreement, as they sought to secure their position.

In Scotland and Wales, an obvious source of strain would be a divergence in political control between their devolved governments and Westminster. This might come about because the nationalists won in Cardiff and Edinburgh, because of a Conservative victory at UK level, or even from a combination of the two. Nationalist victories would not necessarily mean independence for Scotland or Wales since Plaid Cymru does not even have this as its policy and the SNP might be cautious in seeking a mandate for secession. They would, however, require that the relationships with London, which since 1999 have been rather informal, be put on a more formal basis. Intergovernmental concordats, for example, could be invoked more often and the Judicial Committee of the Privy Council be called on to rule on the division of powers. This would create a firmer legal basis for devolution in case law and precedent and move the United Kingdom closer to a written constitution. A Conservative UK government faced with Labour administrations in Cardiff and Edinburgh would raise similar issues, although such Labour administrations might be cautious in pressing constitutional questions for fear of giving encouragement to the nationalists.

Growing policy divergence amongst the central and devolved administrations might also cause strains in the system. Whilst the division of competences in the devolution Acts is reasonably clear, this is based on a practical assumption that these powers will not be exercised to radically different ends. If a UK government were, however, to privatise the National Health Service, this would have massive implications for Scotland, Wales and Northern Ireland. The fiscal transfers corresponding to health spending in England would no longer flow and the devolved assemblies would either have to follow England or else find the resources for public provision elsewhere (which would in practice require new tax powers). If they followed the latter course, there would need to be a strict definition of who would qualify for free treatment. Already such issues have arisen in relation to university fees and free long-term care for the elderly in Scotland. In this way, different entitlements would underpin a distinct form of social citizenship in the various parts of the United Kingdom. The 1998 Scotland and Wales Acts, however, seem based on the assumption that the common British social citizenship forged in the twentieth-century welfare state will be maintained. Northern Ireland is a different case, and British government has been less concerned to preserve the social union there – although one thing on which both communities are agreed is that there should be no reduction below British standards of welfare provision.

Fiscal pressures more generally will lead to demands to reopen the settlement, as suggested above. The Barnett formula, like other aspects of the devolution settlement, was carried over from the old system of administrative devolution and even in its original form was more of a holding operation than a permanent settlement. Of course, provisional arrangements can last a very long time, but it seems unlikely that Barnett will survive in the long run. Opinion polls in Scotland show that the public support greater taxing powers for the Scottish Parliament, as do the SNP, the Liberal Democrats and a section of the Conservative Party. So the informal Barnett mechanism is likely to give way to something more transparent and permanent.

European policy may be another source of friction. As the scope of the EU expands, it extends further into matters under the competence of the devolved bodies, yet the UK government remains in charge. Scottish, Welsh and Northern Irish participation is at the discretion of Whitehall, which also has the final say in the Joint Ministerial Committees. In the event of differences in party control, this kind of cooperative arrangement, also inherited from the pre-devolution days of the Scottish and Welsh Offices, could not easily survive. Parties governing in Scotland and Wales but in opposition at Westminster would not be welcomed into UK delegations in the way Scottish and Welsh ministers have since 1999 and would not be given confidential information. Consequently, a more formalised mechanism would have to be found to give the devolved bodies an input into EU matters, as happens in Germany and Belgium. These are both federal states in which there is a constitutional division of power and in which the federal government cannot proceed in Europe on regional matters without the assent of the regional authorities. Given the asymmetrical nature of the UK reforms and the absence of a government for England, the German or Belgian model could not easily be reproduced, but a formalisation of the position of the devolved governments would represent another move towards a federal type of arrangement. Much also depends on how the EU itself evolves. There have been strong demands, especially in the context of the European Convention and the reform of EU institutions, for a recognised role for 'constitutional regions' or 'regions with legislative powers'. These are bodies like the German Länder, the Spanish Autonomous Communities, Belgian regions and communities, and the devolved bodies of the United Kingdom, who have the full responsibility for implementing EU laws and regulations in important matters such as agriculture, environment or transport. They have been complaining that matters still have to pass through the national level, even if they are represented there in various ways, and that they do not have the opportunity to deal directly with Brussels. These complaints have an obvious applicability to Scotland where the devolution legislation has resulted in whole areas of policy being transferred to the Scottish Parliament and Executive, with no role for Whitehall and Westminster at all. It is therefore likely that any initiative to allow more direct access by these stronger regions to the instances of the EU will be taken up by Scotland, Northern Ireland and Wales. This would represent a further loosening of the UK framework but not necessarily the secession of the nations.

Imitation effects are also likely to lead to changes in constitutional demands. Already there has been pressure in Wales to give the National Assembly the same powers as the Scottish Parliament. Northern Ireland has hitherto been regarded as a case apart, because of the peculiar nature of its politics but, if the peace process succeeds in normalising politics there, then the other devolved bodies may look to it for inspiration. Finally, there is the question of England. So far, English public opinion has been very relaxed about devolution in Scotland and Wales and decidedly supportive of it in Northern Ireland, no doubt secure in the knowledge that the state-wide Parliament is always going to be heavily dominated by the English contingent. Demands for devolution in England so far have focused on regional government, which is more of an internal solution to the question of governing England than a contribution to the reform of the United Kingdom as a whole, since England will continue to have a single legislature and unitary central ministries. If demands were to grow for an English Parliament, however, as the expression of an English nationalism that has hitherto been channelled into the United Kingdom, this would represent a marked step towards federalism, or even the break-up of the state. It therefore remains as true as ever that the key to the future of the state lies not at the periphery but at the centre.

The centre remains one of the missing pieces in the constitutional transformation of the United Kingdom. Federal systems have a clear distinction between state-wide matters, handled by the federation, and local matters, handled by the federated units. Devolution in the United Kingdom has created something equivalent to federated units in Scotland, Northern Ireland and Wales, but has left the centre looking exactly as it did before, including even the presence of the three territorial secretaries of state in the Cabinet. As long as governments refuse to countenance reform at the centre, then a move towards federalism is unlikely. Instead, we will have an evolving and unusual form of union.

A NEW FORM OF UNION

The United Kingdom before 1999 was prepared to concede a great deal of symbolic recognition to its constituent nations, on condition that political power remained firmly in Westminster. Other plurinational states, such as Canada and Spain, have decentralised to their constituent parts but sought to deny the national identity of these parts, and promoted the state as a single nation. Now the United Kingdom has given both symbolic and political recognition to its nations, with the whole held together not by a federal constitution but by the increasingly tenuous doctrine that Westminster retains ultimate control over the whole system. This is not a federal system, therefore, but it has federal elements and, as it adjusts to future strains, it will acquire yet more formalised federal-type mechanisms. It is more usefully seen as the harbinger of a new type of union of nations and regions, each of which finds its own accommodation within the Union. The European context is crucial here, since European integration provides the conditions for loosening the UK frame and giving a new dimension to autonomy. If the European project continues to evolve and deepen, spawning new forms of shared and divided sovereignty, then the plurinational states of Europe may evolve with it, providing a political experiment and new answers to the age-old question of how to reconcile state and nation.

NOTES

1. H.C.G. Mathew, *Gladstone, 1809–1898* (Oxford: Oxford University Press, 1997)
2. M. Keating, The Role of the Scottish MP, PhD thesis, Glasgow College of Technology and CNAA (1975)
3. See D.J. Elazar, *Exploring Federalism* (Tuscaloosa: University of Alabama Press, 1987); J. Mitchell, *Strategies for Self-government: The Campaigns for a Scottish Parliament* (Edinburgh: Polygon, 1996); S. Rokkan and D. Urwin, *Economy, Territory, Identity: Politics of West European Peripheries* (London: Sage, 1983)
4. A.V. Dicey, *England's Case against Irish Home Rule* (Richmond: Richmond Publishing, 1973, first published 1886); idem, *A Leap in the Dark: A Criticism of the Principles of Home Rule as Illustrated by the Bill of 1893*, 3rd edition (London: John Murray, 1912); C. Wilson, Note of Dissent, *Scotland's Government: Report of the Scottish Constitutional Committee* (Edinburgh: Scottish Constitutional Committee, 1970)
5. M. Keating and D. Bleiman, *Labour and Scottish Nationalism* (London: Macmillan, 1979)
6. Tom Nairn, *After Britain. New Labour and the Return of Scotland* (London: Granta, 2000)
7. Mathew, op. cit. (1997)
8. N. MacCormick, *Questioning Sovereignty: Law, State and Nation in the European Commonwealth* (Oxford: Oxford University Press, 1999); idem, Is There a Scottish Path to Constitutional Independence?, *Parliamentary Affairs* 53 (2000) pp.721–36
9. CSA Campaign for a Scottish Assembly, A Claim of Right for Scotland, in O. Dudley Edwards (ed.), *A Claim of Right for Scotland* (Edinburgh: Polygon, 1988)
10. To be precise, the Scottish National Party, Plaid Cymru and the Social Democratic and Labour Party of Northern Ireland are pro-Europe. Sinn Féin is still hostile, as are the extreme unionist parties.
11. C. Tarleton, Symmetry and Asymmetry as Elements of Federalism: A Theoretical Speculation, *Journal of Politics* 27 (1965) pp.861–74
12. The list went on endlessly, as Dalyell filibustered the Scotland Bill.
13. J. Camilleri and J. Falk, *The End of Sovereignty? The Politics of a Shrinking and Fragmenting World* (Aldershot: Edward Elgar, 1991)
14. N. Walker, Beyond the Unitary Conception of the United Kingdom Constitution?, *Public Law* (Autumn, 2000) pp.384–404; idem, Late Sovereignty in the European Union, *European Forum Discussion Paper* (Florence: European University Institute, 2001)
15. M. Keating, *Plurinational Democracy: Stateless Nations in a Post-sovereignty Era* (Oxford: Oxford University Press, 2001)
16. MacCormick, op. cit. (1999)
17. Nairn, op. cit. (2000)
18. Keating, op. cit. (2001)
19. L. Paterson, Changing Views of 'Britain' after Devolution, *Regional and Federal Studies* 12(1) (2002) pp.21–42
20. Keating, op. cit. (2001)

14 Unfinished business: the 'significant others'

Michael O'Neill

HOME RULE ALL ROUND?

Home rule for England has never had the same appeal as it did for the United Kingdom's other constituent nations. The idea was advocated by the Victorian Liberal Party, but with little support let alone serious conviction. The Labour Party in its radical juvenescence flirted with English regional governance, both as a counter-balance to Celtic home rule and as a restraint on the centralised state.[1] The call for home rule 'all round' was little more than an attempt to mollify English objections to proposed home rule for the smaller British nations. The idea never took firm hold on the official mindset and over time Labour became as reconciled to the unitary state as any other party used to exercising the immense power and patronage available to British governments. As such, regional identity in England has remained notional at best, a cultural phenomenon of limited appeal, and one lacking political salience.

English identity, too, has remained problematical, a concept as nebulous throughout the postwar decades as it was during the early experience of nation building. Primary identity for the English population remains national rather than regional or territorial in focus and orientation, though with some recent indications of competition now between its respective English and British expressions. Spatial geographers and other academic specialists toyed with the idea of notional regions as a countervailing corrective to the centripetal pull of the central state.[2] Some pluralist thinkers did once claim that the English would become reconciled to devolution, if only it would be tried there. However, even those who shared this vision acknowledged the difficulty of conjuring meaningful regional identity from such a culturally homogeneous country. As one leading advocate of British pluralism once cautiously observed: 'I am not saying that [regional] feelings . . . are equally strong in all parts of the country, but only that they exist as a foundation on which regional sentiments attached to Regional Authorities could be built'.[3]

Modest administrative functions were relocated from the centre to sub-national governance from the late nineteenth century, but only through the medium of local government. The latter acted primarily as Parliament's agent in the provinces, an arrangement that did lead to some limited administrative autonomy between the 1920s and 1960s. The idea was revived briefly in 1940, but again less as a matter of principle than as an administrative convenience, a response to national emergency. The United Kingdom was organised into twelve regions (nine of them designated in England) for the purpose of managing civil defence, and each one under the jurisdiction of regional commissioners directly responsible to the minister for home security. Neither the new authorities nor their commissioners were well received and the political establishment remained hostile in peacetime to the very idea of ceding any real powers to a sub-national tier of government.

Regionalism did make a partial recovery post 1945. Central government utilised regional arrangements as a convenient administrative locus for the emergent welfare state, and regional bodies operated as administrative units for some devolved central government functions. For instance, the new National Health Service set up regional offices. Even so, regional administration was inchoate, a diverse arrangement lacking in overall coherence.[4] In so far as there was any political motive behind regionalism in postwar England, it was mostly confined to 'seeking to restore popular interest in the existing structures of local government rather than in creating new ones'.[5] Proposals followed in the postwar years for regional bodies to streamline and enhance administrative efficiency, and thereby to boost national economic performance. The Attlee government established development areas and subsequent Conservative and Labour governments both launched development councils under the supervision of the Board of Trade. Later still, the incoming Labour government (in 1964) created regional planning boards as an adjunct of its broad policy objective of improved strategic planning to fulfil national economic goals. There was also an initiative in what might be called 'cultural regionalism', with government assistance and encouragement for events such as regional arts festivals, culminating in the setting up of regional arts councils and the reorganisation of the BBC into regions.

The issue received rather more political attention once devolution became a critical issue in British politics, a response to rising discontent in the territorial nations. The Kilbrandon Report made the connection between increased interest in home rule and the broader public concern over the inexorable trend towards the centralisation of government throughout the twentieth century.

To ensure a more balanced devolution, the Report proposed regional councils for England to offset territorial assemblies elsewhere in the United Kingdom, though only the minority report advocated their parity.[6] The principle of regionalism, if not its routine or consistent practice, was now in the public domain, but the problem of defining boundaries and competences remained unresolved. The 1974 Labour government, though raising the prospect of regional governance in the broad context of the emerging devolution debate, acknowledged the differential context as between 'mere' English regions and the historical territorial nations.[7]

The requirement of a firm cultural underpinning for effective regional governance, providing a clear focus for popular identity and affiliation, is now widely acknowledged. A history of tepid proposals and ad hoc experimentation with British policy agencies has merely served to confirm what most pundits already knew: that there was no natural cultural locus, no obvious geographical boundaries to demarcate distinct English regional identities. This identity deficit in England has weakened both the political demand for, and undermined the organisational impetus to, English regional government.[8] As one commentator has observed: 'the territorial boundaries of the Anglo-Saxon kingdoms . . . had frequently changed even in the Middle Ages [and] barely corresponded to modern geographical ones. The periodic existence of clear territorial boundaries over several centuries is a vital element in the maintenance of an identity. Even Wales, despite its extensive integration with England, had achieved that feat'.[9] The English Tourist Board did indeed attempt to market England's distinctive regions, but these are merely notional entities and they have never been regarded as anything more than 'politically innocuous divisions of the national community'.[10]

How far, then, have the recent constitutional changes altered this situation, improving the prospects for meaningful devolution within England? To what extent have these events increased the potential for a fundamental reform of English governance, or for re-imagining the union state? All is change in the state of the Union except in its dominant English heartland. English public opinion remains, for the most part, convinced about the tried-and-tested union state formula – but for how much longer?[11] On the face of it, devolution for Scotland and Wales does seem to be designed so as to have minimal impact on England's governance. The government gave priority to home rule for the territorial nations rather than crowding the legislative agenda with reform unwanted, for the most part, in England. Yet, even on a cautious evaluation of developments, devolution will have far-reaching consequences for English government.

The *real* locus of power, the critical levers of macro-economic management, the principal source of public expenditure, the fount of national sovereignty, the conduit for relations with the international community, all remain with government at the centre. Nevertheless, the implications of devolution for the structure and governance of the British state are considerable. To unravel a unitary state, reallocating some of its essential powers away from the centre, changes the formal constitutional balance between the constituent polities. It also alters political expectations all round. English public opinion is likely, sooner or later, to respond to territorial demands for constitutional change, not merely by ceding competences but also by asking some fundamental questions about the nature of the political relations between England and 'the others'.

Change, nevertheless, is not likely to be easily forthcoming.[12] There are powerful centripetal pressures operating within English national culture that sustain a residual 'regio-scepticism'. Resistance to the idea of separating out, or to translating parochial expressions of cultural identity into their various components, is deeply embedded. There is a pervasive historical narrative about the idea of governance and statehood with its roots in the influential nineteenth century discourse on the British constitution. This classical narrative rebutted both federalism, and even altogether more modest demands for territorial home rule within the framework of the British Empire, as alien and potentially destructive of national unity.[13] Regionalism, construed here as devolving power away from the centre, was associated with weak government and the lack of international clout, threatening the 'national interest'. In a recent commentary, Richard Weight observes that this outlook has:

> continued to inform English national identity long after it had been rejected elsewhere in Britain. The continuing resistance to regionalism was in effect a defiant last stand against the dissolution of the Anglo-Saxon polity. But regio-scepticism also sprang from the fact that England was one of the first European territories to become a unitary nation state and one of those that survived intact the longest ... In England, the traces left by the Heptarchy were so slight that no region had any of the building blocks of political autonomy, such as a separate Church or legal and educational systems ... Nor, with the exception of Cornwall, did any of them have their own ancient language, as Wales did.[14]

The problem for English regionalism has been that this particular history has shaped, or rather captured, the constitutional imagination. The only 'natural' English region, one possessed of at least the semblance of an ancient identity rooted in popular imagination, is Cornwall. In fact, closer examination of the evidence for this somewhat bold claim reveals a region already well integrated into 'neighbouring' England by the end of the fifteenth century.[15] Moreover, it is a region whose historical identity was less a natural or imagined community than a carefully constructed, manufactured entity: and one that was so 'imagined' only latterly and by a few romantic Victorians.[16]

There have been modest stirrings of regional discontent in other parts of England, but for the most part negatively inspired. This latterday cultural restiveness is again a reactive response, less a drive for identity than an expression of relative deprivation *vis-à-vis* Scotland and Wales as these historical sub-nations of the Union threaten to steal a march on the altogether more anonymous or amorphous English regions. Events, too, have contributed to changing outlooks. English reticence about rethinking the regions' relations with the centre shifted somewhat after 1992 when the Conservatives won power for a fourth consecutive term. A meeting of Labour MPs representing both Scottish and northern English constituencies at Carlisle in November 1987 acknowledged their common economic and social problems, agreeing to mutually endorse each other's campaigns for directly elected assemblies.

ENGLISH NATIONALISM

English nationalism appears, latterly, to be stirring, though for the most part in non-political expressions confined mostly to sporting venues, including the defence of blood sports. Or is otherwise purloined by a small minority of far right and so far marginalised zealots who confuse, for their own purposes, nationality and malignant notions of racial purity. The recent resurgence of rural populism in the form of the so-called countryside movement does indicate some potential for politicising an eccentric idea of English patriotism against what is seen as a metropolitan government with an essentially urban agenda. But this, too, is a disparate movement with an eclectic agenda, one that draws on British-wide rather than specifically English discontents. For the most part, 'Englishness' has not taken off as a mainstream political idea in a country where the prevailing temperament, following the calculus of perceived advantage, prefers to fuse – or confuse – English and British identity.[17] In its most benign expression, 'Englishness' remains nebulous, a notion, a subdued, overly self-conscious and even embarrassed sense of an ancient nation that is much misunderstood, unfairly maligned, and is now besieged by the 'others' in these islands. At its most militant it manifests surly and acerbic xenophobic defiance at the 'demons' of Europe, ungrateful Celts, or other imaginary enemies.

A rather less benign and a potentially more menacing assessment of the import of devolution for England and its citizens may stir once the relatively new experience of power sharing with the territorial polities begins to seep into the political consciousness. For significant changes there certainly will be. There were early signs of English impatience with implied Celtic rebuke during the 1990s as support for devolution gathered momentum. An unprecedented debate began about the most appropriate English response to the identity question that was so exercising the other British nations. But it was a response suffused, as cynical Scots opinion tended to regard it, with familiar English hubris and indeed a degree of implied sanction. As one former Conservative MP defiantly predicted: 'far from having been overtaken or destroyed, English nationalism is actually the most potent of the four nationalisms found on our island . . . I have a hunch that their secret nationalism will resurface powerfully in the century ahead'.[18]

Stirrings there may well be in England as the 'others' strut their stuff on a new political stage. Yet some seasoned commentators remain unconvinced about the political potential for a mainstream as opposed to a minority and/or extreme racist nationalism in England. As Paxman sees the situation, there is now more scope for a new post-national nationalism. For:

> The English are simultaneously rediscovering the past that was buried when 'Britain' was created, and inventing a new future . . . The new nationalism is less likely to be based on flags and anthems. It is modest, individualistic, ironic and solipsistic [and] based on values that are so deeply embedded in the culture as to be almost unconscious. In an age of decaying nation states, it might be the nationalism of the future.[19]

Although this invitation to respond to postmodern sensibilities may be appealing on one level, it may, however, be an unduly optimistic and, indeed, overly idealistic claim. It ignores, on the one hand, growing turbulence in the 'near-abroad', with a widely perceived 'invasion' of alien asylum seekers and economic refugees as Europe's south-eastern borders open to a new wave of migration. It underestimates, too, the impact on public perceptions in England of the ongoing debate about the extent of 'insidious' EU integration that, for many, merely confirms residual fears about continental 'interference' with ancient liberties. Meanwhile, the experience of devolution within these islands, accompanied by a discernible mood of territorial assertiveness beyond once invisible or meaningless internal borders, serves to revive old prejudices and even to foster exaggerated ethnic stereotypes about parasitic or itinerant Celts on the make.

Even in its present and limited format, devolution will move the ratchet of power one or more notches in favour of the territorial polities and, in what is widely perceived to be a zero-sum power game, away from England's former pre-eminence. Of course, we must not exaggerate the extent of the shift in the balance of political power, as between the centre and the constituent parts of the Union. But myths are frequently more potent than 'mere' facts and have the power to influence mindsets, and thereby to shape political perceptions and prescriptions alike.

According to this evaluation, the devolution bargain may seem too unbalanced, stacked against England, for Scotland and Wales retain their secretaries of state and, for the time being at least, their Cabinet rank. England's regions, at best nebulous or nascent, have no such privileged advocate for their territorial interests residing at the very heart of central government. The fiscal arrangements for devolution likewise have the potential for distorting perceptions, for they appear, or may be made to appear by malevolent or merely determined political forces reacting to perceived inequities, to be too one-sided, unduly discriminatory against England and its 'hard-pressed taxpayers'. And as long as the West Lothian Question is avoided and Scotland retains its over-representation at Westminster, the territorial polities appear to some English critics to enjoy the dubious privilege of having their cake and the chance, too, to consume it.

The problem remains, however, of how to accommodate English regional interests within a reformed state – assuming English opinion can be rallied to the devolution cause – and to do so within a framework that does not subjugate Scottish and Welsh interests. What would the constitutional architecture of such a territorially balanced British polity look like? An English parliament cast in the same devolved mould as the other territorial assemblies, and presumably sited in London alongside a reconstituted national (and presumably quasi-federal or even a fully federal) parliament, is one patent solution. But it is one that would probably be a recipe for serious administrative confusion; and without commensurate reform of local government, possibly a recipe, too, for over-government. The idea of an English parliament, or at least in its lesser form of an English grand committee, has certainly gained some support. English nationalists launched the English Parliament Movement in 1996 and organised regular demonstrations outside Westminster. Support amongst the wider populace was recorded in one poll in 1999 at a quite respectable 38 per cent, and by 2001 the number of respondents who identified as English rather than British had also risen from 34 per cent in 1997 to 43 per cent.[20]

The idea was adopted, in turn, by the Conservative Party, seemingly marooned in its own electoral wilderness and looking more than ever like an English political party than a British one, or at least, a party trying to position itself to recapture traditional support in middle England yielded in recent general elections to its opponents. It is debatable, though, just how seriously the Conservative Party has embraced such a narrow focus on the question of political identity. Some far right activists amongst the Conservatives' rank and file membership did attempt to propel the then leader, William Hague, into embracing this idea at the 1998 Party Conference. A flurry of intellectual support on the right has likewise endorsed the idea of English home rule.[21] However, when a senior back-bench Conservative MP did introduce a private member's bill proposing an English parliament, it failed to carry.[22] Stiff resistance remains within the wider Conservative Party to any proposal that might threaten further weakening of the cement of the Union.[23]

Aware, perhaps, of the adverse consequences for the Union of releasing the untamed power of English nationalism, the Conservative Party has preferred instead to pull back from endorsing English home rule. Conservative strategists have certainly recognised the latent, potentially useful, boost for their cause from harnessing the nascent idea of English identity. The party must be seen to respond to this mood, if only to tame it, to prevent it becoming the exclusive preserve of far right extremists with a narrow idea of nationality and an unpalatable racist agenda. Rather than advocating a fully fledged English parliament, mainstream Conservatives have preferred instead to limit the role at Westminster of MPs from the territorial polities, to curtail their voting rights at least in exclusively English matters. There has been discussion, too, of reforming the procedures for transacting purely English business.

This calculated approach has found expression in recent reform proposals. An arrangement, albeit some considerable way short of full parliamentary status, was the Standing Committee on Regional Affairs. This body nevertheless fell into disuse, becoming merely a sounding board without real influence. There is, of course, paradox if not parody in seeking to reconcile the present devolution arrangements with a putative English parliament, for the present territorial institutions represent relatively small populations whereas England has the great preponderance of the United Kingdom's population. The problem of such demographic and institutional imbalance in what would be *de facto*, and possibly *de jure*, a British federation, was acknowledged when the idea was reviewed by the Royal Commission on the Constitution. The Report observed that:

> A federation consisting of four units – England, Scotland, Wales, and Northern Ireland – would be so unbalanced as to be unworkable. It would be dominated by the overwhelming political importance and wealth of England. The English Parliament would rival the United Kingdom federal Parliament; and in the federal Parliament itself the representation of England could hardly be scaled down in such a way as to enable it to be outvoted by Scotland, Wales and Northern Ireland, together representing less than one-fifth of the population. A United Kingdom federation of four countries, with a federal Parliament and provincial Parliaments in the four national capitals, is therefore not a realistic proposition.[24]

Moreover, a parliament for England that represented such a disproportionately large territorial population in marked contrast to the other territorial polities, and that likewise failed to acknowledge the immense variety of interests within the English polity, would merely replicate administrative centralisation and a provincial resentment about political remoteness. These are the very failings of governance that have given political impetus to contemporary regional and devolution movements throughout Europe.

For these reasons, administrative regionalism seems to suggest a more feasible model for devolution in England. On the one hand, it offers a more tenable corrective to excessive centralisation. It also appears to be an appropriate response to the territorial interests concerned not to lose out to the Scots and the Welsh when it comes, for instance, to attracting inward investment or maximising regional clout when determining the policy agenda, whether in Whitehall or in Brussels. In the debate on the reform of the state that has gathered pace in official and academic circles since the 1960s, English regional councils have generally been seen as a useful political counterweight to devolution to the Scottish Parliament and the Welsh Assembly. Although this suggestion was appended only in the minority recommendations in the Kilbrandon Report, and for reasons more to do with political discretion than outright antipathy, this proposal received at the time little by way of official endorsement.

ENGLISH REGIONALISM: WILL THIS DOG EVER BARK?

Kilbrandon's minority conclusions clearly separated the matter of the governance of the English regions from devolution to Scotland and Wales. The passage of time has only confirmed endemic tension between the demand for territorial devolution and official English reticence about that matter. Members representing English constituencies and from every party have used the very fact of this demographic imbalance as a convenient excuse for resistance, to delay, block and otherwise dilute those devolution proposals that did eventually emerge. Objections to the 1978 proposals for asymmetrical devolution mirrored growing concern over what seemed to be the diminishing of English power in the union state. Not that this amounted to a merely mobilised spitefulness, resentment driving a negative attempt to block change: in some quarters, doubts about devolution represented a genuine expression of anxiety about whether a balanced constitution could survive the clamour for change. There was genuine concern, too, to avoid new democratic deficits embedded in asymmetrical arrangements. A signal influence here was the British political establishment's deep-seated Diceyian instincts, the persistent preference for the maintenance of effective political institutions at home, and on that basis of international prestige abroad.

The process of regionalisation has continued, though only as an ad hoc and reactive response to what was regarded at Westminster as specific policy problems.[25] Whether there is sufficient political will for enacting far-reaching regional reform remains to be seen. Thus far there is little real enthusiasm from the main British parties to reform English government in order to assimilate the structure of English governance to both the culture of devolution and the new architecture of territorial institutions now operating in the other constituent nations. The Conservatives in government before 1997 concentrated mostly on improving regional coordination within the unitary state, integrating the regional offices of the Whitehall departments (government offices for the regions, GORs) to facilitate better resource use, more cogent policy initiatives, improved access to European funding. Labour in opposition prevaricated on the 'English Question'. Under cover of a consultation exercise (in itself perhaps a telling indication of its political uncertainty about the matter), the party reviewed local government arrangements, but only with a view to improving their coherence and performance – a leitmotif of government reform on this matter throughout the postwar years.[26]

Labour's considered response here came in the shape of an influential and widely trailed report from the Regional Policy Commission established by

Labour's leadership team in 1995 precisely to review the available options. The Report proposed a primarily economic development strategy to be delivered by regional development agencies (RDAs), to follow the pattern for Scotland and Wales, and with some, albeit indeterminate, suggestions for their 'accountability' via regional chambers.[27] The local/regional arms of national organisations (for instance, the Confederation of British Industry and the Trades Union Congress, and the voluntary sector) were to cooperate in an inward investment strategy, to manage regional economic policy, to coordinate bids for, and deliver project work financed by EU structural funding, and likewise to manage programmes under the Single Regeneration Budget. There was acknowledgement, too, of the need for 'appropriate' regional democratic structures to provide consultation and to facilitate policy implementation and review.

A regional tier set above local government administration was floated as one possible solution for reconciling changes in England with the party's firm commitment to territorial devolution. Predictably, this was refuted by the Conservatives on grounds of cost and bureaucratic duplication. Ironically, it was resisted, too, by Labour's own local government establishment as a 'threat' to their concept of localism and community-based democracy.[28] More cynical observers preferred to see here defiance in the face of a perceived threat to modest but, for all that, rewarding personal power bases.

It is not the case that every local government interest has resisted the logics of contemporary regionalism. There was no consensus, however, about regional governance for England, though rather more agreement about enhancing regional access to the policy process both nationally and in Europe.[29] Some politicians and officials are more receptive to regional planning as a stimulus for investment in infrastructural projects conducive to employment creation and related benefits.[30] Cooperation across restrictive local government boundaries has acquired a new institutional expression with the creation, for example, of the English Regional Association (ERA) in 1993. This belated response to devolution elsewhere in the United Kingdom has lacked a coherent programme. The ERA was, nevertheless, a useful benchmarking exercise, and as such a necessary precursor to formulating a coherent regional structure for England. It brought together regional associations throughout England, promoting best practice, coordinating joint initiatives and sharing expertise, pooling energies in policy domains such as environmental strategy, transport, regional planning initiatives and other sectors where it sought to influence the policy process of central government and Europe alike.

The principal motivation here was not to further devolution per se but rather to foster closer consultation between central government and sub-national interests. Meanwhile, various proposals for a regional tier of governance, democratically accountable to regional electorates in stark contrast to the top-down executive regionalism of current GOR arrangements, began to emanate from local authority think-tanks and consultative arrangements.[31] Concerned to reverse the trend to excessive centralisation that ensued after 1979, John Major's government established in 1994 government offices (GOs) in the regions. These offices combined the regional offices of the Departments of the

Environment, Transport and the Regions, Trade and Industry, and the Training, Enterprise and Education Directorate of the Department for Education and Employment. They provided a sort of 'one-stop shop' for regional interests, public or private, seeking to secure government or EU funding, or to otherwise influence policy at the centre.[32]

The development and coordination of these regional arrangements for England has been inchoate. A cumulative tier of regional authorities and administrative bodies has grown like topsy, but without coherence and defying administrative rationality.[33] It is an arrangement whose outcome is a fragmented and uncoordinated political map reflecting an absence of a clear precept or a coherent design.[34] There was no conjunction, for instance, between those areas covered by the GOs and those of the Next Steps agencies. Nor was there any real sense of joined-up administration, organisational synergy between the agencies that deal with important infrastructure tasks such as health, transport, education, home affairs, law enforcement and agriculture.[35]

These inchoate regional functions are still much more about managing regional expectations than about empowerment. Regionalism represents the preference for managing the delivery of the policy targets of central government, rather than providing a conduit for channelling independent regional preferences up the policy line to the centre.[36] One critical stimulus to recent calls for reform here was apparent concern to establish regional structures capable of responding to the EC's own reformed structural funding initiatives as these were expanded and reorganised after 1988 on a regional, even cross-border, basis. A rather different and altogether more reactive politics seems to be driving developments in England than the more positive momentum that has propelled devolution elsewhere in the United Kingdom.[37]

The Labour government took office in 1997 with a radical agenda for constitutional reform. The new government made some reassuring noises about complementing territorial devolution with a commensurate regionalism for England.[38] But it has faced the very same apathy, the lack of demand, that has confronted every previous attempt to address this awkward issue. Absence of consensus about the most appropriate arrangements has also hindered any clear policy prospectus: a constraint acknowledged by the party's strategists. The incoming secretary of state, John Prescott, repeated in office the pledge of Labour's 1997 general election manifesto that, although committed to the principle of directly elected regional government for England, the demand for this so 'varies across England [that] it would be wrong to envisage a uniform system at this stage'. The government proposed, over time, to introduce legislation to allow the people, region by region, to decide in a referendum whether they want directly elected regional government, but only after clear consent is established.[39] In these circumstances Labour has had little alternative other than to adopt a cautious approach, which in British government procedure usually involves launching an open-ended consultative process.[40] There was the practical consideration, too, about not adding to an already heavy constitutional reform programme.

The Blair government has revisited regionalism as part of its ongoing constitutional reform prospectus, and for much the same reasons as its predecessors, promising greater accountability by the centre to the English regions. Yet it has confronted the very same constraints as its predecessors for the idea still has little appeal in England on its democratic merits, that is as a meso tier of governance standing between the municipal and state levels. The prospect after 1997 of a new government committed to far-reaching constitutional change did encourage English local authorities to mobilise their own resources in order to impact on the debate, but their voice has remained muted. The three pre-existing local government associations did, however, combine in 1997 as the national Local Government Association.

The ensuing White Paper *Building Partnerships for Prosperity* (Cmnd 3814, 1997), proposed regional development agencies, regional chambers indirectly elected by local authorities, and a Greater London Authority headed by a directly elected mayor. These reforms were heralded as a 'first step towards greater devolution in England', anticipating a learning process or an adjustment in popular expectations that 'will help to foster a sense of regional identity and develop a regional capability'.[41] The evidence so far, however, suggests only scant support for these proposals. A poll conducted by MORI for the Rowntree Trust in September 1995 found that 62 per cent of English people remain opposed to devolving greater power to a regional tier of government, with a further 13 per cent wholly unconcerned about the very idea.[42]

A uniform regional tier of governance for England cannot be ruled out, although on present form this will be more as an afterthought, a reactive response to devolution elsewhere in the United Kingdom than any cogent strategy for coordinated governance as between the centre and the English regions.[43] The Labour government has opted for minimal change, endorsing the economic logic rather than the political rationale for regionalism.[44] The government has, for instance, instituted regional development agencies, but these organisations, as with their predecessors, the government offices for the regions which amalgamated and streamlined regional bureaux of the Whitehall departments, are primarily concerned with top-down coordination.[45] The principal objective here is to maximise economic efficiency, to improve competitiveness and to secure more from the EU's structural funds for the regions than to enhance 'bottom-up' empowerment of regional communities. Regional chambers, too, are now on offer, though on an ad hoc and voluntary basis, depending on local demand as determined by regional referenda. At one level, these latest proposals would certainly entail the most far-reaching reform of local government ever enacted in the United Kingdom.[46] But the proposed changes are seen in some quarters as little more than surrogate local government reorganisation, with unitary structures installed only where no additional public expenditure is required.[47]

These proposals confirm a familiar pattern. Ad hoc and incremental adjustment to political pressures and structural changes is the principal driver here rather than clear-sighted constitutional rethinking, and with most emphasis placed on administrative and political considerations rather than on cultural foundations or identity.[48] This is a familiar reactive rather than a considered approach to devolution in British government, though the reform process has at least been set in motion.[49] The assembly for London, for instance, is conceived of rather more as a solution to the challenge of coordinating services in the capital city than as a model for regional government per se. As one commentator sees these latest developments: 'As the English rediscovered their nationhood, regionalism came to be seen for what it mostly was: a pragmatic attempt by politicians on the left and in the centre to placate English resentment about Celtic devolution without further undermining the Union'.[50]

In the meantime, an imbalance between the newly devolved polities with their considerable and prospectively growing appetite for self-government, and the still highly centralised governance of England remains a source of disquiet and even of pique in some quarters of English politics,[51] and especially with those who are perturbed by what they perceive to be privileged treatment for Scotland and Wales.[52] There is simmering discontent amongst English Labour MPs, especially those from northern constituencies where a Campaign for a Northern Assembly has already issued a Declaration of the North, at perceived 'privileged' treatment for the territorial nations with levels of socio-economic deprivation no worse than those in their own areas.[53] The regional dog may not yet be ready to bark, but is surely clearing its throat. A Northern Assembly was launched in 1998.[54] In a somewhat belated response, five of eight designated English regions had by 2000 embarked on publicity campaigns to boost support for regional devolution. These initiatives indicate an emergent political dynamic for English regionalism, although this is hardly yet a movement that attracts wide popular support.

The government published its proposals for assemblies in May 2002,[55] to be established by 2005–06 in those regions opting for them.[56] Even these comparatively modest changes, in comparison with the changes elsewhere in British government, confront formidable obstacles. The main parties remain deeply divided over the issue, as does the local government establishment resistant to abolishing familiar arrangements, most especially the counties. Objections are raised at every level to larger, more remote and impersonal government arrangements threatening additional costs and ever more remote bureaucracy.[57] There are counter-forces, however, that see advantage from larger units bidding for national and EU structural funds.

The acid test for these proposals as an interim stage in a meaningful rather than merely cosmetic exercise in devolution, is how much real power passes to these territorial assemblies from the centre. If the Greater London Authority (GLA) is any yardstick of the government's intent in this crucial indicator, there is little here to excite the radically inclined. The GLA has acquired no significant powers from the centre – not even in secondary legislation – in those public policy domains that determine life chances, for instance in training and further education, planning, and economic regeneration, or in those matters relating to the quality of personal services (notably health and control of restructuring public transport) that are important to citizens everywhere but especially so in a great capital city.[58] Furthermore, London remains dependent for financing these services on raising a share of its revenues from lower-tier local authorities and on grants determined and disbursed from general taxation raised by central government.[59]

The proposal to expand the mayoral system to those local authorities where the electorate opts for this form of civic leadership culminated in a handful of mayoral contests in May 2002. This cross-fertilisation of local government reform within the bigger picture of incipient but limited regionalism merely confirms a familiar reactive and piecemeal approach, rather than a considered and coherent strategy to the reform of British meso-government. It may well be that caution in Whitehall and hesitancy at Westminster denotes deep-seated concern at the centre that further devolution threatens a far-reaching shift in the balance of power between central government and the territorial polities. As with devolution in Scotland and Wales, regionalism in England would significantly alter the balance of power between the territorial components and the centre: not immediately, but ineluctably and in ways not anticipated at the outset. The upshot would almost certainly be something like a neo-federal state, an outcome that has been firmly resisted by those authorities who have addressed this question ever since it was first broached during the Irish home rule and imperial governance crises in the latter years of the nineteenth century.[60]

The option to do nothing, the illusion that these palpable forces for change can simply be ignored, resisted or even rolled back, as some complacent or reactionary opinion advocates, is surely folly. Recrudescence in the face of demands for devolution is as much of a challenge to political stability as the centripetal nationalism that has propelled recent changes in British government. The 'solution' of the Conservative Opposition to the relocation of some power from the centre, by divesting Scots and Welsh MPs of any role in English law making, implies petulance or at least short-sightedness rather than mature reflection on a politically delicate issue.[61] The former Conservative Party leader's approving reference to G.K. Chesterton's die-hard provincialism that summoned up 'the people of England that have not spoken yet' is an imprudent response and one wholly out of step with the times.

The regional issue has recently become linked with the ongoing debate on European integration. Euro-sceptics see the drive by Brussels to empower the regions as iniquitous, a devious plan to bring about the demise of the nation state and to implement a federalist agenda by covert means, though for the most part they harbour a distorted idea about the meaning of European federalism. The publication in 1995 of an official EU map that represented Scotland and Wales as 'merely' British and European regions but omitted to name England, replacing it with its designated European regions, merely confirmed suspicions of conspiracy. Resistance to reduced sovereignty has long been a potent rallying cry of Euro- sceptics, and one that resonates with all manner of opinion across the British ideological spectrum. As long as regionalism remains thus conflated with European integration the idea will prove hard to sell to the English electorate. However, merely appealing to 'little England' sentiments is not the answer to the challenge posed to the Union by territorial nationalism in the other constituent nations. Atavism is no solution to the predicament of how best to accommodate England – so used to hegemony over affairs in these islands and for so long – to the new realities of British, or indeed to the novel demands of European multi-level governance. Retreat into narrow primordial instincts will merely exacerbate the problem of reaching an amicable constitutional settlement appropriate to changing times.

Reform of English governance will almost certainly follow the asymmetrical devolution model devised for the territorial nations. Nor is this model inherently undesirable or unworkable. Elsewhere in the Continent, regional and even quasi-federal arrangements have resulted in asymmetrical political arrangements. In both Belgium and Spain, for instance, the regional constituents have acquired varying degrees of power by negotiating agreement on power sharing with the federal centre. The competences and scope of jurisdiction granted to the new assemblies in Scotland, Wales, and Northern Ireland are likewise variable, meeting particular local needs rather than following a singular rigid pattern. There is no reason, then, to imagine that similar flexibility cannot be replicated in any future design for sub-national governance in what has so far been the chimerical 'English polity'.

TOWARDS MULTI-LEVEL GOVERNMENT? THE IMPACT OF EUROPEAN INTEGRATION

External factors have contributed to the accelerated pace of political change in these islands.[62] Arrangements for representing the regional dimension in the formulation and management of EU macro-economic and structural policy in order to counterbalance the strong centripetal pull exerted by the EU's economic core, the 'golden banana', the geographical heart of the Single Market, invariably spill back into domestic policy-making procedures.[63] The EU offers a fiscal incentive to regional cooperation and in the Committee of the Regions it provides an important institutional arena for the representation of sub-national territorial interests.[64] The reorganisation of the EU's structural funds (in 1988 and 1992) to compensate regions outside the Single Market mainstream, was designed to benefit those member states that formulate a concerted regional strategy.[65] These reforms have, in turn, facilitated the direct participation of the regions in the EU's policy process, though in practice national governments do remain as the principal actors in determining overall policy criteria and are the main conduit for deciding national allocations.[66]

Multi-level governance in the EU facilitates cooperation between the regions and the Commission, with financial and other inducements for regional authorities and agencies to participate in trans-European networks, and to directly liaise one with another within the ambit of the Committee of the Regions. Close observers of EU affairs point, nevertheless, to the clear limits on regional autonomy, even in a Community where the concept of subsidiarity, the idea that policy decisions should be taken at the lowest possible level of government, has become almost a constitutional mantra, a balm for tensions arising between Brussels, the member states and the regions.

Formally enshrined in the Maastricht Treaty, subsidiarity was designed to improve the prospects for regional self-determination – or at least for an independent territorial or local voice, enhancing the role of governance below the level of the nation state. These developments in EU governance have given some encouragement to those in England who advocate at least a comprehensive and coordinate system of administrative regionalism. Regional as well as national business lobbies–the Confederation of British Industry for instance – have pressed for a more coherent regional development strategy to correspond better with more effective regional development strategies elsewhere in the Continent.[67]

The EU dimension has contributed, too, to developments in the United Kingdom's constituent polities. Both the Scots and Welsh nationalist parties initially disapproved of European integration, sharing the widespread concern of some radicals in the other British parties that the EC was merely a 'bankers club', and as such principally concerned with economic efficiency and thus with centralising rather than dispersing power. This instinctive antipathy was mirrored in wider territorial opinion. The Scottish electorate gave the lowest vote of any of the British nations in the 1975 referendum on the question of whether or not to endorse continued EC membership. Yet rising nationalist support for European integration and its various agencies has been, in part, a response to territorial antipathy to what is now perceived to be overweening central power. It also reflects a palpable sense that the government has ignored, or at least discounted, territorial interests in its management of national economic and social policy.[68] The Scottish National Party's election slogan 'Scotland – independent in Europe' is a testament to newfound confidence in devolution as the harbinger of even more far-reaching change.[69]

The role of sub-national government in the policy-setting process in EU matters has certainly been boosted by devolution. Previously, the secretaries of state were the principal voice of territorial interests in the Cabinet and its committees, though usually with far less real influence over agenda setting and resource allocations than the strategically better placed sectoral ministers. Some of the key EU policy domains (for instance, agriculture and fisheries) are now, in whole or in part, devolved to the territorial governments. Nevertheless, the territorial executives have no right in law to participate in the conclusive European Council decisions or in the important comitology negotiations that precede them. No UK policy domain is the exclusive preserve of the devolved administrations, so national ministers continue to be the principal conduit for formulating national negotiating positions and, as such, are bound to reflect broad national interests rather than particular territorial preferences. The disjunction between, on the one hand, the formal accountability for policy available to territorial parliaments, and, on the other hand, their lack of influence in Community policy-making councils remains a problem: a serious instance of democratic deficit. And one that must needs be addressed if the nationalist clamour for outright independence is to be checked.

The solution so far to representing distinct territorial interests within the overall national negotiating position at the EU level has been typically ad hoc: the inclusion of ministers and officials from the territorial executives as members of UK delegations. The problematic of reconciling quite different negotiating positions within a coherent national bargaining position is for the time being somewhat eased by the coincidence of a Labour government at Westminster with Labour-dominated administrations in both Cardiff and

Edinburgh. When this political situation alters, as in time it certainly will do, reliance on a sense of common feeling, or merely the appeal to prudence, may not be enough to contain the differences within these politically heterogeneous national delegations.

Council procedures are likely to compound the problem, for they preclude carrying fundamental policy differences, as between national and sub-national actors, from the national arena into the Council. The voting system in the Council of Ministers, though weighted in relation to national population size, assumes that each member state will exercise its weighted vote singularly for or against the particular policy option before the Council. The logic of Council bargaining similarly reinforces the requirement of a uniform national negotiating strategy, in as much as it operates on the assumption of a clear preference within each of the national delegations. Without that elemental procedure, an already multifarious and inordinately complex decision-making process would simply be unworkable.

Clearly, if UK territorial interests are to have an effective voice in formulating national negotiating positions in EU policy, this must needs be exercised during the early policy-setting stage – before even national representatives participate in the elaborate bargaining in Coreper, or during the comitology negotiations.[70] One avenue that has long been available to territorial interests for exercising influence directly during the EU policy process was to lobby the appropriate directorates-general in the European Commission, the institution formally responsible for proposing policy initiatives. The scope for territorial influence on formulating national policy in response to Commission proposals is rather more tenuous. Present arrangements merely give the territorial executives a right to be consulted, but even then only if they agree to abide by the rules of confidentiality and collective responsibility for a policy position they may not, in the end, endorse.[71] To make this system work requires habits of constraint, a pluralist disposition, and a degree of political maturity that is, for the most part, a rare attribute in adversarial British politics.

EU countries with federal constitutions, and thus the prospect of tiers of governments of different political complexions at the federal and territorial levels, have special procedures expressly designed to manage intergovernmental consultation. These delicate negotiations tend to be embedded in appropriate norms, a culture of positive-sum bargains and trade-offs, consociational arrangements that emphasise conciliation so as to ensure proper balance amongst territorial and national interests, the constituent polities and the centre. The EC treaties do permit sub-national governments to directly represent their views in the Council, but only in those policy matters for which they have exclusive competence. A case in point here is Belgium, where responsibility for language policy rests solely with the regional governments, and likewise the prerogative of the German Länder for education, culture and the arts. As such, the German Basic Law permits a representative of the Länder nominated by the Bundesrat to participate in the German delegation in the Council whenever exclusive Laender competences are the subject of EU policy making.

Of course, these are fully federal states, polities where the norms shaping the conduct of government and politics are predisposed to compromise, attuned to the political arts of managing territorial and cultural diversity.[72] Devolution in Britain is an arrangement some way removed from the consociational norms that facilitate positive-sum transactions, though something can surely be learned from territorial parleying elsewhere. What is required in these novel circumstances is readiness to adapt, to change habits, to engage in collaboration, to practise restraint and tolerance of entrenched difference. Above all, there is a need to exhibit mutual respect across party political and territorial boundaries. These are the essential cultural preconditions for the transactional logics of devolution, and they can hardly yet be said to be securely rooted in British political culture.

NOTES

1. Report of Labour Party Conference, 1918
2. C.B. Fawcett, *The Provinces of England: A Study in Some Geographical Aspects of Devolution* (1917); see also idem, Natural Divisions of England, *The Geographical Journal* (February 1917)
3. G.D.H. Cole, *Local and Regional Government* (1947) pp.154–5
4. C. Harvie, English Regionalism: The Dog that Never Barked, in B. Crick (ed.), *National Identities, the Constitution of the UK* (1991)
5. R. Weight, *Patriots: National Identity in Britain 1940–2000* (2002) p.171
6. Report of the Royal Commission on the Constitution, 1973, paras 1–7
7. *Devolution: The English Dimension – A Consultative Document* (Her Majesty's Government, 1976)
8. C. Moore, Regional Government in the United Kingdom: Proposals and Prospects, *Regional Politics and Policy* 1 (1991)
9. R. Weight, op. cit. (2002) p.595
10. C. Harvie, op. cit. (1991) p.110
11. Ibid.
12. See the broader discussion of British constitutional reform in J. Cornford, On Writing a Constitution, *Parliamentary Affairs* 44 (1991)
13. B. Burrows and G. Denton, *Devolution or Federalism? Options for the United Kingdom* (1980)
14. R. Weight, op. cit. (2002) pp.594–5
15. M. Hechter, *Internal Colonialism: The Celtic Fringe in British National Development, 1536–1966* (1975) pp.64–5
16. B. Deacon, And Shall Trelawney Die? The Cornish Identity, in P. Payton (ed.), *Cornwall Since the War* (1993) pp.206–7
17. R. Rose, *The Territorial Dimension in Politics: Understanding the United Kingdom* (1982)
18. M. Parris, *The Times*, 7 February 1994
19. J. Paxman, *The English: A Portrait of a People* (1998) pp.265–6
20. Gallup poll conducted for the *Daily Telegraph*, 15 April 1999
21. P. Hitchens, *The Abolition of Britain* (1999); R. Scruton, *England: An Elegy* (2000); S. Heffer, *Nor Shall My Sword: The Reinvention of England* (1999) pp.132–3

22. HCD vol. 304, 589–660, 16 January 1998

23. *The Spectator*, 19 September 1998; see also K. Baker, Speaking for England, *The Spectator*, 1 August 1998

24. Cmnd 5460 (1973) para. 531

25. B. Hogwood and M. Keating, *Regional Government in England* (1982)

26. Labour Party, *Rebuilding Democracy, Rebuilding Communities* (1995)

27. *The Report of the Regional Policy Commission* (1996); see also The Labour Party, *A Choice for England: A Consultation Paper on Labour's Plans for English Regional Government* (1995)

28. An argument that figured prominently in the objections of pro-local government advocates. See for instance G.W. Jones, Against Regional Government, *Local Government Studies* (Sept/Oct 1988)

29. J. Mawson, The Re-emergence of the Regional Agenda in the English Regions: New Patterns of Urban and Regional Governance, *Local Economy* 10 (1996)

30. See J. Mawson, The English Regional Debate: Towards Regional Governance or Government?, in J. Bradbury and J. Mawson (eds), *British Regionalism or Devolution: The Challenges of State Reform and European Integration* (1997) pp.189–93, in which he reviewed this rising tide of pressure

31. See, for instance, *Regionalism: The Local Government Dimension*, Association of Municipal Authorities (1995); *A Choice for England* (AMA, 1995); and the proposals of the Constitution Unit, *Regional Government in England* (1996)

32. J. Mawson and K. Spencer, The Government Office for the Regions: Towards Regional Governance?, *Policy and Politics* 25 (1997)

33. J. Tomaney, The Evolution of English Regional Governance, *Regional Studies* 36 (2002); J. Tomaney and J. Mawson (eds), *England: The State of the Regions* (2002)

34. R. Hazell, Regional Government in England: Three Policies in Search of a Strategy, in S. Chen and T. Wright (eds), *The English Question* (2000)

35. B. Hogwood, *Mapping the Regions: Boundaries, Coordination and Government* (1996); see also R. Hazell and P. Jervis, *Devolution and Health*, Nuffield Trust Series no.3 (1998)

36. Policy and Innovation Unit, Cabinet Office, *Reaching Out: The Role of Central Government at the Regional and Local Level* (2000)

37. A. Harding, *Is There a 'Missing Middle' in English Governance?* (New Local Government Network, 2000)

38. The Labour Party, *A Voice for England* (1995); idem, *A New Voice for England's Regions* (1996)

39. HCD 6th series vol. 359 (3 December 1997)

40. J. Tomaney, New Labour and the English Question, *The Political Quarterly* 70 (1999)

41. Cmnd 3814 (1997) p.52

42. 'State of the Nation': The 1995 Joseph Rowntree Reform Trust/MORI Survey, *Scottish Public Opinion* (September 1995)

43. G. Stoker, Is Regional Government the Answer to the English Question?, in Chen and Wright (eds), op. cit. (2000)

44. P. Robinson, Does the Government Really Have a Regional Policy?, in M. Nathan (ed.), *The New Regionalism* (Centre for Local Economic Strategies, 2000)

45. P. Benneworth, Reaching Out, Regional Development Agencies and Evolving Regional Governance, *Regions: Newsletter of the Regional Studies Association* 225 (2000)

46. J. Mawson, The English Regional Debate: Towards Regional Governance or Government? in J. Bradbury and J. Mawson (eds), op. cit. (1997)

47. *Building Partnerships for Prosperity: Sustainable Growth, Competitiveness and Employment in the English Regions*, Cmnd 3814 (1997)

48. For an overview of developments since 1997 see J. Tomaney, The Regional Governance of England, in R. Hazell (ed.), *The State and the Nations: The First Year of Devolution in the United Kingdom* (2000). There is a thought-provoking critique of the devolution arrangements by A. Ward, Devolution: Labour's strange constitutional 'design', in J. Jowell and D. Oliver (eds), *The Changing Constitution* (2000)

49. For an overview of this debate, see Department of the Environment, Transport and the Regions, *Regional Government in England: A Preliminary Review of Literature and Research Findings* (2000)

50. R. Weight, op. cit. (2002) p.720

51. K. Morgan, 'The English Question': Regional Perspectives on a Fractured Nation, *Regional Studies* 36 (2002)

52. The notion of Scottish indebtedness has permeated the debate on Anglo-Scottish relations throughout. See the discussion in C. Lee, *Scotland and the United Kingdom* (1995), and the rejoinder in the review of this book by C. Harvie in *Scottish History Review* (1996)

53. Identity and Politics – The Regional Government Debate in the North East, *Northern Economic Review* 31 (2001)

54. J. Tomaney, Democratically elected regional government in England: The Work of the North East Constitutional Convention, *Regional Studies* 34 (2000)

55. *Your Region, Your Choice: Revitalizing the English Regions*, Cmnd 5511 (2002). For a commentary on the White Paper, see I. Newman and J. Dungey, The Government White Paper, *Your Region, Your Choice: Revitalizing the English Regions*, *Local Economy* 17 (2002); see also, M. Sandford, *A Commentary on the Regional Government White Paper, Your Region, Your Choice: Revitalizing the English Regions* (The Constitution Unit, 2002); and J. Tomaney and P. Hetherington, England Arisen?, in R. Hazell (ed.) *The State of the Nations 2003* (2003); J. Adams and J. Tomaney, *Restoring the Balance: Strengthening the Government's Proposals for Regional Assemblies* (Institute for Public Policy Research, 2002)

56. *The Times*, 4 July 2002

57. E. Balls, Britain's New Regional Policy, in E. Balls and J. Healey (eds), *Towards a New Regional Policy: Delivering Growth and Full Employment* (The Smith Institute, 2000)

58. J. Tomaney, The New Governance of London: A Case of 'Post-democratic' Politics, *City* 5 (2001)

59. J. Tomaney, The Governance of London, in R. Hazell, op. cit. (2000)

60. M. Russel and R. Hazell, Devolution and Westminster: Tentative Steps Towards a More Federal Parliament, in R. Hazell (ed.), op. cit. (2000)

61. See, for instance, the speech *Change and Tradition: Thinking Creatively About the Constitution* by William Hague, the former Conservative Party leader, delivered to the Centre for Policy Studies on 24 February 1998; and idem, *Strengthening the Union after Devolution*, delivered to the same body, 15 July 1999. See also The Conservative Party, *Believing in Britain* (2000) at p.23

62. W. Paterson, Britain and the European Union Revisited: Some Unanswered Questions, *Scottish Affairs* 9 (1994)

63. A. Amin and N. Thrift (eds), *Globalization, Institutions, and Regional Development in Europe* (1994)

64. M. Keating, The Continental Meso: Regions in the European Community, in L. Sharpe (ed.), *The Rise of Meso Government in Europe* (1993)

65. L. Albrechts, F. Moulaert, P. Roberts, E. Swyngedouw (eds), *Regional Policy at the Crossroads: European Perspectives* (1989)

66. I. Bache, *The Politics of European Union Regional Policy: Multi-level Governance or Flexible Gatekeeping?* (Sheffield, 1998)

67. J. Mawson, in J. Bradbury and J. Mawson, op. cit. (1997) pp.188–9

68. G. McCrone, The Scottish Economy and European Integration, *Scottish Affairs* 4 (1993)

69. M. Keating and B. Jones, Scotland and Wales: Peripheral Assertion and European Integration, *Parliamentary Affairs* 44 (1991)

70. P. Hogwood, C. Carter, S. Bulmer, M. Burch and A. Scott, Devolution and EU Policy-making: The Territorial Challenge, *Public Policy and Administration* 15 (2000)

71. *Scotland's Parliament*, Cmnd 3658 (1997) paras 5.4 and 5.12

72. H-G. Gerstenlauer, German Länder and the European Community, in B. Jones and M. Keating (eds), *The European Union and the Regions* (1995)

15 Britishness and politics: towards a federal future?

Michael O'Neill

THE QUESTION OF IDENTITY

Political identity in some degree is always manufactured, and usually with the purpose of sustaining a particular political project.[1] The British project was designed during the course of the eighteenth century principally to legitimise the Union of 1707, and especially to foster in 'North Britain' a commonality of purpose with England. This purpose was rooted in a supposedly shared endeavour with mutual interests binding together the subjects of the Crown in the home islands and in the white dominions of the Empire. At the outset it was, strange to say, the English who were the more reluctant participants in this common project, continuing to regard their northern neighbours as virtually a primitive tribe, or at least as mostly self-seeking and ungrateful freeloaders.

Men of substance and influence in both Scotland and Wales had rather more cause to embrace Britishness than their English counterparts. The English remained reticent about espousing the new British identity, and whilst their Celtic partners 'came to think of themselves as Scottish/Welsh and British, the English refused to adopt a dual national identity. Their scepticism about the Union allowed the Scots the space and time in which to dominate the construction of Britishness in its early crucial years.'[2] In time, the English assimilated British identity and shared in the commonality of purpose that Britishness supposedly represents.

The two failed Jacobite rebellions in the early eighteenth century that had threatened to overthrow the Hanoverian dynasty reinforced English prejudice, notwithstanding the fact that some Scots regiments did remain loyal to the Crown and contributed to the subsequent brutal suppression of these uprisings. The Protestant succession was ensured at Culloden, the Jacobite threat expunged by the ruthless suppression of Catholic dissent and of Gaelic culture and language.[3] Scots played their part, by assimilation and by proving their loyalty to the British State, both during this episode and in the Continental wars that reinforced Britain's status as a world power. Indeed, Scots contributed disproportionately to successful empire building. They were prominent in missionary work, in commercial expansion and in the intellectual, political, commercial, industrial and cultural life of the United Kingdom. Political violence perpetrated by militant Irish nationalists throughout the nineteenth century did sustain a residual sense of Anglo-Saxon superiority over Celtic barbarism, but this was a temporary interlude in the otherwise steady development of a distinctly British identity.

Even so, a discernible sense of cultural hegemony, if not quite internal colonialism, accompanied British nation building.[4] A kindred feeling is difficult to reconcile with clear political dominance, and cultural subjection confirms the status of outsiders, or at least that of supplicants. This was certainly one response to the Union on either side of the border. Early diffidence amongst England's political elite about adopting British identity was softened by a successful strategy of state building during the late eighteenth and throughout the nineteenth centuries. By degrees, this saw the English appropriate Britishness, conflating it with English identity.[5] As James Bryce observed in the 1880s: 'The English had but one patriotism because England and the United Kingdom are to him practically the same thing'.[6]

Tradition and modernity combined over time to cement a distinctive British identity, even though it had a quite different value for its respective constituents.[7] The ceremonial associated with monarchy, successful resistance to Continental threats to national security and the Empire, and the role of Scots and Welsh in defending the Victorian Pax Britannica all helped to embed the idea of British nationhood. The very power, legitimacy and cultural impact of national political institutions, the centrifugal forces released by accelerating social change, underpinned by the impact of mass education, and the growing role of the media and later of electronic broadcasting, all served to consolidate Britain's place in the emergent international order.

There was always some ambivalence amongst the non-English nations about assimilating English norms and institutions. The political bargain of 1707 became the bedrock of the Union, in large part because it seemed to the 'other' nations, the Irish excepted, that there was nothing remotely viable that could, for the time being at least, replace it. Britain's growing international stature, its exceptional military prowess, but above all its prosperity and the prospects for self-improvement by migration to the outposts of the Empire when domestic living standards dipped all served to confirm the tangible benefits of the British project.

Recent shifts in comparative economic advantage between the constituent parts of the Union have confirmed just how much this affective affiliation depended on material benefits. Once economic decline and reduced international standing began to hit the pockets and permeate the consciousness of territorial public opinion, the glue holding the Union together was considerably weakened. The slow deterioration after the Great War of those very industries, located not exclusively but disproportionately in Wales and Scotland, and on which Britain had based its power and claim to international status, heavily undermined the conditional British bargain.

English regions, too, relied for their prosperity on these same declining industries and experienced similar difficulties though with rather less dependence, and thus without the same dramatic impact when they experienced decline. Moreover, there was much greater labour mobility within England because there was less cultural resistance to relocating to the areas of new industrial and commercial opportunity in the English Midlands and the South-East.

The sense of betrayal in the 'other' nations as the terms of this bargain shifted was sharpened, too, by the growing, if misplaced, perception in the non-English regions that central government was better disposed to finance economic reconstruction in England. The very dominance of English interests within Britain's institutions nurtured a mindset of blame and recrimination amongst the territorial publics. This was of course a gradual shift. The economic stimulus provided by the centrally managed wartime economy, and in particular the marked success of an energetic Scottish secretary in securing Treasury investment of some £12 million for improving domestic infrastructure, boosting new jobs by an estimated ninety thousand, assuaged this rising discontent though relief was only temporary.[8]

Wales too enjoyed temporary respite from the seemingly inexorable prewar economic decline. The unemployment statistics tell part of the story. By 1944, Scottish unemployment had dropped from a prewar 15.7 per cent to almost nil and increased to only 2.5 per cent during the early postwar years. In Wales the comparative figures were 21.4 per cent in 1938 and 2.7 per cent in 1951.[9] The political payoff from this new, if fragile, prosperity was summarised by the then Scottish secretary who commended 'a new spirit of independence and hope in national life . . . We met England now without any inferiority complex. We were a nation once again'.[10] But this was still a nation without any effective purchase over its own affairs, and much less so once prosperity evaporated with the end of the postwar boom during the 1960s.

In effect, this short-lived economic revival was little more than an interlude in the long-term decline of the heavy industrial sector on which both Scotland and Wales primarily depended for prosperity, employment and, no less significant, for national self-respect. The accelerated economic decline after 1945 was depicted by Celtic nationalists for their own political purposes as indicating English indifference to, even its gross misgovernment of, territorial affairs. The precipitate loss of the Empire after 1945 closed off the traditional escape route from poverty, and merely served to confirm to the non-English inhabitants of the islands the one-sided nature of the British bargain. There was already some resentment that the contribution of the non-English people to the war effort merited greater recognition by the centre. The business of managing declining public expectations was badly handled too, in as much as 'Scottish and Welsh discontent was addressed haphazardly and in ham fisted fashion, with concessions often accompanied by gaffes which wiped out what little goodwill had been earned. When these measures failed to halt the growth of nationalism the response was surprise and exasperation'.[11]

The Scottish National Party's victory in the Motherwell by-election in 1945 was an early indication that such manifest discontent had the potential to become a demand for fully fledged home rule. The sense here was of a distinct Celtic identity already stirring within the intellectual substratum of the territorial elite, though one yet to take firmer root in popular Scottish culture.[12] Some two-thirds of Scottish and Welsh MPs elected in 1945 took their cue from the popular mood, indicating their support for a degree of devolution. In the meantime, the expansion of state aid and a growing public sector after 1945, along with the reduction of government offices and installations, created some additional employment. But power remained firmly at the centre. The postwar Labour government preferred to manage disbursements centrally from the public purse. And though these block grants did much to improve regional and territorial infrastructure, a steadily deteriorating economy after 1947 confirmed retrenchment in regional assistance, hitting disproportionately hard these territorial outreaches of central government.

The English political establishment displayed complacency more than indifference to these stirrings on the territorial margins. It eschewed any lengthy, let alone serious, reflections about the state of the Union, ignoring occasional interventions by a few discordant but marginalised radical voices. George Orwell, for instance, cautioned against such apparent complacency, the cavalier disregard of nationalist sensibilities, presciently warning that:

> The Scottish nationalist movement seems to have gone almost unnoticed in England . . . In the past, certainly, we have plundered Scotland shamefully . . . The point is that many Scottish people, often quite moderate in outlook, are beginning to think about autonomy and to feel that they are pushed into an inferior position . . . I think that we should pay more attention to the small but violent separatist movements which exist within our own island.[13]

When the issue of territorial governance was eventually addressed it was initially treated by Westminster as merely a facet of embittered postwar party politics, and a minor one at that. The Conservative Opposition tried to discomfit the Labour government in its Celtic heartland by endorsing disillusionment there and promising a review – though by no means an overhaul – of the Constitution. Churchill's assertion in 1949 that 'Scotland is a nation [but] it is only since 1945, under the first socialist majority, that we have seen the policy of amalgamation superseding that of Union',[14] was more a critique of socialist central planning, an attempt to undermine the government's legitimacy amongst its staunchest support base than it was unequivocal acknowledgement of territorial rights.

A similar appeal was directed to Wales, where the Conservative manifesto for the 1950 general election included devolution proposals. The party chairman rather gave the game away, revealing the cosmetic quality of this commitment when he commented that: 'A country for the whole of which the product of a penny rate fetches less than the City of Westminster cannot be expected to pull itself up by its bootstraps'.[15] How this promise was eventually redeemed when the Conservatives returned to power in 1951 reveals an altogether more accurate picture of political intentions.

Responsibility for the Principality's affairs was appended to the home secretary's department. A decision was taken not to publish separate public accounts for Wales following the introduction in 1952 of this same procedure for the Scottish accounts, for it was felt that to publish such sensitive information would merely add to territorial discontents, thereby increasing political pressure on central government given that, in the Treasury's view, Wales remained 'a deficiency region'. When responsibility for Welsh affairs was subsequently relocated in the Ministry of Housing in 1957, the new ministry tellingly found that Whitehall files relating to Wales were almost non-existent.[16]

At this juncture, growing concern about the centre's apparent indifference to special territorial needs in its management of public policy hardly amounted to widespread rebuttal of overarching British identity. In so far as devolution appealed to critics of the union state, it was less as a denial of Britishness and rather more as a means both of venting the authentic territorial voice and for improving democratic empowerment and cultural diversity in an ever more centralised state. What did occur, if gradually and certainly tentatively in these territorial outreaches, was the onset of a mood of questioning the political management from the centre. National sentiment revived even in Wales where once it seemed to have faded away.[17] This in turn prompted Welsh Labour MPs in 1945 and again in 1946 to petition Downing Street for a measure of devolution. Predictably, the request was resisted.[18]

The Labour government had by now abandoned the 1917 commitment to 'all round' devolution, subsequently confirmed as official party policy in 1929. In government for the first time with a large working majority, and by now ideologically committed to central planning, the party leadership forbore from what it saw as merely wasteful of scarce resources by increasing bureaucracy. Labour MPs from both Scotland and Wales continued, nevertheless, to lobby ministers, demanding due consideration for the territorial dimension of public policy. An all-party delegation met with the Prime Minister in 1947.[19] The official response was, however, mere tokenism: a Council for Wales was installed in 1949, but without real powers.

A Campaign for a Welsh Parliament was launched in 1950, collecting over a quarter of a million signatures on a petition, though it was hampered by intra-party factionalism and wound up in 1959. Further perceived slights to Welsh sensibilities sustained nationalist feelings throughout the 1950s. The rejection in 1957 of the Council of Wales's report recommending the establishment of a Welsh Office, and the seemingly peremptory manner with which a majority of English Members voted powers to enable land in Merioneth to be appropriated for building a reservoir for Liverpool, fuelled deep resentment in North Wales. The very language in which such decisions were couched seemed to reflect a lack of cultural sensitivity that boosted national sentiments, if not quite a politicised national identity. The Prime Minister's letter refusing a Welsh Office, for instance, seemed to confirm complacency in London about the state of territorial feelings on such sensitive matters. As Harold Macmillan saw it, Wales was indeed a nation, but one whose historical assimilation with English government required nothing more than improved regional economic opportunities. Wholesale constitutional change was out of the question because:

> the majority of the Welsh people are in agreement that their interests can best be furthered in association with England and the English people; at the same time Wales has not only her own language but her distinctive needs and culture . . . her own history, her own geography, her own hopes, her own life . . . Yet what Wales needs is not isolation from the rest of Britain, but wise understanding of Welsh problems . . . Wales, unlike Scotland, has the same system of law and of local government and of land tenure as England; there is no division or need for division there. The geographic and economic links with England are very strong.[20]

One minor victory for Welsh exceptionalism did confirm a reviving national spirit. Periodic attempts from 1893 to restore the historic Welsh flag and to have it incorporated into the Union flag had been resisted by the British establishment on the grounds that Wales had never enjoyed the status of being a kingdom. The new royal emblem designed to mark the role of the monarchy in Wales for use on public buildings was spurned by its people in preference to the ancient flag of the Welsh Princes. In the end, the Queen was obliged to recognise the ancient red dragon insignia.[21]

A similar tokenism, treating territorial sensibilities more as a public relations exercise than as a matter of political substance, was also apparent in central government's response to Scottish discontents. An inquiry whose aim was officially described in patronising terms by Prime Minister Attlee as placating the alarms of 'our Scottish friends',[22] culminated in a White Paper (1948) that proposed more parliamentary time be allocated to reviewing Scottish legislation.[23]

The government went on the cultural offensive, launching in 1951 a Festival of Britain. But this was an event primarily designed not to restore an overarching British identity already under threat from the geographical periphery, but rather to recapture the wartime sense of national purpose. As one contemporary observer saw it, this event was designed 'to dissipate the gloom that hung like a pea-soup fog above the generation of 1951 . . . [to] emphasize our unity . . . [to] show the world that we were after all a people, cemented together by the gigantic pressures of history, being amused by the same silly things [, that] we had the same sort of character underneath . . . an ancient people formed of many obscure strands'.[24]

The Coronation of 1953, though briefly rekindling a sense of common identity throughout the realm, by no means confirmed any abiding sense of Britishness. Clearly, something had been lost along the way. For many Scots the Coronation ritual, accompanied by frequent references in public discourse to 'the new Elizabethan Age', recalled a powerful English state rather more than it confirmed a pan-British identity. The very term United Kingdom had replaced England in the Coronation oath only as recently as 1937. Moreover, a series of mishaps occurred that affronted more than they assuaged Scots' sensibilities. The Proclamation of Accession itself referred to the new monarch as Elizabeth II though she was in fact the first Queen Elizabeth to reign in Scotland. Postboxes in Scotland bearing the insignia EIIR were vandalised. In direct response, the royal title in Scotland became simply ER, but the damage was already done.

The government also rejected the suggestion of some Scottish peers that the stone of Scone should be temporarily repatriated so that the Queen might be separately crowned in her northern realm. This foreshadowed a subsequent cultural slight over postage stamps. The assistant postmaster-general's proposal in 1955 to issue stamps with separate national symbols for each country of the Union *except* for England pleased no one. The prime minister, Anthony Eden, at first declined the proposal on the grounds that it would merely revive nationalist sentiments. When these stamps were eventually issued in 1956 the decision not to print a distinctive symbol on English stamps seemed merely patronising and brought a protest from the Scottish Office.[25]

The contribution of such perceived affronts to Scottish feelings, and their contribution to an already diminishing sense of British identity, was significant if not yet critical. The 1951 Conservative government, aware of simmering discontent and obliged because of Churchill's promise in Opposition, appointed yet another Royal Commission (1951) with the brief to review prospects for greater territorial self-determination, though home rule was expressly excluded from its remit. The Report of the Commission (1954) recommended a modest increase in the powers of the Scottish Office (notably, over electricity and roads), but without addressing the roots of discontent about the current arrangements for Scotland's governance. The Report did, nevertheless, mark a turning point, at least in official deliberations about the state of territorial relations 'because for the first time an official body of the British State publicly acknowledged that there had been a significant deterioration in Anglo-Scottish relations. What is more, it is argued that the cause of Scottish discontent was due to long-term and deep-seated cultural problems which underlay the political structure of the Union: namely the English tendency to regard Britain as "Greater England".'[26]

Although this Report had little material impact on the architecture of British government, it did at least acknowledge that the cultural glue of Britishness binding the Union since the eighteenth century was weakening. There was also some acknowledgement that political affiliation, the palpable sense of belonging to a common historical endeavour, requires something more substantial to sustain it than efficient economic management, or even the equitable disbursement, of public goods.[27] Instead, the Balfour Report detected 'emotional dissatisfaction' and identified its roots in English 'thoughtlessness and lack of tact and disregard of sentiment'. As a consequence, there was 'a widespread feeling that national individuality is being lost, and the Treaty of 1707 is no longer remembered as the voluntary union of two proud peoples each with their own distinctive national and cultural characteristics and traditions, but rather as the absorption of Scotland by England'.[28]

The remedy proposed to redress this situation betrayed much of the same underlying complacency as in past times. For the most part, the centre seemed content to trade in the debased currency of vacuous platitudes about 'mutual respect' and the expectation that national economic recovery would somehow dissipate territorial anxieties, thereby reducing the appetite for devolution. Complacency at the centre was merely confirmed when the parliamentary debate on the Report was sparsely attended by English Members and with not one minister or shadow minister in attendance. Despite these quite minor dislocations, the general outlook on the state of the Union in the early postwar years was largely one of 'business as usual'. A sense prevailed on all sides that 'the Coronation legitimized the postwar consensus far more than it undermined it . . . Like the Festival of Britain, it was a state celebration of a culturally homogeneous nation, one desperately seeking inspiration from its past in order to revive its fortunes'.[29]

A SHIFTING CULTURAL LANDSCAPE

It remained problematical whether, or in what degree, these national fortunes did indeed revive. By the time the British nation was invited to celebrate the Queen's Silver Jubilee in 1977 much had shifted in the once-settled firmament of British national identity. The role of monarchy as the common cement of national identity in the realm had markedly weakened during the previous quarter-century, notwithstanding the present incumbent's personal popularity.[30] As one commentator has interpreted this event: 'Unlike the Coronation of 1953, the Jubilee offered no coherent vision of who the British were or what direction they should take'.[31] Important here was the fact that national economic decline had continued unabated and indeed had accelerated. Accompanying social and cultural change, in turn, further eroded once-pervasive support for the one institution that had embodied common national currency. The energy that went into celebrating the event, at least in England, was an attempt, by now largely futile, at national denial, 'to persuade, by pomp and circumstance, that no such decline had taken place, or to argue that even if it had, it didn't matter'.[32]

No subsequent event has restored the British project to its former primacy in national affections, not even the brief renaissance in 1982 of the imperial idea, albeit in miniature. Wars and the sense of shared danger they give rise to have long been the customary means for reaffirming the bargain made between the constituent nationalities of the Union. However, not even the jingoistic clamour that surrounded the Falklands War in 1982 could convince the public at large that the nation was in mortal danger. Nor, for that matter, did the equally decisive military encounter with Iraq in 1991. There was no lasting dividend for residual Britishness in either of these brief post-imperial hurrahs. The respective theatres of war were too remote, the threat to the national interests seen as negligible. Media-inspired jingoism and synthetic patriotism could hardly erase deep-seated ambivalence, the dyspeptic mix of hubris and national self-doubt that was the lasting legacy of the 1956 Suez debacle.

Embarrassment and moral outrage in some quarters over the Belgrano incident that saw the loss of life of hundreds of young Argentine conscripts took the shine off victory over Argentina in the South Atlantic. The Queen's decision to absent herself from what many saw as a tasteless victory parade through central London and the Archbishop of Canterbury's apologia for the war merely underlined the mood of public disquiet. Muted celebrations, too, in Scotland and Wales on the occasion of the fiftieth anniversary of VE day, in marked contrast to those in England, further confirmed a loosening of affiliation to a once-pervasive sense of a shared island history. Nostalgia for a 'valiant' past when the islanders had stood alone, defying the threat of Continental invasion, had been an evocative bond that briefly revived an already flagging sense of national identity during the course of the last century. Fifty years on and the generation that had experienced these events had either passed on or was fast ageing. And though this anniversary did evoke nostalgia, for the majority of younger citizens it was as no more than an historic moment, emotionally remote and fast receding, and for many a feature entirely absent from the collective folk memory.

The evidence of opinion surveys and polls substantiates the extent of this fundamental shift in political affiliations. In the survey on nationality conducted in 1985 by the Rowntree Trust, the response to the question about the definition of nationality indicated that some 64 per cent of Scots and 41 per cent of the Welsh felt themselves to be more Scottish/Welsh than British. Or indeed, not to be British at all.[33] This compared with only 25 per cent of English respondents who felt themselves to be more English than British.[34] The Nuffield survey reported similar findings in 1997.[35] Another poll confirmed that the visceral anti-English feeling amongst Scots was as deep-rooted as ever.[36]

The importance of generation shift was quite evident in these findings, with older Scots and Welsh respondents more likely to perceive their primary identity as British. The significance, too, of the economic variable in reconfiguring identity, not least the role of territorial economic decline in recasting political identity, is clear from the polling data.[37] Working class, and by and large poorer, respondents are more likely than middle class subjects to reject British affiliation and to give primacy to territorial identity, though at the same time resisting support for outright independence because of economic uncertainty.[38] These important shifts in the cultural landscape were manifested in changing political preferences, adding real momentum to the movement for devolution throughout the postwar years.[39]

WHITHER IRELAND: RECONCILIATION OR RECALCITRANCE?

Cultural shifts and social change was likewise instrumental in altering once closed minds in Ulster. Sectarianism remains deeply entrenched there, but a new politics based on power sharing by moderates in both communities has been one remarkable outcome of the peace process. If consolidated – a prospect that is far from certain at the time of writing – this will amount to far-reaching change, both in patterns of behaviour and in the political expectations of the two sides. One critical development in this respect is the establishment of a civic forum representing business, labour, the Churches, and social groups, and intended to embed in these critical interstices of civil society those habits and norms appropriate to a non-sectarianism outlook and essential for mutual respect.[40] The impact of these changes on political identity in Ulster over the longer term is more difficult to forecast. The 1998 Agreement has potential for at least institutionalising, if not yet for reconciling, divergent political identities that once threatened to tear the Province apart.[41]

The peace process has at least confirmed the prospects for negotiated political change. There is now acknowledgement on both sides in the north and in Dublin of the right of Ulster's citizens to determine their own political future according to the democratic principle of consent.[42] After the Northern Ireland parliament was suspended in 1972, the guarantee incorporated into the Ireland Act 1949, that Northern Ireland would not be excluded from the United Kingdom without the consent of its parliament, was reformulated. The Northern Ireland Constitution Act 1973 recognised the consent principle through the democratic medium of 'the majority of the people of Northern Ireland voting in a poll' to be held periodically.[43] This same guarantee was reiterated in the Belfast Agreement (1998) allowing for periodic plebiscites every seven years or so to determine whether or not there is majority support for reunion with the Republic.

There is rather more hope than certainty about these outcomes, but even this degree of expectancy is novel in this troubled polity.[44] The assurance about consent may reconcile a majority of unionists to power sharing and even to cross-border cooperation. The demons of republicanism might be exorcised, too, by the benefits accruing from closer regional collaboration at the EU level. And enough Protestants might be persuaded to rethink their once blind allegiance to a Union that is itself embarked on re-evaluating the fundaments of its own constitutional and political order. These aspirations remain wholly conditional, though there is some cause for optimism concerning futures, some encouragement to be drawn from significant attitude shifts in the Republic where growing secularism promises pragmatic politics that may, in turn, soften unionist resistance to dealing with Dublin.[45]

The modernisation of this once parochial society has certainly altered public aspirations there, reshaping in turn its own idea of national identity, and in the process has fundamentally changed the political agenda. The provincialism that once moulded the Republic's economy and determined its statecraft, fuelled by abiding post-independence mistrust of Britain, has been overtaken by events. Prosperity has secularised politics, here as elsewhere in the advanced world, releasing the present generation from the introverted and visceral nationalism of their forebears.

What passes now for radical energy in the Republic is focused less on perpetuating tribal quarrels, or on maintaining an exclusive political identity, and rather more on pursuing contemporary and progressive causes rooted in social and cultural agendas – issues from ecologism to lifestyle choices (divorce, abortion and family planning), so long blocked by the Catholic hierarchy. Impatience with Northern sectarianism, in case unprecedented prosperity and public order suffer by contagion, has also influenced public opinion. So, indeed, have the direct costs of protracted civil unrest. By 1992 the Irish Justice Minister estimated that during the previous year alone, 'the additional security costs for the Republic . . . arising from the Northern troubles would be in the order of £180 millions'.[46] Parties in the Republic that had once set their ideological compass by this tribal quarrel have assimilated to this changed outlook, as all democratic parties with a weather eye for electoral prospects must do. In short, the axis of Irish party politics no longer revolves around old quarrels over relations with Britain. The discourse of politics did take rather longer here to catch up with its everyday practice, but electoral logistics has finally prevailed over ideological bombast. Since the late 1960s the substance of Irish politics – and now its rhetoric too – reflects these social and economic changes. If Dublin has any residual interest in affairs in the North, it is primarily that of a near-neighbour concerned to calm turbulence in its hinterland.[47]

Even more significant for political identity in Ulster is the palpable fact of British retreat from unconditionally maintaining the post-1921 commitment to 'loyalist' Ulster. It is impossible nowadays to imagine a contemporary Conservative leader reminding a mass meeting of Belfast unionists, as Bonar Law did on the eve of the passage of the Home Rule Bill in 1912, that 'once again (as in 1689) you hold the pass for the empire. You are a beseiged city. Does not the picture of the past, the glorious past . . . rise again before your eyes . . . The government have by their Parliament Act erected a boom to cut you off from the help of the British people. You will burst that boom'.[48] Endorsement of, or at least indifference to, the old political order was replaced over time by rising impatience, annoyance at an adamantine refusal to rethink an intransigent politics. The protracted peace process embarked on by John Major's government in the early 1990s, and culminating in the Belfast Agreement under its successor, highlighted the determination of British politicians to finally settle this issue. Significantly, the Prime Minister Tony Blair and his Conservative predecessor John Major campaigned together in Ulster in favour of the peace accord during the 1998 referendum campaign on the Agreement.[49]

At the beginning of 'The Troubles' the sense of British identity amongst unionists markedly deepened. According to one survey, 20 per cent of Northern Protestants in 1968 saw themselves as Irish, a figure that had dropped to barely 3 per cent by 1989.[50] Attempts in some quarters to foster an autonomous Ulster identity as the basis for a claim to statehood, have received scant support. It may well be that this idea of territorial identity in Ireland will be revisited by future generations. Perhaps in the novel context of a quasi-federal Britain, if communal reconciliation takes firmer root, though this outcome, too, is by no means certain.[51]

There are changes, too, on the nationalist side. No longer excluded from power and reassured by the all-Irish dimension to Ulster's governance, the Catholic community may likewise become reconciled to a reformed UK citizenship within a democratic Ulster, and as such, be less attracted to relocating in a Republic where mainstream public opinion has distanced itself from the excesses of Northern republicanism. Recent polling has indicated that a significant minority of Ulster's Catholics does prefer British citizenship to that of the Republic.[52]

The new arrangements do at least facilitate the prospect of a new political culture, even if they do not guarantee it. Tolerance of multiple identities is built into these political arrangements. Article 1 of the Agreement acknowledges, for instance, respect for both British and Irish identities, and indeed inhabitants of Northern Ireland are permitted to hold dual Irish–British citizenship if they so choose. One outcome of these reciprocal shifts may be a dual Anglo-Irish identity, an abandoning of exclusive British or republican/nationalist identities. Reconciliation, education, prosperity, secularism, and, of course, generation change, can all contribute to re-imagining perceptions of what it is to 'belong' to a responsive, representative body politic.[53] The future outcome of this particular form of devolution may be uncertain. What is clear, however, from events here and indeed throughout the United Kingdom, is that for the first time since the early eighteenth century a fundamental reimagination of political identity is under way, though its eventual configuration remains as yet undetermined.[54]

BEYOND DEVOLUTION: TOWARDS A FEDERAL FUTURE?

By way of conclusion we might now venture some tentative thoughts about the possible trajectory of the developments reviewed in the foregoing chapters, in particular what the constitutional outcome of the reimagination of political identity in the United Kingdom discussed above might be. Constitutional reform is a risky business, though the foregoing account indicates that the process was in some significant part a direct response to deep-seated changes in the postwar fabric of British political culture. Complacency about the state of the Union has been overtaken by events. The constitutional order is now a central issue on the national political agenda and is likely to remain so. Of course, there has been and there remains residual resistance to constitutional change. The patent danger of negotiating uncharted change clearly has to be weighed against the perils of paralysis.[55]

The challenge that has confronted British governments is how to reconcile demands for self-determination in ways that reflect a meaningful sense of territorial identity, whilst avoiding the unravelling of the Union. The key here is to accommodate cultural diversity, but without weakening the affective cement that binds the United Kingdom's constituent territories together within an effective national polity.[56] The solution to this conundrum that eventually emerged, that of institutional arrangements based on asymmetrical devolution, mirrors in reverse the haphazard process by which various territorial components were accommodated at various times and in different ways to the overarching idea of the Union.

Clearly, a new politics is emerging with novel rules to be learned.[57] It seems unlikely, however, that this will be an end of the matter. For devolution has fundamentally altered the fabric of the state. Tension might be anticipated between the formal arrangements and the classical assumptions about British government that underwrite these reforms. The case for minimal change is appealing and is easily made in such a long-established and stable polity. The assumption of Westminster's overarching sovereignty permeates the recent constitutional discourse and is likely to continue so to do. There are reassuring allusions in this narrative to the continuing supremacy of the UK Parliament.[58] There is always, nevertheless, the prospect of unanticipated consequences, of disparity between what is expected from the new constitutional arrangements and how things might actually work out in practice. The assumption from some quarters of modest adaptation, to be followed by a future of unalloyed and stable continuity is almost certainly unrealistic. Rather, the devolution legislation of 1998 is the beginning of what will undoubtedly be a protracted process of political change.

This of course implies that Scottish public opinion remains enamoured of its new institutions and the arrangements for territorial government. Disputes over the location and the cost of the new parliament building and personal scandals surrounding some of its leading personnel may have taken some of the gloss off the new political order. To allow this is one thing, but it is far from the full picture.[59] We must not confuse public dismay over local difficulties with widespread disaffection about the new arrangements. They are not one and the same.[60] The polling evidence indicates rather more disaffection with the incumbent Executive than with the Parliament per se.[61] It may well be that public disillusionment with the political establishment will hasten the Scottish National Party's election into government, a nationalist party committed to separatism and outright independence.[62] In any event, the prospect – permitted by the present arrangements – for using reserve powers and residual constitutional authority to enforce London's will in any putative quarrel over respective competences is just the sort of situation designed to galvanise territorial public opinion: to rally it around recalcitrant territorial politicians bent on resisting demands from the centre. As one seasoned observer has perceptively observed, 'such constitutional plans cannot take any regard for the intangible at the heart of government: politics itself.'[63] There will be yet more negotiation and hard bargaining to come.

The aspirations expressed by the growing demand for devolution and the expectations it has raised at the level of territorial politics do indicate unpredictable, though not necessarily turbulent, relations between the centre and the new assemblies.[64] One expert commentator sees the restive dynamic at work in the new intergovernmental arrangement as follows:

> Constitutionally, the Scottish Parliament will clearly be subordinate. Politically, however, it will be anything but subordinate. For the Scotland Act creates a new locus of political power. Its most important power will be one not mentioned in the Act at all, that of representing the people of Scotland. The basic premiss of devolution, after all, is that there is a separate political will in Scotland. The First Minister in Scotland will be seen as an executant of that political will, backed as he or she will be by a popular majority in Scotland . . . In practice, therefore, the First Minister in Scotland is likely to be seen as the real leader of Scottish opinion; he or she is likely to be seen as the prime minister of Scotland . . . In Scotland, then, the supremacy of Parliament will bear a very different and attenuated meaning after the setting up of her parliament. It will certainly not mean the supremacy over 'all persons, matters and things' . . . [for] Westminster, instead of enjoying a regular and continuous exercise of supremacy will possess merely a nebulous right of supervision over this parliament.[65]

There will inevitably be unprecedented political constraints on Westminster's exercise of its supervisory role, or on the exercise of its right to legislate even in the devolved areas as it sees fit. These eventualities will not, however, be determined by formal documents, a straightforward reading of the legislation, but rather by the altogether more problematical exigencies of everyday politics. It is impracticable and indeed improbable to imagine Westminster taking unilateral action whatever the law may say on these matters. Once reassuring nostrums about a singular and overarching British national interest have disappeared for good.[66]

Events do have their own intrinsic momentum and the essentially contingent nature of politics makes for the unexpected. No one can predict with certainty where the process of constitutional change will end. Change may beget more change as the experience of home rule replaces the former disposition for centralised power, and as territorial elites become adept at strategies for maximising autonomy in relations with central government. Tension between agents in these respective levels of government is certain to make for uncertain politics, prompting further redrawing of constitutional boundaries. Territorial elites may demand more autonomy whereas Westminster is just as likely to resist them, promising a war of nerves that will test the effectiveness of current conciliation procedures. Much will depend here on the disposition to goodwill, or on residual empathy between politicians representing the respective interests of both the central and territorial governments.

As with the process of government so with the practice of politics. Territorial elections contested by the British parties even on dedicated territorial policy agendas are bound to impact on the fabric of UK party politics, and in ways not yet anticipated by the principal actors.[67] The very asymmetry of the devolution arrangements, too, might encourage a leapfrogging effect, with less empowered polities – Wales and the putative English regions – pushing to catch up the pace-setters, Scotland and Northern Ireland. Contesting the status quo, the balance of power between the central and territorial tiers of governance is an occupational hazard of power-sharing arrangements that is well illustrated by the history of federalism. Outright separatists, though currently marginalised in territorial politics, will need little excuse for provoking crisis politics, demanding a final reckoning with the Union. All of this amounts to a unique politics. Unprecedented change for sure, a journey without a reliable map though probably still some way short of the crisis once predicted by visceral opponents of devolution, for it would be fatuous to forecast the break-up of the Union on the evidence so far of devolution. On the contrary, one might just as plausibly argue that recent constitutional change represents a timely and indeed an imaginative response to a fast-moving political landscape.

It is clear that the United Kingdom has a new constitutional order;[68] not yet a federal order, but one whose constitutional trajectory points, albeit tentatively, in that direction. For this latest adaptation of the British Constitution to current exigencies 'does more than devolve powers [but] *divides* the power to legislate for Scotland between Westminster and Edinburgh, creating a quasi-federal relationship between the two parliaments'.[69] According to this radical account of the new arrangements, the Judicial Committee of the Privy Council assumes the familiar mantle of judicial review and adjudication, as between the centre and the territorial governments performed by constitutional courts in fully federal polities. And to that extent it further dents the long-established constitutional precept of parliamentary supremacy already eroded by the legal obligations consequent on EU membership.

At the very least, Westminster and Whitehall are required to adjust to a novel constitutional landscape whereby routine 'top-down' governance is moderated, if not replaced, by shared arrangements. Yet more centripetal pressures may come from various directions, and each reinforced by perceived strains on the centre from another part of the state. The most significant cause of stress here would be a significant rise in public support for a more assertive English regionalism. Whether this will take the form of a positive demand for a form of English regionalism spurred on by revived territorial fortunes in the new devolved areas, or more negative resentment at Celtic ingratitude that threatens territorial gridlock or worse, remains to be seen. The next stage of constitutional adaptation will require participants to navigate through the uncertainties of fast-changing events.[70] Another unpredictable and potentially eruptive outcome of asymmetrical devolution is the unforeseen political consequences of tackling head on – or for that matter, not tackling – the inequitable representation of the devolved territories at Westminster and within the central government machinery.[71]

These predictions about the future of British government will be tested only as events unfold. Nevertheless, political logic, and certainly the experience elsewhere of devolving power from the centre, does tend to endorse this unaccustomed account of the new territorial relations. Politics is, of course, a contingent business with unpredictable outcomes. It may even be the case that the current trend to deconcentrate power away from the centre will somehow be reversed. That after flexing territorial muscle the novelty will simply wear off, with old habits restored, leading in turn to a restoration of the unitary state. This outcome, though possible, is unlikely. The sheer political momentum driving the current changes suggests otherwise[72] – and not only in Britain, for reimagining the nation state is a phenomenon that is apparent everywhere in the Continent.[73]

The classic Westphalian state system[74] is under challenge across the Continent and beyond, a trend that reflects a global phenomenon, a structural shift in the locus of governance responding to unparalleled changes in international political economy.[75] The familiar realist paradigm of a world order of exclusive and competing nation states manifesting discrete sovereignty is challenged by what in the theoretical literature tracking these trends one leading political scientist has aptly described as 'cascading interdependence'.[76] The architecture of contemporary governance reflects this advanced state of transnational interdependence, with policy setting and decision making now taking place simultaneously at several levels of the global, regional, national and sub-national polities.[77] British devolution is but one particular manifestation of these generic shifts in the locus of government.

Yet even these prodigious and ubiquitous forces must be viewed from a properly balanced perspective. For whilst the idea of the nation state is severely challenged by forces that are beyond its limited resources to adequately cope with, it continues to exist, drawing not only on a deep reservoir of public loyalty, popular identification and citizens' expectations with regard to ideas about 'good governance', but also on the preferences of influential political elites for exercising their appetite for leadership within manageable political bounds. Nor is this a case of vainly clinging to the wreckage, of misplaced nostalgia. A residual sense of political identity, an abiding need for cultural belonging, let alone the sheer force of habit amongst its stakeholders, precludes the obsolescence of the nation state.

An altogether different impetus is under way in international politics, a response by political elites to current challenges above and below the national polity. A reaction to structural shifts that makes the first duty of those charged with conducting public affairs the nation states' reform, adapting its familiar arrangements so as to better carry out its mission under contemporary circumstances. Change, however, that in no way amounts either to countenancing the nation states' obsolescence through merger with some larger supra-national entity, or hastening its improvident dismemberment into micro-states.[78]

The nation state is everywhere in the process of being reformed and even re-imagined. This remarkable endeavour presents a practical challenge to politicians, as well as testing the theoretical acumen of social scientists to properly explain the prospective trajectories and predict the likely outcomes of contemporary political change.[79] In these islands, and indeed beyond them, political identity is undergoing change as a consequence of the vast challenges and shifts brought about by globalisation. The reform of the British state is best understood within this wider context, as a response in part to insidious global forces. The unitary state proved to be an ineffective because unduly rigid model for the governance of its sub-national territories once they had rediscovered differences both of interest and of identity alongside continuing shared concerns with the metropolitan centre. Dicey's classic, confident but essentially complacent prescription for a centralised union state is now inappropriate and out of kilter with the times.[80] The national state will almost certainly survive, but here as elsewhere in a much changed form. Acknowledging the significance of the territorial dimension is now as crucial to democratic management of affairs in these islands as it is in many other European nation states.

How, then, might the reimagined and reconfigured union state develop in future? One possible solution for the management of accelerated territorial pressures – and a positive alternative to sundering the British state – is to embrace the logic of expanded devolution, and maybe even to anticipate a variant of federalism: an outcome that is now by no means as far-fetched as it appeared to Dicey and his contemporaries, who summarily dismissed the prospect as fundamentally un-British.[81] Indeed, one might agree with the commentator who sees in present arrangements for territorial government just such an impetus towards a federal state. The case made here is that, even in its attenuated form, the dynamics and trajectory of the recent constitutional changes in Great Britain and Northern Ireland since 1998, their likely consequence for British political culture, is the introduction of at least 'the spirit of federalism'. According to this prognosis, the challenge of resolving 'the West Lothian Question, then, draws attention to the fact that devolution will transform Westminster into the quasi-federal parliament of a quasi-federal state.'[82]

Developments elsewhere in Europe seem to reinforce this general tendency. The trend towards regionalism, the gathering momentum behind territorial politics and devolved governance across the Continent is accelerating,[83] encouraged by an EU polity rooted in notions of subsidiarity, variable geometry and similarly spatial metaphors that reflect new and flexible ways of thinking about governance.[84] After all, federalism is the classical solution in liberal but culturally plural polities to the challenge of divesting the centre of excessive power and empowering the constituent territorial parts of the once unitary state. Moreover, this approach could be said to fit the temper of the times. The unitary state was created in an era when central governance functions and collective goals were rather more salient in politics than they currently are in light of new and post-materialist preferences.[85] Public demands for greater local empowerment, the wider acknowledgement now of multiple identities and even of a more cosmopolitan or prismatic concept of citizenship indicate a new political climate.

Political science narratives chart and seek to explain these significant developments in the fabric of politics and governance at every level. The discipline now trades in the novel discourse of post-national identity and cosmopolitan citizenship.[86] It might be rather easier in these circumstances to find a balance between what unites and divides the inhabitants of these islands if we relocate this gathering debate on political identity within the framework of developments in the wider European and global milieux.[87] A new inclusive British citizenship, one that embraces all the composite nations, ethnicities and creeds of these islands, would be a positive step forward in the development of multi-layered identity. The task here is to accommodate political relations, refit the institutions of the state and adapt the processes of government to the medley of multiple, overlapping, and by no means mutually exclusive identities that better depict the contemporary cultural reality of the islands. This is precisely what Linda Colley has alluded to in her observation that:

> Instead of being mesmerised by debates over British identity, it would be far more productive to concentrate on renovating British citizenship, and on convincing all of the inhabitants of these islands that they are equal and valued citizens irrespective of whatever identity they may individually select to prioritise.[88]

The case for a plural polity that reflects this cultural diversity is more easily made now than it was in Dicey's day. And on that same basis, so is the case made for federalism in the United Kingdom as elsewhere. Federalism is a model of government whose time may well have arrived in the Continent that gave rise to centralised authority and hierarchical polities. Conceived by the Enlightenment project as a rational formula for accommodating respect for the pluralism of emergent *status civitatus* with civilised governance, federalism has, at the end of a century where the unitary state failed to strike a judicious balance between order and representation, finally come into its own.[89]

The essence of federalism is the reallocation of power between territorial and central authorities in order to close present and disquieting democratic deficits. Devolution is quite consistent with this logic, though the balance of power here remains for the time being with the centre. As such, it may not satisfy the current mood for reforming the British state and relocating some of its power away from the centre. For one thing, a clear difference of degree remains between the competences of the centre and those of the territorial governments. Devolved government is about sharing power within a unitary state rather than enacting a classic federal separation of powers. To this extent, devolution is not about the unravelling of the unitary state that equates with historical federalism. Or at least, not yet.

As currently constituted, the United Kingdom is some way removed from the sort of crisis politics that requires the dramatic reaccommodation, a constitutional rebalancing of its constituent polities. A root and branch renegotiation of the founding political bargain struck between the Uniteds Kingdom's constituent nations, and requiring the sort of federal compact negotiated in nineteenth-century Switzerland, more recently in Belgium, Spain, and prospectively in Canada and Italy, is still some way off.[90] It may be that this historic Rubicon will never be crossed. Recent events do suggest, however, that we cannot be sure of the eventual outcome. A recent survey commissioned by the House of Lords constitution committee on attitudes to devolution found widespread disquiet both in Scotland and Wales concerning the political outcomes of devolution. This prompted Professor John Curtice in his report to that committee to conclude that:

> It appears that devolution has simply failed to fulfil the political aspirations with which many people in Scotland, Wales and Northern Ireland invested it . . . In the devolved territories it is perceived as having largely failed to take power away from London in the way it was originally anticipated and for the most part is still desired.[91]

One might conclude from this interim evaluation that public pressure will increase for even greater devolution. What began in 1998 was the start of a protracted process of reform rather than a conclusive constitutional settlement, a final outcome. Unparalleled political change is under way and there is serious slippage in the once secure and apparently settled idea of the United Kingdom. Scotland has probably acquired as much independence within the Union as Bavaria enjoys within the German model of cooperative federalism, with Wales receiving altogether less autonomy than Scotland or a Spanish *autonomios communidados* but more self-determination than a French regional council. Northern Ireland, meanwhile, is closer to the Welsh than the Scottish model, except for the peculiarities of the new cross-border bodies and the open promise that its ultimate destiny will be determined by a free vote of its people. Comparisons with devolution elsewhere are bound to be crude, politically charged, and selective. Taken out of historical context they provide only a crude measure of particular circumstances, and far less a reliable guide to future developments.

In this flux an even more novel constitutional architecture than the one currently under construction appears to be a less fanciful outcome now than it once appeared to those foundational thinkers whose ideas became, for the past two centuries and more, the axioms of British constitutional thought.[92] The very least to be said, by way of conclusion, is that an altogether less certain future beckons.[93] The break-up of Britain, once confidently predicted by Tom Nairn,[94] might on this evidence seem to be a less remote prospect now, for there are centripetal as well as centrifugal forces at work too. There is no conclusive evidence that the Scottish people, much less those in Wales, wish to push the logic of devolution to the point of outright separation. Territorial politicians are well aware of the public's sensibilities on this matter and are unlikely, whatever their own ideological preferences, to pursue the inevitable disputes about policy and respective competences to the very brink of political crisis.

Political elites elsewhere in western Europe, both territorial and at the centre, even in polities with much deeper ethnic divisions and clearer cultural disparities than those that emerged in the United Kingdom during the 1960s, have resolved to avoid such cataclysmic breakdown. They have instead sought to reconfigure centre–territorial relations, accommodating diversities and difference within a new constitutional framework to better accommodate these abiding differences. This accommodation of cultural diversity has proved, without exception, preferable to suffering the uncertainties of political instability, and the heavy social and economic costs of territorial political disintegration. This same task faces political elites in Britain, and there is no obvious reason why this same instinct to balance difference with commonality of purpose will not also be the pragmatic outcome of this mutual endeavour.

The process of constitutional accommodation in the United Kingdom has not been an easy one to negotiate. Indeed, it has required a more far-reaching devolution to keep the state intact than was ever anticipated in the nineteenth century when the territorial question first emerged on the political agenda. But in the process of working out these new constitutional arrangements the political establishment at every level has been able to draw on a residual sense of common purpose. This may be a kingdom whose affective cement is altogether weaker now, whose founding compact is certainly undergoing re-imagination, but it is one nevertheless where a sense of shared endeavour is still palpable, where the overarching affinities between its constituent nations remains as a durable bond.

Whether this is accommodation still rooted in an abiding commonality of purpose, a mutual sense of belonging in a common project, and the enduring sense of a shared past is one interpretation of recent events. Another interpretation is that the British bargain rests instead only on sufferance, is merely staid habit, a disposition that evokes little positive enthusiasm amongst its different territorial peoples for the notion of mutual interests and 'common endeavour'. Clearly, the meaning of, the prospects for, the British project is a matter still to be settled in these islands. The outcome of this critical question about how to live together but separately extends the present discourse on the future of the British polity into an uncertain future. Indeed, this is the very challenge of, the opportunity presented by, the current move to devolution in British politics.

NOTES

1. B. Anderson, *Imagined Communities: Reflections on the Origins and Spread of Nationalism* (1983)
2. R. Weight, *Patriots: National Identity in Britain 1940–2000* (2002) at p.5
3. L. Colley, *Britons. Forging the Nation, 1707–1837* (1992) pp.53–4
4. M. Hechter, *Internal Colonialism: the Celtic Fringe in British National Development* (1975)
5. See the discussion in C. Kidd, *Subverting Scotland's Past: Scottish Whig Historians and the Creation of an Anglo-Scottish Identity, 1689–c1830* (1993)
6. Cited in I. McBride, Ulster and the British Problem, in R. English and G. Walker (eds), *Unionism in Modern Ireland: New Perspectives on Politics and Culture* (1996) p.6
7. N. Evans (ed.), *National Identity in the British Isles* (1989)
8. C. Harvie, *No Gods and Precious Few Heroes: Twentieth Century Scotland*, 3rd edition (1998)
9. S. Glynn and A. Booth, *Modern Britain: An Economic and Social History* (1996) pp.91 and 284
10. Quoted in R. Galbraith, *Without Quarter: A Biography of Tom Johnson, 'The Uncrowned King of Scotland'* (1995) p.247
11. R. Weight, op. cit. (2002) p.123
12. See for instance I. Finlay, *Scotland* (1945) p.130
13. G. Orwell, In Front of your Nose 1945–50, reprinted in S. Orwell and I. Angus (eds), *The Collected Essays, Journalism and Letters of George Orwell*, vol. 4 (1970) pp.328–9

14. Conservative Party, *Scottish Control, Scottish Affairs: Unionist Policy* (1949) p.1
15. Lord Wooton, quoted in A. Butt Philip, *The Welsh Question: Nationality in Welsh Politics, 1945–1970* (1975) at p.296
16. R. Weight, op. cit. (2002) at p.220
17. K. Morgan, *Rebirth of a Nation: Wales 1880–1980* (1981) p.376
18. PRO: HO45/21645, statement by the Welsh Parliamentary Labour Party to the Prime Minister, 6 March 1946
19. PRO: PREM8/658, John Taylor (Secretary, Scottish Council of the Labour Party) to Herbert Morrison, 16 June 1947
20. PRO: PREM11/2204, Macmillan to Huw Edwards, 11 December 1957
21. R. Weight, op. cit. (2002) pp.283–5
22. PRO: PREM8/658, Attlee to Morrison, 23 June 1947
23. Cmnd 7308, *Scottish Affairs* (1948)
24. H. Nicholson, After the Festival: A Note for Posterity, *Listener* 46 (1183), (1951)
25. R. Weight, op. cit. (2002) pp.218–19
26. Ibid., p.217
27. V. Bogdanor and W. Field, Lessons of History: Core and Periphery in British Electoral Behaviour: 1910–1992, *Electoral Studies* 12 (1993)
28. Cmnd 9212, *Royal Commission on Scottish Affairs* (1954) p.12
29. R. Weight, op. cit. (2002) p.238
30. T. Nairn, *The Enchanted Glass: Britain and its Monarchy* (1988)
31. R. Weight, op. cit. (2002) p.551
32. D. Cannadine, The Context, Performance and Meaning of Ritual: The British Monarchy and the Invention of Tradition, c.1820–1977, in E. Hobsbawm and T. Ranger (eds), *The Invention of Tradition* (1983) p.160
33. On the question of changing perceptions of primary identity in Wales, see J. Osmond, Welsh Civil Identity in the Twenty-first Century, in D. Harvey, R. Jones, N. McInroy and C. Milligan (eds), *Celtic Geographies* (2002)
34. The State of the Nation: The 1995 Joseph Rowntree Memorial Trust/Mori Survey, *Scottish Public Opinion,* September 1995
35. Cited in J. Curtice, Is Scotland a Nation and Wales Not?, in B. Taylor and K. Thompson (eds), *Scotland and Wales: Nations Again?* (1999) p.127
36. Noted in the NOP poll in the *Sunday Times,* 28 June 1998; J. Curtice, The North–South Divide, *British Social Attitudes Survey* 9 (1992); idem, One Nation Again?, in R. Jowell, J. Curtice, A. Park, L. Brook and K. Thompson (eds), *British Social Attitudes: The 13th Report* (1996)
37. B. Ashcroft, Scottish Economic Performance and Government Policy: A North–South Divide?, *Scottish Government Yearbook 1988* (Unit for the Study of Government in Scotland, Edinburgh, 1988)
38. A. Brown, D. McCrone, L. Paterson and P. Sturridge, *The Scottish Electorate: The 1997 Election and Beyond* (1999) pp.62–3
39. See B. Crick, Essay on Britishness, *Scottish Affairs* 2 (1993)
40. P. Dixon, Consociationalism and the Northern Ireland Peace Process: The Glass Half Full or Half Empty?, *Nationalism and Ethnic Politics* 3 (1997); see also, P. Dixon, Paths to Peace in Northern Ireland (I): Civil Society and Consociational

Approaches, *Democratization* 4 (1997); idem, Paths to Peace in Northern Ireland (II), *Democratization* 4 (1997)

41. J. Loughlin, *Ulster Unionism and British National Identity since 1885* (1995)
42. *The Belfast Agreement*, Cmnd 3883, para. 1(ii)
43. Section 1 Northern Ireland Constitution Act 1973
44. R. Wilford and R. Wilson, Northern Ireland Valedictory?, in R. Hazell (ed.) *The State of the Nations 2003* (2003)
45. P. Mair, Breaking the Nationalist Mould: The Irish Republic and the Anglo-Irish Agreement, in P. Teague (ed.), *Beyond the Rhetoric: Politics, the Economy and Social Policy in Northern Ireland* (1987)
46. *Irish Times*, 23 January 1992
47. C. Coulter, *Contemporary Northern Irish Society* (1999)
48. Quoted in R. Blake, *The Unknown Prime Minister* (London, 1955) p.129
49. *Belfast Telegraph*, 21 May 1998
50. Cited in R. Weight, op. cit. (2002) p.530
51. E. Hazelkorn and H. Paterson, The New Politics of the Irish Republic, *New Left Review* 207 (1994)
52. *Belfast Telegraph*, 21 May 1998
53. D. Birrell, Relative Deprivation as a Factor in Conflict in Northern Ireland, *Sociological Review* 20 (1972); R. MacGinty and R. Wilford, More Knowing than Knowledgeable: Attitudes towards Devolution, in A. Gray *et al.* (eds), *Social Attitudes in Northern Ireland: The Eighth Report* (2002)
54. B. Taylor and K. Thompson (eds), *Scotland and Wales: Nations Again?* (1999)
55. A. Tomkins, *Devolution and the English Constitution* (1998)
56. D. Marquand, The Twilight of the British State? Henry Dubb versus Sceptical Awe, *Political Quarterly* 64 (1993)
57. N. McGarvey, New Scottish Politics, New Texts Required, *British Journal of Politics and International Relations* 3 (2001)
58. *Scotland's Parliament*, Cmnd 3658; section 28(7) The Scotland Act 1998
59. For an early summary of the state of territorial public opinion and its responses to operational devolution, see J. Curtice, The People's Verdict: Public Attitudes to Devolution and the Union, in R. Hazell (ed.) *The State and the Nations: The first year of Devolution in the United Kingdom* (2000); idem, Hopes Dashed and Fears Assuaged? What the Public Makes of it So Far, in A. Trench (ed), *The State of the Nations 2001: The Second Year of Devolution in the United Kingdom* (2001); and idem, Devolution Meets the Voters, in R. Hazell (ed.), op. cit. (2003)
60. P. Sturridge, L. Paterson, A. Brown and D. McCrone, The Scottish Electorate and the Scottish Parliament, in L. Paterson (ed.), *Understanding Constitutional Change*, special edition of *Scottish Affairs* (1998)
61. J. Mitchell *et al.*, Scotland: Maturing Devolution, in A. Trench (ed.) op. cit. (2001) p.73; D. Miller, Scotland's Parliament: A Mini-Westminster or a Model of Democracy?, in A. Wright (ed.), *Scotland: The Challenge of Devolution* (2000); J. Mitchell, What Could a Scottish Parliament Do?, *Regional and Federal Studies* 8 (1998)
62. N. MacCormick, Is There a Constitutional Path to Scottish Independence?, *Parliamentary Affairs* 53 (2000)

63. *The Scotsman*, 19 December 1997

64. J. Mitchell, The Study of Scottish Politics Post Devolution: New Evidence, New Analysis?, *West European Politics* 24 (2001)

65. V. Bogdanor, *Devolution in the United Kingdom* (2001) at pp.288 and 291

66. A. Marr, *The Day Britain Died* (2000)

67. J. Bradbury and J. Mitchell, Devolution: New Politics for Old?, *Parliamentary Affairs* 54 (2001); J. Bradbury, D. Denver, J. Mitchell, L. Bennie, Devolution and party change: Candidate Selection for the 1999 Scottish Parliament and Welsh Assembly Elections, *Journal of Legislative Studies* 6 (2000); A. Brown, designing the New Scottish Parliament, *Parliamentary Affairs* 53 (2000); G. Hassan and C. Warhurst, New Scotland? Policy, Parties and Institutions, *Political Quarterly* 72 (2002)

68. J. Kellas, Some Constitutional Aspects of Devolution, in A. Wright (ed.), *Scotland: The Challenge of Devolutuion* (2000)

69. V. Bogdanor, op. cit. (2001) p.293

70. *The Scotsman*, 19 December 1997

71. *The Economist*, 26 July 1997

72. A. Heath and J. Kellas, Nationalisms and Constitutional Questions, *Scottish Affairs*, Special Issue on Understanding Constitutional Change (1998)

73. I. Duchacek, *The Territorial Dimension of Politics: Within, Among, and Across Nations* (1986)

74. W. Mommsen, The Varieties of the Nation State in Modern History, in M. Mann (ed.), *The Rise of the Nation State* (1990); G. Poggi, *The State: Its Nature, Development and Prospects* (1990)

75. W. Muller and V. Wright, Reshaping the State in Western Europe, *West European Politics* 17 (1994)

76. J. Rosenau, A Pre-theory Revisited: World Politics in an Era of Cascading Interdependence, *International Studies Quarterly* 28 (1984)

77. A. Scott, Declining Autonomy: Recent Trends in the Scottish Economy, *Scottish Government Yearbook 1983* (Unit for the Study of Government in Scotland, 1983)

78. M. Mann, *The Rise and Decline of the Nation State* (1990); idem, Nation States in Europe and Other Continents: Diversifying, Developing or Dying, *Daedelus* 3 (1993)

79. D. Beetham, The Future of the Nation State, in G. McLennan, D. Held and S. Hall (eds), *The Idea of the Modern State* (1993)

80. J. Curtice and B. Seyd, Is Devolution Strengthening or Weakening the UK?, in A. Parl *et al.* (eds), *British Social Attitudes: The 18th Report* (2001)

81. J. Kendle, *Federal Britain: A History* (1997) ch. 2

82. V. Bogdanor, op. cit. (2001) p.235

83. P. Wagstaff (ed.), Regionalism in Europe, *Europa* (1994)

84. J. Hesse and N. Johnson (eds), *Constitutional Policy and Change in Europe* (1995); *The Economist*, 6 September 1997

85. A. Giddens, *Modernity and Self-identity* (1991)

86. There is an abundance of literature on this subject. For a broad overview, see the discussion in K. Hutchings and R. Dannreuther (eds), *Cosmopolitan Citizenship* (1999)

87. J. Rutherford, *Identity: Community, Culture and Difference* (1990); D. Austin and M. O'Neill (eds), *Democracy and Cultural Diversity* (2001)

88. L. Colley, *Observer*, 12 December 1999

89. *Financial Times*, 21 July 1997

90. The Diceyian anti-federalist disposition prevailed amongst the British political elite when constitutional reform resurfaced as a significant issue. See M. Keating, Regionalism, Devolution and the State, in P. Garside and M. Hibbert (eds), *British Regionalism 1900–2000* (1989)

91. *Financial Times*, 30 April 2003

92. J. Mitchell, Towards a New Constitutional Settlement, in C. Hay (ed.), *British Politics Today* (2001)

93. W. Muller and V. Wright, op. cit. (1994)

94. T. Nairn, *The Break-up of Britain* (1977); see also J. Mitchell, Devolution and the End of Britain?, *Contemporary British History* 14 (2000)

Index